BUDDHISM IN PRACTICE

PRINCETON READINGS IN RELIGIONS

Donald S. Lopez, Jr., Editor

TITLES IN THE SERIES

Donald S. Lopez, Jr., *Religions of India in Practice*

Donald S. Lopez, Jr., *Buddhism in Practice*

BUDDHISM

IN PRACTICE

Donald S. Lopez, Jr., Editor

PRINCETON READINGS IN RELIGIONS

PRINCETON UNIVERSITY PRESS

PRINCETON, NEW JERSEY

Published by Princeton University Press, 41 William Street,
Princeton, New Jersey 08540
In the United Kingdom: Princeton University Press, Chichester, West Sussex

Library of Congress Cataloging-in-Publication Data

Buddhism in practice / Donald S. Lopez, Jr., editor.
p. cm. — (Princeton readings in religions)
Includes bibliographical references and index.
ISBN 0-691-04442-2. — ISBN 0-691-04441-4 (pbk.)
1. Buddhist literature—Translations into English. I. Lopez,
Donald S., 1952– . II. Series.
BQ1012.B83 1995
294.3—dc20 94-48201

This book has been composed in Berkeley

Princeton University Press books are printed on acid-free paper and meet the guidelines for permanence and durability of the Committee on Production Guidelines for Book Longevity of the Council on Library Resources

Printed in the United States of America

1 3 5 7 9 10 8 6 4 2

1 3 5 7 9 10 8 6 4 2
(pbk.)

PRINCETON READINGS IN RELIGIONS

Princeton Readings in Religions is a new series of anthologies on the religions of the world, representing the significant advances that have been made in the study of religions in the last thirty years. The sourcebooks used by the last generation of students placed a heavy emphasis on philosophy and on the religious expressions of elite groups in what were deemed the "classical" civilizations of Asia and the Middle East. Princeton Readings in Religions provides a different configuration of texts in an attempt better to represent the range of religious practices, placing particular emphasis on the ways in which texts are used in diverse contexts. The series therefore includes ritual manuals, hagiographical and autobiographical works, and folktales, as well as some ethnographic material. Many works are drawn from vernacular sources. The readings in the series are new in two senses. First, the majority of the works contained in the volumes have never been translated into a Western language before. Second, the readings are new in the sense that each volume provides new ways to read and understand the religions of the world, breaking down the sometimes misleading stereotypes inherited from the past in an effort to provide both more expansive and more focused perspectives on the richness and diversity of religious expressions. The series is designed for use by a wide range of readers, with key terms translated and technical notes omitted. Each volume also contains a substantial introduction by a distinguished scholar in which the histories of the traditions are outlined and the significance of each of the works is explored.

Buddhism in Practice is the second volume of Princeton Readings in Religions. The thirty-three contributors include leading scholars of Indian, Chinese, Tibetan, Japanese, Thai, Burmese, Korean, Nepalese, and Sri Lankan Buddhism, each of whom has provided one or more translations of key works, most of which are translated here for the first time. Each chapter in the volume begins with a substantial introduction in which the translator discusses the history and influence of the work, identifying points of particular difficulty or interest.

Two other volumes of the Princeton Readings in Religions are in press: *Religions of China in Practice* and *Religions of Japan in Practice.* Volumes currently nearing completion are devoted to: Islam in Asia, Islamic Mysticism, and the Religions of Tibet. Future volumes are planned for Religions of Latin America, Religions of Africa, as well as several volumes on Judaism and Christianity.

Donald S. Lopez, Jr.
Series Editor

NOTE ON TRANSLITERATION

Most technical terms and Indic names are provided in Sanskrit. In an effort to reduce confusion, in the case of works translated from Pāli, the Pāli is generally provided at the first occurrence, after which the term or name appears in Sanskrit. Chinese terms appear in pinyin. Tibetan terms are rendered in a phonetic equivalent by the translator, after which the term is provided in Wylie transliteration. Certain common place names and selected terms that have entered into English usage appear without diacritical marks.

CONTENTS

Buddha

Dharma

Saṅgha

CONTENTS BY VEHICLE

As discussed in the Introduction, there are many problems with organizing Buddhist works according to "vehicle." However, a tentative organization is provided below. It would require a long commentary to catalogue all of the inherent ambiguities. For example, the chapter entitled "Āryadeva and Candrakīrti on Self and Selfishness" contains no specifically Mahāyāna content, but because such content appears later in the same text, it is classified as a Mahāyāna work. The same could be said of "A Hymn of Praise to Buddha's Good Qualities." One of the forty-eight chapters is not listed below: "Deaths, Funerals, and the Division of Property in a Monastic Code." This is a work from another of the Hīnayāna schools, the Mūlasarvāstivādin. Hence, it is not Theravāda, although similar rules are found in the Pāli vinaya. Many of the great scholar monks of India who composed some of the famous treatises of the Mahāyāna followed the Mūlasarvāstivādin vinaya. And it is this vinaya which is the monastic code for Tibetan Buddhist monks, who have always regarded themselves as followers of the Vajrayāna.

Mahāyāna

CONTENTS BY COUNTRY

It would seem that organizing the contents of this volume by country of origin would be less equivocal than organizing by vehicle. However, even here there are ambiguities. For example, Atiśa's *Lamp for the Path to Awakening* was composed by Atiśa, a Bengali in Tibet, at the request of a Tibetan prince. Is it an Indian or Tibetan work? Because the colophon states that it was translated into Tibetan by its author (with the aid of a Tibetan monk), it seems that it was composed in Sanskrit, and hence is classed here, not without qualms, as an Indian text.

Burma

China

India

CONTRIBUTORS

Alan Berkowitz teaches in the Asian Studies Program at Swarthmore College.

Daniel Boucher is a graduate student at the University of Pennsylvania.

Robert Buswell teaches in the Department of East Asian Languages and Cultures at UCLA.

Carl Bielefeldt teaches in the Department of Religious Studies at Stanford University.

Roger Corless teaches in the Department of Religion at Duke University.

Ronald M. Davidson teaches in the Department of Religious Studies at Fairfield University.

William Deal teaches in the Department of Religious Studies at Case Western Reserve University.

Hubert Decleer heads the Tibet program of the School for International Training in Kathmandu.

T. Griffith Foulk teaches at Sarah Lawrence College.

Luis O. Gómez teaches in the Department of Asian Languages and Cultures at the University of Michigan.

Paul Griffiths teaches in the Divinity School at the University of Chicago.

William Grosnick teaches in the Department of Religion at La Salle College.

Charles Hallisey teaches in the Committee on the Study of Religion at Harvard University.

Dennis Hirota is Head Translator of the Shin Buddhism Translation Series in Kyoto and Adjunct Professor at the Institute of Buddhist Studies in Berkeley.

Jamie Hubbard teaches in the Department of Religion at Smith College.

Matthew Kapstein teaches in the Department of Religion at Columbia University.

Sallie B. King teaches in the Department of Philosophy and Religion at James Madison University.

Anne C. Klein teaches in the Department of Religious Studies at Rice University.

Karen Lang teaches in the Department of Religious Studies at the University of Virginia.

Todd T. Lewis teaches in the Department of Religious Studies at the College of the Holy Cross.

Donald S. Lopez, Jr. teaches in the Department of Asian Languages and Cultures at the University of Michigan.

Jan Nattier teaches in the Department of Religious Studies at Indiana University.

John Newman teaches in the Division of Humanities at New College of the University of South Florida.

Charles Orzech teaches in the Department of Religious Studies at UNC Greensboro.

Patrick Pranke heads the Bodhgaya program of Antioch University.

Gregory Schopen teaches in the Center for Asian Studies at the University of Texas, Austin.

Daniel B. Stevenson teaches in the Department of Religious Studies at the University of Kansas.

Jackie Stone teaches in the Department of Religion at Princeton University.

Donald K. Swearer teaches in the Department of Religion at Swarthmore College.

George J. Tanabe, Jr. teaches in the Department of Religious Studies at the University of Hawaii.

Sybil Thornton teaches in the Department of History at Arizona State University.

Kyoko Tokuno teaches in the Department of Religious Studies at the University of Oregon, Eugene.

Jonathan Walters teaches in the Department of Religion at Whitman College.

Chün-fang Yü teaches in the Department of Religious Studies at Rutgers University.

BUDDHISM IN PRACTICE

INTRODUCTION

Donald S. Lopez, Jr.

This volume is testimony to the vast scope of Buddhist practice in Asia, past and present. It does not follow a chronological sequence or attempt to represent systematically the various Buddhist traditions. Instead, it offers a selection of texts, in the broadest sense of that term, in order to provide the reader with a sense of the remarkable diversity and range of the practices of persons who over the course of 2,500 years have been identified, by themselves or by others, as Buddhists. In this diversity there are often contradictions, such that the practices of a Buddhist community of one time might seem strange or unfamiliar to a Buddhist community elsewhere. Indeed, one of the questions that this volume seeks to raise is whether one can accurately speak of something called "Buddhism" or "the Buddhist tradition," or whether those terms are better rendered in the plural. At the same time, there is evidence here of often surprising parallels among the practices of Buddhist cultures widely separated by both history and topography, parallels to be accounted for in large part by a constant retrospection to the figure of the Buddha.

The chapters in this volume highlight types of discourse (including ritual manuals, folktales, prayers, sermons, pilgrimage songs, and autobiographies) and voices (vernacular, esoteric, domestic, and female) that have not been sufficiently represented in previous anthologies and standard accounts of Buddhism. Few of the usual canonical texts are here. Moreover, the selections juxtapose materials from different "vehicles," historical periods, and geographical regions that are often regarded as distinct and discontinuous, in an attempt to broaden the range of what we understand Buddhism and the practice of Buddhism to be. The contents and organization of this book are designed to aid in identifying areas of shared concern and continuity, as well as areas of contestation and conflict among the widely varied practices of different Buddhist communities. The texts in which those practices appear, rather than being disinterested reflections of a real world, often reflect an ideal. The ideologies that underlie these ideals and the rhetorics that express them are amply represented here. If this anthology helps us to see Buddhism less as the inevitable unfolding of a distinct and self-identical entity and more as a dynamic process of borrowing, conflict, and interaction between and within traditions that have been identified as Buddhist, it will have achieved its purpose (*siddhārtha*).

This introduction is meant to serve two purposes. First, it will provide a brief historical sketch of the history of Buddhism, in the course of which I will explain how the contents of the volume are, and are not, organized. Second, it will provide a description of some of the Buddhist doctrines that have come to be considered fundamental by the tradition of scholars, both Buddhist and Western.

The life and teachings of the Buddha as they recorded in traditional sources are recounted in some detail below.[1] After the death of the Buddha, the community of his followers is said to have met in a series of councils, each sponsored by a different king, to settle disputes regarding what the Buddha had taught and what rules the monastic order should follow. The Buddha had preached for over forty years to a wide variety of audiences, and there was a concern that those teachings be remembered and preserved before they could be forgotten. This preservation was done orally, with different groups of monks responsible for the memorization and retention of what evolved into a variety of oral canons. None of these was committed to writing until the last decades before the common era, and not in India but in Sri Lanka, some four hundred years after the Buddha's death. Despite the sophisticated mnemonic devices that Buddhist monks employed in preserving these teachings, there can be little certainty as to which of them, if any, were actually the words of the Buddha; there remains debate even about which language the Buddha spoke. Thus, it is no longer tenable to accept the assumption shared by both early Western scholars of Buddhism and Buddhist figures in Southeast Asia (often under Western influence) that what is known as the Theravāda tradition (the tradition of the Elders) found in the Pāli language represents an original Buddhism from which all other forms of Buddhism derived (and sometimes deviated). The original teachings of the historical Buddha are extremely difficult, if not impossible, to recover or reconstruct.

The Buddhist community flourished in India during the Mauryan dynasty (324–187 B.C.E.), especially during the reign of the emperor Aśoka, whose rule extended over most of the Indian subcontinent and who, in a series of rock edicts, professed his faith in the Buddha, his teaching, and the monastic community. Although Aśoka's edicts set forth a generalized morality that allowed him to support many religious groups in his vast kingdom, he is remembered in Buddhist legends as the ideal Buddhist king, deeply devoted to the propagation of the Buddha's teaching and to the support of the monastic community. By the end of Aśoka's reign, Buddhist monks and nuns were established in monasteries throughout the Indian subcontinent, monasteries that were often located near cities and that relied on state support. From this point on, the fortunes of Buddhism in India waxed and waned largely in dependence on the policies of local rulers.

In the first centuries of the common era, a movement, or series of movements, occurred in India that came to be referred to as the *Mahāyāna,* the Great Vehicle. This seems to have begun as a disparate collection of cults centered around newly composed texts and their charismatic expositors, the dharmabhāṇaka. These texts, although composed centuries after the Buddha's death, were accepted by their devotees as sūtras (discourses attributed to the Buddha or spoken with his sanction). Some of the texts, like the *Lotus Sūtra* (discussed below), in addition to proclaiming their own unique potency as the means to salvation, would also praise the veneration of stūpas, the reliquaries in which the remains of the Buddha were enshrined. Other texts, like much of the early Perfection of Wisdom (*prajñāpāramitā*) corpus, would proclaim their superiority to stūpas, declaring themselves to be substitutes for the body and speech of the absent Buddha, equally worthy of veneration and equally efficacious.

It is perhaps best to regard the Mahāyāna as a social movement of monks, nuns, and lay people that began in reaction against the controls exercised by a powerful monastic institution. This movement was responsible for the production and dissemination of a body of literature that challenged the authority of that institution by having the Buddha proclaim a superior and more inclusive path and a more profound wisdom. In subsequent centuries, during which sūtras continued to be composed, the Mahāyāna became not merely a collection of cults of the book but a self-conscious scholastic entity. Adherents of the Mahayana devoted a good deal of energy to surveying what was by then a rather large corpus and then attempting, through a variety of hermeneutical machinations, to craft the myriad doctrines into a philosophical and doctrinal system. In short, it is in this later period that the sūtras, which seem at first to have been recited and worshiped, became the object also of scholastic reflection. The fact that these treatises commonly contain a defense of the Mahāyāna as the authentic word of the Buddha—even treatises composed a millennium after the composition of the first Mahāyāna sūtras—may provide evidence of the minority status of the Mahāyāna in India.

These new movements came to designate themselves by the term "Mahāyāna," the "Great Vehicle" to enlightenment, in contradistinction from the earlier Buddhist schools who did not accept their new sūtras as authoritative (that is, as the word of the Buddha). They disparagingly referred to these earlier schools with the term "Hīnayāna," often rendered euphemistically as the "Lesser Vehicle," although *hīna* means also "inferior," "base," and "vile." Members of these earlier schools, of course, never thought of or referred to themselves as passengers on the Hīnayāna. It has thus become common in Western writing about Buddhism to avoid this term by replacing it with "Theravāda." But the terms "Hīnayāna" and "Theravāda" do not designate the same groups; there is a traditional list of some eighteen Hīnayāna schools with diverse doctrines, only one of which has survived into the present, the Theravāda of Sri Lanka and Southeast Asia, whose works are preserved in the Pāli language.

The term "Mahāyāna" is less objectionable for the reason that it was used self-referentially. Most previous anthologies provide selections from the Pāli texts followed by a sampling from Mahāyāna sūtras, suggesting that with the rise of the Mahāyāna the earlier traditions were both superseded and eclipsed. This is, however, historically inaccurate. The reports of Chinese pilgrims to India in the seventh century indicate that followers of the Mahāyāna and the "Hīnayāna" lived together in monasteries (*vihāras*) and that they all maintained the same "Hīnayāna" monastic vows. The reports further indicate that in many monasteries adherents of the Hīnayāna outnumbered those of the Mahāyāna. Thus, as an alternative to the polemical "Hīnayāna," the term "foundational Buddhism" may be used, referring to the members of Buddhist monastic communities and their supporters who did not accept the legitimacy of the new scriptures composed by followers of the Mahāyāna. As the seventh-century Chinese pilgrim Yijing observed about India, "those who worship bodhisattvas and read Mahāyāna sūtras are called Mahāyāna, while those who do not do this are called the Hīnayāna." The foundational nature and persistence of the Hīnayāna schools in India is often forgotten because of the domination of the Mahāyāna in China, Japan, Korea, Mongolia, and Tibet.

Some five centuries after the rise of the Mahāyāna, another major movement occurred in Indian Buddhism, which was retrospectively designated as the Vajrayāna (the Thunderbolt or Diamond Vehicle). Its origins are even less clearly understood than those of the Mahāyāna. Like "Hīnayāna" and "Mahāyāna," "Vajrayāna" is a retrospective designation, in this case coined to describe a rather disparate set of practices by which the long path to buddhahood could be traversed more quickly than was possible via the Mahāyāna, a path on which various supernormal powers were gained in the process. Some of these practices, such as engaging in behaviors that broke caste taboos, appear to have been borrowed from ascetic movements current in India at the time. Others were developments of themes long present in Buddhist texts, such as the possibility of coming into the presence of the Buddha through visualization practices. Despite the efforts of generations of Buddhist thinkers, it remains exceedingly difficult to identify precisely what it is that sets the Vajrayāna apart. And this difficulty of identifying distinguishing features applies more generally to the issue of distinguishing the Buddhist vehicles, the Hīnayāna, the Mahāyāna, and the Vajrayāna. Adherents of this or that vehicle have much invested in claims to uniqueness. However, one of the purposes of this book is to suggest that these three vehicles share more than is usually assumed.

Anthologies of Buddhist texts have often been organized according to vehicle. One difficulty with such an approach is the almost unavoidable propensity to see the Hīnayāna-Mahāyāna-Vajrayāna sequence as a value-laden development of one kind or another, in which one member of the triad is exalted above the others. According to one view (found especially among European scholars of Buddhism in the nineteenth century), the Hīnayāna (what they called "original Buddhism") was a simple ethical creed of self-reliance, free of ritual elements. In the rise of Mahāyāna, they saw a concession to the masses, in which the Buddha was deified and became an object of worship, and salvation became possible not through diligent practice but through faith in a dizzying pantheon of buddhas and bodhisattvas. The Vajrayāna was an even later development in which, they believed, debased Hindu practices polluted Buddhism until any kind of licentious behavior became accepted.

Another view (found particularly among scholars of Chinese and Japanese Buddhism) also sees the Hīnayāna as an ethical creed, which became an institution of self-satisfied and complacent monks who cared only about their own authority. The Mahāyāna, they believe, was a popular lay movement that sought to restore to the tradition the Buddha's original compassion through the ideal of the bodhisattva, the person who sacrifices his or her own welfare in order to lead all sentient beings in the universe to nirvāṇa. The bodhisattva path is a long one, and requires many millions of lifetimes of practice. According to this view, the Vajrayāna was again a late development, coming at a time when people were no longer interested in dedicating themselves to this protracted path to enlightenment for the sake of others, and imagined that the Vajrayāna provided a shortcut.

Finally, there is the view that sees the Vajrayāna as the pinnacle in the evolution of Buddhism, moving from the austere individualism of the Hīnayāna to the relatively simple compassion of the Mahāyāna, which sees salvation only in the ever-distant future, and finally to the culmination in the Vajrayāna, where buddhahood is possible in this very body and in this very lifetime, not through a suppression of desire and the sensual but through the discovery of ultimate reality even there.

The processes by which Buddhist practices developed through Asia are far more complex than any of these three models suggests. For example, the first model ignores the wealth of rituals and devotional practices found in the Theravāda. The second model ignores the important role played by monks and nuns throughout the history of the Mahāyāna. And the third model places far too much emphasis on the claim of buddhahood in this very lifetime, an important but hardly universal claim of tantric texts. Beyond these specific errors, a more general problem with such an evolutionary (or devolutionary) model is that it suggests that one vehicle ceases or dies out before the next becomes fully formed. Such a suggestion is supported in those anthologies that only provide works from the Pāli "canon," the early collection of works considered by the Theravāda to represent the authentic teachings of the Buddha and his early followers. These anthologies ignore the great mass of literature composed in subsequent centuries in both Pāli and the vernaculars of Southeast Asia, as if the Buddhism of this region essentially ceased its literary output after the fifth century of the common era. Most of the works contained in this volume from Sri Lanka and Southeast Asia date from after this period, and illustrate the continuing vitality of Theravāda Buddhism. In order that readers may see both how an organization by vehicle might be made and how misleading such an organization can be, a table of contents by vehicle is provided.

Buddhist institutions had disappeared in India by the thirteenth century. The reasons for this demise remain much debated. The overt cause was a series of Muslim invasions, beginning in the eleventh century, during which the major monastic centers of northern India were destroyed. There had been persecutions of Buddhism by various Hindu kings in the past, but these had been localized and short-lived, often followed by an infusion of support under another dynasty. In this case, however, no such dynasty arose. It also appears that by the end of the first millennium, the locus of Buddhism in India had become the large monastery, which depended on royal rather than local patronage; the most famous of these was Nālandā, said to have housed ten thousand monks. When such centers were destroyed (as Nālandā was by Turkic troops in 1197), the power and influence of the monastic institutions quickly dissipated. Some scholars argue as well that by this time many Buddhist practices had been incorporated into Hinduism and that the local functions fulfilled by Buddhist monks in the past were being performed by Hindu priests. Historians no longer subscribe to the further claim that Buddhism was already weak during this period due to the degenerating influence of tantra. Indeed, tantric Buddhism has survived in Nepal until the present day in a tradition of Mahāyāna devotionalism officiated by a saṅgha of married priests.

Buddhism is often described as the only pan-Asian religion, the only Asian religion to spread beyond the boundaries of its native culture. This is not entirely accurate. Confucian thought has had a profound influence on Korea and Japan, for example, and Hindu epics, with their gods, demons, and social ideals have shaped the cultures of Southeast Asia. It is true, however, that Buddhism spanned both the Indian and Chinese cultural domains of Asia. But it is important to think not so much of a disembodied dharma descending on another culture from above, but rather of a more material movement—of monks, texts, relics, and icons—along trade routes and across deserts, mountains, and seas.

The Buddha is reported to have exhorted his monks to "go and travel around for the welfare of the multitudes, for the happiness of the multitudes, out of sympathy for the world, for the benefit, welfare, and happiness of gods and humans. No two should go in the same direction." Although this last admonition seems not to have been heeded, it is true that Buddhist "missions" were not large and well-organized movements, and instead often took the form of itinerant monks (or groups of monks) traveling by land and sea in the company of traders and royal emissaries. According to traditional accounts, the first foreign mission was to the island of Sri Lanka, and was led by the son of Aśoka.

In descriptions of Buddhism outside of India, one sometimes encounters the term "Southern Buddhism" to describe the Buddhism of Sri Lanka, Thailand, Cambodia, Burma, Laos, and parts of Vietnam, and the term "Northern Buddhism," used in reference to China, Japan, Korea, Tibet, and Mongolia. It is often said that Southern Buddhism is Theravāda and Northern Buddhism is Mahāyana. This is not historically accurate. Theravāda has been the dominant school of Buddhism in most of Southeast Asia since the thirteenth century, with the establishment of the monarchies in Thailand, Burma, Cambodia, and Laos. Prior to that period, however, many other strands of Buddhism were also widely present, including other Hīnayāna sects, as well as Mahāyāna and tantric groups. The great monument at Borobudur in Java reflects Mahāyāna doctrine, and there are reports of Indian monks traveling to Sumatra to study with Mahāyāna and tantric masters there (see Chapter 42). Indeed, Buddhists texts, icons, and institutions (Hīnayāna, Mahāyāna, and Vajrayāna) were just some of the Indian cultural forms introduced into Southeast Asia by traders and travelers, beginning as early as the fourth century. Buddhist Bengal exerted a strong influence from the ninth through thirteenth centuries, and Sanskrit Mahāyāna and tantric texts were donated to Burmese monasteries as late as the fifteenth century. It was only after the demise of Buddhism in India that the Southeast Asian societies looked especially to Sri Lanka for their Buddhism, where by that time Theravāda was established as the orthodoxy. The monarchs of the kingdoms of Thailand, Burma, Cambodia, and Laos found an effective ideology in Theravāda notions of rulership, often invoking the model of Aśoka.

Just as Southeast Asian Buddhism was not always Theravāda, so "Northern Buddhism" was not always Mahāyāna. The monastic codes practiced in China, Japan, Korea, and Tibet were all derived from the Indian Hīnayāna orders. Furthermore, several of these orders flourished in Central Asia (including parts of modern Iran and Afghanistan), whence Buddhism was first introduced into China via the silk route.

Buddhist monks came to China from the northwest sometime during the first century of the common era. China was the most advanced of the civilizations to encounter Buddhism, as measured in terms of literary culture and the organization of social and political institutions. Unlike Tibet and areas of Southeast Asia, for example, China was not a place to which Buddhist monks brought Indian cultural forms, such as writing, which would powerfully shape the future history of the society. It is sometimes argued that if China had not been suffering a period of political disunity in the first centuries of the common era, Buddhism would never have taken hold. It is also argued that Buddhist institutions tended to be strongest in China when the central government was weakest and that Buddhist institutions existed in a state of atrophy after the Tang. Indeed, the first patrons of the dharma were the leaders of the foreign or "barbarian" dynasties in northern China. However, such claims can be overstated, for the influence of Buddhism on a wide range of Chinese cultural forms, such as vernacular literature, has been and remains profound. It is also often stated that Buddhism did not truly take hold in China until it had been fully "sinified," that is, made Chinese. The chapters from China in this volume (as well as in *Religions of China in Practice*) provide an opportunity to consider the degree to which Chinese Buddhism is Chinese and the degree to which it is Buddhist, as well as an opportunity to ponder the bases upon which such judgments might be made.

Contacts with China brought Buddhist monks into the Korean peninsula in the late fourth century. As elsewhere in Asia, these monks did not simply carry texts and icons, but brought with them many of the products of their own civilization, in this case, that of China. Buddhist institutions thrived especially after the unification of the Korean peninsula under the Silla Dynasty in 668. As had been the case in China and would be the case of Japan, part of the appeal of Buddhism to kings was the claim that worshiping the Buddha, promoting the dharma, and supporting the monastic community would protect the state from foreign invasion and calamity, a view set forth in apocryphal works such as the *Sūtra for Humane*

Kings (translated in part in *Religions of China in Practice*). During this period, a number of Korean monks became influential figures in China, Japan, and even in Tibet.

As in China, Buddhism has been both embraced and condemned in Japan as a foreign religion. In the sixth century, monks from Korea first introduced Buddhist texts and teachings into Japan, which, according to traditional accounts were received with enthusiasm at court (see Chapter 17). Just as Buddhist monks had served as carriers of Indian cultural forms to Southeast Asia, so they brought the products of Chinese civilization to Japan. The Japanese have since looked to China as the source of their Buddhism, and for centuries Japanese monks made the often perilous journey to China to retrieve texts and teachings. These monks, such as the founders of the Tendai and Shingon schools of the Heian period (794–1185), were generally rewarded with imperial support upon their return. During the Kamakura period (1185–1333), when the nation was ruled by a series of military dictators, the shoguns, new sects came to prominence with their patronage. The foremost of these were Zen, Pure Land, and Nichiren, which came to eclipse the previous schools in popular support. In contrast to the more eclectic approach of the Heian sects, each of these three claimed that their single practice offered the only effective means to salvation. Selections from all three appear in this volume.

According to traditional accounts, Buddhist monks did not come to Tibet until the seventh century. As was the case with Japan, Buddhism was initially introduced to the court. Indeed, the Tibetan king is said to have been converted to Buddhism by two princesses—one from China and one from Nepal, but both Buddhists—whom he received in marriage as the result of treaties. The dissemination of Buddhist teachings and institutions in Tibet took place in two waves. The first, during the seventh and eighth centuries, saw royal support for the founding and maintenance of Buddhist monasteries, the invitation of Buddhist teachers from India, and the beginnings of a massive project to translate Buddhist texts from Sanskrit into Tibetan. The Tibetan script is said to have been invented for this purpose. Around 840, a king who was not kindly disposed to the dharma closed the monasteries. He was assassinated four years later by a Buddhist monk, thus ending the Tibetan monarchy. A revival of Buddhism took place in western Tibet almost two centuries later. One of the signal events of this second wave was the invitation of the Indian monk Atiśa (discussed in Chapters 24 and 42). There followed a period of extensive contact with India, when Tibetans went to study at the great monasteries of northern India, often inviting their teachers to come back with them. By the end of the fourteenth century, most of the work of translation had been completed. The Tibetans were able to avoid invasion by the Mongols by serving as preceptors to a succession of Mongol khans, who were the first in a series of foreign patrons for the sects of Tibetan Buddhism. In the seventeenth century, the head of one of these sects, the fifth Dalai Lama, was able to consolidate political power over Tibet with the help of his Mongol patron. A succession of Dalai Lamas (or their regents) continued to rule Tibet until 1959, when the current Dalai Lama was forced to flee to India after the invasion and occupation of his nation by China.

In the history of Buddhism in each of these cultures, it is usually possible to discern two general periods. The first is one of assimilation in which Buddhist practices were introduced, with much attention devoted to the translation of texts, the founding of monasteries (with state support), the establishment of places of pilgrimage, often centered on a relic or icon, and close contact with the culture from which Buddhist cultural forms were being received (for example, India in the case of Tibet, Central Asia in the case of China, China in the case of Japan, Sri Lanka in the case of Thailand, and Tibet in the case of Mongolia). In most cases, the period of assimilation lasted for several centuries. This was followed by a period of adaptation, in which Buddhist forms were more fully integrated into the society and made more distinctively its own. It is during this period that schools developed that did not have precise analogs in Indian Buddhism, local deities were incorporated into the Buddhist pantheon, and Buddhist deities were incorporated into the local pantheon. Of course, the adherents of these new schools and devotees of these local cults would reject the suggestion that their practices could not be traced back directly to the Buddha. This concern with the authentic source of the teaching is evinced in the pan-Asian practice of pilgrimage to Bodhgayā, the site of the Buddha's enlightenment. The history of Buddhism in Asia continues to the present day, as reflected in many chapters of this book.

One element common in other anthologies but largely absent here are philosophical texts. Buddhism has a vast literature dealing with what we term logic, epistemology, and ontology—works that are (depending on one's perspective) as profound or as impenetrable, as rich or as arid, as anything produced in the West. However, like philosophical works in other cultures, Buddhist treatises are the products of a tiny, highly educated elite (largely composed of monks in the Buddhist case) and their works rarely touch the ground where the vast majority of Buddhists have lived their lives. Selections from philosophical works are limited here for two reasons. First, the emphasis of this volume is Buddhism in practice, especially in the more quotidian sense of the term. Second, because Western scholars have shown a strong interest in Buddhist philosophical works over the last century, many translations and studies are already available.

It is important to recall, however, that the Buddhist philosopher was also a Buddhist and, in most cases, a Buddhist monk. He was thus a participant in rituals and institutions that provided the setting for his work. The authors of Buddhist philosophical treatises do not, therefore, fulfill our traditional image of the philosopher engaged in a quest for knowledge "for its own sake," with an overarching concern with logic, rationality, and theoretical consistency. Although these enterprises find an important place in Buddhist traditions, it is also true that for many Buddhist scholastics the faculty of reason provides a relatively superficial awareness, insufficient to the task of directly apprehending the truth. All endeavors in the realm of what might be termed "philosophy" were theoretically subservient to the greater goal of enlightenment, and the ultimate task of the philosopher, at least in theory, was to attain that enlightenment. The Tibetan authors who are regarded as preeminent scholars, for example, devoted great efforts to the performance of tantric rituals or to various sophisticated forms of meditation, in an effort to manifest a fantastic world of benign and malevolent forces, propitiating deities and repelling demons. What we term "philosophy" was but one concern of these authors; a perusal of the titles in the collected works of any of Tibet's most erudite thinkers reveals that among the commentaries on Indian logical treatises and expositions of emptiness are myriad works devoted to tantric ceremonies and visualizations, along with instructions on techniques for drawing maṇḍalas, making rain, stopping smallpox, and manufacturing magical pills. The biographies of the most famous Buddhist philosophers are replete with the most extraordinary events (see Chapter 41). Thus, although there is a large and significant body of Buddhist literature devoted to such issues as the validity of sense experience and inference as sources of knowledge, the study of such texts must be undertaken with careful attention to their contexts, in the broadest sense of the term, so that the ideas and arguments are not regarded as denizens of a free-floating world, whether that world be the history of ideas or the dharma.

The forty-eight chapters of this volume are divided according to the most traditional of Buddhist categories, the three jewels: of the Buddha, the dharma, and the saṅgha, that is, the Buddha, his teachings, and the community of his followers. In Buddhist texts, a Buddhist is defined as someone who takes refuge in these three, and the refuge ceremony is the most widely performed ritual in the Buddhist world. The Buddha, dharma, and saṅgha are called jewels because they are precious and rare. It is said that it is difficult to encounter them in the cycle of rebirth and when they are encountered they are of great value. The notion of refuge suggests two points fundamental to the Buddhist worldview. The first is that sentient beings are in need of protection, of a place of refuge where they can escape from the sufferings of saṃsāra, the cycle of rebirths. The second point is that the three jewels can provide such protection, that they themselves are free from the dangers and vicissitudes of saṃsāra, and thus can offer refuge to others. In the medical metaphor of which Buddhists are so fond, the Buddha is the doctor, the dharma is the medicine, and the saṅgha are the nurses. It is the Buddha who finds the path to liberation and shows it to others. The dharma is the path itself, and the saṅgha are one's companions who offer assistance along the way.

Before discussing the three jewels in more detail, it would be useful here to outline some of the doctrines most basic to Buddhist practices, as they have been understood by Buddhist authors and by Western scholars. Although there are significant variations among Buddhist cultures, Buddhists in Asia generally accept a view of the universe and of the afterlife that originated in India. Some elements of this cosmology seem to have been current in India at the time of the Buddha, whereas others are the results of elaborations by Buddhist thinkers, perhaps including the Buddha himself. The most standard cosmology divides the universe into three realms, called the realm of desire (*kāmadhātu*), the realm of form (*rūpadhātu*) and the formless realm (*arūpyadhātu*).

The realm of desire is the universe inhabited by humans. Its topography is symmetrical, with four islands surrounding a central mountain, Mount Meru (or Sumeru). Ours is the southern island, called Jambudvīpa (Rose-Apple Island). The other three islands are also inhabited by humans (although of different height and lifespan), but are generally regarded as inaccessible; a buddha can become enlightened only in Jambudvīpa. Mount Meru is the abode of a class of beings called *asuras,* often translated as "demigod" or "titan." They are usually depicted as mean-spirited lesser deities who can bring harm to humans. At a higher elevation on and above Mount Meru is the abode of six classes of gods (*deva*) who inhabit increasingly pleasant realms for increasingly long lifespans. The first two godly realms are on Mount Meru itself. The lower is that of the four royal lineages, ruled by the guardians of the cardinal directions. Next is the "Heaven of the Thirty-Three," on the flat summit of Mount Meru, where thirty-three gods abide. Here, as elsewhere, we see Buddhists assimilating elements from rival groups or other cultures, because thirty-three is the traditional number of gods in the *Ṛg Veda.* Although early Buddhists rejected any ultimate power for Vedic deities, such as Indra, they nonetheless incorporated them into their pantheon, acknowledging their worldly powers but placing them on the second lowest rung of their heavenly hierarchy. Indeed, throughout Buddhist cultures, the worship of local deities is not proscribed, unless that worship involves animal sacrifice. Gods are honored for the boons they can bestow. The thirty-three gods live very long lives: their lifespan is one thousand years, but each of their days is equal to one hundred human years. Yet they are not immortal; they are also subject to rebirth. The remaining four heavens of the realm of desire float in the sky above the summit of Mount Meru. It is in the fourth of the six godly realms, called Tuṣita (Joyous) that the future Buddha, Maitreya, waits.

Also inhabiting the realm of desire are, of course, all manner of animal and insect life, as well as a pitiful class of beings called *pretas,* usually translated as "ghosts" or "hungry ghosts." These beings—some of whom are visible to humans, some of whom are not—are depicted iconographically with huge, distended bellies and emaciated limbs. Their throats are said to be the size of the eye of a needle, rendering them constantly hungry and thirsty and forcing them to search constantly for food and drink. The feeding of these beings was seen as a special responsibility of Buddhist monks and nuns. Located far below Jambudvīpa (usually measured from Bodhgayā, the place in India where the Buddha achieved enlightenment) in the realm of desire is an extensive system of hells, some burning hot, others freezing cold. The beings there undergo a variety of tortures, often depicted in gruesome detail in Buddhist texts and paintings.

The realm of form is situated above the realm of desire and is regarded as superior to it. The beings here are gods who experience the pleasures of sight, sound, and touch, but not taste and smell. They are distinguished from the gods of the realm of desire by their greater powers of concentration, which provide deep states of mental bliss. There are four major levels within the realm of form, categorized by the increasing power of concentration of its inhabitants. Even more sublime is the formless realm, where gods exist in states of pure consciousness, without bodies and sense organs. This is considered the most blissful of abodes, yet it does not receive a great deal of attention in Buddhist literature outside the psychological treatises.

This universe has no beginning, although its physical constituents pass through a fourfold cosmic cycle of evolution, stasis, devolution, and vacuity. Mount Meru and its surrounding islands are said to have evolved over a period of eons, during which, according to one of the Buddhist creation myths, they came to be populated. At the beginning of this process, the lifespan of humans is said to have been immeasurable. Human life had an Edenic quality about it: there was no need for food and humans illuminated the world with their own inner light. As the result of curiosity and desire (to taste the milky froth that covered the surface of the earth), humans began to eat, which required that they expel waste. Their bodies developed accordingly, leading eventually to sexual intercourse. Their natural light faded, the sun and moon appeared, and they began to hoard food for themselves, creating private property for the first time; the eventual result was human society. The human lifespan also gradually diminished until it reached an average of one hundred years, at which point the Buddha appeared in the world to teach the dharma. The quality of human life and the human life span will continue to decline until it reaches ten years of age, coinciding with a time of pestilence, poverty, and warfare. All memory of the Buddha and his teaching will have disappeared from the world. The human lifespan will then begin to increase once more, until it reaches eighty thousand years again, at which point the next buddha will appear. At the end of twenty such cycles, this universe will gradually be destroyed and will then enter into a long period of vacuity, after which a new universe will be created. As the current Dalai Lama has said, Buddhists do not believe in one Big Bang, they believe in many Big Bangs.

The realm of desire, the realm of form, and the formless realm are not only locations in the Buddhist universe, they are also places of rebirth. Buddhists conceive of a cycle of birth and death, called *saṃsāra* (wandering), in six realms of rebirth: those of the gods, demigods, humans, animals, ghosts, and hell beings (although sometimes the realm of demigods is omitted). The entire cycle of rebirth in which the creations and destructions of universes is encompassed has no ultimate beginning. The realms of animals, ghosts, and hell beings are regarded as places of great suffering, whereas the godly realms are abodes of great bliss. Human rebirth falls in between, bringing as it does both pleasure and pain. The engine of saṃsāra is driven by karma, the cause and effect of actions. Like adherents of other Indian religions, Buddhists believe that every intentional act, whether it be physical, verbal, or mental, leaves a residue. That residue, like a seed, will eventually produce an effect at some point in the future, an effect in the form of pleasure or pain for the person who performed the act. Thus Buddhists conceive of a moral universe in which virtuous deeds create experiences of pleasure and nonvirtuous deeds create experiences of pain. These latter are often delineated in a list of ten nonvirtuous deeds: killing, stealing, sexual misconduct, lying, divisive speech, harsh speech, senseless speech, covetousness, harmful intent, and wrong view. Wrong view can mean many things in Buddhist thought, but here refers especially to the belief that actions do not have effects. Buddhist texts provide extensive discussions of the specific deeds that constitute these ten nonvirtues and their respective karmic weight. The ten virtues are the opposites of this list: sustaining life, giving gifts, maintaining sexual decorum, and so on.

These deeds not only determine the quality of a given life but also determine the place of the rebirth after death. Depending on the gravity of a negative deed (killing being more serious than senseless speech and killing a human more serious than killing an insect, for example) one may be reborn as an animal, a ghost, or in one of the hot or cold hells, where the life span is particularly lengthy. Among the hells, some are more horrific than others; the most tortuous is reserved for those who have committed one of five heinous deeds: killing one's father, killing one's mother, killing an arhat, wounding a buddha, and causing dissent in the saṅgha.

Rebirth as a god or human in the realm of desire is the result of a virtuous deed, and is considered very rare. Rarer still is rebirth as a human who has access to the teachings of the Buddha. In a famous analogy, a single blind tortoise is said to swim in a vast ocean, surfacing for air only once every century. On the surface of the ocean floats a single golden yoke. It is rarer, said the Buddha, to be reborn as a human with the opportunity to practice the dharma than it is for the tortoise to surface for its centennial breath with its head through the hole in the golden yoke. One is said to be reborn as a god in the realm of desire as a result of an act of charity: giving gifts results in future wealth. Rebirth as a human is said to result from consciously refraining from a nonvirtuous deed, as when one takes a vow not to kill humans. The vast majority of Buddhist practice throughout Asia and throughout history has been directed toward securing rebirth as a human or (preferably) a god in the next lifetime, generally through acts of charity directed toward monks and monastic institutions. Despite repeated admonitions that birth as a god is a temporary state from which one must eventually fall, to be reborn in a lower realm—admonitions such as those made by the twentieth-century Thai monk Buddhadāsa (Chapter 33)—a happy life and an auspicious rebirth have remained goals more sought after than escape from saṃsāra into nirvāṇa. Indeed, much Buddhist literature intended for both monks and lay people has promoted a social ideal, defining the good life and explaining how to lead it, as in Chapter 35.

Rebirth as a god in the realm of form or formless realm is achieved somewhat differently. Because these realms are characterized by deep states of concentration, one must achieve one of those states in this life through the practice of meditation in order to be reborn there in the next. For example, one must reach the third level of concentration in order to be reborn as a god in the third level of the realm of form. Because these states require a specialized and sustained practice, they have been little sought as places of rebirth. The formless realm in particular seems to have been more important as an abode to which non-Buddhist meditation masters could be consigned. For example, such a master may have wrongly imagined that he had achieved the ultimate state and liberation from rebirth, when in fact he was only in the realm of infinite consciousness of the formless realm, from which he would eventually be reborn into a lower abode; liberation is possible only by following the teachings of the Buddha.

In the Mahāyāna sūtras, a further cosmic wrinkle is provided by the description of buddha fields (*buddhakṣetra*) or "pure lands," worlds created by buddhas and presided over by them. Through a variety of pious acts, humans can be reborn in these blissful abodes, where the conditions are ideal for rapid progress on the path to enlightenment. The marvels of the pure lands are described in elaborate detail in certain Mahāyāna sūtras, which tell of every variety of jewel growing from trees, streams of variable temperature for bathing, and soothing breezes that carry sermons appropriate to each listener. Rebirth in one of these lands became a prominent goal of Buddhist practice in India, China, and Japan, where it seemed to serve as either a replacement or a temporary substitute for the purportedly greater goal of buddhahood. In some Mahāyāna sūtras, the notion of the buddha field was given a somewhat different twist with the claim that this benighted world in which humans now live is in reality itself a buddha field; it need only be recognized as such. This view was to be important in tantric Buddhism.

A brief description of the Buddha, the dharma, and the saṅgha follows below, interspersed with references to each of the chapters in this book. The contents are organized under these three headings both to reflect this most traditional of Buddhist categories and to call these categories into question by demonstrating the myriad ways in which Buddhists have answered the questions: Who is the Buddha? What is the dharma? And who belongs to the saṅgha?

The Buddha

Scholars are increasingly reluctant to make unqualified claims about the historical facts of the Buddha's life and teachings. There is even a difference of opinion concerning the years of his birth and death. The long accepted dates of 563–483 B.C.E. have recently been called into question with the suggestion that the Buddha may have lived and died as much as a century later.

The traditional accounts of the Buddha's life are largely hagiographic and tend to include the following narrative. It tells of the miraculous birth of a prince of the warrior (*kṣatriya*) caste in a kingdom in what is today southern Nepal. Astrologers predict that the prince, named Siddhārtha ("He Who Achieves His Goal") will be either a great king or a great religious teacher. His father the king, apparently convinced that dissatisfaction with the world is what causes one's mind to turn to existential questions and the spiritual quest, is determined to protect his son from all that is unpleasant, and keeps him in a palace where he is surrounded by beauty and all forms of sport and delight. Only at the age of twenty-nine does the prince become sufficiently curious about the world beyond the palace walls to venture forth on four chariot rides. During the first he sees an old person for the first time in his life, and is informed by his charioteer that this is not the only old man in the world, but that old age eventually befalls everyone. On the next tour he sees a sick person, on the next a corpse. It is only then that he learns of the existence of sickness and death. On his final chariot ride he sees a religious mendicant, who has renounced the world in search of freedom from birth and death. He decides to follow a similar path and, against his father's orders and leaving behind his wife and infant son, goes forth from the life of a householder in search of liberation from suffering.

Over a period of six years he engages in a number of the yogic disciplines current in India at the time, including severe asceticism, and concludes that mortification of the flesh is not conducive to progress toward his goal of freedom from birth, aging, sickness, and death. He eventually sits beneath a tree and meditates all night. After repulsing an attack by the evil deity Māra and his armies, at dawn he comes to a realization that makes him the Buddha ("Awakened One"), forever free from future rebirth. Exactly what it was that he understood on that full-moon night has remained a source of both inspiration and contention throughout the history of Buddhism. Some accounts say that the content of the enlightenment was so profound that the Buddha was initially reluctant to try to teach it to others, and decided otherwise only after being beseeched by the great god Brahmā, himself subject to rebirth and hence desirous of liberation. In this volume, the life of the Buddha and the content of his enlightenment is recounted in a Thai ritual for consecrating (that is, animating) a statue of the Buddha, and in the lament of the wife he deserted (Chapters 2 and 43).

The Buddha was one of an infinite series of buddhas, all of whom reached their exalted state in the same manner, at exactly the same spot in India under one or another species of bodhi tree. When the Buddha gained enlightenment (*bodhi*), he did so all at once, in an instant, and his realization of the truth was perfect. He also made his momentous discovery by himself, without the aid of a teacher. It was this fact above all that distinguished the Buddha from his enlightened disciples, called *arhats,* in the early tradition. The disciples had to rely on his teachings to realize nirvāṇa, and typically did so only in stages. The Buddha was able to reach his enlightenment on his own and in a single night of meditation because he had previously devoted himself to the practice of virtues such as generosity, patience, and effort over countless previous lifetimes. In one of his previous lives, in the presence of a previous buddha, he had made the firm resolution to become a buddha himself at a future time when the path to liberation had been lost; he had dedicated his practice of virtue over the next eons of rebirth to that goal.

Seven weeks after his enlightenment, the Buddha is said to have walked to the city of Varanasi (Banaras) and to a deer park on its outskirts, where he encountered five renunciates with whom he had previously practiced asceticism. To them he gave his first teaching, usually referred to as the "four noble truths." However, it is not the truths that are noble. The term is perhaps less euphoniously but more accurately rendered as the "four truths for nobles." The term "noble" or "superior" in Sanskrit is *āryan,* the term with which the Indo-European invaders of India had described themselves and which Buddhism appropriated to mean one who is spiritually superior, that is, who has had a vision of a state beyond birth and death. The four things that the Buddha set forth to the five ascetics are known to be true by such people, not by others. Although some Mahāyāna texts dispute that this was the Buddha's very first teaching after his enlightenment, all agree that the teaching of the four truths was of great importance. Over the centuries it has received numerous renditions, the general contours of which follow.

The first truth is that life is inherently unsatisfactory, qualified as it inevitably is by birth, aging, sickness, and death. Various forms of suffering are delineated in Buddhist texts, including the fact that beings must separate from friends and meet with enemies, that they encounter what they do not want, and do not find what they want. The fundamental problem is presented as one of a lack of control over future events; a person wanders constantly from situation to situation, from rebirth to rebirth without companions, discarding one body to take on another, with no certainty or satisfaction, sometimes exalted and sometimes debased. Briefly stated, the problem is change or, as more commonly rendered, impermanence (*anitya*). Because suffering can occur at any moment without warning, even pleasure is in a sense a form of pain, because it will eventually be replaced by pain; there is no activity in which one can engage that will not, in the short or long term, become either physically or mentally painful.

The second truth is the cause of this suffering, identified as action (*karma*), specifically nonvirtuous action, and the negative mental states that motivate such action. As described above, the experience of pleasure and pain is the direct result of actions performed in the past. These actions are motivated by states of mind called *kleśas* (often translated as "afflictions" or "defilements"), the most important of which are desire, hatred, and ignorance. The exact content of this ignorance is again the subject of extensive discussion in Buddhist literature, but it is represented as an active misconception of the nature of reality, usually described as a belief in self (*ātman*). There is, in fact, no permanent and autonomous self in the mind or the body, and to believe otherwise is the root cause of all suffering. It is this imagined self that is inflamed by desire and defended by hatred. As long as one believes in the illusion of self, one will continue to engage in deeds and accumulate karma, and will remain in the cycle of rebirth. This belief in self, in short, is not merely a philosophical problem, but is the cause of the egotism and selfishness that harm others now and oneself in the future through the negative karma they create (see Chapter 32).

The third truth is the truth of cessation, the postulation of a state beyond suffering. If suffering is caused by negative karma, and karma is caused by desire and hatred, and desire and hatred are caused by ignorance, it follows that if one could destroy ignorance then everything caused by ignorance, directly or indirectly, would also be destroyed. There would be a cessation of suffering. This state of cessation is called *nirvāṇa* ("passing away") and, again, a remarkable range of opinion has been expressed concerning the precise nature of this state beyond suffering—whether it is the cessation also of mind and body or whether the person persists in nirvāṇa.

The postulation of a state beyond suffering would be of little interest if there were not some means to achieve it. The fourth truth, then, is the path, the technique for putting an end to ignorance. Diverse renditions of this path are represented in the chapters of this book. One useful way to approach the topic is through the traditional triad of ethics, meditation, and wisdom. Ethics refers to the conscious restraint of nonvirtuous deeds of body and speech, usually through observing some form of vows. Meditation (*dhyāna*), in this context, refers to developing a sufficient level of concentration (through a wide variety of techniques) to make the mind a suitable tool for breaking through the illusion of self to the vision of nirvāṇa. Wisdom is insight, at a deep level of concentration, into the fact that there is no self. Such wisdom is said not only to prevent the accumulation of future karma but eventually to destroy all past karma so that upon death one is not reborn but passes into nirvāṇa. A person who has achieved that state is called an *arhat* ("worthy one"). Two paths to becoming an arhat were set forth. The first was that of the *śravaka* ("listener"), who hears the Buddha's teachings and then puts them into practice. The second was the *pratyekabuddha* ("privately awakened one") who becomes an arhat in solitude.

It is important to reiterate that although many Buddhists throughout history have known the teaching of the four truths in more or less detail, not very many have actively set out to destroy the ignorance of self and achieve nirvāṇa through the practice of meditation. Lay people tended to see this as the business of monks, and most monks tended to see it as the business of the relatively few among them who seriously practiced meditation. Even for such monks, the practice of meditation should be understood as a ritual act in a ritual setting, replete with devotions to the three jewels (see Chapter 16).

If the Buddha taught the four truths, he also must have taught many other things over the course of the four decades that followed his enlightenment. He is renowned for his ability to teach what was appropriate for a particular person, for adapting his message to the situation. Indeed, in the more spectacular descriptions of his pedagogical powers it was said that the Buddha could sit before an audience and simply utter the letter *a* and each person in the audience would hear a discourse designed specifically to meet his or her needs and capacities, in his or her native language. What he taught was represented as a truth that he had not invented but discovered, a truth that had been discovered by other buddhas in the past and would be discovered by buddhas in the future. Importantly, this truth, whatever it may be, was portrayed as something that could be taught, that could be passed on from one person to another, in a variety of languages. It is in this sense that we may speak of a Buddhist tradition. At the same time, the emphasis on the flexibility of the Buddha's teaching helps to account for the remarkable range of practices described as "Buddhist."

According to traditional accounts, at the age of eighty the Buddha died, or passed into nirvāṇa. He is said to have instructed his followers to cremate his body and distribute the relics that remained among various groups of his followers, who were to enshrine them in hemispherical reliquaries called stūpas. For all Buddhist schools, the stūpa became a reference point denoting the Buddha's presence in the landscape. Early texts and the archeological records link stūpa worship with the Buddha's life and especially the key sites in his career, such as the site of his birth, enlightenment, first teaching, and death. A standard list of eight shrines is recommended for pilgrimage and veneration. However, stūpas are also found at places that were sacred for other reasons, often associated with a local deity. Stūpas were constructed for past buddhas and for prominent disciples of the Buddha. Indeed, as suggested in Chapter 38, stūpas dedicated to disciples of the Buddha may have been especially popular because the monastic rules stipulate that donations to such stūpas became the property of the monastery, whereas donations to stūpas of the Buddha remained the property of the Buddha, who continued to function as a legal resident of most monasteries in what was called "the perfumed chamber."

The Mahāyāna stūpa later became a symbol of buddhahood's omnipresence, a center of text revelation, a place guaranteeing rebirth in a pure land. By the seventh century, the practice of enshrining the physical relics of the Buddha ceases to appear in the archaeological record. Instead, one finds stūpas filled with small clay tablets that have been stamped or engraved with a four-line verse that was regarded as the essence of the Buddha's teaching: "The Tathāgata has explained the cause of all things that arise from a cause. The great renunciate has also explained their cessation." Although this pithy statement is subject to wide interpretation, we can see here an intimation of the four truths: the Buddha has identified that suffering arises from the cause of ignorance and he has also identified nirvāṇa, the cessation of suffering. It is said that the wisest of the disciples, Śāriputra, decided to become the Buddha's follower upon simply hearing these words spoken by a monk, in the absence of the Buddha. But of perhaps greater importance in this context is the fact that this statement functions as a slogan, a mantra, and as a substitute for the relics of the Buddha to be enshrined in a stūpa. The teaching has become the teacher (see Chapter 3).

Stūpas were pivotal in the social history of Buddhism: these monuments became magnets attracting monastery building and votive construction, as well as local ritual traditions and regional pilgrimage. The economics of Buddhist devotionalism at these centers generated income for local monasteries, artisans, and merchants, an alliance basic to Buddhism throughout its history. At these geographical centers arrayed around the symbolic monument, diverse devotional exertions, textual studies, and devotees' mercantile pursuits could all prosper. The great stūpa complexes—monasteries with endowed lands, a pilgrimage center, a market, and support from the state—represent central points in the Buddhist polities of Central, South, and Southeast Asia. The great benefits of venerating a stūpa are extolled in Chapter 28.

The Buddha was also worshiped in paintings and statues. The production and worship of Buddhist icons—whether images of buddhas such as Śākyamuni and Amitābha, or bodhisattvas such as Avalokiteśvara and Maitreya—has been a central feature of Buddhist religious life throughout Asian history. As is clear in Chapter 3, the worship of Buddhist icons was promoted by sūtras, and sponsoring the production of an icon was considered an act of great merit, as was bathing an image, a practice that continues in Southeast Asia, China, and Japan. A common goal of both devotional and ascetic Buddhist practice was to recollect the good qualities of the Buddha, which sometimes led to seeing the Buddha "face to face." Images of the Buddha seem to have been important aids in such practices, in part because, far from being a "symbol" of the departed master, images of the Buddha were ritually animated in consecration ceremonies intended to transform an inanimate image into a living deity (see Chapter 2). Icons thus empowered were treated as spiritual beings possessed of magical powers, to be worshiped with regular offerings of incense, flowers, food, money, and other assorted valuables. Buddhist literature from all over Asia is replete with tales of miraculous occurrences associated with such images.

The Buddha was thus the object of elaborate ritual devotions, often accompanied by recitations of his myriad virtues and powers (see Chapter 1). These devotions were later incorporated into a larger liturgy that included the visualization of vast offerings and the confession of misdeeds (see Chapter 14). But not all buddhas were so extraordinary. Indeed, the Japanese Zen master Dōgen went to some lengths to explain why the extraordinary telepathic powers that were supposedly a standard byproduct of enlightenment were not necessarily possessed by enlightened Zen masters in China. The true Zen master is utterly beyond all such categories of Buddhist doctrine (see Chapter 4).

The question arose early as to the object of devotion in the universal practice of taking refuge in the three jewels: the Buddha, the dharma, and the saṅgha. In some formulations, the Buddha was regarded as having a physical body that was the result of past karma; it consisted of his contaminated aggregates (*skandha*), the final residue of the ignorance that had bound him in saṃsāra until his last lifetime. Because that body was the product of ignorance and subject to disintegration, it was not considered suitable as an object of veneration, as the Buddha-jewel. The Buddha was at the same time said to possess certain qualities (also called *dharma*) that are uncontaminated by ignorance, such as his pure ethics, his deep concentration, his wisdom, his knowledge that he has destroyed all afflictions, and his knowledge that the afflictions will not recur. The qualities were later categorized as the eighteen unshared qualities of a buddha's uncontaminated wisdom (see Chapter 1). This "body of [uncontaminated] qualities" was deemed the true object of the practice of refuge. Thus, the term "body" came to shift its meaning from the physical form of the Buddha, corporeal extension in space and over time, to a collection of timeless abstract virtues. In addition, the early community had to account for those fantastic elements in the Buddha's hagiography such as his visit to his mother, who had died shortly after his birth and been reborn in the Heaven of the Thirty-Three. The Buddha is said to have made use of a "mind-made body" for his celestial journey. These notions were later systematized into a three-body theory encompassing the physical body (*rūpakāya*), the body of uncontaminated qualities (*dharmakāya*), and the mind-made or emanation body (*nirmāṇakāya*).

In Mahāyāna literature also there is a doctrine of the three bodies of the Buddha. There we find references to the dharmakāya as almost a cosmic principle, an ultimate reality in which all buddhas partake through their omniscient minds. After the dharmakāya comes the enjoyment body (*saṃbhogakāya*), a fantastic form of a buddha that resides only in the highest pure lands, adorned with thirty-two major and eighty minor physical marks, eternally teaching the Mahāyāna to highly advanced bodhisattvas; the enjoyment body does not appear to ordinary beings. The third body is the emanation body (*nirmāṇakāya*). It is this body that appears in the world to teach the dharma. Thus we can discern an important change in the development of the conception of the Buddha in India: whereas in the earlier tradition, the nirmāṇakāya had been that specialized body employed by the Buddha for the performance of occasional supernormal excursions, in the Mahāyāna there is no buddha that ever appears in the world other than the nirmāṇakāya. All of the deeds of the Buddha are permutations of the emanation body—they are all magical creations, the reflexive functions of the dharmakāya. These functions are by no means random. Indeed, the biography of the Buddha is transformed from the linear narration of a unique event into a paradigm, reduplicated precisely by all the buddhas of the past, present, and future in twelve deeds: descent from the Joyous Pure Land, entry into his mother's womb, being born, becoming skilled in arts and sports as a youth, keeping a harem, taking four trips outside the city that cause him to renounce the world, practicing austerities for six years, sitting under the bodhi tree, defeating Māra and his hosts, attaining enlightenment, turning the wheel of doctrine, and passing into nirvāṇa.

The effects of this final deed have long been felt by Buddhist communities. Their sense of loss was not limited to the direct disciples of the Buddha but has been expressed by generations of future followers, often in the form of the lament that one's negative karma caused one to be reborn someplace other than northern India during the lifetime of the Buddha, that one's misdeeds prevented one from joining the audience of the Buddha's teaching. A standard part of Buddhist rituals became the request that other buddhas not pass into nirvāṇa but remain in the world for an eon, which they could do if they wished (see Chapter 14). Such a request to the current Dalai Lama of Tibet, regarded by his followers as a buddha, is translated in Chapter 12.

The absence of the Buddha has remained a powerful motif in Buddhist history, and remedies have taken a wide variety of forms. In Burma, secret societies, with possible antecedents in tantric traditions, concentrate their energies on kinds of supernormal power that the mainstream tradition regards with some suspicion. Specifically, they engage in longevity practices to allow them to live until the coming of the next buddha, Maitreya (see Chapter 30). In China and Japan, rituals constructed around the chanting of the name of the buddha Amitābha offer a means of being delivered at death into the presence of a buddha who is not present here but is present now, elsewhere, in the western paradise of Sukhāvatī (see Chapters 31 and 48).

With the absence of the historical Buddha, a variety of substitutes were conceived to take his place. One such substitute was the icon, as we already noted. Another was the written text of his teaching, the sūtra, described below. In the absence of the Buddha, the transcendent principle of his enlightenment, sometimes called the buddha nature, became the subject of a wide range of doctrinal speculation, devotion, and practice. This impersonal principle, which made possible the transformation of Prince Siddhārtha from an ignorant and suffering human being into an omniscient and blissful buddha, was most commonly referred to as the *tathāgatagarbha. Tathāgata,* "One Who Has Thus Come [or Gone]" is one of the standard epithets of the Buddha. *Garbha* has a wide range of meanings, including "essence" and "womb," which were exploited in works like the *Tathāgatagarbha Sūtra* (translated in Chapter 7), a popular and influential Mahāyāna work which declared that this seed or potential for buddhahood resides equally in all beings, and it needs only to be developed. A related work, translated in Chapter 8, states that everything in the universe contains in itself the entire universe, and that, therefore, the wisdom of a buddha is fully present in each and every being. Such an impersonal principle was not only an important point of doctrine but could also be the object of devotion and praise, prompting the Japanese monk Myōe to address an island as the Buddha. In so doing, Myōe, who had desired to go to India, was able to find the Buddha in Japan (see Chapter 6).

There is a vacillation in the metaphors and similes employed in these texts as if between two models of the means of making manifest the buddha nature, of achieving enlightenment. One model regards the buddha nature as something pure that has been polluted. The process of the path, therefore, is a gradual process of purification, removing defilements through a variety of practices until the utter transformation from afflicted sentient being to perfect buddha has been effected. Other tropes in these texts, however, do not suggest a developmental model but employ instead a rhetoric of discovery: buddhahood is always already fully present in each being. It need only be recognized. It was this latter model that exercised particular influence in the Chan and Zen schools of China and Japan, which were at least rhetorically dismissive of standard doctrinal categories and traditional practices. Such an attitude is evident in the homily of an early Japanese Zen teacher (see Chapter 15). And in Tibet, the most ancient Buddhist school spoke of a first buddha, a primordial buddha who is the fundamental embodiment of enlightenment. A widely recited hymn to this buddha is found in Chapter 5.

One of the earliest substitutes for the Buddha was the wisdom by which he became enlightened and, by extension, the texts that contained that wisdom. This wisdom was called the "perfection of wisdom" (*prajñāpāramitā*). In part because it was this wisdom that metaphorically gave birth to the Buddha and, in part, because the word *prajñāpāramitā* is in the feminine gender in Sanskrit, this wisdom was anthropomorphized and worshiped as a goddess, referred to sometimes as Prajñāpāramitā, sometimes as "the Great Mother." But not all of the important female figures in Buddhism have been anthropomorphized principles. In Chapter 10, the eighth-century queen of Tibet is identified as a female buddha, and the tantric symbolism of her vagina as the source of enlightenment is set forth. Chapter 9 tells the story of Gotamī, not the Buddha's metaphorical mother, but his aunt and foster-mother (his own mother died shortly after his birth). She was instrumental in convincing the Buddha to establish the order of nuns, and her life story has served as a female parallel to the life of the Buddha. The account of her passage into nirvāṇa included here clearly mimics the story of the Buddha's death.

Perhaps the most popular substitute for the absent Buddha, however, was the bodhisattva. The Buddha is said to have been able to remember all of his past lives, and he is said to have employed his prodigious memory to recount events from those lives. The Buddha's remarkable memory provided a scriptural justification for the appropriation of a diverse body of folklore into the canon. The Jātakas ("Birth Stories"), of which there are over five hundred, were transformed from an Indian version of Aesop's Fables into the word of the Buddha by a conclusion appended to each story, in which the Buddha represents the tale as the recollection of one of his former lives and inevitably identifies himself as the protagonist ("in that existence the otter was Ānanda, the jackal was Maudgalyāyana, the monkey was Śāriputra, and I was the wise hare"). In these tales, the Buddha is referred to as the *bodhisattva,* a term widely etymologized in later literature, but which generally means a person who is intent on the attainment of bodhi, enlightenment. If very few Buddhists felt that they could emulate the Buddha in his last life by leaving their families, living the life of an ascetic, and practicing meditation, the stories of the Buddha's previous lives provided a more accessible model. Stories of the Bodhisattva's deeds of generosity, morality, patience, and perseverance against great odds have remained among the most popular forms of Buddhist literature, both written and oral, and both in the Jātaka tales and in another genre called Avadāna, an example of which is translated in Chapter 11.

In the early Mahāyāna sūtras, the bodhisattva's deeds were represented not merely as an inspiration but as a model to be scrupulously emulated. Earlier in the tradition, the goal had been to follow the path set forth by the Buddha and become liberated from rebirth as an arhat. But in the Mahāyāna, the goal became to do not what the Buddha said but what he did: to follow a much, much longer path to become a buddha oneself. It seems that, at least in the time of the Buddha, it had been possible to become an arhat in one lifetime. Later Mahāyāna exegetes would calculate that, from the time that one made buddhahood one's goal until buddhahood was achieved, a minimum of 384×10^{58} years was required. This amount of time was needed to accumulate the vast stores of merit and wisdom that would result in the omniscience of a buddha, who was able to teach the path to liberation more effectively than any other because of his telepathic knowledge of the capacities and interests of his disciples. It was not the case, then, that bodhisattvas were postponing their enlightenment as buddhas; instead, they would forego the lesser enlightenment of the arhat, which offered freedom from suffering for oneself alone, in favor of the greater enlightenment of a buddha, whereby others could also be liberated.

Formal ceremonies were designed for taking the vow to become a bodhisattva and then follow the long bodhisattva path to buddhahood in order to liberate others from saṃsāra. This included the promise to follow a specific code of conduct (see Chapter 39). At those ceremonies, the officiant, speaking as the Buddha, would declare that a particular disciple, at a point several eons in the future, would complete the long bodhisattva path and become a buddha of such and such a name, presiding over such and such a pure land. So, with the rise of the Mahāyāna we see the goal of enlightenment recede to a point beyond the horizon, but with the millions of intervening lives, beginning with this one, consecrated by the Buddha's prophecy that these present lives are a future buddha's former lives, part of a buddha's story and thus sacred history.

But the bodhisattva was not simply an object of emulation; the bodhisattva was also an object of devotion, for if the bodhisattva had vowed to liberate all beings in the universe from suffering, all beings were the object of the bodhisattva's compassionate deeds. The bodhisattvas mentioned in the Mahāyāna sūtras were worshiped for the varieties of mundane and supramundane succor they could bestow—bodhisattvas such as Mañjuśrī, the bodhisattva of wisdom; Kṣitigarbha, who as Jizō in Japan rescues children, both born and unborn; Maitreya, the bodhisattva who will become the next buddha; and most of all, Avalokiteśvara, the most widely worshiped bodhisattva, who takes a female form as Guanyin in China (see Chapter 13) and Kannon in Japan, and who in Tibet takes human form in the succession of Dalai Lamas (see Chapter 12).

Yet another substitute for the absent Buddha is to be found in the Vajrayāna, in which rituals (called *sādhana,* literally, "means of achievement") are set forth in which the practitioner, through a practice of visualization, petitions a buddha or bodhisattva to come into the practitioner's presence. Much of the practice described in tantric sādhanas involves the enactment of a world—the fantastic jewel-encrusted world of the Mahāyāna sūtras or the horrific world of the charnel ground. In the sūtras, these worlds appear before the audience of the sūtra at the command of the Buddha, as in the *Lotus Sūtra,* or are described by him, as in the Pure Land sūtras. In the tantric sādhana, the practitioner manifests that world through visualization, through a process of invitation, descent, and identification, evoking the world that the sūtras declare to be immanent, yet only describe. The tantric sādhana is, in this sense, the making of the world of the Mahāyāna sūtras here and now. Tantric sādhanas usually take one of two forms. In the first, the buddha or bodhisattva is requested to appear before the meditator and is then worshiped in the hope of receiving blessings. Two popular sādhanas of this type, to the female bodhisattva of compassion, Tārā, are translated in Chapter 27. In the other type of tantric sādhana, the meditator imagines himself or herself to be a fully enlightened buddha or bodhisattva now, to have the exalted body, speech, and mind of an enlightened being. Those who become particularly skillful at this practice, it is said, gain the ability to appear in this form to others. The case of a manifestation as a wrathful buddha is translated in Chapter 42.

Dharma

Before the Buddha passed away, it is said that he was asked who would succeed him as leader of the community. He answered that his teaching should be the teacher. That teaching is most commonly referred to with the name *dharma,* a word derived from the root *dhṛ,* "to hold," a term with a wide range of meanings. Indeed, ten meanings of *dharma,* including "path," "virtue," "quality," "vow," and "nirvāṇa" were enumerated by a fifth-century scholar. Nineteenth-century translators often rendered *dharma* as "the law." But two meanings predominate. The first is the teaching of the Buddha, creatively etymologized from *dhṛ* to mean "that which holds one back from falling into suffering." The second meaning of dharma, appearing particularly in philosophical contexts, is often rendered in English as "phenomenon" or "thing," as in "all dharmas lack self."

The ambiguities encountered in translating the term are emblematic of a wide range of practices that have been regarded as the teaching of the Buddha. And because the Buddha adapted his teachings to the situation and because (at least according to the Mahāyāna), the Buddha did not actually disappear into nirvāṇa but remains forever present, works that represented themselves as his teaching (which begin with the standard formula, "Thus did I hear") have continued to be composed throughout the history of Buddhism. The term "Buddhist apocrypha" has generally been used to describe those texts composed outside of India (in China, for example) which represent themselves as being of Indian origin. Yet strictly speaking all Buddhist texts, even those composed in Indian languages, are apocryphal because none can be identified with complete certainty as a record of the teaching of the historical Buddha. This has, on the one hand, led to a certain tolerance for accepting diverse doctrines and practices as Buddhist. Sometimes new texts were written as ways of summarizing what was most important from an unwieldy and overwhelming canon. In some cases, these new texts represented themselves as the words of the historical Buddha (see Chapter 25); in other cases, essays were composed in poetry and prose with the purpose of explicating for a newly converted society the most essential teachings from a bewildering scriptural tradition (as in Chapter 24).

The absence of the Buddha did not merely occasion the creation of substitutes for him. Over the course of the history of Buddhism in Asia, it also portended crisis, notably in a variety of texts that responded to the notion of the decline of the dharma. Within a century or two after the Buddha's death, there were predictions of the eventual disappearance of the dharma from the world. Various reasons were given for its demise, ranging from a general deterioration in human virtue to the fact that the Buddha had agreed to admit women into the order.

These texts, like most Buddhist sūtras, are set at the time of the Buddha, and the dire circumstances that signal the demise of the dharma are expressed in terms of prophecies by the Buddha of what will happen in the future. We can assume that the authors of the sūtras were in fact describing the events of their own day, usually including the corrupt and greedy behavior of monks, the persecution of Buddhism by the state, or the threat posed by foreign invaders. Some works of this genre not only prophesied decline of the dharma but offered prescriptions so that decline could be averted. Chapter 21 is a Chinese work that criticizes the traditional practice of offering gifts to monks and monasteries, and advocates acts of charity directed instead toward the poor, the orphaned, the aged, the sick, and even animals and insects. Chapter 23, composed at the time of the first major incursion of Muslim armies into northern India, foretells an apocalyptic war in which Buddhist forces will sweep out of the Himalayas to defeat the barbarians and establish a utopian Buddhist kingdom. In the case of the text translated in Chapter 20, there is no such threat. Instead, the text may be addressed to a community whose very security and complacency would allow the eventual disappearance of the dharma.

When works such as these were composed to respond to a particular historical circumstance, it was sometimes necessary to account for the fact that there had been no previous record of such a text. It was explained that the text translated in Chapter 26 had been found locked inside an iron stūpa, having been placed there long ago to be discovered at the appropriate time. The fact that the version which eventually reached China seemed little more than an outline was the result of an unfortunate circumstance: the larger and more comprehensive version of the work had inadvertently been thrown overboard on the sea journey from India to China. Likewise, the Tibetan ritual text of the Great Bliss Queen (Chapter 10) is an example of a Tibetan genre of texts known as *gter ma* (treasures). It is believed that the Indian tantric master who visited Tibet in the late eighth century, Padmasambhava, and his followers buried texts all over Tibet, knowing that they would be uncovered at an appropriate time in the future.

As one might imagine, there were those who found such claims fantastic, and the Mahāyāna was challenged by the foundational schools for fabricating new sūtras and distorting the Buddhist teaching. A sixth-century Mahāyāna author, Bhāvaviveka, summarizes the Hīnayāna argument that the Mahāyāna is not the word of the Buddha: the Mahāyāna sūtras were not included in either the original or subsequent compilations of the word of the Buddha; by teaching that the Buddha is permanent, the Mahāyāna contradicts the dictum that all conditioned phenomena are impermanent; because the Mahāyāna teaches that the buddha nature is all-pervasive, it does not relinquish the belief in self; because the Mahāyāna teaches that the Buddha did not pass into nirvāṇa, it suggests that nirvāṇa is not the final state of peace; the Mahāyāna contains prophecies that the great early disciples will become buddhas; the Mahāyāna belittles the arhats; the Mahāyāna praises bodhisattvas above the Buddha; the Mahāyāna perverts the entire teaching by claiming that the historical Buddha was an emanation; the statement in the Mahāyāna sūtras that the Buddha was constantly in meditative absorption is unfeasible; by teaching that great sins can be completely absolved, the Mahāyāna teaches that actions have no effects, contradicting the law of karma. Therefore, the opponents of the Mahāyāna claim, the Buddha did not set forth the Mahāyāna; it was created by beings who were demonic in order to deceive the obtuse and those with evil minds.

Centuries earlier we find implied responses to these criticisms in the Mahāyāna sūtras themselves, side by side with the assertions that the Hīnayāna found so heretical. The most influential defense of new sūtras as authoritative teachings of the Buddha is found in the *Lotus Sūtra,* with its doctrine of skillful means (*upāya*). In that work the validity of the Mahāyāna and the Mahāyāna vision of buddhahood is defended by the use of parables. Because the *Lotus* is the most influential of Buddhist texts in all of East Asia, it is worthwhile to consider some of these.

The *Lotus Sūtra* must somehow account for the fact that the Mahāyāna has appeared late, after the Buddha had taught a path to nirvāṇa that had already been successfully followed to its terminus by his original disciples, the great arhats such as Śāriputra, Maudgalyāyana, and Kāśyapa. If the Mahāyāna is the superior teaching why had it not been evident earlier? Several of the parables place the fault with the disciples themselves. Thus, in the parable of the hidden jewel, a man falls asleep drunk in the house of a friend who, unbeknownst to him, sews a jewel into the hem of his garment. The man awakes and goes on his way, only to suffer great poverty and hardship. He encounters his friend, who reveals the jewel, showing him that he had been endowed with great wealth all the while. In the same way, the disciples of the Buddha have constant access to the path to supreme enlightenment but are unaware of it; they are bodhisattvas unaware of their true identity. Again, the Buddha compares his teaching to the rainfall that descends without discrimination on the earth. That this rain causes some seeds to grow into flowers and some into great trees implies no differentiation in the rain but rather is due to the capacities of the seeds that it nurtures. Thus, the teaching of the Buddha is of a single flavor but benefits beings in a variety of ways according to their capacity. The Buddha knows the abilities and dispositions of his disciples and causes them to hear his dharma in a way most suitable to them.

Other parables employ a more radical strategy of authorization, suggesting that the Hīnayāna nirvāṇa is but a fiction. The oft-cited parable of the burning house tells of a father distraught as his children blithely play, unaware that the house is ablaze. Knowing of their respective predilections for playthings, he lures them from the inferno with the promise that he has a cart for each waiting outside, a deer-drawn cart for one, a goat-drawn cart for another, and so on. When they emerge from the conflagration, they find only one cart, a magnificent conveyance drawn by a great white ox, something that they had never even dreamed of. The burning house is saṃsāra, the children are ignorant sentient beings, unaware of the dangers of their abode, the father is the Buddha, who lures them out of saṃsāra with the teaching of a variety of vehicles—the vehicle of the śrāvaka, the vehicle of the pratyekabuddha, the vehicle of the bodhisattva—knowing that in fact there is but one vehicle, the buddha vehicle whereby all beings will be conveyed to unsurpassed enlightenment. And the Buddha tells the parable of the conjured city, in which a skillful guide leads a group of travelers on a long journey in search of a cache of jewels. Along the way, the travelers become exhausted and discouraged and decide to turn back. The guide magically conjures a great city in the near distance, where the travelers can rest before continuing toward their ultimate goal. The travelers enter the city where they regain their strength, at which point the guide dissolves the city and announces that the jewel cache is near. The travelers are those sentient beings who are weak and cowardly, intimidated by the thought of traversing the long Mahāyāna path to buddhahood. For their benefit, the Buddha creates the Hīnayāna nirvāṇa, more easily attained, which they mistakenly believe to be their final goal. He then announces to them that they have not reached their ultimate destination and exhorts them on to buddhahood, revealing that the nirvāṇa they had attained was but an illusion.

Thus, the claim to legitimacy of the earlier tradition is usurped by the Mahāyāna through the explanation that what the Buddha had taught before was in fact a lie, that there is no such thing as the path of the arhat, no such thing as nirvāṇa. There is only the Mahāyāna (also called the *ekayāna*, the "one vehicle"), which the Buddha intentionally misrepresents out of his compassionate understanding that there are many among his disciples who are incapable of assimilating so far-reaching a vision. But what of those disciples of the Buddha who are reported in the early sūtras to have become arhats, to have passed into nirvāṇa—what of their attainment? In an ingenious device (found also in other Mahāyāna sūtras) the great heroes of the Hīnayāna are drafted into the Mahāyāna by the Buddha's prophecies that even they will surpass the trifling goal of nirvāṇa and go on to follow the Mahāyāna path to eventual buddhahood. The first such prophecy is for the monk Śāriputra, renowned in the works of the foundational tradition as the wisest of the Buddha's disciples, who is transformed into a stock character in the Mahāyāna sūtras as one who is oblivious of the higher teaching. When his ignorance is revealed to him, he desires to learn more, coming to denounce as parochial the wisdom that he had once deemed supreme. The champion of the Hīnayāna is shown to reject it and embrace that which many adherents of the foundational tradition judged to be spurious. Thus the early history of the movement, already highly mythologized into a sacred history, was fictionalized further in the Mahāyāna sūtras, and another sacred history was eventually created. To legitimate these newly appearing texts, their authors claimed the principal figures of the earlier tradition, indeed its very codifiers, as converts to the Buddha's true teaching and central characters in its drama. The early story of Gautama Buddha and his disciples, preserved in the Pāli canon and already accepted as an historical account by the "pre-Mahāyāna" traditions, is radically rewritten in the *Lotus* in such a way as to glorify the *Lotus* itself as the record of what really happened. Such rewriting recurs throughout the history of the Buddhist traditions in the perpetual attempt to recount "what the Buddha taught."

And who is this Buddha that the *Lotus Sūtra* represents? In the fifteenth chapter, billions of bodhisattvas well up out of the earth and make offerings to the Buddha. The Buddha declares that all of these bodhisattvas who have been practicing the path for innumerable eons are in fact his own disciples, that he had set each of them on the long path to buddhahood. The bodhisattva Maitreya, who has witnessed this fantastic scene, asks the obvious question. He reckons that it had only been some forty years since the Buddha had achieved enlightenment under the tree at Bodhgayā. He finds it incredible that in that short period of time the Buddha could have trained so many bodhisattvas who had progressed so far on the path. "It is as if there were a man, his natural color fair and his hair black, twenty-five years of age, who pointed to men a hundred years of age and said, 'These are my sons!' " Maitreya, representing the self-doubt of the early Mahāyāna and reflecting the Hīnayāna critique, is deeply troubled by this inconsistency, fearing that people who hear of this after the Buddha's passing will doubt the truth of the Buddha's words and attack his teaching.

It is at this point that the Buddha reveals another lie. He explains that even though he is widely believed to have left the palace of his father in search of freedom from suffering and to have found that freedom six years later under a tree near Gayā, in fact, that is not the case. He achieved enlightenment innumerable billions of eons ago and has been preaching the dharma in this world and simultaneously in myriad other worlds ever since. Yet he recognizes the meager intelligence of many beings, and out of his wish to benefit them resorts to the use of skillful methods (*upāya*), recounting how he renounced his princely life and attained unsurpassed enlightenment. And, further recognizing that his continued presence in the world might cause those of little virtue to become complacent and not ardently seek to put his teaching into practice, he declares that he is soon to pass into nirvāṇa. But this also is a lie, because his lifespan will not be exhausted for many innumerable billions of eons.

Thus, the prince's deep anxiety at being confronted with the facts of sickness, aging, and death, his difficult decision to abandon his wife and child and go forth into the forest in search of a state beyond sorrow, his ardent practice of meditation and asceticism for six years, his triumphant attainment of the liberation and his imminent passage into the extinction of nirvāṇa—all are a pretense. He was enlightened all the time, yet feigned these deeds to inspire the world.

But we should not conclude that once the *Lotus* and other Mahāyāna sūtras declared the superiority of the bodhisattva path, the supremacy and authority of the Mahāyāna was finally and unequivocally established. Defenses of the Mahāyāna as the word of the Buddha remained the preoccupation of Mahāyāna scholastics throughout the history of Buddhism in India (see Chapter 34). Nor should we assume that teachings were ranked only as Hīnayāna and Mahāyāna. Even sects that exalted the *Lotus Sūtra* above all others, for example, could disagree about whether there was more than one true practice, one true sūtra, one true buddha. In Japan, a dispute over the meaning of "original enlightenment" in what is called the Matsumoto Debate led to a bloody conflict in 1536 that involved thousands of troops on each side (see Chapters 18 and 19). In China, the promotion and control of sacred scripture was the prerogative of the highest imperial offices. A sect that came into conflict with this authority, the "Teaching of the Three Stages," had its texts declared heretical and banned from the official collection of Buddhist texts (see Chapter 22).

One of the purposes of this volume is to suggest that the significance of Buddhist texts does not lie simply in their doctrinal or philosophical content but in the uses to which they have been put. We find, for example, in Chapter 29 that the Abhidharma (literally, "higher dharma," sometimes rendered as "phenomenology"), a class of Buddhist scriptures concerned with minute analyses of mental states, is chanted at Thai funerals. Contained in virtually every Mahāyāna sūtra was a proclamation of the marvelous benefits that would accrue to those who piously handled, recited, worshiped, copied, or circulated the text itself—again, the teaching had become the teacher. Ritual enshrinement and devotion to the sūtra as a vital embodiment of the dharma and, in a certain sense, as a substitute for the Buddha himself was instrumental to the rise of the disparate collections of cults of the book that came to be known as the Mahāyāna. In China, no text was more venerated than the *Lotus,* and tales were told of the miracles that attended its worship (see Chapter 36).

The importance of texts in Buddhism derives in part from the fact that the tradition represents the Buddha as being eventually persuaded to teach others after his enlightenment. This suggests that the dharma is something that can be passed on, something that is transmittable, transferable. The Buddha is said to have spoken not in Sanskrit, the formal language of the priests of his day, but in the vernacular, and he is said to have forbidden monks from composing his teachings in formal verses for chanting. The implication was that the content was more important than the form. This led to the notion that the dharma could be translated from one language to another, and the act of translation (and the sponsorship of translation) has been regarded throughout Asia as one of the most pious and meritorious acts that could be performed. It was therefore common for Buddhist kings and emperors to sponsor the translation of texts from one language into another: from Sanskrit into Chinese, from Sanskrit into Tibetan, from Tibetan into Manchu, from Pāli into Burmese, and so on. Adding to this notion of translatability was the fact that the primary objects of Buddhist devotion—texts, relics, icons—were all portable; stories of the transportation and enshrinement of a particularly potent image of the Buddha figure in the histories of almost all Buddhist cultures. We should not conclude, however, as Buddhists sometimes do, that the dharma is something self-identical and transcendent, that showers over the cultures of Asia, transforming and pacifying them. In Chapter 17, for example, Buddhism is portrayed as a Korean possession that can be offered in tribute to the Japanese court as a means of protecting the state. It is this universalism of the Buddhist dharma with its plastic pantheon into which any local deity could easily be enlisted, its doctrine of the Buddha's skillful methods for accommodating conflicting views, and its claims about the pervasive nature of reality that have made it a sometimes useful ideology for rulership and empire.

Buddhism has indeed transformed Asia, but it has been transformed in the process. We may consider even whether there ever was some entity called "Buddhism" to be transformed in the first place. What cannot be disputed is that if Buddhism exists, it is impossible to understand it outside the lives of Buddhists, outside the saṅgha.

Saṅgha

The last of the three jewels is the saṅgha, "the community." Technically taken to mean the assembly of enlightened disciples of the Buddha, the term more commonly connotes the community of Buddhist monks and nuns. In the rules governing the ordination ceremony, the saṅgha is said to be present when four fully ordained monks are in attendance. However, in its broadest sense the saṅgha is the whole body of Buddhist faithful. The selections in this section fall under two broad categories. The first deals with monastic life or, more specifically, life organized by vows. The second deals with the lives of Buddhists.

As mentioned earlier, Buddhist practice was traditionally subsumed under three headings: ethics (*śīla*), meditation (*dhyāna*), and wisdom (*prajñā*). Ethics, which in this context refers to refraining from nonvirtue through the conscious control of body and speech, was regarded as the essential prerequisite for progress in meditation and wisdom. It was the element of the triad most widely practiced both by lay people and monks and nuns, and this practice generally took the form of the observance of vows. Since in Buddhist ethical theory karma, both good and bad, depended not on the deed but on the intention, if one could make a promise not to kill humans, for example, and maintain that promise, the good karma accumulated by such restraint would be far greater than had one simply not had the occasion to commit murder. From the early days of the tradition, therefore, elaborate systems of rules for living one's life, called *vinaya,* were established, along with ceremonies for their conferral and maintenance. Lay people could take vows not to kill humans, not to steal, not to commit sexual misconduct, not to lie about spiritual attainments (for example, not to claim to be telepathic when one actually was not), and not to use intoxicants. Novice monks and nuns took these five vows, plus vows not to eat after the noon meal (a rule widely transgressed in some Buddhist cultures through recourse to the evening "medicinal meal"), not to handle gold or silver, not to adorn their bodies, not to sleep in high beds, and not to attend musical performances. Fully ordained monks (*bhikṣu*) and nuns (*bhikṣunī*) took many more vows, which covered the entire range of personal and public decorum, and regulated physical movements, social intercourse, and property. Monks and nuns convened twice monthly to confess their transgressions of the rules in a ceremony and reaffirm their commitment to the code, with transgressions carrying punishments of various weights. The gravest misdeeds entailed expulsion from the order, whereas others could be expiated simply by confessing them aloud. In Buddhist traditions across Asia, ritual maintenance of these monastic codes has served as the mark of orthodoxy, much more than adherence to a particular belief or doctrine. Indeed, it is said that the teaching of the Buddha will endure only as long as the vinaya endures.

The Buddha and his followers were probably originally a group of wandering ascetics. However, they adopted the practice of other ascetic groups in India of remaining in one place during the rainy season. Wealthy patrons had shelters built for their use, and these shelters evolved into monasteries that were inhabited throughout the year. It seems that early in the tradition, the saṅgha became largely sedentary, although the tradition of the wandering monk continued. Still, the saṅgha was by no means a homogeneous community. The vinaya texts describe monks from a wide variety of social backgrounds. Mention is made of monks from all four of India's social castes. There were also a wide variety of monastic specialties. The vinaya texts describe monks who are skilled in speech, those who memorize and recite the sūtras, those who memorize and recite the vinaya, and those who memorize and recite lists of technical terms. There are monks who live in the forest, who wear robes of felt, who wear robes made from discarded rags, who live only on the alms they have begged for, who live at the foot of a tree, who live in a cemetery, who live in the open air, who sleep sitting up, and so on. There were also monks who specialized in meditation, monks who served as advisors to kings, and monks responsible for the administration of the monastery and its property. One of the tasks of this administrator was to insure that the wandering monks were not given mundane work, that meditating monks not be disturbed by noise, and that monks who begged for alms received good food. Whether they wandered without a fixed abode or lived in monasteries, monks and nuns that lived in a designated region, called a *sīmā,* were to gather twice a month to confess and affirm their vows communally, a ceremony that laypeople also attended.

Throughout the Buddhist world, monks and laypeople have lived in a symbiotic relationship: the laity provide material support for monks while monks provide a locus for the layperson's accumulation of merit (by supporting monks who maintained their vows). The rules and regulations in the vinaya texts were meant to govern the lives of Buddhist monks and to structure their relations with the laity. Monks in the vinaya literature are caught in a web of social and ritual obligations, are fully and elaborately housed and permanently settled, and are preoccupied not with nirvāṇa, but with bowls and robes, bathrooms and buckets, and proper behavior in public. Some of these details are found in Chapter 37, which sets forth the rules governing daily life in a Chinese monastery. The saṅgha was also a community where disputes arose and had to be settled. Because it is said that the Buddha only prescribed a rule in response to a specific misdeed, the vinaya texts often provide the story of that first offense and the Buddha's pronouncement of a rule against such behavior in the future. Chapter 38 provides a selection of his rulings in disputes concerning the funerals of monks and the distribution of their sometimes considerable property.

There were also rules for nuns, although these receive much less attention in the vinaya literature. According to several traditions, the Buddha was approached early in his career by his aunt and step-mother, Mahāpajāpatī (called Gotamī in Chapter 9), at the head of a delegation of women who wished him to institute a Buddhist order of nuns. The Buddha initially declined to institute such an order. But when the Buddha's cousin and personal attendant, Ānanda, asked him whether women were able to attain the fruits of the practice of the dharma, the Buddha unhesitatingly answered in the affirmative and agreed to establish an order for women. However, the same text states that if the Buddha had not agreed to establish an order for nuns, his teaching would not disappear from the world so quickly. The rules for nuns are both more numerous and stricter than those for monks, and placed nuns in a position of clear subordination to monks. For example, seniority in the order of monks and nuns is measured by the length of time one has been ordained, such that someone who has been a monk for five years must pay respect to a monk of six years, even if the first monk is chronologically older. However, the rules for nuns state that a woman who has been a nun for one hundred years must pay respect to a man who was ordained as a monk for one day. The difficulties entailed in maintaining the strict nuns' vows and a lack of institutional support led to the decline and eventual disappearance of the order of nuns in India, Sri Lanka, and Southeast Asia, and to an order of novices alone (rather than fully ordained nuns) in Tibet. The tradition of full ordination for women was maintained only in China.

Throughout the development of the Mahāyāna and the Vajrayāna, the rules for monks and nuns seem to have remained fairly uniform and the adherents of the new vehicles seem to have seen no contradiction between the monastic life and the practices of the Mahāyāna and the Vajrayāna. But if we understand the vinaya not as that which restricts individuals and their actions but as that which creates them, we will not be surprised that additional vows were formulated for the bodhisattva and the tantric practitioner, and that rituals which mimicked the monastic confession ceremony were designed for their administration. The vows of a bodhisattva included not only the vow to liberate all beings in the universe from suffering but also to act compassionately by always accepting an apology, not to praise oneself and belittle others, to give gifts and teachings upon request, and so on. Those who took the bodhisattva vows also promised never to claim that the Mahāyāna sūtras were not the word of the Buddha (see Chapter 39).

Vajrayāna practice also entailed extensive sets of vows. Chapter 39 provides a translation of a Tibetan ritual text for the confession of infractions to tantric vows. As mentioned above, it was common for Buddhist monks, especially in late Indian Buddhism and in Tibet, to hold bodhisattva and tantric vows in addition to their monk's vows. In the case of the more advanced tantric initiations, which involved sexual union with a consort, this presented problems, for monks were bound by the rule of celibacy. Whether or not monks were permitted to participate in such initiations became a question of some gravity when Buddhism was being established in Tibet, and a famous Indian monk and tantric master composed a text that dealt with this issue. That text is translated in Chapter 24.

The second type of selection found in this section are stories of Buddhists from across Asia. Some of these accounts are ancient, like the life story of a "miraculous and strange" Chinese monk of the sixth century (Chapter 46); some are modern, like the autobiographies of Japanese Buddhist women after the Second World War (Chapter 40). Some are hagiographies of famous masters, and some tell of miraculous voyages (Chapter 42); others recount the deathbed visions of devotees of Amitābha (Chapter 48). Some of the biographies are highly stereotyped with often transparent agendas (Chapter 44). Part of the ambiguity of assigning chapters to one of the three jewels is evident here; the reader may consider which of these members of the saṅgha might also be considered as buddhas or bodhisattvas.

Other works contained in this section confront quite specific historical dilemmas, such as that of Japanese Pure Land priests whose task it was to insure rebirth in the pure land but who were sometimes ordered into battle themselves (Chapter 47). There are also tales of travel. Because of the portability of relics, texts, and icons, sacred sites were established across the Buddhist world and pilgrimages to those sites was a popular form of Buddhist practice throughout Asia. Pilgrimage was sometimes to a stūpa associated with the life of the Buddha; Bodhgayā, the site of the Buddha's enlightenment, has drawn pilgrims from the outer reaches of the Buddhist world for centuries. Particularly powerful buddha images also attracted pilgrims; it was not uncommon for pilgrims from as far east as Manchuria and as far west as the Mongol regions of Russia to travel to Lhasa, the capital of Tibet, to visit the statue of the Buddha there. They would travel on foot or on horseback; the most pious would proceed by prostration—bowing and then stretching their bodies on the ground before rising, taking one step forward and prostrating again, along the entire route. In China, mountains believed to be the abodes of munificent bodhisattvas were (and are) popular destinations of communal pilgrimages. Chapter 13 provides some of the songs sung by women pilgrims in modern China, who reported a variety of reasons for making the pilgrimage: to insure a good harvest, to protect the silkworms, to promote the health of family members and domestic animals. But we should not assume that Buddhist travel was always directed from the periphery to the center. Chapter 42 recounts the story of a renowned Buddhist scholar who left one of the great monastic universities of India on a perilous sea voyage to Sumatra, where the preeminent teacher of the practice of compassion was said to reside. Nor was travel always so concerned with what or who was to be found at the end of the journey; the Japanese monk Ippen saw travel itself as essential to his practice of devotion to Amitābha (Chapter 45).

This book makes available for the first time works that have hitherto been neglected in the representation of Buddhism to the West, works that do not easily fit into the categories under which the Buddhist traditions have been previously understood—categories such as chronology, country, vehicle, or philosophical school. Because this volume represents above all the practices of Buddhists, it has been organized according to the most traditional of Buddhist categories: the three jewels. This is a category, however, which is not without its own ambiguities. In reading the chapters that follow and in noting under which of the jewels they have been placed, therefore, the reader is asked again to consider: Who is the Buddha? What is the dharma? And who belongs to the saṅgha?

Note

1. The historical survey that follows is drawn largely from Joseph M. Kitagawa and Mark D. Cummings, ed., *Buddhism and Asian History* (New York: Macmillan, 1989), a collection of the most recent scholarship on Buddhist history. Readers are referred there for more detailed histories and bibliographies of sources.

Buddha

—1—

A Hymn of Praise to the Buddha's Good Qualities

Paul J. Griffiths

The Buddha has been an object of devotion, praise, and homage from the beginning of Buddhist history. The presence of the Buddha in the world, in the person of Gautama Śākyamuni in India about 2,400 years ago, has always been regarded by Buddhists as a matter of such surprising and wonderful good fortune that these are the only possible responses. Relatively early Buddhist texts are full of descriptions of such attitudes to Śākyamuni, and later literary works and iconographic representations went to much trouble to give detailed pictures of the good qualities that make the Buddha worthy of such devotion. The hymn of praise translated here is an example of such an attempt.

The historical individual Śākyamuni to whom the honorific title "Buddha" ("Awakened One") is given was, according to the systematic thinkers of the Buddhist tradition, only one of many buddhas. There have been many buddhas active in this world before Śākyamuni, and there will be many after him. Also, there were many buddhas in various forms active in other worlds at the very same time when Śākyamuni was active in our world, just as there are many buddhas active now in various worlds other than ours. Although Śākyamuni is the paradigmatic buddha for us since he is the one closest to us in time and space, he is neither the only buddha to have been the object of devotion by Buddhists nor even, perhaps, the buddha to have received the most attention, praise, and homage.

Although buddhas have been and are so numerous, they all share some characteristics; in fact, it is the possession of these common properties that makes it sensible to call them all buddhas. Buddhist theorists began to show an interest in listing and defining these common properties from a very early period. Some of these lists are no more than standardized sets of epithets applied to the Buddha, short strings of honorifics employed whenever Buddha is mentioned. So, for example, Śākyamuni is often dignified by calling him "Thus Gone, Worthy, Fully and Completely Awakened, Accomplished in Knowledge and Virtuous Conduct,

Well Gone, Knower of Worlds, Unsurpassed Guide for Those Who Need Restraint, Teacher of Gods and Humans, Awakened, Blessed," a litany of titles that rolls sonorously from the tongue in Sanskrit. This litany can be applied to any buddha, since all buddhas have these properties. Other lists of common buddha properties are much more extensive, and are given poetic form, intended to be learned, recited, and used as objects of meditation or as aids to visualizing the Buddha's perfections. It is such a list that is translated below.

The seventeen verses that form the heart of this list are found in at least two different Buddhist texts, the *Mahāyānasūtrālaṅkāra* ("Ornament of the Sacred Texts of the Great Vehicle"), and the *Mahāyānasaṅgraha* ("Summary of the Great Vehicle"). Both were written in India and in Sanskrit by the fourth century of the common era; the problems surrounding the dating of Indian Buddhist texts are sufficiently intractable to make any more precise dating impossible. The fact that these verses are found in different texts strongly suggests that they had a life of their own, independent of any of the larger works in which they are now embedded. This impression is confirmed by the fact that the canonical collection of Buddhist texts preserved in the Tibetan language contains these verses as an independent work. It seems reasonable to conclude that these seventeen verses praising the Buddha's good qualities were in liturgical use by Buddhists in India by the beginning of the common era, and that they were thought sufficiently important to be included in different written works over the next several centuries, and given detailed exposition in those works. Apart from this, unfortunately, we do not know how Buddhists in India used these verses in their ritual and meditational life.

Each of the seventeen verses in the hymn has essentially the same structure. The Buddha, apostrophized reverentially in the second person singular, is described as the possessor of a number of desirable properties, and the verse ends with the refrain "Homage to you!" (*namo'stu te*). The good qualities mentioned in the verses are of a fairly general kind: the Buddha is said to sympathize with all beings (verse 1), to tame their passions (verse 3), to know what they do (verse 6), to remove their doubts (verse 17), and so forth.

The larger written works in which these verses are now embedded typically provide prose comments upon each verse, sometimes brief and sometimes very extensive. In these comments each verse is taken to refer to one or more of a series of buddha properties defined with much greater precision and elaboration, and if these properties are added up we find that the hymn as a whole is taken by the commentators to provide a poetic summary of 206 good qualities possessed by the Buddha.

This large number is divided by the commentators into twenty-one major categories, some with only one member and one with as many as eighty; and each of the seventeen verses is related to one or more of these twenty-one categories. Each of the longer prose works in which the verses are now embedded contains comments of this kind, some more elaborate and some less, but all are in essential agreement as to which members of the more elaborate list—206 properties in twenty-one major categories—are to be referred to which verse.

In the translation that follows I provide my own brief comments upon each verse, drawing on the expositions referred to in the preceding paragraph, in an attempt to show how the Indian commentators understood the verses and linked them to the detailed scholastic categories. Since these categories have many members and are highly technical, I have been able to do no more than give a broad indication of their major divisions and meanings. Further details can be pursued by consulting the works mentioned below. It will be obvious that the verses typically do not contain the technical terms used by the commentators to link them with the categories of the more detailed list, and that there is a certain artificiality and arbitrariness to these connections. The verses can be read and savored independently; doing so will provide something of their religious flavor. But it should also be emphasized that the combination of the devotional fervor of these verses with the dry technicality of the scholastic categories—only hinted at in my expository comments—opens a window of great value upon Buddhist attitudes to and systematic thought about the Buddha in the early centuries of the common era in India; these attitudes and this systematic thought were together of fundamental importance for all later Buddhist theorizing about the person and work of the Buddha.

The translation of the verses given here is made from the Sanskrit text of the *Mahāyānasūtrālaṅkāra,* given in Sylvain Lévi, ed. and trans., *Mahāyāna-Sūtrālaṃkāra: exposé de la doctrine du grand véhicule selon le système Yogācāra,* 2 vols. Bibliothèque de l'École des Hautes Études, Sciences Historiques et Philologiques, vols. 159, 190 (Paris: Librairie Ancienne Honoré Champion, 1907, 1911), I: 184–88.

Lévi's French translation of these verses, together with one of the prose commentaries (*Mahāyānasūtrālaṅkārabhāṣya*) is in II: 299–306, of the same work. A French translation of the same verses in the context of the *Mahāyānasaṅgraha* is in Étienne Lamotte, ed. and trans., *La somme du grand véhicule d'Asaṅga (Mahāyāna-Saṃgraha),* 2 vols. Publications de l'Institut Orientaliste de Louvain, vol. 8 (Louvain-la-Neuve: Institut Orientaliste de l'Université Catholique de Louvain, 1973), II: 290–304. The Tibetan text of the verses is given in I: 88–90, of the same work.

More recently, see Paul J. Griffiths et al., *The Realm of Awakening: A Translation and Study of the Tenth Chapter of Asaṅga's Mahāyñasaṅgraha* (New York: Oxford University Press, 1989), pp. 123–69, 299–335. The second volume of Gadjin M. Nagao's *Shōdaijōron: wayaku to chūkai [Mahāyānasaṅgraha:* A Japanese Translation and Commentary], 2 vols. (Tokyo: Kodansha, 1982, 1987) also contains the Sanskrit text of these verses, together with a translation into Japanese and some exegetical remarks (also in Japanese).

A Hymn of Praise to the Buddha's Good Qualities

You sympathize with sentient beings;
You aspire to unite, to separate, and not to separate;
You aspire to happiness and well-being.
Homage to you!

verse 1, qualities 1–4, category 1

This verse is taken to refer to the Buddha's four "immeasurables," namely, his friendliness, his compassion, his gladness, and his equanimity, as these are directed toward all sentient beings. The Buddha wants the happiness and well-being of all, and so aspires to unite them with happiness, to separate them from suffering, and not to separate them from what happiness they already possess. The immeasurables, then, are among the Buddha's perfections of attitude toward all non-buddhas; they are immeasurable because they are extended to all equally and without limit. They provide the basis for the Buddha's salvific action.

You are liberated from all obstacles;
You are the sage who masters the entire world;
Objects of awareness are pervaded by your awareness;
Your mind is liberated.
Homage to you!

verse 2, qualities 5–30, categories 2–4

Each of the first three lines of this verse is taken to refer to a series of altered states of consciousness produced by the Buddha's meditational practice. The first line is taken to refer to the Buddha's eight "liberations," by means of which the Buddha is liberated from all obstacles to proper cognition—knowing the way things are—and proper affective condition—reacting with emotional appropriateness to such knowledge. The second line is taken to refer to the Buddha's eight "spheres of mastery," by means of which the Buddha attains complete control over his own mental life, learning to manipulate and alter at will the images in which it consists. And the third line of the verse is taken to refer to the Buddha's ten "spheres of totality," by means of which the Buddha can extend his awareness to the limits of possibility, so coming to be aware of everything and obtaining a kind of omniscience (on which see verse 16). The commentators provide a good deal of information about the meditational techniques designed to bring these states into being. The verse as a whole thus refers to the Buddha's perfections of cognition and affect, necessary prerequisites for his salvific action.

You tame all the passions of all sentient beings, without any remainder,
You remove the passions and take pity on the passionate.
Homage to you!

verse 3, quality 31, category 5

This verse is taken to refer to the Buddha's "noncontentiousness," by virtue of which he is able to remove the passions of sentient beings, without at the same time himself being the object of any such passions. This is a centrally important property of the Buddha's perfections of action, connected as it is with one of the main goals of the entire Buddhist path, which is the removal of passions. The second line tells us that the Buddha is opposed only to passions, not to those who have them; and the commentaries, in explaining this, liken the Buddha to a physician who removes fevers or possession by demons, but who shows nothing but compassion to those who have such troubles.

> You are spontaneous, unattached, unimpeded, and concentrated;
> You always and only dispose of all questions.
> Homage to you!
>
> verse 4, quality 32, category 6

This verse as a whole is taken to refer to the Buddha's awareness that results from his original vow to become the Buddha. The first line lists some properties of this awareness, and the second shows its salvific effects: precisely as a result of possessing such awareness, the Buddha is able to do nothing other than remove the questions and doubts of non-buddhas, and so to help such beings on their way toward buddhahood. The emphasis on spontaneity is a thread that runs throughout this hymn. The Buddha does not act with deliberation or analysis; rather, his perfections of knowledge and affect mean that he does everything without forethought or the possibility of error, as a spontaneous outflow of his own nature—just as a mirror spontaneously reflects images with perfect accuracy.

> Your mind is always unimpeded with regard to the support and that which is supported—which are what is taught;
> And with regard to speech and awareness—which are what does the teaching;
> You are always a good teacher.
> Homage to you!
>
> verse 5, qualities 33–36, category 7

This verse is taken to refer to the Buddha's four "specific understandings." These are special cognitive capacities by means of which the Buddha understands, as the first line of the verse has it, "what is taught," which is to say the doctrine (*dharma*) itself ("the support"), as well as its meaning (*artha,* "that which is supported"). The idea is that Buddhist teaching is expressed in words and has meaning, and that the Buddha has complete understanding of both. These are the first two of the four specific understandings. The other two—speech and awareness—are mentioned in the second line. The commentators explain these understandings in terms of the Buddha's unobstructed and complete mastery over the words necessary to teach the doctrine in any natural language, and also in terms of his mastery over the rhetorical conventions necessary for the effective use of such languages. The Buddha is thus both omnilingual and a rhetorician of unparalleled skill, and so is "always a good teacher."

> When approaching sentient beings through their words,
> And upon knowing their conduct in regard to their coming, going, and deliverance,
> You instruct them well.
> Homage to you!
>
> verse 6, qualities 37–42, category 8

This verse is taken to refer in summary fashion to the Buddha's six supernatural knowledges. The commentators present slightly different versions of this sixfold list, and so interpret the verse somewhat differently from one another. But they are in broad agreement that the Buddha's powers of clairvoyance, clairaudience, and telepathy enable him to know everything about what sentient beings do, what their previous lives were, and when and how they will reach nirvāṇa ("knowing their conduct in regard to their coming, going, and deliverance"). Such knowledges provide the Buddha with what he needs to "instruct them well," and so here too we find reference to the Buddha's cognitive powers as a necessary condition for his salvific action. The Buddha's knowledge enables him to tailor his teachings and actions with precision to the needs of each sentient being.

> Upon seeing you, all embodied beings recognize you as a noble person;
> You inspire devotion merely by being seen.
> Homage to you!
>
> verse 7, qualities 43–154, categories 9–10

With this verse we find mention for the first time of the Buddha's perfections of physical appearance when he is active in the world as teacher. These perfections are sufficiently striking that they are capable of eliciting "devotion" (*prasāda*) simply by being seen; they are traditionally divided into two categories, the thirty-two major and the eighty minor physical perfections. The standard list of these marks is too long to be given here, but examples of the major marks are: the Buddha has "thousand-spoked wheels with hubs and rims" on the soles of his feet, his penis is sheathed, his skin is golden, he has forty even teeth with no spaces between them, and so forth. Some of these marks are visible upon statues of the Buddha; they are all meant to incite those who see them to the practice of the path, and to do so by creating in them feelings of reverential awe.

> You have attained mastery in taking up, maintaining, and forsaking,
> In magical transformation and development,

And in concentration and awareness.
Homage to you!

verse 8, qualities 155–58, category 11

This verse is taken to refer to the Buddha's four "purifications," which are really four kinds of mastery. The first, referred to in line one, means that buddhas, as one of the commentators puts it, "are born whenever they want; that when they are born they live as long as they want; and that they relinquish life at whatever time they want." The Buddha thus has complete control over his life span. The second of the four purifications is the Buddha's mastery over his mental life: he can create and manipulate the mental images in which that life consists at will rather than being subject to it, as most of us are. Finally, in line three, the third and fourth of the Buddha's purifications are mentioned: these are his mastery over various kinds of meditational practice ("concentration"), and over various kinds of "awareness" that result from such practice. The keynote throughout is control: the Buddha is not subject to uncontrollable influences outside himself, but rather is the controller of them all. There are important connections here with the good qualities mentioned in verse 2.

You shatter the demon who deceives sentient beings
About what is expedient, about refuge, about purification, and about deliverance through the Great Vehicle.
Homage to you!

verse 9, qualities 159–68, category 12

This verse is taken to treat the Buddha's ten powers, powers that come from the Buddha's awareness of the way things are. These powers enable the Buddha to counter the demonic deceiver Māra, who is always attempting to mislead human beings about what is salvifically effective. Māra's deceptions operate in four main areas: first, what is salvifically effective ("expedient"); second, what is a proper religious "refuge"; third, which religious practices will purify the individual ("purification"); and fourth, which "vehicle" (*yāna*) or tradition of Buddhist practice is most likely to lead to nirvāṇa. In each area the Buddha has the power to counter Māra's false teachings with true ones because the Buddha always knows what is the case. So, for instance, Māra might teach that it is salvifically expedient to believe that there is a god who liberates human persons; the Buddha, using the power that comes from his awareness of what is and is not possible (*sthānāsthānajñānabala*, the first of the ten powers) counters this with the teaching that there is no god who can do this.

You teach awareness, abandonment, deliverance, and that which makes obstacles,

For the benefit of self and other.
Homage to you!

verse 10, qualities 169–72, category 13

This verse is taken to refer to the Buddha's four "fearlessnesses." The Buddha is fearless or confident initially about his own perfection in knowing what needs to be known ("awareness"), and in having disposed of those obstacles that need to be disposed of ("abandonment"). These are the fearlessnesses that concern what benefits the Buddha himself; in virtue of possessing them the Buddha sees, for example, "no possibility that any god or demon can justly accuse me of not having completely realized something," as one of the commentators puts it. The Buddha is also quite confident that his teaching to others, both about what will result in deliverance for them, and about what would create obstacles for them were they to go on doing it, is perfect and beyond reproach. There is a connection here with the idea of spontaneity: the Buddha's action is free from deliberation in part because he does not need to consider in advance whether or not he will betray some imperfection by acting heedlessly. Since he has no imperfections, such a betrayal cannot happen.

You speak with resolve in the assemblies,
You are free from the two defilements,
You have nothing to guard against, you forget nothing, you gather together communities.
Homage to you!

verse 11, qualities 173–78, categories 14–15

This verse is taken to refer to the Buddha's guardlessnesses and mindfulnesses. It is in virtue of the former that the Buddha is able to "speak with resolve" among assembled hearers: he can do this because he has no need to guard his actions, words, or thoughts against possible improprieties. The Buddha is also "free from the two defilements" in the sense that he feels neither attachment to responsive listeners nor repugnance for unresponsive ones. Finally, it is the Buddha's mindfulness, his ability to pay constant attention to the needs of those to whom he is speaking (and so to "forget nothing") that gives him the ability to "gather together communities," and thus to teach all those with whom he comes into contact in the most appropriate and effective manner possible.

Your actions are never without omniscience everywhere, whether setting out or at rest;
Your omniscience always corresponds to reality.
Homage to you!

verse 12, quality 179, category 16

This verse is taken to refer to the Buddha's complete "destruction of propensities" for inappropriate action, a condition understood to require unbroken "omniscience" (see also verse 16) on the Buddha's part. The Buddha, that is to say, always knows fully and precisely what he is doing, and so his actions are never subject to unacknowledged or unconscious "propensities." We might say that the Buddha is never subject to unconscious urges or motivations: what he does makes fully evident what he is. The commentators give some colorful examples of what it would be like to act under the influence of such unacknowledged propensities. For example, a certain individual who had reached a kind of awakening but who had not completely disposed of his propensities is thereby said to have "decked himself out with finery because of the effects of his propensities produced by having been a prostitute in many previous lives."

> When you do what needs to be done for the benefit of sentient beings,
> you waste no time;
> What you do is never fruitless;
> You are without forgetfulness.
> Homage to you!
>
> verse 13, quality 180, category 17

This verse is taken to refer to the Buddha's "nonforgetfulness," which is to say his constant awareness of and attention to everything that needs to be done for sentient beings and his constant and complete efficacy in doing it. One of the commentators puts this with splendid conciseness: "The state of nonforgetfulness means that the Buddha effectively does, at the proper moment, what needs to be done, whenever, wherever, and however it needs to be done . . . moreover, the Buddha is not forgetful of any action, object, or means for performing all those actions for his attention is always present."

> You behold the entire world six times each day and night;
> You are endowed with great compassion;
> You aspire to well-being.
> Homage to you!
>
> verse 14, quality 181, category 18

This verse is taken to refer to the Buddha's "great compassion" for all sentient beings, a quality already mentioned in verse 1. "Six times each day and night" means simply all the time; the phrase mentions a standard Indian division of the twenty-four hours into six equal periods. The third line of this verse is identical with part of the third line of verse 1. Here, as there, the point is that all the Buddha's salvific action can properly be understood under the rubric of compassion.

You far surpass all hearers and solitary awakened ones
In performance, attainment, awareness, and action.
Homage to you!

verse 15, qualities 182–99, category 19

This verse is taken to refer to the eighteen qualities uniquely possessed by the Buddha, qualities that differentiate him from those other beings who have attained some kind of awakening (*bodhi*), but who are not fully and completely awakened (*samyaksambuddha*). The list of eighteen such qualities is long and detailed. It comprises: first, what the Buddha does while active in the world, his "performance"; second, those "attainments," such as concentration and zeal, which have accrued to him as a result of his past salvifically effective actions; third, his "awareness," which is in all respects perfect; and fourth, his "action," which is spontaneously without fault in all its physical, verbal, and mental aspects. There is a polemical point to the elaboration of this list by the commentators: the Buddha must be shown to be superior to all other possible candidates for the reception of reverential homage, including those "solitary awakened ones" (*pratyekabuddha*) who are awakened to the truth as the Buddha is, but who are not yet quite free from all unconscious tendencies toward improper thought, speech, or action. Such beings must still guard themselves against error, while the Buddha no longer needs to do so (see also verses 10–11).

You have attained great awakening in all aspects through the three bodies;
You cut off the doubts of all sentient beings everywhere.
Homage to you!

verse 16, quality 200, category 20

This verse is taken to refer to the Buddha's special omniscience, an omniscience that knows all things in all their "aspects" (see also verse 12). Such omniscience is attained and employed through the "three bodies," which are: the body of dharma (*dharmakāya*), a term used to denote what the Buddha essentially and changelessly is; the body of enjoyment (*sambhogakāya*), which is the Buddha as he is visible and accessible in the various heavenly realms; and the body of magical transformation (*nirmāṇakāya*), a term used to describe the immense variety of specific buddhas active and available in worlds like ours. It is through these bodies, and through the omniscience that is manifest in what they do, that the Buddha performs his salvific function, which is to "cut off the doubts of all sentient beings everywhere" (see also verse 4).

You have no grasping, no fault, no turbidity, no stagnation, no vacillation, and no verbal proliferation toward all things.
Homage to you!

verse 17, qualities 201–6, category 21

The six terms predicated of the Buddha in this verse are taken to refer to the Buddha's mastery of the six perfections. The Buddha has "no grasping" because he is perfect in giving (*dāna*); "no fault" because he is perfect in morality (*śīla*); "no turbidity" because he is perfectly zealous (*vīrya*); "no stagnation" because he is perfect in patience (*kṣānti*); "no vacillation" because he is perfect in meditation (*dhyāna*); and "no verbal proliferation toward all things," which is to say that he does not improperly impose reified categories of thought and speech upon reality as a result of his perfection in wisdom (*prajñā*).

—2—

Consecrating the Buddha

Donald K. Swearer

Images of gods and other sacred persons figure prominently in various forms of popular religious practice. Although the figure of the Buddha seems not to have been depicted in the earliest Buddhist iconography, by the first century of our era images of the Blessed One occupy a prominent place in Buddhist devotional ritual. Scholarly opinion varies regarding the origin and function of the Buddha image, but it is reasonable to assume that from the beginning Buddha images represented two interconnected aspects of the person and the story of the Buddha: the knowledge of the dharma [Pāli *dhamma*] attained at his nirvāṇa [Pāli *nibbāna*], and the supermundane powers associated with the renunciant practices linked with that extraordinary attainment. Buddha images have continued to convey these meanings in culturally specific forms up to the present day.

In contemporary northern Thailand, an elaborate ceremony is held to consecrate Buddha images prior to their installation in temples or other buildings. During the ceremony various ritual acts infuse into the image the wisdom and power associated with Prince Siddhārtha's [Pāli Siddhattha] victory over Māra and his attainment of enlightenment. Monks chant in Pāli or preach in northern Thai several texts including the *Buddha Abhiṣeka (Consecrating the Buddha [Image])*. The text rehearses the life of the Buddha as the Bodhisattva (Pāli *bodhisatta*), Prince Siddhārtha. The narrative focuses, in particular, on the Buddha's enlightenment, the path leading up to this achievement, and the power of the extraordinary states of consciousness (Pāli *ñāṇa*; Sanskrit *jñāna*) associated with the Buddha's enlightenment. The translation of the term ñāṇa, poses special difficulties. It may denote "knowledge" and is often so translated. In our text, however, the term points to a state of extraordinary or transcendental consciousness, a state of awareness or knowing involving a state of being. Thus, the Buddha attains to various ñāṇas that define or characterize the power of his buddhahood.

The text discusses at some length aspects of the Buddha legend found in later Pāli canonical and commentarial texts, most of which postdate the Aśokan age, such as *Chronicle of the Buddhas (Buddhavaṃsa)*, *Basket of Conduct (Cariyāpiṭaka)*,

Birth Stories of the Buddha (Jātaka), and the Pāli life of the Buddha (*Nidāna Kathā*). Although legendary lives of the Buddha, such as *Nidāna Kathā, Buddhacarita,* and *Lalitavistara,* may differ in details, students familiar with them will recognize the story of the Buddha recounted in the *Buddha Abhiṣeka.* Major topics of these texts that appear in the *Buddha Abhiṣeka* include the following: the attainment of buddhahood after the achievement of eons of moral perfection, which make the Buddha of popular cult a field of meritorious power; the realization of trance states or meditative absorptions; and the extraordinary spiritual powers realized by the Buddha in these higher states of consciousness. The text also provides a summary of various seminal Theravāda teachings such as causality and interdependent coarising, the three characteristics of existence (impermanence, not-self, suffering), the four noble truths (suffering, the cause of suffering, the cessation of suffering, and the path to the cessation of suffering), the four paths (stream-enterer, oncereturner, never-returner, and arhat [Pāli *arahant*]) and their fruits, the law of moral causality and the consequences of rebirth in various Buddhist hells, and the various forms of sensory attachment leading to those states of punishment.

We should see the *Buddha Abhiṣeka* not simply as a later noncanonical, popular construction of the Buddha, but as a portrayal of the variegated meanings the Theravāda tradition has attributed to its founder. Much about this portrayal conflicts with the modern predilection to make the Buddha into a "rational renouncer" who espoused a universal message of human suffering. From a historical perspective this modern interpretation of Prince Siddhārtha's realization of buddhahood should not exclude other tales, but should take its place among the many stories the Theravāda tradition has told about the Buddha.

As an oral text preached or chanted within a ritual context, the *Buddha Abhiṣeka* serves several different functions. It provides an abbreviated summary of the life of the Buddha derived from Pāli canonical and commentarial texts; it links the life of Prince Siddhārtha with the lineage of previous buddhas recounted in the *Buddhavaṃsa* and *Cariyāpiṭaka,* and the moral perfection attained through previous bodhisattva rebirths, such as Prince Vessantara. Perhaps most importantly, the ritual infuses these elements into the Buddha image, a material object representing the story, wisdom, and power of the person of the Buddha.

This translation is based primarily on a version currently preached during the Buddha image consecration ceremony at monasteries throughout the Chiang Mai valley of northern Thailand. The text is of the vohāra genre, a vernacular (that is, a Tai Yuan or northern Thai) exposition of a text in which the Pāli progenitor appears in the omnipresence of Pāli words and phrases. Not infrequently, these texts appear to be written as a commentary, an explanation / exposition (in the vernacular) of a sūtra (Pāli *sutta*). Our text is a redaction edited by Mahābunkhit Wajarasāt, a major publisher of sermons and other types of texts purchased and then presented to the saṅgha on various auspicious, merit-making occasions. Prior to the twentieth century lay donors would commission a monk or a layperson to inscribe a text on bundles of palm leaves or to calligraph a text on heavy mulberry paper folded in accordion fashion. Today this custom has virtually disappeared. Instead, the lay donor purchases a facsimile printed on heavy brown paper folded in the rectangular shape of a bundle of palm leaves. Because Mahābunkhit and the other major publishers—most of whom were former monks—in the towns of Lampang and Chiang Rai edit or redact these texts from older palm leaf or mulberry paper copies, they function as unofficial transmitters and transformers of the Theravāda textual tradition in northern Thailand.

A second text consulted was a palm-leaf manuscript from the Duang Dī monastery in Chiang Mai. It was copied in 1576 C.E. in the town of Chiang Saen, one of the early Tai Yuan political and cultural centers. The Mahābunkhit edition abbreviated the traditional text represented by the Duang Dī monastery copy, but in other respects is remarkably similar to the content of the sixteenth-century manuscript. Pāli manuscripts of the *Buddha Abhiṣeka* are also found in northern Thai monastery collections and appear in *The Royal Book of Chants* compiled in the nineteenth century during the reign of King Mongkut. In northern Thailand the *Buddha Abhiṣeka* is always preached in the northern Thai vohāra form, but when it is chanted the Pāli version is used.

Consecrating the Buddha

The Buddha, our great teacher, the Enlightened One, out of his great compassion for all beings, practiced the thirty perfections. His resolve to realize the perfections began with his first birth and continued throughout his countless lifetimes. In his birth as Vessantara he practiced the perfection of generosity, relinquishing even his wife and children. After his death as Vessantara, the Enlightened One was reborn in Tuṣita heaven [the fourth level of the heavenly realm]. There the deities of the countless universes met and addressed him saying, "O, thou of great resolve, the appropriate time has come for you to be reborn in the realm of human beings in order to be enlightened as the Buddha." Then, the Bodhisattva departed from Tuṣita heaven and was born into the family of the king of the Śākyas, having been carried in his mother's womb for ten months. Upon his birth he faced the north, took seven steps, and gazed in all directions declaring, "I am supreme in the three worlds."

The Enlightened One lived as a layman [Prince Siddhārtha] for twenty-nine years. One day, while traveling in his pleasure gardens, he chanced upon four sights: an old person, a sick person, a corpse, and an ascetic. He was so moved by this experience that he gave away all his belongings and departed to become a hermit, residing in the forest on the bank of the Anomā River. There he practiced austerities for six years. On the full moon day of Viśākhā he received an offering from the maiden Sujātā, which he consumed while sitting on the bank of the Nerañjarā River. That day the Buddha cast his golden begging bowl in the river where it [miraculously] floated upstream. In the evening the Bodhisattva, taking eight clusters of kuśa grass given to him by the brahman Sotthiya, went to the auspicious bodhi tree growing beside a road built by the gods. Spreading the grass under the tree he seated himself and made the following vow, "I shall sit here and not move from this place until I am freed from all defilements and from all forms of evil." Then, facing eastward as the sun set, he conquered the forces of Māra. Afterwards, the Bodhisattva sat in meditation practicing breathing awareness, alternating exhaling and inhaling short and long breaths. While engaged in the mindfulness of breathing, he comprehended both physical and mental suffering, overcame bodily and mental formations, and experienced both physical and mental rapture. His mind was so concentrated that it was freed from the four kinds of feeling: mental and physical suffering, and mental and physical happiness. He perceived the impermanence of all things, the nature of nirvāṇa, and the freedom from all passion and suffering. While Prince Siddhārtha was investigating breathing meditation he experienced supreme bliss. Persevering in this practice, he concentrated his mind so intently that he was freed from all sensual pleasure and material pleasure. Free from all taint of evil, he attained the first stage of meditative absorption, a state composed of thought-conception (*vitakka*) and discursive thinking (*vicāra*), physical and mental nonattachment, and the rapture of bliss. He reached the second level of absorption, eliminating both *vitakka* and *vicāra* and attaining the rapture of supreme bliss. He experienced physical and mental joy as a result of unwavering concentration (*samādhi*), realizing a wisdom characterized by equanimity, by five kinds of rapture and without avarice. The third stage of absorption (*jhāna*) combines equanimity, unwavering mindfulness, and contentment. Prince Siddhārtha, having attained this third jhāna, contemplated the fourth, in which both mundane happiness and suffering and all feelings of joy and grief are eliminated. He was completely suffused with equanimity, freed from suffering and filled with pure mindfulness. The Bodhisattva Siddhārtha attained serenity and purity, totally eliminating the 1,500 major defilements and all the minor defilements. He took delight only in the good and was never tempted by the eight worldly elements.

Regarding the higher spiritual powers, the Lord realized the mental state in which he was able to recall his previous lives. During the first watch of the night he recalled the family of his birth, the color of his complexion, his diet, his experiences of happiness and suffering, the span of his life, his death and rebirth. He recalled the nature of each of his previous lives until his present existence. Then Siddhārtha firmly resolved to become pure and to rid himself of the least trace of defilement. With his mind pacified and pure, he was not overcome by the eight worldly elements [gain, fame, praise, happiness, and their opposites]. In the second watch he entered the absorption in which he gained the knowledge of death and rebirth of all things.

Prince Siddhārtha, seeing all beings with the divine eye, transcended all human and godly capabilities. He then spoke as follows:

"Some people harbor evil thoughts, do evil deeds, and speak evil words.

Because of their evil thoughts they condemn the saints, and they reject the four noble truths. When such human and divine beings die, they are reborn in hell, where they experience suffering in the four fearful realms. But when those of pure action and pure heart who lead a virtuous life and do not condemn the saints die, they will be reborn in heaven."

The Bodhisattva, realizing that those who die and are reborn experience the consequences of their action, whether good or evil, with the good being rewarded with good and the evil with evil, sat in meditation, uninfluenced by the eight worldly factors. At that time the Bodhisattva came to understand the nature of all compounded things which, because of ignorance continually die and are reborn. Attachment to consciousness comes from attachment to mental formations, which in turn comes from attachment to name and form. Because of the six kinds of contact there arise the six spheres of sense consciousness and the six different kinds of feeling. Grasping for existence comes from attachment, which leads to birth, old age, lamentation and suffering. The cessation of this process is the complete cessation of dharmic formations: the cessation of consciousness leads to the cessation of mental formations; the cessation of mental formations leads to the cessation of name and form; the cessation of name and form leads to the cessation of the six sense spheres; the cessation of the six sense spheres leads to the cessation of the six modes of contact; the cessation of the six modes of contact leads to the cessation of the six kinds of feeling; the cessation of feeling leads to the cessation of grasping, old age, and rebirth.

The Bodhisattva Siddhārtha, attaining the knowledge-state of insight meditation with a wisdom like the radiance of a great diamond, perceived the three characteristics of existence—impermanence, suffering, and not-self—and the nature of the cause and effect of all things. Then the Lord reached the knowledge of the noble (*ariya*) lineage and the knowledge that conforms to reaching the state of stream-enterer. There he overcame the limitations of speculative views, doubt and perplexity, and all of the ten fetters [false view of individuality, doubt and perplexity, adherence to rules and rituals, sensual lust, irritation, attachment to the realm of form, attachment to formless realms, conceit, distraction, ignorance] which constitute the body of ignorance.

In the transcendental state of consciousness of the stream-enterer, its contemplations and its fruits, the Lord perceived the four noble truths: The existence of suffering, the cause of suffering, the cessation of suffering, and the way to the cessation of suffering. In the transcendental state of insight consciousness, he further contemplated the three characteristics of existence. He realized the state of consciousness of the final stage of insight knowledge and the purification associated with wisdom, thereby achieving the condition of the once-returner. Again he contemplated the four noble truths and the nature of suffering, which characterizes the cycle of birth and death. He realized that grasping is the cause of suffering; that the end of rebirth is the end of suffering; and, that there is a path to the end of suffering. In the transcendental state of insight consciousness, the Lord contemplated the three characteristics of existence of all compounded things.

At this point the Lord reached the state of the never-returner in which he overcame all sensual desire, lust, and ill-will. This was the transcendental state of consciousness of the fruit of the never-returner. In the transcendental state of consciousness of the contemplations, the Lord perceived the four noble truths: that rebirth (*saṃsāra*) is suffering (*dukkha*); that grasping (*taṇhā*) is the cause of suffering; that nirvāṇa is the cessation of suffering; and that there is a path to the cessation of suffering. The Lord understood these truths thoroughly. In the transcendental state of insight consciousness he understood the three characteristics of existence and thus attained to the transcendental state . . . of arhatship. Hence, the Lord realized the transcendental state of consciousness of the fully Enlightened One. His course was completed. He had achieved the transcendental state of the fruit of arhatship, the transcendental state of the contemplations, and so on.

The Bodhisattva Siddhārtha perceived the four noble truths through the transcendental states of knowing the path and the contemplations, being purified from the effects of saṃsāra. Together with all the previous buddhas he came to know the truth of suffering.

In his enlightenment the Bodhisattva Siddhārtha achieved the condition of omniscience, becoming the foremost in the world of human beings and gods, of Māra and Brahmā, and in the realm of religious practitioners. He fully realized that this was the end of rebirth (*saṃsāra*). He attained to the state of sublime bliss while seated under the bodhi tree, proclaiming, "Having realized the endlessness of saṃsāra, I have destroyed all grasping (*taṇha*)."

"O, housebuilder (*gahakāra*) [That is, *taṇhā*, the maker of this body of ignorance]! Before I was enlightened I traveled through many cycles of birth and death, and for an infinite number of lifetimes I experienced suffering. O, housebuilder! Now I have seen you. Hereafter you will not build a house [that is, the five aggregates]. Having broken the crossbeams and destroyed the peak of the roof of that house, I have attained to nirvāṇa, and am freed from all conditions. I have attained to the transcendental state of the destruction of the intoxicants in which all grasping is destroyed."

The Tathāgata reached the supermundane state through perseverance and effort. As one in whom the passions are extinct, the Tathāgata burned up all demerit, and through his wisdom realized the dharma of cause and not-cause. During the first watch of the night all of the Tathāgata's doubts disappeared.

At that time the Buddha was able to recall his previous lives. His heart was pure. Devoid of defilements, he resisted the eight worldly factors [gain and loss, fame and obscurity, blame and praise, happiness and pain]. In the middle watch he was able to see the death and birth of all beings through the divine eye superior to all human beings and gods.

"O, brāhmaṇas, all beings who are subject to evil karma, those who speak and think in evil ways, will be reborn in hell, and will suffer in the four hells after their death. Those, on the other hand, who act and speak in beneficial ways, upon death will be reborn in the realm of bliss."

The Buddha knew the condition of the life and death of all beings: those who are stubborn, those who are superior and inferior, those who are beautiful and ugly, those who are punished in hell and who are rewarded in heaven because of their karma. Then the Buddha, having attained enlightenment, was suffused with calm and established in the good so that he was not influenced by the eight worldly factors. In the middle watch of the night he attained to this state of omniscience.

At that time he understood the nature of conditioned reality and of rebirth caused by ignorance, which in turn is caused by mental formations, which in turn depends upon consciousness, mind-body, the six senses, contact, sensation, thirst, clinging, coming-to-be, birth, old age and death. . . . [The next two paragraphs are omitted because of redundancy.]

In the transcendental state of insight awareness the Blessed One contemplated the three characteristics of existence. The following day he . . . eliminated all of the intoxicants, ignorance, the bonds, and the five hindrances. Then, attaining to the transcendental state of the fruit of arhathood, he perceived the four noble truths by means of the transcendental state of consciousness of the path and the contemplations, namely, that the cycle of birth and death is suffering. This noble truth has been realized by all of the noble ones, and in eliminating grasping they have eliminated suffering. They have also eliminated the cause of suffering, and realized the unconditioned state which is nirvāṇa. That is the cessation of suffering. The "practice leading to the cessation of suffering" is called [in Pāli] the *dukkha-nirodha-gāmini-paṭipadā*. . . . [Next two paragraphs omitted because of redundancy.]

In the last watch of the night the Buddha reflected both forward and backward on the law of interdependent coarising: that ignorance is the cause of the mental formations; that mental formations cause consciousness [and so on]; that birth is the cause of old age, death, grief, and lamentation; and that all physical and mental suffering arises accordingly. The Buddha, thereby coming to know the cause and cessation of all forms of suffering and suffused with supreme bliss exclaimed, "O, housebuilder! Having identified you as the builder of this house, no longer will you be able to construct the five aggregates. All construction materials composing the 1,500 defilements have been totally destroyed. Even the pinnacle of the house is gone. I have reached nirvāṇa which is beyond cause and effect, the cessation of all defilements and the supreme transmundane state. All demerit has been burned up. I have entered the higher meditative absorptions and am devoid of all the intoxicants. The Tathāgata, greater than all beings, has a radiance more brilliant than the sun shining in a cloudless sky."

The Tathāgata, he who is without physical blemish and is devoid of doubt, reached the further shore of enlightenment. He overcame all evil, abided in the bliss of the six kinds of seclusion and realized nirvāṇa. He was without anger, cared for all living beings, was free from desire, and dwelt in supreme bliss.

The Buddha, filled with boundless compassion, practiced the thirty perfections for many eons (four *asaṅkheyya* and one-hundred thousand kalpas), finally reaching enlightenment. I pay homage to that Buddha. May all his qualities (*guṇa*) be invested in this Buddha image. May the Buddha's boundless omniscience be invested in this image until the religion (*sāsana*) ceases to exist.

May all of the transcendental states of the Blessed One—analytical insight, perseverance, the four perfect confidences, the forty paths—a total of seventy-seven different properties be invested in this image. May the boundless concentration (*samādhi*) and the body-of-liberation of the Buddha be invested in this image for five thousand years during the lifetime of the religion. May the supermundane reality discovered by the Buddha during his enlightenment under the bodhi tree be invested in this image for the five thousand years of the religion. May all of the miracles performed by the Buddha after his enlightenment in order to dispel the doubts of all humans and gods be invested in this image for all time. May the powers (*guṇa*) of the reliquary mounds miraculously created by the Buddha at the places of his enlightenment in order that both humans and gods might worship him be invested in this image for five thousand rains-retreats.

May the Buddha's boundless virtue (*guṇa*) acquired during his activities immediately after his enlightenment be stored in this image forever. May the knowledge contained in the seven books of the *Abhidharma* [Pāli *Abhidhamma*] perceived by the Buddha in the seven weeks after his enlightenment be consecrated in this image for the rest of the lifetime of the religion. May the power acquired by the Buddha during the seven days under the ajapāla tree, the seven days at the Mucalinda pond, and so on, be invested in this Buddha image for five thousand rains-retreats. The Buddha then returned to Ajapālanigrodha, where he preached the eighty-four thousand teachings. May they also be stored in this Buddha image. May the Mahābrahma who requested that the Buddha preach come into this image.

The Buddha then went to Varanasi, where he preached his first discourse. May the transcendental state of knowledge embodied in this text be instilled in this Buddha image. The Buddha observed the rains-retreat in the Deer Park where he ordained Yasa. May the supernatural power of that event be stored in this image. The Buddha preached to the ascetics headed by Uruvela Kassapa and his brothers together with their retinues. May the supernatural power of that conversion be invested in this Buddha image for five thousand rains-retreats. The Buddha then entered Kapilavastu in order to teach his relatives and performed many miracles such as flying through the air and walking on a pure crystal road. May the supernatural power of that occasion be instilled in this Buddha image for the lifetime of the religion.

Mahākassapa Thera approached the Buddha and asked him about the tradition of the buddhas (*buddhacarita*). The Buddha then preached the *Cariyā-*

piṭaka to him. May the transcendental truth of this text become a part of this Buddha image for the remainder of the life of the religion. The Buddha, the conqueror of Māra, descended from the air and sat under a mango tree where he preached to the people of the Śākya clan in order for them to pay their respects to him. May the supernatural power of that event be invested in this Buddha image. The Buddha, referring to the miracle of the Pokkhara rainfall during the time of Prince Vessantara, preached the *Mahāvessantara Jātaka*. May the supernatural power of that text also be instilled in this Buddha image for five thousand rains-retreats.

Then the Buddha entered Sāvasthi and stayed at the Jetavanārāma. He received this land out of his great compassion for the lay disciple, Anāthapiṇḍika. There he preached to both human beings and gods. May the supernatural power of that occasion be invested in this Buddha image. The Buddha preached out of compassion for all living beings. May all of his teachings be instilled in this Buddha image for five thousand rains-retreats.

The Buddha performed numerous marvelous acts and taught continually, ordaining monks for the first time into the noble path. May all the gods, together with Indra, Brahmā, Māra, and all people protect this Buddha image, as well as the relics and the religion for five thousand years for the welfare of all human beings and gods.

—3—

Sūtra on the Merit of Bathing the Buddha

Daniel Boucher

This *Sutra on the Merit of Bathing the Buddha* is a short text—a little over a page in the standard Chinese Buddhist canon—that was translated into Chinese, presumably from Sanskrit, by the famous monk and pilgrim Yijing (635–713 C.E.). Yijing was born near modern Beijing and entered the monastic order at age fourteen. Because the monastic rules of his order were incomplete in China, he set out for India from Canton by boat in 671 in search of a complete vinaya (monastic code). He arrived at Śrīvijaya (modern Sumatra) where he studied Sanskrit before continuing to Nālandā, the premier Indian monastic university. Having spent ten years studying in India, he returned to China in 689 and spent his remaining years translating the texts he had acquired. The *Sūtra on the Merit of Bathing the Buddha* was translated in 710 at the Dajian fu ("Great Sacrificial Blessings") Temple.

The authenticity of this text is far from certain. There is neither an extant Sanskrit version nor any known Tibetan translation. Furthermore, it is possible that Yijing may have himself constructed this "translation" by drawing from two related texts already known in China. In 705—just five years before Yijing's translation—the Indian monk Manicintana translated the *Sūtra on the Merit of Bathing the Image,* which parallels Yijing's text quite closely, with the addition in the latter of the four-line dharma-relic verse. This dharma-relic verse was found in a similar context—the consecration of miniature stūpas (funerary monuments)—in the *Sūtra on the Merit of Building a Stūpa* rendered into Chinese in 680 by the Indian translator Divākara. It could be argued that Yijing's *Sūtra on the Merit of Bathing the Buddha* reflects a synthesis of themes from two texts already known in China in translation.

It was not uncommon for Chinese Buddhists to produce apocryphal sūtras under the guise of translations from Sanskrit—the criterion for an "authentic" Buddhist text. Such texts could be made to argue for a particular doctrine or sectarian position in China or, as was often the case, they could attempt to legitimate the sponsoring political regime. There does not appear to be any such motive behind Yijing's text. Regardless of the history of the text underlying Yijing's translation, there is considerable evidence that the practices it describes reflect actual Indian Buddhist practice—something that can seldom be said for the vast majority of Indian Buddhist texts. A brief discussion of these practices and their implications will throw light on the developing conceptions of the Buddha in the medieval period.

The *Sūtra on the Merit of Bathing the Buddha* is primarily concerned with the appropriate methods of rendering homage to the Buddha. The sūtra begins with the Pure Wisdom Bodhisattva asking three questions: How does the Buddha acquire his glorified body? What offerings should living beings make when in the presence of the Buddha? And what merit will accrue from this homage? The Buddha responds with two sets of answers: one describing attendance upon the living Buddha, and the other describing how the Buddha is to be worshiped after his death.

In the first case, the Buddha enumerates the perfections and virtues he has cultivated that resulted in the accomplishment of his purified body. By offering incense, flowers, food, drink, and so forth to the Blessed One, and by bathing his body, one can produce unlimited merit that will eventually lead to enlightenment. Note that the text does not espouse the cultivation of particular virtues or contemplative practices for the attainment of enlightenment. Ritual attendance upon the Buddha—fulfilling his corporeal needs—is sufficient.

The majority of the text is, understandably, preoccupied with ways of worshiping the deceased Buddha—a problem all historically founded traditions face. The sūtra picks up here by explaining the nature of the Buddha's body. It is threefold; the Buddha—as all buddhas before and after him—has a dharma body (*dharmakāya*), a glorified body (*saṃbhogakāya*), and a manifestation body (*nirmāṇakāya*). The development and history of these three bodies is a long, complicated, and not entirely understood feature of Mahāyāna Buddhism. Their appearance in this text seems to be aimed at demonstrating the compatibility of the philosophical conception of the Buddha (as an historical manifestation of an eternal body of truth) with the widely held belief that the Buddha was still fully—and physically—present at his shrines and could therefore still be ritually approached.

To begin with, the text specifies that in order to worship the Buddha, one should worship his relics. The worship of the Buddha's relics (his bodily remains after cremation) enshrined in a funerary mound (*stūpa*) goes back to the early period of Buddhism—possibly although not necessarily to the Buddha's death itself. Numerous stūpas within and outside of India were believed by the faithful to contain some remnant of the Buddha's body.

By the sixth or seventh century, the practice of enshrining the corporeal relics of the Buddha ceases to appear in the archeological record. Instead we begin to find at Buddhist sites numerous clay tablets that were stamped or engraved with the four-line verse epitome of the Buddha's teaching on causality. This is the very dharma-relic verse Yijing's translation recommends as an alternative to a corporeal relic. Yijing, in fact, described this cultic practice in the account he wrote of his travels to India:

> [People in India] make [incense] paste caityas [another term in this context for stūpa] and paste images from rubbings. Some impress them on silk or paper, and venerate them wherever they go. Some amass them into a pile, and by covering them with tiles, they build buddha-stūpas. Some erect them in empty fields, allowing them to fall into ruin. Among the monks and laity of India, they all take this as their practice. Furthermore, whether they build images or make caityas, be they of gold, silver, bronze, iron, paste, lacquer, brick, or stone; or they heap up sand like snow, when they make them, they place inside two kinds of relics. One is called the bodily relic of the Great Teacher; the second is called the dharma-verse relic on causation. This verse goes as follows:
>
> All things arise from a cause.
> The Tathāgata has explained their cause
> And the cessation of the cause of these things.
> This the great ascetic has explained.
>
> If one installs these two [relics], then one's blessings will be extremely abundant. This is why the sūtras, expanded into parables, praise this merit as inconceivable. If a person builds an image the size of a bran kernel or a caitya the size of a small jujube, and places on it a parasol with a staff like a small needle, an extraordinary means [is obtained] which is as inexhaustible as the seven seas. A great reward [is obtained] which, pervading the four births, is without end. Details of this matter are all given in other sūtras.
>
> *Taisho,* 2125; vol. 54, p. 226c.

The *Sūtra on the Merit of Bathing the Buddha* would appear to be one of these "other" sūtras.

The development and history of the use of this dharma-verse is not entirely clear. The Buddhist tradition appears to have struggled since early times between two tendencies: to locate the Buddha in his physical presence, especially as left behind in his corporeal relics; and to identify the "true" Buddha as the dharma, his teachings. The former inspired the stūpa cult; the latter devalued the physical body of the Buddha in favor of his career as teacher, typified by canonical passages in which the Buddha states: "He who sees the dharma sees me; he who sees me sees the dharma." More specifically, the teachings on causality (that is, the twelve-fold chain of dependent coproduction; Sanskrit *pratītyasamutpāda*) were viewed as the very heart of the Buddha's message and remained the subject of rigorous commentary and debate. In the medieval period, the essence of the Buddha's teaching on causality—his dharma par excellence—was located in a single four-line verse from the scriptures. By depositing this "essence" in the traditional shrine of the Buddha's corporeal relics, these Buddhists were able to bring together and harmonize the two tendencies suggested above—tendencies that reflect two different conceptions of the Buddha, one concrete and physically present, the other abstract and metaphorically present.

In addition to relic worship, Yijing's translation commends the construction and ritual bathing of the Buddha image. The construction of Buddha images dates from several centuries after the earliest record of the stūpa cult and its origins remain obscure and controversial. Some look for foreign, especially Greco-Roman, influence in the first sculptured statues from the Indo-Greek regions of northwest India around the turn of the common era. Others locate the first images in India proper as continuations of indigenous artistic traditions. By the sixth or seventh century, the image cult was fully incorporated into Buddhist practice—both lay and monastic. Yijing describes a ritual treatment of the Buddha image in his travel account that has much in common with the ritual in the *Sūtra on the Merit of Bathing the Buddha:*

> In cultivating the foundation of devotion, nothing exceeds the three honored ones (the Buddha, his teachings, and the monastic community); in dedicating oneself to the pursuit of contemplation, how could anything surpass the four noble truths? Nevertheless, the principles of truth are profound and worldly affairs obstruct simple minds. Bathing the holy image is practical for the sake of universal succor. Although the Great Teacher is extinguished, his image is still present. One should venerate it with an elevated mind as if the Buddha were still here. Some may place incense and flowers [before the image] every day, enabling them to produce a pure heart. Others may constantly perform the bathing ritual, completely cleansing their tenebrous karma. Those who apply their thoughts to this practice will automatically receive their unmanifested reward. As for those who exhort others to do it, the merit they have already produced will be compounded. Those who seek blessings should set their minds on this.
>
> Moreover, all the monasteries of the Western Regions [especially India and Central Asia] bathe the noble image. Every morning the monastic director sounds the bell. He spreads a jeweled awning over the courtyard of the monastery. At the side of the [image] temple are arranged jars of incense. He takes the gold, silver, bronze, or stone image and places it inside a basin made of bronze, gold, wood, or stone. He orders the female musicians to play their music while he smears the image with ground incense and bathes it with scented water. He rubs it with a clean, white cloth, and afterwards puts it back in the temple, furnishing it with floral decorations. This then is the custom of the majority of monasteries and the task of the revered director of monastic affairs. In the same manner the monks individually bathe the noble image within their respective cells. Each day they all perform the essentials without deficiency.
>
> *Taishō* 2125; vol. 54, p. 226b

The third question asked by the Pure Wisdom Bodhisattva concerns the merit that accrues from performing these reverential acts. Attendance upon the living Buddha as well as attendance upon his shrine or image after his death are both stated to produce infinite merit and blessings. In fact this merit is efficacious enough to lead one to enlightenment and "the other shore," a typical Buddhist expression for nirvāṇa. But the text also describes a number of other benefits from these ritual performances: prosperity, protection, and comfortable old age in this life; fortunate rebirth—especially the avoidance of a female body—and perpetual encounters with buddhas in future lives.

Western students of Buddhism have generally regarded ritual attainment of enlightenment and desires for prosperity and fortunate rebirth as indicative of lay Buddhist interests and goals. This is contrasted with the presumption that monastics seek enlightenment strictly through contemplative practices and a strict moral life—the so-called "true" path expounded by the Buddha. Such a dichotomy is not supported by much of the evidence. Yijing's travel log, for example, specifically describes activities taking place in the monasteries. Although we do not want to detract from the importance of meditation and related practices for Buddhist mendicants, this is certainly only part of the picture. The vast majority of our data suggests that an array of practices were available to and taken up by monks and nuns of all periods. Not all of these practices were necessarily complementary. Many, in fact, may have been in competition with one another, reflecting competing conceptions of how the presence of the departed teacher—be it the legacy of his teachings or his bodily remains and representation—was to be maintained and, importantly, to be encountered. Such tensions inspired repeated attempts over time to harmonize these various strands of the tradition. The *Sūtra on the Merit of Bathing the Buddha* might be described as one of these attempts. The translation has been made from *Taishō shinshū daizōkyō* (Tokyo, 1924–1934), 698; vol. 16, pp. 799c–800c.

Suggestions for Further Reading

For a brief discussion of Yijing's translation and its relationship to related texts, see Ryojun Mitomo, "An Aspect of Dharma-śarīra," *Indogaku bukkyōgaku kenkyū (Journal of Indian and Buddhist Studies)* 32.2 [64] (1984); (4)–(9) (in English). For a complete translation of Yijing's travel account, describing the many practices he personally witnessed, see I Tsing, *A Record of the Buddhist Religion as Practiced in India and the Malay Archipelago,* translated by J. Takakusu (London, 1886; reprint Delhi: Munshiram Manoharlal, 1966).

For a more detailed discussion of both the literary and archeological development of the dharma-verse relic, see Daniel Boucher, "The *Pratītyasamutpādagāthā* and Its Role in the Medieval Cult of the Relics," *Journal for the International Association of Buddhist Studies* 14.1 (1991), 1–27.

For some general information on the stūpa cult, see among others David L. Snellgrove, "Śākyamuni's Final Nirvāṇa," *Bulletin of the School of Oriental and African Studies* 36 (1973), 399–411. An anthology of papers of mixed quality has appeared in Anna Libera Dallapiccola and Stephanie Zingel-Avé Lallemant, eds., *The Stūpa: Its Religious, Historical and Architectural Significance* (Wiesbaden: Franz

Steiner Verlag, 1980); see also Gregory Schopen, "Burial 'Ad Sanctos' and the Physical Presence of the Buddha in Early Indian Buddhism: A Study in the Archeology of Religions," *Religion* 17 (1987), 193–225.

One of the few scholarly treatments of the ritual of bathing the Buddha is Ferdinand Lessing, "Structure and Meaning of the Rite Called the Bath of Buddha According to Tibetan and Chinese Sources," in Soren Egerod and Else Glahn, eds., *Studia Serica Bernhard Karlgren dedicata* (Copenhagen, 1959), pp. 159–71.

Sūtra on the Merit of Bathing the Buddha

Thus have I heard. At one time the Blessed One was in Rājagṛha, on Vulture's Peak, together with 1,250 monks. There were also an immeasurable, unlimited multitude of bodhisattvas and the eight classes of gods, nāgas, and so forth, who were all assembled. At that time, the Pure Wisdom Bodhisattva was seated in the midst of this assembly. Because he aspired to extend compassion toward all sentient beings, he thought: "By what means do the buddhas, tathāgatas, obtain the pure body, furnished with the marks of the great person?" Again he thought: "All classes of living beings are able to meet the Tathāgata and approach him with offerings. The blessings that are obtained are without measure or limit. I do not yet know, however, what offerings living beings will make or what merit they will cultivate after the death of the Tathāgata so as to bring about those roots of good merit that quickly lead to final, supreme enlightenment." After thinking this, he then arose from his seat and bared his right shoulder; having bowed his head at the feet of the Buddha, he knelt upright, with palms in salutation, and spoke to the Buddha, saying, "World-Honored One, I wish to ask questions and hope that you deign to acknowledge them." The Buddha said, "Noble son, I will teach according to what you ask."

At that time, the Pure Wisdom Bodhisattva spoke to the Buddha, saying, "By what means do the buddhas, tathāgatas, perfectly enlightened ones obtain the pure body, furnished with the marks of the great person? Also, all living beings are able to meet the Tathāgata and approach him with offerings. The blessings that are obtained are without measure or limit. I have not yet discerned what offerings living beings will make or what merit they will cultivate after the death of the Tathāgata so as to bring about those good qualities that quickly lead to final, supreme enlightenment."

At that time, the World-Honored One said to the Pure Wisdom Bodhisattva: "Excellent, excellent, that you are able for the sake of future beings to bring forth such questions! Now listen carefully, reflect on this well, and practice as I say. I will explain for you in detail."

The Pure Wisdom Bodhisattva said, "So be it, World-Honored One. I dearly wish to listen."

The Buddha explained to the Pure Wisdom Bodhisattva: "Noble son, you should know that because giving, morality, patience, vigor, meditation, and wisdom; benevolence, compassion, delight, and indifference; liberation and the knowledge and experience of liberation; the [ten] strengths and the [four] confidences are all the characteristics of the Buddha and are all various kinds of knowledge, virtue, and purity, they are the purity of the Tathāgata.

"If the buddhas, tathāgatas, are in this way given various offerings with a pure heart—incense, flowers, gems, garlands, banners, parasols, and cushions—displayed before the Buddha, multifariously adorning him, and the marvelously scented water is used to bathe his noble form, the dark smoke of the burning incense will carry your mind to the dharma realm. Furthermore, if you celebrate the extraordinary merit of the Tathāgata with food and drink, percussion and stringed music, you will manifest the superb vow to direct [your mind] to the supreme ocean of omniscience. The merit thereby produced will be immeasurable and without limit; it will be perpetually continued [through successive rebirths] to the point of enlightenment. Why is this? The blessed wisdom of the Tathāgata is inconceivable, infinite, and unequaled.

"Noble son, all buddhas, world-honored ones, have three bodies. They are known as the dharma body (*dharmakāya*), the glorified body (*saṃbhogakāya*), and the manifestation body (*nirmāṇakāya*). After my nirvāṇa, if you wish to do homage to these three bodies, then you should do homage to my relics. But there are two kinds: the first is the bodily relic; the second is the dharma-verse relic. I will now recite the verse:

> All things arise from a cause.
> The Tathāgata has explained their cause
> And the cessation of the cause of these things.
> This the great ascetic has explained.

"If men, women, or the five groups of mendicants would build an image of the Buddha; or if those without strength would deposit one as large as a grain of barley, or build a stūpa—its body the size of a jujube, its mast the size of a needle, its parasol equal to a flake of bran, its relic like a mustard seed—or if someone writes the dharma-verse and installs it inside the stūpa, it would be like doing homage by offering up a rare jewel. If in accordance with one's own strength and ability one can be truly sincere and respectful, it [the image or stūpa] would be like my present body, equal without difference.

"Noble son, if there are beings who are able to make such excellent offerings, they will glorify themselves by achieving the fifteen superb virtues. First, they will always be modest. Second, they will manifest a mind of pure faith. Third, their hearts will be simple and honest. Fourth, they will cleave to good friends. Fifth, they will enter a state of passionless wisdom. Sixth, they will constantly encounter buddhas. Seventh, they will always maintain the correct teaching. Eighth, they will be able to act according to my teaching. Ninth, they will be reborn in pure buddha fields according to their wishes. Tenth, if they are reborn among men, they will be noblemen of great families; being respected among men, they will produce joyous thoughts. Eleventh, being born among men, they will naturally set their minds on the Buddha. Twelfth, an army of demons will not be able to harm them. Thirteenth, they will be able in the final age to protect and maintain the true dharma. Fourteenth, they will be protected by the buddhas of the ten directions. Fifteenth, they will be able to quickly obtain the five attributes of the dharma body."

At that time, the World-Honored One uttered these verses:

After my death
You will be able to honor my relics
Some will build stūpas
Or images of the Tathāgata.
At the place of the image or stūpa,
One who anoints that spot of ground
With various incenses and flowers
Scattering them over its surface,
Uses pure, beautifully scented water
To pour onto the body of this image,
Offers it various flavorful drinks and foods,
Fully maintaining it with oblations,
Eulogizes the virtue of the Tathāgata
Which is endlessly difficult to conceive;
Through the wisdom of skillful means and the supernatural power [of the Buddha],
Such a one will quickly reach the other shore [of nirvāṇa].
He will obtain the diamond body
Complete with the thirty-two marks of a great person
And the eighty minor signs of excellence.
He will ferry the multitude of living beings [to the shore of nirvāṇa].

At that time, the Pure Wisdom Bodhisattva, having heard these verses, addressed the Buddha saying, "Future living beings will ask, 'Why bathe the image?" ' The Buddha answered the Pure Wisdom Bodhisattva: "Because you will equal the Tathāgata in producing right mindfulness. You will not be attached to the two sides that deceive people with 'emptiness' and 'being.' You will long insatiably for virtuous conduct. The three emancipations, morality, and wisdom will be constantly sought to escape the endless cycle of birth and death. You will produce great compassion toward all living beings. You will aspire to obtain and quickly perfect the three kinds of bodies.

"Noble son, I have already expounded for your sake the four noble truths, the twelve conditioned co-productions, and the six perfections. And now I teach the method of bathing the image for your sake and the sake of the various kings, princes, ministers, concubines, princesses, gods, nāgas, men, and demons. Among the various types of homage, this [the bathing of image] is the best. It excels the giving of the seven jewels equal to sands of the Ganges.

"When you bathe the image, you should use oxhead sandalwood, white sandalwood, red sandalwood, or aloewood incenses. You should burn Mountain Top Tulip incense, 'Dragon's Brain' incense, Ling-ling [Mountain] incense, and so forth. On the surface of a clean stone, you should grind these to make paste; use [this paste] to make scented water and place it in a clean vessel. At a clean spot, make an altar with good earth, square or round, its size suited to the circumstances. On top establish the bathing platform, and place the Buddha image in the middle. Pour on the scented hot water, purifying and cleansing it, repeatedly pouring the pure water over it. The water that is used must be completely filtered so as not to cause harm to insects. Drops from two fingers of the water with which you bathed the image should be taken and placed on your own head–this is called 'good luck water.' Drain off the water onto clean ground without allowing your feet to tread upon it. With a fine, soft towel wipe the image, making it clean. Burn the above-named incenses, spreading the aroma all around, and put the image back in its original place.

"Noble son, the consequence of performing this bathing of the Buddha image is that you and the great multitude of men and gods will presently receive wealth, happiness, and long life without sickness; your every wish will be fulfilled. Your relatives, friends, and family will all be at ease. You will bid a long farewell to the eight conditions of trouble and forever escape the fount of suffering. You will never again receive the body of a woman, and will quickly achieve enlightenment.

"When you have set up the image and burned the various incenses, face the image, clasping your palms together in pious salutation, and recite these praises:

> I now bathe the Tathāgata.
> His pure wisdom and virtue adorn the assembly.
> I vow that those living beings of this period of the five impurities
> May quickly witness the pure dharma body of the Tathāgata.
> May the incense of morality, meditation, wisdom, and the knowledge and experience of liberation
> Constantly perfume every realm in the ten directions.
> I vow that the smoke of this incense will likewise
> Do the Buddha's work [of salvation] without measure or limit.
> I also vow to put a stop to the three hells and the wheel of saṃsāra,
> Completely extinguishing the fires and obtaining the coolness [of relief]
> So that all may manifest the thought of unsurpassed enlightenment
> Perpetually escaping the river of desires and advancing to the other shore [of nirvāṇa]."

The Buddha finished expounding this sūtra. At this time, there were among this assembly an immeasurable, unlimited number of bodhisattvas who obtained stainless concentration. The countless gods obtained never lapsing wisdom. The multitude of śrāvakas (lit. "hearers," a title for the early disciples of the Buddha) vowed to seek the fruits of buddhahood. The eighty-four thousand living beings all manifested the thought toward unexcelled, complete enlightenment.

At that time, the Pure Wisdom Bodhisattva said to the Buddha: "World-Honored One, being fortunate to receive the compassion and pity of the great teacher [the Buddha], we shall teach the method of bathing the image. I will now convert kings, ministers, and all those of good faith, cheer, or merit. Every day I will bathe the noble image to procure great blessings. I pledge to always receive and carry out with pleasure the *Sūtra on the Merit of Bathing the Buddha.*"

—4—

Reading Others' Minds

Carl Bielefeldt

One of the earliest and best-known Japanese Zen masters is Dogen (1200–1253). Born to the nobility, he became a Tendai monk in his youth; later, he visited Kenninji, the monastery founded by the Zen pioneer Eisai, and eventually made his way to China, accompanying one of Eisai's disciples. On the mainland, he spent four years studying at the Jingde Monastery on Mount Tiandong, where he became a disciple of the Tiandong abbot Rujing. He returned to Japan in 1127 and soon established the Kōshō Monastery on the outskirts of Kyoto. After teaching there for more than a decade and collecting a fair number of disciples, he withdrew with his followers to the relatively isolated province of Echizen (modern Fukui), where he founded the Daibutsuji, the monastery at which he would live out the rest of his days. This institution, which Dōgen later renamed Eiheiji, became one of the headquarters of Sōtō Zen, the school that still looks back to him as its founding patriarch.

Unlike most of the early Japanese Zen figures, Dōgen was a prolific author. His reputation rests especially on a collection (originally several collections) of essays known as the *Treasury of the Eye of the True Dharma (Shōbō genzō)*. These works, prepared over many years for his monks at Kōshōji and Eiheiji, represent a highly original and notoriously difficult body of Buddhist writing. Composed in the vernacular Japanese but incorporating much of the language of the Song Chinese Zen texts, they range broadly in subject matter from highly abstruse metaphysical reflection to concrete religious admonition and ritual instruction, historical discussion and personal recollection. The title of the collection, *Treasury of the Eye of the True Dharma,* is a technical term denoting the Zen tradition, especially as preserved in the literature recording the sayings of the Zen masters. The representative essays in Dōgen's *Treasury* are typically developed in the form of commentaries on such sayings, selected to elucidate a particular Buddhist theme. Though the practice of giving brief, often playfully critical, remarks on the sayings of one's predecessors was well established in Song Zen circles, Dōgen's comments tend to be considerably more sustained and discursive than most; though his points are often obscure and his arguments odd, more than most of his Zen contemporaries he does try to articulate in some detail his particular Buddhist vision.

The *Shōbō genzō tashintsū*, translated here as *Reading Others' Minds*, is one of the later essays in the *Treasury*, composed, according to its colophon, in 1245 at Dōgen's Daibutsu Monastery. It is not perhaps so philosophically engaging or so artfully crafted as some of his earlier, more famous pieces, but it is representative of much of his writing and deals with themes central to his religion. Perhaps more than any one else in Zen tradition, Dōgen's religion was centered on the practice of seated meditation (*zazen*), what he sometimes liked to call "just sitting" (*shikan taza*). Indeed, so fixed was his faith in this practice that he regularly identified it as the very essence of Buddhism, the "treasury of the eye of the true dharma" itself, the "marrow of Bodhidharma" transmitted by all the authentic patriarchs of Zen. As the very essence of Buddhism, seated meditation was, according to Dōgen, more than a psycho-physical exercise intended to still the mind, focus the attention, and generate spiritual insight; it was rather an expression of the enlightened state itself, the actualization of the universal "buddha nature" that the Zen teachings had long held was inherent in all beings. Thus, as Dōgen liked to say, seated meditation was beyond the human intention to "make a buddha"; it was rather the "act of a buddha," the "performance," or "conduct," of a buddha.

The identification of religious practice with the higher acts of a buddha has affinities with, and was no doubt historically influenced by, the tantric teachings popular among Dōgen's Japanese contemporaries; but for Dōgen himself, this truth was the exclusive preserve of the Zen tradition and indeed of those few masters within the tradition who had the eye to see the ultimate implications of the Zen teachings. Such masters were no mere spiritual "commoners," nor even advanced spiritual adepts; they were one with ultimate reality itself and, as such, beyond the reaches of ordinary experience and understanding, beyond even the stages of the Buddhist spiritual path and the categories of Buddhist soteriological doctrine. It is this transcendent status of the authentic Zen master that is celebrated in our text here.

The title theme of *Reading Others' Minds* concerns an interesting and recurrent issue in the Zen literature. Throughout the history of Buddhism, from its earliest days in India, it was widely assumed that contemplative adepts, whether Buddhist or not, could develop paranormal psychic powers. In a standard formulation found across a variety of Buddhist texts, it was said that one who had mastered the basic trance states of the four dhyānas could cultivate five kinds of powers, known collectively as the "superknowledges" (*abhijñā*), or in East Asian usage as the "spiritual penetrations" (*jinzū*): physical transformations and psychic travel, paranormal vision (including knowledge of the future), paranormal hearing, knowledge of others' thoughts, and knowledge of previous lives (both one's own and others'); to these was often added a sixth, more soteriologically significant, power that was reserved for realized Buddhist adepts: knowledge of the exhaustion of the "cankers," or spiritual afflictions.

The Zen tradition, of course, took its very name from the practice of dhyāna, and the monks of this tradition were supposed to be specialists in meditation. Hence, they were naturally expected, both in theological circles and in the popular imagination, to have access to the powers said to accrue to the contemplative, and in fact the hagiographic literature of the Zen masters includes accounts of their extraordinary, often miraculous powers. At the same time, the Zen doctrine claimed a "sudden" practice based solely on an enlightened state of "no-mind." Since the practice was sudden, it took one directly from the mundane world of ordinary experience to the ultimate emptiness of all things, thus obviating the mediating path of traditional spiritual exercises; since it was based solely on the ultimate state of no-mind, it looked down on all lesser states of mind—even the spiritual states of the contemplative and the paranormal knowledge derived from them—as trivial and irrelevant. Thus we see in the literature of Zen a continuing need to distance the religion from the expectations of Buddhist tradition and emphasize the superiority of its practice to the powers of the contemplative. Dōgen, who put such stress on seated meditation, was particularly sensitive to this need, as is clear from his treatment of the transcendental Zen master in *Reading Others' Minds*.

The clash between the expectations of the tradition and the "sudden" style of Zen is dramatically portrayed in the root text on which Dōgen is commenting—the story of the spiritual contest between the mind-reading Indian pundit, the Tripiṭaka Master "Big Ears," and the mind-boggling Chinese Zen master, the National Teacher Huizhong. The Zen master boggles the pundit's mind because his own mind does not fit the latter's image of the spiritual practitioner: it is at once scandalously at home in the most secular, most natural experience and yet at the same time completely free from all experience. Meanwhile, the Tripiṭaka Master remains stuck, as it were, in the sacred realm "between" these two freedoms, with the merely supernatural powers of the entrancing (and entranced) "fox spirit."

Huizhong, a disciple of the famous Sixth Patriarch, was well known in Zen circles, and was himself sometimes said to have mind-reading powers; the tale of his defeat of the Tripiṭaka Master (actually only one version of a popular story) was the subject of comment by many later masters. Dōgen takes up a number of these comments and rejects them all: first, because they assume that the contest in the story concerns mind reading, rather than the Buddhist understanding of the ultimate nature of things; second, because they assume that the Indian scholar might have some inkling of the Zen master's mind. This latter point he argues along two lines: first, that the ability to read minds is an insignificant Indian trick, with no power to get at the mind in any important sense; second, that the mind of the authentic Zen master, even when it is at play in the world, is not something that can be got at. Finally, Dōgen seems to conclude, in a rather obscure argument, that if we want to talk in serious Buddhist terms about reading others' minds, we shall have to question the very categories of mind and body, self and other.

Reading Others' Minds is not the most difficult of Dōgen's writing, but Dōgen's writing is always difficult, and there are passages in this text about which readers disagree and for which the translation must be considered tentative. This English version seeks to preserve something of the difficulties and ambiguities of Dōgen's style by retaining as far as possible its elliptic, sometimes puzzling syntax and its peculiar, sometimes enigmatic diction, and resisting the temptation to "cook" the text with interpolation or paraphrase; terms or passages that seem particularly odd or problematic in the English are sometimes set off by quotation marks or amplified by brief explanation in square brackets. The translation is based on the text edited by Terada Tōru and Mizuno Yaoko, in *Dōgen,* vol. 2, *Nihon shisō taikei* 13 (Tokyo: Iwanami Shoten, 1972), pp. 282–92.

Reading Others' Minds

The National Teacher [Dazheng] Huizhong [d. 775 C.E.], of the Guangzhai Monastery in the Western Capital [Changan], was a native of Juji, in the province of Yue [modern Zhejiang]; his family name was Ran. After receiving the mind seal [of enlightenment from the Sixth Patriarch], he stayed at Dangzi Valley, Mount Baiyai, in Nanyang [modern Henan], where for more than forty years he never descended from his monastery. Word of his spiritual practice reached the imperial capital, and in the second year of the Shangyuan era [761] of the Tang Emperor Suzong [r. 756–762], an imperial commissioner, Sun Zhaojin, was dispatched to summon him to the capital. There he was received with the respect due a teacher and installed in the Xichan cloister of the Qianfu Monastery. Upon the ascension of the Emperor Daizong [r. 762–779], he was reinstalled in the Guangzhai Monastery, where for sixteen years he taught the dharma in accord with the spiritual needs of his audiences.

During this time, a certain Tripiṭaka Master from the Western Heavens [India] named Daer [Big Ears] arrived in the capital, claiming to have achieved the wisdom eye [that knows] the minds of others. The emperor ordered the National Teacher [Huizhong] to test him.

As soon as the Tripiṭaka Master saw the Teacher, he bowed and stood [respectfully] off to his right side.

The Teacher asked him, "You have the penetration of others' minds?"

"It's nothing much," he answered.

"Tell me," said the Teacher, "where is this old monk right now?"

The Tripiṭaka Master said, "Reverend Preceptor, you are the teacher to a nation; how could you go off to Xichuan to watch the boat races?"

The Teacher asked again, "Tell me, where is this old monk right now?"

The Tripiṭaka Master said, "Reverend Preceptor, you are the teacher to a nation; how could you be on the Tianjin bridge watching the playing monkeys?"

The Teacher asked a third time, "Tell me, where is this old monk right now?"

The Tripiṭaka Master said nothing for awhile, not knowing where the Teacher had gone.

The Teacher said, "This fox spirit! Where's his penetration of others' minds?"

The Tripiṭaka Master had nothing to say.

A monk asked Zhaozhou [778–897], "I don't understand why the Tripiṭaka Master Daer couldn't see where the National Teacher was the third time. Where was he?"

Zhaozhou said, "He was on the Tripiṭaka Master's nose."

A monk asked Xuansha [835–908], "If he was on his nose, why didn't he see him?"

Xuansha said, "Because he was too close."

A monk asked Yangshan [803–887], "Why didn't the Tripiṭaka Master Daer see the National Teacher the third time?"

Yangshan said, "The first two times were 'the mind that plays across objects.' After that, he entered 'the samādhi of the personal enjoyment [of enlightenment]'; that's why the Tripiṭaka Master couldn't see him."

Duan of Haihui [1025–1072] said, "If the National Teacher was on the Tripiṭaka Master's nose, why would it be hard to see him? What he doesn't realize is that the National Teacher was in the Tripiṭaka Master's eye."

Xuansha summoned the Tripiṭaka Master, saying, "Tell me, did you really see [his mind] the first two times?"

[Of this,] the Chan Master Mingjue Zhongxian of Xuedou [980–1052] said, "Defeated! Defeated!"

From long ago there have been many "stinking fists" who offered remarks and comments on the case of the National Teacher Dazheng [Huizhong] testing the Tripiṭaka Master Daer, but in particular we have these five old fists. Yet, while there is a sense in which each of these five venerable worthies may be "on the mark, right on the mark," there is much in the conduct of the National Teacher that they do not see. The reason is that until now everyone has thought that the Tripiṭaka Master correctly knows the whereabouts of the National Teacher the first two times he is asked. This is a major error by our predecessors—one that their successors should not fail to realize. My doubts about these five venerable worthies are of two sorts: first, that they do not know the National Teacher's basic intention in testing the Tripiṭaka Master; second, that they do not know the National Teacher's body and mind.

When I say that they do not know the National Teacher's basic intention in testing the Tripiṭaka Master, I mean this: that his basic intention in initially saying, "Tell me, where is this old monk right now?" is to test whether the

Tripiṭaka Master has the eye to see the Buddha's dharma—to test, that is, whether he has the penetration of others' minds [as understood] in the Buddha's dharma. If at that point the Tripiṭaka Master had the Buddha's dharma, when he is asked "Where is this old monk right now?" he would have some "way out of the body," some "personal advantage." The National Teacher's saying "Where is this old monk right now?" is like his asking "What is 'this old monk'?" "What time is 'right now'?" His question "Where?" means "Where is here?" There is a reason behind his asking what to call this "old monk": a national teacher is not always an "old monk"; an "old monk" is always a "fist." That the Tripiṭaka Master Daer, though he came all the way from the Western Heavens, does not understand this is because he has not studied the way of the Buddha, because he has only learned the ways of the infidels and the two vehicles.

The National Teacher asks again, "Tell me, where is this old monk right now?" Here again the Tripiṭaka Master only offers worthless words.

Again the National Teacher asks, "Tell me, where is this old monk right now?" This time the Tripiṭaka Master is silent for a while but is at a loss and has no reply. Then the National Teacher rebukes him, saying, "This fox spirit! Where's his penetration of others' minds?" Yet though he is thus rebuked, the Tripiṭaka Master still has nothing to say, no reply, no "penetrating passageway."

Yet our predecessors all think that the National Teacher's rebuke of the Tripiṭaka Master is only because, although the Master knows the Teacher's whereabouts the first two times, he does not know and cannot see [where the Teacher is] the third time. This is a big mistake. The National Teacher rebukes the Tripiṭaka Master because from the beginning the Tripiṭaka Master has never seen the Buddha's dharma even in his dreams, not because although he knows the first two times he does not know the third time. In short, he rebukes him because, while claiming to have attained the penetration of others' minds, he does not know that penetration.

First, the National Teacher tests him by asking whether there is the penetration of others' minds in the Buddha's dharma. He answers, "It's nothing much," suggesting that there is. Afterwards, the National Teacher thought to himself, "If we say there is the penetration of others' minds in the Buddha's dharma, if we attribute this penetration to the Buddha's dharma, this [that is, answers of this sort (?)] is what it's like. If there's nothing brought up in what we have to say, it's not the Buddha's dharma." Even if the Tripiṭaka Master had something to say the third time, if it were like the first two times, it would not be anything to say; he would be rebuked for all [three answers]. The National Teacher questions him three times in order to ask again and again whether the Tripiṭaka Master has really heard his question.

My second point is that none of our predecessors have known the body and mind of the National Teacher. The body and mind of the National Teacher is not something that Tripiṭaka dharma masters can easily see, can easily know; not something reached by those on the "ten ranks of the holy and three ranks of the wise"; not something understood by the "virtually enlightened, heir apparent" [to buddhahood]. How could a commoner scholar of the Tripiṭaka know the full body of the National Teacher?

We should get this principle fixed [in our minds]. To say that a scholar like the Tripiṭaka Master could see or could know the body and mind of the National Teacher is to slander the Buddha's dharma; to consider that [the National Teacher] stands shoulder to shoulder with the masters of the sūtras and commentaries is the extreme of madness. Do not think that those types who seek to get the penetration of others' minds can know the whereabouts of the National Teacher.

The penetration of others' minds is a local custom of the country of the Western Heavens, and there are occasionally types there who cultivate it. We have never yet heard accounts of an edifying example of such types having verified the Buddha's dharma on the strength of their penetration of others' minds, without depending on production of the "thought of enlightenment" and the right view of the Greater Vehicle. Even after practicing the penetration of others' minds, they must, like ordinary commoners, go on to produce the thought of enlightenment and cultivate the practice, and thereby themselves verify the way of the Buddha. If one could know the way of the Buddha simply on the strength of the penetration of others' minds, all the holy men of the past would have first cultivated this penetration and used it to know the fruit of buddhahood; yet this has never happened in all the appearances in the world of a thousand buddhas and ten thousand patriarchs. If it cannot know the way of the buddhas and patriarchs, what good is it? It is useless to the way of the Buddha.

Those who have the penetration of others' minds and ordinary commoners who do not are equal; they are the same in both maintaining the buddha nature. Those who study the Buddha's [dharma] should not think that those with the "five penetrations" or the "six penetrations" of the infidels and two vehicles are superior to the ordinary commoner. Those who simply have the mind to pursue the way and who would study the Buddha's dharma are superior to those with these penetrations. They are like the kalaviṅka bird, whose voice even inside the shell is superior to that of other birds.

Moreover, what is called in the Western Heavens the penetration of others' minds is better described as the penetration of others' thoughts. Even if it can manage to be conscious of the arising of thoughts, it is quite at a loss when thoughts have not arisen. This is really quite laughable. The mind is not necessarily thoughts; thoughts are not necessarily the mind. And when the mind is thoughts, the penetration of others' minds cannot know this; when thoughts are the mind, the penetration of others' minds cannot know this.

This being the case, the five penetrations or six penetrations of the Western Heavens are all quite useless, not the equal of "cutting the grasses and cultivating the paddies" in our country. Therefore, from Cīnasthāna [China] to the east, the worthies of the past have not cared to cultivate the five penetrations or six penetrations, since they have no use. Even a six-foot jewel is useful, but the five or six penetrations are useless. [As the old saying reminds us,] a "six-foot jewel" is not a treasure, but an "inch of time" is pivotal. For those who value that inch of time, who would cultivate the five or six penetrations?

Thus we should have very firmly fixed [in our minds] the principle that the power of the penetration of others' minds cannot reach the boundaries of the Buddha wisdom. To think nevertheless, as do our five venerable worthies, that the Tripiṭaka Master knew the whereabouts of the National Teacher the first two times he was asked is greatly mistaken. The National Teacher is a buddha and patriarch; the Tripiṭaka Master is a commoner. How could there be any question of their seeing each other?

First, the National Teacher asks, "Tell me, where is this old monk right now?" There is nothing hidden in this question; what it has to say is fully apparent. That the Tripiṭaka Master might not understand it is not so bad; that the five venerable worthies do not hear it or see it is a serious mistake. [The text] says that the National Teacher asked, "Where is this old monk right now?" It does not say that he asked, "Where is this old monk's mind right now?" or "Where are this old monk's thoughts right now?" This has something to say that we should definitely hear and understand, see and take to heart. Nevertheless, [our worthies] do not understand or see it; they do not hear or see what the National Teacher has to say. Therefore, they do not understand the body and mind of the National Teacher, for it is having something to say that makes him a national teacher; without something to say he would not be a national teacher. How much less, then, can they understand that the body and mind of the National Teacher are not big or small, self or other. They might as well have forgotten that he has a head or a nose.

Though the spiritual conduct of the National Teacher be unceasing, how could he "figure to make a buddha"? Therefore, he should not be compared with a buddha. Since the National Teacher has the body and mind of the Buddha's dharma, we should not measure him by the practice and verification of the spiritual penetrations, we should not hem and haw over the notion [that he is in a trance state] of "severing considerations and forgetting objects." He is not something that can be determined by either deliberating or not deliberating. It is not the case either that he has or does not have the buddha nature; it is not the case that his is the [buddha's] "body of empty space." This kind of body and mind of the National Teacher is something entirely unknown [to any of our five venerable worthies]. In the community of [the Sixth Patriarch, Huineng of] Caogi, apart from [the disciples] Qingyuan and Nanyue, only this National Teacher Dazheng was a buddha and patriarch.

Now we need to question all our five venerable worthies.

Zhaozhou says that the Tripiṭaka Master could not see the National Teacher because the latter was "on his nose." This saying has nothing to say. How could the National Teacher be on the Tripiṭaka Master's nose? The Tripiṭaka Master does not yet have a nose. If we admit that the Tripiṭaka Master has a nose, then the National Teacher should see him. Even if we admit that the National Teacher does see him, this would only mean that they are "nose to nose"; it would not mean that the Tripiṭaka Master and the National Teacher see each other.

Xuansha says [that the Tripiṭaka Master did not see the National Teacher the third time] "because he was too close." To be sure, this may be "too close," but it still has not hit it. What is this "too close"? I am afraid that Xuansha still does not understand "too close," has not studied "too close." I say this because he understands only that there is no seeing each other in "too close"; he does not understand that seeing each other is "too close." We have to say that, in terms of the Buddha's dharma, he is the "farthest of the far." If we say that [the National Teacher] is too close only the third time, then he must have been too far away the first two times. Now, I want to ask Xuansha, "What is it that you call 'too close'? Is it a fist? Is it an eye? From now on, do not say that there is nothing seen 'too close.' "

Yangshan says, "The first two times were 'the mind that plays across objects.' After that, he entered 'the samādhi of the personal enjoyment [of enlightenment]'; that's why the Tripiṭaka Master couldn't see him." Yangshan, while being from the Eastern Earth [China], you have a reputation in the Western Heavens as a little Śākyamuni, but your saying here is a big error. "The mind that plays across objects" and the "samādhi of the personal enjoyment [of enlightenment]" are not different; hence, we cannot say that [the Tripiṭaka Master] does not see him by reason of some difference between these two. Therefore, though you set up "the mind that plays across objects" and "the personal enjoyment [of enlightenment]" as the reasons, saying this is no saying. If you say that when I enter "the samādhi of the personal enjoyment [of enlightenment]," others cannot see me, then "the personal enjoyment [of enlightenment]" would not be able to verify itself, and there could be no cultivation and verification of it. Yangshan, if you think that the Tripiṭaka Master really sees, if you believe that he really knows the Teacher's whereabouts the first two times, you are not yet a man who has studied the Buddha's [dharma]. The Tripiṭaka Master Daer does not know or see the whereabouts of the National Teacher, not only the third time but the first two times as well. Judging from the level of this saying, we have to say not only that the Tripiṭaka Master does not know the National Teacher's whereabouts but that Yangshan does not yet know either. Let us ask Yangshan, "Where is the National Teacher right now?" If he thinks to open his mouth, we should give him a big shout.

In Xuansha's summons [to the Tripiṭaka Master], he says, "Tell me, did you really see [his mind] the first two times?" These words sound like they are saying what needs to be said, and Xuansha should learn from his own words.

But granted that this phrase has its value, it seems to be saying only that [the Tripiṭaka Master's] seeing is like not seeing. Hence, it is not right. Hearing this, Zhongxian, the Chan Master Mingjue of Mount Xuedou, said, "Defeated! Defeated!" We may say this when we have taken what Xuansha says as a [significant] saying but not when we take his saying as not a saying.

Duan of Haihui says, "If the National Teacher was on the Tripiṭaka Master's nose, why would it be hard to see him? What he doesn't realize is that the National Teacher was in the Tripiṭaka Master's eye." This also only discusses the third time and does not criticize, as it should, the fact that [the Tripiṭaka Master] never sees [the National Teacher] the first two times. How can [Duan] know whether the National Teacher is on his nose or in his eye? If this is what he says, we have to say that he has not heard the words of the National Teacher. The Tripiṭaka Master still does not have a nose or eyes. Even if we were to say that he does maintain eyes and nose, if the National Teacher were to enter them, the Tripiṭaka Master's eyes and nose would immediately burst. Since they would burst, they are not a cave or cage for the National Teacher.

None of our five venerable worthies knows the National Teacher. He is the old buddha of his age, the tathāgata of his world. He illumined and properly transmitted the "treasury of the eye of the true dharma" of the Buddha; he surely maintained the "eye of the soapberry" [from the seeds of which the Buddhist rosary is made]. He properly transmitted [these eyes] to "his own buddhahood" and to the "buddhahood of others." Though we may say that he studied together with the Buddha Śākyamuni, he studied at the same time as the seven buddhas [of which Śākyamuni was the last] and, in addition, studied together with all the buddhas of the three ages [of past, present, and future]. He realized the way before the King of Emptiness [the ruling buddha of the eon when all is reduced to emptiness]; he realized the way after the King of Emptiness; he practiced together and realized the way precisely with the Buddha King of Emptiness. Though we may say that the National Teacher naturally made this Sahā world his domain, his Sahā is not necessarily within the dharma realm; it is not within the entire world of the ten directions. The rulership of the Buddha Śākyamuni over the Sahā domain does not usurp or hinder the National Teacher's domain. Similarly, for example, the way is realized numerous times, by the earlier and later buddhas and patriarchs one after the next, without their usurping or hindering each other. This is the case because all realizations of the way by the earlier and later buddhas and patriarchs are "hindered by" the realization of the way.

From the evidence that the Tripiṭaka Master Daer does not know [the whereabouts of] the National Teacher, we should get clearly and firmly fixed [in our minds] the general principle that the śrāvakas and pratyekabuddhas, the Lesser Vehicle types, do not know the boundaries of the buddhas and patriarchs. We should clearly understand the point of the National Teacher's rebuke of the

Tripiṭaka Master. It does not make sense that, although being a national teacher, he would rebuke [the Tripiṭaka Master] if the latter knew [his whereabouts] the first two times and failed to know only the third time: [for purposes of the test of his powers] knowing two out of three is knowing it all, in which case he should not be rebuked. Even if he were rebuked, it would not be for failing to know at all; hence, from the Tripiṭaka Master's perspective, it would be the National Teacher who is humiliated [by the test]. Who would trust the National Teacher if he rebuked [the Tripiṭaka Master] for failing to know only the third time? [On the contrary,] the Tripiṭaka Master could have rebuked the National Teacher on the grounds that he did have the power to know [the latter's whereabouts] the first two times.

The point of the National Teacher's rebuke of the Tripiṭaka Master is this: he rebukes him because from the beginning, throughout all three times, he does not know the National Teacher's whereabouts, his thoughts or his body and mind; he rebukes him because he has never seen, heard, learned, or studied the Buddha's dharma. It is because of this point that, from the first time to the last, [the National Teacher] questions him with exactly the same words. When on the first question the Tripiṭaka Master answers, "Reverend Preceptor, you are the teacher to a nation; how could you go off to Xichuan to watch the boat races?" the National Teacher does not acknowledge the answer, saying, "Indeed you did know where this old monk was." Instead, he simply repeats himself, asking the same question three times. Without understanding or clarifying the reason behind this, for several hundred years since the time of the National Teacher, the elders in all directions have been giving their arbitrary comments and explanations of the reasons [behind the story]. Nothing that any has said so far has been [true to] the original intent of the National Teacher or in accord with the point of the Buddha's dharma. What a pity that each of these "venerable old awls," one after the next, has missed [the meaning of the story].

In the Buddha's dharma, if we are going to say that there is the penetration of others' minds, there should be the penetration of others' bodies, the penetration of others' fists, the penetration of others' eyes. If this is the case, there should also be the penetration of one's own mind, the penetration of one's own body. And once this is the case, the penetration of one's own mind is simply one's own mind itself taking up [itself]. If we express the matter in this way, one's own mind itself is the penetration of others' minds. Let me just ask, then, "Should we take this as the penetration of others' minds, or should we take it as the penetration of one's own mind? Speak up! Speak up!" Leaving that aside, "you got my marrow" [as Bodhidharma said in acknowledging the enlightenment of his disciple Huike] is the penetration of others' minds.

Treasury of the Eye of the True Dharma 73.

Presented to the assembly the fourth day of the seventh month of the third year of Kangen [1245], at the Daibutsu Monastery in the province of Etsu.

—5—

The Prayer of the Original Buddha

Matthew Kapstein

The Nyingmapa (Rnying-ma-pa) sect stands in a distinctive relationship to all other traditions of Tibetan religion. As its name, which literally means the "Ancients," suggests, the school maintains that it uniquely represents the ancient Buddhism of Tibet, introduced during the reigns of the great kings of Tibet's imperial age, during the seventh to ninth centuries C.E. In contradistinction to the organized Bön (Bon) religion, which claims to be the pre-Buddhist religion of Tibet, it identifies itself as a purely Buddhist tradition; in contrast to the other Tibetan Buddhist schools and in harmony with Bön, however, it insists upon the value of an indigenous Tibetan religious tradition, expressed and exalted within a unique and continuing revelation of the Buddha's doctrine in Tibet.

The following features of Nyingmapa Buddhism are particularly noteworthy in the present context. The primordial buddha Samantabhadra (in Tibetan, Kuntuzangpo [Kun-tu-bzang-po], the "Omnibeneficient"), iconographically depicted as a naked buddha of celestial blue color, is regarded as the supreme embodiment of buddhahood (shared with Bön). The highest expression of and vehicle for attaining that buddha's enlightenment (which is equivalent to the enlightenment of all buddhas) is the system of meditational teaching known as the "Great Perfection" (Dzokchen [Rdzogs-chen], also shared with Bön). The paradigmatic exponent of this teaching, and indeed of all matters bearing on the spiritual and temporal well-being of the Tibetan people, is held by Nyingmapas to be the immortal guru Padmasambhava, the apotheosis of the Indian tantric master who played a leading role in Tibet's conversion to Buddhism during the eighth century, and who is thought to be always present to intercede on behalf of his devotees.

This emphasis on the figure of Padmasambhava is distinctively Nyingmapa, though the cult of Padmasambhava claims many adherents belonging to the other sects of Tibetan Buddhism as well. Moreover, since the eleventh century the teachings of Padmasambhava have been held to be continually renewed in forms suitable to the devotee's time, place, and circumstances; the agents for such renewal are the "discoverers of spiritual treasure" (called *tertön* [*gter-bton*] in Tibetan), thought to be embodiments of, or regents acting on behalf of, Padmasambhava. In this form the tradition of "spiritual treasure," called *terma* (*gter-ma*), is distinctly Nyingmapa, though non-Nyingmapa terma are also known, particularly among the followers of Bön.

Although the Nyingmapa adhere, as do other Tibetan Buddhists, to tantric forms of ritual and contemplative practice, their tantric canon is altogether distinctive, incorporating a great quantity of literature whose authenticity is challenged by many adherents of the other Tibetan Buddhist schools, as is the authenticity of their special teaching of the Great Perfection.

In the selections below we meet one of the most influential of the "discoverers of spiritual treasure," Ngödrup Gyeltsen (Dngos-grub-rgyal-mtshan), also called Rikdzin Gödemchen (Rig-'dzin rgod-ldem-can) (1337–1408 C.E.). The hidden texts he is said to have discovered form the basis for the tradition of the Northern Treasure, an important Nyingmapa subsect whose headquarters were established at the monastery of Dorje Trak (Rdo-rje-brag), to the south of Tibet's capital, Lhasa. The Fifth Dalai Lama (1612–1682), usually called "the Great Fifth" by Tibetans owing to his tremendous impact on Tibetan political and cultural life, was very partial to the teachings of the Northern Treasure tradition, whose hierarchs had enjoyed close relationships with his family.

The first selection, from *The Nyingma School of Tibetan Buddhism: Its Fundamentals and History* by Dudjom Rinpoche (1904–1987), the late head of the Nyingma School and one of its leading modern authors, is a capsule summary of Ngödrup Gyeltsen's biography, illustrating several of the features commonly found in the lives of the treasure finders: the assertions that he is the incarnation of one of Padmasambhava's personal disciples, that miraculous or unusual characteristics and abilities became apparent even during his childhood, that he came into the possession of a special inventory indicating the nature of the treasures he was destined to discover, and, finally, that he revealed these hidden works under exceptional circumstances, and set them down in a form that would be accessible to the world at large (for the original scrolls are almost always thought to be written in an arcane code, decipherable only by the designated discoverer).

The second selection, *The Prayer of Great Power,* is the most popular of Ngödrup Gyeltsen's treasures, and is recited daily by tens of thousands of Tibetans, and on special occasions by many more. Drawn from a long series of works devoted to the Great Perfection system, the four-volume *Penetration of Samantabhadra's Intention,* it introduces us to the special Nyingmapa conception of the original buddha, and the characteristic teaching of the Great Perfection, which holds that by coming to recognize the nature of awareness (*rig-pa*), and by resting in that recognition, the highest enlightenment may be effortlessly won.

The prayer makes use of three of the basic categories of Buddhist philosophical thought: ground, or the essential nature of reality; path, which is the course followed until enlightenment is attained; and result, the attainment of enlightenment itself. Here the path, and likewise the result, are described in terms of the contrast between the original buddhahood of Samantabhadra, and the path through saṃsāra that sentient beings must pursue, as a result of their lack of enlightened awareness. Samantabhadra's primordial enlightenment gives rise to emanations of peaceful and wrathful deities, buddhas who counteract the coarse emotions born of unawareness that bind ordinary beings to rebirth in the six painful destinies of saṃsāra.

Throughout the prayer, qualities that arise owing to the very nature of the ground are referred to as "self-emergent," "self-manifest," and the like. That is to say, they arise from the ground in and of itself, naturally, without depending on other, extraneous causes and conditions. Because the unsullied, pristine awareness of the buddha's enlightenment may arise in this way, we need only learn to recognize it: there is nothing we can do to cause it to come into being. Because this enlightenment is grounded in our essential nature, when it is indicated to us we become, in a sense, powerless not to become buddhas.

The "Summary Biography of Ngödrup Gyeltsen" has previously appeared in Dudjom Rinpoche, Jikdrel Yeshe Dorje, *The Nyingma School of Tibetan Buddhism: Its Fundamentals and History,* annotated translation by Gyurme Dorje and Matthew Kapstein, 2 vols. (Boston: Wisdom Publications, 1991), pp. 780–783. "The Prayer of Great Power" has appeared in my article "The Amnesic Monarch and the Five Mnemic Men," in Janet Gyatso, ed., *In the Mirror of Memory* (Albany: SUNY Press, 1992), pp. 239–269. See these works for full citations of the Tibetan texts translated below. I wish to thank the editors and publishers mentioned for permission to reproduce brief sections from these writings here.

Summary Biography of Ngödrup Gyeltsen

Ngödrup Gyeltsen, the great master of enlightened awareness and treasure finder, was the reincarnation of Nanam Dorje Düjom, an important disciple of Guru Padmasambhava, and one of the three treasure finders renowned as supreme emanations. He was born, attended by extraordinary omens, on Tuesday February 11, 1337, into the household of Namolung, which hailed from the district of Thoyor Nakpo, to the northeast of Mount Trazang. He was the son of the master Düdül, who belonged to an unbroken lineage of accomplished masters of the rites of the wrathful deity Vajrakīla, descended from the clan of the Horpa king Kurser, an epic hero. In accordance with a prophecy, when Ngödrup Gyeltsen was in his twelfth year three vulture feathers grew from the crown of his head, and five when he was at the age of twenty-four. Therefore, he became universally known as Rikdzin Gödemchen, the "Vulture-quilled Master of Enlightened Awareness." During his youth he attained the limits of study, reflection, and meditation upon all the Nyingmapa doctrinal cycles that were the doctrines of his forefathers.

There was one Zangpo Trakpa of Manglam who had discovered, in Gyang Yönpolung, the texts on eight doctrinal topics, including one called the *Essential Inventory Which Treats the Essence of the Esoteric Instructions in Seven Sections*. He realized that these were required as supplements to the treasures to be revealed at Lhadrak, and for this reason he offered them to the great master of enlightened awareness Gödemchen, sending them through Tönpa Sonam Wangchuk. Accordingly, on Sunday April 19, 1366, on the summit of Mount Trazang, at the three stone pillars of Dzengtrak Karpo, Rikdzin Gödemchen found the key to three great treasures and one hundred minor treasures, and at that place he concealed a substitute treasure, so as to satisfy the local protective deities. That treasure ground, which was then left as it was, is known today as Lungseng, "Windy Hollow." Even at present, new shoots sprout there at the beginning of each new year.

At dusk on Sunday June 14 of that same year, in the cave of Zangzang Lhadrak, Rikdzin Gödemchen discovered a great, profound treasure containing five treasure chambers in separate compartments inside a square, blue treasure chest. From the maroon core treasure chamber in the center he extracted three paper scrolls and three kīlas [daggerlike ritual spikes] wrapped in maroon silk; from the white conch treasure chamber to the east, the *Doctrine Which Ascertains the Causal and Fruitional Aspects of Deeds, of Which the Intention is Vast as Space;* from the yellow gold treasure chamber to the south, the *Doctrinal Cycle of the Four Aspects of Ritual Service and Attainment Which is Luminous like the Sun and Moon;* from the red copper treasure chamber to the west, the *Doctrine of Auspicious Coincidence Which is Like a Sandalwood Tree;* and from the black iron treasure chamber to the north, the *Doctrine Which Pulverizes Enemies and Obstacles, and Which is Like a Poisonous Plant*. In short, he found countless doctrines, the *Penetration of Samantabhadra's Intention* foremost among them, and many sacramental objects. Because each of the five treasure chambers held one hundred doctrinal topics, there were five hundred in all. He established the texts according to the yellow scrolls he discovered, and those of their branches, and propagated them among worthy recipients. In this way, his doctrinal teaching eventually pervaded all the regions of Tibet.

The Prayer of Great Power

Tsitta A! [Heart-mind A!]

Then the original buddha Samantabhadra recited this special prayer, concerning the powerlessness of sentient beings in the round of saṃsāra not to become buddhas:

> Ho! All phenomenal possibilities—
> The round and transcendence—

One ground, two paths, two results—
A miracle of awareness and unawareness!
By the aspiration of the Omnibeneficient
May the buddhahood of all be perfectly disclosed
In the fortress of reality's expanse.
The ground-of-all is unconditioned,
A self-emergent, open expanse, ineffable,
Without even the names of both "round" and "transcendence."
Being aware of just that is buddhahood,
While sentient beings, unaware, wander the round.
May all sentient beings of the three realms
Be aware of the ineffable significance of the ground.

For I, the Omnibeneficient,
Am the significance of the ground,
without cause or condition.
Awareness, self-emergent, from the ground that's just that,
Imputes no fault, outer or inner,
by exaggeration or depreciation.
It is free from the dark taint of forgetfulness,
And so unsullied by self-manifest fault.
In abiding in self-presenting awareness,
There is no terror though the three worlds be afraid;
There is no desire for the five sensual pleasures.
In nonconceptual cognition, self-emergent,
There are neither concrete forms nor the five colors.
The unimpeded radiant aspect of awareness
Has the five pristine cognitions in its sole essence.
As the five pristine cognitions mature,
The original buddhas of five families emerge.
The horizon of pristine cognition expanding thereafter,
Forty-two buddhas emerge.
The expressive power of the five pristine cognitions arises,
And the sixty blood-drinkers emerge.
So the ground-awareness experiences no error.

Because I am the original buddha,
By reciting my aspiration,
May the sentient beings of the round's three realms
Know the face of self-emergent awareness
And expand the horizon of great pristine cognition.

My emanations are incessant,
Radiating inconceivably by hundreds of millions,
Variously revealing how each is trained according to need.

By the aspiration of my compassion,
May all sentient beings in the round's three realms
Be set free from the six classes' abodes.

At first, sentient beings, in error,
Awareness of the ground not arising,
Suffer total forgetfulness and oblivion.
Just that is unawareness, the cause of error,
Overcome by which, as in a faint,
Cognition, in terror, wanders intoxicated.
Thus dividing self and other, enmity is born.
As its residues develop by stages,
The round emerges in evolutionary sequence;
The five poisonous afflictions expand therefrom;
The activity of the five poisons is incessant.
Therefore, because error's ground within sentient beings
Is forgetful unawareness,
By my aspiration as a buddha,
May all sentient beings of the three realms
All know by themselves their own awareness.

Co-emergent unawareness
Is cognition in forgetful oblivion.
Imputative unawareness
Is the apprehension of self and other as two.
Co-emergent and imputative unawareness together
Form error's ground for all sentient beings.
By my aspiration as a buddha,
May all sentient beings in the round
Find the thick darkness of forgetfulness dispelled,
Dualistic cognition removed,
And then know the proper face of awareness.
Dualistic intellect is doubt.

When subtle obsessive attachment arises,
Its residues densely ramify in sequence.
Food, wealth, clothing, abode, and friends,
The five sensuous objects and loving relations—
You are tormented by passionate desire for what pleases.
These are worldly errors;
Apprehended, apprehender, and act have no final end.
When the fruit of obsessive attachment matures,
Embodied as a ghost wracked by craving,
You are born to terrible hunger and thirst.
By my aspiration as a buddha,

May sentient beings engaged in desire and obsessive attachment
Neither renounce the torment of desire,
Nor adhere to desire and obsessive attachment,
But, by letting cognition relax in its proper domain,
May they seize the proper domain of awareness,
And acquire all-comprehending pristine cognition.

Directed to the appearance of outer objects
There proceeds a subtle, frightened cognition;
When the residues of hatred spread forth,
Coarse enmity and violence are born.
When anger's result has matured,
You suffer in the inferno of hell.
By the power of my aspiration as a buddha,
May all sentient beings of the six destinies,
Whenever fierce anger is born,
Neither adhere to nor reject it,
But relax in their proper domain,
And by seizing the proper domain of awareness,
May they acquire clarifying pristine cognition.

When your mind becomes inflated,
There's the thought to debase, in competition with others.
The thought of fierce pride being born,
You suffer combat between self and other.
When the result of that action matures,
Born a god, you are liable to fall and to die.
By my aspiration as a buddha,
May self-inflated sentient beings
Relax cognition in its proper domain,
And by seizing the proper domain of awareness
Acquire equanimity's pristine cognition.

Owing to ramified residues of dualistic grasping,
There are tortured deeds of self-praise, blame of others;
Violent competitiveness develops
And you are born in the murderous antigods' abode:
The result, a fall into hellish abodes.
By the power of my prayer as a buddha,
May those born competitive and violent
Not engage in enmity, but relax in their proper domains,
And by seizing the proper domain of awareness
Realize the pristine cognition of unimpeded enlightened activity.

The result of forgetfulness, apathy, and distraction,
Oblivion, dullness, forgetfulness,

Unconsciousness, laziness, and stupidity
Is to roam as an unprotected beast.
By my aspiration as a buddha
May the luster of mindful clarification arise
In the darkness of insensate stupidity,
And bring acquisition of nonconceptual pristine cognition.

For all the sentient beings of the three realms
Are equal to me, the buddha of the universal ground.
Forgetful, they've drifted into bewilderment's ground,
And so now are engaged in meaningless deeds:
The six deeds are like the bewilderment of dreams.
I am the original buddha:
To train the six destinies by my emanations,
By my aspiration as the Omnibeneficient,
May all sentient beings, none excepted,
Become buddhas in reality's expanse!

Aho!
In the future a powerful yogin,
With unbewildered awareness, self-clarified,
Will recite this powerful prayer,
And all sentient beings who hear it
Will disclose buddhahood within three lives.
During solar or lunar eclipse,
At times of thunder or earthquake,
During the solstices or at New Years,
He will recreate himself as Samantabhadra.
If this is uttered so that all may hear,
Then all the sentient beings of the three realms,
Because of that yogin's prayer,
Will be successively released from suffering
And swiftly attain buddhahood!

From *The Tantra which Teaches the Great Perfection, the Penetration of Samantabhadra's Intention,* the nineteenth chapter, which teaches the powerlessness of sentient beings not to become buddhas, on reciting the Prayer of Great Power.

—6—

Myōe's Letter to the Island

George J. Tanabe, Jr.

Myōe Shōnin ("Holy Man of Clear Wisdom") was born in 1173, also the year of Shinran's birth. Unlike Shinran, who pioneered a new form of Buddhist teaching and practice, Myōe was a Shingon monk who tried to revive the traditional Kegon Sect, which, by his time, had failed to maintain itself as a viable form of Buddhism. Myōe was convinced that the abstruse doctrines of Kegon still made sense, and that the times called not for new forms of Buddhism but a return to older forms.

There were several elements to the traditional forms of Buddhism that Myōe wished to revive. One was the precepts, the rules that prescribed in great detail how monks and nuns should live their lives. For Myōe the precepts were not just rules to be followed but the means by which one could live as Śākyamuni did. What the precepts preserved was the lifestyle of Śākyamuni; since he wished to return to the very source of Buddhism, Myōe advocated the precepts as a blueprint for recreating the Buddha's India. Twice he planned to travel all the way to India, but he never succeeded in carrying out his plans. The first time he was thwarted by illness, and his second attempt was aborted by an oracle from the Kasuga deity, who told Myōe that Japan was as good as India. Myōe agreed and used his imaginative powers to envision his environment as the land of the Buddha.

Visions were also an essential element in traditional Buddhism, and Myōe was extremely skilled in the art of meditation, which for him was a technique for producing visions. Myōe kept a record of his meditative visions—dreams, he called them—and even provided his own interpretations. The primary sources for his dreams and visions were the scriptures, which themselves were often the products of other visionaries. The scriptures are full of fantastic happenings that obviously cannot be explained in any rational fashion.

Myōe himself recognizes that the very act of writing a letter to an island is a fanciful act that others would call crazy. Yet that very act, as well as the content of the letter, is an expression of the idea of nonduality. The island and the Buddha are one, an inanimate object is a living being, and all things are fused together as one. Myōe, of course, knows that this is a preposterous idea, and is content to let it be called crazy since he also knows that preposterous ideas cannot be explained. He criticizes his contemporaries for not being sympathetic with the even more preposterous times in the past when it was usual for people to dig holes in the ground and speak into them. These days, he says with deliberate irony, people are "irrational." Far from being eccentric in writing a letter to an island, Myōe was acting out the central fantasy of Mahāyāna Buddhism: all things are one.

Myōe was also called Kōben ("Highly Articulate"), the name he used to sign the letter. Kōben was a gifted writer and left, in addition to the usual technical writings of monks, a large corpus of poems and essays. In these writings he makes it clear that doctrines were meant to be seen as visions and, even more importantly, transformed into waking reality. He lived as best he could the life of nonduality, and it is equally true to say that he meant waking reality to be transformed into doctrinal visions. The scriptures were not filled with myths and symbols, but were literally true: flowers really did fall as rain. It was the real world that was a symbol, that is, an emblem for something else; and Karma Island, which one can actually visit in Yuasa Bay in Wakayama prefecture, was, in addition to being an ordinary island, the extraordinary body of the Buddha. Ultimately, there were no symbols for Myōe. The island did not stand for the Buddha, it really was the Buddha. Myōe was articulate to the point of being a total literalist, and he therefore did not suffer from the kind of doubts other Buddhists had about the meaning of statements asserting the identity of each thing with everything.

This translation is from Hiraizumi Akira, ed., *Myōe Shōnin denki* (Tokyo: Kōdansha, 1980), pp. 65–68.

Further Reading

See George J. Tanabe, Jr., *Myōe the Dreamkeeper* (Cambridge: Harvard University Press, 1993).

Myōe's Letter to the Island

Dear Mr. Island:
How have you been since the last time I saw you? After I returned from visiting you, I have neither received any message from you, nor have I sent any greetings to you.

I think about your physical form as something tied to the world of desire, a kind of concrete manifestation, an object visible to the eye, a condition perceivable by the faculty of sight, and a substance composed of earth, air, fire, and water that can be experienced as color, smell, taste, and touch. Since the nature of physical form is identical to wisdom, there is nothing that is not enlightened. Since the nature of wisdom is identical to the underlying principle of the universe, there is no place it does not reach. The underlying principle of the universe is identical to the absolute truth, and the absolute truth is identical to the ultimate body of the Buddha. According to the rule by which no distinctions can be made between things, the underlying principle of the universe is identical to the world of ordinary beings and thus cannot be distinguished from it. Therefore, even though we speak of inanimate objects, we must not think of them as being separated from living beings.

It is certainly true that the physical substance of a country is but one of the ten bodies of the Buddha. There is nothing apart from the marvelous body of the radiant Buddha. To speak of the teaching of nondifferentiation and perfect interfusion of the six characteristics of all things—their general conditions, specific details, differences, similarities, formation, and disintegration—is to say that your physical form as an island consists of the land of this nation, which is one part of the body of the Buddha. In terms of the characteristic that things differ, we can speak of you also as the other nine bodies of the Buddha: the bodies of living beings, the body of karmic retribution, the bodies of those who listen to the teachings, the bodies of those who are self-enlightened, the bodies of bodhisattvas, the bodies of buddhas, the body of the truth, the body of wisdom, and the body of emptiness. Your own substance as an island is the substance of these ten bodies of the Buddha, and since these ten bodies are all fused together, they exist in a state of perfect union. This is the epitome of Indra's net, and goes beyond explanation because it far transcends the boundaries of conscious knowledge.

Therefore, in the context of the enlightenment of the ten buddhas in the Kegon sect, the underlying principles of you as an island can be thought of as the nondifferentiation between the karmic determinations of who we are and where we live, the identical existence of the one and the many, Indra's net that intertwines all things, the inexhaustibility of everything, the universality of the world of truth, the perfect interfusion that cannot be explained, and the complete endowment of the ten bodies of the Buddha in all things. Why do we need to seek anything other than your physical form as an island since it is the body of the radiant Buddha?

Even as I speak to you in this way, tears fill my eyes. Though so much time has passed since I saw you so long ago, I can never forget the memory of how much fun I had playing on your island shores. I am filled with a great longing for you in my heart, and I take no delight in passing time without having the time to see you.

And then there is the large cherry tree that I remember so fondly. There are times when I so want to send a letter to the tree to ask how it is doing, but I am afraid that people will say that I am crazy to send a letter to a tree that cannot speak. Though I think of doing it, I refrain in deference to the custom of this irrational world. But really, those who think that a letter to a tree is crazy are not our friends. We will keep company with the Sovereign Master of the Sea, who searched for Treasure Island, and will live on the great ocean, making crossings to islands. Our friend will be the Ocean Cloud Monk with whom we will play to our heart's delight. What more could we want?

Having visited you and carried out my religious practice as I wanted to, I am firmly convinced that you, more than some wonderful person, are truly an interesting and enjoyable friend. Having observed the ways of the world for some time now, I think it suitable that there were those in the past who followed the custom of digging a hole in the ground and speaking into it.

These are all ancient matters. These days no one does anything like this, but when we speak of it there is a certain yearning that we have for it. However, I now practice the precepts of a community of monks who are living in the realm of the one truth. We do not serve the interests of friends living on the outside; neither do we have a mind for embracing all living beings. All in all, however, I do not think that this sin is a sin at all.

At any rate, I should like to write to you again at a later time.

With deepest respect,
Kōben

After this letter was written, the messenger asked, "To whom shall I deliver this letter?" Myōe replied, "Simply stand in the middle of Karma Island; shout in a loud voice, 'This is a letter from Myōe of Toganoo!'; leave the letter; and return."

—7—

The *Tathāgatagarbha Sūtra*

William H. Grosnick

The *Tathāgatagarbha Sūtra* is a short but extremely influential Mahāyāna Buddhist text that was probably composed sometime around the middle of the third century C.E. It is the sūtra that introduced into the Mahāyāna tradition the notion of the tathāgatagarbha, the idea that all beings have latent within themselves all the virtues of a buddha (*tathāgata*), but that those virtues are hidden by a covering (*garbha*) of passion and anguish (the so-called kleśas of greed, anger, lust, confusion, and so on). The central message of the sūtra is that when those kleśas are removed, the buddhahood that is potential in all beings will be revealed.

The idea of the tathāgatagarbha was later to form the nucleus of the concept of buddha nature (*buddhadhātu*) in the Sino-Japanese Buddhist tradition. And concepts of both the tathāgatagarbha and the buddha nature underwent extensive doctrinal development in important Mahāyāna sūtras and influential commentaries. But whereas later treatises generally give a highly philosophical interpretation to the tathāgatagarbha, it is doubtful that any such sophisticated understanding was intended by the author(s) of the *Tathāgatagarbha Sūtra*. In the *Tathāgatagarbha Sūtra*, the concept of the tathāgatagarbha is promulgated primarily to inspire beings with the confidence to seek buddhahood, and to persuade them that despite their poverty, suffering, and bondage to passion, they still have the capacity to attain the ultimate goal of Mahāyāna Buddhism, the perfect enlightenment of the Tathāgata.

The term *tathāgatagarbha* has often been translated by Western scholars as "matrix of the tathāgata," but "matrix" does not exhaust the wide range of meanings of the Sanskrit term *garbha*. The author of the *Tathāgatagarbha Sūtra* seems to have been well aware of this, since he employs many of these different meanings of garbha in the various similes with which he illustrates the meaning of the tathāgatagarbha. In its most common usage, garbha means "womb," and the eighth simile of the sūtra likens the tathāgatagarbha to an impoverished, vile, and ugly woman who bears a noble, world-conquering king in her womb. But garbha can also mean "fetus," so the garbha in the eighth simile may also refer to the son who is within her womb. Garbha can also refer to the calyx of a flower, the cuplike leafy structure that enfolds the blossom, and the image in the sūtra's opening scene of conjured buddha forms seated within lotus flowers seems to be predicated on this meaning. Garbha can also mean "inner room," or "hidden chamber," or "sanctuary" (as in the garbhagrha of a Hindu temple, which houses the image of the deity, or the rounded dome [*garbha*] of a Buddhist stūpa, which houses the precious relics of the Buddha). It is probably this meaning of garbha that the author of the sūtra intends in the fifth simile of the sūtra, when he speaks of the tathāgatagarbha as being like a hidden chamber or a secret store of treasure hidden beneath the house of a poor man. (The Chinese may have had this simile in mind when they chose the term *tsang,* "secret store," to translate *garbha*). Garbha can also refer to the outer husk that covers a fruit or seed or, by extension, to the seed itself. The third and sixth similes of the sūtra, which compare the tathāgatagarbha to the useless husk surrounding an edible kernel of wheat and to the mango pit that can grow into the most regal of trees, make direct use of this sense. Finally, garbha can refer to the inside, middle, or interior of anything, and it is this widest meaning that the author of the sūtra is employing when he likens the tathāgatagarbha to gold hidden inside a pit of waste, to honey hidden inside a swarm of angry bees, or to a golden statue hidden inside a wrapping of dirty rags or within a blackened mold.

The majority of the *Tathāgatagarbha Sūtra*'s similes portray something extremely precious, valuable, or noble (such as buddhas, honey, kernels of wheat, gold, treasure, golden statues, or future princes), contained within something abhorrent and vile (such as rotting petals, angry bees, useless husks, excrement, poor hovels, dirty rags, soot-covered molds, and impoverished, ugly women). So the central meaning of the tathāgatagarbha concept is clear: within each and every person there exists something extremely valuable—the possibility of becoming a tathāgata—but that valuable potential for buddhahood is hidden by something vile—the sufferings and passions and vicissitudes of life. But to carry the interpretation further and to look for a deeper meaning to the tathāgatagarbha concept of this early text would probably be wrong, for when one looks more closely at the various similes used to illustrate the tathāgatagarbha, certain inconsistencies begin to emerge. For example, although most of the similes portray the precious reality within as something already complete in itself, two of the similes clearly indicate that the precious reality will only reach its perfected state in the future. The conjured buddhas within the lotus flowers are already fully enlightened, the honey and the wheat kernel are already edible, the gold in the waste pit is already pure and in no need of refinement, and the golden statues are already fully cast, whereas, by contrast, it will take many years for the embryo in the poor woman's womb to become a world conqueror, and more years still for the mango pit to become a full-grown tree.

The text translated is the Chinese translation by Buddhabhadra, *Taishō shinshū daizōkyō* (Tokyo, 1924–1934), 666, vol. 16, pp. 457a1–460b20.

The Mahāvaipulya Tathāgatagarbha Sūtra

Thus have I heard. At one time the Buddha was staying on the Vulture Peak near Rājagṛha in the lecture hall of a many-tiered pavilion built of fragrant sandalwood. He had attained buddhahood ten years previously and was accompanied by an assembly of hundreds and thousands of great monks and a throng of bodhisattvas and great beings sixty times the number of sands in the Ganges River. All had perfected their zeal and had formerly made offerings to hundreds of thousands of myriad legions of buddhas. All could turn the irreversible wheel of the dharma. If a being were to hear their names, he would become irreversible in the highest path. Their names were Bodhisattva Dharma-Wisdom, Bodhisattva Lion-Wisdom, Bodhisattva Adamantine Wisdom (Vajramati), Bodhisattva Harmonious Wisdom, Bodhisattva Wonderful Wisdom, Bodhisattva Moonlight, Bodhisattva Jeweled Moon, Bodhisattva Full Moon, Bodhisattva Courageous, Bodhisattva Measureless Courage, Bodhisattva Transcending the Triple World, Bodhisattva Avalokiteśvara, Bodhisattva Mahāsthāmaprāpta, Bodhisattva Fragrant Elephant, Bodhisattva Fine Fragrance, Bodhisattva Finest Fragrance, Bodhisattva Main Treasury, Bodhisattva Sun Treasury, Bodhisattva Display of the Standard, Bodhisattva Display of the Great Standard, Bodhisattva Stainless Standard, Bodhisattva Boundless Light, Bodhisattva Bestower of Light, Bodhisattva Stainless Light, Bodhisattva King of Joy, Bodhisattva Eternal Joy, Bodhisattva Jeweled Hand, Bodhisattva Treasury of Space, Bodhisattva King of Light and Virtue, Bodhisattva Self-Abiding King of Dhāraṇīs, Bodhisattva Dhāraṇī, Bodhisattva Destroying All Ills, Bodhisattva Relieving All the Ills of Sentient Beings, Bodhisattva Joyous Thoughts, Bodhisattva Satisfied Will, Bodhisattva Eternally Satisfied, Bodhisattva Shining on All, Bodhisattva Moon Brightness, Bodhisattva Jewel Wisdom, Bodhisattva Transforming into a Woman's Body, Bodhisattva Great Thunderclap, Bodhisattva Spiritual Guide, Bodhisattva Not Groundless Views, Bodhisattva Freedom in All Dharmas, Bodhisattva Maitreya, and Bodhisattva Mañjuśrī. There were also present bodhisattvas and great beings just like them from countless buddha lands, whose number equaled sixty times the number of sands in the Ganges River. Together with an uncountable number of gods, nāgas, yakṣas, gandharvas, asuras, garuḍas, kinnaras, and mahoragas [all divine and quasi-divine beings], they all gathered to pay their respects and make offerings.

At that time, the Buddha sat up straight in meditation in the sandalwood pavilion and, with his supernatural powers, put on a miraculous display. There appeared in the sky a countless number of thousand-petaled lotus flowers as large as chariot wheels, filled with colors and fragrances that one could not begin to enumerate. In the center of each flower was a conjured image of a buddha. The flowers rose and covered the heavens like a jeweled banner, each flower giving forth countless rays of light. The petals all simultaneously unfolded their splendor and then, through the Buddha's miraculous powers, all withered in an instant. Within the flowers all the buddha images sat cross-legged in lotus position, and each issued forth countless hundreds of thousands of rays of light. The adornment of the spot at the time was so extraordinary that the whole assembly rejoiced and danced ecstatically. In fact, it was so very strange and extraordinary that all began to wonder why all the countless wonderful flowers should suddenly be destroyed. As they withered and darkened, the smell they gave off was foul and loathsome.

But at that point the World-honored One realized why the bodhisattvas were perplexed, so he addressed Vajramati ("Adamantine Wisdom"), saying, "O good son. If there is anything in the Buddha's teaching that perplexes you, feel free to ask about it." Bodhisattva Vajramati knew that everyone in the whole assembly was perplexed, and so addressed the Buddha, saying, "O World-honored One, why are there conjured buddha images in all of the innumerable flowers? And for what reason did they ascend into the heavens and cover the world? And why did the buddha images each issue forth countless hundreds of thousands of rays of light?" Everyone in the assembly looked on and then joined his hands together in respect. At that point, Bodhisattva Vajramati spoke in verses, saying:

Never ever have I witnessed
A miraculous display like today's.
To see hundreds of thousands and millions of buddhas
Seated in the calyxes of lotus flowers,
Each emitting countless streams of light,
Filling all the fields,
Scattering the dirt of false teachers,
Adorning all the worlds!
The lotuses suddenly wilted;
There was not one which was not disgusting.
Now tell us,
Why did you display this conjured vision?
We see buddhas more numerous than
The sands of the Ganges,
And incalculable transfigured forms.
Never before have I seen
The like of what I am witnessing now.
I wish you would give us a clear explanation.

At that time the World-honored One spoke to Vajramati and the other bodhisattvas, saying, "Good sons, there is a great vaipulya-sūtra called the '*Tathāgatagarbha.*' It was because I wanted to expound it to you that I showed you these signs. You should all listen attentively and ponder it well." All said, "Excellent. We very much wish to hear it."

The Buddha said, "Good sons, there is a comparison that can be drawn between the countless flowers conjured up by the Buddha that suddenly withered and the innumerable conjured buddha images with their many adornments, seated in lotus position within the flowers, who cast forth light so exceedingly rare that there was no one in the assembly who did not show reverence. In a similar fashion, good sons, when I regard all beings with my buddha eye, I see that hidden within the kleśas of greed, desire, anger, and stupidity there is seated augustly and unmovingly the tathāgata's wisdom, the tathāgata's vision, and the tathāgata's body. Good sons, all beings, though they find themselves with all sorts of kleśas, have a tathāgatagarbha that is eternally unsullied, and that is replete with virtues no different from my own. Moreover, good sons, it is just like a person with supernatural vision who can see the bodies of tathāgatas seated in lotus position inside the flowers, even though the petals are not yet unfurled; whereas after the wilted petals have been removed, those tathāgatas are manifested for all to see. In similar fashion, the Buddha can really see the tathāgatagarbhas of sentient beings. And because he wants to disclose the tathāgatagarbha to them, he expounds the sūtras and the dharma, in order to destroy kleśas and reveal the buddha nature. Good sons, such is the dharma of all the buddhas. Whether or not buddhas appear in the world, the tathāgatagarbhas of all beings are eternal and unchanging. It is just that they are covered by sentient beings' kleśas. When the Tathāgata appears in the world, he expounds the dharma far and wide to remove their ignorance and tribulation and to purify their universal wisdom. Good sons, if there is a bodhisattva who has faith in this teaching and who practices it single-mindedly, he will attain liberation and true, universal enlightenment, and for the sake of the world he will perform buddha deeds far and wide."

At that point, the World-honored One expressed himself in verses, saying:

It is like the wilted flowers;
Before their petals have opened,
One with supernatural vision can see
The unstained body of the Tathāgata.
After the wilted flowers are removed,
One sees, without obstacle, the Teacher,
Who, in order to sever kleśas,
Triumphantly appears in the world.
The Buddha sees that all kinds of beings
Universally possess the tathāgatagarbha.
It is covered by countless kleśas,
Just like a tangle of smelly, wilted petals.
So I, on behalf of all beings,
Everywhere expound the true dharma,
In order to help them remove their kleśas
And quickly reach the buddha way.
I see with my buddha eye
That in the bodies of all beings
There lies concealed the buddhagarbha,
So I expound the dharma in order to reveal it.

"Or good sons, it is like pure honey in a cave or a tree, surrounded and protected by a countless swarm of bees. It may happen that a person comes along who knows some clever techniques. He first gets rid of the bees and takes the honey, and then does as he will with it, eating it or giving it away far and wide. Similarly, good sons, all sentient beings have the tathagatagarbha. It is like pure honey in a cave or tree, but it is covered by kleśas, which, like a swarm of bees, keep one from getting to it. With my buddha eye I see it clearly, and with appropriate skillful techniques I expound the dharma, in order to destroy kleśas and reveal the buddha vision. And everywhere I perform buddha deeds for the benefit of the world." Thereupon the World-honored One expressed himself in verses, saying:

It is just like what happens when the honey in a cave or tree,
Though surrounded by countless bees,
Is taken by someone who knows a clever technique
To first get rid of the swarm.
The tathagatagarbha of sentient beings
Is like the honey in a cave or tree.
The entanglement of ignorance and tribulation
Is like the swarm of bees
That keep one from getting to it.
For the sake of all beings,
I expound the true dharma with skillful means,
Removing the bees of kleśas,
Revealing the tathāgatagarbha.
Endowed with eloquence that knows no obstacle,
I preach the dharma of sweet dew,
Compassionately relieving sentient beings,
Everywhere helping them to true enlightenment.

"Or, good sons, it is like a kernel of wheat that has not yet had its husk removed. Someone who is impoverished might foolishly disdain it, and consider it to be something that should be discarded. But when it is cleaned, the kernel can always be used. In like fashion, good sons, when I observe sentient beings with my buddha eye, I see that the husk of kleśas covers their limitless tathāgata vision. So with appropriate skillful means I expound the dharma, to enable them to remove those kleśas, purify their universal wisdom, and to attain in all worlds the highest true enlightenment." Thereupon, the World-honored One expressed this in verses, saying:

It is just like what happens when all the kernels,
The husks of which have not yet been washed away,
Are disdained by someone who is impoverished,
And said to be something to be discarded.
But although the outside seems like something useless,
The inside is genuine and not to be destroyed.

After the husks are removed,
It becomes food fit for a king.
I see that all kinds of beings
Have a buddhagarbha hidden by kleśas.
I preach the removal of those things
To enable them to attain universal wisdom.
Just as I have a tathāgata nature,
So do all beings.
When they develop it and purify it,
They quickly attain the highest path.

"Or, good sons, it is like genuine gold that has fallen into a pit of waste and been submerged and not seen for years. The pure gold does not decay, yet no one knows that it is there. But suppose there came along someone with supernatural vision, who told people, 'Within the impure waste there is a genuine gold trinket. You should get it out and do with it as you please.' Similarly, good sons, the impure waste is your innumerable kleśas. The genuine gold trinket is your tathāgatagarbha. For this reason, the Tathāgata widely expounds the dharma to enable all beings to destroy their kleśas, attain true enlightenment, and perform buddha deeds."

At that time the World-honored One expressed himself in verses, saying:

It is just like what happens when gold is submerged
In impure waste, where no one can see it.
But someone with supernatural vision sees it
And tells people about it, saying
'If you get it out and wash it clean,
You may do with it as you will,'
Which causes their relatives and family to all rejoice.
The Well-departed One's vision is like this.
He sees that for all kinds of beings,
The tathāgata nature is not destroyed,
Though it is submerged in the muddy silt of kleśas.
So he appropriately expounds the dharma
And enables them to manage all things,
So that the kleśas covering the buddha nature
Are quickly removed and beings are purified.

"Or, good sons, it is like a store of treasure hidden beneath an impoverished household. The treasure cannot speak and say that it is there, since it isn't conscious of itself and doesn't have a voice. So no one can discover this treasure store. It is just the same with sentient beings. But there is nothing that the power of the Tathāgata's vision is afraid of. The treasure store of the great dharma is within sentient beings' bodies. It does not hear and it is not aware of the addictions and delusions of the five desires. The wheel of saṃsāra turns and beings are subjected to countless sufferings. Therefore buddhas appear in the world and reveal to them the dharma store of the tathāgata in their bodies. And they believe in it and accept it and purify their universal wisdom. Everywhere on behalf of beings he reveals the tathāgatagarbha. He employs an eloquence which knows no obstacle on behalf of the Buddhist faithful. In this way, good sons, with my buddha eye I see that all beings possess the tathāgatagarbha. And so on behalf of bodhisattvas I expound this dharma." At that point, the Tathāgata expressed himself in verses, saying:

It is like a store of treasure
Inside the house of an impoverished man.
The owner is not aware of it,
Nor can the treasure speak.
For a very long time it is buried in darkness,
As there is no one who can tell of its presence.
When you have treasure but do not know of it,
This causes poverty and suffering.
When the buddha eye observes sentient beings,
It sees that, although they transmigrate
Through the five realms of reincarnation,
There is a great treasure in their bodies
That is eternal and unchanging.
When he sees this, the Buddha
Teaches on behalf of all beings,
Enabling them to attain the treasure-store of wisdom,
And the great wealth of widely caring for one another.
If you believe what I have taught you
About all having a treasure store,
And practice it faithfully and ardently,
Employing skillful means,
You will quickly attain the highest path.

"Or, good sons, it is like the pit inside a mango (*āmra*) fruit which does not decay. When you plant it in the ground, it grows into the largest and most regal of trees. In the same manner, good sons, when I look at sentient beings with my buddha vision, I see that the tathāgatagarbha is surrounded by a husk of ignorance, just as the seeds of a fruit are only found at its core. Good sons, that tathāgatagarbha is cold and unripe. It is the profound quiescence of nirvāṇa that is brought about by great wisdom. It is called the truly enlightened one, the tathāgata, the arhat, and so on. Good sons, after the Tathāgata has observed sentient beings, he reveals this message in order to purify the wisdom of bodhisattvas and great beings."

At that point, the World-honored One expressed himself in verses, saying:

It is just like the pit of a mango fruit
Which does not decay.
Plant it in the earth

And inevitably a great tree grows.
The Tathāgata's faultless vision
Sees that the tathāgatagarbha
Within the bodies of sentient beings
Is just like the seed within a flower or fruit.
Though ignorance covers the buddhagarbha,
You ought to have faith and realize
That you are possessed of samādhi wisdom,
None of which can be destroyed.
For this reason I expound the dharma
And reveal the tathāgatagarbha,
That you may quickly attain the highest path,
Just as a fruit grows into the most regal of trees.

"Or, good sons, it is like a man with a statue of pure gold, who was to travel through the narrow roads of another country and feared that he might be victimized and robbed. So he wrapped the statue in worn-out rags so that no one would know that he had it. On the way the man suddenly died, and the golden statue was discarded in an open field. Travelers trampled it and it became totally filthy. But a person with supernatural vision saw that within the worn-out rags there was a pure gold statue, so he unwrapped it and all paid homage to it. Similarly, good sons, I see the different sentient beings with their many kleśas, transmigrating through the long night of endless saṃsāra, and I perceive that within their bodies is the wondrous garbha of the tathāgata. They are august and pure and no different from myself. For this reason the Buddha expounds the dharma for sentient beings, that they might sever those kleśas and purify their tathāgata wisdom. I turn the wheel of the dharma again and again in order to convert all worlds."

At that point, the World-honored One expressed himself in verses, saying:

It is like a traveler to another country
Carrying a gold statue,
Who wraps it in dirty, worn-out rags
And discards it in an unused field.
One with supernatural vision sees it
And tells other people about it.
They remove the dirty rags and reveal the statue
And all rejoice greatly.
My supernatural vision is like this.
I see that beings of all sorts
Are entangled in kleśas and evil actions
And are plagued with all the sufferings of saṃsāra.
Yet I also see that within
The dust of ignorance of all beings,
The tathāgata nature sits motionless,

Great and indestructible.
After I have seen this,
I explain to bodhisattvas that
Kleśas and evil actions
Cover the most victorious body.
You should endeavor to sever them,
And manifest the tathāgata wisdom.
It is the refuge of all—
Gods, men, nāgas, and spirits.

"Or, good sons, it is like a woman who is impoverished, vile, ugly, and hated by others, who bears a noble son in her womb. He will become a sage king, a ruler of all the four directions. But she does not know his future history, and constantly thinks of him as a base-born, impoverished child. In like fashion, good sons, the Tathāgata sees that all sentient beings are carried around by the wheel of saṃsāra, receiving suffering and poison, but their bodies possess the tathāgata's treasure store. Just like that woman, they do not realize this. This is why the Tathāgata everywhere expounds the dharma, saying, 'Good sons, do not consider yourselves inferior or base. You all personally possess the buddha nature.' If you exert yourselves and destroy your past evils, then you will receive the title of bodhisattvas or world-honored ones, and convert and save countless sentient beings."

At that point, the World-honored One expressed himself in verses, saying:

It is like an impoverished woman
Whose appearance is common and vile,
But who bears a son of noble degree
Who will become a universal monarch.
Replete with seven treasures and all virtues,
He will possess as king the four quarters of the earth.
But she is incapable of knowing this
And conceives only thoughts of inferiority.
I see that all beings
Are like infants in distress.
Within their bodies is the tathāgatagarbha,
But they do not realize it.
So I tell bodhisattvas,
'Be careful not to consider yourselves inferior.
Your bodies are tathāgatagarbhas;
They always contain
The light of the world's salvation.'
If you exert yourselves
And do not spend a lot of time
Sitting in the meditation hall,

You will attain the path of very highest realization
And save limitless beings.

"Or, good sons, it is like a master foundryman casting a statue of pure gold. After casting is complete, it is inverted and placed on the ground. Although the outside is scorched and blackened, the inside is unchanged. When it is opened and the statue taken out, the golden color is radiant and dazzling. Similarly, good sons, when the Tathāgata observes all sentient beings, he sees that the buddhagarbha is inside their bodies replete with all its many virtues. After seeing this, he reveals far and wide that all beings will obtain relief. He removes kleśas with his adamantine wisdom, and reveals the buddha body like a person uncovering a golden statue."

At that point, the World-honored One expressed himself in verses, saying:

It is like a great foundry
With countless golden statues.
Foolish people look at the outside
And see only the darkened earthen molds.
The master foundryman estimates that they have cooled,
And opens them to extract their contents.
All impurity is removed
And the features clearly revealed.
With my buddha vision
I see that all sentient beings are like this.
Within the mud shell of passions,
All have the tathāgata-nature.
By means of adamantine wisdom,
We break the mold of kleśas
And reveal the tathāgatagarbha,
Like pure, shining gold.
Just as I have seen this
And so instructed all the bodhisattvas,
So should you accept it,
And convert in turn all other beings.

At that point, the World-honored One spoke to Vajramati and the other bodhisattvas and great beings, saying, "Whether you are monks or laypersons, good sons and daughters, you should accept, recite, copy, revere, and widely expound this *Tathāgatagarbha Sūtra* for the benefit of others. The virtues that you will derive from it are inestimable. Vajramati, if there were a bodhisattva who, for the sake of the buddha path, worked diligently and assiduously, or who cultivated spiritual powers, or who entered all of the samādhis, or who desired to plant the roots of virtue, or who worshiped the buddhas of the present, more numerous than the sands of the Ganges River, or who erected more seven-jeweled stūpas than there are sands in the Ganges River, of a height of ten yojanas [one yojana equals about nine miles] and a depth and breadth of one yojana, or who set up in those stūpas seven-jeweled couches covered with divine paintings, or who daily erected for each buddha more seven-jeweled stūpas than there are sands in the Ganges River, and who presented them to each tathāgata and bodhisattva and śrāvaka in the assembly, or who did this sort of thing everywhere for all the present-day buddhas, whose number is greater than the sands of the Ganges River, or who erected fifty times more jeweled stūpas than there are sands in the Ganges River and who presented them as an offering to fifty times more buddhas and bodhisattvas and śrāvakas in the assembly than there are sands in the Ganges River, and who did this for countless hundreds and thousands and tens of thousands of eons, O Vajramati, that bodhisattva would still not be the equal of the person who finds joy and enlightenment in the *Tathāgatagarbha Sūtra,* who accepts it, recites it, copies it, or even reveres but a single one of its metaphors. O Vajramati, even though the number of good roots and virtues planted by those good sons on behalf of the buddhas is incalculable, it does not come to a hundredth or a thousandth or any possible calculable fraction of the number of virtues attained by the good sons and daughters who revere the *Tathāgatagarbha Sūtra.*"

At that point, the World-honored One expressed himself in verses, saying:

If there is a person seeking enlightenment
Who listens to and accepts this sūtra,
And who copies and reveres
Even a single verse,
The subtle and profound garbha of the Tathāgata
Will instantly come forth, accompanied with joy.
If you give yourself to this true teaching
Your virtues will be incalculable.
If there is a person seeking enlightenment
Who has attained great spiritual powers,
And who desires to make an offering
To the buddhas of the ten directions
And to the bodhisattvas and śrāvakas of the assembly,
The number of which is greater
Than the sands of the Ganges,
A hundred million times incalculable;
If for each of the buddhas
He constructed a marvelous jeweled stūpa
Ten yojanas in height
And a breadth of forty li [one li equals about one-third of a mile],
Within which he would bestow a seven-jeweled seat,
With all the marvels
Appropriate for the august Teacher,
Covered with divine pictures and cushions,

Each one with its own unique designs;
If he offered to the buddhas and the saṅgha
An incalculable number of these,
More than the sands of the Ganges River,
And if he offered them
Without ceasing day or night
For hundreds and thousands
And tens of thousands of eons,
The virtues he would obtain in this manner
Could not be compared with
The far greater virtues of
The wise person who listens to this sūtra,
Who accepts even a single metaphor from it
And who explains it for the benefit of others.
Beings who take refuge in it
Will quickly attain the highest path.
Bodhisattvas who devote their thought
To the profound tathāgatagarbha,
Know that all beings possess it
And quickly attain the highest path.

At that time the World-honored One again addressed Bodhisattva Vajramati, saying, "An incalculable time far back in the distant past, longer ago than many inconceivable countless eons, there was a buddha who was called the Eternally Light-Bestowing King, the Tathāgata, the Arhat, the Truly Enlightened One, the One Possessed of Shining Actions, the One Who has Well Transcended the World, the Master Who Has Grasped the Highest, the Hero of Harmony, the Teacher of Men and Gods, the Buddha, the World-honored One. O Vajramati, why was he called the Eternally Light-bestowing King? When that buddha was originally practicing the bodhisattva path and descended as a spirit into his mother's womb, he always gave off light which penetrated and illuminated in an instant even the tiniest atoms of all the thousands of buddha worlds in the ten directions. Any being who saw this light was filled with joy. His kleśas were destroyed; he became endowed with the power of form; his wisdom was perfected; and he attained an eloquence which knew no obstacle. If a denizen of hell, a hungry ghost, an animal, King Yama, Lord of the Dead, or an asura saw this light, all of his rebirths in evil realms were cut off and he was born as a god. If any god saw this light, he attained irreversibility in the highest path and was endowed with the five supernatural powers. If anyone who had attained irreversibility saw this light, he attained unborn dharma-patience and the fifty dhāraṇīs [incantations] of virtue. Vajramati, all the lands illuminated by that light became stately and pure, like translucent porcelain, with golden cords marking out the eightfold path, luxuriant with the fragrance of various kinds of jeweled trees, flowers, and fruits. Light breezes blew gently through them, producing soft, subtle sounds that expounded freely and unrestrainedly the three jewels, the bodhisattva virtues, the power of good roots, the study of the path, meditation, and liberation. Beings who heard it all attained joy in the dharma. Their faith was made firm and they were forever freed from the realms of evil rebirth. Vajramati, because all the beings of the ten directions were instantly enveloped in light, at six o'clock every morning and evening they joined their palms together and offered worship. Vajramati, until the time he attained buddhahood and nirvāṇa without a remainder, the place where that bodhisattva issued forth from the womb always shone with light. And after his final nirvāṇa the stūpa in which his ashes were kept also gleamed with light. Consequently, the inhabitants of the heavenly realms called him the Eternally Light-bestowing King. Vajramati, when the Eternally Light-bestowing King, the Tathāgata, the Arhat, the Universally Enlightened One, first attained buddhahood, among his dharma-disciples there was a bodhisattva named Boundless Light, as well as a group of two billion other bodhisattvas. The great being Bodhisattva Boundless Light turned toward the spot where the Buddha was and asked about the *Tathāgatagarbha Sūtra,* and the Buddha expounded it. He was in his seat for fifty long eons. And because he protected the thoughts of all the bodhisattvas, his voice reached everywhere in the ten buddha worlds, even down to the smallest atoms, and it spread to hundreds of thousands of buddha lands. Because of the numberless different backgrounds of the bodhisattvas, he presented hundreds of thousands of metaphors. He called it the *Mahāyāna Tathāgatagarbha Sūtra.* All the bodhisattvas who heard him preach this sūtra accepted it, recited it, and practiced it just as it had been explained. All but four of the bodhisattvas attained buddhahood. Vajramati, you must not regard them as exceptional. How could Bodhisattva Boundless Light be different from you? You are identical with him. The four bodhisattvas who had not yet attained buddhahood were Mañjuśrī, Avalokiteśvara, Mahāsthāmaprāpta, and you, Vajramati. Vajramati, the *Tathāgatagarbha Sūtra* has an abundant capacity. Anyone who hears it can attain the buddha path."

Then the Buddha again expressed himself in verse, saying:

> Countless eons ago
> A buddha named King of Light
> Always shone forth great light
> And illumined innumerable lands everywhere.
> Bodhisattva Boundless Light
> First attained the way under that buddha,
> And requested this sūtra.
> The buddha accordingly preached it.
> All those who encountered it were victorious,
> And all those who heard it
> Attained buddhahood,
> Except for four bodhisattvas.

Mañjuśrī, Avalokiteśvara,
Mahāsthāmaprāpta, and Vajramati—
These four bodhisattvas
All formerly heard this dharma.
Of them, Vajramati
Was the most gifted disciple.
At the time he was called Boundless Light
And had already heard this sūtra.
When I originally sought the way
At the lion standard marking the buddha place,
I too once received this sūtra
And practiced it as I had heard it.
Because of these good roots,
I quickly attained the buddha path.
Therefore all bodhisattvas
Ought to uphold and preach this sūtra.
After you have heard it
And practiced just as it has been explained,
You will become buddhas just like I am now.
If a person upholds this sūtra,
He will comport himself like the World-honored One.
If a person obtains this sūtra,
He will be called 'Lord of the Buddhadharma,'
And then, on behalf of the world, he will protect
What all the buddhas proclaim.
If anyone upholds this sūtra,
He will be called 'The Dharma King,'
And in the eyes of the world
He will deserve to be praised
Like the World-honored One.

Then, when the World-honored One had finished expounding this sūtra, Vajramati, together with the four groups of bodhisattvas, the gods, the gandharvas, the asuras, and the rest, rejoiced at what they had heard the Buddha explain, and they practiced it as they had been told.

—8—

The Whole Universe as a Sūtra

Luis O. Gómez

The following selection is a translation of two versions of a single passage from a Mahāyāna sūtra entitled "The Teaching Regarding the Source from Which Tathāgatas Arise" (*Tathāgatotpattisaṃbhava-nirdeśa;* here *Tathāgatotpatti,* for short). This sūtra is not preserved in any complete Indian version; only short quotations occur here and there in the Sanskrit literature. Three different versions of the sūtra survive, however, as part of a monumental collection preserved in Chinese and Tibetan translations, and known as the *Buddhāvataṃsaka Sūtra.* This collection is commonly known in the West as the *Avataṃsaka Sūtra* or by its Chinese and Japanese names: *Hua-yen jing* and *Kegon kyō,* respectively.

The *Tathāgatotpatti* describes the way in which the knowledge and enlightenment of buddhas is present in all sentient beings, in fact, in all things, and is therefore accessible to all as "the source from which tathāgatas will arise." This is a common theme in the doctrine known as *tathāgatagarbha.* This is the idea that buddhahood is somehow inherent or innate to all sentient beings as a pure and enlightened core underlying the deluded mind. As part of the *Avataṃsaka Sūtra* collection, however, the *Tathāgatotpatti* may be seen also as expressing two themes common to that collection: first, that all things reflect each other perfectly, so that every thing in the universe may be said to contain in itself the whole universe, and, consequently, that the ultimate reality and the wisdom of a buddha are present in each and every being.

The short section translated below occurs as part of a description of ten intuitions or understandings that accompany the enlightenment of bodhisattvas. According to the passage, all bodhisattvas realize that truth is already present "in every particle of dust in the universe." Stated in this way, this is a common enough theme; but in the present extract the idea is developed with a metaphor that has interesting connotations for our understanding of what a religious text or image is, and what it means to interpret, render, or imagine religious truths. The whole universe is represented on a text or a canvas (depending on which version we use), but this representation is itself contained in every particle of dust in the universe. With this tantalizing image the text can lead us to reflect on the relationship between text and interpretation, or between representation and reality.

Of the two extracts translated below, the first and longer selection is a translation of Buddhabhadra's Chinese version of the whole section explaining the bodhisattva's "tenth intuition" in the *Buddhāvataṃsaka, Taishō shinshū daizōkyō* (Tokyo, 1924–1934), 278, vol. 9, pp. 623c23–624a26, 625a6–13. There are parallels in Śikṣānanda's translation, *Taishō shinshū daizōkyō* 279, vol. 10, pp. 272c5–29, 273b15–22; and in Dharmarakṣa's translation of the *Tathāgotpattisaṃbhava, Taishō shinshū daizōkyō* 291, vol. 10, pp. 607c3–608a13. In this Chinese version, the *Tathāgatotpatti* is book 32 of the *Avataṃsaka Sūtra* (corresponding to book 43 in the Tibetan translation, Peking edition).

The second, and shorter, passage included below is an English translation of a Sanskrit version of the same passage that is quoted in the commentary to the *Ratnagotravibhāga*, a treatise on the tathāgatagarbha doctrine of uncertain authorship (Sāramati?) and date (4th–5th centuries C.E.). This version includes only the central simile describing the "tenth intuition." The *Ratnagotravibhāga*, of course, uses the passage to argue for the tathāgatagarbha doctrine. Thus, the *Ratnagotravibhāga* introduces the selection translated below with the following comment: "The immaculate qualities of a buddha are forever found even in [that human state called] the stage of profane, ordinary people, which is a stage that is totally defiled and afflicted. [These immaculate qualities] are found there without qualification or distinction. This is something inconceivable." See the *Ratnagotravibhāga-uttaratantra-śāstra*, edited by E. H. Johnston (Patna: Bihar Research Society, 1950), pp. 22–24.

The Whole Universe Contained in a Sūtra

Moreover, Son of the Buddha, there is no place where the knowledge and wisdom of the Tathāgata does not abide. There is not a single sentient being, and no single body of a sentient being, that is not endowed with the knowledge and wisdom of the Tathāgata. Still, because sentient beings see things contrary to what they are, they do not know this wisdom of the Tathāgata. Only when they abandon their deluded, contrary views, will omniscience, the knowledge that needs no teacher, the unimpeded knowledge, arise [for them].

Son of the Buddha, it is as if there were a sūtra scroll, as large as this world system of three-thousandfold multi-thousand worlds. And on this [scroll] would be recorded all things without exceptions in this world system of three-thousandfold multi-thousand worlds. And the two-thousandfold multi-thousand worlds would be recorded in full detail on this [scroll], including all things in the two-thousandfold multi-thousand worlds. And the single-thousand worlds would be recorded in full detail on this [scroll], including all things in the single-thousand worlds.

And whatever is in the [realm] of the four guardian deities and below would be recorded in full detail on this [scroll], including all things in the [realm] of the four guardian deities and below.

And whatever is found on Mount Sumeru would be recorded in full detail on this [scroll], including all things on Mount Sumeru.

And whatever is in the [realm] of the earth deities would be recorded in full detail on this [scroll], including all things in the [realm] of the earth deities.

And whatever is in the [realm] of the deities of the realm of desire would be recorded in full detail on this [scroll], including all things in the [realm] of the deities of the realm of desire.

And whatever is in the [realm] of the deities of the realm of form would be recorded in full detail on this [scroll], including all things in the [realm] of the deities of the realm of form.

And whatever is in the [realm] of the deities of the formless realm would be recorded in full detail on this [scroll], including all things in the [realm] of the deities of the formless realm.

This sūtra scroll [thus containing] the world system of three-thousandfold multi-thousand worlds would be contained in a minute particle of dust. And every particle of dust [in the universe] would in the same way [contain a copy of this sūtra scroll].

Now, at one time, there would appear in the world a certain person who had clear, penetrating wisdom, and was endowed with a perfectly pure divine eye. And this person would see the sūtra scroll inside [every] particle of dust, and it would occur to this person, "How can this vast sūtra scroll be present in [every] particle of dust, yet it does not benefit sentient beings in the least? I should gather all my energy and devise a means to break open a dust particle and let out this sūtra scroll, that it may benefit all sentient beings." Thereupon this person would find the means to break open a dust particle, let out the sūtra scroll so that it could benefit all sentient beings.

Son of a Buddha, this is the way it is with the wisdom and knowledge of the Tathāgata. This wisdom is without [limiting] characteristics and without impediments, it is present in the body of every sentient being; and yet foolish living beings [persisting in their] deluded, contrary views, do not know, do not see [this wisdom], and do not put their faith and trust in it. Then the Tathāgata surveys all sentient beings with his unimpeded, pure divine eye, and having examined them, exclaims, "Isn't it strange, strange indeed, how the wisdom of the Tathāgata is present in the body [of every sentient being] and yet they do not know or see it! I will teach these [sentient beings] so that they may awaken fully in the noble path. I will free them of deluded conceptions, of contrary views, and from the fetters of [worldly] impurity; then they will see that the Tathāgata's wisdom is present in their own bodies, that they are no different from a buddha."

The Tathāgata thereupon teaches these sentient beings how to practice the eightfold noble path, and they abandon false, erroneous, and contrary views. Having abandoned contrary views, they [are able to] see the wisdom of a tathāgata, they become equal to buddhas, and [are able to] benefit sentient beings.

Son of a Buddha, this is the tenth [intuition] of bodhisattvas mahāsattvas, [by which bodhisattvas] perfectly practice, know, and perceive the mind of the perfectly awakened, who are tathāgatas and arhats.

> It is as if in the heart of a minute particle of dust
> Were present a vast sūtra scroll,
> As large as the three-thousandfold world,
> [Yet] bringing no benefit to any living being.
> Then this one person
> Would arise in the world,
> Who would break a speck of dust, let out the scroll,
> And benefit the whole world.
> It is the same with the Tathāgata's wisdom.
> All sentient being possess it;
> [But] contrary views and deluded thoughts hide it,
> So that sentient beings cannot see it or know it.
> [Then] the Tathāgata instructs sentient beings
> On how to cultivate the noble eightfold path,
> So that they can remove all the veils [of delusion],
> And finally attain awakening.

The Universe Painted on a Canvas

[Son of the Conqueror,] there is no living being whatsoever in the mass of living beings [in the universe] who is not pervaded by the whole knowledge of the Tathāgata. Yet, because of [our] grasping at [preconceived] notions, [we are] not able to discern this knowledge of the Tathāgata. But if we abandon [our] grasping at [such] notions, the knowledge of the all-knowing, the knowledge of the self-made, is manifested unattached and unhindered.

O Son of the Conqueror, it is as if there were an immense canvas the size of the three-thousandfold, multi-thousand world system; and on this immense canvas one were to paint the three-thousandfold, multi-thousand world system in its entirety. The great earthly plane would be [painted] to the measure of the great earthly plane; the two-thousandfold world system would be [drawn] to the measure of the two-thousandfold world system; the thousandfold world system to that of the thousandfold world system; the plane of the four continents to that of the plane of the four continents; the great ocean to the measure of the great ocean; the Rose-Apple continent to the measure of the Rose-Apple continent; the Pūrva-Videha continent to that of the Pūrva-Videha continent;

the Godavarī continent to that of the Godavarī; the Uttarakuru continent to that of the Uttarakuru; the [Great Mount] Sumeru would be [drawn] to the measure of [Mount] Sumeru; the abodes of the gods on earth to the measure of the abodes of the gods on earth; the abodes of the gods of the realm of desire to the measure of the abodes of the gods of the realm of desire; the abodes of the gods of the realm of form to the measure of the abodes of the gods of the realm of form. [The text omits the formless realm.] And this immense canvas would correspond in extent, detail, and proportions to the three-thousandfold, multi-thousand world system.

Furthermore, this immense canvas would be folded into a single atomic particle of dust. And, in the same way that this immense canvas was folded into a single atomic particle of dust, similar immense canvases would be enclosed in every single atom of dust [in the universe].

Now, a certain person would appear, knowing, alert, discerning, intelligent, and endowed with the analytic faculty necessary for comprehending [the nature of this reality]. And this person would have purified his divine eye, perfectly, so that it was most lucid. With that divine eye this person would look with discernment [at a particle of dust], [and perceive] that although this immense canvas is present in its entirety here [in this] minute, atomic, particle of dust, this is of no avail to any living being. Thus it would occur to him: "If I could only break open this particle of dust, by means of the force and strength of my energy, and turn this immense canvas into a support and sustenance for the whole world!" Producing the force and strength of his energy, he would break open that particle of dust with a minute pestle (*vajra*), and would turn the immense canvas into a support and sustenance for the whole world, in accordance with his [original] intention. And as he had done with this particle of dust he would do with all the rest.

In the same way, O Son of the Jina, the knowledge of the Tathāgata, the measureless knowledge, the knowledge that supports and sustains living beings, in its entirety pervades every instant of thought in the mind of all living beings. And every single series of thoughts in the mind of [every] living being is [manifested] to the measure of the knowledge of the Tathāgata. Yet, childish beings, bound by their grasping at notions do not know this, do not discern this, do not experience this, do not perceive directly this knowledge of the Tathāgatas. Therefore, the Tathāgata, looking at the abodes of all living beings in the dharmadhātu with his unhindered and unattached Tathāgata knowledge, reflects with astonishment: "Alas, these living beings fail to discern the knowledge of the Tathāgata as it is, yet the knowledge of the Tathāgata pervades all of them. If only I could remove all of the fetters which these beings have fashioned with notions [by instructing them] with a noble instruction on the path, so that once they have undone the great knot of notions using the power that arises from the noble path, they may themselves come to recognize the knowledge of the Tathāgata, and become equals of the Tathāgata."

By means of the Tathāgata's instruction on the path, living beings undo the fetters formed by notions. And when the fetters formed by notion are cast aside, there remains this measureless knowledge of the Tathāgata, the support and sustenance of the whole world.

— 9 —

Gotamī's Story

Jonathan S. Walters

The *Gotamī-apadāna* is the story of Buddha's maternal aunt and foster-mother, Mahāpajāpatī Gotamī. "Gotamī's Story" is part of a collection of moral biographies called *Apadāna*, which is contained in the canon's "Miscellaneous Division" (*Khuddaka-nikāya*). The *Apadāna* was composed in India during about the last two centuries B.C.E. Most of it consists of autobiographies ascribed to about forty early Buddhist nuns (*Therī-apadāna*) and about five hundred and fifty early Buddhist monks (*Therāpadāna*).

The *Apadāna* stories are extensions of two earlier collections of Pāli verses (*gāthā*), which some scholars date to the time of Buddha himself, called "The Monks' Verses" (*Theragāthā*) and "The Nuns' Verses" (*Therīgāthā*). These are also included in the "Miscellaneous Division" of the Pāli canon, and are supposed to have been uttered by the Buddha's most famous disciples after they had become saints (*arhats*). The *Apadāna* takes these pithy ancient verses and weaves them into elaborated stories about the monks and nuns who are believed to have uttered them.

The *Apadāna* was produced in a period of great change and expansion in Buddhist history. Imperial unification of the Indian subcontinent by Aśoka Maurya in the third century B.C.E., and the privileged place held by Buddhists in the Mauryan and some subsequent Indian empires, left Buddhism in the post-Aśokan period, the period of the *Apadāna*, considerably different from what it had been during the pre-Aśokan period, the period to which the "The Monks' Verses" and "The Nuns' Verses" belong. What had been primarily a renunciate religion, focused upon monks and nuns devoting their lives to imminent achievement of nirvāṇa, became after the Aśokan impetus an international, universal, religion.

The early paradigms—saints who renounce the world and attain nirvāṇa—were not immediately appropriate for the bulk of society newly included within Buddhism's post-Aśokan universal embrace, who would not renounce the world in the present life but would instead continue to produce karma and, consequently, future existence. The early paradigms seemed relevant only to those near the end of the path, who were already putting an end to karma and rebirth; how did they apply to common people who remain in the world of attachments, unwilling to leave it? The answer demonstrates a remarkable logic: if the biographies of the Buddha and his monks and nuns in this life provide models of and for the end of the path, then biographies of their previous lives, the stories of what they did when they too were commoners, should provide models of and for a person at the beginning of the path. This insight of the second and first centuries B.C.E. stimulated the composition of the *Apadāna* stories, which focus upon the previous lives of the monks and nuns in light of their present achievements.

All the moral biographies in the *Apadāna* share a basic structure: the monk or nun in question states: "In a previous life I met such-and-such buddha, performed such-and-such pious deed, experienced such-and-such happiness in heaven and on earth, and finally was born in the time of Gotama [Sanskrit Gautama] Buddha to experience the true happiness of nirvāṇa." The catalogue of all these previous lives of all those saints produced a virtual blueprint for the new universal society, representing every major city and kingdom in the "India" Aśoka first established, every occupation and station in life, every age, every caste, every type of being (male and female, animals and deities, as well as humans). In every situation there was, and is, an opportunity for piety whose rewards include heavenly bliss and nirvāṇa in the time of the coming buddha, Maitreya ("Love").

In the *Apadāna* we can see more than soteriology at work; different biographies incorporate and inscribe new calculations of time, new geographies and cosmologies, new forms of political activity. The moral biographies of the nuns, including "Gotamī's Story," address, further, certain problems that had emerged concerning the role of women in Buddhist practice. On the one hand, the nuns provided paradigmatic counterparts to the monks; without them one-half of universal society, the female half, would have been excluded from the new revelation of universal soteriology. On the other hand, the nuns' stories, which were most likely composed by women, unmistakably combat misogynist attitudes that continued among Indian Buddhists despite the Buddha's own apparent egalitarianism.

Later Buddhist authors would find even more relevance in these biographies for the societies in which they lived. These stories generated such wide-ranging discourses as political philosophy, law, and personal and social ethics. Some of the insights from texts like the *Apadāna* were repeated and enlarged; some were discarded. Likewise, some retellings of the stories were in prose rather than verse, meant for study rather than recitation. But through their many incarnations these stories have remained alive in the hearts and imaginations of Theravāda Buddhists to this day.

"Gotamī's Story" is a good example of the *Apadāna* genre. One of the most elaborate individual texts in that collection, it exemplifies many characteristic themes and styles: elaborate frame stories; alliteration, rhyme, and word-play; previous buddhas and times ancient enough to boggle the minds even of modern geologists; highly developed epithets for the Buddha; good deeds bearing fruit in nirvāṇa; elaborate biographical detail; supernormal powers and the performance of miracles; the divine pantheon (in subservience to the Buddha and Buddhists); devotion to the Buddha; articulation of his teachings; and, as one of the nuns' biographies, vindication of woman's religiosity.

But its very complexity renders "Gotamī's Story" unique among the moral biographies. The set pattern of these tales—the good deed in the time of a previous Buddha, details of the heavenly and earthly delights enjoyed as a result of that deed, and its ultimate blossoming in the attainment of nirvāṇa—concludes with a three-verse chorus that categorizes the various achievements common to all Buddhist saints (*arhats*). In "Gotamī's Story" this chorus appears not once but twice, and in the body of the text rather than at the end of it (verses 76–78, 125–27). These choruses indicate that the text includes within itself two "mini-apadānas" (verses 68–78, 95–127). Unlike most of the other texts in the *Apadāna,* Gotamī is not the only subject of her own autobiography. Instead, she transmigrates with five hundred other nuns who, in addition to various monks, the Buddha, laywomen, and deities—and a pervasive narrative overvoice—join her as speakers in "Gotamī's Story," which in effect becomes a full-fledged drama. Odder still, the focus of this biography is not life but death. All the other moral biographies end with these saints very much alive and singing about their own achievements. Gotamī and the five hundred nuns, on the other hand, die, leaving the Buddha to boast their achievements for them (verses 179–89).

Although "Gotamī's Story" flashes back to events in Gotamī's youth and numerous previous lives, all the action in the text occurs on the day of Gotamī's death. In brief, she decides on that very day (as do the five hundred nuns) to pass out of existence, which causes an earthquake. After consoling her followers she proceeds to the monastery where the Buddha is staying in order to inform him of her decision and secure his permission, which he grants in a pithy verse (verse 48). She next announces her decision to Nanda ("Delight," her son), Rāhula ("Fetter," the Buddha's son) and Ānanda ("Joy," the Buddha's personal secretary). The first two, already arhats fully detached from worldly ties, are unmoved, but Ānanda, still in training, weeps at the news. Consoling him, Gotamī tells the first "mini-apadāna," which recapitulates the story thus far. Then the Buddha, who is still present, asks Gotamī to put on a show of her miraculous powers as a lesson to those who doubt that women can achieve the highest states of spiritual perfection (verse 79), and she complies with great finesse (verses 80–92). She proceeds to tell the second mini-apadāna in order to inform the assembled folk, astonished by her miracles, how she had achieved this great power (verses 95–127). She takes final leave of the Buddha, returns to her own convent, and passes out of existence with the nuns (verses 145–52). The text concludes with a colorful description of Gotamī's funeral and the homage paid to her by the entire universe (verses 155–89).

Aspects of Mahāpajāpatī Gotamī's biography as known from other Pāli sources, too, are woven into the narrative structure of "Gotamī's Story." She was born in Devadaha ("Divine Lake"), the daughter of a Śākya nobleman and his wife (verse 115). Her family went to the Śākya capital Kapilavastu ("Red's Field") where her father's kinsman Suddhodhana ("Clean Gruel"), the future father of the Buddha, was king (verse 115). Gotamī's elder sister, Māyā ("Illusion"), married Suddhodhana and became the Buddha's mother (verse 2), but she died when the Buddha (Prince Siddhārtha) was an infant. Gotamī subsequently took her sister's place as the Buddha's wet-nurse and, as the fecund imagery of "Gotamī's Story" reveals, she was thus de facto the Buddha's actual mother (verses 31–36, 60, 117, 158–60, 170–71, 181). After Prince Siddhārtha became the Buddha, Gotamī hounded him until he consented to establish an order of nuns parallel to the monks' order (verse 45), of which she became the preeminent leader (verses 46, 105). She died in Vesali, at the age of 120.

Gotamī's death was her ultimate achievement, for, as "Gotamī's Story" makes clear, it was no ordinary death. She had achieved the goal of nirvāṇa, so death for her was final release from the tedium of future birth and death in saṃsāra. This religious death, the attainment of nirvāṇa, is clearly the central theme in "Gotamī's Story." The text is rich with plays on the verbal forms of the Pāli word for nirvāṇa (*nibbāna,* lit. "blown out"), which I have reproduced in the translation by consistently rendering them with forms of the English verb "to go" (especially "go out," which preserves the literal meaning of *nibbāna*). Gotamī's death is not called "death" but "the great going out" (*parinirvāṇa;* Pāli *parinibbāna*). The text develops rich metaphors for this religious death: it is the journey to a great city (verse 11) where one who has gone cannot be seen (verses 67, 159), comparable to a fire that has gone out leaving no trace of where it went (verses 148, 152, 181, 182, 187).

In addition to nirvāṇa itself, "Gotamī's Story" explains, exemplifies, and mentions numerous other Buddhist themes: the central doctrine of the impermanence and essencelessness of all things (verses 56–57, 59–60, 138, 144, 151, 153, 179–80), the four noble truths (verse 21), the nature and powers of arhats (verses 76–78, 124–30, 183–88), the contrast of "form-body" and "dharma-body" (verses 31–33), meditative states of consciousness (verses 145–47), the auspicious marks of a buddha (verses 39, 41, 42, 52) and various cosmological perspectives. This somewhat indirect, but simple, means of teaching abstract concepts serves the obvious intention of the author(s) to encourage listeners to become more Buddhist by following Gotamī's example: to understand what she understood, and to act with her biography as their inspiration (verses 27–29, 188–89).

In particular, "Gotamī's Story" addresses itself to Buddhist women, from nuns striving for nirvāṇa here and now to laywomen (verses 20–29, 142–44) and goddesses (verses 13–17) for whom the goal remains more remote. She is explicit that they should follow her in following the Buddha's path (verses 28–29), affirms that even as children females have attained the most exalted states (verses 65–66), and puts on her show of miracles to demonstrate how much a woman can achieve (verse 79). She parodies some typical views of women even as she undermines them with her great achievements (verses 43–47), and suggests that the liberation of nirvāṇa transcends normal filial duties (verses 34–38).

This special focus on woman's religiosity is apparent in many of the nuns' biographies found in the *Apadāna.* The paradigmatic examples provided by the famous nuns in their varied previous lives defined woman's place within the new universal soteriology. "Gotamī's Story" alone documents the soteriological efficacy of deeds performed by herself in a former birth as a slave woman, a rich man's daughter, and a powerful goddess. But a problem remained for Buddhist women which is addressed only by "Gotamī's Story," and which constitutes its real uniqueness. In the karmically black and white world of the *Apadāna*, males and females tread parallel yet distinct paths. Men were always male in previous lives; women always female. This is the reason that the monks' biographies were not suitable paradigms for that half of universal society which is not male.

But what woman could stand in apposition to the Buddha himself? The Buddha did not merely attain nirvāṇa, he attained parinirvāṇa, that "great going out" which, attained by few, points out the goal to many. The Buddha's "great going out" opened the door to arhatship, guaranteeing the finality of the monks' nirvāṇa. What of the nuns' path? Whose "great going out" guarantees that the nirvāṇa of nuns, too, is final?

The answer of course is Gotamī, for as we have seen already, in "Gotamī's Story" she does not attain merely nirvāṇa but parinirvāṇa (verses 38, 74, 75, 173, 179–80). She is the female counterpart of the Buddha, the founder and leader of the nuns' order who parallels (though does not supersede) Gotama, the founder and leader of the monks' order. Gotamī is represented as the Buddha for women. This helps make sense of some of the oddities in "Gotamī's Story." For example, her biography is collective because her own achievement, like a buddha's, is realized only by assuring the salvation of others, as well. Another oddity is that she is always called "Gotamī," which is merely her clan name; her given name, Mahāpajāpatī, is never used in the body of the text. Yet in all other Theravādin writings, both before and after "Gotamī's Story," she is consistently referred to as "Mahāpajāpatī" or "Mahāpajāpatī Gotamī." But the name took on special significance for the *Apadāna* author(s), concerned with portraying Gotamī as a female Buddha: "Gotamī" is, grammatically speaking, the exact feminine equivalent of the name Buddha was known by, "Gotama."

This apposition of Gotama and Gotamī, the Buddha and the Buddhī, is apparent in various situations within "Gotamī's Story" itself. It is even clearer when the text is compared with the canonical telling of the Buddha's own "great going out," "The Book of the Great Decease" (*Mahāparinibbānasutta*). This famous narrative, which some scholars consider the very heart of ancient Buddhism, is mimed step by step in "Gotamī's Story," explicitly illustrating that what Gotama was for men, Gotamī was for women. In the "Gotamī's Story" description of Gotamī's funeral, which is designated "better" than the Buddha's own (verse 173), she appears to be the very center of the universe. From the perspective of the author(s) of "Gotamī's Story," for religious women this is not far from the truth.

This translation is made from Mary E. Lilley, ed., *The Apadāna of the Khuddakanikāya*, vol. 2 (London: Pāli Text Society, 1927), pp. 529–43. The names of the speakers have been added by the translator.

Further Reading

The following translation of "Gotamī's Story" represents the only *Apadāna* biography of a monk or nun ever published in a Western language. For a more detailed analysis of *Gotamī-apadāna* and its intertextual location see my article "A Voice from the Silence: the Buddha's Mother's Story," *History of Religions* 33 (May 1994), 358–79. My "Stupa, Story and Empire: Constructions of the Buddha Biography in Early Post-Aśokan India," in Juliane Schober, ed., *Sacred Biography in the Buddhist Traditions of South and South-east Asia* (Honolulu: University of Hawaii Press, forthcoming) reviews scholarship on the *Apadāna* and related texts and provides further detail about their socio-historical location. But the "Monks' Verses" and "Nuns' Verses," translated into English verse as well as literal English prose, have been published by the Pāli Text Society and can be found in major libraries. A good introduction to the study of Buddhist women is Diana Paul's *Women in Buddhism* (Berkeley and Los Angeles: University of California Press, 1979), in which she surveys the condition of women under early Buddhism and explicates a Mahāyāna Buddhist attempt at creating a female Buddha that parallels (though differs from) the Theravādin attempt represented by "Gotamī's Story." A more detailed account of women in Theravāda Buddhist literature is I. B. Horner's *Women under Primitive Buddhism* (New York: E. P. Dutton, 1930).

Gotamī's Story

Narrator: One day the world's bright lamp,
the charioteer of men,
dwelt in Mahāvana Hall
among Vesali's gabled huts. (1)

The victor's mother's sister then,
the nun Great Gotamī,
dwelt in that white and lovely city
with saintly nuns five hundred. (2)

Gone off alone, she reasoned thus:

Gotamī: I cannot bear to look upon
the Buddha's final passing,
nor that of his two chief disciples,
nor Rāhula ["Fetter"], Ānanda ["Joy"], and Nanda ["Delight"]. (3)

Ending life's constituents
and letting go, I shall go out:

permitted by the greatest sage,
by he who is the whole world's lord. (4)

Narrator: The five hundred nuns there,
Khemā ["Peace"] and the rest,
reasoned that very thing out:
that same thing they too reasoned out. (5)

And then there was an earthquake;
the gods' thunder roared.
Weighed down by grief the goddesses
who dwelt there wailed and wept. (6)

The nuns all came to Gotamī
and bowed their heads upon her feet
while questioning her thus: (7)

Nuns: In solitude, sister, we were dampened with tears;
the solid earth trembled, the gods' thunder roared.
There it's as though someone's crying is heard:
What does this mean, Gotamī? (8)

Narrator: Then she said to all of them
just what she'd reasoned out,
and all of them then also said,
that's what they thought, too. (9)

Nuns: If this is what you want, sister—
the unsurpassed pure going out—
then, pious one, with his assent,
we all will go out too. (10)

Along with us you left your home
and also left the world.
Again together all of us
to great nirvāṇa city go! (11)

Narrator: She said, "what is there to be said
to women who are going out?"
Then, with all of them, quit the ashram. (12)

Gotamī: Forgive me, goddesses dwelling here:
I take my last glance at the ashram. (13)
I'll go to unconditionedness
where death and decay are both absent,
and one doesn't meet the unpleasant,
nor get cut off from pleasant things. (14)

Narrator: The Buddhist goddesses, not free of passion,
wailed in grief when they heard that speech.

Goddesses: Alas! Meritless women are we, (15)
this ashram has become empty:
the victor's heirs, no longer seen,
are like the stars at daybreak. (16)

Gotamī goes to nirvāṇa,
so do her five hundred;
she's like the Ganges flowing toward
the sea, with all her tributaries. (17)

Narrator: The faithful laywomen came outside
at seeing them go down the road
and bent down at their feet to say: (18)

Laywomen: Your good fortune, does it please you?
To go and leave us destitute
is something that you should not do.

Narrator: Thus lamented the ladies, distressed, (19)
so Gotamī spoke this sweet song,
attempting to dispel their grief:

Gotamī: Enough with all your crying, children:
today's a day to laugh! (20)

Suffering is understood;
the cause of suffering allayed.
I've experienced cessation;
I've cultivated the path. (21)

I have worshiped the teacher,
and done what the Buddha taught;
laid down the heavy load,
and loosed the ties to life. (22)

The reason for which I went forth
from home to homelessness
is finally attained by me:
destroying all the fetters. (23)

The Buddha and his splendid truth
are still around, complete.
So now's the time I should go out:
do not grieve for me, children! (24)

Kondañña, Ānanda, Nanda, and more,
Rāhula and the victor remain.
The monks are now all cheerful and close;
the conceit of the heretics slain. (25)

The famed one in Okkāka's clan
has crushed Māra ["Death"], the god of death.
Now children, isn't this the time
for me to reach nirvāṇa? (26)

My wish I've had for very long
today will be fulfilled.
This is the time for drums of joy!
Why are you crying, children? (27)

If you all have love for me,
and if you all appreciate
the dharma's great stability
then strong and fervent you should be. (28)

The great Buddha made women nuns
only at my beseeching.
So if you love me, be like me,
and follow after him. (29)

Narrator: Preaching thus to those women,
preceded by the nuns,
she proceeded to the Buddha's place
then worshiped him and said: (30)

Gotamī: Well-gone-one, I am your mother;
you're my father, O wise one.
Lord, you give the truth's pure pleasure!
Gotama, I'm born from you! (31)

It was I, O well-gone one,
who reared you, flesh and bones.
But by your nurturing was reared
my flawless dharma-body. (32)

I suckled you with mother's milk
which quenched thirst for a moment.
From you I drank the dharma-milk,
perpetually tranquil. (33)

You do not owe a debt to me
because I brought you up.

Great sage, to get a son like you
sates all desire for sons. (34)

Mothers of kings, like Mandhātā,
are sunk into existence sea.
Across this ocean of becoming
is how far, son, you have helped me. (35)

Women can obtain with ease
the names "Chief Queen," "King's Mother."
The hardest name of all to get
is "Mother of the Buddha." (36)

O hero, I attained that name!
My only aspiration's this:
be they minute or massive ones,
to fulfill all duties to you. (37)

I wish to go out totally,
abandoning this body;
grant me permission, hero, guide,
O ender of dis-ease. (38)

Stretch forth your feet, like lilies soft,
marked with the wheel, goad, and flag;
I will bend to worship them,
my son, with all my love. (39)

Show your body to me;
it's like a heap of gold.
A good look at your body,
then off I go to peace, O guide. (40)

Narrator: The victor bared his lovely body
marked with the auspicious marks.
It was as though a pale sun
emerged from a dark evening cloud. (41)

She put her head down on his feet
which looked like lotuses in bloom,
upon his soles, where wheels were marked
like young suns' shining rays. (42)

Gotamī: I'm bowing to the sun for men,
the banner of the solar clan.
After this, my final death,
I'll not see you again. (43)

It is thought, chief of the world,
that women are all flawed.
If there should be some flaw in me,
compassion-mine, forgive it. (44)

I begged you, over and again,
for women's ordination.
If that is somehow fault in me
forgive it, bull of men. (45)

Having gotten your permission
I taught and I instructed nuns.
If I have given bad advice
forgive it, lord forgiveness. (46)

Unforgivable? Forgive!
Why should I praise my virtue now?
What more is there to say to you
when I am going to nirvāṇa? (47)

The Buddha: Those in my order, pure and faultless,
made ready to escape the world
are like the crescent moon at dawn
which, fading, sees destruction. (48)

Narrator: The other nuns among them worshiped
The Buddha and fell at his feet
then sat there, gazing at his face
like stars and moon around Mount Meru. (49)

Gotamī: My eyes and ears weren't satisfied
to see you or to hear you speak.
But now that I've become perfect
my mind is quenched by dharma-taste. (50)

O bull of men, when you roar forth,
debunking the assembled sophists,
those there who get to see your face
are fortunate to do so. (51)

O battle-ender, fortunate
are they who worship your fine feet
which have broad heels, extended toes
and golden nails upon them. (52)

Fortunate indeed are they,
O best of all the men,

who hear your anger-slaying words,
so cheerful, friendly, sweet. (53)

I am fortunate, great hero,
intently I worship your feet.
The existential desert's crossed;
the dharma makes me shine. (54)

Narrator: She told the monks of her intention,
those who were devout,
and worshiped Rāhula, Ānanda, Nanda.
She spoke like this to them: (55)

Gotamī: I've had it with this body,
needing others, and hard to control;
this sick house like a serpent's lair
is pastured for old age and death,
and covered with suffering's slime.
Therefore I want to go out now;
give me permission, children. (56–57)

Narrator: Nanda and the auspicious Rāhula,
free of grief and defilement,
wise, unmovingly steadfast,
reflected on the way things are: (58)

Rāhula and Nanda:
Greed for real things, all conditioned,
is worthless as banana wood.
It is impermanent and fleeting,
only an unreal mirage. (59)

Conditioned things? Impermanent!
Gotamī, the victor's aunt,
the one who nursed the Buddha goes,
leaving behind no trace. (60)

Narrator: Ānanda was still in training.
He loved the Buddha, but he was sad.
Standing there and shedding tears,
he piteously wailed: (61)

Ānanda: Gotamī is going, smiling;
soon the Buddha too will go
to nonexistence, called nirvāṇa,
like a fire without fuel. (62)

Narrator: Gotamī spoke to Ānanda,
who was weeping in this way:

Gotamī: My son, intent on serving the Buddha,
your wisdom's deep, as is the sea.
And so you really shouldn't mourn
when the time to laugh has come!
With your assistance, son, I reached
the goal toward which I strived: nirvāṇa.
At your request, son, he ordained us;
do not be distressed, my child:
your toil is bearing fruit. (63–65)

That state which is not seen by elders
nor by non-Buddhist teachers
is witnessed by some Buddhist girls
when they are only seven. (66)

Take your final look at me,
preserver of the Buddha's word.
My son, I'm going to that place
where one who's gone cannot be seen. (67)

Once, when he was preaching dharma,
the chief guide of the people sneezed.
And then, compassionate, I spoke
these words of blessing to him: (68)

"Enjoy long life, great hero!
Remain an eon, sage!
For the sake of all the world
don't dare grow old or die." (69)

The Buddha then replied to me,
who'd spoken to him thus:
"A buddha never should be blessed
as you would bless me, Gotamī." (70)

"How then," I asked, "O all-knower,
should thus-gone ones be blessed?
And how should buddhas not be blessed?
Tell all of that to me." (71)

He said, "Look close at my disciples,
in harmony, and vigorous,
energetic, resolute,
that's how to bless a buddha." (72)

Then I returned to our ashram
and thought it out alone:
"The lord who ended re-becoming
is pleased by monks and nuns at peace. (73)

"Well then, I'll go out utterly;
don't let me see a hindrance!"
Thinking thus, and having seen
the seventh of the sages, (74)

I announced to that instructor,
"It's time for my great going out"
and then he granted me permission:
"Know that it's the time!" (75)

Defilements gone, I've abolished existence;
I am now like an elephant cow
who, breaking every single fetter,
dwells without constraint. (76)

Being in the Buddha's midst
was pure profit for me:
I attained the three special knowledges:
The Buddha's teaching is achieved! (77)

The four analytical knowledges,
the eight deliverances,
the six higher knowledges experienced:
The Buddha's teaching is achieved! (78)

The Buddha: Yet still there are these fools who doubt
that women too can grasp the truth.
Gotamī, show miracles,
that they might give up their false views. (79)

Narrator: Gotamī bowed to the lord
then leaped into the sky.
Permitted by the Buddha, she
displayed her special powers. (80)

She was alone, then she was cloned;
cloned, and then alone.
She would appear, then disappear;
she walked through walls and through the sky. (81)

She went about unstuck on earth
and also sank down in it;

she walked on water as on land,
without breaking the surface. (82)

Cross-legged, she flew like a bird
across the surface of the sky.
With her body she controlled
the space right up to God's own home. (83)

She made the earth a canopy;
Mount Meru was its handle.
And, twirling her new parasol,
she walked around the sky. (84)

It was as though six suns arose:
she made the world fume.
As though it was the end of time,
she garlanded the earth in flames. (85)

She held mounts Meru, Mandara,
Daddara, and great Muccalind—
all of them, in a single fist,
like tiny mustard seeds. (86)

She concealed with finger's tip
the makers of both day and night
as if her necklace had as gems
a thousand suns and moons. (87)

From her tiny palm that held
the waters in the four great seas,
she rained forth a torrential rain
like an apocalyptic cloud. (88)

She made appear up in the sky
a world-ruler with cortège.
She showed [Viṣṇu as] the Lion and Boar
and Garuḍa, his eagle mount. (89)

Alone, creating magically
a measureless chapter of nuns
she made them disappear again,
then said this to the sage: (90)

Gotamī: This one who's done the work, hero,
your mother's younger sister,
attained the goal, eyeful one,
and now worships your feet. (91)

Narrator: Her miracle display complete,
that nun descended from the sky,
paid homage to the world's lamp,
then sat down at one side. (92)

Gotamī: A century and score from birth:
great sage, that is my age.
That much is old enough, hero,
O guide, I'll now go out! (93)

Narrator: Astonished, with hands clasped in praise,
folks then said this to Gotamī:

Layfolk: Your prowess has been shown sister
in supernormal miracles. (94)

Narrator: Gotamī then told them all
how she had come to be a saint.

Gotamī: There was a seer of all things,
the Buddha Padumuttara ["Best Lotus"].
That guide was born into the world
one hundred thousand eons ago. (95)

I too existed at that time,
born in a clan of ministers.
We lived in Haṃsavatī ["Swan-filled"] town,
quite rich, with many servants. (96)

Once, when tagging on with father—
surrounded by a group of slaves—
along with a large retinue,
I approached that bull of men. (97)

The victor like autumnal sun,
surrounded by aura ablaze,
was raining forth, a dharma-cloud,
like king of all the gods. (98)

Seeing him, my mind was pleased
and then I heard his lovely voice:
that guide for men was making his
aunt chief of all the nuns. (99)

Hearing this, for one whole week,
I sponsored lavish donations.
I gave a lot of the requisites
to the chief and his disciples. (100)

I fell down prostrate at his feet,
aspiring to that rank,
and then the greatly mindful one,
the seventh sage, said this: (101)

The Buddha "Best Lotus":
This one who for a week has fed
the world's guide and disciples:
I shall relate the fate of her;
listen to my words! (102)

In one hundred thousand eons,
born into Okkāka's clan,
the one whose name is Gotama
will be the master in the land. (103)

Rightful heir to his great teachings,
transformed by his truth,
the woman Gotamī will be
his female disciple. (104)

She will be his mother's sister,
The Buddha's wet-nurse all his life.
And she'll attain preeminence
among the senior nuns. (105)

Gotamī: Hearing that, I felt true bliss,
and then I spent my whole life
serving the Buddha requisites.
And when I died I was reborn (106)

among the highest gods who lived
in Tāvatiṃsa ["Thirty-Three"] heaven.
In all delights and riches I
outshone the others in ten ways: (107)

with my shape and sound and smell,
and with my taste and feel,
in terms of lifespan and complexion
and happiness and fame (108)

I shone, attaining supreme power.
And then I was seen in the place
of the most favored of the queens
of him, the king of gods. (109)

Transmigrating now here, now there,
I was blown on by karma-wind

and born into a slaves' village
in the king of Kāśi's realm [Banaras]. (110)

Every day there were five hundred
dwelling in that very place.
There I became the wife of him
who was the eldest of them all. (111)

Five hundred self-enlightened ones
entered our village for alms.
I was very glad to see them,
as were all the women. (112)

We formed ourselves into a guild
and served them for four months.
We gave to them monastic robes;
we women with our husbands then (113)

transmigrating, passed on from there
and went to Tāvatiṃsa.
And now, in this, my final life,
I was born in Devadaha ["Divine Lake"]. (114)

My father was the Śākyan Añjana ["Jet Black"];
my mother was Sulakkhanā ["Well Marked"].
We left there for Kapilavastu ["Red's Field"],
staying with Suddhodana ["Clean Gruel"]. (115)

All the other Śākyan women
also went there then.
But of them all I was the best;
I was the Victor's nurse. (116)

My son, once he had left the world
became the Buddha, the instructor.
Afterwards I too went forth
with the five hundred women. (117)

I witnessed the joy of peace
[attained] by the male Śākyan heroes.
They were the men who formerly
had been born as our husbands. (118)

They were the doers of good deeds
and seized the crucial moment.
Pitied by the well-gone one,
they all became great saints. (119)

Narrator: The other nuns who were still there
rose up into the air.
and came together, just like stars,
those great women then shone. (120)

They displayed some miracles,
just as ornaments of every kind
are shown by craftsmen who are skilled,
especially by goldsmiths. (121)

Having shown these miracles,
diverse and numerous,
and having pleased the sage debater
with his assembly at that time (122)

they all descended from the sky
and worshiped him, the seventh sage;
obtaining the chief man's consent,
they sat down in that place. (123)

Nuns: Hey, hero, it was Gotamī
who pitied all of us.
Perfumed by your good karma
we slew the imperfections. (124)

Defilements gone, we've abolished existence
and now we are like elephant cows
who, breaking every single fetter,
dwell without constraint. (125)

Being in the Buddha's midst
was pure profit for us:
we attained the three special knowledges:
The Buddha's teaching is achieved! (126)

The four analytical knowledges,
the eight deliverances,
the six higher knowledges experienced:
The Buddha's teaching is achieved! (127)

We've mastered all the miracles,
and the "divine-ear" faculty.
Great sage, we're masters of the knowledge
of what is stored in others' hearts. (128)

We know all of our former lives;
"divine-eye" now is purified.

With every imperfection gone,
we won't be born again. (129)

We understand meanings and doctrinal things,
etymology and how to preach.
Great hero, it was in your presence
that our knowledge was produced. (130)

O guide, you are surrounded by
us all with loving hearts.
Great sage, now give us your consent
to go and reach nirvāṇa. (131)

Right now we're going out!

Narrator: The Victor said, "What can I say
to women who are going out?
Know that it's the time!" (132)

Gotamī and all the nuns
paid homage to the Victor.
Then from their seats they all rose up
and went away from there. (133)

With all the people the great man,
the wise one, chief of all the world,
followed after his own aunt
until she reached the gate. (134)

Then Gotamī fell to the ground
beneath the world's kinsman's feet,
and with all of the other nuns
she worshiped them once more. (135)

Gotamī: This is my last look
at the lord of the world;
your face, a fountain of ambrosia,
won't be seen again. (136)

No more homage to your soft feet;
I won't touch them again.
O hero, chief of all the world,
today I go to nonexistence! (137)

Who needs your face and body,
with things such as they are?
Everything conditioned changes;
it provides no comfort. (138)

Narrator: She, having gone along with them
back to her own "nuns' lair,"
sat down with legs crossed on each other
in her own auspicious seat. (139)

The laywomen residing there,
adorers of the Buddha's word,
heard her rustlings about,
so those foot-worshipers approached, (141)

pounding fists hard on their chests
and crying piteous tears.
Grieving, they fell to the earth
like creepers cut off at their roots. (142)

Laywomen: O lady, bestower of the refuge,
please don't leave us for nirvāṇa.
Bowing down our heads, we all
are begging this of you. (142)

Gotamī: One of them was energetic,
a laywoman faithful and wise.
While gently stroking that one's head
I spoke these words to her: (143)

"Enough, enough depression child;
free yourself from Māra's snares!
Everything existent changes;
shaking, it's lost in the end." (144)

Narrator: Then having sent them all away,
she entered the first altered state;
the second, yes, and then the third,
and then she reached the fourth of them. (145)

In order, moving higher still:
the plane of space-infinity
the plane in which perception's pure
and that where nothingness is seen. (146)

Gotamī reversed the order,
backward reaching all these states,
the last one first, the first one last,
and then back to the fourth. (147)

Rising up, she went out
like a fuelless lamp's flame.

There was a great earthquake;
lightening fell from the sky. (148)

The thunder rumbled loudly,
the deities there wailed;
a shower of flowers from the sky
rained down upon the earth. (149)

Meru, king of mountains, shook
just like a dancer on the stage;
the great ocean was greatly grieved
and he was weeping in distress. (150)

The gods, snake gods, and demons too,
and even Brahmā [God], in awe,
said, "This one now is all dissolved;
in flux indeed is all that is." (151)

The other women who were there,
who practiced the Buddha's teachings,
they too went out just like the flames
in lamps with no more fuel. (152)

"Alas! Attachments end up cut!
Alas! Conditioned things all change!
Alas! Life ends up in destruction!"
Just like this the people wailed. (153)

Then Brahmā and the deities
approached the seventh sage
and acted as one ought to act
in such a situation. (154)

And then the Buddha told Ānanda,
whose knowledge was an ocean,

The Buddha: Go now, Ānanda, tell the monks
my mother's reached nirvāṇa. (155)

Narrator: Ānanda, who had lost his joy,
his eyes filled up with tears,
announced, while choking on the words:

Ānanda: Now assemble, all you monks, (156)

who are out of east or in the south
or in the west, or in the north;
listen to my words, you monks
who are the Buddha's heirs. (157)

This Gotamī who carefully
reared up the sage's body,
is gone to peace, no longer seen,
just like the stars at sunrise. (158)

Her destination now is reached;
her name alone remains.
Even the Buddha, who has five eyes,
cannot see where she went. (159)

Each who has faith in the Well-Gone One
and each who is the sage's pupil
ought to come, that Buddha's son,
to honor Buddha's mother. (160)

Narrator: The wise monks living far away
heard that, then they came with speed.
Some came by the Buddha's majesty,
some by their own great power. (161)

The folks there raised a funeral bier
where Gotamī now lay,
inside a shiny gabled hut
of golden color, lovely. (162)

The four great gods lifted it up,
each corner one supported,
while their king and all the other
gods stood in the gabled hut. (163)

The cosmic builder, Viśvakarma ["Universal Maker"]
erected many gabled huts:
five hundred of them, which were all
the color of autumnal suns. (164)

And all the nuns there in those huts
had been laid out on biers,
hoisted up on god-shoulders,
lined up in proper order. (165)

A canopy up in the sky
was stretched out over everything.
The sun and moon and all the stars
were drawn on it in gold. (166)

Flags of different sorts were raised,
a floral carpet laid;

and incense rose into the sky
like blossoms from the earth. (167)

The real sun and moon and stars
were sparkling and seen by all,
and even though it was high noon
the sun cooled like the moon. (168)

The gods made offerings of garlands
scented with divine perfume
and worshiped Gotamī with song,
with music, and with dance. (169)

The snake gods, demons, and Brahmā,
according to their powers,
made offerings as best they could
for the Buddha's gone-out mother. (170)

All the Buddha's daughters there,
gone out, were carried off.
And after them came Gotamī
the wet-nurse of the Buddha. (171)

Proceeding, worshiping the mother,
came forth gods and men;
the snake gods, demons, and Brahmā,
then Buddha and disciples. (172)

The Buddha's great nirvāṇa, good,
but not as good as this one:
Gotamī's great going out
was positively stellar. (173)

Ānanda: O monks, we will not see the Buddha
at his own great nirvāṇa;
the Buddha's here at Gotamī's,
and monks like Śāriputra ["River's Son"]. (174)

Narrator: Then they built the funeral pyres
made out of fragrant wood,
and sprinkled them with sweet perfume;
being set afire, they burned. (175)

Each part of them had been consumed;
only bones remained then.
At that time Ānanda spoke
words giving rise to deep emotion. (176)

Ānanda: Gotamī is gone, no life,
and now her body's burnt.
The indication is that soon
the Buddha too will leave. (177)

Narrator: Ānanda put all her bones
into her begging bowl,
then, urged to do so by the lord,
he gave them to the Buddha. (178)

Taking them up with his hands,
the seventh sage then spoke:

The Buddha: Even the trunk of a huge timber tree,
however massive it may be,
will break to bits, eventually.
Thus Gotamī, who was a nun,
is now gone out completely. (179–80)

It is so marvelous a thing:
my mother who has reached nirvāṇa
leaving only bits of bone
had neither grief nor tears. (181)

She crossed this ocean of existence,
grieving not for others left;
she now is cool, she's well gone out:
her torment now is done. (182)

Know this, O monks, she was most wise,
with wisdom vast and wide.
She was a nun of great renown,
a master of great powers.
She cultivated "divine-ear"
and knew what others thought.

In former births, before this one,
she mastered "divine-eye."
All imperfections were destroyed;
she'll have no more rebirths. (183–85)

She had purified her knowledge
of meaning and the doctrines,
of etymology, and preaching;
therefore she did not grieve. (186)

An iron rod aglow in fire
cools off and leaves no ash.

Just like the flame once in the rod,
it's not known where she went. (187)

Those who are emancipated
cross the god of lust's deluge;
those with solid happiness
do not get born again. (188)

Therefore be lamps for yourselves;
go graze in mindfulness.
With wisdom's seven parts attained,
you all should end your woe. (189)

—10—

The Great Bliss Queen

Anne C. Klein

Yeshey Tsogyal (Ye shes mtsho rgyal) is identified as a queen of the eighth-century Tibetan king Tri-srong-day-tsen (Khri srong lde bstan). Tibetans regard her as a fully enlightened buddha who appeared as an ordinary Tibetan girl so that people of her country might easily form a relationship with her, visualize her, and attain enlightenment through conjoining this visualization with the Nyingma Great Completeness teachings that were preserved by her. The Nyingma tradition, which alone among the Tibetan orders adds the title Great Bliss Queen to her name, reveres her also as a manifestation of the Indian goddess of sound, the muse of learning and literature, Sarasvatī. She is also identified with the female bodhisattva Tārā, and with the Buddha's own mother. In addition, she is considered an emanation, or appearance in ordinary form, of a female buddha known as Vajravārahī, "the Adamantine Sow." In her resplendent form as Vajravārahī, however, she is not accessible to ordinary persons. Thus, her appearance in Tibet as a daughter of the Karchen family was "for the sake of those who, for the time being, do not see her Vajravārahī form as a fully perfected deity. Among the practices of the guru [Padmasambhava] especially intended for Tibetans there are many whose chief deity is [the Great Bliss Queen] Yeshey Tsogyal." (Do-drup-chen III, *Rig 'dzin yum ka,* 474.2ff.) From the hagiographical literature we can discern that she is venerated for two quite different reasons. On the one hand, she is the acknowledged preserver of the tradition that she embodies. On the other, she is an exemplary religious seeker who triumphs over the most difficult challenges in accomplishing her goal of demonstrating a path to enlightenment. In many ways, her story is like that of a hero—alone, overcoming obstacles—even though the principles her story puts forward undermine that model of highly individuated, oppositional accomplishment.

According to her hagiography, Yeshey Tsogyal was born under miraculous circumstances. The sound of a Sanskrit mantra echoed in the air, her mother gave birth painlessly (as had the Buddha's mother) and a nearby lake increased vastly in size—hence, perhaps, the name "Queen (*gyal*) of the Lake (*tso*) of Primordial

Wisdom (*yeshey*)." Tsogyal was sought after by such a multitude of suitors that, in order to prevent fighting from breaking out among them, a specially appointed council determined that she would marry no one unless an emperor himself should ask. The suitors dispersed, whereupon two great princes arrived with treasure to ask for her hand. Her parents left the choice to her, but would not listen to her pleas to remain free of marriage altogether. This part of her biography is the quintessential narrative of an abused woman.

> Although I begged them earnestly, my parents were adamant. "There are no finer palaces in the known world than the residence of these two princes," my father told me. ". . . I will give you to one of these princes." . . . I was involuntarily led out of the house. The instant I stepped outside, the rivals rushed toward me. . . . [One] caught me by the breast and attempted to lead me away. However, I braced my legs against a boulder so that my feet sank into it like mud. To move me was like trying to move a mountain, and no one succeeded. Then those fiendish officials took a lash of iron thorns, and stripping me naked they began to whip me. (Keith Dowman, trans., *Sky Dancer: The Secret Life and Songs of the Lady Yeshe Tsogyel* [London: Routledge and Kegan Paul, 1984], p. 16)

Finally forced to join the entourage, she petitions the buddhas for protection. The men guarding her fall asleep and she escapes, becoming the object of a widespread search. To bypass the riotous claims on her by the two princes, she is eventually given to the emperor himself in marriage. This was the famous religious king Tri-song-day-tsen (740 to c. 798 C.E.), then in the process of encouraging the growth of Buddhism in Tibet, to which end he invited Padmasambhava from India. In this context, both Tsogyal and Padmasambhava are positioned on the side of Buddhism against the earlier religious traditions of Tibet. At one point Tsogyal debates with her mirror image from an earlier layer of Tibetan culture, the female Bön practitioner Bönmo Tso, whose name means "the Female Bön [of the] Lake." The particular tradition Yeshey Tsogyal champions, the Great Completeness, is the one major system of thought and practice shared by Nyingma and the Bön down to this day.

She is the nurturer and distributor of these teachings, which she dispenses through the ages like "timely messages" for those intent on emulating her state of realization. In describing her role as preserver of the teaching, one liturgical commentary makes an explicit connection with women's roles, noting that in the world it is the man who seeks wealth and the woman who keeps it safely, both activities being required if wealth is to increase.

Yeshey Tsogyal is thus in part depicted as a kind of sublime housekeeper. She is also a model of zestful energy, courage, and perseverance. One passage from her hagiography describes an incident early in her practice: "I sat where I was, totally detached, thought-free. 'She must be a yeti,' they cried, and proceeded to shoot their arrows at me, beat me with their clubs, stab at me with their spears, and slash at me with their knives. But no matter in what way they attacked me or with what weapons, they caused absolutely no harm to my body. They gave me the name Invulnerable Tibetan, and not knowing what to do they dispersed to their homes." (Dowman, *Sky Dancer,* p. 84) Yeshey Tsogyal did not passively endure degradation and worse; the context of this passage emphasizes that she was beyond danger or discomfort precisely because of her actively cultivated realization. Praise of Tsogyal as a fully accomplished yoginī, emphasizing her extraordinary influence and charisma, is meant as an incentive to others. According to Tsogyal, some time after this event the king

> invited me to Samye [the first Buddhist monastery in Tibet] . . . the translators, courtiers, ministers, and queens led by the king, Mutri Tsenpo, all paid me honor and served me with humility . . . fifteen hundred new monks were ordained at one time, and [the king] appointed the Indian sage Kamalaśīla as the new abbot. I gave instruction to the newly ordained monks, and they went to Chimphu to begin their meditation, which bore nothing but positive results. (Dowman, *Sky Dancer,* p. 137)

This characterization is notable, for although Tsogyal is venerated as a preserver of the Great Completeness traditions, and in this role mirrors one element of Tibetan women's role in their own families, she is not limited to this role. To see her only as a preserver would be too narrow, even on the mythic level, and would make impossible the kinds of symbolic representations associated with her in the liturgical literature. Her other activities, miraculous and otherwise, fall mainly into two categories: her arduous ascetic practices (remaining on a glacier for three years with scarcely any food or clothing, for example), and bringing enlightenment to others through personal instruction and example. These are classic elements to be found in any Buddhist story of liberation. There is little particularly "female" here. The close relationship with a guru, which is particularized in Tsogyal's biography as her consortship with Padmasambhava, fits the classic pattern. She also, however, seeks her own male consorts, one of whom she ransoms with gold given her for the miraculous act of raising a Nepali child from the dead. Most central is her status as an enlightened buddha. And, like other figures described by the Mahāyāna, from Śākyamuni on down, it is said that although she seemed to develop her realization through depending on her teacher and through strong effort, she had actually been enlightened prior to her birth in Tibet as Yeshey Tsogyal.

The Great Bliss Queen has for centuries been a major figure among Nyingma practitioners. The liturgy, or root sādhana, of the Great Bliss Queen ritual, known as "The Glorious Blissful Garland," is found in the three-volume collection known as the *Root Cluster of the Great Spacious Sphere's Heart Essence* of Jig-may-ling-pa, inspired, like the other works in the collection, by his vision of the fourteenth-century Long-chen-rab-jam. Numerous explications of this liturgy exist; the most elaborate (214 folios) is the *Commentary on the Practice Emulating the Sky Woman, the Great Bliss Queen, from the Great Spacious Sphere Heart Essence Tradition of Long-chen-ba.* This text is more popularly known by the brief title *Ra Ṭīk* or *Commentary by Ra* since its author, a disciple of Jig-may-ling-ba's from Central Tibet, was known as the Ra teacher (*Ra ston*), Ra being a clan or family name. The Ra teacher, also known as Ngawang Denzin Dorje, was an abbot of the Great Completeness Monastery mentioned above. Another important work is by the third Do-drup-chen Rinboche, *Notes on the Basic Text for Emulating the Mother Knowledge Bearer, the Great Bliss Queen—A Lamp Clarifying the Good Path of Great Bliss.*

This translation opens with excerpts from Do-drup-chen's work, a sample of the hagiographical literature on the Great Bliss Queen. It is translated from: Jig-may-den-bay-nyi-ma ('Jigs-med-bstan-ba'i nyi-ma, also known as the third Do Drup Chen Rinboche), *Rig 'dzin yum ka bde chen rgyal mo'i sgrub gzhung gi zin bris bde chen lam gzang gsal ba'i gron me* ("Notes on the Basic Text for Emulating the Mother Knowledge Bearer, the Great Bliss Queen: A Lamp Clarifying the Good Path of Great Bliss"), in *The Collected Works of Do-drup-chen* (Gantok, Sikkhim: Do-drup-chen Rinboche III, 1975), Vol. 5. Citations to "Do-drup-chen III, *Rig 'dzin yum ka*" in the introductory section also come from this source. The second set of selections are from the *Ra Ṭīk,* and exemplify the Tibetan understanding of her symbolism and ritual importance. They are translated from Ngawang Denzin Dorje (Ngag-dbang-bstan-'dzin-rdo-rje, 18th century), *kLong chen snying gi thig le'i mkha' 'gro bde chen rgyal mo'i sgrub gzhung 'grel ba rgyud don snang ba* ("Commentary on the Practice Emulating the Sky Woman, the Great Bliss Queen, from the Great Spacious Sphere Heart Essence Tradition of Long-chen-ba"), also known as *The Ra Commentary*. In working on these translations I read both these texts with Tulku Thondup, who is himself closely associated with the present and fourth Do-drup-chen. I am grateful to Tulku Thondup for his collaboration in this work.

Further Reading

On gender issues in Buddhism, see the following: José Ignacio Cabezón, ed., *Buddhism, Sexuality, and Gender* (Albany: SUNY Press, 1992); I.B. Horner, *Women under Primitive Buddhism* (New York: E. P. Dutton, 1930); Anne C. Klein, *Meeting the Great Bliss Queen: Buddhists, Feminists, and the Art of the Self* (Boston: Beacon Press, 1995); and Janice D. Willis, ed., *Feminine Ground: Essays on Women in Tibet* (Ithaca: Snow Lion Publications, 1989).

Tsultrim Allione, *Women of Wisdom* (London: Routledge & Kegan Paul, 1984) contains short biographies of important Tibetan women practitioners. Janet Gyatso, ed., *In the Mirror of Memory: Reflections on Mindfulness and Remembrance in Indian and Tibetan Buddhism* (Albany: SUNY Press, 1992) is an exemplary discussion of *dhāraṇī,* and see also her article, "The Development of the *Gcod* Tradition" in *Soundings in Tibetan Civilization,* edited by M. Kapstein and B. Aziz (Delhi: Manohar, 1985). *Gcod* is associated with one of the most famous female Tibetan practitioners, Ma-jig Lab-drön (Ma-gcig lab-sgron, b. 1031). There is a discussion of practices preliminary to Dzogchen meditations, including *gcod* and meditative rituals similar to that described here, in Khetsun Sangpo, *Tantric Prac-*

tice in Nyingma (Ithaca: Snow Lion Publications, 1986 [reprint of Rider & Company 1982 edition]).

Selection from *Notes on the Basic Text for Emulating the Mother Knowledge Bearer, the Great Bliss Queen*

The teacher Vajradhara emanated inestimable maṇḍalas of immutable sky women in order to lead disciples quickly—like magic—to the buddha ground through the path of great bliss. . . . One hundred yojanas [one yojana is about nine miles] from [Bodhgayā] is a country known as Tibet, where there came to be an accumulation of auspicious circumstances relating to the environment and beings, as indicated below. For there [appeared] the emanation body of the superior Manjuśrī as the venerable Tri-srong-day-tsen, and many varieties of most excellent and fortunate subjects such as Ding-dzin-sang-bo [who advised the king to invite Vimalamitra to Tibet] of the Nyang family, who was definitely to become Vajrasattva in that very life. There were also preceptor lamas on the buddha ground such as the great blissful one, the Lotus-Born [Padmasambhava], who actually came forth as Amitābha, [the embodiment of] immutable speech, taking on the aspect of an accomplished knowledge bearer. And there were local deities such as twelve female protectors of the teaching, the twelve members of Cakrasamvara's retinue, who took rebirth among the worldly female spirits.

At this time, many accomplished yoginīs arrived, such as the Mon [a reference to people from the Tibeto-Indian, Bhutanese, and Sikkimese borders] Tashi-kyi-den [one of the five chief consorts of Padmasambhava] and Dorjay-tsho of the Shel-gar family. Among these, the one who came to be like the topmost ornament of a victory banner was the noblewoman, Yeshey Tsogyal, born in the family of the Kharchen king. She is the venerable superior Lady Tārā, the ruler of all the lotus and action lineages, a sky woman, the actual Vajravārahī, mother of the buddhas, the basis of emanation who is the source of [other] sky women equal in number to the dust particles of Mount Meru. . . .

The rich spacious sphere, the vajra yoginī, due to her merciful compassion for the disciples of this area [Tibet], made a prayer petition before the great Lotus Master for the turning of limitless wheels of the doctrine of secret mantra and collected his spoken word. So that the continuum of these volumes would not vanish, she requested the concealing of innumerable treasures which could not be damaged by humans, nonhumans, demons, or the elements.

Having done this, she offered the following prayer and mental seal [meant to affect the minds of those who would discover these hidden texts in the future]: "May these [teachings] meet with those fortunate beings who have a karmic connection with them so that they may arise in accordance with the time and situation of master and disciples." . . . [In this way] Yeshey Tsogyal opened the door of the sacred buried texts for many recoverers of texts. . . . For this reason, it is also stated in the *Scripture on Ethics ('Dul ba lung):*

> A householder's wife said: "My good lord, if you seek and I save,
> This house will be wealthy and prosper before long."

Accordingly, in the world, a woman maintains the fund of resources, in the same way that when the sustainer sayings (*dhāraṇī, gzungs*) which hold and accumulate the doctrine manifest as tantric deities, they do so in the form of female deities. Therefore, they are called female sustaining protectors, maṇḍalas of sustaining, and so forth. . . .

Beyond this, because she came for the sake of protecting beings through excellent deeds of the highest path, secret and quick, her strands of blessings are great and potent. Among the practices of the guru [Padmasambhava] especially intended for Tibetans, there are many whose chief deity is Yeshey Tsogyal. . . .

Also, those many practices which were left behind especially for emulating her are like sending timely messages for the sake of maintaining Tibetans who would make effort at such emulation. There were many continually emerging general treasure troves of, for example, fierce tantras, and [ritual] substances, as well as teachings and specific methods for emulating the venerable lady herself, images [which she blessed and empowered as her own representatives], manuscripts, as well as substances for attainment.

These are still emerging. It can be understood from the prophecies of many authoritative sacred recovered texts that these treasures are great signs, and that if one is able to accomplish through effort the practice by which one emulates her, and [accomplish] the mantra of this chief female yoginī, one's actual attainments will arise unobstructedly, and there will be a nondegeneration of blessings in a bad era such as this one. . . .

When doing recitation [of her mantra for the purpose of emulating her], through combining [your visualization of yourself as Yeshey Tsogyal] with a visualization at your heart of Vajravārahī, who is profound in achieving supreme feats, one is bound to receive the inconceivable wisdom of clear light. When initiating activities one will unobstructedly have the actual attainment of various activities through incorporating [a visualization of] the superior Lady Tārā, who is swift to accomplish ordinary activities. When taking empowerment, one will simultaneously complete all three empowerments [of the three deities, due to these being bestowed within your incorporation of the three], the external [Tsogyal], the internal [Tārā], and the secret [Vajravārahī]. . . . The *Empowerment Text, Blessings of the Mother* says:

> Within a single rite, these three are completed:
> The blessings of the yoginī [Yeshey Tsogyal],
> The permission [associated with Lady Tārā], and
> The bestowal of the empowerments [associated with Vajravārahī].

[These teachings] are not given to those whose pledges have degenerated.
If publicized to persons other than
Those who are practicing, [the giver] will be punished.

Note that this text itself is not secret, however, and it does not contain actual instructions for meditation.

Selection from *the Ra Ṭīk*

The author opens his text by commenting on the refuge prayer of the Yeshey Tsogyal liturgy, and in the process gives a rare explanation of the very important term "ḍākinī," a category of female wisdom-being of whom Yeshey Tsogyal is the unparalleled example. The bold italic type in this section indicates words from the liturgy on which his comments are based. After this refuge, we translate here select portions from the ritual. These focus on reflections that precede visualization, and the visualization of the maṇḍala and of the Great Bliss Queen herself.

EXPLANATION OF THE WORLD VESSEL, THE ENVIRONMENT, AS THE SPACIOUS SPHERE OF FIVE MOTHER-CONSORTS

All appearances are the expanse of the five mother-consorts.

All that appears as the external container—the world—is naturally pure; it is the spacious sphere of the five families of mother-consorts.

All constituents of earth or hardness are pure, the sphere of the mother-consort, the female buddha Locanā [consort of Vajrasattva].

All constituents of water or softness are pure, the spacious sphere of the mother-consort Māmakī [consort of Ratnasambhava].

All constituents of fire or heat are pure, the spacious sphere of the mother consort Pāṇḍaravāsinī ["the White-clad One," consort of Amitābha].

All the constituents of wind or movement are pure, the spacious sphere of the mother-consort Samaya-Tārā [consort of Amoghasiddhi].

All constituents of space or atmosphere are pure, the spacious sphere of the mother-consort Dhātvīśvarī [consort of Vairocana].

VISUALIZATION OF THE MAṆḌALA AS THE PALACE; THE SINGLE FUNDAMENTAL ORB OR GREAT BLISS

A celestial mansion beyond causes and conditions,
The door which is the expanse of reality and the single, fundamental drop.

Appearances and beings are also the endlessly pure maṇḍala. This maṇḍala passes beyond an aspect that is cultivated or visualized by way of a mantra which [acts as] a causal condition for visualization; for example, *bhruṃ* which, according to the lower tantras, is a flawless root causal mantra. [*Bhruṃ* is the seed syllable of the celestial mansion; in the lower tantras one visualizes this as a cause of the visualized mansion, while in highest tantra this seed syllable is not required. (Tulku Thondup)]

The great wisdom—the basic condition—is the fundamental drop, the "truth dimension." Externally, its shape is completely round [signifying] its passing beyond the corners of the eight extremes of the elaborations [as truly existent production, cessation, permanence, annihilation, coming, going, being truly one or truly many]. Internally it has a semicircle [signifying] the taming of living beings through the activity of empowerment. [The four activities of pacification, taming, increase, and wrath are typically symbolized by a circle, semicircle, square, and triangle, respectively.] Its single door is [symbolically] the expanse of reality (*chos dbyings, dharmadhātu*)—an extinguishment of the extremes, and a freedom from the enumeration of one and many. . . .

[Explaining the meaning of the maṇḍala,] The *Source of Everything [Chos thams cad kun byed rgyal po,* one of the major early Nyingma tantras] says:

> The center is the essence of the flawless meaning [of emptiness].
> The circle possesses the completion of cyclic existence and nirvāṇa as very blissful.
> This central circle is the root of all, the essence [of the deities] in the maṇḍala.
> Realize that all maṇḍalas are completed in this one.

In the center of that mansion of flaming great bliss . . .

The female organ [*bhāga*] of the Vajra Queen is the place of abiding of the thoroughly perfected body whose nature it is to unite the seven limbs of great bliss. [This female organ] is triangular in shape, signifying body, voice, and mind, or the three doors of liberation. In order to embody the union of method and wisdom, its outside is white and the inside blazes with red light. Because the good qualities of the thorough joy and so forth expand more and more, the upper portion opens more broadly [than the base of the triangle].

Vimalamitra says:

> The mansion, the sphere of reality,
> Is known as the bhāga, [symbolized by two triangles in a symbol known as] the source of phenomena (*chos 'byung*).
> [It signifies] the expanse of reality that is without limits or center.
> It is asserted as the excellent abode. . . .

Padma[sambhava] says:

> The five elements are [the five deities of] the five [buddha] families. The five mother-consorts themselves are [the peaceful] Samantabhadrī and [the

wrathful] Dro-di-sho-ri (*kro-dheśvarī*). The bhāga of that mother-consort is the mansion, the expanse of reality. Within the sphere that is the pistil of the lotus [the *bhāga*], the five wisdoms, together with the maṇḍala—the glorious wisdom drop—[of semen] are enlightened in this womb of the mother-consort [that is, they are enlightened in the expanse of reality, the *dharmadhātu*)].

At present, replicas [that is, persons now becoming buddhas] also abide inseparably here in the bhāga of the mother-consort. [All buddhas, and all others who become enlightened, metaphorically take birth in the womb of Samantabhadrī—Tulku Thondup, oral commentary]. All the buddhas who come in the future will come through this bhāga. Therefore, this womb [*bhāga*] of the mother-consort—reality—is the source of all buddhas. It is the basis of all coming and going, the place of arising of all existents. Because it is the play of the various wisdoms, it is the womb of the mother-consort. . . .

The Great Commentary [a famous full-length commentary on the *Kālacakra Tantra* by Dri-med 'od] says:

> The letter *eh*, the great secret [ḍākinīs], the lotus, and the source of phenomena, the element of space, the abode of great bliss, the lion's throne, and the bhāga [all] express emptiness through secret names.

[These terms] are said to be of the same meaning, synonyms. . . .

> *Atop the filament inside an opened water lotus*
> *On a seat which is a sun disc . . .*

> The [word] *gesar* [filament or pistil] which [refers to] the lotus that arises in water is a rough [Tibetan] approximation of [the Sanskrit word] *kesar*. Due to the youthfulness of the antlers [on the flower's filament, the lotus] is opened and blossoming. This signifies that, like the lotus which dwells in mud without wearing the faults of mud, so [the sky woman Yeshey Tsogyal, the Great Bliss Queen], although she dwells in cyclic existence (saṃsāra) for the sake of living beings, does not wear its faults. Moreover, [the Great Bliss Queen] is seated upon a dais made of a sun disc, [signifying] the primordial, spontaneous clear light in the truth dimension of the mind.

VISUALIZING THE CHIEF SKY WOMAN

> *. . . The chief sky wisdom woman*
> *In the sphere of the truth dimension [is] Samantabhadrī,*
> *In the [pure] land of the thoroughly perfected body, Vajrāvarahī.*
> *[She is] the emanation body Yeshey Tsogyal.*

The female chief of all the sky women, upon a sun-disc dias, is the truth dimension, naturally free from elaborations, the unproduced sphere. She is

Samantabhadrī, reality, the natural state of the youthful vase body, the internal clear light, the great bliss which possesses the excellence of all aspects. . . .

She [the chief sky woman] shows whatever emanation body will tame any given [person] just as, for example, the full moon in the sky gives rise to reflections in different water vessels. . . .

With one face, two hands, and the color of her body is red.
Naked, her feet evenly on the ground, with one foot forward,
[Her expression is] very desirous, with a laughing face

. . . From the beginning, all phenomena that have the aspect of status of natural spontaneous occurrence are of one taste in the actual state of reality. For this reason [the Great Bliss Queen] has a single face. Her two hands signify the method—great compassion—and wisdom—emptiness. The red color of her body signifies her taming of disciples through the lotus lineage, the essence of the discriminating wisdom that thoroughly purifies desire.

Because [she] purifies the two obstructions, her form is naked, free of the clothing of conceptuality that characterizes subject and object. She has the youthful appearance of a sixteen-year-old, due to having completed the four joys.

Her manner of standing, with her two feet evenly placed, is due to her not dwelling in an extreme qualified by either mundane existence or the pacification [into the] actual state. As a sign of her activities for the sake of living beings, she poses in the manner of advancing slightly.

Although the conceptual bonds of all ordinary desires are completely severed, she displays [an expression of] very great desire, due to the force of her compassion for all living beings who, not realizing their own nature, which is the buddha womb, engage in the various errors of cyclic existence. However, because from the beginning the essential nature of all living beings is manifestly enlightened, she is shown as smiling and laughing because she observes that [they have] a nature that does not possess miserable, mistaken, cyclic existence as its own [natural] characteristic.

In her right hand is a small drum made of skulls
Which she plays, holding it at ear level.
In her left hand is the handle of a curved blade,
Holding this at her side, she stands most proudly
Her bhāga is extended, and her breasts swell forth.

The skull held in her right hand [signifies] selflessness and that which is self-arisen due to the nature of the method, great compassion. The backs [of the two skulls forming the drum] signify cyclic existence and nirvāṇa. These are joined in the sphere [of reality]. A connecting hollow in the small drum links [the two skulls], signifying [that cyclic existence and nirvāṇa share] the nature of a single reality that is free of discarding and adopting. [The drum] faces outward, in the manner of exhorting the mind of one's own compassionate lama, the head of one's [buddha] family, who is exhorted by the [drum's] two whips [representing] the conventional and ultimate minds of enlightenment. She sounds the drum at ear level.

Her left hand, hanging downward and holding a [knife] handle, signifies the excising of subject and object—the ignorance which is the root of cyclic existence—by means of the curved knife of emptiness, the natural condition which is a realization of selflessness, [that is, of] whose nature is the wisdom free from the eight elaborations.

She has a prideful posture in the completely perfect sphere [of reality], with her [right hand holding the knife] resting on her waist signifying the generation of blissful wisdom which is the quick path of secret mantra.

In order to train desirous disciples, she is adorned with swelling breasts which remain at the youthful age of sixteen years, with extensive waves of bliss that are the secret bhāga. . . .

In general, she is adorned with jeweled necklaces, bracelets, and so forth; more specifically, she has precious stones that are renowned as ornaments of youth or of children. Her draping necklace [of jewels] interspersed with flowers reaches to her secret region. [The text continues with elaborate descriptions of her adornments and their symbolism.]

Her middle eye gazes [upward] into space.
Her [right] thoroughly perfected body eye tames living beings.
Her [left] emanation body eye summons the three realms.

Her truth dimension eye—the empty essence—gazes into the heart of the leading family lama [Padmasambhava, and through the fourfold bliss and wisdom], their minds becoming one. [Her gaze] fills the wisdom sphere [both a symbol and a method for achieving the truth dimension.]

The right eye of the five wisdoms—the nature of the thoroughly perfected body—gazes directly into its own pure land, [which means that] clear appearances will ripen as body and wisdom, completing the deeds for taming living beings.

Her left eye of the emanation body, [which signifies] the compassion that trains disciples, appropriately gazes downward. It summons and exhorts disciples in the three realms of cyclic existence who are attached to their own continuum as self. . . . Through such powerful and fearful actions [Yeshey Tsogyal and oneself] liberate cyclic existence into the spacious sphere. . . .

Because she has purified birth in its own place, her flesh is soft; because she has purified sickness in its own place, her waist is thin and pliant; because she has purified death in its own place, her body is taut and supple. Because her mind is unwavering and straight, she is elastic; because she has purified aging in its own place, she has an intrinsically soft and youthful body. These are the five good qualities of her essence.

Because the good qualities of her major and minor signs are unalloyed and pristine, she is stainless, and thus her color is clear. Because of the complete extinguishment [of conceptuality], she has a bright and brilliant complexion. Because her brightness is pleasing, it is spontaneously appealing, and because it outshines living beings, it has a great glow. These are the four good qualities of aspects. *The Secret Essence (Guhyagarbha)* says:

> Having a youthful mode, with coiled tender limbs,
> Possessed of brilliance, spontaneously appealing and with a great glow . . .

> *The complete maṇḍala of tantric deities*
> *Are included in her body.*

In the shape of the sky woman's body all the hosts of deities in the maṇḍalas of the four sets of tantra are completed by way of being guests, some [present] explicitly, some implicitly. . . .

> *At her heart, in the spacious sphere of the glorious knot*
> *[Are] the birthless, self-arisen, thoroughly established deities*
> *In the center of a five-spoked wheel.*

Just as the 2,002 buddhas of the three times [of this eon] become perfected on the immutable seat in Magadha, Bodhgayā, so the place where the natural condition of the mind, the essence of the tathāgatas, which is not categorized into any of the three times, is enlightened, is on the vajra seat of the doctrine wheel in her heart. Therefore, the basis for the emanation and dissolution of all the stages of visualization and completion is located in her heart. . . . Where do these exist? In the center of her heart's empty interior, in the clear white channel, the central of the eight channels [that cross each other at the heart, that is] in the mansion where dwell the five Samantabhadric [All-Good Buddha] families, the basis of the natural mind of enlightenment.

It is said that when the clear aspect of one's mind is gathered [as in death], there will arise all the visions of the pure land of nirvāṇa. Therefore, because the heart is the place from which all good qualities arise, the glorious know it is the natural producer of the aggregates and constituents. [This is so] primordially, without being produced by the mind in the spacious sphere; this is the abode of the appearances of the thoroughly established deities in a single wheel. The five primordial wisdoms which are the spokes of that abode have as their center the inconceivable primordial wisdom.

—11—

Story of Siṃhala, the Caravan Leader

Todd T. Lewis

The *Siṃhalasārthabāhu Avadāna* is a popular Buddhist story that draws upon a narrative adventure spanning all Indic folklore, for a similar tale is found in the Prakrit Jain canon. In its Buddhist incarnations, this story found its way across Asia.

As indicated by its title, an avadāna (significant deed) is a form of Buddhist literature that imparts religious instruction through stories of the actions of a bodhisattva or other spiritually advanced being. One of the earliest collections of such stories, a Sanskrit text called the *Avadānaśataka* ("One Hundred Avadānas"), was written by the second century C.E. Later avadāna texts drew heavily upon this work and on one like it, Aśvaghoṣa's *Sūtrālaṃkāra.* The most popular collection was the *Divyāvadāna* ("Heavenly Stories"), and the *Story of Siṃhala* translated here follows this genealogy. Later Buddhist versions were also translated in Khotanese, Tibetan, Chinese, and Japanese Buddhist texts. The modern Newari recension probably can be traced back through the early *Divyāvadāna* to the Mahāyāna version of the *Guṇakāraṇḍavyūha,* a late (sixteenth century?) Sanskrit text devoted to Avalokiteśvara. Buddhist artists of different eras have depicted this story: it is found on a third-century stone pillar at Mathura, in Cave 17 at Ajanta, and in Central Asia, as well as in Burma, Angkor, Borobudur, and Nepal.

The *Siṃhalasārthabāhu Avadāna* highlights the merchant class in ancient South Asia, a group especially important in the history of Buddhism and often featured in Buddhist popular literature, both Hīnayāna and Mahāyāna. Monks traveled with the caravans, allied with artisans and merchants plying the diaspora trade networks. This mode of livelihood, relying on business acumen, capital, diplomatic skill, and ethnic partners stationed in strategic venues, was a pervasive phenomenon from late antiquity onward, both globally and in South Asia. By the Gupta era, many Buddhist monasteries were granted land and also had extensive economic ties with their surrounding communities; the administrative practices of monastic officials—such as lending money and warehousing goods—created a symbiotic relationship with traders. The missionary success of Buddhist monasticism was clearly linked to the devotion and patronage of this class.

The text is an exemplary tale depicting many facets of Mahāyāna Buddhism in practice: the main hero is identified as an earlier incarnation of Śākyamuni; the savior deity taking the form of the white horse is Avalokiteśvara; the ritual lauded at the end, the eight-day observance (*aṣṭamī-vrata*, the name referring to the eighth day of the lunar fortnight), is still a popular Mahāyāna ritual of devotion to Avalokiteśvara in Nepal.

In its most straightforward message, the text is a morality or karma-retribution tale that emphasizes the dire consequences of damaging stūpas. This concern with stūpa veneration spans all Buddhist schools. More strictly Mahāyāna in tone is the utter necessity of relying on the saving grace of the bodhisattva, whose help is necessary to avoid falling prey to worldly temptations that undermine the spiritual life. On yet another level, the text underlines the importance of ethnic loyalty, an especially poignant message for diaspora merchants who (like the hero) spent months away from home and who often faced temptation. Modern Nepalese Buddhists all point out how this text (and many other Mahāyāna avadānas) must also be understood symbolically: that is, the rākṣasīs (demonesses) are really symbols of the five senses (*indriyā*); if uncontrolled, they lead to ignorance, delusion, and destruction. This message is conveyed with vivid directness and dramatic force in the narrative.

The text can also be read for its injunctions on Mahāyāna Buddhist kingship, with the hero showing the exemplary traits of protection, compassion, generosity, and ritual leadership focused on Avalokiteśvara. The ethos of Buddhist royalty is poignantly shown in the king's conquest of the rākṣasīs in the final section: after effectively organizing and leading his army, the hero inspires them to fight bravely. In victory, he responds compassionately to the pleas of the vanquished; foregoing massacre, he effectively banishes the rākṣasīs to a distant place and conquers their territory in the name of justice and Buddhist order.

Other discourses in the story hold forth rather bluntly on women as dangerous to the superior man's spiritual life. The text joins many other Buddhist sūtras in providing evidence of the celibate, male monastic's sexist disdain for the female gender.

This selection has been translated from Bhikṣu Sudarśan, ed., *Siṃhasārthabāhu va Kabīr Kumāryā Bākhaṃ* (Kathmandu: Cvasāpāsā, 1967).

Further Reading

See generally Mary Cummings, *The Lives of the Buddha in the Art and Literature of Asia*, Michigan Papers on South and Southeast Asia 20 (Ann Arbor: University of Michigan Center for South and Southeast Asian Studies, 1982). On avadāna literature, see John Strong, "The Transforming Gift: An Analysis of Devotional Acts of Offering in Buddhist Avadāna Literature," *History of Religions* 18:3 (1979), 221–37, and on this avadāna's role in Nepalese Buddhism, see Todd T. Lewis, "Newar-Tibetan Trade and the Domestication of the Siṃhalasārthabāhu Avadāna," *History of Religions* 33:2 (1993), 135–60. On trade and the merchant class, see Philip D. Curtin, *Cross-Cultural Trade in World History* (Cambridge: Cambridge University Press, 1984); Todd T. Lewis, "Himalayan Frontier Trade: Newar Diaspora Merchants and Buddhism," in Martin Brauen et al., eds., *Anthropology of Tibet and the Himalaya* (Zurich: Volkerkundemuseum, 1993), pp. 165–178; and Himanshu P. Ray, *Monastery and Guild: Commerce under the Satavahanas* (Delhi: Oxford University Press, 1986). On Buddhist royalty, see David Snellgrove, "The Notion of Divine Kingship in Tantric Buddhism," *Studies in the History of Religions* 4 (1959), 204–18. And on male monastics' attitude toward women, see Diane Y. Paul, *Women in Buddhism: Images of the Feminine in the Mahāyāna Tradition* (Berkeley and Los Angeles: University of California Press, 1985).

The Story of Siṃhalasārthabāhu

In the town Siṃhalakalpa ruled by Siṃhakeṣara, a son named Siṃhalasārthabāhu was born to Siṃhalasārthabāha. Once he grew up, the son thought that he should leave the traditional family jewelry business, and said to his parents, "O mother and father, we should not give up our family business. I shall go across the Ratnākar Sea to trade."

Having heard the son say, "Bid me farewell!" both parents felt distressed and replied, "O son Siṃhalasārthabāhu, we are now old. We already possess innumerable properties. You should be content, stay here and enjoy the riches we already possess. Why are you so eager to abandon gold, gems, and other wealth to risk great misery? Why go to this Ratnākar? The troubles along the way to Ratnākar are so many: after passing through many villages and countries, you will reach a great forest. In that forest there is danger from many lions, tigers, wild animals, and also from thieves. In some places you must tolerate great cold and high temperatures. Furthermore, since you are an immature young man, your body is still delicate. O son, please do not talk about going to Ratnākar."

Having listened to his parents' objections, Siṃhalasārthabāhu replied respectfully, "O mother and father, in the world the effects of the karma written on the forehead will unfold, no matter where I go. How can you regard me as an accomplished man if I merely enjoy the wealth earned by my parents? How can one become an accomplished man if he does not earn a living from his own labor? How can one perform the duty of meritorious giving (*dāna*)? For this additional reason I must go. Please, both of you, do not worry. For undertaking a mission of dharma, certainly no troubles will befall me. Give me your blessings and let me be off!" After respectfully gesturing to his mother and father, he touched their lotuslike feet; and having taken leave with their auspicious blessings, he assembled five hundred less one attendants, who speedily prepared elephants, horses, donkeys, camels, and so on, loaded the luggage, then departed in the northern direction, toward Ratnapura.

Later, however, they committed the evil deed of destroying caityas along the way, and Saturn intervened. Despite Saturn's intervention, having crossed many villages, towns, rivers, and mountains, they eventually reached the shore of the Brahmaputra River. From the result of destroying caityas [shrines] at that time, Siṃhalasārthabāhu, having seen the oceanlike Brahmaputra River, cautiously restrained the 499 and called out and hired a boatman named Karnadhara; after respectfully gesturing to the broad Brahmaputra, Siṃhalasārthabāhu and attendants embarked in his boat and started to cross the mighty river.

When they reached the middle of the river, a very terrible wind arose and began to capsize the boat. Seeing the danger of sinking with the boat and fearing their possible deaths, the five hundred attendants addressed their leader: "O Siṃhalasārthabāhu, we five hundred attendants along with you are about to go to our deaths in the middle of this very river! Here and now is there any means by which [we can] be rescued? Please tell us immediately!" Siṃhalasārthabāhu quickly replied, "O attendants! In times of the greatest trouble, the only one capable of rescuing [us] is the glorious triratna [three jewels]; there is no other in the world. Take refuge in the triratna!" But due to the transgression of destroying caityas along the road, they could not concentrate their minds, or even pronounce the name of the triratna; they could only pronounce the name of their own family deities [Hindu deities that protect the group]. As a result, Siṃhalasārthabāhu and the 499 attendants fell into the sea as the boat broke into small pieces. At that time, by the strength of their own limbs, they crossed the great river and reached an island shore [where] they laid under campaka trees, making great lamentations, crying and weeping loudly. Remembering their love of their own country again, they sighed out sadly.

At that time, the rākṣasīs from the town of Ratnapura on Tamradvīpa Island saw the 499 attendants who had fallen into the river and who had climbed up on the banks with their own hands and who were making lamentations beneath campaka trees. Delighted, the rākṣasīs of Ratnapura joined together to appear as maidens possessing the spotless beauty of sixteen-year-olds looking like the youthful, beautiful Ratidevī [the wife of the Indic god of desire, Kāma]. Having become immensely alluring, they reached the place where Siṃhalasārthabāhu and the 499 attendants were resting beneath the campaka trees. All of the rākṣasīs were delighted; with smiles and expressions captivating to look at, they spoke sweet charming words to Siṃhalasārthabāhu and the rest, and proposed, "O masters, having overcome disaster in the great river, why do you have such gloomy faces, anxious minds, and uncertainty? For what reason is this so? From where have you come? Which is your country? What trouble [occurred] such that you are in this place by the river? Tell us the details." Saying "O master," they inquired of Siṃhalasārthabāhu, showing great affection.

Having listened thus to the rākṣasīs' speech and having felt spellbound, Siṃhalasārthabāhu responded, "O beautiful ones! I am no other than Siṃhalasārthabāhu the merchant, son of Siṃhalasārthabāha from the town of Siṃhalakalpa in Jambudvīpa. Including me, there are five hundred in all. Carrying loads of different kinds of trade goods, we were unable to cross the broad river: when our boat reached the middle a very terrible wind came from the opposite direction and broke up the boat. We and our goods fell into the river and everything was washed away. We ourselves by our own strength made it here. And so sitting under these campaka trees, we are remembering our families at home. We feel great sorrow, O beautiful ones."

So having heard his speech, the rākṣasīs in their beautiful female forms made a request: "O masters, how great is our fortune to hear this! We have lived in the country called Ratnapura and we also happen to have come here seeking virile men, since we are now fully mature and beautiful. By our good luck we have taken sight of you." They implored them, "Please come to our Ratnapura and make love to us who are happily in our adolescence. Do make love to us in all the different ways."

Having been persuaded by various means, Siṃhalasārthabāhu and the other attendants each escorted one woman and carried her to her own dwelling. Having fed them with different divine foods, given them many types of gold, jewels, and ornaments, at night the rākṣasīs made love to them and kept them there every night. After seven days of enjoying lovemaking and all love sports, the rākṣasīs in the form of beautiful women happened to fall asleep.

Now at that time, Śrī Śrī Śrī Ārya Avalokiteśvara—who lends assistance with compassion to poor suffering men in the world—saw Simhalasārthabāhu and his entourage deluded and imprisoned in the grip of the rākṣasīs in Ratnapura on Tamradvīpa Island. Feeling compassion, Avalokiteśvara thought, "My miserable children are imprisoned in the grip of the evil-souled man-eating rākṣasīs of Tamradvīpa." Vowing to help these people, Śrī Śrī Śrī Ārya Avalokiteśvara immediately entered the lamp placed in the room of Siṃhalasārthabāhu on Tamradvīpa, for the purpose of discoursing with him, and so made the lamp flicker. Having seen the lamp flicker, Siṃhalasārthabāhu was surprised and focused on the lamp alone.

For a second time, Avalokiteśvara made the lamp flicker. Having seen the lamp flicker again, Siṃhalasārthabāhu asked, "O lamp! Why do you flicker? Who is it who has come into the lamp? What is your purpose in coming? Please tell me this and let me know the reason!" Śrī Avalokiteśvara answered, "O Siṃhalasārthabāhu! How little do you know! They are not really beautiful women: they are evil-souled ones and man-eating rākṣasīs as well. These rākṣasīs will most certainly devour all of you. You must escape as soon as possible."

Having heard these words and feeling terror, he prayed respectfully again [to the lamp] and said, "O lord of the lamp, how have you come to know this? Is it really true?" and then he respectfully saluted the lamp. Śrī Lokeśvara replied, "O Siṃhalasārthabāhu, if you do not believe me, go and look in the cell called Āyaśa in the southern direction."

Following this advice, that very night Siṃhalasārthabāhu went out alone in the southern direction, holding his sword.

Having arrived at the Āyaśa cell, he saw a house without doors or windows. He also heard peoples' voices only. Feeling great surprise, he climbed a tree and looked in. Having heard peoples' cries, he climbed higher up the campaka tree and asked, "O people! Who are you and why are you living here?"

They responded, "O sir, having come for Ratnākar trade, while we were crossing the Brahmaputra a very terrible wind blew and broke up our boat, and we fell into the river. And when we emerged from the water, we fell into the grip of rākṣasīs from Ratnapura. We had sex and love play with them, but then they came to know of other traders on the road. They threw us down into this Āyaśa cell and come to eat us every day." They also added, "What is to be done, O great man, and who are you?"

Siṃhalasārthabāhu listened to them and replied, "O people, I am none other than the son of Siṃhalasārthabāha called Siṃhalasārthabāhu from Jambudvīpa. I also came to trade in Ratnākar. I have come to see who you are here and what things there are. I have come to investigate." Having replied in this way and heard as much as he needed to, he returned.

After returning to his own room, Siṃhalasārthabāhu saluted the still-burning lamp with joined palms and addressed the deity, "O lamp, O divine one! By your grace I have looked in the Āyaśa cell. Guide us [to know] how we can be saved. You have to protect us." He ended his petition with a respectful gesture.

Dwelling in the lamp, Śrī Avalokiteśvara replied, "O Siṃhalasārthabāhu! If you are determined to return to Jambudvīpa, I will show you how. Listen: the means of crossing the Brahmaputra River is there on the bank of the river. A compassionate soul is living there called Vārahaka, a great horse. This one living there [will be] eating white-medicine herbs and rubbing his back on the gold sand bank. This one will call upon you and what will he say? 'Who is willing to go across the river? I will send you across.' At that time all of you must go before him, make three circumambulations around him with joined hands, touch your heads to his lotuslike feet, and make this request: 'O protector! O lord! O Vārahaka! O noble horse who is a store of compassion: please take us across the broad river.' And at that time, having aroused the compassion of the supreme lord, he will transport you across the ocean." After instructing him, Śrī Ārya Avalokiteśvara vanished in an instant.

Afterwards, Siṃhalasārthabāhu climbed into bed in order to sleep alongside the rākṣasī. At that time, the rākṣasī awoke and asked, "O master! Where have you been? Your body feels very cold." Siṃhalasārthabāhu replied, "My dear beauty, due to answering the call of nature, I had to go out. For this reason my body became very cold." Saying this, he convinced the rākṣasī by his lie. After that, Siṃhalasārthabāhu felt disgust at having slept with the rākṣasī who appeared beautiful. And so the night passed. And once dawn came, Siṃhalasārthabāhu met the 499 attendants outside the town in a grove, after finishing the daily routine of ablutions and rituals. He addressed them, "O attendants!

I will make a speech on one topic. Listen! If you say 'What is this about?' [it concerns] your beloved ones here, your very own wives. How much do they love you? How much do they care? What do they feed you? You must tell me the details in all honesty."

Having heard this, the leader of Siṃhalasārthabāhu's attendants smiled and answered merrily, "O leader! O brave one! Master! By your grace and by the influence of your great and good fortune we have come to enjoy such sensual pleasures with the beautiful ones of Ratnapura." Another one [from the group] said, "O brave one! To have had the chance to enjoy sex and such lovemaking, etc., . . . how fortunate we are to have been so divinely blessed! We have no desire at all to leave this, our own great fortune, and return to Jambudvīpa." Another said, "O leader, my beloved wife, having put on different jewels and ornaments, honored me happily and allowed me such delightful sexual dalliance with her." And yet another said, "O Siṃhalasārthabāhu! My wife, having put on clothes and special royal robes of different types, allowed me to enjoy the sexual pleasure of her tender body." And another, "O brave one! By the fruit of what merit have we enjoyed the pleasures of the celestial nymphs of Ratnapura? We have certainly settled here happily and with the greatest respect. Such kinds of pleasure, even for those kings living in all realms, must be rare. Again, even Indra with Indrāyanī rarely obtains such pleasure in Amarāvatī heaven. In this world, the illusion of love prevails. Again, it is rare for Śrī Kṛṣṇa with Rādhikā to enjoy such sexual pleasures. O leader! For this reason, if we were to return to Jambudvīpa, we would not obtain such pleasures. We will stay here forever and do not want to return."

The attendants all made similar statements, narrating their own many pleasures. Having heard the remarks of his attendants, Siṃhalasārthabāhu told them, "O companions! Although they seem to be beloved ones, only if you do not tell this secret to your own wives will our lives be saved. Listen and I will explain. And how is this? We have left our own country and homeland, including family, wealth, property, friends, and neighbors, and have come to this Ratnapura. If you wish to return and see these faces ever again, I will tell you how." Feeling horrified at hearing this, they inquired, "O Siṃhalasārthabāhu! What happened? What is it? Even though we love them, we will not tell them. O master, please tell us."

Siṃhalasārthabāhu replied, "All these women are not who they appear to be. They are, in fact, man-eating rākṣasīs of Tamradvīpa. They are not human. You must not be deceived, even though they give you all sorts of sensual pleasure, jeweled goods, endless delight, and say 'My own master,' undoubtedly they will devour us. It is absolutely certain. For this reason, for the good of everyone, you must keep it a secret."

Having listened again and felt the horrifying fear of death, they joined their hands and touched their heads to Siṃhalasārthabāhu's feet and pleaded with him, "O protector! How did you come to know that these women are the rākṣasīs of Tamradvīpa? Can it be true? How can we rescue ourselves? Have we arrived at death's door? Are there any means of saving us from death? You must give us instructions on how to cross the river and go back to Jambudvīpa." They answered him with great urgency and sighed deeply.

Having listened to their speech, again Siṃhalasārthabāhu spoke, "You should not feel great worry, O attendants! Be patient. Patience in the face of misery is called for and all of you must do exactly as I say. On the shore of the Brahmaputra River, on a gold sand beach is a compassionate one, king of horses, called Vārahaka, who will convey us across." Having given instructions, Siṃhalasārthabāhu and all the attendants went to their places with their own beautiful ones.

And later, after returning to their own houses and having enjoyed different foods, at night they enjoyed and made love to their beautiful wives. At that time, the beautiful ones asked their own men, "O master, in the daytime today where did you go for amusement? Have you been out to see gardens of different types? Have you brought [us] different types of flowers, fruits, and vegetables?"

Responding to their wives' queries, they answered, "O beautiful ones, we did not see any of these things. After four days we will go to see [them]. [Now] prepare and give us some rice and other foods."

Having heard their answer, the wives replied teasingly, "O masters! Where did you really go? How is it that you did not see any gardens, flowers, fruits, and so on?" Later on, those attendants while sitting in their own places, remembering the danger of death, sat deeply sighing. And so the women, seeing them taking deep breaths, said to them, "O masters! Why are you now and then sighing so? What trouble has arisen? Please tell us."

At that time, Siṃhalasārthabāhu and the 499 attendants told their own beautiful ones, "O, dear beloved ones, there is no other reason for our heavy sighs than having remembered our mothers, fathers, sons, daughters, wives, relatives, and friends from our homeland. Feeling attachment for them, we have passed a long period of time absent from our own country." Having answered in this way, even though worried, they tried to brighten up their faces as much as possible.

At that time, the rākṣasīs, looking at the faces of their own men and smiling, enticed them; revealing the youthful curves of their bodies, they spoke tenderly to them and asked, "O masters! O greatly beloved ones! Why are you frequently sighing after remembering your wives, sons, etc., in your own country, Jambudvīpa? Here in this Ratnāpur Nagar of Tamradvīpa, isn't there everything here? Living here are many different cows, buffalo, horses, elephants, camels, she goats, sheep, deer, stags, yaks, musk deer, and so on, and all species. There are also all varieties of fruits and vegetables. All kinds of flowers are here: fragrant, night-blooming, and so on. There are all sorts of scented things, too, such as musk, camphor, saffron, sandalwood, herbs, cardamom, cloves, nutmeg, betel nut and betel leaf, and so on. And again there are all sorts of delightful places such as gardens, stone fountains, pleasure groves, and so on. And there are birds of every variety such as peacocks, swans, and so on, as well as butterflies all with sweet voices that are lovely to listen to. So delightful is this place! Why do you long for your own country in spite of the charms of Ratnapura? You are in command of all of this and our beautiful adolescence, so enjoy yourselves," they said clearly.

Having listened to the rākṣasīs' words, though worried about the danger of death, the men [still] enjoyed their rākṣasīs sexually in the night and fell asleep.

And so, feeling very worried and anxious, just as a hungry one longs for food, a sick one for a doctor's face, a devotee for the deity, a cakora bird for the moon, so they waited for the four days to pass.

Thereupon after four days passed, they went about the daily rituals and had their own women prepare their meals. On the evening of the fourth day, they went to sleep.

At dawn on the next day, in their own houses they recalled the deities in their daily ritual. After eating and having gathered up their equipment and food, they went off, making a pretense of seeing the pavilions and ponds, all to mislead them. Having said good-bye to their wives, they remembered their own kula devatās [family deities]. After this, Siṃhalasarthabahu and the 499 attendants arrived outside the town. And at that time, all of them gathered together and hastily went to the Brahmaputra shore with the golden sand. Then the black-eared king of horses Vārahaka arrived nearby. When he saw the arrival of Siṃhalasārthabāhu and the five hundred merchants, he stood up from the golden sand, shook his body three times, and called out, "I will carry across all those wishing to cross the river to Jambudvīpa."

Having heard the horse's words, they circumambulated him three times, touched their heads, and greeted him reverentially. Then Siṃhalasārthabāhu addressed him, "O noble king of horses, you must protect us who are living in the grip of the evil rākṣasīs of Ratnāpur Nagar in Tamradvīpa. If you do not protect us, surely they will devour us. O compassionate one, for this reason we have come for refuge to your feet. Please look upon us compassionately and send us across the Brahmaputra." This all the men repeated with tears falling from their eyes.

Having heard this request and feeling compassion, the horse again spoke, "O five hundred merchants, if you have the wish to go across the river to Jambudvīpa, I will send you across. Until you reach the other side, you must remember the triratna and not look back. If you obey this, I will deliver all of you to the other side."

They listened and again touched the horse's feet with their heads and said respectfully, "O supreme lord, king of horses, we will certainly not cease reciting the names of Śrī Buddha, dharma, and saṅgha. Nor will we look back. We are poised at the mouth of death, so please send us across the river."

Having heard their plea, the glorious horse became large and said, "O Siṃhalasārthabāhu and you 499 attendants! All of you get on my body and pronounce the names of the triratna." Having heard this instruction, they touched their heads to his feet and got on the horse's back, remembering their own family deities.

Making the sound "Hu-nu-num," the horse then accelerated like the wind and soon reached the middle of the great river. But noticing the noise, the rākṣasīs realized that Siṃhalasārthabāhu and the rest were crossing the river and one called out, "O sisters! The five hundred traders we have taken as husbands are all escaping across the ocean. Now let us go and devour them." They called to one another, and revealing their true forms produced the wild crying sound "kilikila." Lighting up the sky in many ways, they went flying in the air.

Flying up close to them, the rākṣasīs made lamentations as to elicit sympathy and used endearing, lovely words which created the illusion of enchantment and love. From behind them, they cried, "O masters! Where are you going? Are you leaving us with youthful figures, whose longings you have satisfied in Ratnapura? Where are you going? Why are you disgracing us? What misery has arisen! O masters! Why are you going, abandoning your royal robes and sensual pleasures, forgetting the virtues of heavenlike Ratnapura, forsaking our love? O husbands, beloved ones, lords of life! Being unable to subdue the longing for enjoyment and the various ways of sex, we have followed after you. Let us accompany you to your country. If you will not do so, then just look back a little, show us just a little glimpse of your faces. How can you abandon our love and not give us even a glimpse of your faces? We will be helpless! Because of you, we will die! We never thought that you could be so cruel!" They cried on and on with these and other love-inducing words, speaking to them as they followed [behind] in the sky.

Remembering the sensual pleasure and enjoyments, each and every attendant was unable to ignore the rākṣasīs' endearing words. One by one, each looked back at them. From the evil karma of destroying the caityas along the road, those who glanced back fell into the river. And right after falling down, each rākṣasī swooped over her own husband, plucked him from the sea by the hair, and took him to the bank. There they devoured all of them.

But due to the compassion of Ārya Avalokiteśvara, Śrī Śrī Śrī Karuṇāmaya, from the effect of performing the eighth-day observance (*aṣṭamī vrata*), and from having taken refuge in the noble triratna, it was Siṃhalasārthabāhu alone who still held on to the mane of the horse Aśvarāja [with one hand] so that he could embrace the neck [with the other]. Only he crossed the great river.

Having reached the other shore and having climbed down from the horse's body, he went around the horse three times, touched the horse's feet, joined his hands, and said respectfully, "O Karuṇāmaya, king of horses! I am the only one who has had good fortune. Although lying in the mouth of the rākṣasīs, from the grace of the triratna and from your grace, I have crossed the great river. I have reached Jambudvīpa. You must always protect me!"

The horse replied, "O Siṃhalasārthabāhu! For the merit of taking the name of the triratna you were protected from the rākṣasīs. Now go to the town called Siṃhakalpa in Jambudvīpa and have sight of your parents' own feet, always take refuge in the triratna. Perform the aṣṭamī vrata. Whenever you are in danger, I will protect you. In the future, you will be the king of Siṃhakalpa."

And having given him different blessings and after he handed over the kingdom of Siṃhakalpa to Siṃhalasārthabāhu, the king of horses immediately vanished, giving a sacred vision (*darśana*) of Śrī Avalokiteśvara in the sky.

And so after the king of horses gave many instructions, Śrī Avalokiteśvara made his own luminous flame go up into the sky like a fire and then he [too] disappeared. Feeling awe for that deity, Siṃhalasārthabāhu joined his hands for as long as he could see, then did an eightfold salutation. Then, holding a sword in his hand, he started off alone toward Jambudvīpa and came upon a dense forest.

At that moment, all the rākṣasīs of Tamradvīpa circled around their leader who was Siṃhalasārthabāhu's wife and said to her, "We have just finished eating our own husbands who fell back into the river. Yet you alone let your husband escape and he was not eaten. That one will go to Jambudvīpa and tell this news to everyone. If others hear his tale, who else will come to our place? There will be no food in the future. If you do not go and devour that Siṃhalasārthabāhu, we will eat you."

Once she heard their ultimatum, the head rākṣasī felt afraid and said, "O younger sisters! Please do not say that you will devour me. It is certain that I will return after having eaten that husband Siṃhalasārthabāhu." After convincing them, the head rākṣasī flew into the sky. Having assumed her beautiful form, she appeared in front of Siṃhalasārthabāhu, frightening him. But Siṃhalasārthabāhu, seeing the rākṣasī before him, quickly took his special sword in hand and when he started to chop at her, that rākṣasī ran away in fear.

Soon the rākṣasī saw other traders who had come there from many countries. She assumed her beautiful form and went nearby. After seeing such a beautiful one and feeling amazed at seeing the woman's face, they said, "O younger sister! Who are you! Why are you living alone in this unpleasant dense forest?" She answered, "O elder brother traders! For one trying to escape great danger, there is nothing other than the triratna so I have come for refuge in the triratna. O brothers! What can I do feeling such great misery?" After saying this, she took deep breaths like those of the male and female serpent deities (*nāgas*), made a gloomy face, and then sighed deeply again. Then the merchants said, "O younger sister! Where have you come from? What evil has befallen you? Whose daughter are you? Who are your friends? You must tell us in detail."

After she heard the traders' request, she produced tears in her eyes, joined her hands, and spoke politely, "O traders, what to do? It is so that in Ratnapura kingdom of Tamradvīpa, I was a princess. My father gave me in marriage to Siṃhalasārthabāhu when he was trading [there]. Now this Siṃhalasārthabāhu, after having enjoyed marital bliss with me for several months in my parents' country, announced [one day] to my father, 'Now I am returning to my own country. Farewell!' and brought me here. Then we were shipwrecked and only we crossed the river by our own strength. All the wealth given by my parents—gifts, jewels, and so on—was washed away. After this, Siṃhalasārthabāhu scolded me saying, 'O evil woman, having crossed the river with you, I was almost lost. With such an unlucky woman I will not go anywhere. If I do go on with you who has such bad luck, I will surely die. You must not come along with me. Wherever you wish to go, be off! And I will be off to where I please.' [After he said this] I tried many means of changing his mind, but I could not. Today I have been left alone in this dense forest. What to do? Thus, traders, you must see my husband for me and convince him to love me again."

After hearing her request, they said, "All right, we will do so," and soon they came upon Siṃhalasārthabāhu and addressed him. They made perfunctory conversation and [finally] said, "O Siṃhalasārthabāhu! There is a king's daughter of Ratnapura: after choosing her and bringing her to this dense forest, why did you abandon her? It is rare to find a woman who does not make a mistake and they are powerless. You must forgive her and take her along." So having heard the traders' speech, Siṃhalasārthabāhu replied, "O traders and friends! This woman is no princess, nor did I bring her along. This very woman is in fact a rākṣasī who feeds upon men living in Tamradvīpa."

Having heard Siṃhalasārthabāhu's response, the traders again spoke, "O Siṃhalasārthabāhu, O friend! How did you come to learn that in fact this woman is a rākṣasī? From whom did you hear this? Is it really true? You must tell us truthfully." Siṃhalasārthabāhu replied after this, "O friends, this woman is really a rākṣasī," and he started then to tell the story in detail. After hearing this tale, the traders were very frightened and they quickly returned to their own countries.

Then, Siṃhalasārthabāhu took his sword in hand and went alone toward the country Siṃhalakalpa in Jambudvīpa. After reaching his own house, touching the feet of his parents, and exchanging formalities, he wept. "O mother and father, all of the goods and properties you gave to me—they all are lost. Also, the 499 attendants sent with me, they fell into the hands of the Tamradvīpa rākṣasīs and died. I have come home safely due to your virtue and the influence of the glorious triratna. What to do?" After saying this, he respectfully related the tale in detail.

Both mother and father listened to this, sobbed, breathed deeply, and looked anxious. Looking at their son's face, they replied, "O son, O jewel of the family! It is our good fortune to have the opportunity to see you again. Beset by such trouble and such great misfortune, you have escaped. O son! Of what consideration is the lost property? Although the goods we gave are all gone, do not worry at all! In our house, there remains a great portion of wealth that we have earned. Having command over this property, take pleasure in making meritorious gifts [*puṇya dāna*]. O son, although some wealth was lost, there is the ability to make it back again. If a son like you is lost, what can be recovered thereafter? At the time when we are old, a son is like a walking stick; when the eyes cannot see, he is like a guide; at the time of death, he is the one to light the cremation fire; and he is the one to do the last rites [*piṇḍa dāna*] and who sends [us] to a heavenly abode. So, dear son, do not worry and feel happy."

Soon afterwards, the rākṣasī who was driven off in the Tamradvīpa forest arrived into the Siṃhakalpa city with a beautiful baby whose face and traits resembled Siṃhalasārthabāhu, though he was made with delusion power [*māyā*]. At that time, she went about asking in every neighborhood of the country, "O people! Where is the house of Siṃhalasārthabāhu?" The people then escorted her to his house and she reached there. While staying near the house door, having placed the illusory baby in her lap, she silently produced tears so as to elicit sympathy from the others and sat silently.

The people then asked who the beautiful woman was. "O beautiful sister, where are you from? Who are you? Who is the father of this baby? What sorrows have befallen you?" She responded, "O people, having wondered about whose son this might be, please look!" Hearing this, the people replied, "O beautiful woman, looking at this baby's appearance, it seems to have the resemblance of Siṃhalasārthabāhu, son of Siṃhalasārthabāha. It is his son, is it not? Or else is it another's son? Why are you staying here?"

The rākṣasī replied, "O people! I am the princess of Ratnapura, a kingdom of Tamradvīpa. Not long ago, Siṃhalasārthabāhu traded in Ratnapura, my father gave me to him in marriage. After we lived several months in my father's country, I was brought by him to his own country. Once we reached the river bank and began to cross the water, the boat sank and by our own strength we reached shore. After that, having said I was an evil one, he left me in the forest. What to do? For the sake of this very child, I have come to this place, inquiring all along the way, facing great troubles. O people, having put myself in your graces, speak to my husband and convince him to love me."

Having listened to her account, the people went to Siṃhalasārthabāhu and related what the woman said, "O Siṃhalasārthabāhu! Having married this woman who seems to be a heavenly nymph, a blameless woman of Tamradvīpa, why did you abandon her in the forest? Even if blameworthy, forgive her. Welcome this princess who has a son and please keep her inside your home." Siṃhalasārthabāhu replied, "O beloved friends and fellows! This very woman is not a Tamradvīpa princess. I never married her nor is this child mine. This one is in fact made from māyā. This very woman is a rākṣasī from Tamradvīpa." This he told to the people.

After they heard his answer, the people, unable to convince Siṃhalasārthabāhu, went to his father, Siṃhalasārthabāha, and said, "O Siṃhalasārthabāha! You are famous among the people as a virtuous one. Your son Siṃhalasārthabāhu, after marrying a Tamradvīpa princess and fathering a son, then accompanied both but later abandoned them in the forest. Together with the baby, this princess is knocking at your door. After hearing her request to convince him, we tried but failed persuade your son. You must convince your son to take this princess into your house." Hearing the people's words, Siṃhalasārthabāha realized their truth and called his son, saying, "O son Siṃhalasārthabāhu! Having married a princess of Tamradvīpa and fathering a son, why did you abandon them in the forest? Where will a blameless woman go? Therefore, forgive all her mistakes, admit them together into the house, and love her."

Having listened to his father's words, Siṃhalasārthabāhu touched his father's feet and said "O father! This woman is not one I took in marriage, nor is she a princess from Tamradvīpa, nor is this child mine. This woman is undoubtedly a rākṣasī and this child has been created by her māyā. This very rākṣasī, having completely eaten all of our attendants, has returned to eat me as well." Hearing this response, both the mother and father responded, "O son, all women are rākṣasīs. Therefore, after forgiving her faults, you must love her." Hearing their command, Siṃhalasārthabāhu replied angrily, "O mother and father! If you do not believe me, then you may love her. If you say that this woman will be kept in this house, I will go away from here. Go ahead then and accept her in this house!"

Noting the son's anger, the parents replied, "O son, having driven out a son, what is the use of a daughter-in-law? After you recover, there can be many brides." And so they came down from the house, held her by the neck, pushed her along from near the door, and cast her out.

Having been driven away by Siṃhalasārthabāhu's parents, she took her child and reached the gate of King Siṃhakeṣara's palace, while sobbing and making great lamentations. She placed the child on her lap and made her appearance fascinatingly beautiful for the people. At that moment, many people, including the ministers who were coming to see the king, saw this beautiful woman; feeling greatly surprised and deluded, they quickly went up to King Siṃhakeṣara and made a request, "O King Siṃhakeṣara, on this very day, a beautiful, youthful woman with child is staying at your door. Whether she is a heavenly maiden, a serpent deity beauty, or else a heavenly nymph, we don't know. Please consider her case."

At that time, therefore, the king listened to their account and responded, "O ministers, admit this beautiful one inside. I will consider her case." And so the ministers escorted the woman to the king's presence. Then King Siṃhakeṣara saw the beautiful one; overcome by lust, he remained silent for an instant.

Having looked at the beautiful one's face, the king responded in a soft and pleasant voice, "O beautiful one! Where do you come from? And whose son is this? Why have you come to stay at the palace door? What trouble has befallen you? You must explain everything in detail." Then with tears in her eyes, the beautiful rākṣasī made whimpering sounds in her throat which aroused compassion at merely seeing her. She then touched the king's feet and spoke in a voice inspiring compassion, "O King Siṃhakeṣara, what to do? My suffering is just as I say: I am an unfortunate princess of Tamradvīpa. At the time when Siṃhalasārthabāhu went to trade in Ratnapura, my father gave me in marriage to him. Therefore, having brought me along on the way to cross the river, our boat sunk and then we fell into the water. Saying, 'How unlucky is this woman I have brought, who has made us fall into the river,' he left me. Then I gave birth in the forest and together with this son I went to find Siṃhalasārthabāhu's house. There his father and mother both grabbed me by the neck and threw me out. O great king! I have come to you for refuge. You must make my husband love me."

Having heard the beautiful one's story, the king called for his chief policeman and said, "O chief of police, you go and bring Siṃhalasārthabāhu here." They did as they were commanded.

Seeing Siṃhalasārthabāhu before him, the king spoke, "O Siṃhalasārthabāhu! Having married this princess of Tamradvīpa, and after fathering this child, why did you abandon them in the forest? Do not treat women such as this unjustly. Although she may be faultworthy, forgive her as you must love and accept her." Siṃhalasārthabāhu replied, "O King Siṃhakeṣara! I did not take this woman in marriage. She is not a Tamradvīpa princess nor is this child my son. This one here is a rākṣasī and she has produced this child through māyā; having come from Tamradvīpa, she intends to eat me also." This is how he answered the king respectfully, giving this detailed account.

Caught by his desire, the king replied, "O Siṃhalasārthabāhu! All women are rākṣasīs. Having forgiven them, love them. If you do not really like her, then turn her over to me. Relegate her to me and I will keep her." Hearing this, Siṃhalasārthabāhu replied, "O king, this woman here is without doubt a rākṣasī. I cannot turn her over to you. Having considered this statement go ahead and do [what you wish]." The king, having heard Siṃhalasārthabāhu's warning, but feeling desire for the beautiful pubescent one, carried her to his private quarters.

After going home, Siṃhalasārthabāhu dwelt happily and enjoyed himself. King Siṃhakeṣara, having enjoyed sensual pleasures with the beautiful one, felt the delusion of happiness. The rākṣasī satisfied the wishes and desires of the king; having covered him with a net of delusion, she ensnared him more deeply with each passing day.

But one night, after completely satisfying the king's desire for pleasure, the rākṣasī made the king, all his family, and the people living in the private quarters fall into a deep sleep. In the night she flew up into the sky, returned to Tamradvīpa, went to the place where her rākṣasī friends were and said, "O younger sisters! After eating just Siṃhalasārthabāhu, is that enough? In Siṃhakalpa town, I have made King Siṃhakesara and all of the people in the royal family fall into a deep sleep. Let us go and devour the king and all the others." And after all the rākṣasī friends flew and reached the king's palace, they devoured all the people there, including King Siṃhakeṣara. After finishing, all the rākṣasīs returned.

Once dawn broke, many vultures, kites, and crows, and so on, were circling in the sky around and above the royal palace. At this time, the chief policeman and ministers came to pay homage to the king and [other] royal officials. They then noticed that the palace doors were closed. Seeing the flocks circling above, they asked, "What has happened in the royal palace?" They cried out with all the people. After Siṃhalasārthabāhu heard the news, he came out of his house holding the sword in his hands, and went to the place where all the ministers were assembled at the palace. There he said, "O ministers, here in the palace, the king and all of the rest of the people have been completely eaten. Go quickly and bring a ladder. We will go and look. Hurry up!" After having heard this speech, the ministers and policemen raised a commotion; crying and sobbing, they brought the ladder, and leaned it against the palace wall.

Then Siṃhalasārthabāhu, with sword in hand, climbed the ladder, went up to the balcony, and cursed the rākṣasīs, driving [the remaining] rākṣasīs away. Once they saw the glint of Siṃhalasārthabāhu's sword, the rākṣasīs felt terrified and flew up and away to Tamradvīpa. Siṃhalasārthabāhu and all the others then went inside the palace and unlocked the doors. There they saw slaughtered the king, queen, and all the people living in the palace. The ministers and police were upset and made lamentations. They mourned and cleaned up the palace and ritually purified it.

After some days, the ministers called upon all the country's paṇḍits, astrologers, and the senior men and women to assemble. On that occasion they held a discussion, and the chief minister said, "O subjects! Our king and queens were eaten by rākṣasīs and killed. And so there is no natural successor. How to proceed? Without a king, the people will not be sustained." He asked, "Who will succeed our king?" And the people replied, "O minister! What to do? Having sought a [natural] successor for this king, we feel that there is no one to offer the kingship to except Siṃhalasārthabāhu. There is no one else. For what reasons? He has the knowledge of different hand weapons, projectile weapons, different scripts; he is generous, compassionate, and devoted to the four gods. If we make him king, he would be the sort of king who would always serve the triratna and [show] great virtue. And he would make all of the people happy."

All having agreed, they went to Siṃhalasārthabāhu's house. Having knelt with left knee on the ground, with joined hands they said, "O Siṃhalasārthabāhu! We have no king right now. As there is no natural successor to this king, so we must choose another. A country without a king will not remain a country. Please become king and sustain the people. You must come and look after the kingdom."

Siṃhalasārthabāhu replied, "O ministers! I am of the trading caste. I am one who has lived by commerce. If I took up the responsibility of the kingdom, I could not do it. For me to be king is not suitable. Think again and look for another one suitable to be the king."

The ministers replied respectfully, "O Siṃhalasārthabāhu! Except for you we do not have another fit to be made king. In all our opinions, we see the necessary traits in you. Please mount the [royal] lion's throne!" Then he went to the throne and received the royal initiation; during the royal coronation, he became known as Siṃhalarājā.

Thereafter in Siṃhakalpa town, the [new] king looked after his subjects like sons and caused them to serve the Buddha, dharma, and saṅgha and to observe the śrī aṣṭamī vrata so that most enjoyed happiness and peace.

One day, the king called upon his minister and said, "O minister, organize a strong army four divisions. We will go to defeat the rākṣasīs of Tamradvīpa and rule Ratnapura." After successfully assembling the fourfold army, he informed the king. Then Siṃhalarājā called together the strong four-division army—elephant chariots, horse chariots, horsemen, and infantry—and assembled the hand weapons, projectile weapons, bows, arrows, maces, lassos, hammers, axes, nooses, elephant discuses, mantra weapons, and fire weapons, and so forth. He also raised many umbrellas, flags, and banners, and after having the martial musical instruments played, bid auspicious farewell. In this way, Siṃhalarājā departed to do battle facing Tamradvīpa.

He passed through many countries, villages, mountains, and rivers, then crossed the Brahmaputra and had his army camp near Tamradvīpa. As they reached there, all the flags that the rākṣasīs of Ratnapura had raised fluttered ominously. Seeing this happen, all felt amazed and terrified. The senior rākṣasī then spoke, "O younger sisters! From ancient times, the flags have never fluttered like this. This fluttering we have not heard or seen before. On this day, an evil omen has occurred. What was that? Siṃhalarājā, King of Siṃhakalpa town, might have come to destroy us. Make ready the hand and projectile weapons!" The leader called upon all the rākṣasīs, "Let us go, let us go! We all must go and fight! Come let us defeat them!" Having armed themselves with weapons, they assumed their dreadful forms, projected out their fangs, displayed their red eyes, and raised up their hair. They made noises indicating extreme agitation and yelled loudly in such a way that the frost there turned to hail.

After they made noises like those made by a dark cloud, Siṃhalarājā noticed them, united his four-division army, and sent them into battle.

Then, having gone forth as their king commanded, all in the four-division army fought fiercely against the rākṣasīs. Once the rākṣasīs saw this army ready for battle, they became enraged and descended onto the battlefield; some showed their fighting skill with fire arrows, mantra weapons, and arrows; others, suspended in the air, wielded discuses, tridents, maces, swords, and so on. They all did battle, crying out. Seeing the rākṣasīs using various weapons, the soldiers of Siṃhalarājā yelled out in many ways, made their weapons empowered with mantras, and fought on. Some got into the elephant chariots and some [stood] on the ground. All showed their own skills in battle as they fought.

If one asks what happened on that afternoon, it became dark just as on the night of a dark fortnight when a cloud covers the earth and when lightening roars and the rain falls. Only the flashing of many weapons was visible and arrows fell like a rain deluge. Shouting was heard amidst the darkness. At last, due to the influence of the aṣṭamī vrata, the power of the king's boldness, and the four-division army's bravery, Siṃhalarājā finally turned back the rākṣasīs.

Though the rākṣasīs revealed their own skills in fighting, they finally could not fight on. Several rākṣasīs ran away; staying at a distance and feeling afraid, they only looked on. Several others threw down their weapons, joined their hands, and bowed at the feet of Siṃhalarājā. Feeling afraid, they spoke in a manner betraying their terror, "O master Siṃhalarājā, after we saw that you had come to wage war, we also came to fight. But due to your bravery, we have lost our ability to wage war and so have come to your feet for refuge. You must pardon the crimes by those who are helpless. This is because we are not equal to one with your fighting skill. To kill women like this is not ethical. It is a great sin, O Mahārājā!" they said respectfully, touching their heads to his feet and joining their hands. They praised him saying, "Thinking we are not your worthy rivals, to us you have become a great compassionate one, a virtuous one, one who has the highest knowledge of merit, who is also a great benefactor and learned, devoted to the gods . . . you who have become popular among the people as 'The One Who is an Endless Store of Favors.' And O master, these unkillable women cannot be virtuous or avoid committing crimes. Having forgiven all our mistakes, after manifesting compassion and grace, you must protect us!" Weeping in many ways, they beseeched him.

After hearing the rākṣasīs' humble requests, [the king] felt great compassion and replied "O rākṣasīs! After seeing all of your crimes, you deserve to be killed immediately. But what to do? If, having understood what I say, you obey me then I will heed your plea." The rākṣasīs joined their hands, touched his feet, arranged their shawls respectfully, and said with respect, "O gracious mahārājā, leader of Siṃhalakalpa! We certainly shall do as you say. Wherever you say 'stay there' we certainly will stay there. Please protect us."

Siṃhalarājā then replied to their plea, "O rākṣasīs, up until now you have lived in Tamradvīpa in Ratnapura. I have just completely conquered this kingdom. And in this land I have conquered, you should not live. You must never come here, so go and live in a dense forest in a far-off land. If you ever return to this town, I will certainly kill you all." Having given this ultimatum and bid them farewell, he left. According to Siṃhalarājā's command, each rākṣasī took an oath never to come there again and to leave for a distant forest. Then they ran off.

Then, O Śākyamuni Tathāgata, the rākṣasīs from this very city called Ratnapura did go to a different land. King Siṃhalarājā, after making victory banners and calling many people of different countries, gave shelter to the people in Ratnapura. Promoting the religious life among them, he caused the people to serve the Buddha, the dharma, and the saṅgha and conveyed the highest importance of the aṣṭamī vrata of Amoghapāśa Lokeśvara, and sponsored its performance. He also set up the professions, law and order, and trade and then showed them the jewel, silver, and gold mines. He also established a statue of himself. Having shown the path of happiness to the people, he addressed them, "O people! Formerly this place was called Tamradvīpa, but now I have conquered it and so it will be called Siṃhaladvīpa in the future. And this name will become famous. You who live in this country called Siṃhaladvīpa must remember the triratna and observe the aṣṭamī vrata and so live in peace and happiness. I am returning to the kingdom of Siṃhakalpa in Jambudvīpa; I will show the dharma to the people and live happily there." Having given this assurance to the people of the Siṃhaladvīpa kingdom, Siṃhalarājā departed for Jambudvīpa.

At that time, having reached the shore of the Brahmaputra River, in order to have the army cross, he made a boat and called it "Syāmkarṇa," placed an image of the king of horses on it and so made Syāmkarṇa famous. After crossing over with his four-division army, he returned to Siṃhakalpa and taught the dharma to people living in various places and countries.

Once he reached there, he called together the ministers, officials, and others, saying, "O people! From the grace of the Śrī Śrī Śrī Triratna and the influence of the aṣṭamī vrata, I conquered the rākṣasīs of Tamradvīpa and made the name of Siṃhaladvīpa famous. From today on, all of the people will recall the Śrī Śrī Śrī Triratna and observe the bright fortnight aṣṭamī vrata of Lokeśvara." Following the king's command, the ministers and others all remembered the triratna and prepared the holy aṣṭamī vrata; making their minds compassionate, they lived happily. From the merit of remembering the triratna and the influence of the aṣṭamī vrata, in Siṃhakalpa town there was always and everywhere abundant food, virtuous conduct, and timely rainfall; and diseases, dangers, unhappiness, troubles, thieves, thugs, and evil ones were all eliminated; and only virtuous, artistic, learned, and auspicious people lived there. The king, ministers, officials, and all the people cultivated virtuous minds, served the triratna, and found [both] pleasure and happiness.

—12—

A Prayer for the Long Life of the Dalai Lama

Donald S. Lopez, Jr.

The Buddha is said to have remarked to his attendant and cousin, Ānanda, that a buddha has the power to prolong his life almost indefinitely. Ānanda, however, did not take the hint and beseech the Buddha to live for an eon. Some time later the same day, the Buddha announced to Ānanda that he would die three months hence. Ānanda immediately reminded the Buddha of his earlier remark and implored him not to pass into nirvāṇa but rather remain in the world for the welfare of all beings. The Buddha explained that he would have prolonged his life if Ānanda had only asked him earlier, but that now it was too late, the time for making such a request had passed. His impending death, says the Buddha, is the fault of Ānanda, and he goes on to remind him of all the times in the past that he had suggested to Ānanda that he could live for an eon, and that each time Ānanda had failed to ask him to do so (see *Dīgha Nikāya* II.115–20). The death of the Buddha was sorely felt by the community and, in a certain sense, Buddhists have been seeking means of coping with the absence of the Buddha ever since.

With the rise of the Mahāyāna and the belief that multiple buddhas are accessible through various devotional and meditational practices, a simple three-part liturgy, called the *triskandhaka,* was developed. The first part was the confession of past misdeeds to the buddhas and bodhisattvas. The second part was the admiration of their meritorious deeds. The third part seems to have been designed to insure that Ānanda's mistake not be repeated: it is a prayer that the buddhas remain in the world and not pass into nirvāṇa. This tripartite ritual was eventually expanded to include seven elements: obeisance, offering, confession, admiration, entreaty not to pass into nirvāṇa, supplication of the buddhas and bodhisattvas to teach the dharma, and dedication of the merit of performing the preceding toward the enlightenment of all beings. This sevenfold practice, presented most famously in the opening twelve stanzas of "Prayer of Samantabhadra" (*Bhadracaryāpraṇidhāna*) of the *Avatamsaka Sūtra,* became a standard part of almost any Mahāyāna practice, often serving as a prolegomenon to a meditation session.

In Tibet this entreaty to the buddhas to remain in the world developed from a standard component of daily prayers to a separate genre of literature, called *zhabs brtan*. The term literally means "steadfast feet," suggesting that the buddhas remain with their feet firmly planted in this world. From Indian tantric Buddhism, the Tibetans received the notion that during this degenerate age, after the passing away of Śākyamuni, it is the spiritual teacher, the guru, who will serve as the Buddha's substitute. Prayers for "steadfast feet" or long-life prayers are hence composed for one's teacher.

The work translated below is the best known of all Tibetan long-life prayers. It is a modern work, composed for the present Dalai Lama, Tenzin Gyatso (1935–). The prayer was composed by his two tutors. Since the seventeenth century, the Dalai Lamas have been regarded as the physical incarnations of the bodhisattva of compassion, Avalokiteśvara, who has assumed the special task of protecting and sustaining the Tibetan people. Tibetans believe that Avalokiteśvara has taken human form throughout Tibetan history, as kings prior to the introduction of Buddhism, and later as great Buddhist teachers.

Tibetan Buddhism (which extends far beyond Tibet into Nepal, Mongolia, and parts of China and Russia) appears to be unique among Buddhist traditions for its belief in the repeated incarnation of Buddhist teachers. Like all Buddhists, the Tibetans believe in rebirth, the powerless wandering in saṃsāra, due to the power of desire, hatred, and ignorance. And like Mahāyāna Buddhists, the Tibetans believe that buddhas can appear in whatever form they choose to best benefit sentient beings. What is unique about Tibetan Buddhism, however, is the belief (dating perhaps from the twelfth century) that a particular teacher, regarded by his followers as a buddha, can be identified after his death in the form of a newborn child. The term that Tibetans use to describe such being is tulku (*sprul sku*), which literally means "emanation body," the body of a buddha that appears in the world. These emanation bodies or incarnate lamas are believed to take human form again by their own compassionate wish, and not because they are subject to the laws of karma and rebirth.

By the time of the Chinese invasion of Tibet in 1950, there were some three thousand "lines" of incarnate lamas in Tibet, the most famous of whom was the Dalai Lama. The Dalai Lama line began in the fifteenth century, when the next incarnation of a scholar of the Geluk (dGe lugs) sect was discovered. It was the third incarnation of this scholar who was given the name "Dalai Lama" ("Ocean Teacher") by the Mongol chieftain Altan Khan in 1578. His two previous incarnations were then retrospectively regarded as the first and second Dalai Lamas. The current Dalai Lama is the fourteenth in the line.

The prayer translated below is written in the highly ornate style typical of the genre. It is filled with allusions to a wide variety of deities and doctrines, only several of which can be elucidated here. The first six stanzas follow a similar pattern, with elaborate description of a class of exalted beings, ending with an identical plea that the Dalai Lama, "the protector of the Snowy Land, Tenzin Gyatso, [will] remain steadfast for hundreds of eons without destruction." The first stanza is dedicated to the lamas or teachers, both one's own teachers and the lineage of teachers. Next, the tutelary deities (*yi dam*) are beseeched. These are the buddhas in their tantric forms, some beneficent, some horrific, who are the focus of tantric practice, both as objects of devotion and as the deities with whom one identifies in visualization. The next three stanzas are directed to the three jewels. Next the heroes and ḍākinīs ("literally "sky goers") are beseeched. These are special deities who aid tantric yogins in their practice. Finally, an appeal is made to the protectors of the dharma, wrathful deities who defend Buddhism and its adherents. After two long summarizing stanzas, the prayer concludes with four stanzas of more general prayers, asking that all the wishes of sentient beings be granted, that they be liberated from suffering, and that they forever receive the blessings of Avalokiteśvara, of whom the Dalai Lama is the human embodiment. Here, Avalokiteśvara is referred to as Padmapāṇi, "He Who Holds a Lotus."

This long-life prayer is known by heart by almost all of the 120,000 Tibetans living in exile, as well as by many thousands more who remain in Tibet. It is recited (sometimes by an audience of tens of thousands) on all occasions when the Dalai Lama gives a public teaching or presides at a ceremony, as well as at other ceremonies and festivals.

The translation is from *Bla ma'i rnal 'byor dang yi dam khag gi bdag bskyed sogs zhal 'don gces btus* (Dharmsala, India: Tibetan Cultural Printing Press, 1977), pp. 133–38.

Further Reading

For a translation of the "Prayer of Samantabhadra," see William Theodore deBary, *The Buddhist Tradition in India, China, and Japan* (New York: Modern Library, 1969), pp. 172–78. For a study of Tibetan genre of *zhabs brtan,* see José Cabezón, "Firm Feet and Long Lives: the Zhabs brtan Literature of Tibetan Buddhism" in José Cabezón and Roger Jackson, ed., *Tibetan Literature* (Ithaca, N.Y.: Snow Lion Publications, 1995).

The Melody of Immortality Attained

A Prayer Beseeching the Compassion of the Ocean of the Three Supreme Ones in Order that the Crown Jewel of Saṃsāra and Nirvāṇa, the Supreme Refuge and Protector, the Lord of Conquerors, the Supreme All-Knowing and Seeing One, May Have Steadfast Feet as the Protector of the Teaching and of Transmigrators, that the Great Waves of His Wishes be Spontaneously Achieved

Oṃ svastī
When we pray with strong yearning

To the assembly of kind lamas, direct and lineaged,
The three secrets of the billions of conquerors without exception
The magical drama which appears in whatever way will tame [sentient beings],
The wish granting jewels, source of all goodness and saṃsāra and nirvāṇa,
Bless the life of the protector of the Snowy Land, Tenzin Gyatso,
To remain steadfast for hundreds of eons without destruction,
That his wishes be spontaneously achieved.

When we pray with strong yearning
To all the assembled tutelary gods,
The stainless magical cloud of the wisdom of great bliss
United with the expanse of the perfectly clear dharmadhatu,
Appearing in countless resident and residence maṇḍalas,
Bless the life of the protector of the Snowy Land, Tenzin Gyatso,
To remain steadfast for hundreds of eons without destruction,
That his wishes be spontaneously achieved.

When we pray with strong yearning
To all the billions of conquerors of the three times
The gods of gods endowed with the ten powers,
Their qualities of abandonment and realization are complete,
Reflections of their deeds play constantly in oceans of transmigratory realms, bringing benefit,
Bless the life of the protector of the Snowy Land, Tenzin Gyatso,
To remain steadfast for hundreds of eons without destruction,
That his wishes be spontaneously achieved.

When we pray with strong yearning
To the collection of the excellent dharma of the three vehicles
Which brings certain liberation from the three realms,
The treasury of jewels of enlightenment, the supreme peace,
The glory of virtues, uncontaminated, immovable, auspicious
Bless the life of the protector of the Snowy Land, Tenzin Gyatso,
To remain steadfast for hundreds of eons without destruction,
That his wishes be spontaneously achieved.

When we pray with strong yearning
To the entire saṅgha of superior beings, knowing and liberated,
Inseparable from the vajra city of liberation,
Endowed with the wisdom that comprehends the truth directly,
Who most heroically destroy the engines of saṃsāra,
Bless the life of the protector of the Snowy Land, Tenzin Gyatso,
To remain steadfast for hundreds of eons without destruction,
That his wishes be spontaneously achieved.

When we pray with strong yearning
To the assembly of heroes and ḍākinīs of the three abodes,
Who assist those who practice the auspicious path of yoga,
Through delightful play in myriad poses of bliss and emptiness,
In the ḍākinī lands and the charnel grounds,
Bless the life of the protector of the Snowy Land, Tenzin Gyatso,
To remain steadfast for hundreds of eons without destruction,
That his wishes be spontaneously achieved.

When we pray with strong yearning
To the ocean of protectors of the teaching, endowed with the eye of wisdom,
Who place the knotted seal of the order of Vajradhara
Inseparably upon the matted hair of their heads,
Who have the skill to guard the teaching and those who uphold the teaching,
Bless the life of the protector of the Snowy Land, Tenzin Gyatso,
To remain steadfast for hundreds of eons without destruction,
That his wishes be spontaneously achieved.

Thus, by the power of praying respectfully from the depths of the heart with great strength,
To the supreme infallible sources of refuge,
May the supreme Ngawang Losang Tensin Gyatso,
The sole protector of the transmigrators of the Snowy Range—
We who are afflicted with the unceasing pain of the degenerate age—
Remain ever steadyfast, immovable for oceans of eons
On the vajra-essence throne utterly free from destruction,
His three secrets [of body, speech, and mind] not disintegrating, not changing, not disappearing.

May the burden of the great waves of deeds of all the billions of conquerors,
That he bears on his courageous shoulder,
The all-benefiting deeds with an essence of jewels,
Be spontaneously achieved according to [his] wish.

By the power of that, may the door to the sky of the auspicious age of fulfillment,
Be ever opened to the springtime that relieves the weariness of the embodied,
And may the auspicious sign that the teaching of the Subduer has spread in all directions
Reach the peak of saṃsāra and nirvāṇa.

May the stream of ambrosia of the blessings of Padmapāṇi
[Avalokiteśvara]
Ever fructify as our strength of heart
And having served him through offering the fulfillment of his word,
May we cross the ocean of Samantabhadra's supreme deeds.

Through the waves of blessing of the conquerors and their excellent
children
And the infallible truth of dependent arising
And by the power of my pure intention,
May all the aims of my prayers be easily and quickly achieved.

—13—

Chinese Women Pilgrims' Songs Glorifying Guanyin

Chün-fang Yü

Although Guanyin (Avalokiteśvara) is a great bodhisattva mentioned in many Buddhist sūtras, the Chinese people know her primarily through her human manifestation, Princess Miaoshan ("Wondrous Goodness"). The legend of Miaoshan and its relationship with the pilgrimage center Fragrant Mountain (Xiangshan) in Henan Province has received considerable scholarly attention. The earliest written version of the myth is dated to 1100 C.E., and a few years later, in 1104, a stele recording the same legend was erected at the Upper Tianzhu Monastery in Hangzhou, another important pilgrimage center of Guanyin worship. A popular religious text, *The Precious Scroll of Fragrant Mountain (Xiangshan baojuan)* provides a detailed account of the princess's religious struggles and her eventual transfiguration into Guanyin. Ordinary men and women in China came to know the story by reading and listening to the chanting of this text. Later, during the Ming and Qing dynasties, between the fifteenth and nineteenth centuries, plays were written and performed, making the story even more well known.

We do not know when the *Precious Scroll of Fragrant Mountain* was first written. The earliest extant version was dated 1773. According to the preface, a monk of the Upper Tianzhu Monastery was visited by another monk on September 17, 1103, and was instructed to write down the story of Guanyin for the sake of universal salvation. He wrote the text based on what the mysterious visitor told him and then had a vision of Guanyin herself carrying the pure vase and green willow. Sometime later, a female great being (*nütashi*) gave the text to a certain monk who was staying in retreat on Mount Lu and told him to disseminate it among people who were spiritually too immature to practice Chan. The popular text of *Precious Scroll* provides many details about the life of Miaoshan / Guanyin not found in earlier versions of the story. The preface clearly places the time of composition at the beginning of the twelfth century, when the myth first took shape. The following is a summary of the story:

Princess Miaoshan was the third daughter of King Miaozhuang, who ruled a mythical kingdom at an unspecified time. She was born on the nineteenth day of the second month (this is the source for the celebration of the "birthday" of Guanyin observed by lay devotees and on the monastic calendar). She kept a vegetarian diet from childhood and, unlike her two elder sisters who accepted the husbands chosen by their father, refused to get married when she became a teenager. This rebellion so angered the father that he first imprisoned her in the imperial garden and then sent her to do hard labor under the bidding of nuns at the White Sparrow Monastery. When she refused to relent, the father had the monastery burned down, killing the five hundred nuns. Miaoshan survived, but the king sentenced her to die by strangulation. The order was carried out, her corpse was carried by a mountain deity to the Forest of Corpses. While her body lay lifeless there, Bodhisattva Dizang (Sanskrit Kṣitigarbha) conducted her spirit on a tour of the hells, where she preached a sermon to the hellish beings and enabled them to achieve rebirth in the Western Paradise. Fearing that the hells would soon be emptied of their denizens, Lord Yama asked her to go back to the world of the living. She then went to Xiangshan and practiced religion for nine years. By then, caught up by his evil karma, the king contracted a terrible disease that no doctor could cure. Miaoshan took the disguise of a monk and came to visit her father. She predicted that only the medicine made of the eyes and hands of one who was without hatred could cure him, and then directed the king's servants to look for the "Great Immortal" at Xiangshan. When they arrived, she cut off her arms and gouged out her eyes for them to take back to the father. The king indeed became well after taking the medicine and decided to offer thanks to his savior. When the royal party arrived, first the queen and then the king recognized the eyeless and armless sage to be no other than their own daughter. The king was so moved that he immediately repented his earlier sins and became converted to Buddhism. He made a loud wish that Miaoshan should be restored to the condition of "fully eyed and fully armed," whereupon she announced that she was actually the bodhisattva Guanyin.

Pilgrimages to cultic centers of Guanyin worship have constituted an important religious phenomenon since the medieval period. Hangzhou, with its several hundred Buddhist monasteries, attracted large numbers of pilgrims every spring. To accommodate the large influx of pilgrims, merchants also flocked to the city to trade. Descriptions of the "Pilgrims' Fair" appeared frequently in travel accounts and local gazetteers of Hangzhou from the seventeenth century on. In the spring of 1987 I went to Hangzhou to interview pilgrims, and studied the rituals of pilgrimage to Upper Tianzhu Monastery as a participant-observer. The catchment area for Hangzhou pilgrims covered southern Jiangsu and northern Zhejiang. Jiangsu pilgrims came by chartered boats, spending two nights on the boat, one coming and one returning, and two nights at an inn in Hangzhou that catered exclusively to them. Zhejiang pilgrims, on the other hand, came by chartered buses and spent about three days and two nights in Hangzhou. The pilgrimage business had become so good in recent years that inns had cooperated with steamship and bus companies to serve the needs of transportation and housing of Hangzhou pilgrims. These people identified themselves as working for "religious tourism enterprises."

Pilgrims came to Hangzhou in groups consisting mainly of middle-aged and elder women. They were farmers and silkworm raisers. Because the retirement age for them was fifty for women and sixty for men, the overwhelming majority of the pilgrims were over fifty. The cost of the trip was generally borne by themselves and contributions made by their children. But some communes actually encouraged their retired farmers to go on pilgrimage, and reimbursed their tour expenses upon their return.

Pilgrims came to Hangzhou in groups that were led by group leaders who took care of practical matters. Some groups also had a spiritual leader called "Buddhist leader" (*fotou*) who knew how to chant scriptures, sing pilgrimage songs and go into trance, become a living bodhisattva who could speak for Guanyin, and practice healing among fellow pilgrims. The women pilgrims wore pieces of red cloth with their group names written in ink on their left arms. They also wore distinctive head coverings that provided them with their regional identities. Those from Suzhou and Kunshan in Jiangsu Province, for instance, covered their heads with colorful towels. Those from elsewhere wore square kerchiefs of either green or deep blue. Colored yarns binding their hair had symbolic meanings: red indicating that the husband was alive, white that he had died recently, black that he had died two years previously, and blue that he had died three years previously. It was desirable for a pilgrim to come to Hangzhou for either three years or five years in a row: the first year for the benefit of her father, the second year for her mother, the third year for her husband, the fourth year for herself, and the fifth year for her children. Pilgrims kept a vegetarian diet, starting with the evening meal before they left home and lasting until their return. If they came with their husbands, they slept in separate quarters. Even their married children back home should observe the taboo against eating meat and having sex, for otherwise some untoward accident would happen to their traveling parents or mothers. They could resume their normal way of life only upon the safe return of the pilgrims.

When asked why they came to Hangzhou, the usual answer was that this was the custom. They felt "at peace" only after they had offered incense at Upper Tianzhu, knowing that the crop would have a good harvest, the silkworms would be safe, domestic animals and members of the household would be healthy and prosperous. The majority of informants did not mention making or fulfilling vows. In fact, coming to Hangzhou was as much for fun as for religious reasons. They used the term "enjoying the spring outing with the excuse of worshiping the Buddha" (*jiefo yuzun*) to describe their trip. But the sightseeing and shopping were reserved for the second day. The first thing they did after they disembarked from the boat or the bus was to head straight for Upper Tianzhu. The Pilgrims' Way leading to the temple from Lingyin Monastery, the starting point, is about three Chinese miles, and it must be covered on foot. Once inside the Upper Tianzhu, they busied themselves with lighting candles and incense, burning spirit money, having their yellow incense bags and incense belts stamped with the seals of the monastery, and having their own names and those of their loved ones entered in the temple's subscription book. They usually spent half an hour to an hour doing these things, depending on the size of the group.

Even though the temple ground was filled with visitors, pilgrims always stayed with their own group and never mingled with other groups. The sense of communitas stressed so much by Victor Turner was found among members of the same group, but strikingly absent between different groups, which usually had nothing to do with each other. In large groups composed of people from different villages, new friendships were often formed after spending four days together. The sense of camaraderie and fellowship was especially strong at night in the inn. After they returned to the inn around four in the afternoon, they relaxed in the evening by visiting each other, sharing gossip and laughter, exchanging stories about Guanyin, and singing pilgrims' songs together.

The stories they told about Guanyin all came from the *Precious Scroll of Fragrant Mountain*, but with some strong local coloring. It is characteristic of all the pilgrims' songs which are called "Guanyin sūtra" (*Guanyin jing*) that the singer shifts identity between that of a worshiper and that of Guanyin herself. This is perhaps because the songs were originally created by the "living bodhisattvas" who became Guanyin in their trances. The songs told the story of Miaoshan / Guanyin, praised her for her religious dedication, and envied her independence and freedom resulting from her refusing to be married. In the following, I translate two pilgrims' songs.

Further Reading

See Chün-fang Yü, "P'u-t'o Shan: Pilgrimage and the Creation of the Chinese Potalaka," in *Pilgrims and Sacred Sites in China*, edited by Susan Naquin and Chün-fang Yü (Berkeley and Los Angeles: University of California Press, 1992), 190–245. On the legend of Miaoshan, see Glen Dudbridge, *The Legend of Miao-shan*, Oxford Oriental Monographs, no. 1 (London: Ithaca Press, 1978); and idem, "Miao-shan on Stone," *Harvard Journal of Asiatic Studies* 42:2 (December 1982), 589–614.

Seven-fold Guanyin Sūtra (*Qipin Guanyin jing*)

Sung by a forty-five-year-old "living bodhisattva" from Tongxiang, Jiangsu Province

Bodhisattva Guanyin has entered my body.
On the nineteenth day of the second month, Mother gave birth to me.
On the nineteenth day of the sixth month I went up to heaven.

Having arrived in heaven, I turned around.
And sat in the main hall wearing a crown of pearls on my head.
Beating on the wooden fish I go everywhere.
Without a home and without any worries I worship the Third Sister.
The Third Sister does not want food to eat.
The Third Sister does not want clothes to wear.
The Third Sister wants to go to the Ninth Cloud beyond the empyrean to become a living immortal.
First I want to cultivate an affinity with a thousand people.
Second I want to cultivate an affinity with ten thousand people.
Immortals are originally made of ordinary mortals.
Yet ultimately ordinary mortals' hearts are not firm.
Green grasses by the roadside serve as the Buddha hall.
An immortal's boat lands by the sea shore.
Breadfruit trees grow on all four sides.
Three thousand buddhas fell into the lotus pond.
The four guardians come in two pairs.
Someone taught me the Guanyin Sūtra.
Every morning I rinse my mouth and chant seven times.
Having chanted seven times, I see Guanyin.
Adoration of the Buddha, Amitābha.

Guanyin Sūtra (*Guanyin jing*)

Sung by a 59-year-old woman pilgrim from Jiangyin, Jiangsu

Wearing a crown of pearls and striking
A hand-held wooden fish, I go everywhere to proselytize.
I ask buddhas of the ten directions:
Which road leads to spiritual cultivation?
In the west, there is no other than King Miaozhuang.
There is a truly chaste woman in the household of King Miaozhuang.
First, she does not have to bear the ill humor of her parents-in-law.
Second, she does not have to eat the food of her husband.
Third, she does not have to carry a child in her womb or on her arms.
Fourth, she does not need a maid to serve her.
Every day she enjoys peace and quiet in her fragrant room.
Turning over the cotton coverlet, she sleeps on the bed alone.
Stretching out her legs, she went into the Buddha hall.
Pulling in her feet, she withdrew into the back garden.
For the sake of cultivation, she suffered punishment by her parents.
But now, sitting on the lotus throne, she enjoys blessings.
Over and over again, I chant the Guanyin Sūtra
On the first and fifteenth, I receive the offering of incense.
Adoration to the Buddha, Amitābha.

Dharma

—14—

A Mahāyāna Liturgy

Luis O. Gómez

Buddhism is not lacking in rites of passage, calendric rituals, and festivals, but some Buddhist rituals are meant to be performed at the discretion of individuals and more than once, even on a daily basis. The following selection is a sampling from a classical Mahāyāna liturgy meant to be performed once as a rite of passage (the adoption of the vows of the bodhisattva) and repeatedly as a rite of confirmation or affirmation (as a way of cultivating the mind-set of a bodhisattva and as the starting point for other practices).

The selection is from the first four chapters in Śāntideva's *Bodhicaryāvatāra* (about seventh century C.E.). This text, in over seven hundred stanzas divided into ten chapters, is meant as an "introduction" (*avatāra*) to the bodhisattva path. It outlines the main practices of Mahāyāna conceived as stemming from an initial grasping of "the thought of awakening" (*bodhicitta*), growing in the practice of "the precepts" (*saṃvara* or *śikṣā*), and culminating in the perfect practice of compassion and wisdom. Briefly stated, "the thought of awakening" is threefold: the first instant of thought in which a person conceives of the possibility or desirability of seeking buddhahood for the sake of all living beings; the subsequent will to seek buddhahood; and the attitudes and mind-set that accompany the quest for buddhahood. Often "the thought of awakening" is considered to be somehow identical with enlightenment (awakening) itself. For Śāntideva, the first moments of the thought of awakening have to be protected and nurtured until they grow into full-blown awakening. The prescribed forms of behavior that protect and nurture the thought of awakening are "the precepts," a notion that encompasses ritual, demeanor, mental attitudes, monastic rules, and moral principles. The precepts form the basis for the practice of the perfections: perfect generosity, perfect morality, perfect patience, perfect energy, perfect meditation, and perfect discernment. The passages selected emphasize the importance of devotion, worship, and ritual in first consolidating the thought of awakening and laying the foundation for the practice of the precepts.

Perhaps the most important connection between the ritual and the ideal conduct of the bodhisattva is the vow (*praṇidhāna*): a solemn promise to pursue the goal of perfect awakening (that is, full buddhahood), in order to relieve the suffering of all living beings. In a certain manner of speaking, the ritual may be seen as a frame for this solemn vow. But it is also possible to see the liturgy as a variant on the "dedication of merit," perhaps the most common and most important form of Mahāyāna ritual. In this interpretation (which could be justified by quoting several passages from the following selection), the ritual is a means toward acquiring merit and then relinquishing it, dedicating it to one's own awakening and to the awakening of all living beings. Conceived in this manner, the ritual is a skillful means toward increasing merit and detachment.

The basic structure of the ritual described in this text is used in many other texts and is sometimes called "the sevenfold incomparable worship" (*saptavidhā anuttarā pūjā*), although the liturgy often has more or less than seven parts, and although there is some disagreement as to what the seven parts should be. The structure of the liturgy has some scriptural basis in Mahāyāna texts like the Bhadracarī-praṇidhāna (in the *Gaṇḍavyūha Sūtra*) and the Triskandhaka (in the *Upālipariprcchā* and other Mahāyāna sūtras). This structure is also represented in many tantric rituals (see Chapter 27).

The *Bodhicaryāvatāra* was very popular, at least in monastic circles, during the later Mahāyāna period in India (about eighth to thirteenth centuries C.E.). It also had a lasting influence in Tibet, where Śāntideva's ritual formulas have been incorporated into actual liturgies. The *Bodhicaryāvatāra* is often quoted by the Dalai Lama as an important authority on the cultivation of compassion. It has been translated a number of times into modern languages, including thrice into English and twice into German and French.

The passages from the *Bodhicaryāvatāra* included in the following selection are complemented here with selected portions of a late commentary by Prajñākaramati (about eleventh century C.E.). These extracts serve to illustrate the concerns and tenor of scholastic interpretations of the ritual and the style and tone of classical Indian commentaries. They are translated from the edition of La Vallée Poussin, Bibliotheca India (Calcutta: Bibliotheca Indica, 1902–1914), which contains both Śāntideva's verses and Prajñākaramati's commentary. On occasion the Tibetan text in the Peking edition of the Tanjur had to be consulted to fill lacunae in the extant Sanskrit text. Needless to say, all headings have been introduced to help punctuate a text that is very terse and disconnected.

Selections from Śāntideva

FROM THE FIRST CHAPTER

The first chapter explains the value of the thought of awakening, and recommends that one should cultivate it. It also extols the virtues of those who have had and have cultivated the thought of awakening. It concludes (stanza 36) with the author paying homage to these persons, who, of course, are the bodhisattvas.

(I.36) I bow before the bodies of those [beings] in whom is born the jewel of the sublime thought. I take refuge in these mines of bliss, from which one receives happiness even when one offends them.

FROM THE SECOND CHAPTER

The second chapter picks on the theme of worship and begins a long description, mostly in the first person, of a ritual of worship and self-consecration.

Reverential salutation (vandana)

(II.1) To acquire the jewel that is this thought, I worship duly the tathāgatas, the pure gem of the true dharma, and the sons of the awakened, oceans of virtue.

Worship and offering (pūjana)

(II.2) For an offering I will avail myself of all the flowers, fruits, and medicinal plants, all the treasures that there are in the universe, of whatever waters flow, clear and sweet, (II.3) of mountains rich in fine gems, forests that charm with calm, their creepers shining with loads of flowers, their trees bent by the weight of fruit. (II.4) From the world of the gods and the other celestial beings I will take perfumes and incenses, the wish-fulfilling tree and the gem-bearing trees. I will take ponds adorned by lotus flowers, made more lovely by the song of the swan. (II.5) The grains of the fields, wild and cultivated, as well as any other treasure I may find in the immeasurable ends of space, by which one may adorn the venerable buddhas—all these treasures that have no owner (II.6) I make my own in thought, and I offer them to the bulls among the sages, and to their sons. May they, who deserve the best offerings and are endowed with the greatest pity, accept this offering of mine, out of compassion for me. (II.7) I have no merit of my own, I am only a poor beggar. Apart from this universe of ownerless treasures I have nothing with which to adore them. Therefore, may the protectors, who only desire the good of others, accept this offering through their own powers and for my sake.

Offering of self

(II.8) I also offer myself without constraints to the conquerors and to their sons. "Take me as your property, O sublime beings. Devoutly I become your slave. (II.9) As your possession, I will devote myself without hesitation to bringing good to living beings. And I will free myself from my past faults, and will not incur in further wrongdoing."

Act of worship

(II.10) In perfumed bathing halls, beautified by columns that shine with encrusted pearls, with awnings that shine with garlanded pearls, and with floors of shining pure crystal, (II.11) full of urns inlaid with fine gems, full of delicate flowers and perfumed waters, there shall I prepare a bath for the tathāgatas and their sons, accompanied by music and song. (II.12) With incomparable and pure garments, impregnated with the smell of incense, I wipe clean their bodies, and then give them select, perfumed tunics, dyed in exquisite colors. (II.13) With delicate heavenly clothing, soft to the touch, of many colors, and with fine ornaments, I cover Samantabhadra, Ajita [Maitreya], Mañjughoṣa, Lokeśvara [Avalokiteśvara] and the other bodhisattvas. (II.14) With the best perfumes that fill a billion worlds with their scent I anoint these [bodhisattvas, who are] monarchs among the sages, whose bodies shine with the brightness of well purified, burnished and polished gold.

(II.15) With all kinds of lovely and sweet-smelling flowers—such as mandarava, blue lotus, or jasmine—and with gracefully woven garlands I worship the monarchs among the sages, who are most worthy of worship. (II.16) I cense them with clouds of incense that charm the senses with thick, penetrating scent. And I offer them food—hard and soft—and the most varied drinks. (II.17) On golden, lotus-shaped trays I present to them lamps inlaid with precious stones. On floors sprinkled with perfumed waters and powders I strew delicate flowers.

(II.18) I also offer these benevolent ones heavenly chapels arrayed in shining clouds adorning the heavenly directions, bedecked with festoons of pearls and rubies, embellished by hymn and song. (II.19) Over the heads of these great sages I spread out tall and beautiful parasols made of precious stones, strung together with pearls, with graceful golden handles.

(II.20) May these pleasing clouds of offerings rise, these clouds of music and song, which delight all living beings. (II.21) May flowers, jewels, and other offerings rain without interruption upon the three jewels of the true dharma, and upon their shrines (*caitya*) and images.

(II.22) As Mañjughoṣa and the other bodhisattvas adore the conquerors, so do I adore the tathāgatas, protectors, and their sons. (II.23) With hymns that are melodious seas I praise these oceans of virtue. May these clouds of hymn and song reach them directly.

Worship of the three jewels

(II.24) I bow before the awakened ones of the three times, the dharma and the sublime congregation, with as many prostrations as there are atoms in all the [buddha-] fields. (II.25) I pay homage to all stūpas and shrines, and to [sacred] sites associated with [the lives of] the bodhisattvas as well. I bow before all teachers, as well as before all venerable ascetics.

Triple refuge

(II.26) I take refuge in the awakened, until I have attained the heart of awakening. I take refuge in the dharma, and in the community of the bodhisattvas.

Repentance and confession

(II.27) I address with joined palms the perfectly awakened ones who dwell in all the directions of the universe, and the bodhisattvas of great compassion. (II.28) All the evil that I, a true beast, have committed or have had someone else commit in my beginningless transmigrations, or in this very same life, (II.29) and the evil that I have approved of, all this that I have done out of delusion for my own harm, all this evil, I now confess burning with remorse. (II.30) Every violation, of body, word, or thought that out of negligence I have committed against the three jewels, or against my mother, or father, or others who are equally deserving of my respect—(II.31) every grave transgression that I, an evildoer corrupted by various vices, have committed—all I confess now, O guides. . . .

Contrition and meditation on death

(II.35) What I love and what I hate have been many times the cause of my evil deeds. I did not examine this: that one day I will have to depart and leave everything behind. (II.36) What I love will cease to be, what I hate will be no more. I too will cease to be. Everything will cease to be. . . .

(II.42) When the messengers of Yama [the king of the underworld] take hold of me, where will I find a [true] relative or friend? Then merit is the only protection, but I have not gathered any. (II.43) Because of my attachment to this transient life, not perceiving the danger, heedless, I have accumulated many misdeeds, O protectors. . . .

(II.45) How will I feel when the terrible messengers of Yama take hold of me, consumed by fever and fear, sunken in my own excrement? (II.46) My terrified eyes will look in vain in all directions for a means of escape. Which kind being will then become my savior from this terrifying danger? . . .

Refuge

(II.48) Right away I must take refuge in the powerful world protectors, the conquerors who are devoted to caring for the world, those who keep away all causes of fear. (II.49) I also take refuge in the dharma that they have understood, which destroys all danger in the sphere of transmigration. I likewise take refuge with sincere faith in the community of the bodhisattvas.

(II.50) Confused with fear, I turn to Samantabhadra. I also surrender myself to Mañjughoṣa. (II.51) Terrified, I call with anguished voice upon the protector Avalokita whose actions are all moved by pity. Let him protect this evildoer! (II.52) Searching for my salvation, I call with true faith upon the noble Akāśagarbha, Kṣitigarbha and all those who have great pity. (II.53) I pay homage to Vajrapāṇi, the one who carries the vajra, whose mere presence is enough to scatter away in terror Yama's messengers and other beings of hell.

(II.54) I have heedlessly ignored your prescriptions, and now, terrified by these dangers, I seek refuge in you. Hasten to destroy this threat! (II.55) One should not disobey the instructions of a physician, even if it is for fear of a common and short illness, how much [less should one ignore them] when one is afflicted by the four hundred four diseases! (II.56) For a single one of them would exterminate all the human beings on [this land of ours,] the Rose Apple Continent (Jambudvīpa), and in the whole universe there is no cure for any of them. (II.57) Yet I ignore the advice of the all-knowing physician who cures all these pains. How pitiful is this endless delusion of mine! . . .

(II.59) "Death shall not come today"—I have no reason for feeling so smug. The time when I will cease to be most surely will come. (II.60) Who will give me shelter? How will I escape? Surely I will cease to be. How can my mind be at ease? (II.61) Is it perhaps that something of value remains of those things that perished after I enjoyed them—attachment to which led me to ignore the advice of the teachers? (II.62) When I will have left the world of the living, as well as friends and relatives, and when I depart alone to I know not where, what good will come from those things that I have loved and those that I have hated? (II.63) Therefore I must day and night remain mindful of this reflection: from evil necessarily follows suffering, how shall I escape from it?

Confession

(II.64) Whatever faults I, deluded fool that I am, have committed, be they shunned by natural law or by prescription [in the monastic code], (II.65) I confess them all before the protectors, palms joined, with repeated prostrations. For I fear the pains [that will result from my transgression]. (II.66) Let the guides recognize my faults as faults. It was not noble conduct, protectors. I will not repeat this conduct.

FROM THE THIRD CHAPTER

The "standard" order of the Mahāyāna liturgy continues in chapter 3 of the *Bodhicaryāvatāra,* culminating in the bodhisattva's vow and dedication of merit.

Rejoicing in the merit of others

(III.1) With delight I rejoice that all living beings acquire the merit that quells the pains of evil destinies. May all suffering beings reach happiness! (III.2) I rejoice that living beings can become free from the suffering of transmigration and I rejoice that the perfect ones are in possession of buddhahood or bodhisattvahood. (III.3) I rejoice in the arising of the thought of awakening in those who adopt the teaching, for this thought is an ocean whose tide brings bliss, whose depths hold the treasure of [everything that is] beneficial to all sentient beings.

Entreaty

(III.4) Palms joined in prayer, I entreat all awakened ones in all the directions that they light the lamp of dharma for those who, in the darkness of their own delusion, fall into the abyss of suffering.

Supplication

(III.5) Palms joined in prayer, I plead with the conquerors who seek the final rest of nirvāṇa, that they remain in the world of transmigration for an infinite number of cosmic ages, that this world may not remain blind.

Dedication of merit

(III.6) With the merit that I have achieved in this manner through all of these [acts of devotion] may I be the one who relieves the entirety of the suffering of all sentient beings.

Self-surrender

(III.7) Let me be medicine, physician, and nurse for the sick, until I have put an end to all illness. (III.8) May I bring an end to the torments of hunger and thirst with rivers of food and drink, and may I myself become food and drink when the minor cosmic cycle ends with a great famine. (III.9) May I become inexhaustible wealth for the poor. May I remain at their side ready to satisfy each one of their needs. (III.10) All bodies, property, and merit that I have acquired in the past, the one I have now, and the ones that I may acquire in the future, I surrender them all with indifference for the benefit of all living beings. (III.11) Nirvāṇa means renunciation of all things, and my mind seeks this peace. If I must renounce all, it would be better to surrender it to living beings.

(III.12) I relinquish my person to the whims of all embodied beings; let them hurt me, insult me, cover me with dust without ceasing, (III.13) let them use my body as their toy, let them laugh at it and enjoy themselves with it. I have given them my body, why should it be my concern any more? (III.14) Let them have it to do whatever is pleasing to them, but let them never suffer any harm on my account. (III.15) Rather, if because of me their hearts are driven to anger or anxiety, let these same feelings become in every occasion the cause for their attainment of all merit. (III.16) May all those who slander me, injure me or scoff at me, and all other beings share in awakening.

(III.17) May I become protector for those who have no protection, caravan leader for travelers, a ship, bridge, or ford for those who seek to reach the other shore, (III.18) a lamp for those who seek light, a bed for the tired, a slave for those embodied beings who need slaves. (III.19) May I become a wish-fulfilling jewel to all embodied beings, a horn of plenty, a powerful magical formula, the universal remedy, the tree of desires, the cow of plenty. (III.20) Just as earth and the other [elements] render service, in multiple ways, conforming to their desires, to the numberless living beings that inhabit infinite space, (III.21) may I in the same manner, in numberless ways, serve as sustenance for this universe of living beings filling the breadth of space, for as long as they have not reached satisfaction and peace.

The vow

(III.22) "Just as the sugatas in the past took possession of the thought of awakening and established themselves progressively in the discipline of training of the bodhisattvas, (III.23) today I produce the thought of awakening for the good of the world. In this way I shall train successively in the various levels of this discipline."

In praise of the thought

(III.24) Once the man of wisdom has taken possession of the thought of enlightenment in this manner, he shall exalt that same thought repeatedly in the following manner, in order to secure its subsequent growth: (III.25) "Today my birth bears fruit, and my human existence becomes profitable; today I have been born in the family of the tathāgatas, now I become a son of the awakened. (III.26) From today on I must act according to the customs of my family, so that no stain will fall on this immaculate lineage. (III.27) "It is as if a blind man were to find a jewel in a pile of dung. In the same way, I know not how, this thought of awakening has arisen in me. (III.28) This elixir has arisen to vanquish death in the world. It is the inexhaustible treasure that will alleviate thirst in the world. (III.29) It is the unsurpassed medicine that will allay the sufferings of the world. It is the tree under which the tired world can rest from its wanderings through the roads of existence. (III.30) It is like a bridge open to all travelers that they may cross beyond the evil destinies. This moon of the thought of awakening has arisen to freshen with its light the heat of the afflictions of the world. (III.31) It is an immense sun that dissipates the darkness of worldly ignorance. It is the fresh butter produced by the churning of the ocean of milk of the true dharma. (III. 32) The caravan of men, which travels through the roads of existence, hungering for pleasure and happiness, finds here the banquet of bliss, in which all those who come to it become satiated. (III. 33) "Today, before the perfect ones, I invite the whole world to the condition of awakening, and, at the same time, to happiness. May gods, asuras, and all living beings rejoice."

FROM THE FOURTH CHAPTER

Having concluded the liturgy, Śāntideva explains the importance of using this ritual as a basis for other dimensions of Buddhist practice. Only the first stanza of the fourth chapter is included here, by way of conclusion, to illustrate the connections that Śāntideva sees between the thought of awakening, ritual, and the rest of the bodhisattva practice.

(IV.1) The son of the conquerors who in this manner has taken firm hold of the thought of awakening should tirelessly make a constant effort to avoid violating the precepts.

Selections from Prajñākaramati's Commentary

According to Prajñākaramati, the order of the liturgy begins with the last stanza of the first chapter in which Śāntideva pays obeisance to the bodhisattvas. This is, presumably, "the act of veneration" (or reverent salutation: *vandana*), the first moment in every act of worship, which is defined minimally and technically as a reverent bow or prostration.

FROM THE FIRST CHAPTER

(I.36) The author of this treatise, expressing himself [as having] a strong faith in those who have already generated the thought of awakening, pronounces [the last stanza of this chapter, I.36] as he pays obeisance to [bows before] these persons. "Before the bodies," that is, before their persons, "I bow," I salute [them] by prostrating [myself before them].

FROM THE SECOND CHAPTER

(II.1) [The author,] having understood correctly that it is extremely difficult to obtain the favorable conditions [that allow us to practice the path,] as [he explained in the previous chapter], and knowing well the advantages of [developing] the thought of awakening, turns [his sight and mind] toward buddhas and bodhisattvas, in order to consolidate [his] grasp of the thought of awakening. He proceeds to explain the proper order of the liturgy consisting in reverent salutation, worship, taking of refuge, confession of sins, rejoicing in the merit [of sentient beings], entreating and petitioning the buddhas, and dedicating [thought and merit] to the attainment of awakening.

[In the first stanza of this chapter, II.1] . . . "to acquire" is to take possession; this means to bring forth and foster the thought that is [here compared to] a jewel. To "worship . . . the tathāgatas," that is, to worship the buddhas, the blessed ones . . . This refers to the [first of the three treasures,] the treasure that is the Buddha. [The phrase] "the pure gem of the true dharma" is [the dharma] as it is defined in the [scriptural] tradition. . . . This refers to [the second of the three treasures,] the treasure that is the dharma. And, lastly, "the sons of the awakened" are his legitimate sons, called "oceans of virtue," because they are [inexhaustible] mines of virtue [like] the ocean [holds mines of] precious gems—this is the company of those led by the noble Avalokiteśvara, Mañjuśrī, and the rest. This refers to [the third of the three treasures,] the treasure that is the saṅgha. With this begins the ritual of worshiping the three treasures.

(II.6) "Make my own in thought," take possession with the mental faculty. "I offer them to the bulls among the sages," I give them to those who among sages [lead and command, like] a bull [in a herd of cows]. "Together with their sons," together with the host of the bodhisattvas. "May they . . . accept this offering of mine," may they receive as their own all the offerings I now present in worship. "Who deserve the best offerings," the buddhas and bodhisattvas, who are the worthy vessels for incomparable gifts and offerings. "Endowed with the greatest pity," that is, their only concern is to provide all living beings with all that is for their benefit and happiness. "Out of compassion for me," feeling sympathy for this destitute, suffering being, that I am. This also means, feeling a favorable disposition toward me.

This is all very well, but why is it that he only makes mental offerings in this manner, and does not present actual objects of offering? With this doubt in mind, the author [then presents his seventh stanza, II.7].

(II.7) "I have no merit of my own," therefore, "I am only a poor beggar." Merit is possible when there is an abundance of good acts; but since [I] lack such [abundance], "I have nothing with which to adore them," "apart from this universe" [which is ownerless, and which I now imagine]. "Therefore," [may the protectors accept this offering] "for my sake"—knowing that I wish I had more merit. [That is, may] the blessed ones, "who only desire the good of others," who only seek [to give others] all that is for their benefit and happiness, because they possess the greatest compassion, . . . accept this offering that I present to them.

But I also have at my disposition my whole person. Thinking "I will offer this [too]" the author then presents [the eighth stanza].

(II.8) I also give "myself . . . to the conquerors. "Without constraints," in every respect. "And to their sons" as well I give myself and all that belongs to me. Accept me, O you who are like bulls among human beings. "I become your slave," adopt the condition of a slave. [In other words, I do it] not seeking compensation or recompense, but "devoutly," out of devotion, because [I feel for them] the highest esteem and respect, that is to say, [I do this] because my mind is overtaken by faith and trust in them.

(II.24) Next he pronounces the act of worship consisting in homage to the [three] treasures: Buddha, dharma, and saṅgha.

As many buddha fields as there are in the ten directions, and as many atoms as there are in all these fields, [this is] the number of prostrations [with which he worships] the tathāgatas "of the three times," that is, of the past, the present, and the future. [Now, what are these buddhas] associated with? "With the dharma and the sublime congregation." The supreme among all assemblies, the highest, the congregation of the bodhisattvas. . . .

(II.25) Then he pays homage to the stūpas of the tathāgatas. The meaning [of this stanza] is this: "I pay homage to [all] the stūpas, those that contain relics as well as those that do not, in all the main and the secondary heavenly directions, above, below and across." And also to "sites associated with the bodhisattvas," places [connected with stories of] Jātakas and Avadānas, and various births [of bodhisattvas]. "Venerable," that is, the buddhas, who are worthy of veneration. This is why [the ritual] is said to consist of veneration and worship.

(II.26) Next he will pronounce the confession of sins, preceded by the taking of refuge in the three treasures. "Refuge" means the same thing as haven. [Taking refuge or] "going for refuge" means observing and protecting the authority of these [three treasures]. The import [of this notion] is that one who goes for refuge to these [three treasures] does not contravene their authority.

"The heart of awakening" (*bodhimaṇḍa*): the word "heart" or "cream" (*maṇḍa*) means "essence" or "core," as in the expression "the cream of the ghee." Accordingly, "until [I have attained] the heart of awakening" means "until true awakening," that is, "for as long as I have not attained perfect, full, awakening."

(II.27)"I address," indicates that one should pronounce [this confession] facing buddhas and bodhisattvas, with sincere intention and self-reflection. "With joined palms" refers to the physical signs and basis [for the sincere intention]. "Joined palms" means with the hands cupped [and held together]. . . .

(II.64) Then, convinced [as explained above] of the connection between his actions and the fruits [he experiences,] he begins by confessing to having transgressed repeatedly, due to an obstinate clinging [to error].

"Fool," not understanding; "deluded," blinded by ignorance. "Whatever [faults]" [I have committed], with body, speech, or thought. "Be they shunned by natural law," that is, those [deeds] defined by the ten unwholesome types of action, such as the taking of life, [taking possession of what has not been given to us,] and so on. "By prescription," that is, the prescriptions contained in those precepts adopted by the blessed ones, such as eating at forbidden times, and so on.

(II.65) "I confess them," manifesting the verbal signs and basis [for repentance]; "palms joined," the physical signs and basis. "With repeated prostrations" expresses the extreme intensity and agitation of his mind.

FROM THE THIRD CHAPTER

(III.1) Now, immediately following the confession, he presents the act of rejoicing at the merit [of all sentient beings]. . . . "With delight I rejoice," I celebrate with a bright and composed mind. Rejoicing is also of three kinds: in mind, body, and speech. . . .

(III.2) Having expressed his joy in the [good] karma [that generates merit] in the world, [that is, in the round of transmigration, in the next stanza,] he expresses delight in [the good karma that bears fruit] outside of the world system, [in liberation]. "Free from the suffering of transmigration" refers to the awakening attained by those who are mere disciples (*śrāvaka*) or to that attained by solitary buddhas (*pratyekabuddha*). "Bodhisattvahood" is the condition that is the cause for [human beings becoming] blessed ones. "Buddhahood" is the fruit.

(III.4) In order to explain the entreaty, the author [then presents the next stanza, III.4]. "That they light the lamp of dharma" for those living beings who are wrapped in the darkness of ignorance, unable to distinguish what is the path from that which is not the path: may [the buddhas] light the lamp that is the teaching of the dharma. . . .

(III.5) In order to illustrate the supplication, [he presents stanza III.5]. Because they have already attained what they set out to attain, [buddhas naturally] want to go into complete nirvāṇa, [their final rest]. "I plead [with them]" that they stay for endless cosmic ages: "that [the world] may not remain blind," rendered senseless on account of its ignorance of the path, as explained above.

(III.6) Immediately after the supplication, he explains the dedication [of merit in stanza III.6]. With the performance of "all of these" ritual [acts of devotion], as explained above in proper order—worship, confession, rejoicing, etc.—[one gains merit]. "With the merit" or meritorious actions "accomplished," "through [the power of] this merit, may I be," may I become, "for all sentient beings," all breathing beings, "the one who relieves the entirety of their suffering.". . .

(III.19) "A wish-fulfilling jewel," a particular kind of gem that grants whatever one wishes. "A horn of plenty," a [magical] vessel that grants its possessor whatever object he might wish for. . . . "A powerful magical formula," a potent mantra having the power to cause success in any enterprise whenever it is pronounced. "Universal remedy," a medicinal herb that allays all fevers and aches. "The tree of desires," a certain kind of tree that satisfies all of one's desires. "The cow of plenty," which produces a milk that satisfies [whatever one] yearns for.

(III.20–21) "The earth and the other," "earth" [means here] the generous ground [we tread]. With the addition of the phrase "and the other" [the whole clause means] the four great elements: [earth,] water, fire, and wind. Just as these provide a place on which to lie, nourishment, a basis for the roots of grain to grow in, . . . in the same manner may I too provide sustenance to all living beings in multiple ways. "For as long as they have not reached satisfaction and peace," for as long as they all have not been released from the suffering of transmigration.

Therefore, the person who wishes to attain awakening should give away [all] of these [things], beginning with the person's own being and self. And this [kind of] generosity has been explained in detail [in Śāntideva's own] *Śikṣā-samuccaya.*

Thus, on this same point, [regarding detached generosity,] it is said in the *Bodhisattvaprātimokṣa:*

> Again, Śāriputra, the bodhisattva should conceive of all things as belonging to others, and should not make a possession of anything whatsoever. And why is this so? Because appropriating [anything] is [the greatest] danger.

All of the above, beginning with [the first words of the second chapter (II.1)], "To acquire the jewel that is this thought," is meant to explain the practice by which one adopts the precepts [that consolidate] the thought of awakening. One becomes committed and focused on the [practice of these precepts] once one has done [the following]: once one has performed [the ritual] as described above, beginning with the act of worship; once one has given away as a gift [all that one has] beginning with one's own person; once one has understood the virtues of the thought of awakening and taken to heart how very difficult it is to obtain the favorable conditions [that allow us to practice the path]; once one has planted firmly the roots of faith; once one has felt compassion for [all] living beings [knowing that they] have no one to rescue them and nowhere to go, and once one has consequently disregarded one's own happiness and made one's own the suffering of others; once one has in view only [the goal of] buddhahood and the means to attain it, with a mind that is resolutely set on saving all these living beings.

(III.22) [The author then] proceeds [to take the vow] in order to give rise to [the thought of awakening,] the thought of perfect and full awakening. [He does so,] with the intention of releasing all living beings from all forms of suffering.

["Just as the sugatas,"] or, just as they understand how one should take possession. [On the phrase,] "the thought of awakening," "awakening" means buddhahood: the full comprehension of the fact that all things are without a self-nature, an understanding that follows the complete abandonment of the veils [of mental affliction and confusion]. This point will be explained abundantly in [Śāntideva's ninth chapter,] the chapter on discernment. [As to the word] "thought" in the present context, [it is used] in the sense of "resolve" or "determination," that is, the setting of one's mind on the goal of obtaining buddhahood, which consists of [the following mental resolution]: "I will become a buddha, in order to provide all living beings with that which is for their benefit and happiness."

Once the first half of the stanza has stated in this manner the way in which one gives rise to the thought of awakening, the text [in the second half of the stanza] points to the adoption of the precepts that constitute the discipline of training [of the bodhisattvas]. . . . The point is that this discipline of the bodhisattva should always be practiced by the bodhisattva who has given rise to the thought of awakening.

[In his commentary to the first stanza of the fourth chapter (IV.1), Prajñākaramati explains that the liturgy is an integral part of the practice of the bodhisattva path, and ties in ritual practice with the cultivation of meditation and wisdom:]

FROM THE FOURTH CHAPTER

(IV.1) [The author] explained above in detail the [ritual practice] that follows [the initial thought of awakening]. He then introduces the stanza beginning with the words "The son of the conquerors" in order to make the point that one should not act against the precepts, because only those who adopt the full practice as the heart [of their religious life can gain] possession of awakening. "In this manner" [refers to the repeated practice of] the ritual described above, by which the bodhisattva holds on firmly to the thought of awakening, and thus strives earnestly in [the practice of] the bodhisattva's precepts of training (*śikṣā*). This means that someone who becomes a bodhisattva must be capable [of following] the precepts of training.

"Effort" means cultivation (*bhāvanā*). Consequently, this is not effort applied to conditions contrary [to the goal of awakening]; it means to apply effort or strive earnestly toward that [goal]. "Tirelessly" means without indolence.

As it is said in the noble *Gayāśirṣa,* "The bodhisattva who adopts full practice as the heart [of their religious life] attains awakening, not the one for whom full practice is not the heart [of religious life]." . . . Now, if bodhisattvas are to train even in matters pertaining to those precepts [that bring merit] in this world, how much more should they [train] in [those practices that bear fruit] beyond the world of transmigration, such as meditation and wisdom! Otherwise, how could they bring about in every way the well-being of all living beings?

Now, this [full practice] of the bodhisattvas is, in brief, a practice consisting of skillful means (*upāya*) and discernment (*prajñā*). It is not only discernment, nor is it only skillful means. Of these two, skillful means are all the wholesome [roots planted by bodhisattvas,] beginning with the elements of attraction and the perfection of giving, but excluding discernment. That is to say, skillful means are the wholesome roots that contribute to the acquisition of a bodhisattva's exalted conditions, such as the purification of the fields, the great enjoyment, the perfect retinue, the maturation of living beings, the illusory bodies, and so on. Discernment, on the other hand, is the cause of the unerring, definitive knowledge of the true nature of these same means. For a full exposition of the meaning of this, one should consult the *Bhāvanākrama* of Kamalaśīla.

—15—

A Discussion of Seated Zen

Carl Bielefeldt

One of the most important pioneers of Japanese Zen was the Kamakura-period figure Enni (or Ben'en, 1202–1280). Originally a monk of the Tendai school, he took up the study of the newly imported Zen religion under a disciple of Eisai (or Yōsai) and then spent several years in China, where he trained under the prominent master Wuzhun Shifan. Upon his return to Japan in 1241, he won the support of the powerful court politician Kujō Michiie, was appointed by Michiie as the founding abbot of the great new monastic complex Tōfukuji, and became instructor to both emperor and shōgun. Such was his renown that he was posthumously honored by the imperial title National Teacher First of Sages (Shōichi Kokushi).

Unfortunately, little of Enni's Zen teaching is preserved for us. We know that, like his forebear Eisai, he retained broad interests in other forms of Buddhism, especially the esoteric tantric systems popular in his day. Aside from a brief collection of his sayings, his teachings on Zen are best known from a little tract usually referred to simply as *A Discussion of Seated Zen (Zazen ron)*. This is a work in a genre that might be called "vernacular homily" (*kana hōgo*), which was often used by the first Japanese Zen teachers to spread the new faith among their countrymen. Hence, the text has received its more formal alternative title: *A Vernacular Dharma Talk by the National Teacher Shōichi of Tōfuku (Shōichi kokushi kana hōgo)*.

Enni's *Discussion* is usually said to have been written for his lay patron, Michiie, but there is reason to doubt this tradition. In fact, the origin of the work is quite mysterious. The vulgate version as we now know it was not published until the seventeenth century and differs considerably from a recently discovered early manuscript. Moreover, whatever their differences, both these versions are largely reworkings of material in another text of the same title, written in Chinese and attributed to the first Song Zen missionary to the Kamakura, Lanqi Daolong (Rankei Dōryū, 1213–1278), who arrived in Japan only a few years after Enni's return. This fact in itself, however, does not necessarily mean that Enni's work is spurious; for, whoever wrote the first version of the *Discussion,* it was probably not the Chinese master Daolong: both the content and style of this text seem clearly to stamp it as a work of Japanese authorship.

Throughout the brief introduction and two dozen questions and answers that comprise the vulgate version of the *Discussion,* we find a number of interlocking themes that recur in other early Japanese texts on Zen. These themes, as well as the language through which they are discussed, remind us less of the contemporaneous Chan literature of the Southern Song than of the old Tang writings of early Chan long familiar to Japanese Tendai scholars. At the outset of the text, Zen is defined as the "buddha mind," a name by which the Zen teachings had long been known in Japan and a term that is central to the entire argument of the *Discussion.* The "buddha mind" as used here designates at once the ultimate reality, or "emptiness," of all things and the enlightened state, or knowledge of that reality, characteristic of a buddha.

Since Zen is this buddha mind, it represents the very essence—both the highest truth and final goal—of all Buddhism. Since the buddha mind is empty of all "marks," or distinguishing characteristics, it cannot be described; since Zen specializes in this mind alone, it is beyond (and looks down on) all other forms of Buddhism that seek to describe reality and the means to its knowledge. Hence, like much of traditional Chan literature, the *Discussion* is dismissive of the standard categories of Buddhist teaching and the traditional practices of the bodhisattva path.

Since the buddha mind is the reality of all beings, the enlightened state of a buddha is our own true nature—a "subliminal self-consciousness," so to speak, of ultimate reality that is present in all awareness, however seemingly distorted or "afflicted"; since Zen is concerned only with this enlightened state, it has no need to overcome afflictions or gain virtues but only calls on us to see our natures and be our true selves. In the *Discussion,* this call takes two forms regularly found in the classical literature of early Chan: one that urges the reader to a "sudden awakening," or recognition of the truth of the buddha mind; the other that enjoins what might be called the "imitation" of the markless character of that mind through the cultivation of a state of detached, preconceptual awareness called "no-mind" or "no-thought."

The rather uneasy relationship between these two forms is probably reflected in the text's seeming ambivalence toward its title theme of *zazen,* a term I have rendered here "seated zen." The word *zen,* of course, derives from a Chinese term for *dhyāna* and can be rendered "meditation"; the word *zazen* is widely used for Buddhist contemplative practice and usually translated as "seated meditation." At the outset, the *Discussion* identifies Zen as the "school of seated meditation" and the traditional Buddhist "gate of meditation," and it goes on to identify the practice of zazen with buddhahood itself. Yet, like many of the texts of early Chan, it also emphasizes that Zen is beyond seated meditation and strongly rejects the notion that this practice should be seen as the focus of Zen religious life. Given this ambivalence, I have opted in the following English version of the text to leave the term *zen* untranslated.

The translation is based on the vulgate text of the *Discussion* published as *Shōichi kokushi kana hōgo,* in *Zenmon hōgo shū,* vol. 2 (rev. ed., Tokyo: Kōyūkan, 1921), pp. 411–22. For ease of reference, I have supplied section numbers to the text.

A Vernacular Dharma Talk by the National Teacher Shōichi of Tōfuku

The school of seated zen is the way of the great liberation. All the various dharmas flow out from this gate; all the myriad practices are mastered from this way. The mystic functions of wisdom and psychic powers are born from within it; the life of men and gods have opened forth from within it. Therefore, the buddhas have resided in this gate, and the bodhisattvas practice it and enter into this way. Even those of the Lesser Vehicle and non-Buddhists practice it, although they do not yet accord with the true path. All the exoteric and esoteric schools have their self-verification by attaining this way. Therefore, the [Third] Patriarch [of Zen] has said [in *Believing in the Mind* (*Xin xin ming*)], "All the wise men of the ten directions enter this school."

[1.] Q: Why do you say that this zen gate is the root of all the teachings?

A: Zen is the buddha mind. The precepts are its outer marks; the teachings are its explanation; the recitation of the [Buddha's] name is its device. These three spiritual practices have all come from the buddha mind. Therefore, this school represents the root.

[2.] Q: The dharma of zen has no-marks as its essence. How, then, [does it explain] the appearance of the spiritual virtues, and what does it take as the verification of seeing one's nature?

A: One's own mind is the buddha. What spiritual virtue is there beyond this? And what verification should we seek beyond the recognition of our own minds?

[3.] Q: If we cultivate this one mind, this is but one practice. If we cultivate the myriad practices and good works, how could the merit from this be inferior to that of one practice?

A: An ancient has said [in the *Song of Enlightenment* (Zheng daoge)], "When you suddenly recognize the zen of the Thus Come One, the six perfections and the myriad practices are complete within your own body." Thus, the one dharma of zen includes all dharmas. Even in the secular world, we have the saying, "Myriad talents cannot match one mind." Therefore, although we cultivate myriad practices, if we do not put an end to the delusion of one mind, we will not attain awakening; and, if we are not awakened, how can we become buddhas?

[4.] Q: Why are we to cultivate this buddha-mind school? Even if we do so, it is not certain that we will attain awakening; and, if it is not certain, what use is there in cultivating it?

A: Because this school is the way of inconceivable liberation, for one who but hears it, it forms the surpassing cause of enlightenment; and if he cultivates this school, it represents the ultimate of the buddha mind. The buddha mind is basically without delusion or awakening; it is the mystic practice of [Śākyamuni's] six years of erect sitting in the Snowy Mountains that is clear in this school. Even if you have not attained the way, when you do seated zen for one period, you are a one-period buddha; when you do seated zen for one day, you are a one-day buddha; when you do seated zen for one lifetime, you are a lifetime buddha. To have this kind of faith is to be one of great faculties, a great vessel of the dharma.

[5.] Q: In practicing this way, how are we to employ our minds?

A: The buddha mind is without marks and without attachments. The *Diamond Sūtra* says that the buddhas are free from all marks. Therefore, where we have no-mind and no-thought in the midst of the four attitudes of walking, standing, sitting, and reclining, this is the true employment of the mind, the true concentrated effort.

[6.] Q: This kind of cultivation is difficult to believe in and difficult to practice. How would it be if one were to seek the merits of reading the sūtras and reciting spells (*dhāraṇī*), or keeping the precepts, or recollecting the Buddha and calling his name?

A: The sūtras and spells are not words: they are the original mind of all beings. They are speech, intended for those who have lost their original minds, that teaches through various similes in order to bring about awakening to the original mind and put an end to birth and death in delusion. One who awakens to his original mind and returns to the origin reads the true sūtra. If we keep on reciting words with the mouth and say that this is the ultimate, are we then supposed to get warm by saying "fire" when we are cold, or get cool by saying "breeze" when we are hot? Or when we are hungry, are we supposed to get full by intoning the name of the food that we want? Therefore, though we say "fire" all day, it will not make us warm; though we say "water" all night, it will not wet our mouths. Words and speech are like the picture of a rice cake: though we intone them with our mouths our entire lives, our hunger will not be assuaged. What a pity that the ordinary man, his deluded concepts of birth and death deeply [rooted], is always thinking of attainment in regard to the dharmas. This is great stupidity. To practice all dharmas without the mind of attainment is called the prajñā of the Great Vehicle. This is the wisdom of the buddhas, immaculate and without concepts. Because this wisdom cuts the root of birth and death, it is called the sword of prajñā.

[7.] Q: If we do not accumulate the merits and good spiritual roots [of the bodhisattva path], how can we become a buddha, perfectly endowed with the myriad virtues?

A: One who seeks buddhahood through accumulating the merits and good roots may become a buddha after three great incalculable eons; but one who cultivates [the Zen way of] direct pointing at a person's mind, seeing his nature and becoming a buddha, [knows that he] is himself [a buddha] from the beginning: it is not that he initially verifies the fruit of buddhahood.

[8.] Q: Then does one who cultivates zen reject the power of the merits and good roots?

A: Although he cultivates the good roots for the sake of benefiting others, since he has no aspirations, he does not seek merits. For he has no-mind at all times.

[9.] Q: If this no-mind represents the ultimate, who is it that verifies the seeing of his nature and awakening to the way?

A: The ultimate no-mind means to put a stop to all wrong knowledge and bad views, all the discriminations of thinking. Since it does not produce any [false] view of cultivation, it does not aspire to become a buddha; since it does not produce any view of social intercourse, it does not rejoice in respect and reputation; since it does not produce any view of love and hate, it makes no distinction of intimacy and distance between self and other. Do not think of any good or bad—such [a person] is called the one on the way of no-thought. This way is not something known to the ordinary person or those on the two vehicles [of the śrāvaka and pratyekabuddha].

[10.] Q: In the [Buddhist] teachings, the merits of the myriad good works and practices are often explained; why is it that the merit of no-mind is not directly explained?

A: Since the bodhisattvas of original enlightenment already value and understand it, it is not explained. This is the sense of the *Lotus Sūtra* statement, "Do not teach this sūtra among those without wisdom." Although the teachings have eighty-four thousand dharma gates, if we seek their source, they do not go beyond the two dharmas of form and emptiness. "Form" means the substance of the four great [physical elements] and five aggregates; "emptiness" is the nature of the afflictions and enlightenment. Because this body has shape, it is called "form"; because the mind is without shape, it is called "emptiness." In all realms, there is nothing to be explained beyond this body and mind.

[11.] Q: Are the shape and substance of the four great [elements] originally something deluded or something awakened?

A: There is from the beginning no distinction of ignorance and enlightenment in either body or mind. Everything merely appears provisionally, like a dream or an illusion. Do not think about any of the myriad things.

[12.] Q: The two vehicles also have this no-mind, as well as enlightenment and nirvāṇa. How is the Great Vehicle different?

A: From the start, the arhats of the śrāvaka and pratyekabuddha [vehicles] consider body and mind as the afflictions and hate them. They seek to extinguish body and mind, becoming like dead trees, tiles, and stones. Though they practice in this way, they [merely] become heavenly beings in the formless realm. This is not the true dharma; it is [merely] the fruit of the Lesser Vehicle. The no-mind of the Great Vehicle is not the same.

[13.] Q: Do the bodhisattvas of the Great Vehicle have this way of no-mind?

A: Until they reach the tenth stage [of their path], bodhisattvas have the afflictive and cognitive obstacles and therefore do not yet accord [with no-mind]. [To say that they have] the afflictive obstacles means that, because until the tenth stage they have aspirations to seek the dharma, they do not accord with their original lot. It is only when they attain the virtual enlightenment [following the tenth stage] that they reach this way of no-mind.

[14.] Q: If it is difficult even for the bodhisattvas to accord with it, how could beginners easily accord with this way?

A: The true dharma is inconceivable. The establishment of the three ranks of the wise and ten ranks of the holy [that define the stages of the bodhisattva path] is for the sake of those of dull spiritual faculties. Those of acute faculties awaken to the true enlightenment of no-mind when they first produce the thought [of seeking supreme enlightenment at the outset of the bodhisattva path].

[15.] Q: Why is it that, though one who sees his nature and awakens to the way is immediately a buddha, he does not have the psychic powers and radiance [of a buddha] or show the mystic functions [of a buddha] that would distinguish him from the ordinary person?

A: Because this body has been constructed from past deluded conceptions, though we see our nature, it does not show the psychic powers and radiance. Yet, is it not a psychic power to master the six dusts [of the senses] and the deluded conceptions? Without depending on difficult, painful practices, without passing through the three great incalculable eons, to cut off birth and death, see directly one's nature and become a buddha—this is the mystic function. To use the light of wisdom of the immaculate dharma body to save all beings from the darkness of ignorance—what use is there in any radiance beyond this? To want psychic powers other than the great wisdom and penetration is the way of Māra and the non-Buddhists. Foxes have psychic powers and transformations, but should we honor them? Just cultivating no-mind, we should extinguish at once the three great incalculable eons and abruptly see our natures and become buddhas.

[16.] Q: What kind of wisdom are we to use to awaken to the meaning of seeing our natures and becoming buddhas?

A: The knowledge gained by studying the sūtras and treatises is called [the knowledge of] seeing, hearing, recognizing, and knowing. This may be knowledge for the ordinary, stupid person, but it is not true knowledge. To recognize the inherent buddha nature by turning the light around and shining it back is called the wisdom eye. We use this wisdom eye to see our natures and become buddhas.

[17.] Q: What is this inherent buddha nature? And what do you mean by "turning the light around and shining it back"?

A: All beings have a self-nature. This nature is intrinsically without arising or cessation; it constantly abides without change. Therefore, it is called the inherent self-nature. Both the buddhas of the three worlds [of past, present, and future] and all beings have this nature as the dharma body of the original ground. The radiance of this dharma body fills the entire dharma realm, turning the light and shining it back on the darkness of the ignorance of all beings. Where this light does not reach is called Māra's realm of ignorance. In this realm of Māra dwells the spirit of the afflictions, seeking to devour the dharma nature. Those injured by this spirit of the afflictions, believing that their deluded thoughts are their original mind and taking delight in the seeds of desire, revolve through the four [kinds of] births in the three evil [destinies]. When will they ever cut off birth and death?

[18.] Q: Birth and death arise from deluded thoughts. If one awakens to the source from which deluded thoughts arise, will birth and death naturally stop?

A: Throughout the twenty-four hours of the day, beings are perverted by deluded thoughts, and their original buddha nature is naturally buried by the afflictions. It is like the bright moon hidden by clouds. Once they have awakened to the source of these thoughts, it is like the bright moon emerging from the clouds. It is like the mirror that, when clean, clearly reflects the myriad images. It has full mastery in regard to all dharmas and, though facing the myriad objects, suffers not so much as a hair's breadth of defilement. This is because the original buddha nature has freedom of psychic power.

[19.] Q: What does it mean to say that, in employing the mind in seated zen, we "should not think of any good or bad"?

A: This phrase will directly cut off the root source of birth and death. Do not think it is limited to seated zen. One who reaches [understanding of] this phrase is a buddha without beginning or end, is [practicing] zen whether walking, standing, sitting, or reclining.

[20.] Q: What are big thoughts and small thoughts?

A: Small thoughts are thoughts that arise from conditions; big thoughts are [the three poisons of] the desire, aversion, and delusion of beginningless birth and death. One who stops the thoughts of the three poisons, big and small, only in seated zen, one who lacks the authentic mind of the way, does not clarify the root source of the beginningless birth and death and does not exhaust the consciousness characterized by the three poisons. When one has clarified this root source, the afflictions become bodhi, the three poisons become the three pure precepts [of avoiding evil, cultivating good, and benefiting others], birth and death become the beginningless nirvāṇa, and the six dusts become the six psychic powers.

[21.] Q: The mind of one who has long cultivated seated meditation will clearly be pure, but how should one just beginning to cultivate put a stop to the perversions of deluded conceptions?

A: Do not detest the perversions of deluded conceptions; just clarify the nature of the mind. Because we are confused about the one mind, we think that, where in fact it is originally pure, there are the perversions of deluded conceptions. For example, though during sleep we see various things in our dreams, when we wake from the dreams, all these become merely deluded conceptions to us. When we awaken to the one mind, all things are empty, and not a single thing remains.

[22.] Q: What does it mean to say "the afflictions are bodhi; birth and death are nirvāṇa?

A: The afflictions mean stupidity and ignorance; bodhi means the buddha nature of all beings. Beings, not knowing their own buddha nature, seek it outside themselves; they see good and bad outside themselves and form attachments to the marks [of things]. This is great stupidity. Then those who abandon these marks and seek their own buddha nature may produce some view of clear awakening and, when they have some slight measure of difference from ordinary men, often become proud of themselves and fall into the way of Māra. This is ignorance. Not knowing that the one mind is originally no-mind, we rouse the mind to seek the mind and, in the process, produce the ongoing perversions. This is the seed of birth and death. When we have awakened to the fact that from the beginning the one mind neither arises nor ceases, then there is no distinction between self and other, there is no good or bad, no love or hatred; we are completely no-thought and no-mind. This is what is meant by "birth and death are nirvāṇa." Failing to awaken to the root source of the one mind, we lose our constant self and obscure our buddha nature. If we seek the source of the afflictions, [we find that] they are like dreams, illusions, bubbles, or shadows. Arriving at the fact that the one mind is originally pure is [what is meant by] "the afflictions are bodhi." And when we reach the source of the one mind, the radiance of inherent wisdom will be manifest. At this time, the myriad dharmas will be at rest, and we will attain the import of the ultimate emptiness of all the buddhas. For example, suppose there is a dark cave, into which the light of the sun and moon does not reach; yet when we take a lamp into it, the darkness of long years is naturally illuminated. Similarly, when the dark night encounters the light of the moon, space naturally becomes bright without changing its substance. The dharmas of the mind are like this: when beings, lost in the dark of ignorance and afflictions, encounter the light of wisdom, they are naturally purified without changing body or mind. This is what is meant by saying "the afflictions are bodhi; birth and death are nirvāṇa."

[23.] Q: Although the nature of the mind constantly abides without changing, and buddhas and sentient beings are one and equivalent, sentient beings, who have yet to master and awaken [to this fact], cannot avoid suffering and, for this reason, must cultivate and awaken to the way. Now, after they have seen their natures, should they still employ the mind [in cultivation]?

A: The oneness and equivalence [of buddhas and sentient beings] is what is illumined by wisdom. The teachings of the sūtras are like a finger pointing at the moon. If we have not yet seen the moon, we should rely on the finger; after we have seen the moon, the finger is of no use. When we have yet to awaken to the buddha mind, we should rely on the teachings; when we recognize the buddha mind, the eighty thousand dharma gates are all clearly apparent in one mind. After we have awakened to the one mind, there is no use for a single teaching. The words of the patriarchs are like a tile used to knock on a gate. Before you enter the gate, you take up the tile; once you have entered the gate, why take up the tile? Therefore, so long as we have not awakened to the original meaning of the buddhas and patriarchs, we should take up and examine the expression "see your nature and become a buddha." When we have already opened the gate of the great liberation and thoroughly awakened to the original meaning of the buddhas and patriarchs, [we recognize that] seeing one's nature is nothing special and becoming a buddha cannot be grasped. There is no buddha, no sentient being; from the beginning there is not a single thing, and the three worlds cannot be grasped.

[24.] Q: When we face the end without having clarified the import of "seeing our natures and becoming a buddha," how should we employ the mind at the last?

A: When one mind arises, there is birth and death; when there is no-mind, there is no body that is born, and when there is no-thought, there is no mind that ceases. When there is no-thought and no-mind, there is no birth and cessation whatsoever. This body is like the dew that forms on the grass: the dew is originally without subjectivity. When we stop the mind that thinks we have a body and turn toward the fact that from the beginning there is not a single thing, when we do not think that there is either birth or death and have no-mind and no-thought, this is equivalent to the great nirvāṇa of all the buddhas of the three worlds. Although the good and bad marks appear to us in their variety, we should take no notice of them. If we produce even a hair's breadth of mind, it is the seed of cyclic existence. If we just cultivate no-mind and do not forget it, whether walking, standing, sitting, or reclining, there is no special way to employ the mind at the last. When we truly reside on the way of no-mind, [we go] like blossoms that fall and leaves that scatter before the wind, like the melting of frost and snow in the morning sun. What is there that employs the mind in such events as these? When we truly attain no-mind, there are no three realms [of existence] or six paths [of rebirth], no pure lands or defiled lands, no buddhas, no beings, not a single thing.

Of this mind that resides on the way of no-mind and puts a stop to birth and death, the Buddha said at the last [in the *Nirvāṇa Sūtra*], "All constructed things are impermanent; they are dharmas that arise and cease. When arising and ceasing cease, their calm cessation is joy." "All constructed things are impermanent" refers to the conditioned dharmas of all beings; they are all like dreams, illusions, reflections, like the moon in the water. "They are dharmas that arise and cease" means that, from sentient beings to plants, all things that are born necessarily die; and further, the mountains, rivers and great earth of this world will break down and disappear in the end. All dharmas, wherever they are established, are dharmas that arise and cease. This is merely birth and death from the ongoing transformations of one thought; none of it is real. "When arising and ceasing cease" means that when, based on [the fact that] the original lot of all beings is immaculate and without marks, we reach the source of our original marklessness, the beginningless, endless birth and death, coming and going, cease all at once, and the openness of the mind is like empty space. "Their calm cessation is joy" means that the buddhas are no-mind, beings are no-mind, mountains and rivers and the great earth, the myriad phenomena all arrayed are no-mind. When all beings are no-mind, hell is no-mind, paradise is no-mind; there is no joy and no sadness. Trusting in the way like this, we see all dharmas without seeing them in the mind, we hear all things without hearing them in the mind; and so too with the minds of tasting and smelling. Just have no-mind in all circumstances. The mind of no-mind is the original teacher of all the buddhas of the three worlds. It is the cardinal buddha. The realization of this original buddha of no-thought is what is called the supreme perfect enlightenment of the buddhas. To awaken to the meaning of this is what is called "their calm cessation is joy." Trusting in the dharma like this and abandoning this body, we should not think of any dharma for a single thought.

With all respect.

A Discussion of Seated Zen intimately revealed to the Great Minister Kujō by the National Teacher Shōichi.

—16—

The Way to Meditation

Donald K. Swearer

The following essay on samatha (concentration) meditation was written by Bhikkhu Pannawong [Pali Pannavaṃsa] (B.E. 2424–2499 [1871–1956 C.E.]), the founder of Wat Sī Pun Yūn in the district of Lamphun, northern Thailand, and a distinguished monk of a generation prior to the invasive impact of modernization and Westernization in northern Thailand. Pannawong was a student of a highly revered teacher in the Lamphun area, Khrūbā Khamphira [Pāli Gambhira] and it is surmised that the type of meditation taught by Pannawong represented the instruction of his teacher. There is substantial additional evidence that the method espoused in the text represents the type of meditation generally practiced in the Lamphun area prior to the resurgence of vipassanā (insight) meditation in the modern period promoted, in particular, by disciples of the northeastern Thai monk, Acharn Mun, and Thai students of the Burmese meditation teacher, Mahasi Sayadaw. It has been reported, for example, that prior to World War II, it was customary for monks and novices in northern Thailand to use meditation beads, an essential device in the practice of samatha meditation as taught in the text under consideration.

Later Theravāda tends to make a sharp distinction between trance—or concentration—meditation, leading to psychic powers, and insight meditation, which promotes a direct comprehension of the true nature of things. Earlier Pāli texts mute this distinction. In contemporary practice Burmese teachers make a more precise distinction between the two than do Thai teachers. Pannawong's text defies a clear textbook distinction between trance and insight types of meditation.

Although comparison with other Theravāda meditation treatises is beyond the scope of this introduction, there is clearly a general indebtedness to Buddhaghosa's *Visuddhimagga,* a text frequently found in monastery palm-leaf manuscript collections in northern Thailand. Buddhaghosa structures the *Visuddhimagga* around virtue (*sīla*), concentration (*samādhi*), and wisdom (*paññā*). Bhikkhu Pannawong's text is a much abbreviated adaption of the samādhi section of the *Visuddhimagga.* Some *Visuddhimagga* topics, such as concentration on the ten loathsome states of the body, are merely listed in Pannawong's "Way to Meditation." Others, such as concentration on the immaterial states, are omitted altogether. Over 30 percent of Pannawong's text deals with recollecting on or focusing one's awareness on the triple gem (or three jewels), in particular, the Buddha. Consequently, the text conveys a devotional feeling, a sense that meditation as a soteriological strategy opens the meditator to the transforming power of the Buddha, the dharma (Pāli dhamma), and the saṅgha. The text, therefore, serves as an example of the essential linkage between recollection and meditation. The tendency of western Buddhist meditators, in particular, to remove meditation from its ritual-devotional context represents what some scholars of Theravāda Buddhism have characterized as a "Protestantizing" of the tradition.

Two important topics in the Pannawong text not included in this translation are recollecting the thirty-two parts of the body and their repulsiveness, and developing the four divine abidings—loving kindness, compassion, altruistic joy, and equanimity. Also omitted are two sections of a more analytical nature, one on insight and the other on dwelling in the dharma. These sections emphasize the impermanent (*anicca*), unsatisfactory (*dukkha*), and not-self (*anattā*) nature of all compounded things.

The treatise was written in B.E. 2445 (1900 C.E.), when Pannawong was still a young monk. The following essay is an exegetical translation from a *samut khoi* (heavy mulberry paper folded in accordion style) 28 cm. × 10½ cm., fifty-five pages in length. The text was composed in Pāli and Tai Yuan (northern Thai) and written in the Tai Yuan script. The importance of both languages as a vehicle of recollection is particularly noteworthy. Although in this text visualization plays a role in the process of contemplative recollection, language, rather than visualization, is the focus of meditation. It re-calls or re-collects the characteristics of the Buddha and his teaching, the loathsomeness of the body, the positive mental states of loving-kindness and compassion, and the impermanent, unsatisfactory, and not-self nature of things. In this regard, it is noteworthy that the mantralike conclusion to "Dwelling in the Dharma" states that by firmly establishing the three syllables—Ah (*anicca*), A (*dukkha*), Di (*anattā*)—in their minds, meditators will overcome suffering and reach nirvāṇa (Pāli nibbāna).

Further Reading

On the distinction between trance and insight types of meditation, see the introduction to Edward Conze, *Buddhist Meditation* (London: George Allen and Unwin, 1956). See also Donald K. Swearer, "Control and Freedom: The Structure of Buddhist Meditation in the Pali Suttas," *Philosophy East and West* 23:4 (October 1973), 435–54. On the linkage between recollection and meditation, see Paul Harrison, "Commemoration and Identification in *Buddhānusmṛti*," in Janet Gyatso, ed., *In the Mirror of Memory* (Albany: SUNY Press, 1992), pp. 215–38.

The Way to Meditation
by Bhikkhu Pannawong

Whoever practices meditation, whether a yogin, layperson, or a monk, who desires the fruits of meditation from both trance (*samatha*) and insight (*vipassanā*) should begin with certain dedicatory preparations. Take puffed rice and flowers and divide them into five groups. Then take five pairs of candles, or if not five then three; if you do not have three then two or even one will be all right; if you cannot afford candles, then only take the puffed rice and flowers. If these are not accessible, then simply dedicate yourself by placing your ten fingers and palms together in the shape of a lotus bud and prostrating three times with the forehead, forearms, and knees touching the ground before the Buddha image, the reliquary, the bodhi tree, or your meditation teacher. Do this with a humble heart filled with faith, respect, and joy repeating, "Now, O five precious ones headed by the fully enlightened Buddha, I, who am just beginning in the pursuit of true wisdom, desiring to practice meditation, place these five offerings of puffed rice and flowers in this bowl out of respect for the five gems [Buddha, dharma, saṅgha, meditation subject, teacher]. Out of your compassion may you accept these offerings. May the merit accrued from this endeavor become those qualities which will enable me to reach nirvāṇa; may my aspirations succeed in every way; may I be released from worry and danger; may I live comfortably and have a long life; and may I work for the welfare of the Buddhist religion until the end of my life."

Then prostrate three times and say: "I pay homage to the Buddha who, having seated himself under the bodhi tree and defeated Mara and his great retinue, became fully enlightened. Attaining unlimited vision he became incomparable among everyone in this world.

"I pay homage to the dharma, the noble eightfold path, the direct means to nirvāṇa, which brings peace to humankind and release from the cycle of life and death.

"I pay homage to the saṅgha which is pure, worthy of noble offerings, having pacified sensual attachments and suppressed all defilements, is pure and endowed with virtue.

"I salute the Buddha with his immeasurable virtues; I salute the dharma well proclaimed by the great sage; I salute his disciples, the saṅgha; I salute the meditation subject which is the very means to reach nirvāṇa; I salute the teacher who gives the meditation subject and shows me the way to nirvāṇa.

"O, Blessed One! If I have foolishly or carelessly done something wrong against the five gems in the past or in the present, knowingly or unknowingly, through body, speech, or mind, and now realize the wrong I have committed, I will refrain from it for the sake of the dharma. O, Venerable One! May the five gems, in particular the Buddha through his compassion, accept and forgive my fault. I will refrain from all future wrongdoing." Then repeat the following:

"To worship the Buddha brings great power; to worship the dharma brings great wisdom; and to worship the saṅgha brings great material gain. By paying respects with incense, flowers, and candles to those who are worthy of veneration, the Buddha or his noble disciples who have surmounted the hindrances, who have suppressed sorrow and grief, and who have reached a state of utter peace, by such an act of worship may I have the opportunity to see the Maitreya (Pāli Metteyya) Buddha. May I, while traveling in the cycle of birth and death, not be reborn in the lower worlds before the Maitreya Buddha, now being worshiped by the gods, appears. May this merit enable me to reach nirvāṇa."

Having repeated this the meditator prostrates three times and then worships the triple gem with the words [in Pāli], "So it is that he is well preached, well trained. . . ." Find a place that is quiet and uncrowded. Enter there and sit in a meditation posture, putting the right foot on the left thigh and the left foot on the right thigh with the legs firmly against the ground. Sitting upright, put the two hands together in front of the forehead, and repeat three times, "Namo buddhāya, namo dhammāya, namo sanghāya" ["Homage to the Buddha, the dharma, and the saṅgha"]. Then repeat three times [in Pāli]: "The Buddha, the world refuge, having defeated the five Māras and realized enlightenment, proclaimed the four truths and turned the wheel of dharma. By proclaiming this truth may the auspicious victory be mine." Afterward repeat three times [in Pāli]: "Just as a man who wants to tame a calf should tie it at the stake, so should [a meditator] vigilantly tie his mind to the mind objects." [Followed by, in Pāli]:

"Homage to the Blessed One, the Worthy One, the Fully Enlightened One. I dedicate my self, my body, and my life to the Enlightened One." Say this once and then repeat three times: "Appamāno buddho; appamāno dhammo; appamāno sangho" followed by one recitation of the translation in Thai, "The Buddha, the dharma, and the saṅgha have virtue beyond measure." Then recite, "Buddho me nātho; dhammo me nātho; sangho me nātho; kammaṭṭhānam me nāthem; kammaṭṭhānadāyakācariyo me nātho," three times [and then repeat in an elaborated Thai translation]: "The Buddha is my refuge; the nine supramundane dharmas [the four paths and their corresponding fruits plus nirvāṇa] and one pariyattidhamma [the Pāli canon] are my refuge; the two saṅghas, that is, the noble saṅgha and ordinary saṅgha, are my refuge; the two meditation subjects, that is, trance and insight are my refuge; the two teachers, that is, those who propagate the Buddha's teaching and those who teach all the meditation subjects are my refuge." Afterward repeat three times [in Pāli, and then in Thai:] "O Blessed One, now I beg the recollection of the Buddha which is the noblest of all. May I be free from all suffering. May the Buddha through his compassion give me the recollection of the Buddha. May rapture and concentration arise in my body and my mind in this seated meditation posture." Afterward repeat three times [in Pāli]: "I take up this holy life; I take up this act of meditation"; [followed by three recitations of the Buddha's auspicious qualities].

Place the hands in the lap, the left under the right, recollecting [first in Pāli and then in Thai, based on the *Akaravatta Sutta*]:

"Thus, the Blessed One is worthy of receiving the offerings of men and gods, having destroyed all defilements by his own wisdom;

"the Blessed One has discovered all things rightly and by himself;

"the Blessed One is endowed with eight kinds of clear vision and fifteen kinds of virtuous conduct;

"the Blessed One is well-gone to nirvāṇa, a place of surpassing worth; the Blessed One knows the world in all ways;

"the Blessed One surpasses men and gods in virtue, concentration, and wisdom;

"the Blessed One tames and guides men to be disciples, and establishes them in the righteous way, the four noble truths;

"the Blessed One teaches men and gods by means of the here and now, of the life to come, and of the ultimate goal, nirvāṇa;

"the Blessed One discovered the four profound, noble truths by himself and awakened others to them;

"the Blessed One is endowed with special, incomparable attributes and qualities which arouse joy in those who see them."

Repeat three times [in Pāli]: "O, the worthy, fully enlightened Buddha!"] and then take the rosary and hold it before the forehead, repeating: "Buddho, Buddho" for a hundred or a thousand beads. Recollect the Buddha's virtue, "Buddho," [saying in Thai]: "The Enlightened One discovered the four profound, noble truths, and he freed himself from the fetters of Māra, that is to say, ignorance and desire; he also freed all beings from them; he overcame by himself the suffering of the cycle of birth and death and also helped others to surmount it. The Enlightened One is endowed with special attributes."

Alternate between this recollection and counting beads. Stop after completing one rosary [108 beads]. Then repeat the same thing again and again. Rapture and tranquility will surely arise through the power of the extraordinary virtue of the Buddha.

The meditator who takes up the recollecting the Buddha meditation subject should respectfully recollect and establish a strong faith in the Buddha's virtues, recalling their extraordinary and immeasurable quality. A strong faith in the Buddha's virtues is one that persists even in the face of someone who threatens, "Don't believe in the Buddha or I'll cut off your head." With such an unshakable faith one who meditates on the Buddha's virtues realizes rapture and tranquillity.

FIVEFOLD RAPTURE

The fivefold rapture—minor rapture, momentary rapture, flood of rapture, uplifting rapture, and pervading rapture [*Visuddhimagga* 143]—will surely appear to the meditator who recalls the recollecting the Buddha meditation subject and who is endowed with five faculties of faith, mindfulness, effort, tranquillity, and wisdom. When minor rapture arises in meditators it will make their hair stand on end but then gradually disappear; when momentary rapture arises, the meditator is suffused with a sudden happiness that disappears as quickly as lightning; when the flood of rapture arises the meditator's body is flooded with the feeling of joy, which will gradually disappear like the tossing of the waves of the sea. When uplifting rapture arises it is very strong; it makes the whole body shake and tremble. The meditator will fall to the left or to the right, bow down, clap hands and feet, sit down, stand up, and then run around filled with strange emotions. The meditators will cry and laugh and will not be able to shut their eyes or mouths. The veins will protrude and the blood feel both hot and cold. The body will feel as if it is expanding and will levitate the length of a finger span, a cubit, an arm's length, or one wa [two meters]; or, the meditator may [experience the sensation of] diving down into the water.

The signs mentioned above are all a consequence of the fourth uplifting rapture. They are not a cause for worry, not a sign of madness or insanity, and are not disruptive. Instead, they are the power of rapture which is good and occurs through the Buddha's power in accord with the meditator's accumulated merit. If women, men, laymen, or monks encounter the aforementioned uplifting rapture, they must not be worried or doubtful. All these signs are positive. Those who practice meditation arduously will surely encounter all aspects of the above-mentioned aspects of uplifting rapture. Some may encounter only one or two aspects, but for those with highly trained minds the power of uplifting rapture will be very strong. For those who have a little training the power of uplifting rapture will be moderate.

One should strive for the arising of uplifting rapture but then should not cling to it when it appears, in order that pervading rapture may have a chance to arise. Thus, the meditator who attains a powerful uplifting rapture should reflect: "Now I have abandoned uplifting rapture. May it vanish completely from my mind and my body. May only stable rapture and tranquillity arise in my heart." Repeat this three times. One should resume meditation when the uplifting rapture has arisen and disappeared. If it appears again, the meditator should strive as before to abandon it until it has absolutely vanished. . . .

When the pervading rapture arises it fills the body with happiness, pervading the whole body in the same way as water flows into and fills ponds and rivers. Upon the arising of pervading rapture, *upacārasamādhi* [access concentration] emerges. This samādhi suppresses the disorder and unrest of the mind, and the mental faculties function quite slowly. It is a stable, unshakable, and joyful state. The mind will rest firmly and tranquilly on one's chosen contemplation object. Access concentration will occur to the meditator only by means of recollecting the Buddha meditation. Ecstasy trance (*appaṇāsamādhi*) will not arise [without it]. Recollecting the Buddha meditation is very powerful and meritorious.

When the meditator continuously reflects on the Buddha's virtues, his mind fully occupied by "Buddho," he will not be overwhelmed by lust, hatred, or delusion. The hindrances will be uprooted by the Buddha's virtues. Rapture, peace, happiness, and tranquillity will vanish when one attains the access trance. The monk who arduously develops recollecting the Buddha will attain an unlimited faith and wisdom as if he were with the Buddha. Fear and anxiety, shame and dread will be overcome as though the meditator were standing before the Buddha himself. He will be unable to do wrong; his body will be a shrine of buddha virtues; he will be as worthy of worship as a reliquary. If he finally realizes the fruit of arhatship, he will surely go to a peaceful place [that is, nirvāṇa]. Thus, the monk filled with wisdom and devoid of carelessness should take up and develop recollecting the Buddha as prescribed above. The meditation subject of recollecting the Buddha is finished [explained].

RECOLLECTION OF THE DHARMA

If meditators want to develop the recollection of the dharma, with hands raised before [their faces] and held together in the shape of the lotus bud they should chant: "*Buddho me nātho, dhammo me nātho, sangho me nātho*" ["I take refuge in the Buddha . . ."] three times and then recite the Dhammābhithuti or Stanzas of Praise to the Dharma three times. They should then rest their hands on their laps and repeat: "The nine noble supramundane dharmas together with the knowledge of the three scriptures [the sūtras (Pāli sutta), vinaya, abhidharma] which prevent those who practice them earnestly from going to hell and which bring all beings to a good reward, are well proclaimed by the Buddha." The dharma is excellent in the beginning, the middle, and the end, perfect and pure in meaning and detail, and capable of destroying all defilements. [The dharma is]: sandiṭṭhiko—seen by the noble ones by their own wisdom; akāliko—uninterrupted by the time, [and], brings instant reward; ehipassiko—challenges others to come and see the Buddha's path; opanayiko—leads the mind [to the knowledge that] the Buddha developed the path and discovered nirvāṇa by himself. Then repeat "bhagavatā dhammao" three times and recite "dhammo dhammao" repeatedly for a hundred or a thousand times. Conclude by recollecting the virtue of the true dharma as follows: "The nine supramundane dharmas together with the knowledge of the three scriptures prevent those who practice them earnestly from going to hell. Instead, they bring all beings to a good place, destroy all defilements and bring all beings to a good place." The meditation subject of recollecting the dharma is now finished [explained].

RECOLLECTION OF THE SAṄGHA

If meditators want to develop the recollection of the virtues of the community of the Buddha's disciples, they should recite, as in the case of the dharma, [the Saṅghābhithuti or Stanzas in Praise of the Saṅgha; in these verses the monastic order is said to be an "incomparable field of merit for the world"] three times.

Then rest [the raised and folded] hands on the lap and repeat [the following Pāli verses] three times, followed by one recitation of [the Thai translation]:

"Bhagavato sāvakasaṅgho—The community of the Blessed One's disciples, supaṭipanno—has entered on the good way;

"Bhagavato sāvakasaṅgho—The community of the Blessed One's disciples, ujupaṭipanno—has entered on the straight way through their mouth, body, and heart;

"Bhagavato sāvakasaṅgho—The community of the Blessed One's disciples, ñāyapaṭipanno—has entered on the way with nirvāṇa as the aim;

"Bhagavato sāvakasaṅgho—The community of the Blessed One's disciples, sāmīcipaṭipanno—has entered on the proper way of those who are worthy of proper acts of veneration;

"Yadidam cattāri purisayugāni—Four pairs of people represent the first path and its fruition, the second path and its fruition, the third path and its fruition, and the fourth path and its fruition.

"Esa [bhagavato] sāvakasaṅgho—They represent the community of the Blessed One's disciples, āhuṇeyyo—worthy to receive gifts given by those who believe in the world hereafter;

"Bhagavato sāvakasaṅgho—The community of the Blessed One's disciples, pāhuṇeyyo—is fit for donations prepared and presented with honor;

"Bhagavato sāvakasaṅgho—The community of the Blessed One's disciples, dakkhiṇeyyo—is fit for offerings given by those who expect the three fruitions [stream-enterer, once-returner, never-returner];

"Bhagavato sāvakasaṅgho—The community of the Blessed One's disciples, añjalīkaraṇīyo—is fit for reverential salutation by men and gods;

"Bhagavato sāvakasaṅgho—The community of the Blessed One's disciples, anuttaram puññakkhettam lokassa—is an incomparable field of merit for the world just as the rice field is good for rice cultivation."

Recite [in Pāli]: "The well-trained disciples of the Blessed One" three times; "the Blessed One's disciples" three times; "saṅgho saṅgho" repeatedly up to a hundred or a thousand times, and then recollect the virtues of the saṅgha as follows:

"Sāvakasaṅgho—The community of the Blessed One's disciples has entered the straight path with nirvāṇa as the aim through the body, the mouth, and the heart." The meditation subject of recollecting the saṅgha is finished [explained].

The subsequent sections of the text are similar in style. They admonish the meditator to recollect: the thirty-two bodily parts from the hairs on the head to the urine; loving kindness toward oneself; loving kindness toward all beings; compassion toward all beings; altruistic joy toward all beings; equanimity toward all beings; purity of insight; purity of release from all doubt; insight into the impermanent (*anicca*), unsatisfactory (*dukkha*), and not-self (*anattā*), nature of the self (*nāmarūpa*); the dharma, recognizing that the path to purity is the recognition that all compounded things are impermanent, unsatisfactory, and not-self; the ten kasiṇa or signs of contemplation; ten loathsome states of the body; and the ten recollections. Eight of the ten recollections are identical with Buddhaghosa's final list of meditation subjects. Pannawong substitutes recollection of cessation for recollection of the body, and recollection of the four divine abidings for recollection on peace. In the *Visuddhimagga* the section on recollecting the divine abidings follows the ten meditation subjects.

—17—

Buddhism and the State in Early Japan

William E. Deal

The *Nihon shoki* (or *Nihongi,* "Chronicle of Japan") is Japan's second oldest extant written record. It chronicles the history of Japan from creation to 697 C.E. This text is of particular importance because it narrates the introduction of Buddhism to Japan in 552 C.E. and follows the course of Buddhism's reception among the ruling elite. The *Nihon shoki* was compiled, in part, to legitimate the imperial family's claims to power and authority over an emerging Japanese nation. By the time it was compiled in 720 C.E., Buddhism had already become an important part of the lives of many of the aristocracy, and Buddhist texts, images, and rituals were utilized in the rhetoric of national unity expressed in the text. As the *Nihon shoki* makes clear, Buddhist worship and control of its ecclesial institutions were contested issues between the imperial family and other aristocratic families vying for positions of power and influence. There are numerous Buddhist themes that appear in the *Nihon shoki,* but those connecting Buddhism and politics are particularly important. In these passages, Buddhist rituals often have both spiritual and political implications.

Part of the initial struggle over whether or not to accept Buddhism was couched in terms of the indigenous gods (*kami*) and their "feelings" toward the Buddha, a foreign kami. This debate mirrored the struggle for political power in the court between the Soga family, who were supporters of Buddhism, and families traditionally associated with Shintō, such as the Mononobe and Nakatomi. Buddhism must have represented a powerful threat to the existing Shintō hierarchy, and its power and influence at court. Buddhism, of course, won the day, but not without a struggle, as the passages translated below clearly show.

It is likely that as Buddhism was gaining popularity among certain aristocratic families, the imperial family needed to take control of this powerful ideology. The *Nihon shoki* represents Buddhism as a "commodity" that could be offered in tribute from the Korean king to the Japanese emperor, and as something for the imperial family to accept or deny on the basis of consultation with other aristocratic families. Other sources indicate that Buddhism was probably brought to Japan by envoys and traders before its official date of introduction, but by presenting Buddhism as the prerogative of the imperial family, this powerful and authoritative continental religion was officially placed in the custody of the ruling elite.

In addition to the connection between Buddhism and internal politics, the *Nihon shoki* depicts the strong connection between Japan and Korea. Japan had laid claim to parts of Korea since the sixth century, and many entries from the *Nihon shoki* make note of the difficulties of this relationship. Despite the apparent military and political advantage that Japan had over parts of Korea, early Japanese Buddhists needed the assistance of Korean monks to make sense of the many texts, images, and rituals that were central to the Buddhist tradition. One of the ways in which Korean kingdoms paid tribute to the Japanese was by sending them Buddhist teachers and Buddhist ritual implements and images. Korean Buddhists thus played a pivotal role in the propagation of Buddhism in Japan, both in terms of expounding Buddhist teachings and in taking leading roles, often through imperial appointment, in the development of monastic institutions and ecclesial rules. For instance, in 624 C.E., the *Nihon shoki* reports that the Korean monk Ekan was appointed archbishop. We are left to wonder if this was because there were not yet enough qualified Japanese monks to fill positions of authority in the Buddhist hierarchy.

Once Buddhism was accepted in Japan, the ruling elite found it in their best interest to control the increasing power of the monasteries. There are several passages that report the efforts of the government to control ecclesial power through monastic regulations. One of the incidents that led to stronger control occurred in the year 623 C.E., when a priest is reported to have struck his grandfather with an ax. This incident prompted Empress Suiko to insist on the implementation of monastic laws and a system of monk-superintendents to oversee the monasteries and enforce monastic laws, thereby ensuring state control of Buddhist institutions. The extent of imperial control over Buddhism is suggested in a passage from 689 C.E. in which permission to take Buddhist vows must be secured from the empress.

Nihon shoki passages suggest that there was not always a strong distinction drawn between the activities and functions of monastics and bureaucrats. Priests sometimes served as political envoys, and government bureaucrats were involved in Buddhist activities such as overseeing temple construction, preparing festivals for temples, and making votive images for the sake of an empress's illness.

Buddhist rituals were often connected to the national interest. Rituals held a central place in the spirituality of early Japanese Buddhists and extended to political concerns. For instance, Buddhist rituals were often utilized to combat the ravages of nationwide epidemics and to end excessive rain that threatened the agricultural foundations of the early Japanese economy. The national interest and the personal interests of individual aristocrats overlapped, and Buddhism flourished, in part, because of the patronage of the rich and powerful. Monks and nuns were often invited to imperial palaces to participate in Buddhist assemblies sponsored by aristocrats. Monastics would also conduct rituals meant to cure a sick emperor or other powerful officials.

Finally, it should be pointed out that women apparently played a prominent role in the early history of Japanese Buddhism. Nuns were given important responsibilities for carrying out Buddhist rituals, and were sent to Korea to learn more about Buddhism so that they could bring back to Japan a deeper understanding of the dharma. Soga no Umako, the powerful aristocrat and promoter of Buddhism, is portrayed as holding the nuns in great esteem and reverence, providing them with temples and other necessities of the monastic life.

The translations here are based on Sakamoto Tarō, Ienaga Saburō, Inoue Mitsusada, and Ōno Susumu, eds., *Nihon shoki,* Vol. 2, Nihon Koten Bungaku Taikei 68 (Tokyo: Iwanami Shoten, 1965). Bureaucratic ranks, lists of names of otherwise unknown people, alternative readings for names, and other such material has sometimes been omitted from the translations in the interest of readability. This translation has utilized the Japanese pronunciation of Korean names and places. The translated passages are arranged in chronological order.

Selections from the *Nihon shoki*

552 C.E. Winter, 10th Month

King Seimei of the Korean kingdom of Kudara (also known as King Sei) dispatched Kishi, Nurishichikei, and other retainers to Japan. They offered as tribute a gold and copper statue of Śākyamuni Buddha, ritual banners and canopies, and several volumes of sūtras and commentaries. In a separate declaration, King Sei praised the merit of propagating and worshiping the dharma, stating, "This dharma is superior to all the others. It is difficult to understand and difficult to attain. Neither the Duke of Chou nor Confucius was able to comprehend it. This dharma can produce immeasurable, limitless meritorious karmic consequence, leading to the attainment of supreme wisdom. It is like a person who has a wish-fulfilling gem whose every desire is granted. The jewel of this wonderful dharma is also like this. Every prayer is answered and not a need goes unfulfilled. Moreover, from distant India all the way to China this teaching has been followed and upheld. There is no one who does not revere it. Accordingly, I, King Seimei, your vassal, have humbly dispatched my retainer Nurishichikei to the Imperial Kingdom of Japan to transmit and propagate this teaching, thereby effecting what the Buddha foretold, 'my dharma will spread to the east.' "

This very day the emperor heard this declaration and leapt with joy. He declared to the Korean envoys, "From ancient times to the present we have not heard of such a fine dharma as this. Nevertheless, we cannot ourselves decide whether to accept this teaching." Thereupon the emperor inquired of his assembled officials, "The Buddha presented to us from the country to our west has a face of extreme solemnity. We have never known such a thing before. Should we worship it or not?"

Soga no Iname humbly responded: "The many countries to the west all worship this Buddha. Is it only Japan that will reject this teaching?"

Mononobe no Okoshi and Nakatomi no Kamako together humbly responded: "The rulers of our country have always worshiped throughout the four seasons the 180 deities of heaven and earth. If they now change this and worship the deity of a foreign country, we fear that the deities of our country will become angry."

The emperor declared, "I grant to Soga no Iname the worship of this Buddha in order to test its efficacy."

Soga no Iname knelt down and received the statue. With great joy, he enshrined it in his home at Owarida and devotedly performed the rituals of a world renouncer. He also purified his home at Mukuhara and made it into a temple.

Later, an epidemic afflicted the country and cut short the lives of many people. With the passing of time, more and more people died of this incurable disease. Mononobe no Okoshi and Nakatomi no Kamako together humbly addressed the emperor: "Previously, the counsel we offered went unheeded. As a result, this epidemic has occurred. Now, before it is too late, this situation must be rectified. Throw away the statue of the Buddha at once and diligently seek future blessings."

The emperor responded: "We will do as you have counseled."

The emperor's officials took the Buddha statue and threw it into the waters of the Naniwa canal. They then set fire to the temple in which it was enshrined and burned it to the ground. At this time, although the winds were calm and the sky cloudless, suddenly a fire broke out in the great hall of the Imperial Palace.

577 C.E. Winter, 11th Month, 1st Day

The king of the Korean kingdom of Kudara presented the Japanese envoy Prince Ōwake and his entourage, who were returning to Japan, many volumes of sūtras and sūtra commentaries, a precept master (*risshi*), a meditation master (*zenji*), a nun, a mantra master (*jugon no hakase*), a Buddhist statue maker, and a temple architect, six people in all. They came to be installed at Ōwake's temple in Naniwa.

579 C.E. Winter, 10th Month

The Korean kingdom of Shiragi dispatched an envoy to present tribute to Japan that included a Buddhist statue.

584 C.E. Autumn, 9th Month

Minister Kabuka returned from the Korean kingdom of Kudara, bringing with him a stone statue of Maitreya Buddha. Minister Saeki also returned with a Buddhist statue. This same year, Soga no Umako requested these two statues. He then dispatched Kuratsukuri no Tsuguri Shimedachito and Ikebe no Atai Hita to seek out and bring back practitioners of the dharma. It was only in

Harima Province that they discovered a former Korean monk who had returned to lay life by the name of Eben. Soga no Umako made him his dharma teacher and allowed Shima, the daughter of Shimedachito, to become a nun. She was eleven years old and took the Buddhist name Zenshin. Two of Zenshin's disciples also became nuns: Toyome, Ayahito no Yabo's daughter, who took the Buddhist name Zenzō, and Ishime, Nishikori no Tsubu's daughter, who took the Buddhist name Ezen. Umako, in accord with the Buddha's dharma, reverenced the three nuns. Umako placed Hita no Atai and Shimedachito in charge of the three nuns and commanded them to make offerings of clothing and food. He built a Buddha hall to the east of his house and enshrined there the stone image of Maitreya. Umako had the three nuns prepare offerings of food for a Buddhist assembly. At this time, Shimedachito discovered a relic of the Buddha on the food offering bowl and presented it to Umako. Umako, as a test, placed the relic on an anvil, brandished an iron hammer and pounded the relic. The anvil and hammer were completely smashed, but the relic remained intact. Umako then threw the relic into water, and, following his mental wish, it would either float or sink. As a result, Umako, Ikebe no Hita, and Shimedachito developed a deep faith in the Buddha's dharma and never neglected Buddhist rituals. Umako also built a Buddha hall at his home in Ishikawa. It is from these events that the Buddha's dharma had its beginning in Japan.

584 C.E. Spring, 2nd Month, 15th Day

Soga no Umako built a stūpa to the north of Ōno no Oka and conducted a Buddhist assembly with offerings of food. Shimedachito placed the Buddha relic that he had previously discovered on the top of the stūpa's central pillar.

584 C.E. Spring, 2nd Month, 24th Day

Soga no Umako became sick. A diviner was summoned to explain his condition: "This illness is a curse, the will of the Buddha who was worshiped in your father Iname's day." Hearing this, Umako dispatched a family member to report the diviner's words to Emperor Bidatsu. The emperor proclaimed, "In accord with the diviner's words, worship your father's deity, the Buddha." Umako, receiving this proclamation, worshiped the stone image of Maitreya and prayed for a long life. At this time, an epidemic broke out throughout the country and many people died.

584 C.E. 3rd Month, 1st Day

Mononobe no Moriya and Nakatomi no Katsumi addressed Emperor Bidatsu: "Why did you not follow the advice we offered you? Since the reign of your father, Emperor Kinmei, until your present reign, epidemic has been rife in the land and the nation's people may die out. There is no doubt that this is entirely due to the propagation of the Buddha's dharma by the Soga family."

The emperor declared, "It is evident what must be done. The Buddha's dharma must be abandoned."

584 C.E. 3rd Month, 30th Day

Mononobe no Moriya went to the Soga temple, cut down the stūpa and set fire to it. He also burned the Buddha statue and the Buddha hall. He had the charred remains of the statue thrown into the Naniwa canal. On this day, although there were no clouds, there was wind and rain. Mononobe no Moriya wore a raincoat. He censured Soga no Umako and his followers for practicing the dharma and caused their hearts to fill with shame. Mononobe no Moriya also dispatched Saeki no Mimuro to summon Zenshin and the other nuns who had been provided for by Umako. Umako did not dare disregard this order, and, with tears of sorrow, called the nuns and handed them over to Mimuro. Government officials immediately stripped them of their monastic robes, arrested them, and had them whipped at the Tsubakichi post town. . . .

Once again there was an outbreak of smallpox that killed many people throughout the country. Those suffering from smallpox exclaimed, "It is as if our bodies are being burned, or beaten, or smashed!" While thus crying with despair, they died. Old and young alike secretly said to one another, "Surely this epidemic is retribution for burning the Buddha statue."

584 C.E. Summer, 6th Month

Soga no Umako said to Emperor Bidatsu, "My sickness is not yet healed. If I do not receive assistance from the power of the Buddha, recovery will be impossible." The emperor proclaimed to Umako, "You alone may follow the Buddha's dharma, but such practice is prohibited to others." Accordingly, the three nuns were returned to Umako, who joyfully received them. Lamenting these unprecedented events, Umako bowed down to the ground in homage to the three nuns. Umako rebuilt the temple, welcomed the nuns into it, and, as an offering, provided for their needs. (According to another source, Mononobe no Moriya, Ōmiwa no Sakō, and Nakatomi no Iware together plotted to destroy the Buddha's dharma. They tried to burn the temple and stūpa, and to throw away the Buddha image. Umako interceded and this plan was not carried out.)

585 C.E.

Emperor Yōmei placed his faith in the Buddha's dharma and revered the Way of the Gods (Shintō).

587 C.E. Summer, 4th Month, 2nd Day

Emperor Yōmei performed the rice-harvesting ritual on the river bank at Iware. This day, the emperor became sick and returned to the palace. His ministers in attendance, the emperor addressed them, saying, "I desire to take refuge in the three treasures [the Buddha, the dharma, and the saṅgha]. Deliberate on this matter." The ministers entered the court and considered the emperor's words. Mononobe no Moriya and Nakatomi no Katsumi opposed the emperor's plan, saying, "Why turn away from our national deities and revere a foreign deity? Since ancient times we have never heard of such a thing." Soga no Umako said, "We must follow the emperor's wishes and assist him with his plan. Who would consider a different course of action . . . ?"

The emperor's smallpox grew increasingly severe. When the end of his life drew near, Kuratsukuri no Tasuna, Shimedachito's son, came forward and addressed the emperor: "I, for the sake of the emperor, desire to renounce the world and practice the Buddha's path. I will also construct a sixteen-foot statue of the Buddha and build a temple." The emperor was greatly saddened and moved by these words. The sixteen-foot wooden image of Buddha and attendant bodhisattva images that are now housed in Sakata Temple in Minabuchi are those that Kuratsukuri no Tasuna spoke of.

The emperor died in the great hall of the palace on the 9th day.

587 C.E. Summer, 6th Month, 21st Day

Zenshin and the other nuns said to Soga no Umako: "Renouncing the world takes the precepts as its foundation. We therefore desire to go to the Korean kingdom of Kudara to study and receive the precepts." This month envoys from Kudara came to Japan and Soga no Umako asked them, "Take these nuns to your country and teach them the precepts. When they have completed their studies send them back to Japan." The envoys replied, "When we return to our country we will speak to the king. It will not be too late to have you send the nuns at that time."

588 C.E. Spring, 3rd Month

This year the Korean kingdom of Kudara dispatched envoys and Buddhist priests to Japan with the Buddha's relics as tribute. Kudara also sent government officials with tribute of relics of the Buddha, a precept master and other priests, temple carpenters, stūpa roof makers, tile makers, and a painter of Buddhist pictures. Soga no Umako asked the Kudara priests how to receive the Buddhist precepts. He entrusted Zenshin and the other nuns to the Kudaran envoys and sent them to Kudara to study Buddhism. . . . Umako began construction of the temple Hōkōji.

590 C.E. Spring, 3rd Month

Zenshin and the other nuns who went to study Buddhism in Kudara returned to Japan, taking up residence at the temple Sakuraidera.

590 C.E. Autumn, 10th Month

People entered the mountains to gather wood to be used for Buddhist temple construction. This year the following women renounced the world and became nuns: Zentoku, daughter of Ōtomo no Sadehiko, and the Korean wives of Ōtomo no Sadehiko, Shiragi-hime who became known as Zenmyō, and Kudara-hime who became known as Myōkō. Men of Chinese descent also renounced the world, as did Tasuna, the son of Kuratsukuri no Shimedachito. Tasuna was known as Tokusai, the dharma teacher.

593 C.E. Autumn, 9th Month

This year, construction was begun of the Temple of the Four Heavenly Kings (Shitennōji) at Arahaka in Naniwa.

622 C.E. Autumn, 7th Month

The Korean kingdoms of Shiragi and Mimana dispatched envoys to Japan to present as tribute a Buddhist image, a gold stūpa, Buddha relics, a large flag used in esoteric rituals, and twelve small ritual flags. The image of Buddha was enshrined at the temple Utsumasa-dera in Kadono. The relics of the Buddha, the gold stūpa and the ritual flags were consecrated at the temple Shitennōji.

623 C.E. Summer, 4th Month, 3rd Day

A monk took an ax and struck his grandfather. When Empress Suiko learned of this, she summoned the Ōomi, Soga no Umako, and issued the following imperial edict: "A world renouncer should earnestly take refuge in the three treasures [the Buddha, dharma, saṅgha] and fully uphold the rules of monastic conduct. How can one, without repentance, easily commit evil acts in violation of the precepts? Now I have heard that there is a monk who struck his grandfather. Therefore, gather together all the monks and nuns of the various temples and question them. If what I have heard is true, serious punishment must be meted out."

Accordingly, the monks and nuns of the various temples were assembled and questioned. The monk who had violated the precepts, as well as all the other monks and nuns, were about to be punished. At this time, the monk Kanroku from the Korean kingdom of Kudara presented a memorial to the empress, saying: "The Buddha's dharma came from India to China, and, three hundred years later, China transmitted it to Kudara. A mere hundred years after this King Seimei of Kudara heard of the wisdom of the Emperor Kinmei and offered in tribute a statue of the Buddha and sūtras. Since then, not even one hundred years have passed so that at this time the monks and nuns have not yet learned the monastic precepts and easily violate them. As a result, the monks and nuns are afraid because they do not know what is right. I respectfully request that the monks and nuns who have not violated the precepts be pardoned and not punished. This would be an act of great merit." Thereupon, the empress granted this request.

13th Day. The following edict was issued: "Even followers of the way violate the dharma. How then can the laity be instructed? Therefore, from this time forward, we will appoint an archbishop and bishop who shall oversee the monks and nuns."

17th Day. The monk Kanroku was appointed archbishop and Kuratsukuri no Tokushaku was appointed bishop. This same day, Azumi no Muraji was appointed head of the dharma.

Autumn, 9th Month, 3rd Day. There was a review of temples, and the monks and nuns. The reason temples were built, and the reasons why monks and nuns entered the Buddhist path, as well as the year, month, and day of entry, were recorded in detail. At this time, there were 46 temples, 816 monks, and 569 nuns: in total, 1,385 people.

624 C.E. Spring, 1st Month, 7th Day

The king of the Korean kingdom of Kudara sent as tribute to Japan the monk Ekan, who was appointed archbishop.

645 C.E. 1st Year

Emperor Kōtoku revered the Buddha's dharma, but he reviled the Way of the Gods (Shintō), as is evidenced from his cutting down the trees of the Ikukunitama Shrine.

645 C.E. 1st Year, 8th Month, 8th Day

A messenger was dispatched to the temple Ō-dera ["Great Temple," perhaps a reference to the Asuka-dera]. Gathering the monks and nuns together, he pronounced an imperial edict: "In the thirteenth year of the reign of Emperor Kinmei, King Mei [Seimei] of the Korean kingdom of Kudara offered the Buddha's dharma in tribute to Japan. At this time, the ministers were united in their desire not to accept it. Only Soga no Iname placed faith in the dharma. Thus, the emperor decreed to Soga no Iname that he would be allowed to revere the dharma. In the reign of Emperor Bidatsu, Soga no Umako, out of respect for the deeds of his father, deeply revered the Buddha's dharma. However, some ministers did not place faith in the dharma and tried to destroy it completely. Emperor Bidatsu issued an edict to Soga no Umako decreeing that he should revere the dharma. In the reign of Empress Suiko, Soga no Umako constructed sixteen-foot embroidered and copper images of the Buddha on her behalf. He extolled the Buddha's teaching and revered the monks and nuns. We now wish to reiterate our desire to revere the Buddha's true teaching and to shine widely the light of this great dharma. Therefore, we appoint the following priests dharma teachers: The Korean dharma masters Fukuryō, Eun, Jōan, Ryōun, and Eshi, and the temple heads Sōmin, Dōtō, Erin, and Emyō. We separately appoint dharma teacher Emyō the head priest of the temple Kudara-dera. These dharma teachers will thoroughly instruct the monastic community and lead them in the practice of the Buddha's teaching so the Buddha's dharma is properly followed. From the emperor to the managerial class, we will all assist in the building of temples. We will now appoint temple head priests and lay administrators. Temples will be visited to determine the actual situation pertaining to monks and nuns, their servants, and their rice fields. All findings will be presented to the emperor." Thereupon, Kume no Omi, Miwa no Shikobu no Kimi, and Nukatabe no Muraji Oi were appointed heads of the dharma.

650 C.E. Winter, 10th Month

This month work was begun on a sixteen-foot embroidery image of the Buddha with his attendant bodhisattvas, the eight Buddhist protective deities, and thirty-six other images. This year Ōkuchi received an imperial edict to carve one thousand Buddhist images.

651 C.E. Spring, 3rd Month, 14th Day
The sixteen-foot embroidery image of the Buddha was completed.

651 C.E. Spring, 3rd Month, 15th Day
The former empress Kōgyoku invited ten dharma teachers and held a Buddhist assembly with offerings of food.

651 C.E. Winter, 12th Month, Last Day
More than 1,200 monks and nuns were invited to the Ajifu palace to read the entire Buddhist canon (*issaikyō*). That evening, more than 2,700 lamps were lit in the palace garden and sūtras were read.

671 C.E. Winter, 10th Month, 8th Day
One hundred Buddhist statues were consecrated in the imperial palace.

677 C.E. Autumn, 8th Month, 15th Day
A great Buddhist assembly with offerings of food, accompanied by a reading of the Buddhist canon, was held at the Asuka-dera. Thereupon, Emperor Temmu stood at the south gate of the temple in reverence to the three treasures. At this time, the emperor decreed to the assembled aristocrats to present one person each to renounce the world. These world renouncers were all ordained in accordance with the emperor's wish without regard to gender or age. Accordingly, they all participated in the assembly.

679 C.E. Winter, 10th Month, 13th Day
Emperor Temmu issued an edict prescribing regulations concerning the monastic garb of monks and nuns, the color of their robes, and the horses and attendants that accompany them in the streets.

679 C.E. Winter, 10th Month, 17th Day
This month Emperor Temmu issued an edict decreeing: "Monks and nuns always reside in temples and uphold the three treasures. But when they get old and sick they suffer from lying for a long time in their narrow quarters, unable to move about. They pollute the purity of the temple. Therefore, from now on, their family or friends will construct one or two small dwellings in the empty spaces on temple grounds where the elderly can nourish their bodies and the sick can take medicine."

680 C.E. Winter, 11th Month, 12th Day
The empress was sick. Emperor Temmu vowed on her behalf to begin building the temple Yakushiji. In accord with this vow, one hundred people entered the Buddhist path. As a result, the empress recovered.

680 C.E. Winter, 11th Month, 26th Day

Emperor Temmu was sick. Therefore, one hundred people entered the Buddhist path. He quickly recovered.

683 C.E. Autumn, 7th Month, 5th Day

This summer, for the first time, monks and nuns were invited to the palace for the rainy season retreat. Accordingly, thirty people of pure conduct were chosen to renounce the world.

683 C.E. Autumn, 7th Month, 20th Day

There was a drought that began this month and lasted until the eighth month. The Korean monk Dōzō successfully prayed for rain.

685 C.E. Spring, 3rd Month, 27th Day

It was decreed that every household in every province would construct a Buddhist altar to enshrine a Buddha image and sūtras for the purpose of worship and making offerings.

685 C.E. Summer, 5th Month, 5th Day

Emperor Temmu traveled to Asuka-dera and offered precious jewels in reverence to the Buddha.

685 C.E. Autumn, 9th Month, 24th Day

Because Emperor Temmu was sick, sūtras were chanted for three days at the temples Daikandaiji, Kawahara-dera, and Asuka-dera. Accordingly, rice was given to the three temples in varying amounts.

689 C.E. Spring, 1st Month, 3rd Day

Maro and Kanaori, sons of Shiriko of Michinoku province, requested permission to take the tonsure and become monks. Empress Jitō issued an edict decreeing, "Although Maro and Kanaori are young, they are refined and unselfish. Having arrived at this point in their lives, they wish only to eat vegetarian food and observe the monastic precepts. In accord with their request, they are granted permission to renounce the world and practice the Buddhist path."

691 C.E. 2nd Month, 1st Day

Empress Jitō issued an edict to her ministers decreeing: "In the reign of Emperor Temmu Buddha halls and sūtra repositories were constructed and every month the six precept-keeping days were observed. The emperor would from time to time dispatch his attendants to inquire about these matters. My reign will also be like this. Therefore, endeavor to revere the Buddha's dharma."

691 C.E. Summer, 6th Month, 19th Day

An imperial edict was issued, saying: "This summer's rainfall has been excessive. We fear that this will most certainly cause damage to the crops. From morning until evening we worry about where the fault lies for this situation. Ministers and officials are forbidden to drink alcohol and eat meat. Be virtuous and repent your transgressions. The monks and nuns of all the temples in the capital and the surrounding provinces will chant sūtras for five days. It is hoped that these measures will be effective in ending the rain."

694 C.E. Summer, 5th Month, 11th Day

One hundred copies of the *Golden Light Sūtra* (*Konkōmyōkyō;* Sanskrit *Suvarṇaprabhāsottama-sūtra*) were sent to the provinces. They are to be read, without fail, every year on the eighth day of the first month. Gifts to the monastics for rendering this service will be provided for from the resources of each province.

696 C.E. Winter, 12th Month, 1st Day

An imperial edict was issued decreeing that the *Golden Light Sūtra* be read, and that, accordingly, on the last day of the twelfth month of every year ten people of pure conduct will be ordained into Buddhism.

697 C.E. Autumn, 7th Month, 29th Day

Ministers and officials held a dharma assembly for the consecration of Buddhist images at the temple Yakushiji.

—18—

Original Enlightenment Thought in the Nichiren Tradition

Jackie Stone

The *Lotus Sūtra,* with its universal promise that "all shall attain the buddha way," has long been revered in the Japanese Buddhist tradition and has inspired numerous interpretations. For centuries it was transcribed, recited, and lectured upon for the sake of worldly benefits, protection of the nation, eradication of sins, rebirth in the Buddha's pure land, and the attainment of buddhahood. Two major Buddhist traditions claim it as their central scripture: Tendai (Chinese Tian-tai) Buddhism, introduced to Japan by Saichō (767–822) in the early ninth century and closely associated with the nobles of the court, and Nichiren Buddhism, which began in the medieval period with the Buddhist teacher Nichiren (1222–1282) and drew many of its early adherents from the rising warrior class.

The writings presented here all interpret the *Lotus Sūtra* as enabling one to realize enlightenment "in this lifetime," rather than over the course of successive births. They have been handed down for centuries within the Nichiren tradition as Nichiren's own writings, yet they reflect little that is considered unique to his thought, and in fact stand much closer to the medieval Tendai tradition from which Nichiren Buddhism emerged. Today, many Japanese scholars of Nichiren Buddhism question whether Nichiren wrote them at all. Regardless of authorship, however, these texts hold considerable interest for the study of *Lotus Sūtra*-related Buddhism in Japan, both philosophically—for their view of what enlightenment entails—and historically, in showing how a major Tendai discourse, that of original enlightenment thought, was incorporated into the Nichiren tradition.

By around the late eleventh to early twelfth centuries, Tendai monks had begun to write down and expand upon an earlier oral tradition interpreting the *Lotus Sūtra* as a unique statement of what they termed the doctrine of original enlightenment (*hongaku hōmon*). Simply put, this means that expressions such as "attaining enlightenment" are merely a manner of speaking, for enlightenment is not something to be "attained" as though it were somehow apart from oneself. Rather, one is enlightened inherently, and has only to realize it. This claim rests on traditional Mahāyāna notions of nonduality: Delusion and enlightenment, ultimate reality and the mundane phenomenal world are mutually dependent categories; hence they have no independent existence apart from one another, and in an ultimate or ontological (as opposed to an experiential) sense, cannot be distinguished. Original enlightenment thinkers extended this logic of nonduality to assert that ordinary persons, although they do not realize it, are buddhas just as they are. Original enlightenment thought collapses the conventional, linear model of Buddhist practice as a progression through successive stages of spiritual development spanning many lifetimes, by which the ordinary person is gradually transformed into a buddha. Rather, enlightenment is defined as direct insight into the identity of oneself at this moment and the ultimate reality—an insight which, Tendai writings suggest, can be gained, lost, and regained any number of times. One practices Buddhism, not to "attain" enlightenment as a goal external to oneself, but to see—and then to establish the insight—that one is enlightened already. In this moment of insight, one's entire experience of the phenomenal world is transvalued and infused with meaning, as all transient things, just as they are, are seen to manifest ultimate reality. As Nichiren wrote in an early work much influenced by this idea: "When we attain the enlightenment of the *Lotus Sūtra*, our own body, subject to birth and death, is precisely unborn and unperishing. And the land is also thus. The oxen, horses, and other animals in this land are all buddhas, and the grasses and trees, sun and moon, are all the holy saṅgha [Buddhist community]."

In the Tendai tradition, the original enlightenment doctrine was for a long time cast in the form of a secret teaching. This can probably be attributed partly to the influence of Shingon esoteric Buddhism, which stresses secret transmission; partly to the attempts of Tendai teaching lineages to enhance the prestige of their doctrine by surrounding it with an aura of secrecy; and partly to a legitimate concern that the original enlightenment doctrine could easily be misconstrued to mean that, since one is a buddha already, Buddhist practice is therefore unnecessary.

Tendai Buddhists sought to assimilate a wide range of practices to the *Lotus Sūtra*, including various forms of meditation, sūtra recitation, esoteric rites, and devotional practices. A radically different approach was taken by Nichiren, originally a Tendai monk, who initiated a new tradition that would eventually bear his name. Nichiren shared with the Pure Land Buddhist teacher Hōnen (1133–1212) and other Buddhists of his day a conviction that the world had entered the final dharma age (*mappō*), a period of decline when attaining enlightenment by means of traditional practices was thought to be all but impossible. He was therefore concerned to find an easily accessible way by which all men and women could obtain salvation in this degenerate era. Like Hōnen, Nichiren propounded a single way of practice, one that he claimed was universally and exclusively valid and contained the benefits of all other good practices within itself. This practice was simply cultivating faith in the *Lotus Sūtra* and chanting its daimoku or title in the formula "Namu myōhō renge kyō." *Myōhō-renge-kyō* (Chinese *Miao-fa lian-*

hua jing), is the title in Japanese pronunciation of the *Lotus Sūtra*—literally, "Sūtra of the Lotus Blossom of the Wonderful Law [Dharma]." In Tendai Buddhism, this title had come to designate not only the name of the sūtra but ultimate reality itself. *Namu,* from Sanskrit *namas,* is an expression of devotion. For Nichiren, the words "Myōhō renge kyō" contained the enlightenment of the eternal buddha spoken of in the *Lotus Sūtra* and were thus the seed of buddhahood for all people of the final dharma age. In the act of chanting "namu myōhō renge kyō" with faith, he taught, one receives the seed of buddhahood, thus accessing the eternal buddha's enlightenment—the ultimate reality that is the truth of the *Lotus Sūtra*—and attaining buddhahood in this very body.

How far Nichiren himself espoused the original enlightenment doctrine is hard to determine, as it is not possible in all cases to distinguish genuine from apocryphal texts in the body of writings that the Nichiren tradition has attributed to him. Indisputably authentic works, such as those that have survived in Nichiren's own handwriting, collectively suggest that although Nichiren was strongly influenced by this idea in his earlier years, the emphasis of his mature teaching was not the originally inherent nature of enlightenment even prior to practice but rather the absolute necessity of faith in the *Lotus Sūtra* and the chanting of its title as the sole way of salvation in the final dharma age. Nevertheless, some of the writings traditionally handed down as his work link the two emphases, interpreting Nichiren's practice of chanting the daimoku in terms of original enlightenment thought. Many of those writings questioned by modern scholars as possibly apocryphal fall into this category. At this point, it is not certain whether they might indeed be Nichiren's writings, dating perhaps from his early years when he was still strongly influenced by the medieval Tendai original enlightenment discourse, or whether they are forgeries by those scholar-monks within some of the later Nichiren communities who maintained close ties with Tendai institutions and tended to interpret Nichiren's teachings in terms of the Tendai original enlightenment doctrine. Not all Nichiren Buddhist denominations now value these writings equally: the academic wing of Nichirenshū tends to treat them as secondary texts, whereas Nichiren Shōshū continues to regard them as authentic works of Nichiren. All three pieces included here belong to this problematic group. They should be read with the idea in mind that they may represent not so much Nichiren's thought as one of several interpretations that developed within the later Nichiren tradition.

The first text is abridged from a much longer essay called the "The Division of Teachings Established by All Buddhas throughout Time" ("Sanze shobutsu sōkanmon kyōsō hairyū"). It contains little that would relate it explicitly to Nichiren's teaching but is typical rather of Tendai original enlightenment thought, to which it serves as a good introduction. Its central image, the contrast between dreaming and waking as a metaphor for the difference between ordinary deluded consciousness and the enlightened state, has a long history in Buddhism, whose very name comes from the Indic root *budh,* "to wake up." In this writing, however, it is given a unique twist: "Dreaming" is shown to include not only ordinary deluded consciousness but also conventional views of enlightenment as a state that has to be reached in the future or acquired as though it were something external to oneself. Teachings that advocate steadily accumulating virtue and eradicating mental defilements as the way to liberation—a view of the path equated here with the Buddha's pre-*Lotus Sūtra* teachings—are said to concern only "the good and evil that occur in dreams." They must be revalued in light of the *Lotus Sūtra,* which is intended in contrast to "rouse the beings into the waking reality of original enlightenment." Enlightenment is presented not as the gradual eradication of defilements but as direct insight into the identity of one's own mind with the unconditioned, ultimate reality. This is illustrated in the text with a modified version of the famous butterfly dream of the Chinese sage Zhuang-zi. Just as a person when dreaming and the same person when awake are not separate persons, so ordinary people and the Buddha are not separate beings. Nevertheless, the distinction between delusion and enlightenment, although without ontological status, is empirically real, just as the experience of dreaming differs significantly from that of waking. Hence the need for Buddhist practice to transform one's consciousness and "wake up" to the fact of being enlightened originally.

The second and third pieces explicitly link the notion of original enlightenment to the practice of chanting the daimoku advocated by Nichiren, presenting it as the direct way of realizing one's inherently enlightened nature. The first of these two pieces is the concluding section of an essay called "The Ten Suchnesses" ("Junyoze ji"), a reworking of a Tendai piece long attributed to—though probably not the work of—Genshin (942–1017), dealing with original enlightenment ideas. The section included here was added when the earlier work was adapted for Nichiren Buddhist needs to explain original enlightenment in terms of the daimoku. The division of practitioners into three levels of capacity as seen in this text is more typical of Tendai thought than of Nichiren, who stressed merely that the *Lotus Sūtra* saves everyone equally. However, the idea expressed here, that a single utterance of the daimoku contains the merit of reciting the entire sūtra, can be found in writings known to be indisputably those of Nichiren.

The third piece, "Becoming a Buddha in this Single Lifetime" ("*Isshō jōbutsu shō*") is a complete essay, traditionally said to date from the early years of Nichiren's teaching career. Whether or not it is in fact his work, this writing stresses an idea of considerable importance in his thought, namely, the immanence of the Buddha's pure land in this present world. Nichiren vehemently objected to the position of Hōnen and other Pure Land Buddhists who urged their followers to aspire to rebirth in the buddha Amida's pure land in the western quarter of the universe. Because the subjective realm (the individual) and the objective realm (the land that the individual inhabits) are nondual, Nichiren asserted, when the individual realizes buddhahood, that person's world becomes the buddha land. For Nichiren, the realization of the pure land in the present world was no mere subjective insight but would bring about a concrete transformation of the visible realm, making it peaceful and harmonious. This strand in Nichiren's teaching no doubt underlies the fact that many modern Nichiren movements have been associated with programs of political action and social reform.

Brief mention should be made of the Tendai terminology used in these texts.

Enlightenment is sometimes described as realizing the identity of oneself and the universe or cosmos. This is expressed with such statements as "the ten realms are one's body and mind," meaning that the ten realms of existence, from hell-dwellers to buddhas, into which Tendai cosmology divides the world, are all inherent in oneself—an expression of the identity of the practitioner with the totality of all that is. At other times, the moment of insight is described as a consciousness of the identity of oneself with ultimate reality, or with its personification as a cosmic buddha. A typical expression would be that "oneself is the tathāgata of original enlightenment who possesses three bodies in one"—meaning that the practitioner is identified with the perfect tathāgata (buddha) who possesses all three kinds of bodies that buddhas in the Mahāyāna may have: the physical body (corresponding to compassion), the subtle body (corresponding to wisdom), and the dharma body, or ultimate reality itself.

The translations are from Risshō Daigaku Nichiren Kyōgaku Kenkyūjo, ed., *Shōwa teihon Nichiren Shōnin ibun,* 4 vols. (Minobu-chō, Yamanashi Prefecture: Minobusan Kuon-ji, 1952–59; revised 1989; abbreviated as *STN*. The first piece is excerpts from *STN* 2:1686–1705. The second piece is from *STN* 3:2031–33; the third is from *STN* 1:42–45.

Further Reading

On Nichiren, see Philip Yampolsky, ed., with Burton Watson, trans., *Selected Writings of Nichiren* (New York: Columbia University Press, 1990), which contains the "five major writings" accepted by all Nichiren denominations as Nichiren's most important essays, and Alicia and Daigan Matsunaga, *Foundation of Japanese Buddhism,* Vol. 2, *The Mass Movement* (Los Angeles and Tokyo: Buddhist Books International, 1976), pp. 137–81. On Tendai original enlightenment thought, see Tamura Yoshirō, "The Critique of Original Awakening Thought in Shōshin and Dōgen," *Japanese Journal of Religious Studies* 11:2–3 (1984), 243–66, and "Japanese Culture and the Tendai Concept of Original Enlightenment," *Japanese Journal of Religious Studies* 14:2–3 (1987), 203–10.

Of Dreams and Waking Reality

Now the sacred teachings of the Buddha's lifetime were all expounded over a period of fifty years and constitute what is termed the body of sūtras. They may be divided into two categories: those the Buddha expounded in order to instruct others, and those he expounded as "self-practice" [that is, the direct expression of his own enlightenment]. Those of the first category, the sūtras for instructing others, are the scriptural teachings that the Buddha expounded for a period of forty-two years before preaching the *Lotus Sūtra.* They are termed the provisional teachings and are also called skillful means. . . . Among the ten realms of existence, they correspond to the first nine realms [from hell-dwellers to bodhisattvas, which represent the unenlightened states]. And in terms of dreams and waking reality, they concern the good and evil that occur in dreams. Dreams correspond to the provisional, while the waking state corresponds to the true. Dreams are temporary phenomena having no substantial nature; that is why they are termed provisional. Waking reality constantly abides and is the unchanging essence of the mind; therefore, it is termed true. The various sūtras of the first forty-two years set forth matters of good and evil occurring in the dream of birth and death, and on that account, they are called provisional teachings. They are the scriptural teachings of preparatory, expedient means, by which the Buddha sought to entice and lead the dreaming beings, in order to startle and rouse them into the waking reality of the *Lotus Sūtra.* . . . Because the dream of birth and death is provisional, without self-nature or substance, it is the model of transient things. Therefore, it is termed a false conception. The waking reality of original enlightenment is genuine; because it is the mind separated from birth and extinction, it is the model of true reality. Therefore, it is called the true aspect. Making clear the two words "provisional" and "true" in this light, one should understand the distinction within the sacred teachings of the Buddha's lifetime between the provisional teachings expounded in order to instruct others and the true teaching that represents the Buddha's self-practice. . . .

In the case of the provisional teachings, one may exert himself in difficult and painful practices and think that he has at last contrived to become a buddha, but this is only a provisional buddhahood obtained in a dream. When contrasted with the waking reality of original enlightenment, it is in fact not buddhahood at all. Because no buddha ever obtained the ultimate fruit of enlightenment through these provisional teachings, we speak of the teaching existing but not the person. And could even the teaching be real? One who gives precedence to these provisional teachings and practices them goes astray with respect to the meaning of the sacred teachings. The Buddha Śākyamuni [Sage of the Śākyas] taught and left behind for us proof that one cannot become a buddha through the provisional teachings, thus enabling the beings of the last age to open their wisdom and understanding.

Living beings of the nine realms are in the midst of the sleep of ignorance at each thought-moment. Submerged in the dream of birth and death, they forget the waking reality of original enlightenment. Attached to rights and wrongs in a dream, they move from darkness into darkness. Therefore, the Buddha entered our dream of birth and death, placing himself on the same level as the deluded beings, and by means of the language used in dreams enticed the dreaming beings, leading them gradually by expounding matters concerning the distinction between the good and evil that occur in dreams. . . . All these teachings concern the rights and wrongs, good and evil, occurring within the dream of birth and death in the nine realms. From the standpoint of the *Lotus Sūtra*, they are all to be regarded as false views and heretical teachings. . . .

As to the second category of teaching, that of the Buddha's self-practice, this refers to the *Lotus Sūtra*, preached over a period of eight years. This sūtra expounds the original mind of waking reality. However, because the thoughts of the beings were habituated to the mind-ground of dreaming, the Buddha borrowed the language used in dreams to teach the waking reality of the original mind. Thus the words of the sūtra are the language used in dreams, but its intent is to teach the original mind, which is waking reality. Such is the aim of the text of the *Lotus Sūtra* and its commentaries. If one fails to understand this clearly, he will surely go astray concerning both the sūtra and the commentarial texts.

Nevertheless, because even the doctrines of dreams, the teachings for instructing others, are doctrines concerning the virtuous functions inherent in the original mind of waking reality, one takes these teachings of dreams and incorporates them into the mind of waking reality. Therefore, even the doctrines of dreams, the expedient means for instructing others that were expounded over a period of forty-two years, are contained within the waking mind that is the *Lotus Sūtra*, and apart from this mind, there is no teaching. This is called the "opening and integration" of the provisional teachings into the *Lotus Sūtra*. It is just as the many streams flow into and are contained within the great ocean. . . .

Birth and death are principles of the dream of transmigration [saṃsāra]. They are false conceptions, perversions. When by means of the waking reality of original enlightenment we inquire into the nature of our mind, we will find no beginning that is to be born, and therefore, no end that is to die. Is this not precisely the mind liberated from birth and death? It cannot be burned in the fire at the eon's end, nor will it rot in a flood. It cannot be cut by swords, nor shot by bow and arrows. It can fit within a mustard seed, yet the mustard seed will not expand nor will the mind contract. It can fill all of space, yet space is not too broad, nor is the mind too narrow.

To turn one's back on good is termed evil; to turn one's back on evil is termed good. Apart from the mind, there is neither good nor evil. That which is neither good nor evil is termed neutral. Good, evil, or neutral—apart from these three, there is no mind, and apart from the mind, there are no categories [dharmas]. Therefore, good and evil, the pure land and the defiled land, the common mortal and the sage, heaven and earth, large and small, east and west, south and north, the four subsidiary directions, above and below, all originate where the path of language is cut off and the workings of conceptualization are extinguished. It is in the mind that one discriminates and forms concepts, expressing them in language; thus, apart from the mind, there is neither discrimination nor nondiscrimination. Words are what cause mental conceptions to reverberate as they are given utterance through the voice. . . .

The inconceivable nature of the mind is the conclusion and essence of the sūtras and treatises. One who awakens to and knows this mind is called "tathāgata" [a buddha; literally, "thus come," meaning one who comes from the realm of truth]. When one awakens to and knows it, the ten realms of existence are all his body, the ten realms are his mind, and the ten realms are his form. This is because the tathāgata of original enlightenment is our body and mind. When one does not know this, that is called ignorance. The word "ignorance" (Chinese *wuming*, Japanese *mumyō*) is read as being "without illumination." It is not being clearly awakened to the nature of our mind. When one awakens to and knows it, it is called the ultimate reality [dharma nature]. Thus ignorance and ultimate reality are but different names for the one mind. Though the names or designations are two, the mind is only one mind. Accordingly, ignorance is not something to be cut off, for if one cuts off the ignorance of the dreaming mind, he will lose the mind of waking reality. In general, the intent of the perfect teaching [that is, the *Lotus*] is not to eradicate even so much as a single hair's-breadth of delusion. Therefore, it is said that all phenomena [dharmas] are themselves the Buddhist law. . . .

When one considers the matter in this way, the mind while dreaming may be likened to delusion, and the mind while waking may be likened to enlightenment. When on this basis one awakens to the sacred teachings of the Buddha's lifetime, he will understand as follows: When one has dreams, though they are false and empty and leave no trace, they trouble his mind so that he breaks into a sweat and wakes with a start. Thereupon he finds that he himself, his house, and his sleeping chamber are all in a single place, and are no different from what they were. Although we see with our eyes and conceive in our minds these two matters, the falsehood of dreams and the reality of waking, the place where they occur is but a single place; the person who experiences them is but a single person; and yet there remains the difference between these two, falsehood and reality. By this, you should know that our mind, which beholds the dream of birth and death in the nine realms, and the waking mind that is the constantly abiding buddha realm, do not differ. The place where one beholds the dream of birth and death in the nine realms is the very place of the waking reality of the buddha realm that constantly abides. The mind is not a different mind, nor are the places distinguished. Yet dreams are in all cases false affairs, while waking reality is in all cases true.

The *Great Calming and Insight* [Chinese *Mohe zhi-guan*, of the Tian-tai founder Zhi-yi] tells the following story: "Long ago, there was a man named Zhuang-chou. In a dream, he became a butterfly and passed a hundred years. His sufferings were many and his pleasures few. At last he broke into a sweat and woke with a start, whereupon he found that he had not become a butterfly, a hundred years had not passed, and there had been neither sufferings nor pleasures; all were falsehoods, deluded thoughts." . . . The Zhuang-chou who dreamed he had become a butterfly was not a different person from the Zhuang-chou who, on waking, realized that he had not. When we think of ourselves as ordinary beings in the realm of birth and death, that is a distorted view, a distorted thought, like Zhuang-chou dreaming that he had become a butterfly.

But when we realize that we are the tathāgata of original enlightenment, that is like Zhuang-chou returning to himself. It is the attainment of buddhahood in this very body. This does not mean that one attains buddhahood in the form of a butterfly. Because conceiving of oneself as a butterfly is a falsehood, therein one cannot speak of attaining buddhahood; it would be out of the question. But when we understand that ignorance is like the dream butterfly, our distorted ideas will also be like yesterday's dream, false conceptions without self-nature or substance. Who would believe in and embrace birth and death in an empty dream, and give rise to doubts concerning the buddha nature, the nirvāṇa that constantly abides? . . .

When one perceives the oneness of his own mind and the Buddha's body, he will at once become a buddha. Therefore, the commentary on the *Great Calming* states, "All the buddhas, by perceiving that their own mind did not differ from the buddha mind, were able to become buddhas." This is called the "contemplation of the mind" [Chinese *guan-xin,* Japanese *kanjin,* a basic Tendai meditation]. When one realizes that his own mind and the buddha mind are really one mind, then there is no evil karma that can obstruct him at the moment of death, and no false thinking that can detain him in the saṃsāric realm. Because he knows that all teachings [dharmas] are precisely the Buddhist law [dharma], he has no need of a good teacher to instruct him. With each thought, each word, each act, each behavior, in any of the four modes of conduct—whether walking, standing, sitting, or lying down—in all cases, his conduct is perfectly united and of one essence with the buddha mind. Thus he becomes a person of autonomy, without fault or restriction. This is what is meant by "self-practice."

Because one abandons such conduct of autonomous self-practice and dwells instead in the mind of one-sided thoughts arising from ignorance and false conceptualizing that are utterly without substance, and thus turns his back on the teachings and instruction of all buddhas throughout time, he moves from darkness into darkness, ever going against the Buddha's teaching. How sad, how grievous! But if at this moment he were to come to himself, rectify his thinking and return to his enlightenment, he would know that there is no becoming a buddha in this very body apart from himself. . . .

This lifetime, no matter what, you should awaken from the dream of birth and death and return to the waking reality of original enlightenment, severing the bonds of birth and death. From now on, do not ensconce in your heart the doctrines found in dreams. Let your one mind be united with the buddhas throughout time and carry out the practice of the *Lotus Sūtra,* attaining enlightenment without obstruction.

The difference between the two kinds of teachings, that of the Buddha's self-practice and those for instructing others, is as clear as though reflected in a mirror without any obscurity. Such is the testimony of all buddhas throughout time. Keep this secret! Keep this secret!

The Power of the Daimoku

Whether good or evil, not a single hair's-breadth of anything is to be found apart from our own body and mind. This being the case, we ourselves are precisely the tathāgata of original enlightenment, possessing the three bodies in one. One who thinks this buddha exists outside oneself is called an unenlightened being, deluded, an ordinary person, while one who knows the Buddha to be oneself is called a tathāgata, awakened, a sage, a wise person. When we awaken to and clearly perceive the matter in this way, then our own person will within this lifetime manifest the tathāgata of original enlightenment. This is called "becoming a buddha in this very body."

To illustrate, in spring and summer one prepares and plants his fields, so that in autumn and winter he can gather the harvest into the granary and use it as he wishes. To wait from spring until autumn seems a long time, but since it will arrive within the year, one can manage to wait. Similarly, to enter this awakening and manifest the buddha may seem to take a long time, but within this single lifetime you will do so, becoming in your own person a buddha possessing the three bodies in one.

Even among those who enter this path, there are those of superior, intermediate, and lesser faculties, yet they will all alike manifest buddhahood within this single lifetime. Those of superior faculties perfect their awakening and manifest it on hearing the wonderful law of the *Lotus Sūtra*. Those of intermediate faculties can manifest it in a day, a month, or a year. Those of lesser faculties do not advance in any way and seem to be blocked, yet because enlightenment is certain within this lifetime, when such a person approaches the hour of death, then—just as one wakens from the various dreams that have appeared to him and returns to the waking state—the twisted logic and the false conceptualizations and distorted ideas of birth and death that he has held until this moment will vanish without a trace, and he will return to the waking reality of original enlightenment. Gazing around at the universe [dharma realm], he will see that it is all the Buddha's Land of Tranquil Light, and that his own person, which he has habitually despised as base, is the tathāgata of original enlightenment endowed with the three bodies in one. Of the rice that ripens in autumn, there are three strains: that which ripens early, that which ripens in mid-autumn, and that which ripens late, but it is all harvested within the year. In like manner, though people possess the distinctions of superior, intermediate, and lesser faculties, they will all alike within this single lifetime comprehend that they and the buddhas and tathāgatas are of one substance and without duality.

As for the marvelous essence of the *Lotus Sūtra:* When we inquire into what sort of essence it is, we find that it is the eight-petaled white lotus blossom that is the true nature of our mind. This being the case, our own essential nature is called the *Lotus Sūtra (Myōhō-renge-kyō)*. This is not the name of a sūtra but rather, one's own essence. When we understand this, we at once become the *Lotus Sūtra*. Because the *Lotus Sūtra* represents the Buddha's words in which he summoned forth and manifested the essence of ourselves, we ourselves are precisely the tathāgata of original enlightenment, possessing the three bodies in one. When we awaken to this, the false conceptualizing of distorted ideas to which we have accustomed ourselves since the beginningless past until the present will all be dispersed like yesterday's dream, vanishing without a trace.

When you believe this and chant "Namu myōhō renge kyō" even once, then that is awakening to the *Lotus Sūtra* and reciting its entirety in accordance with its teaching. Chanting "Namu myōhō renge kyō" ten times is equivalent to ten recitations of the entire sūtra; a hundred times, to a hundred recitations; and a thousand times, to a thousand recitations. One who believes in this way is called a person who practices in accordance with the sūtra's teaching. Namu myōhō renge kyō.

Becoming a Buddha in This Single Lifetime

Now if you wish to stop the beginningless cycle of birth and death and, this time round, attain the supreme wisdom without fail, you must contemplate the wonderful principle originally inherent in all living beings. "The wonderful principle originally inherent in all living beings" is precisely the *Lotus Sūtra* *(Myōhō-renge-kyō)*. Therefore, chanting [the words "Namu] myōhō renge kyō" is contemplating the wonderful principle originally inherent in living beings. Because the *Lotus* is the king of sūtras, true and correct in text and principle, its words and letters are themselves the true aspect, and the true aspect is itself the wonderful law (*myōhō*). The "wonderful law" is that which expounds and reveals the meaning of one mind being all phenomena. That is why this sūtra is called "the wisdom of the buddhas." "One mind being all phenomena" means that both the land, or object, and the individual, or subject, the body and the mind, of all beings in every realm of existence, as well as insentient beings including grasses and trees, the sky and earth, not excepting even a particle of dust, are all encompassed in the mind in a single thought-moment, and this mind in a single thought-moment permeates the universe; this interpenetration at each moment of the mind and the phenomenal realm is what we mean when we speak of "the myriad things." When one awakens to this principle, that is called "one mind being all phenomena." However, even if you chant and uphold the *Lotus Sūtra,* if you think this law is apart from your own mind, it is not the wonderful law but some inferior teaching. If it is some inferior teaching, it is not the present sūtra, and if it is not the present sūtra, it is an expedient means, a provisional doctrine. And if it is a teaching of expedient means or provisional doctrines, then it is not the direct path of attaining buddhahood, and if it is not the direct path of attaining buddhahood, then one cannot become a buddha, even if one should practice over the course of many lifetimes and long eons. Becoming a buddha in this one lifetime would then be impossible. Therefore, when you chant the wonderful law and recite the *Lotus Sūtra,* you should arouse deep faith that "Myōhō renge kyō" refers to your own mind at each thought-moment.

Never should you think that the eighty thousand sacred teachings expounded by the Buddha in his lifetime, or the buddhas and bodhisattvas throughout time and space, exist apart from your own mind. Even though you may study Buddhism, if you fail to perceive the mind-nature, you can never separate yourself from birth and death. If you seek the way apart from the mind, then even if you perform all manner of practices and good deeds, you will be like a poor man who calculates his neighbor's wealth by day and night but does not gain so much as half a cent thereby. Thus we read in a commentary by Chan-ran of the Tian-tai school that "if one fails to contemplate the mind, one's heavy sins will not be eradicated"—a judgment that, if one fails to perceive the nature of the mind, one's practice will become an endless painful austerity. Thus people like this have been shamed as those who study the Buddhist teachings only to become followers of heterodox ways. As the *Great Calming and Insight* of Zhi-yi states, "Although they study the Buddhist teachings, they in fact are no different from those who hold external views."

This being the case, whether one chants the Buddha's name, reads from the sūtra rolls, scatters flowers, or lights incense, in every case, the merit and good roots formed by such acts are inherent in one's thought-moment. You should take faith in this. In this regard, the *Vimalakīrti Sūtra* makes clear that if one seeks the liberation of the buddhas in the mental functions of living beings, then the beings are none other than enlightened wisdom, and birth and death are none other than nirvāṇa. We also read there that when the minds of the beings are defiled, their land is also defiled, but when their minds are pure, the land is also pure. Thus we find there that whether we speak of the pure land or of the impure land, these are not two separate lands; the distinction depends solely on the good or evil of our minds.

The same holds true whether we speak of the beings or of the Buddha. While deluded, one is called an ordinary being, and when awakened, one is called a buddha. To illustrate, even a tarnished mirror, when polished, will appear like a jewel. The mind which right now in this thought-moment is deluded by ignorance is a tarnished mirror. But if one polishes it, it will surely become the bright mirror of ultimate reality. Arouse faith deeply and day and night, morning and evening, polish the mirror of the mind without neglect. How should you polish it? Simply chanting "Namu myōhō renge kyō" is what is meant by "polishing."

Now, what is the essential meaning of "wonderful," or *myō?* "Wonderful" refers simply to the inconceivable nature of our mind at each thought-moment; "inconceivable" means that thoughts cannot grasp it nor words express it. This being the case, on inquiring into the nature of the mind as it arises at each thought-moment, if we try to say that it exists, it has neither form nor substance that would verify such an assertion, but if we try to say that it does not exist, various thoughts arise and thus repudiate this claim. We are not right in thinking that it exists, nor would we be correct in thinking that it does not exist. The dual terms "existence" and "nonexistence" cannot express it, and the dual concepts of existence and nonexistence cannot grasp it. Neither existence nor nonexistence, yet encompassing both, it is the subtle essence that is the sole reality of the middle way, whose inconceivability is termed "wonderful." This wonderful mind is also termed the law [dharma, *hō*]. When the inconceivability of this doctrine is expressed by analogy to concrete realities, it is called the lotus blossom [*renge*]. When one realizes that one moment of the mind is wonderful, one will know by extension that other moments of the mind are wonderful, too; this realization is called the wonderful sūtra [*kyō*].

This being the case, the *Lotus* is the king of sūtras, expounding that the essence of our mind, which produces thoughts of both good and evil, is the essence of the wonderful law. Thus it is called the direct path of attaining buddhahood. If you have deep faith in this and chant "Myōhō renge kyō," there can be no further doubt about your attaining buddhahood in this single lifetime. Therefore, the *Lotus Sūtra* states, "After my nirvāṇa, truly one should receive and keep this sūtra. Such a person, with respect to the buddha way, is assured; there can be no doubt." Never give way to doubt but by all means carry out the faith that will enable you to become a buddha in this single lifetime. Namu myōhō renge kyō, Namu myōhō renge kyō.

—19—

The Matsumoto Debate

George J. Tanabe, Jr.

With the demise of the government of the Kamakura shoguns in the mid-fourteenth century, the center of power shifted back to Kyoto. The old capital city was once again bustling with political activity, and the temples and shrines were likewise busy places. The religious landscape in Kyoto had been changed with the rise of the Nichiren sect, which had established itself firmly among the merchants and craftsmen. By the mid-fifteenth century, over half of the merchants of Kyoto were said to have been members of the Nichiren sect. The traditional Tendai and Shingon sects did all they could to oppose the spread of Nichiren Buddhism in the capital, but Nichiren Buddhism thrived despite the constant persecutions from the main Tendai temples.

Persecution was an important part of Nichiren's own mentality and religion, and it continued to be a significant stimulus as well as barrier to the Nichiren movement. Since the *Lotus Sūtra* itself said that the propagators of this scripture would be persecuted, persecution proved its truthfulness. Despite the opinion held by many Nichiren priests that propagation should be through peaceful compromise, the movement derived much of its strength from those who practiced forceful proselytization. This aggressive style typically included criticism of the government for not promoting the Nichiren faith and the *Lotus Sūtra,* and the officials often felt compelled to reprimand their clerical critics. The Nichiren priest Nisshin (1407–1488), for instance, incurred the wrath of one of the Ashikaga shoguns, who made him wear a cooking pot on his head to silence him. The effect was advantageous to "Pot-headed Nisshin," as he was called, for he instantly became famous.

By the sixteenth century, the Nichiren sect had twenty-one large temples in Kyoto and its environs, and it enjoyed power and influence in the capital city. Partly in response to the peasant uprisings associated with the True Pure Land sect, Nichiren believers staged their own rebellion in 1532 and gained control of much of Kyoto. The leaders of this Lotus uprising were from upper-class merchant and warrior families, all of whom were interested in forming ties with other local leaders to protect themselves against the spread of the peasant uprisings, and, of course, against the influence of the Tendai establishment, which maintained large forces of warrior priests. Despite this formidable enemy, Nichiren Buddhists managed to control Kyoto for nearly five years. In 1536, however, the Tendai establishment had had enough, and they struck back fiercely to destroy the Nichiren movement.

The impetus for striking back was a seemingly innocuous debate. Nichiren Buddhists were long accustomed to debating rival factions within their sect as well as those from other schools. Even lay persons were experienced in debate, and it was just such a person who touched off a debate with a Tendai priest on a bright spring day in 1536. A certain Matsumoto Shinsaemon Hisayoshi was sightseeing in the capital when he passed a temple in which a Tendai priest named Keō ("Lotus King") was delivering a lecture on the topic of how to become a buddha by reciting mantras. Matsumoto stopped and listened with great interest, and then interrupted Keō with a series of questions that made up the debate.

The details of what became a heated exchange have been reported in several texts, most lucidly in *The Matsumoto Debate*. This lively text is not entirely trustworthy, and mentions people and events for which there is no corroborating evidence. Some details may be inaccurate, but the main issues are clear, the most important of which was that Keō lost the debate for failing to defend himself against Matsumoto's charges that he was making unreasonable claims drawn from teachings other than the *Lotus Sūtra*. The *Lotus Sūtra* is the primary scripture for both the Nichiren and Tendai sects, but Matsumoto successfully charged Keō with the error of compromising the one and only truth of the *Lotus Sūtra* by mixing it with other teachings. The Hiei monks, upon hearing of the outcome of this unexpected and rude intrusion, were affected only by the embarrassing fact that Keō lost, not by the implication that their recognition of Matsumoto's victory would mean that he had the better arguments. Good arguments are good only for the winners.

Both sides prepared carefully for conflict. The Nichiren temples fortified themselves within defensive perimeters formed by trenches. The Tendai forces laid the groundwork for their action by first securing the support of other temples in Kyoto and even in Nara. The long standing rivalry between the Tendai temples at Miidera and Mount Hiei was suspended by mutual consent so that considerable numbers of warrior monks at both temples could join forces against their common enemy. Shipments to and from the city were tightly controlled, guards were posted at predetermined places, a system of rewards and punishments for bravery and treachery was established, and lines of communication were defined so that consultation could take place throughout the campaign. Somewhere between 30,000 to 150,000 warrior monks were amassed on the Tendai side, while the Nichiren temples had an estimated 20,000 troops.

The battle lasted for five days. The superior Tendai army swept through the city and completely destroyed the twenty-one Nichiren temples. Despite the battle plan to limit the attack to the Nichiren temples, fighting inevitably spread, with the result that the southern part of the city below the Third Avenue was burned. Despite the fact that the Tendai forces were the attackers, the blame for the war is placed on the Nichiren side. The battle is now referred to as the Lotus Rebellion of the Tembun Period: losers in war are always labeled rebels, even if they are winners in debate.

In the following selection, the Nichiren layman Matsumoto challenges the Tendai priest on several grounds. The first issue he raises is that of sectarian fidelity. Tendai priests, he says, should not be adopting the teachings of the Shingon or Pure Land schools. Matsumoto also raises the issue of whether the doctrine of becoming a buddha in this body can be realized in fact. The rational character of this argument is clear, as it is in Matsumoto's later charges that Shingon rituals for the protection of Emperor Antoku and the Retired Emperor were powerless and useless. Matsumoto also argues that certain Tendai and Shingon ideas cannot be found in the teachings of the Buddha. The significance of this argument is enormous, for it predates by several centuries the same conclusion that was drawn by Tominaga Nakamoto (1715–1746) in his controversial theory that Mahāyāna Buddhism could not have been preached by the Buddha. Matsumoto and Tominaga both argue that such widely divergent views could not have been taught by a single person, who should have a certain degree of integrity in his thinking. It is clear from even this small sampling of Buddhist debate that argumentation was practiced at a sophisticated level in medieval Japan, and that it consisted of a complex mixture of rational analysis and superstitious belief.

The translation is from Imatani Akira, *Tembun Hokke no ran* (Tokyo: Heibonsha, 1989), pp. 180–88.

The Matsumoto Debate

Matsumoto: I understand you to say that the Tendai sect of Mount Hiei to which you belong is based solely on the Great Master of the Transmitted Teaching [Saichō], but your practice is based only on the prescriptions of the Shingon school, which teaches the possibility of becoming a buddha in this body. This teaching of becoming a buddha in this body is found originally in the *Lotus Sūtra,* but not in other scriptures. Since the entire text of the *Lotus Sūtra* is the truth, why should you have to seek a method in another school for becoming a buddha?

Keō: The source for what you say is the Devadatta Chapter of the *Lotus Sūtra.* It speaks of the Dragon King's daughter becoming a buddha, but that was possible during the time when Śākyamuni was still alive. This is not the case with people who are living in this age when Buddhism is in decline. Our school recognizes that the Great Master of the Extensive Teaching [Kūkai], the founder of the Shingon school, manifested the figure of one who became a buddha in his actual body. How can you doubt this? You should submit yourself to our teaching.

Matsumoto: It is said that the Great Master of the Extensive Teaching became a buddha in his own body, but I doubt if this is true. In what year and month is it said that he became a buddha? During the fifty years of Śākyamuni's life when he preached the scriptures, he never spoke of becoming a buddha when he explained the Shingon teachings. It is even more impossible for the Great Master of the Extensive Teaching to become a buddha in the age of the artificial truth. Your story about the Great Master of the Extensive Teaching becoming a buddha appears in the *Phonetic Meanings of the Peacock Scripture,* a commentary written by Shinzei, a disciple of the Great Master. Shinzei became a heretic, and is the one referred to as the abbot of Kakimoto and the abbot of the province of Kii. He was overcome by an indecent love for the Princess of the Tinted Mansion, and became a ghost or, as some say, a long-nosed goblin when he died. The evidence for the Great Master becoming a buddha is given in a work woven by this Shinzei, and is something about which one can only laugh. Any evidence for the teaching of the Buddha cannot be considered apart from the golden words of Śākyamuni himself. To speak of becoming a buddha in a way that Śākyamuni himself did not explain is precisely what the *Scripture on Nirvāṇa* calls the preaching of the devil. What kind of a priest are you to spread such false theories and fool the people?

Keō: Śākyamuni is not the only buddha. In addition to the preachings of Śākyamuni, there is the *Scripture on the Great Sun* preached by the Great Sun Buddha. This scripture contains what can be called the ultimate enlightenment of a buddha. You probably did not know this.

Matsumoto: What kind of a buddha is this Great Sun Buddha? There is not supposed to be anyone else besides Śākyamuni who preaches the teachings. Are you saying there are two buddhas who have preached the teachings? If that is the case, then one of those two buddhas must be the devil king mentioned in the *Scripture on Nirvāṇa.*

Keō: The Great Sun Buddha is the buddha of transcendent truth. The *Scripture on the Great Sun* is an esoteric scripture of the Buddha's enlightenment. It is not a part of the exoteric scriptures or the great collection of scriptures which tell what Śākyamuni taught during the forty-two years of his career. The Great Sun Buddha is the buddha of transcendent truth and is therefore not something for the ordinary person to know. You should shut your mouth.

Matsumoto: No, I will not shut my mouth just for that. Now there are two kinds of esoteric scriptures: those for dark secrets and those for subtle secrets. Dark secrets hide that which is bad or defective. Subtle secrets hide that which is good or, for example, precious things. Does the *Scripture on the Great Sun* speak of women, evil persons, hearers of the teachings, and self-taught disciples becoming buddhas? The Buddha applies his compassion equally: all beings will become buddhas. Therefore what the *Lotus Sūtra* refers to as esoteric is the Buddha's secret treasury according to the Chapter on Infinite Life, the treasury of all the buddhas according to the Chapter on the Preachers of the Teaching, and "the marvelous teaching in all of the secret treasuries of the Buddha" according to the Chapter on Supernatural Powers. All of these point to the matter of the subtle secrets. Although you speak of the treasured secrets of the Shingon school, it has no provision for women, evil persons, hearers of the teachings, and self-taught disciples to become buddhas. It can furthermore be said that the Chinese Shingon Master Yixing ["Single Practice"] stole the Tendai meditation of visualizing three thousand worlds in a moment of thought and secretly added it to the Shingon school, calling it another teaching of the Buddha, which is not to be found in the exoteric scriptures preached during the forty-two years of the Buddha's career. What is really happening here is that he is fabricating another buddha, and this is a terrible defect that establishes a teaching of dark secrets. It is a fearsome enemy of the Buddha's teaching.

You may speak of the Great Sun Buddha, or of the buddha of transcendent truth, but in either case it comes down to the person of Śākyamuni. Now the buddha of transcendent truth refers to pure wisdom, which has no basis for assuming a form visible to the eye. Originally there were no attempts to give it a name. Because you have tried to give it a name, all kinds of unreasonable problems arise. Have you not created a weird situation? In all cases it is a matter of the mind of the Buddha. You give it a name and call it the buddha of transcendent truth. The buddha of transcendent truth has no form, so how can something that has no physical body give sermons?

The *Lotus Sūtra* of our Nichiren school is the king of all scriptures, so how can this foremost of all scriptures be considered third-rate? How can it be spoken of as empty speculation? If we carefully consider what you say, we will have to conclude in the end that the *Scripture on the Great Sun* was not preached by Śākyamuni. What do you make of this? You set up an empty theory, fabricate another buddha, and make a heresy out of his teachings of the four periods of his forty-two year career. This is why Nichiren spoke of Shingon as a teaching that is destroying our country. Furthermore, the Shingon subsect at Negoroji in Kii province makes fun of Śākyamuni as being the sandal bearer for the Great Sun Buddha, and ridicules the idea that he was the one and only buddha. They are guilty of the five deadly sins. In explaining your position, you are also guilty of the same sins. What do you say to this?

Keō (did not answer for a while).

Matsumoto: Mount Hiei and the Enryakuji temple to which you belong are situated naturally on three peaks, and comprise the place where the Great Master of the Transmitted Teaching [Saichō] transposed Mount Tien-tai from China, established the ordination platform, and built three thousand huts as a manifestation of the three thousand worlds seen in a single moment of thought. You, however, propagate the teaching of the Shingon school. Is this in accord with the original intentions of your founder, the Master of the Transmitted Teaching? Even if you are going against his original intentions, can this be the teaching of a subsect? What about this, Mr. Priest Keō?

Keō (red in the face): Our Mount Hiei is where Saichō's successor, the Great Master of Compassionate Enlightenment [Ennin], practiced the mysteries of Shingon Buddhism with refinement; and it has expanded with the protection of all the gods and good deities. It can be said to be in accord with the Buddha's intention and is consonant with the Buddha's heart and mind. That is why it is considered to be a Shingon mountain. Ennin had a miraculous dream in which the arrow of wisdom flew out from his chest and hit the Sun Deity. You will probably doubt this precisely because you are vulgar in a big way. You should shut up.

Matsumoto: You may say that you are in accord with the Buddha's intentions, but since the arrow of wisdom hit the Sun Deity dead center, will our country not fall into the darkness of night? That is why Nichiren spoke of Shingon's destruction of the country.

Keō: Earlier you spoke of the destruction of the country several times, but what evidence do you have for Shingon's destruction of the country?

Matsumoto: Well, then, let me speak of the actual evidence for the destruction of the country. The times of Emperor Antoku and the Retired Emperor Gotoba are cases in point. Emperor Antoku was supported by the Taira clan and had prayers offered for the defeat of the commander Minamoto Yoritomo in the eastern provinces. At that time, the chief abbot of your Tendai sect, Myōun ["Clear Cloud"], primarily used Shingon methods to pray for Yoritomo's defeat; but to the contrary Emperor Antoku was defeated along with the Taira clan, and he drowned at Dan-no-ura in the western seas. Yoritomo was only an imperial retainer, and the Son of Heaven was the last in a line of emperors. All the gods and good deities were supposed to have protected Emperor Antoku, but the *Lotus Sūtra* was despised because of Shingon and was reviled as being third-rate empty speculation. Therefore they were not in accord with the mind and heart of the Buddha, and all the gods and good deities abandoned them. This is what I mean by the destruction of the country.

After Emperor Antoku, Emperor Gotoba abdicated as sovereign and ruled through the Office of the Retired Emperor. At that time, he planned to attack the regent Hōjō Yoshitoki in the east, and had Jien ["Perfect Compassion"], the chief abbot of the Tendai establishment at Enryakuji, along with monks from Ninnaji and Onjōji, perform Shingon and Tendai rituals for the defeat of Yoshitoki. It is said that these rituals were for the subjugation and death of a person, and for sending that dead person to the pure land to become a buddha. This is a ritual carried out in fifteen stages, and has been an important ritual ever since the Great Master of the Extensive Teaching [Kūkai] and the Great Master of Compassionate Enlightenment [Ennin] brought it back from China. It has been kept a secret ritual that is not widely performed in this degenerate age of the end of the Buddhist teaching. In order to subjugate Yoshitoki, prayers were carried out from the eighth to the fourteenth days of the sixth month of 1221 at the Purple Imperial Palace with the expectation that the subjugation would be successfully carried out. On the seventh day of the ritual, the Retired

Emperor Gotoba and his retainers were arrested by Hōjō soldiers and exiled to Oki and other provinces. Forty-one monks and three hundred and four assistants who had offered prayers were captured alive, while several thousand others were executed. The attempt to subjugate Yoshitoki hardly lasted more than thirty days, in which they tried to destroy the country through the performance of rituals. This is actual evidence. What do you think?

Keō (remained silent with nothing to say for a long time).

Matsumoto: Well, now, Shingon speaks of becoming a buddha, but there is no such thing. You should shut your mouth. Or perhaps Your Eminence knows of people in this degenerate age who have become buddhas?

Keō: What a man of such capricious words! No matter how much they pray, people in this degenerate age will find it difficult to become buddhas through their own efforts. They must graciously rely on help given through the other power of the buddhas.

Matsumoto: That does not make much sense. The efficacy of using one's own power to recite just a phrase or hymn from the *Lotus Sūtra* is superior to relying on the other power of a buddha.

Keō: And which preaching of the Buddha is that?

Matsumoto: Well, at the beginning of the ten parables section in the Medicine King Chapter of the *Lotus Sūtra,* it says that the greatest merit is achieved by reciting the *Lotus Sūtra* through one's own power, and that the acceptance of one phrase or one hymn of the marvelous teaching of the *Lotus Sūtra* is superior to reverence given to the other power of the buddhas. Therefore, the recitation of one hymn by oneself is superior to salvation through the other power of Amida Buddha. This is the teaching of the Buddha. Furthermore, the Parable Chapter of the *Lotus Sutra* says that if you commit the crime of slandering the *Lotus Sūtra,* you will fall into hell and tumble in and out of rebirths there for countless eons without being able to escape. Despite this experience of suffering, you will not only be reborn a beast, but will also be reborn as a foul-smelling filthy person hated by people, who will throw stones at you. The story of your life is one of being severed from the seed of the Buddha, and therefore you must suffer this kind of retribution. Well, now, how are you going to answer this? You, eminent priest, speak of petitioning the buddha of the other power. Amida's original vow about the other power, however, is a teaching of those in the Pure Land sect, who recite the name of Amida. Could it be that Your Eminence is practicing Pure Land Buddhism?

Keō: No, not at all. All of the buddhas are the same. Śākyamuni, the Great Sun Buddha, and Amida Buddha are all of equal value. That is why I speak of relying on the power of the buddhas. Nichiren's belief was such that he slandered Amida Buddha and said that the Pure Land sect was the teaching of the hell of unending suffering. He is really a criminal guilty of making light of the buddhas. Therefore Nichiren encountered various persecutions, which were the punishments meted out by the Buddha in his own mysterious way. Well, now, Shinsaemon; what will you do now?

Matsumoto: Your Eminence has said this much; I also have something to say. The *Lotus Sūtra* is the king of all scriptures and was ranked by Śākyamuni as first in superiority. Kūkai ["Sky and Sea"], the founder of your Shingon sect, lowered it from number one to number three, and belittled the *Lotus Sūtra* as empty speculation. Hōnen slandered it as a difficult practice, calling for throwing away the mind of self-assertion, shutting the gate of zen meditation, leaving aside all practices, and casting out wisdom. What kind of sin does this offense amount to? The answer is clearly stated in the scriptures. This is the sin of blasphemy against the one and only Buddha. Should you, eminent priest, not think that this is a sin? This is why we say that the teaching of Shingon destroys the country. Hōnen was exiled not for the sake of the Buddha's teaching. He reverted to being a lay person, and took on the secular name of Fujii Motohiko. His followers, Sasshō and Shōkaku, were beheaded at Rokujō Kawara in Kyoto. This is nothing other than actual evidence for the punishment meted out by the Buddha in his own mysterious way.

You referred to the persecutions inflicted on Nichiren, but these were not persecutions of him as a person, but were persecutions that originated with the *Lotus Sūtra*. You may wonder about this, but the features of Nichiren's persecution were predicted by Śākyamuni in the *Lotus Sūtra*. This being the case, if Nichiren's persecution were not for the sake of the Buddha's teaching, then what was it for? We can see in the golden words of Śākyamuni that those who propagate the *Lotus Sūtra* in this world of the degenerate age will meet with danger and persecution. In the Chapter on the Preachers of the Teaching in the *Lotus Sūtra*, the Buddha speaks of how much jealousy and envy there were in the world while he was still alive. How much more likely will it be for there to be jealousy and envy after the Buddha is gone! It is said, for example, that birds are jealous of other birds that have food and will try to take it away from them. The persecution suffered for the sake of the *Lotus Sūtra* is not a persecution that can be called persecution. What of this?

Keō: As is the habit of secular people, you are very clever with your tongue.

—20—

A Prophecy of the Death of the Dharma

Jan Nattier

As far back as our sources can take us, Buddhism has taught that all things that emerge in time and consist of separate components (in technical terms, all "conditioned" phenomena) are subject to eventual destruction. And with remarkable consistency, Buddhists have applied this general theory not only to mundane things but even to the duration of their own religion. Within a century or two after the death of the Buddha, detailed accounts began to emerge predicting not only the eventual "death of the dharma" but also the cause and the approximate time of its destruction. Some of these accounts grew into full-fledged prophecies, of which the story found in the text translated here became one of the most influential.

It is difficult to establish with certainty the date or provenance of any Indian Buddhist text, but internal evidence and the testimony of the Chinese sources (the earliest Chinese translation of this prophecy dates to the late 3rd / early 4th century C.E.) point to its emergence in or around northwest India during the period 100–250 C.E. No Indian version of the prophecy has survived, but a total of thirteen different recensions of the tale have been preserved in such languages as Chinese, Tibetan, Khotanese, and Mongolian.

A comparison of these versions allows us to track the gradual evolution of the form and content of the prophecy. Originally it was not attributed to the Buddha at all but to a monk named Kātyāyana—that is, it was considered a "tradition," not a canonical scripture. Over the course of time, however, Kātyāyana's name was dropped, the prophecy was placed in the mouth of the Buddha, and (in the version translated here) the bodhisattva Candragarbha was introduced as the Buddha's interlocutor. Likewise, we see a gradual shift in the timetable for the duration of Buddhism from earlier to later versions of the text: whereas the oldest versions predict that Buddhism will have a lifespan of one thousand years (following the death of the Buddha), later versions of the same prophecy extend this figure to fifteen hundred and then to two thousand years.

Most interesting, perhaps, are the shifts in the names of the foreign invaders who set in motion the chain of events leading to the eventual destruction of the Buddhist religion. The majority of versions of the prophecy list these as the Greeks, Sakas, and Parthians, who did in fact invade northwest India during the period from the second century B.C.E. through the first century C.E. In other versions, however, we see certain adjustments in the list, made to reflect the local ethnic makeup and changing political configurations. Thus we have a second- or third-century version of the prophecy (which seems to stem from Bactria) in which the list consists of Rome, Iran, and the Parthians, and in some of the latest recensions of the text (dating from around the eighth century C.E. and probably composed in Khotan) we find such figures as the Chinese, the Tibetans, and the Turks. Such adaptations provide evidence of the long-lasting popularity of the text, and of its amenability to adjustment in light of new historical circumstances.

Although we will probably never know who composed this prophecy of the destruction of Buddhism (unless it was indeed a monk named Kātyāyana, which is of course a possibility), we can determine at least a few things about the circles in which it originated. First of all, it is quite clear that the prophecy originated among Mainstream (non-Mahāyāna) Buddhists. Although some of the latest recensions of the text (including the one translated here) have introduced isolated Mahāyāna motifs into the story, this is not true of any of the older versions of the story, and in no case is any Mahāyāna element essential to the plot. Judging from the apparent affiliations of the surviving versions of the prophecy, it seems most likely that it was composed by members of either the Dharmaguptaka or the Sarvāstivādin order; this is only a hypothesis, however, and cannot be proven on the basis of the materials currently at our disposal.

Finally, a word is in order concerning the apparent motivation behind the composition of this text. What could have led Buddhists (for there is no doubt that this prophecy was composed, and subsequently preserved and transmitted, by Buddhists and not by their opponents) to write a scripture predicting the demise of their own religion? It has been customary to point to the persecution of the Buddhist community as the motive for such prophecies of decline. Our text offers no support for such an interpretation, however; the foreign invaders are successfully defeated by the king of Kauśāmbī, and the debacle resulting in the annihilation of the Buddhist community comes as a direct result of the king's generosity toward the saṅgha. A careful analysis of our prophecy, in fact, suggests another possibility: that it is addressed to an all-too-prosperous Buddhist community whose very comfort and complacency can lead to the watering down—and in fact, the eventual extinction—of the dharma. (The fact that many versions of this prophecy—though not the one translated here—contain exhortations to uphold and practice the basic Buddhist teachings while the opportunity exists would support this interpretation.) The probable time and place of composition of our text, northwestern India during the "golden age" of the Kushan dynasty, would harmonize well with such a scenario.

The version of the prophecy translated here is based on a Tibetan manuscript copy that dates from around the ninth century C.E.: *Sangs-rgyas Shag-kya-thub-pa' [la] / byang-cub-sems-dpa' sems-dpa'-chen-po Zla-ba' snying-pos zhus-pa-las lung-bstan-ba,* based on the Dunhuang manuscript kept in the Stein Collection of the India Office Library, text no. J601.1; corresponding to Narthang no. 343, Peking no. 1025, Derge no. 356, Lhasa no. 364, and Stog Palace vol. 81, pp. 474–86. I have regularized the spelling of the proper names, which had become significantly altered in transmission and fluctuate even within this manuscript. As the title shows, in this recension the prophecy had been incorporated into a larger work, entitled the *Candragarbha-paripṛcchā-sūtra,* "The Inquiry of Candragarbha." This manuscript, however, included only the prophecy section (translated in full here), which apparently was still circulating independently. No Tibetan version of the remainder of "The Inquiry of Candragarbha" has been preserved.

Further Reading

See David W. Chappell, "Early Forebodings of the Death of Buddhism," *Numen* 27 (1980), 122–53; Étienne Lamotte, *History of Indian Buddhism,* translated by Sara Webb-Boin, pp. 191–202 (Louvain: Institut Orientaliste, 1988); and Jan Nattier, *Once Upon a Future Time: Studies in a Buddhism Prophecy of Decline* (Berkeley: Asian Humanities Press, 1991).

From the "Inquiry of the Bodhisattva Candragarbha to the Buddha Śākyamuni": The Prophecy

Once the Buddha, the Lord Śākyamuni, was staying on Mount Khadiraka [a mythical mountain, said to be one of the "great mountains" surrounding Mount Meru], and powerful beings of all kinds—the bodhisattvas of the ten directions with their attendants, and arhats, gods, nāgas, yakṣas, gandharvas, asuras, kiṃnaras, māhoragas, garuḍas, Māra the Evil One, and the rest—had assembled there. Then a ray of light issued from the space between Śākyamuni Buddha's eyebrows, and it completely permeated the four continents: Videha in the east, Jambudvīpa in the south, Aparagodanīya in the west, and Uttarakuru in the north. It shone equally on the great mountains with Mount Meru at the center, on ordinary mountains, woods, valleys, caves, and ravines. And all four continents became illuminated and fully visible, as clear as the palm of one's own hand.

And from those same rays of light there emerged a host of buddha images, luminous and of various colors and shapes. And all beings—bodhisattvas, nāgas, and the rest—saw them, and were amazed.

Then the four great kings [the guardians of the four cardinal directions]—Vaiśravaṇa and the rest—said to the Lord Śākyamuni, "Why was a ray of light like this produced?" And the Lord replied, "After I have attained nirvāṇa, the scriptures of my true dharma (*saddharma*), my relics, and my images will emerge like this. All these I will entrust to you. Protect them!"

Then the bodhisattva Candragarbha said to the Buddha, "O Lord, it is a great kindness on your part to entrust the true dharma to the four great kings after you have entered nirvāṇa. After the nirvāṇa of the previous buddha, the reflection of the true dharma (*saddharma-pratirūpaka*) disappeared after only seven years. How long will the true dharma last after you have attained nirvāṇa?" The Lord replied, "It is good that you have asked this question. Listen well, and I will explain. After I have attained nirvāṇa, the reflection of the true dharma will last for two thousand years."

Then the bodhisattva Candragarbha asked, "O Lord, how will the true dharma finally disappear? What will cause it to decline, and who will bring it to an end?"

The Lord replied, "After I have attained nirvāṇa, during the first five hundred years there will be many living beings who will practice my teachings and attain liberation. During the second five hundred years there will be many who will practice meditation (*samādhi*). But even though kings and ordinary people will believe in and practice the true dharma, eventually such people will become few. During the third five hundred years there will appear many teachers who instruct people in the true dharma, serve as leaders for living beings, and cause them to attain liberation. But śrāvakas and arhats will become few. Kings, ministers, and ordinary people will be reduced to merely listening to the teaching; they will not take it to heart and practice it, nor will they exert themselves, and their faith will decrease. The protectors of the true dharma will be displeased, and the power and influence of those who do not believe in the true dharma will increase. The kings of this world will lead armies to and fro in battle against one another, and the forces of evil will increase.

"Then, as to the fourth five hundred years, during the first three hundred years the protectors of beings who live according to the true dharma—the gods, nāgas, and the rest—will not stay in this world, but will go elsewhere to spread the true dharma. And even those beings who do practice the dharma will not do so according to the basic dharma texts. Because their efforts are small, their attainments will be few. The four primary colors and their derivatives will decline, and the sense of taste and the rest will diminish. And epidemics, animal diseases, and famine will appear.

"During the final two hundred years, even monks will not practice in accordance with the true dharma. They will seek worldly profit and fame; their compassion will be meager, and they will not live according to the law of the land. They will put down and malign those who do practice in accordance with the true dharma, and will steal their valuables and necessities. Relying on assassins of kings, they will even grasp at kingship. Acting as royal messengers, they will go about seeking profit. They will sow discord between kings and their subjects, and seek for ways to trade and make a profit. Even those who do practice the true dharma will not do so having truly taken it to heart. Rather, they will occupy themselves with all sorts of frivolous talk, casual activities, and playful vacuities.

"Then all the gods and nāgas who delight in the dharma will abandon the place where monks of the kingdom act in such a way, while the faction of those who obstruct the dharma—the party of Māra and so on—will appear there, and their power and influence will increase. Kings, ministers, and the rest will decline in faith; they will no longer see any difference between virtue and vice, and they will do harm to the true dharma. They will steal and usurp the treasures belonging to the three jewels, and they will not shrink from evil deeds. They will gradually destroy images and stūpas, and the materials used for worship will diminish.

"At that time there will still be a few monks and householders who will practice the true dharma without error, and because of their merit there will be a few fortunate places where rain will fall in the proper season and where human and animal diseases will be few. But for those who do not live in this way, all sorts of suffering and unhappiness will arise.

"At that time three great Indian and non-Indian kings—named 'Greek,' 'Parthian,' and 'Saka'—will appear, and they will not practice the true dharma. Leading armies and waging war, they will annihilate many territories in the west and north. They will destroy and set fire to stūpas, temples, and so on in those territories, and will steal and usurp the materials used for worship and the treasures belonging to the three jewels. These three kingdoms will inflict various kinds of harm on one another, and all three of their kingdoms will become unhappy.

"Subsequently, the three kings will join forces, and having united the many divisions of their armies, they will seize and take control of the countries of India. At that time they will take over the countries on this side of the Ganges River: Gandhāra, Madhyadeśa, and so on.

"At that time, on the other, southern side of the Ganges, in the country of Kauśāmbī, a son will be born to a king named Mahendrasena. He will be named Duṣprasaha ["Hard to Bear"], and he will be born with an iron mole between his eyebrows and with his arms covered with blood from the elbows down. At the same time, sons will be born to five hundred of the king's ministers, all with their hands bloody from the wrists down. And at the same time, to the king's horse there will be born a foal that is able to speak. And that night a rain of blood will fall from the sky.

"Then King Mahendrasena will ask a seer who possesses the five supernatural powers, 'The birth of sons to my retinue, the birth of this marvel to my horse, and the falling of a rain of blood—what sort of omens are these?' And the seer will reply, 'Your son will soak this land of Jambudvīpa with blood. And afterward your son will become the ruler of all of Jambudvīpa.'

"Twelve years after the birth of the prince, the assembled armies of the three kings—Greek, Parthian, and Saka—numbering three hundred thousand in all, will invade the country of King Mahendrasena. And due to the incursions of these vast armies into his kingdom the king will be cast down, and will be in distress. Duṣprasaha will ask his father, 'Father, why are you so unhappy?' And his father will reply, 'I am unhappy because the armies of these three kings have appeared in our country.' And the son will reply, 'Father, do not despair! I will take on these armies.' And the father will reply, 'So be it.'

"Then the prince and the five hundred sons of the ministers will assemble an army of two hundred thousand and send it forth. And during the ensuing battle the iron mole between the eyebrows of the prince will grow prominent and his entire body will become like iron; and he will fight, filled with wrath.

"The army of Duṣprasaha will be victorious, and upon their return his father will say, 'Son, it is good that you have fought with the armies of the three kings and been victorious. From now on, you take over my kingdom. As for me, I shall go forth [as a renunciant].' And so instructed, the son will take over the kingdom. After fighting with the armies of the three kings for a period of twelve years, Duṣprasaha will destroy all their forces. Having captured the three kings, he will put them to death. And from then on, he will be the great king of Jambudvīpa.

"Then the young king will say to his ministers, 'I am glad to be the king of Jambudvīpa, but one thing still disturbs me.' And the ministers will reply, 'What is it that makes you unhappy?' The king will reply, 'I am unhappy because of my great sin of having killed so many living beings. What can I do to eradicate this sin?' And the ministers will reply, 'In the country [actually the city] of Paṭaliputra there is a dharma master who knows the Tripiṭaka, living in a hermitage. His name is Śiṣyaka, and he is the son of the brahman Agnidatta. If you invite him here, he will be able to wipe out your offense.'

"Then the king will be delighted, and he will send a summons to Śiṣyaka the monk, who will come into the presence of the king. Then the king will bow before Śiṣyaka the preceptor and ask him, 'These sins that I have committed—how can they be eradicated?' And the preceptor will reply, 'O great king, if you honor the three jewels and take refuge in them for a period of twelve years, your sins will be wiped out.'

"Then the king will send a summons to all the monks of Jambudvīpa, and they will all come together and assemble on the other side of the Ganges River, where the king of Kauśāmbī is. And as a result, the other regions of Jambudvīpa will become devoid of practitioners of the dharma.

"When the monks assemble, many will have perished along the way, and only one hundred thousand will arrive at the king's court. Those monks who have died en route will have been carried off by wild animals, human savages, water, and so on. But when the remaining monks do arrive, the king will offer them a religious feast, and will honor them with offerings.

"At that time, the monks will exchange news with one another, asking 'Where is your preceptor? Where have your disciples gone? Where are your companions and fellow-practitioners?' And having heard the news that many of their number were killed by tigers, lions, and human savages, or carried off by water, or struck by illness, the monks will all be distressed, and they will be overcome with tears and will beat their breasts. Then the king will exhort them, 'Don't cry! Don't be upset!' But the monks will not heed him. And in distress the king will turn his face to one side and fall asleep.

"And while he is sleeping, the king will make the following vow: 'There is no refuge in these worldly monks. May I meet an arhat face to face!' And when he has made this vow, a god of this world [that is, the realm of desire] will reveal the following to him in a dream: 'On Mount Gandhamādana there is living Sūrata, the son of Sudhana. If you invite him here, he will eradicate your sin and remove your doubts.' And having dreamed this dream, when the king awakes he will again send out a messenger. And having been invited, the arhat will come to Kauśāmbī. And the king will honor him and bow down before him.

"Then, on the evening of the fourteenth day of the month, some newly arrived monks among the assembled monks will ask Śiṣyaka, knower of the Tripiṭaka, to expound the vinaya. But Śiṣyaka will reply, 'What use has a person who is blind, and has no nose or ears, for a mirror? What will he be able to see? Even if I expound the vinaya, you will not act in accordance with it. What is the use of expounding the vinaya to those who do not keep the Buddhist precepts?'

"But when he has said this, Sūrata the arhat will speak like the roar of a lion: 'From the time when I first accepted the Lord Buddha's precepts until this day, I have not harmed so much as a blade of grass. Do not say such words. Expound the vinaya!' And when Sūrata says this, Śiṣyaka the preceptor will realize that Sūrata is indeed an arhat. And being deeply ashamed, he will not say a word.

"Then a monk named Aṅgada, who is a disciple of Śiṣyaka, will rise up and shout angrily at Sūrata the arhat, 'How can you say such a thing to my preceptor? You don't keep the precepts, and you don't know the vinaya! So why do you despise my preceptor who possesses the Tripiṭaka?' And seizing a doorbolt, he will strike and kill the arhat.

"At that time a dharma-loving yakṣa named Dadhimukha will appear, vajra in hand, and will say to Aṅgada the monk, 'How could you kill an arhat?' And hurling the vajra, he will kill him. Then a monk named Kedara will strike and kill Śiṣyaka the preceptor. Then the monks will all kill one another, and not a single one will remain alive.

"Then gods, nāgas, and the other heavenly protectors of the dharma will be displeased, and their tears will fall as a rain of blood and fire. The sky will turn yellow and black, and there will be thunder and lightning. What looks like black smoke will pour forth from the star named Dhumaketu, and the moon, stars, and constellations will grow dim. And the gods of the Trayastriṃśa heaven, Mother Mahāmāyā [the mother of Śākyamuni Buddha; according to tradition she died seven days after his birth] and the rest, together with their numerous attendants, will gather up the colored robes of the monks and carry them off.

"Then the king will say, 'What is the cause of this great hue and cry?' And his attendants will tell him, 'The monks have fought and killed one another.' And the king will be greatly distressed; he will get up and go at dawn to the temple outside his castle. And when he arrives there, he will see that some of the monks have their heads cut off, some have their legs cut off, some have their eyes plucked out. And seeing them dead in these various ways, the king will find the bodies of the arhat and of Śiṣyaka the preceptor, knower of the Tripiṭaka. And placing one under each arm, he will say, 'The arhat was my mother! Śiṣyaka was my dharma treasury! Since these two have passed away, from now on I do not care even for my own body and life. As to my kingdom, I shall give it to whoever wants it.' And when he has said this his eyes will darken, and he will become blind.

"Then the ministers will take pity upon the king, and in order to ease his suffering they will disguise five hundred men as Buddhist mendicants. They will not cut their hair and beards with a razor, but will burn them with fire. Since the one hundred and ten kinds of dyes will also have disappeared at that time, the five hundred mendicants will be unable to obtain monastic robes, and they will put on black and red animal hides. And having disguised themselves as mendicants, they will go before the king.

"Then the ministers will say to the king, 'Five hundred mendicants have arrived!' And the king will be delighted. His sight will be restored, and when he looks at the mendicants, he will not see that they are all dressed in animal skins, and that their hair and beards have not been shaved, but are burned with fire. The king will be overjoyed and will command his attendants, 'Bring me the materials for doing homage to the three jewels!' But when the king asks the mendicants questions, they will not know a single thing about the dharma. And the king will be overcome with suffering, and will burst into tears. Then he will take all the dead bodies of the mendicants and will cremate them and do homage to them.

"Then at that time the true dharma will disappear completely from Jambudvīpa. Then gold will turn to bad silver and stone, silver will turn to brass, brass will turn to copper, and jewels and pearls will turn to horn. And of the six flavors of food, four—sweet and so on [sour, salty, astringent]—will disappear. And only two—the bitter and the pungent—will remain."

—21—

The Book of Resolving Doubts Concerning the Semblance Dharma

Kyoko Tokuno

The *Book of Resolving Doubts Concerning the Semblance Dharma (Xiangfa jueyi jing)* is a Buddhist apocryphon dating from the mid-sixth century. C.E. The term "apocrypha" in this context refers to Buddhist texts written in China and modeled upon translations of Indian and Central Asian scriptures. Because of their indigenous origins, these texts were traditionally called "spurious scriptures" and the majority of them were proscribed from the Buddhist canon. Consequently, they remained dispersed and uncollected for centuries. Little was known about the content of such texts until the discovery of the Dunhuang manuscript cache at the turn of this century, which included recensions of many of these proscribed materials. The burgeoning research on this corpus revealed the startling fact that many of the scriptures most important in the Chinese tradition were in fact not translations of Indian texts at all, but instead were actually of Chinese origin.

The doctrines and practices described in Chinese Buddhist apocrypha are the culmination of a protracted process of adaptation and assimilation of imported Indian Buddhist ideologies with the indigenous Chinese *Weltanschauung*. Furthermore, the overwhelmingly popular orientation of these scriptures has proven to be a treasure-trove of information for the study of Buddhism among the people at large. Most studies of Chinese Buddhist history have been concerned mainly with the theoretically oriented Buddhism of religious specialists and scholarly elites within the Buddhist ecclesia. In order to understand the full range of the Chinese manifestations of Buddhism, however, Buddhism as accepted, interpreted, and practiced at the local level cannot be ignored. When "apocryphal" or "spurious" scriptures are acknowledged to be an integral and organic part of Chinese Buddhism, it no longer seems appropriate to refer to these texts using such pejorative terms, but rather a more neutral designation such as "indigenous Chinese scriptures."

Resolving Doubts claims to be the Buddha's last sermon before entering complete quiescence (*parinirvāṇa*), a scenario that is well attested in canonical scriptures. The theme of the Buddha's discourse is the imminent demise of the Buddhist religion: the Buddha prophesies the advent of a period of semblance dharma, when monks will disregard the teachings and violate the precepts. This misconduct will induce the lay followers of the religion to lose their reverence for the three jewels of Buddhism (the Buddha, the dharma, the saṅgha). Ultimately, the conduct of all Buddhist followers and others will degenerate and the decline of the religion and society will soon follow. The text outlines strategies to cope with this socio-religious crisis.

The notion of the decline and imminent demise of Buddhism, also of Indian Buddhist origin, permeated Chinese Buddhism from the fifth century onward. This eschatological concern was one of the principal impulses behind the compilation of indigenous Chinese scriptures, which was one expression of the efforts among Chinese Buddhists to confront the religious crisis they believed to be facing them. *Resolving Doubts* is just such an example of an attempt to ensure the survival of the religion by composing a new scripture that would specifically address the severity of the times and offer measures necessary to survive them.

The apocalyptic prophecy contained in *Resolving Doubts* mainly addresses the degenerate condition of Buddhist followers, both ordained and lay. The cause of that degeneration includes transgression of specific precepts of their religion. The worst culprits are evil monks who fail to observe the precepts, cultivate the spiritual path, transmit the teachings to others, or convert others, who are greedy for fame and material gain, and who harbor hatred and jealousy toward those few noble monks who are keeping their religious vocations. Moreover, lay adherents are also called to task for showing disrespect toward the three jewels of Buddhism, inviting only a few selected monks to vegetarian feasts, failing to repair old religious edifices, selling Buddhist images for profit, and ignoring the lay precepts. Such criticisms are directed at all strata of society, from kings and high officials to merchants and other householders.

Resolving Doubts' emphasis on precepts is a common theme in indigenous Chinese scriptures. The purpose of these injunctions is twofold. First, as with all Buddhist preceptive texts, canonical and apocryphal alike, precepts are said to provide a model for ethically appropriate behavior. The injunctions against engaging in wrong livelihoods, meat eating, drinking intoxicants, and so forth, all have such an edifying role. But second, *Resolving Doubts* seems to use some of these rules as a means of conveying certain messages or criticisms regarding contemporary religious issues and social conditions. Injunctions that are not attested in other Indian Buddhist sources were most likely intended to fulfill this function. These include the usurpation of objects belonging to the monastic community by the laity, or the taxation of monastic properties or expropriation of its resources by governmental authorities. But even some of its precepts that have their antecedents in earlier preceptive materials may also be addressing conditions that Buddhism specifically faced during the sixth century. Thus the preceptive aspect of *Resolving Doubts* is a clever blend of traditional edifying precepts with critiques—disguised as injunctions—on contemporary religious and social conditions.

The only Buddhists who will be able to resist the perverse tendencies of this degenerate time will be bodhisattvas who actively strive to benefit other sentient beings out of their loving-kindness and compassion. One of the major themes of the text is to describe the single most efficacious religious practice during this corrupt age: universal giving. Unlike most Indian Buddhist texts, *Resolving Doubts* specifies that the optimal recipients of charity were not the monks but instead the impoverished, the orphaned, the aged, the sick, and even animals and insects. Such recipients are called the field of compassion, which this scripture defines as the most excellent field of merit (*puṇyakṣetra*) for Buddhists to cultivate. This attitude toward the act of giving and its ideal recipients is an innovation unique to this scripture.

The practice of giving had been advocated since the early days of Buddhism. Charity was seen as one of the essential religious activities of the laity, who were expected to supply the monks with their requisites of food, clothing, shelter, and medicine. Indeed, the viability of the Buddhist monastic institution was almost entirely dependent upon the largess of the laity. The recipients of one's charity were called a field of merit, for they were the source from which merit accrued to the donor through his or her charitable deeds. The amount of merit received by a donor was determined by the spiritual status of the recipient, and hence the Buddha and his disciples in the monastic order were considered to be the most meritorious field for giving. Such material sacrifice on the part of the laity was motivated by the goal of generating enough merit to ensure rebirth in the heavens. The earliest stratum of Indian Buddhist scriptures, in fact, explicitly instructs the laity to practice giving and to observe precepts in order to obtain heavenly rebirth.

Later in Mahāyāna scriptures, giving becomes one of the perfections (*pāramitā*, along with morality, patience, energy, concentration, and wisdom), the essential elements in the practice of the bodhisattvas, whose great compassion motivated them to seek the salvation of all sentient beings. Mahāyāna scriptures refute the conception that a donor obtains merit from his charitable deeds in direct proportion to the spiritual status of the recipient. Some texts in this branch of Buddhism say, for example, that there are no distinctions in the quality of the various fields of merit: parents and teachers, the poor and the indigent are as deserving fields of merit as are the monks. Still other scriptures claim that the merit deriving from giving depends not on the recipient but on the quality of mind of the donor himself.

Resolving Doubts adopts the Mahāyāna conception of giving, and modifies it to meet specific needs. It asserts that the underprivileged in society are the worthiest recipients of donations, surpassing even the three jewels of Buddhism. The central message of the text was intended, in effect, to repudiate the exclusiveness of the original conception of giving, which specified members of the order as the principal beneficiaries of charity. It issues a clarion call for all Buddhists, clergy and laity alike, to pay attention to neglected segments of society, rather than simply take care of their own. The significance of giving is also upgraded so that the cultivation of the other five perfections is said to be contingent upon giving; in fact, the text goes so far as to suggest that buddhahood can be attained solely through the practice of giving. Such a claim is indeed a radical departure from the traditional Buddhist conception of giving.

Resolving Doubts also includes an array of doctrinal ideas drawn from major Indian Mahāyāna scriptures then available in Chinese translation, as well as from a fifth-century apocryphon, the *Book of Brahmā's Net (Fanwang jing)*. The ideas include the apophatic characterization of the Thus Come One (*Tathāgata*) and sentient beings—in terms of what they lack or are empty of—and the insubstantiality of all phenomena. The doctrinal ideas included seem often to be afterthoughts and appear rather incongruous. Still, their presence was vital if this indigenous scripture was to be successful in passing itself off as an authentic translation of an Indian Buddhist text.

One of the more important influences *Resolving Doubts* exerted in the development of Chinese Buddhism was on the Sect of Three Stages (*Sanjie jiao*), whose teachings were based on the eschatological notion of the imminent demise of Buddhism (see Chapter 22). One of the most important scriptures written by the sect, which described this degenerate age of the dharma, was the *Yoga Dharma Mirror that Exposes Transgressors (Shi suofanzhe yuqie fajing jing)*, a text closely based on *Resolving Doubts*. This sect is perhaps best known for developing the institution of the Cloister of the Inexhaustible Treasury (*Wujinzang yuan*), which gathered public contributions and distributed them for religious and altruistic purposes. This activity was also clearly influenced by *Resolving Doubts*, which had praised the notion of collective giving over individual donations: the most meritorious manner of giving was said to be for all persons to offer what they could regardless of their financial or social status, and the needy would receive according to their needs from those pooled resources. Other evidence of the long-term influence of *Resolving Doubts* is found in the writings of such Buddhist thinkers in China and Japan as Zhiyi (538–597), Jizang (549–623), Hōnen (1133–1212), and Dōchū (d. 1281), as well as in a scripture of religious Daoism, the *Book of the Repository of Knowledge on the Sea of Voidness of the Most High One Vehicle (Taishang yisheng haikong zhizang jing)*.

The translation here is from *Foshuo xiangfa jueyi jing, Taishō shinshū daizōkyo* (Tokyo, 1924–1934), 2870; vol. 85, pp. 1335c–1338c.

Book of Resolving Doubts Concerning the Semblance Dharma

Thus I have heard. At one time the Buddha was on the bank of the Vatī [a kind of tree] River between the twin sal (*sāla*) trees, [where] he had completed the ordination of Most Splendid (Subhadra). All the congregation—great bodhisattvas [beings intent on enlightenment], disciples, great Brahmā kings, dragons, spirits, and all the [earthly] kings—gathered together solemnly.

At that time the World-honored One announced to the congregation: "The great quiescence (*parinirvāṇa*) has already been extensively expounded; and I have already described all the buddha lands in the ten directions for the bodhisattva Universal Expanse (Puguang). If anyone in the congregation has doubts, he should ask about them promptly, for the supreme jewel of the dharma will before long be obliterated." Upon hearing these words of the Buddha, the congregation wailed, sobbed, and choked with tears, unable to control themselves. Only those who achieved deliverance through realization did not give rise to sorrowful affection.

At that time there was a bodhisattva named Constant Donor (Changshi) in the congregation. Relying on the awesome spiritual power of the Buddha, he rose from his seat, joined his palms before the Buddha, and spoke these words: "There is something I would ask, but I am afraid it might break the heart of the Sage. I only wish that the Thus Come One would not consider [me to be] at fault." The Buddha told Constant Donor: "I, the Thus Come One, have already delivered [you from] the eight worldly concerns [such as gain and loss, and so on]; what do you need to worry about?" The bodhisattva Constant Donor replied to the Buddha: "World-honored One. After the Thus Come One leaves this world, no sentient being will ever again see the form-body of the Thus Come One, or hear the true dharma. In future generations, during the period of the semblance dharma, the good dharma will gradually decline and evil activities will flourish. Instruct all the sentient beings as to what meritorious virtues are the most excellent at such a time."

At that time, the World-honored One told the bodhisattva Constant Donor: "Excellent, excellent. Future sentient beings are extremely pitiable. Why so? Although all the sentient beings will arduously practice, they will not comprehend the right principle. [Therefore] although they increasingly add to their performance of meritorious [deeds], the fruit they obtain will be infinitesimal. Son of good family! In future generations, monks, nuns, laymen, laywomen, kings, vassals, merchants, householders, and brahman priests will slight my dharma and be disrespectful toward the three jewels, and [consequently] will be devoid of truthfulness. Although they perform numerous good deeds, [since their purpose is] to seek name and gain, or to surpass others, they will not have even one thought of renouncing the world.

"Son of good family! In the future, at the time of the semblance dharma age, immeasurable disasters and calamities and loathsome events [will occur]. What are they? All the clergy and laity will not be conscious about the rules of the dharma. [For example], a donor might arrange a gathering to invite monks, but he will dispatch men to guard the gates and protect the doorways in order to screen out [uninvited] monks and not allow them to join the gathering. If impoverished beggars wish to enter seeking food, [the guards] again will bar their passage and not allow [them to enter]. This sort of gathering merely wastes food and drink, and is devoid of the slightest portion of wholesomeness.

"Furthermore, there will be sentient beings who only wish for their own goodness, and do not edify other sentient beings; seeing others carry out good [deeds], they cannot rejoice, which would augment their small allotment [of goodness]. The merit of such people will be minute and inferior.

"Moreover, there will be sentient beings who will see other ancient reliquaries, images, and scriptures that are ramshackle or ruined, but will be unwilling to repair them. Then they will say: 'These were not built by my ancestors. What is the use of fixing them? I would much rather build a new one myself.' Son of good family! It is better that sentient beings repair old ones than build new ones—the merit [of the former] is extremely great.

"Moreover, there will be sentient beings who see other people congregate and carry out meritorious activities; but, merely seeking name and fame, they will exhaust family wealth and use it for donation. But when they see the impoverished and the orphaned, they will curse them and drive them away without offering even one iota of help. Sentient beings like this are called 'those whose performance of good deeds is perverted.' They are ignorant and insane in cultivating merit, and are called 'unjust producers of merit.' Such people are extremely pitiable, [for] though their use of wealth [for donation] is abundant, the merit they obtain will be extremely minute.

"Son of good family! I once told the congregation that even if a person, over an infinite number of lives, were to make offerings to all the buddhas of the ten directions, and all the bodhisattvas and disciples, it would not be as good as a person giving a mouthful of drink and food to an animal. The merit accruing therefrom is superior to the former by one million or ten million times, immeasurably and infinitely. Son of good family! The reason that I have expounded giving everywhere in the scriptures is because I aspired to have renunciates and householders cultivate thoughts of loving-kindness and compassion and give to the impoverished, the orphaned and the aged, and even to starving dogs. But none of my disciples understand my intention, and hence they give only to the field of reverence (*jingtian*) and do not give to the field of compassion (*beitian*). The field of reverence is the jewels of the Buddha, dharma, and monks. The field of compassion is the poor, the orphaned, the aged, and even ants. Of the two fields of merit, the field of compassion is more excellent.

"Son of good family! Even if, moreover, there were a person who, with his abundant wealth, carried out giving single-mindedly from the time of his birth until old age, [his charity still would] not be as good as a multitude of people, regardless of whether they are poor or rich, noble or lowly, clergy or laity, together exhorting and influencing one another to each take a little of their resources and accumulate them at one place and, as needed, donate them to the poor, the orphaned, the aged, and those suffering from malignant diseases and serious illnesses. The merit [thus acquired] will be extremely great. Even when [such people] do not donate [personally], the merit of giving is generated every moment, limitlessly. The merit [acquired] by practice of giving alone will be extremely minute [compared to this].

"Son of good family! In future generations, all my disciples will delight in fine clothes and dine on delicacies. They will covet profit and gain, which they will avariciously accumulate. They will not cultivate thoughts of compassion, but only harbor hatred. Seeing others do good, they will criticize and envy them, saying, 'This person pursues wrong livelihood and [his purpose in doing good is] to curry favor and to seek fame and gain.' If they see someone giving alms to the poor and to beggars, they again will be enraged and think, 'Why should a renunciate give alms? He only has to cultivate the practices of meditation and wisdom. What is the use of these hurly-burly, futile affairs?' Those who produce such thoughts are the retinue of the devil and at the end of their life they will fall into the great hell, where they will pass through progressive torments. Escaping hell, they will fall into the realm of hungry ghosts, where they will suffer great afflictions. Upon emerging from the hungry ghosts, they will be reborn as dogs for [as long as] five hundred births. Upon emerging from the [realm of] dogs, they will always be reborn among the poor or the lowly for five hundred generations, constantly afflicted by hunger and other sorts of sufferings. There will not be even a moment of satisfaction. Why is this? It is because, when they see others give, they do not rejoice.

"Son of good family! My attainment of buddhahood is all due to practicing giving since time immemorial, in order to succor impoverished and distressed sentient beings. All the buddhas of the ten directions also attained their buddhahood by [practicing] giving. This is why giving is placed at the head of the six perfections whenever I have expounded them in the scriptures.

"Son of good family! Suppose there is a person whose legs are both broken: even if he wants to walk a long way, he cannot go. Monks are also like this person. Even if they spend eons as innumerable as the sands of the Ganges practicing the five perfections, if they do not practice giving, they will not be able to arrive at the other shore of quiescence (*nirvāṇa*).

"Son of good family! If [a monk] does not practice giving, then his precepts are not genuine; if his precepts are not genuine, then he will have no compassionate thoughts; if he lacks compassion, then he cannot persevere; if he lacks perseverance, he will not exert spiritual effort; if he does not exert spiritual effort, he will not practice meditation; if he does not practice meditation, he will not posses wisdom; if he does not possess wisdom, he will constantly be taken advantage of by immeasurable intruding afflictions.

"Son of good family! This teaching of giving is what all the buddhas of the three times [past, present, and future] have each revered. For this reason, of the four means of conversion [giving, kind speech, benefiting others, emulation of religious training], the means through wealth is by far the most excellent.

"Son of good family! Sometimes I preach the observance of precepts, and at other times I preach perseverance. Or again sometimes I commend meditation, while at other times I commend wisdom. Or again sometimes I commend ascetic practices. Or again sometimes I commend contentment. Or again sometimes I commend disciples. Or again sometimes I commend bodhisattvas. In such a way [my teaching] varies in accordance with the differing potential [of people]. In the future, all the evil monks will not comprehend these intentions of mine and each will adhere to his own view, attacking one another [over who is] right or wrong, and thereby destroying my teaching.

"Moreover, all the evil monks will be in the lecture seat expounding the teachings of the scriptures. [But their exposition] will not penetrate to the profundity of my intentions, [and instead] they will grasp the meaning on the basis of the phraseology and defy the truth, the supreme and true dharma. [These evil monks] will incessantly utter self-praise: 'The purport of my exposition is in accordance with the intent of the Buddha. Other masters of the dharma deceive the clergy and laity.' One who speaks thus will eternally be submerged in the ocean of suffering.

"All the evil monks, seeing others practice meditation, will furthermore say, 'This person is ignorant like a tree stump. Without understanding the scriptures and treatises, what will he practice? What is the use of cultivating himself through religious practice?' One who says this will [be afflicted by] calamities eon after eon.

"All the evil monks will vilify each other for fame and gain. Some of the evil cultivate merit without relying on scriptures and treatises. Naturally, they follow their own views and take what is not as what is, unable to discriminate what is wrong from what is right. To anyone they face, be it clergy or laity, they say, 'We are competent to know what is right, and we are competent to see what is right.' You should be aware that such persons will in no time destroy my dharma.

"All the evil monks furthermore observe the monastic discipline, but they do not understand the profound import of the discipline (*vinaya*). They would say, 'The Buddha allowed meat eating in the discipline.' Son of good family! If I had expounded the idea of meat eating, disciples and self-enlightened ones (*pratyekabuddha*) as well as bodhisattvas on the lower stages [of spiritual progress] would have been perplexed, and common people and monks would have slandered [this idea] upon hearing it. Hence it is altogether inconceivable that the discipline allows meat eating.

"Son of good family! Since my first attainment of the path up to the present day, all those cases in which my disciples, here or there, accepted meat and ate it are those which common people saw as actually eating meat. Moreover, there are sentient beings who see all the monks seeming to eat meat. Moreover, there are sentient beings who know that when monks eat meat they enter deep within the immeasurable gate of counteractive techniques (*pratipakṣa*). Innumerable monks will eradicate subtle defilements; innumerable monks will eradicate average defilements; innumerable monks will eradicate serious defilements; innumerable monks will deliver sentient beings, whom they enable to enter the path to buddhahood. The edification of the Thus Come One is inconceivable, [for] ever since I attained buddhahood, none of my disciples has yet consumed or devoured the flesh of sentient beings.

"As for the cases in the discipline where I allowed meat eating, you certainly should know that this flesh was not born from the four great [elements of earth, water, fire, and wind]; it was not born from the womb, nor from the egg, nor from moisture, nor spontaneously born; it was not united with consciousness, nor united with the life force. You should know that nowhere in this world is there such flesh.

"Son of good family! In the future, all evil monks, wherever they are, will expound the scriptures and monastic rules. [However,] they will understand the meaning [of the scriptures and so on] according to the phraseology, without being aware that the Thus Come One had concealed secrets [in those phrases]. Son of good family! There were no such cases where the Buddha allowed his disciples to eat the flesh of sentient beings after his appearance into the world. If [the disciples] ate meat, then why would they be named for great compassion?

"Son of good family! Each of the infinite number of people in today's assembly sees [the Thus Come One] differently. Some see the Thus Come One entering complete quiescence (*parinirvāṇa*); others see the Thus Come One dwelling [in this world] for an immeasurable number of eons. Some see the Thus Come One as six feet tall; others see him as small-bodied; others see him as big-bodied. Some see his enjoyment body sitting in the sea of the lotus-womb worlds, where he expounds the discourse on the mind-ground for one hundred trillion Śākyamuni buddhas. Some see his dharma body as equal to the expanse of space and without distinctions, marks, or hindrances, pervading the realm of the dharma. Some see this place, the sal grove, as all earth, pebbles, grass, trees, rocks, and walls; others see this place as immaculately embellished with gold, silver, and the seven precious jewels; some see this as the place where all the buddhas of all time periods wandered; some see this place as the inconceivable buddha realm, which is the true essence of the dharma.

"Son of good family! All the buddhas appearing in this world, and all their deeds, whether wandering or cenobitic, are completely separate from worldly marks; and yet they are not separate from the worldly dharma that reveals the true marks. What the Thus Come One expounded includes myriad teachings. And every character and every phrase he explicated, and every syllable he uttered, can catalyze each and every sentient being to obtain different [teachings] according to their varying types of births and varying types of basic natures. The special teachings of the Thus Come One are inconceivable: they are not something of which the disciples and self-enlightened ones are aware. The Thus Come One, utilizing his power of autonomy, edifies sentient beings surreptitiously or explicitly, depending on the capacity [of the individual]. During the period of the semblance dharma, all evil monks will not understand my intention; they will adhere to their own views and propagate the twelve divisions of the scriptures. [These evil monks] will grasp the meaning of [the scriptures] according to the phraseology and will offer definitive explanations. You ought to know that these people are reproved by the buddhas of the three time periods for quickly destroying my dharma.

"Son of good family! All the buddhas propounded the dharma by constantly relying on two truths. When they expound the dharma of mundane truth, it does not deviate from the ultimate truth, and they allude to the familiar in order to represent the abstract [as in the example of] using images to portray the obscure. Evil monks are unable to comprehend this intent and will slander and not believe it. They will grasp at the meaning according to the [surface] features, and pass through eons, receiving afflictions. These monks will also give themselves titles, saying, 'I am a master of the dharma,' 'I am a master of the discipline,' or 'I am a master of meditation.' It is precisely these three types of people who annihilate my dharma. These three types of people talk about each others' faults and criticize each other. These three types of people will enter hell like a shot arrow."

At that time the bodhisattva Constant Donor addressed the Buddha, saying, "World-honored One. When will such monks appear?"

"Son of good family! One thousand years after my extinction the evil dharma will gradually flourish. One thousand and one hundred years after [my extinction] all the evil monks and nuns will fill all of the Rose Apple Continent (Jambudvīpa; India). Not cultivating the virtues of the path, many will seek wealth, practicing only what is not the dharma. Many of them will accumulate the eight types of impure objects [slaves, gold, silver, grain, cattle, sheep, elephants, horses]. Even without possessing ten virtues himself [which allow him to perform novice ordinations], [a monk will] keep two novices, or before his ten years [after receiving full ordination] are completed, he will ordain novices [as fully ordained monks]. Because of these causes and conditions, all the laymen will come to slight and despise the three jewels. From that time onward, every one of the clergy and laity will vie with one another in constructing reliquaries and temples, which will entirely fill the world. Reliquaries, temples, and images will be everywhere: some in mountain groves and open fields, some at roadsides, some in alleys and in stinking, filthy, despicable places. [Even if reliquaries and so on are] falling into ruin, no one will repair them. At such a time, even if the clergy and laity construct reliquaries and temples and make offerings to the three jewels, they will not have reverence toward the three jewels. They will invite monks to stay at the monasteries without providing them with drink and food, clothing, bedding, and medicine. On the contrary, they will instead go ahead and borrow and beg [from the monks they invite] and devour the food belonging to the monastic community, without fearing the suffering of the three [evil] destinies [animals, hungry ghosts, hell denizens]. At such a time, all the lay followers, whether noble or lowly, will have no desire to offer any support whatsoever to the monks and will encroach upon [the monasteries], creating disorder without desiring to protect [monks]. People such as these will fall for an eternity into the three [evil] destinies.

"Son of good family! In future generations no civil officials will believe in merit and demerit, and they will steal away the monks' possessions by taxation. Or they will tax livestock and grain, and even worthless things. Or they will order about the serfs belonging to the three jewels. Or they will ride around on the cattle and horses of the three jewels. No civil official should either strike the serfs and animals of the three jewels, or receive reverence from the serfs of the three jewels. [If the civil officials do any of the above,] they will all reap calamitous faults. How is it possible that they should drive or strike [what belongs to the monastic community]? I declare to all civil officials! If you would avoid taxation at the place of the king of death [Yama rāja], then take care not to tax monks. If you wish to tax renunciates, then you will obtain immeasurable demerits.

"Son of good family! At such a time, if all the clergy and laity would perform meritorious activities, they should give to the orphaned, the aged, the impoverished, and those stricken with malignant illness. Moreover, they should repair broken and damaged reliquaries and temples, as well as all kinds of images. Do not question whether you have been given permission yourself or whether others have been given permission. [If] everyone performs repairs in accordance with their individual capacity, then the meritorious virtue of those people will be inconceivable, because they will repair just the old without futilely constructing anything new.

"Son of good family! Why in future generations will all the lay followers slight and look down upon the three jewels? It is precisely because monks and nuns do not conform to the dharma. While their bodies may be robed in the garment of the dharma, they belittle principle and trivialize conditionality. Some, furthermore, will engage in trade in the marketplace to support themselves. Some, furthermore, will tread the roads conducting business to seek profit. Some will engage in the trades of painters and artisans. Some will tell the fortunes of men and women, and divine various types of auspicious signs and evil omens. They will consume alcohol and under its influence become disorderly, sing, dance, or play music. Some will play chess. Some monks will preach the dharma obsequiously and with distortion in order to curry favor with the people. Some will recite magical spells to cure others' illnesses. Some will, furthermore, practice meditation, but since they cannot focus their minds, they will employ heterodox methods of meditation in order to divine fortunes. Some will practice acupuncture and moxibustion (moxa cautery) and various other types of medicine as a means of getting clothing and food. These are the causes and conditions which prompt the laity not to feel reverence [toward the three jewels]. The only exception will be bodhisattvas who benefit sentient beings."

Then the World-honored One told the bodhisattva Constant Donor: "Son of good family! In future generations, among the clergy and laity, there will be various wicked people who construct images of me or of bodhisattvas and sell them for profit in order to support themselves. All the clergy and laity, not knowing [what constitutes] merit and demerit, will purchase those images and make offerings to them. Both [those who sell and purchase] images incur demerit [as a result of which] they will be constantly sold by others for as long as five hundred generations.

"Son of good family! In future generations sentient beings will construct images that will lack all the characteristics [of a buddha or bodhisattva]. Some will be only the torso, some will have incomplete hands and feet, and the ears, nose, eyes, and mouth will all be incomplete; they will have only the rough appearance [of an image]. Some will build reliquaries without installing images. Even if there are broken reliquaries and damaged images, they still will not repair them. The demerit that such people incur will be immeasurable.

"Son of good family! In future generations, every monk, and so forth, will restrict his living accommodations to himself or his group in order to keep out all the monks of the four directions. They will impose food restrictions to have one meal in one day, ten days, or five, four or three days. When the lives of these monks come to an end, they will fall into hell [or be reborn] as hungry ghosts or animals, experiencing infinite suffering. Furthermore, there will be monks and even novices who consider the things of the monastic community to be their own and appropriate them as they please, eat them at wrong hours, or give them away to their friends. These monks and novices will never hear the dharma even though one thousand buddhas appear in this world; and they will remain in the three [evil] destinies without any opportunity to repent. If one dwells or sojourns with such people, all activities of the dharma, such as the fortnightly confessional, will be incorrectly performed, and will all inevitably incur demerit.

"Son of good family! Even if someone were to commit all of the four serious sins [sexual intercourse, grand theft, murder, lying about supernatural powers] and the five heinous acts [patricide, matricide, killing an enlightened person, injuring a buddha, fomenting schism in the order], he is easily succored and [his sins] can be repented. But if someone appropriates from the monastic community even one strand of hair or one grain of millet and eats it at wrong hours, or takes it and gives it away as he pleases, then he will be eternally submerged in the ocean of suffering without any chance of escape, or he will obtain all sorts of vexation in this world. If one dwells or sojourns with people like this, he will incur sins day and night.

"Son of good family! In future generations, there will be various lay followers who are not aware of merit and demerit. Then they will sell to others the buddha images, scriptures, banners, and [artificial] flowers made by their ancestors or by themselves, and use them to support their wives and children. These also should not be bought. At such a time, all the civil officials and those who have authority will arrest these people, and should punish them severely and banish them from the kingdom.

"Son of good family! In future generations, monks, nuns, laymen and laywomen, kings, vassals, empresses, and consorts will transgress prohibitions and precepts, knowing neither shame and dread nor repentance. These causes and conditions will defile the dharma and make it impure.

"Son of good family! In future generations, all the evil monks will be attached to their dwelling places, just like laypeople. They will guard their own lodgings and be unable to move once every three months according to [the changes] of the seasons. When they see other monks keep their robes and alms bowls at hand in their lodging and move when the ninety-day sojourning period is completed, all these evil monks will say in unison, 'These monks have wavering intentions and are vexed with various duties; they have gone crazy and lost their minds. [That is why] they move around so often.' Those who speak in this manner will incur immeasurable demerits.

"Son of good family! In future generations when all types of evil have arisen, all the clergy and laity should cultivate and train themselves in great loving-kindness and great compassion. Patiently accepting the vexation of others, one should think, 'Since time immemorial, all sentient beings have been my father and mother; since time immemorial, all sentient beings have been my brother, sister, wife, children, and relatives. This being the case, I will have loving-kindness and compassion toward all sentient beings, whom I will succor according to my ability. If I see beings who are suffering, I will devise various contrivances [in order to save them], without concern for my own body and life.

"At such a time, kings, vassals, mayors, village heads, influential merchants, brahman priests, and powerful monks should admonish them so as to help save them from backsliding. With the aid of these influences, one will never allow evil people to create difficulties, or allow evil people to appropriate and snatch away one's possessions. The merit of people who aid [others] in this manner can never be fully described.

"At such a time, the merit of giving compassionately to the impoverished, the orphaned, the aged, all those in distress, and even to ants, will be most excellent. Son of good family! If I were to expound comprehensively the merit and virtue of giving to orphans, the impoverished, and those afflicted by illness, then [it would take] inexhaustible eons and still not be completed. As the time for my quiescence has arrived, I have expounded it for you in brief."

At that time, all the congregation heard the Buddha describe the various calamities [that are to occur] in future generations, at the end of the semblance-dharma period. [Upon hearing this,] their body hair stood on end and they cried and wailed, unable to control themselves. The Buddha told the congregation: "Stop! Do not lament. It is the fixed principle of the world that good necessarily contains evil and prosperity necessarily involves decline."

The Buddha, furthermore, told the bodhisattva Constant Donor: "Let us put this matter aside. By what marks do you observe the Thus Come One; by what marks do you observe a sentient being?" The bodhisattva Constant Donor addressed the Buddha: "World-honored One. I observe that the Thus Come One does not come from the past, does not arrive at the other shore [of enlightenment], and does not dwell in between. He is neither existing nor nonexisting, neither appearing nor disappearing, neither formed nor formless, neither conditioned nor unconditioned, neither permanent nor transitory, neither having outflows nor free from outflows. He is equal to empty space, and commensurate with the nature of the dharma. We do not see the Thus Come One expound a single phrase of the dharma from his first attainment of the path until his quiescence, or anytime in between. However, all sentient beings see [him] appear and disappear to expound the dharma in order to succor people. The realm of the Thus Come One is inconceivable, uncognizable through consciousness, unknowable through knowledge. He transcends the three times, and yet is not separate from the three times. It is only the Thus Come One, who has awakened himself to this dharma. I observe the Thus Come One in this manner.

"World-honored One. I now observe the [material] marks of four great elements of all sentient beings. They are like clouds in the sky, like heat waves in the hot season, like a heavenly musician's city, like a phantom, like a mirage, like a hamlet in the sky, like a reflection in a mirror, like the moon in water, like an echo in an empty valley. Feelings, perception, volition, and consciousness are all like this. World-honored One. The [mental] marks of sentient beings are inconceivable. They are not something that the disciples, the self-enlightened ones, or the bodhisattvas in the lower stages [of spiritual advancement] can know. World-honored One. The marks of sentient beings neither come nor go, are neither existent nor nonexistent, are neither internal nor external, neither come from somewhere nor go anywhere. And yet [sentient beings] are revolving in perpetual transmigration, incurring afflictions in vain.

"Since time immemorial, sentient beings have been deeply attached to the view that the self exists; and due to their attachment to the self, they compound their craving, [according to] the dharma of the twelvefold chain of dependent origination. Thus, they incur afflictions unceasingly throughout the long night [of transmigration]. The marks of sentient beings are intrinsically ethereal. On account of these causes and conditions, great compassion arises in the bodhisattvas.

"World-honored One. All the good and evil actions of all sentient beings are merely produced by the one mind; they are not residual phenomena. These are the marks of sentient beings as I observe them."

At that time, the Buddha addressed the bodhisattva Constant Donor: "Excellent, excellent. You have expounded the dharma joyfully. The explanation you have now given would be approved of by all the buddhas. The bodhisattva who practices the four means of conversion and the six perfections [giving, morality, patience, energy, meditation, and wisdom] should observe the marks of sentient beings in such a way.

"Son of good family! When a bodhisattva practices giving, he does not observe [whether the recipient is] a field of merit or not a field of merit; if he sees poor and suffering sentient beings, then he will give to all of them. When practicing giving, one should undertake the following contemplation: 'I see neither recipient, nor donor, nor the thing given. These three matters are all nonsubstantial, [and hence I am] equanimous and nonattached toward them.' Why so? [It is because] all elements of reality are devoid of either self or anything belonging to a self. When [a bodhisattva] practices giving, he neither is hopeful for present rewards nor hopeful for the future pleasures [contingent on rebirth among] humans or gods. [A bodhisattva] seeks great enlightenment only for sentient beings. Because he wishes to comfort and gladden incalculable sentient beings, he practices giving. Because he aspires to embrace all evil sentient beings and cause them to abide in wholesome phenomena, he practices giving. He furthermore makes this observation: 'The marks of the realm of enlightenment and the marks of the realm of sentient beings are both ethereal.' He relies on words and letters and consequently delivers sentient beings, and attains enlightenment. [But] in the true dharma, there is neither attainment nor realization.

"Son of good family! It is like a person who dreams about various events at night. He might dream that his own body is imprisoned by officials, undergoing all sorts of torment. He suffers great vexation, and then later obtains liberation. He again finds himself dreaming that he has become the prince of a great state, and now has power and autonomy and enjoys great pleasure. Then he thinks in his dream, 'I formerly suffered such afflictions but now I am free, enjoying great pleasure.' Having thought this, he suddenly wakes from his sleep, and does not know where the events of suffering and pleasure are. Just as the events in a dream neither exist nor do not exist, so it is for all the elements of reality. This sort of contemplation is called 'right contemplation.' "

When [the Buddha] expounded this teaching, immeasurable numbers of bodhisattvas attained the stage of buddhahood; immeasurable numbers of bodhisattvas attained the stage of imminent buddhahood; immeasurable numbers of bodhisattvas, according to what they had cultivated, each attained excellent progress; immeasurable numbers of humans and gods attained the four stages of fruition; immeasurable numbers of disciples entered the bodhisattva stage; immeasurable numbers of various species of sentient beings aroused the thought of enlightenment.

"Son of good family! If in future generations the four types of disciples are able to hear this scripture, then they will have thoughts of joy. The meritorious virtues they obtain will be immeasurable and boundless."

The Buddha told Ānanda and all the congregation: "Receive and retain well [this scripture], and be prudent that it not be lost and forgotten. This scripture is entitled *Resolving Doubts Concerning the Semblance Dharma* and is also entitled *The Salvation of the Widowed and Orphaned*. Receive and retain it."

At that time, having heard the exposition of the Buddha, the great congregation received it wholeheartedly and reverently paid respects and withdrew. All together they solemnly prepared the implements for [the Buddha's] cremation. Their grief shook heaven and earth.

—22—

A Heretical Chinese Buddhist Text

Jamie Hubbard

Although the Buddhist tradition is well known for its nondogmatic or even anti-authoritarian attitude toward the notion of a scriptural orthodoxy, it is equally true that Buddhists everywhere have gone to great lengths to secure just such a textual orthodoxy. This was especially true in China, where promotion and control of sacred scripture was the prerogative of the highest imperial offices. The Teaching of the Three Levels is an example of a Buddhist movement that ran afoul of this canon-creating authority, with the result that its texts were declared heretical and banned from the official collection of Buddhist texts.

The Teaching of the Three Levels took form during the turbulent last years of the North-South dynasties and the early years of the reunification of the Chinese empire under the Sui dynasty. The three hundred years of continuous warfare and cultural change that preceded the Sui unification saw both imperial suppressions of the Buddhist church and the emergence of new and indigenous expressions of Buddhist doctrine, practice, and institutions. Indeed, it was one of the most fertile epochs in Chinese Buddhist history, setting the patterns for the more formal systematizations of later dynasties. Xinxin (540–594), the founder of the Teaching of the Three Levels, incorporated many of those new directions in his movement, and, precisely because they were singled out as heretical and their texts wholly excised from the orthodox canon, their study sheds much light on an early stage of these Chinese contributions to the Buddhist tradition that survive in other schools and teachings.

Undoubtedly reflecting the chaotic times of its birth, the Teaching of the Three Levels looked upon humankind as totally bereft of the noble qualities of virtue, wisdom, and compassion taught in the many Buddhist sūtras and commentaries. As their name implies, they described our spiritual capacities in terms of three levels, each successively more degenerate and lacking in capacity for practice or realization. In this description they tapped into both an extensive Buddhist literature describing the decline of the Buddha's teachings and the widespread mood of apocalyptic expectation that figured prominently in Daoist as well as Buddhist movements during the North-South dynasties. The notion of three levels was a harbinger of the more popular three times of the Buddha's teachings that became a standard in East Asia. The Indian roots of the idea of the decline of the Buddha's teachings are to be found in a concern for doctrinal orthodoxy, a theme that continued to dominate the later Mahāyāna development of the concept (the *Lotus Sūtra,* or the *Mahāparinirvāṇa Sūtra,* for example). Reflecting its origins in a concern for scriptural precision and authority, the teaching that prevailing spiritual capacities of humankind were vastly lower than those of the Buddha's time meant that particular attention to scriptural sources was required. Although on one level the decline of the dharma concerns our spiritual capacities to understand and realize the teachings of the scriptures, the usual function of this idea was an apologetic or polemic principle of interpretation, a hermeneutic by which the tradition ascertained its relation to scripture taught to a different audience in an earlier time and more hallowed place. Thus in East Asian Buddhism the decline of the dharma became a yardstick by which to measure the efficacy or appropriateness of various sūtra traditions. Just which sūtras and which buddhas were the most appropriate refuge for the community of Buddhists that lived in such a degenerate time?

It is significant, however, that the Three Levels movement and the idea of the decline of the dharma that it taught continued after the difficult times of its birth; both were extremely influential during the Tang dynasty as well, a golden period of Chinese Buddhist development. Indeed, the notion of the decline of the dharma is an important and powerful feature of East Asian Buddhism to this day. One probable reason for the ability of the Three Levels movement to outlive the crisis mentality that figured in its birth is that it was not specifically apocalyptic, that is, it did not predict an actual end to the world as we know it and a return to purity through the advent of a savior. Although both Buddhists and Daoists did make such prophesies (Maitreya, the next Buddha predicted to appear in our world, frequently fulfills this sort of yearning), the Teaching of the Three Levels, like the emerging Pure Land traditions, taught a more existential form of spiritual decline. It taught that the degeneration of the dharma was a congenital disease of the human condition rather than a strictly chronological "fall." Perhaps this was related to the Chinese dating of the decline which, in adding a definite "final period of the dharma" to a looser Indian scheme of decline, allotted to it a duration of ten thousand years, a traditional Chinese number connoting "forever." The question was therefore not what to do about our historical situation but rather how to deal with the predicament in terms of practice. It would be interesting to compare this shift from a central concern for historical events to an existential or inward understanding of salvation and knowledge with changes in Judeo-Christian eschatological expectations.

In addition to this pessimistic understanding of humankind's spiritual capacity, however, there was another, highly optimistic, view of our spiritual capacity that gained widespread acceptance during the same time. This is the idea that the essential nature of all living beings is the same as the nature of a buddha and all beings will in fact one day attain the full enlightenment of the Buddha. This doctrine, known as the doctrine of buddha nature, was particularly popular in the south, taught in the same *Mahāparinirvāṇa Sūtra* that predicted the final days of the Buddha's teachings, and it is this universal and noncategorical affirmation of spiritual dignity that is the concern of the text translated here. It should also be noted that because the descriptions of buddha nature and the closely related "matrix of enlightenment" (*tathātgatagarbha*) are so similar to the notion of the eternal and joyous self of the "heretical" non-Buddhists, these teachings have been controversial from their inception, and many Buddhist traditions have refused to consider them among the highest truths of the Buddha. Nonetheless, this tradition gained considerable influence throughout the Buddhist world and represents a significant parallel to the equally influential notion of the decline of the dharma.

Incorporating these two widely influential doctrines, the Three Levels movement was immediately popular in the capital city of Changan, and counted among its patrons powerful statesmen, imperial princes, and Empress Wu. Based on the teaching of the bodhisattva's infinite compassion and the holographic universalism of the *Huayan Sūtra,* it also established a mutual aid society known as the Inexhaustible Storehouse. Located at the Huadu Temple in Changan, this charitable organization attracted both donors and the needy from all corners of China, and was the forerunner of the pawnshop and other temple-based lending institutions in East Asia.

Although its writings had been included in the scripture catalogs from as early as 597, and in spite of the popularity of its Inexhaustible Storehouse, the texts and practices of the Three Levels movement were proscribed by imperial order on five occasions between 600 and 725, with the result that the movement finally died out and all of its texts were lost, no longer copied and circulated as part of the official canon. It is hard to know the exact causes of such persistent imperial hostility, although they probably include such factors as the social criticism implicit in the notion of the decline of the dharma, which reflected as poorly on our worldly activities as on our spiritual capacities (and perhaps impugned the imperial competence to determine orthodoxy as well), the economic success and popularity brought by the Inexhaustible Storehouse, and, perhaps more than anything, the proximity of followers of the movement to power (their first suppression, in 600, occurred immediately after the fall from power of their patron Gaojiong, whose home had become the movement's headquarters and later the home of their Inexhaustible Storehouse). At any rate, the ephemeral nature of orthodoxy and the political nature of religious establishment is clearly shown in the treatment accorded the movement of the Three Levels.

The Refuge of the Four Buddhas of the Universal Dharma is the tentative title given to a manuscript fragment discovered in a cave in the Central Asian oasis of Dunhuang and taken to the British Museum in the early 1900s by the British explorer Sir Aurel Stein. Because the texts of the Three Levels movement were long ago declared noncanonical and hence not copied or included within monastic libraries, it was a momentous discovery when this text, lacking a title or author, was recognized by the Japanese scholar Yabuki Keiki as a text of the Three Levels movement. Together with some fifteen other texts discovered at Dunhuang and in Japan, we were given for the first time a look at the doctrines of this influential movement.

As noted above, the texts of the Three Levels movement were excised from the orthodox canon for political rather than doctrinal reasons or questions about their textual lineage. Indeed, it would be very hard to characterize the text translated here as anything but orthodox. It regularly cites the most influential Buddhist sūtras as its authorities (fourteen direct references to some seven different sūtras in fewer than three pages of manuscript) and gives them what, by the late sixth century, was a far from controversial reading. Although, as indicated above, the teaching of the "matrix of enlightenment" has always been debatable, it is fundamentally an affirmative approach to truth and wisdom, offering descriptions of reality not in negative terms of what it is lacking or empty of (apophatic description, typical of the *Perfection of Wisdom* corpus and the Mādhyamika school), but rather in positive terms of what it is (catophatic description, more typical of the devotional, tantric, *Mahāparinirvāṇa,* and *Lotus* traditions). Our text promotes a description of this ultimate reality that moves from a rather abstract discussion of the nonduality of enlightenment and delusion within the universe of all things (*dharmadhātu*) to the very concrete practice of looking upon all beings at this very moment, in their phenomenal nature, as fully enlightened buddhas, no different from their ultimate natures. For people of degenerate capacity, unable to accurately distinguish truth from untruth, this universality of the buddha nature was deemed the appropriate place of refuge.

The text opens with a description of the matrix of enlightenment (*tathāgatagarbha*) as congruent with all phenomena, utilizing classic Mahāyāna Buddhist terms of emptiness and nonduality, such as the nonproduction of substantial things, neither increase in enlightenment nor decrease in delusion in spite of the destruction of suffering and its cause, ultimate and provisional reality neither the same nor different, and the like. This is illustrated with a simile of waves that are neither the same as nor different from the water from which they arise. The text is careful to tell us, however, that though the waves are constituted by water, it is not the water per se but rather the "winds of ignorance" that cause the waves to arise. The metaphor breaks down at this point, though, because if the matrix of enlightenment is coterminous with all phenomena, it should naturally include the "wind of ignorance" as well. Therefore the text further equates the matrix of enlightenment with the storehouse consciousness, the realm of consciousness that supports both wisdom and ignorance. Although this move to incorporate consciousness within the structure of the matrix of enlightenment is found in Indian texts such as those cited here, this notion became especially influential in East Asia through the works attributed to the great translator Paramārtha (499–569), in particular the *Treatise on the Awakening of Faith in the Mahāyāna,* and the later Japanese development of the notion of "original enlightenment" (*hongaku*).

After this description of the matrix of enlightenment, the text moves to both a more positive characterization of this reality and a more concrete description of its efficacy as the "true cause" of the enlightenment of living beings. This aspect is called the buddha nature, possessed by all living beings, and it is characterized by the four perfected qualities (*guṇapāramitā*) of permanence, bliss, great self, and purity—notions that are applicable to the truth of what exists or is not empty (*aśūnya*), that is, nirvāṇa, but not applicable to what is empty (*śūnya*), that is, saṃsāra. Thus buddha nature, we are told, is both "truly empty" and at the same time "profoundly existent." In such a degenerate time as the present, the text tells us, it is like a treasure house that causes our liberation. As such degeneracy and such liberation are only relevant to suffering sentient beings, the text also claims that the nonsentient does not have this enlightenment potential, a position generally repudiated in East Asian, especially Japanese, Buddhism.

The third aspect treated is the inevitable future realization of buddhahood by all those sentient beings possessed of the nature of a buddha, an important theme of the *Lotus Sūtra,* perhaps the most popular and influential sūtra in East Asia. This is an even more concrete evocation of the nonduality of nirvāṇa and saṃsāra, and the circle is completed in the fourth aspect considered, the practice of perceiving all living beings according to their ultimate nature rather than their provisional nature, that is, perceiving all living beings as buddhas right now. Based on the *Huayan Sūtra,* the notion of the "perceived buddha" led to another oft-mentioned practice of the Three Levels, that of bowing to even dogs met on the street, cherishing them with the thought that they in fact are at this very moment the embodiment of the full enlightenment of the Buddha.

As noted, the larger context of this teaching of the "Four Buddhas of the Universal Dharma" is the Three Levels doctrine of the appropriate refuge for the third, degenerate level of human capacity. Just as the doctrine and practice appropriate for living beings of each capacity differ, so too does the refuge of the Buddha. Thus, for example, although a being of superior wisdom living in the first level may successfully take refuge in a single buddha (Amida), for beings of no wisdom at all of the third level this would be tantamount to slandering all the other buddhas as less than effective! Hence the appropriate sanctuary is that of the "universally true and universally correct buddha." Thus the buddha jewel for the third level consists not only of all buddhas, but also of all living beings, who, though still thoroughly enmeshed in false views, attachments, and desires, are nonetheless perceived as no different from fully enlightened buddhas.

This tendency to insist that living beings blinded by their own delusions must look only to the purity and truth-value of the nonduality of nirvāṇa and saṃsāra is the basis of the Three Levels' concept of universality, shared with both the Tiantai and the Huayan schools. Indeed, the Three Levels movement declared that, considering our prejudices, ignorance, and greed, we have no hope of discerning particular or relative levels of truth and falsity, so it is preferable to rely on the universality of truth declared in the scriptures. It must be added, however, that at the same time it taught the present buddhahood of all living beings, this was restricted to other living beings; one's own faults were to be recognized, austerities and charity were to be vigorously cultivated, and Three Levels followers segregated themselves from others within the monastery. As noted above, they also operated the most famous example of Chinese Buddhist social welfare, the Inexhaustible Storehouse of the Huadu Temple. Thus, while on the one hand looking to the ultimate, nondiscriminated level of existence as the basic reality of all things, they also advocated a variety of specific practices for the biased, intolerant, and quarreling beings of the third level.

The translation is from Yabuki Keiki, *Sangaikyō no kenkyū* (Tokyo: Iwanami, 1927 [reprint 1974]), appendix pp. 201–206.

Further Reading

For a more detailed discussion of the text translated here, see Jamie Hubbard, "Absolute Delusion, Perfect Buddhahood," in Griffiths and Keenan, eds., *Buddha Nature: A Festchrift in Honor of Minoru Kiyota* (Tokyo and Los Angeles: Buddhist Books International, 1990). The other essays in the volume discuss buddha nature and the matrix of enlightenment (*tathāgatagarbha*) in various other contexts. For an extended treatment of the Buddhist tradition of the decline of the dharma, see Jan Nattier, *Once Upon A Future Time* (Berkeley: Asian Humanities Press, 1991). See also Robert Buswell, ed., *Chinese Buddhist Apocrypha* (Honolulu: University of Hawaii Press, 1990) for essays dealing with a range of issues surrounding apocryphal Buddhist texts, including two articles on the Movement of the Three Levels.

The Refuge of the Four Buddhas of the Universal Dharma

THE BUDDHA AS THE MATRIX OF ENLIGHTENMENT

[Truth and untruth] are neither different nor the same. [Nonetheless, truth and untruth] are one as well as different, while being neither one nor different. Although separated from attachments, the truth of the universe produces the untruth of the universe; therefore, untruth is dependent upon truth. But truth is not independent, because it is eternally dependent on untruth; neither does untruth arise independently, because it is dependent upon truth. Again, the matrix of enlightenment and all of saṃsāra, the essence and the forms, are also like this [that is, neither the same nor different]. Like gold and the ornaments made from gold, the essence and forms are forever the same. Again, the matrix of enlightenment and the phenomenal forms of the universe, the essence and forms, are forever different, as dust and moisture are always distinct, yet neither different nor not different. The *Scripture of the Lion's Roar of Queen Śrīmālādevī* says: "If there is no doubt about the matrix of enlightenment when it is covered by the innumerable stores of defilements, then there will be no doubt concerning the body of truth which is free of those innumerable stores of defilements."

Further, the *Scripture of the Lion's Roar of Queen Śrīmālādevī* teaches that "the matrix of enlightenment is the basis of the repeated cycles of birth and death; because of this matrix of enlightenment the original limits are taught to be unknowable. Because the matrix of enlightenment is the basis, we speak of the cycle of birth and death, and this is called well-spoken. Birth and death are taught as worldly convention, but neither birth nor death is found in the matrix of enlightenment. The matrix of enlightenment is the matrix of the universe, the matrix of the truth-body, the supreme matrix of the transcendent, the matrix whose self-nature is pure." It is wholly quiescent, truly ultimate, and forever separated from all false thoughts and delusion. Yet the untruth of the universe continues to be dependent upon the truth of the universe. The phenomenal forms of the universe continue to be dependent upon the matrix of enlightenment, just as the water is the basis of the many waves. Because there is the matrix of enlightenment there are the phenomenal forms of the universe, as there are many waves because of the water.

The matrix of enlightenment has the form of saṃsāra, the repeated cycle of birth and death. "Birth" is the arising of new phenomenal form; "death" is the extinction of old phenomenal form. As with the water and the waves, [the matrix of enlightenment and the repeated cycles of birth and death] arise together and end together. Nonetheless, the water neither arises nor comes to an end. Dependent upon the water, the form of the wave arises and falls. When the new wave arises, the old wave ceases. The phenomenal forms of the universe, therefore, are none other than the matrix of enlightenment, and there is no other essence outside of this essence and these forms. It is like the waves that are nothing other than the water, yet outside of those waves there is no other water.

However, the myriad phenomenal forms of the universe arise because of good and evil actions, not because of the matrix of enlightenment, as the true cause of the arising of the many waves is the wind, not the water. Again, the virtues of the matrix of enlightenment function throughout the universe together with the phenomenal forms as their base, support, and foundation. It is like the virtue of the water whose essence and function permeate the waves as the basis of all of the waves. Nonetheless, the matrix of enlightenment is different from the myriad phenomenal forms that arise dependent upon it—the matrix of enlightenment alone is the essence, the phenomenal forms are not the essence, as the essence of water is different from the many waves. Only the water is water, the waves are not the water. Similarly, the truth of the essential nature of the matrix of enlightenment both functions and does not function in relation to the myriad phenomenal forms. It is like the purity of the essence of the water, which both functions and does not function with respect to the waves [insofar as all waves arise from and consist of water, the water functions vis-à-vis the waves, yet it is the wind that actually causes the waves to arise, and not the water per se].

Again, this essence is called the storehouse consciousness. Therefore the last book of the *Ghanavyūha Sūtra* says, "the Buddha has taught the matrix of enlightenment as the storehouse consciousness. Delusory thinking cannot know that this matrix is the storehouse consciousness." There are two basic explanations with regard to this, that of the principle and the mind. The matrix of enlightenment is the principle, and worldly consciousness is the mind. The matrix is true, and consciousness provisional. It is also called the four unconditioned noble truths: although suffering and its cause are destroyed, nothing is actually destroyed. Although the truths of extinction and the path are obtained, nothing is actually obtained. Therefore, because nothing is actually destroyed or obtained, there is neither increase nor decrease. It is also called the one truth because it is ultimate and true, with neither destruction nor attainment. It is also called the one foundation because it is the unsurpassed foundation of all practice and understanding in the universe. It is also called suchness in itself, because it is equal and nondual. It is also called the totality of the universe because there is neither increase nor decrease. It is also called the store-consciousness because it appropriates and stores all the various phenomena.

The matrix of enlightenment and the conditions and forms have no beginning or end, and thus truth and untruth are dependent upon each other, neither separate nor distinct. Therefore the *Laṅkāvatāra Sutra* states in a simile that "the storehouse consciousness is like the expansive ocean and waves. Because of violent winds the great waves arise, which roll ceaselessly over the depths. The ocean of the store-consciousness is eternally abiding, and that which is aroused by the wind is the world of objects. It is the waves of consciousness that arise, jumping and dancing about." Sometimes the true is changed into the untrue, like a multitalented actor. Sometimes the untrue is transformed into the true, like a golden ornament. The true cause [that is, matrix of enlightenment] and the conditioned cause [that is, conditioned phenomena] are both the same and different, like milk, cream, and clarified butter. Truth and untruth both take shape within the same matrix like the ocean and the waves. The one vehicle [of the buddhas] and the three vehicles [of the bodhisattva, the śrāvaka, and the pratyekabuddha] are both the same and different, like the Anavatapta Lake and the eight rivers that flow from it. All of these causes and conditions are thoroughly explained in various similes within the sūtras. Therein it is taught that the matrix of enlightenment gives rise to the cause and fully ripens the fruit, changing the small into the great and transforming the common into the noble. All this is due to the efficacious power of the Buddha as the matrix of enlightenment.

THE BUDDHA AS BUDDHA NATURE

The second item is the buddha that exists within all living beings as the nature of a buddha. Some texts talk of this buddha nature as a principle, while others speak of it as something acquired. Some speak of this nature as the cause of enlightenment and others as a result. Now, in clarifying this we only rely on the thirty-eighth juan of the *Nirvāṇa Sūtra* which illuminates the buddha nature as the "true cause." Therein it states that all of the living beings of the universe, ordinary persons as well as sages, have this nature, as do all of the buddhas and bodhisattvas. Thus, from the perspective of the result, the name is established and called buddha nature. However, this buddha nature is neither cause nor result. Existing as the cause it is termed cause, existing as the result it is termed result.

Related to the former concept of the matrix of enlightenment, just as "observe" and "watch" are different words but both mean "to see," with regard to conditions there is a slight difference in meaning [between the Buddha as the matrix of enlightenment and the Buddha as the nature of the buddha in all living beings]. Buddha nature is so called because it includes the permanence of the fruits of buddhahood throughout the universe as well as the permanence of the causes of buddhahood throughout the universe. Wholly embracing everything from the fruits of buddhahood down to its causes, it is termed the Buddha as buddha nature.

Book thirty-six of the *Nirvāṇa Sūtra* says that the buddha nature is not one thing, nor ten things, nor one hundred, one thousand, nor even ten thousand things, nor up to the as-yet-unattained highest perfect enlightenment; the totality of all of the good, evil, and neutral are all called buddha nature. Buddha nature is the perfection of the four qualities: the truly permanent, truly blissful, truly self, and truly pure. Eternal because it never changes, pure because it is without defilement, true self because it is self-abiding. Because buddha nature is unsullied by defilements, while revolving and changing in saṃsāra according to conditions it remains unsullied though in the midst of defilements. Within the person of an ordinary being it is mixed with defilements, like bloodied milk—the śrāvakas [disciples] are like milk, the pratyekabuddhas [solitary buddhas] like cream, the bodhisattvas like yogurt, and the various buddhas and tathāgatas like clarified butter. Although the level of practice of the commoner and the noble differ, with regard to the quality of the nature of the true cause of buddhahood they do not differ but are the same. Although the buddha nature abides due to its essential nature, this nature is yet without essence. Emptiness is none other than existence, and existence none other than emptiness; neither momentary nor eternal; one nor different; removed from the bifurcations of subject and object, it transcends the four logical alternatives and the eight negations.

In the twenty-eighth book of the *Nirvāṇa Sūtra* the bodhisattva Sinhanada asked about the meaning of the buddha nature. The answer is that the seeds of all of the buddhas, the highest perfect enlightenment, and the middle path are called buddha nature. The sūtra also says that "the buddha nature is called the emptiness of the ultimate meaning and the emptiness of ultimate meaning is wisdom. One who merely talks about emptiness sees neither the empty nor the nonempty, but the wise one sees both the empty and the nonempty. Empty are all things in saṃsāra, but the nonempty is great liberation. When one sees everything as empty but does not see that which is not empty, it is not called the middle path. Self and no-self are also like this. For these reasons the middle path is called buddha nature. Because the buddha nature is without change, it is eternal." The *Nirvāṇa Sūtra* further says: "The śrāvakas and pratyekabuddhas only see emptiness, but they do not see that which is not empty—this is not called the middle path." Further, buddha nature is called the truth of ultimate meaning, because it dwells eternally without change. Because it is separated from all phenomenal forms, it is as well called the emptiness of ultimate meaning. Because it is separated from all delusion and darkness it is also called wisdom and illumination. Ungraspable and unrestricted, yet one can realize it. One should not rely on a person with wordy explanations but no insight.

Buddha nature is also called the diamond contemplation, because it cannot be destroyed. Buddha nature is also called nirvāṇa, because it neither arises nor ceases. It is also called buddha nature because it is the realization of enlightenment. It is also called the dharma nature, because it is that which upholds the norm. It is also called the principle of the saṅgha because it is without error. The sūtra says that if a person only has faith in the three jewels of Buddha, doctrine, and community without having faith in the one nature of these three jewels, it is called incomplete faith. Because it is not simply nonexistent like the horns of a rabbit, it is called truly empty; yet because it is not simple nothingness like vacuous space, it is also profoundly existent. Again, the *Huayan Sūtra* calls it the formless because it is the unobstructed wisdom in sentient beings. It is also called the "mind's gateway to suchness," because it is intrinsically unchanging. It is also called the "unborn and the undying," because the nature of the true conditions and true manifestations of the physical and mental (that is, buddha nature) dwells eternally. It is also called the "buddha nature that abides of its own nature," because the nature of original enlightenment is uncaused. It is also self-nature, because nirvāṇa is intrinsically quiescent. It is also self-nature, because wisdom is originally pure and removed from ignorance. It is also called the reality limit, because the essence of the buddha nature is true and not like vacuous space. It is also called suchness in itself, because the nature of the principle is without change. It is not to be found in the five psycho-physical components, the eighteen bases of existence, or in the twelve entrances of cognition, yet neither is it to be found separated from the five psycho-physical components, the eighteen bases of existence, or the twelve entrances of cognition. It is not to be found within living beings nor separate from living beings. It is neither eternal nor not eternal, because it contains both the eternal and the impermanent. It is also called the king of wonderful medicines, because it is able to remove the disease of living beings' passions. It is also called the treasure house that benefits living beings, as the *Nirvāṇa Sūtra* teaches with a simile about a rich man who, in a time of famine, when wealth is hard to come by, opens his treasure house and shares it with all—so too, within this world of passions in the time of the counterfeit doctrine, when living beings are totally perverse and the pure doctrine is exhausted, when the extreme evil of the five heinous crimes increases, leading to the lowest hell of no respite, when perverted views arise and everybody is quarreling with one another and living beings who hold the twelve heterodox views are everywhere, when the dharma is endangered, this, the treasure house of the Buddha's doctrine is opened and shared by all—this is what is meant by the buddha nature as the "true cause." All of the living beings of the universe, those of base and noble spirit alike, all possess this nature [of a buddha], excluding only the grasses, trees, walls, broken tiles, and so on. The sūtra teaches the difference between those things that have no buddha nature and those that have buddha nature: "That which is without buddha nature is the earth, trees, tiles, and rocks; that which is distinct from these nonsentient things are all said to have buddha nature."

It is only because of ignorance that the gold within the dross is not discovered. If one wishes to have insight, then through emptiness of self and emptiness of phenomena one must dispel belief in the ego-self and the self of things; when fixed in equanimous quiescence, clearly illuminating the identity of principle and phenomena, foul and pure, essence and form, and when the mind that follows the object is suppressed, then one will eliminate the self and identify with others. Hearing this without hearing, seeing this without seeing, this is well-seen.

THE FUTURE BUDDHA

The essence gives rise to the conditioned, and the practices are pursued according to the conditions—all are the practices of the matrix of enlightenment, the practices of the buddha nature. The tree includes the bud and truth includes untruth—thus all practices are those of the universal bodhisattva of the one vehicle. With the full completion of the practices, the fruits of buddhahood are realized. Because the Buddha as the matrix of enlightenment and the Buddha as buddha nature exist within the bondage of ignorance and the realm of causality, there is likewise the future realization of buddhahood. Therefore, this aspect is termed the "future buddha."

We rely on the *Lotus Sūtra,* which teaches that the bodhisattva Never Despise (Sadāparibhūta) worshiped all among the four classes of beings, that is, monks, nuns, male and female lay devotees, as the same because they possess the true essence of the matrix of enlightenment and buddha nature. Therefore he told them, "You all practice the path of the bodhisattva and in the future will become buddhas," hence this aspect of the refuge of the universal buddha is termed the "future buddha."

THE PERCEIVED BUDDHA

Because all living beings in the universe are none other than the Buddha as the matrix of enlightenment, the Buddha as the buddha nature, and the future buddha, the forms of living beings are not different from the true buddha. This is called the "perceived buddha."

According to the "Chapter on Clarifying the Dharma" in the eighth book of the *Huayan Sūtra,* the superior and inferior levels of living beings are all to be thought of as the Buddha. Although we may speak of the many levels of living beings and their differences, from the point of view of their essence they are all the Buddha as the matrix of enlightenment, the Buddha as the buddha nature, and the future buddha; they should, therefore, all be respected with the thought that indeed they *are* buddhas. According to the fourth book of the *Daśacakra Sūtra,* we are taught to respect equally the three kinds of monks, that is, those with no precepts, those who break the precepts, and those who keep the precepts, with the thought that they are the true buddhas. Although we may talk of the difference between holding the precepts and breaking the precepts, because the Buddha as the matrix of enlightenment is the same as the Buddha as the buddha nature and the future buddha, they are one and not two. Therefore, you should respect all, perceiving them as true buddhas, and this is termed "perceived buddha."

These four buddhas comprise a single buddha, and thus these four buddhas clarify the essence of the eightfold doctrine [as taught within the *Sūtra on the Teaching of Vimalakīrti,* which teaches that "all are to be revered as buddhas"].

—23—

Eschatology in the Wheel of Time Tantra

John Newman

The Wheel of Time Tantra (*Kālacakra-tantra*) was the last Buddhist revelation produced in India. Although it draws on all the preceding developments of Indian Buddhism, the Wheel of Time is in many respects unique. Among the Wheel of Time's special features are its adaptation of a Hindu myth as part of its strategy of self-legitimation, and its emphasis on the ancient theory of the identity of the macrocosm (the universe) and the microcosm (the individual human being). Both of these elements play a role in the eschatology—the account of the end of time—of the Wheel of Time.

The Wheel of Time Tantra originated in north India early in the eleventh century C.E., at a time when Buddhism was subject to two significant threats. On the one hand, Buddhism was gradually losing its ongoing competition with Hinduism for allegiance and support. On the other hand, the early eleventh century saw the first major incursion of Islam, a religious and political force that eventually hastened the demise of Buddhism in northern India. The eschatology of the Wheel of Time reflects these historical circumstances: it presents a prophetic vision in which Buddhism, allied with a subordinated Hinduism, triumphs over the "barbarian" religion of Islam in a final apocalyptic war.

To understand the eschatology of the Wheel of Time we must first examine the earlier Hindu myth of Kalki. According to the devotees of Viṣṇu, this god manifests on earth in the form of ten sequential incarnations, nine of which have already appeared. It is prophesied that the future tenth incarnation of Viṣṇu, Kalki, will appear at the end of the current age of decadence, when conditions have reached their very nadir. Humans will degenerate into a state of barbarism in which greed and malice will control every action; the basest forms of self-gratification will replace virtue and morality. Worst of all from the point of view of the followers of Viṣṇu, the caste system will be violated, and outcastes will subjugate and oppress the brahmans. At the end of the cosmic cycle, when evil has almost entirely eclipsed good, the brahman warrior Kalki will be born in the village of Sambhala. Leading an army of brahmans, Kalki will annihilate the outcastes and barbarians, establishing a new golden age of righteousness, prosperity, and social order.

The Wheel of Time Tantra borrowed the Hindu myth of Kalki and adapted it to current religious and political conditions. The Buddhist refashioning of the prophetic myth says the Buddha taught the Wheel of Time Tantra to Sucandra, the bodhisattva emperor of the vast Central Asian empire of Sambhala. The eighth successor to the throne of Sambhala, Yaśas, unified all of the brahman families of Sambhala within a single Buddhist Adamantine Vehicle clan. For this he was given the title Kalkin, which in the Buddhist myth means "chieftain." To this day the Kalkins of Sambhala reign in their Central Asian paradise on earth, preserving the Wheel of Time teachings from the forces of barbarism without. At the end of the current age of degeneration, when the barbarian Muslims have overrun the earth outside of Sambhala, the last Kalkin, Cakrin, will assemble a great army headed by the kings of Sambhala and the Hindu gods. Kalkin Cakrin and his army—elephants, chariots, cavalry, and infantry—will come out from Sambhala to eradicate the forces of Islam. After the great Armageddon, when the barbarian horde has been obliterated, Cakrin will return to Sambhala to initiate a new age of perfection. Buddhism will flourish, people will live long, happy lives, and righteousness will reign supreme.

So much for the exoteric presentation of the Buddhist myth. The Wheel of Time explains that the external war with the barbarians is illusory; the Buddha taught it merely as a skillful means to attract the allegiance of Hindu brahmans. In fact, the external war will simply be a magical display Kalkin Cakrin will conjure up to overwhelm the arrogance of the Muslims: through meditative concentration he will radiate countless magic horses that will captivate the minds of the barbarians, causing them to convert to Buddhism. Furthermore, the actual war will not take place in the macrocosm—the outside world—it will occur within the microcosm—the body of the practitioner of the Wheel of Time Tantra.

The real war is the struggle between the forces of enlightenment and ignorance that characterizes the path of the yogin, the tantric practitioner. When the yogin achieves adamantine gnosis, the transformative wisdom that is the goal of the Wheel of Time path, he or she overcomes the inner barbarism that creates the evils of existence. In this esoteric, allegorical interpretation of the myth, the war between Kalkin and Islam symbolizes the radical illumination of the yogin in which correct understanding of reality dispels the darkness of ignorance.

Like many other prophetic, eschatological traditions, the Wheel of Time Tantra responded to contemporary religious, social, and political tensions by projecting them and their resolution onto an idealized future. The Buddhist author of the Wheel of Time was greatly troubled by the decline of Buddhism vis-à-vis Hinduism, and by the ominous appearance of marauding Muslim armies on the western borders of India. Earlier Buddhist eschatology (the prophecy of the future buddha Maitreya) provided no clear solution to these problems, so the Wheel of Time presented its own creative response. By adapting a Hindu myth to counter the threat of Islam, the Buddhists hoped to draw Hindus into the Buddhist camp to face a new common enemy. Whereas the Hindu myth of Kalki was devised to assert the caste privileges of the brahmans, the Buddhist myth attempted to unite all Indians against a foreign invader. Although this strategy met with no great success in India, the myth of the Kalkins of Sambhala lives on among the Tibetan and Mongol followers of the Wheel of Time.

The exoteric myth of a Buddhist holy war against Islam may be powerful propaganda, but it creates tension within the Buddhist tradition itself. Buddhism is perhaps best known for its adherence to the principle of nonviolence, and Kalkin Cakrin's annihilation of the Muslim barbarians appears directly to contradict this. The conflict is resolved in two ways. The violent war, which the Wheel of Time Tantra first describes in glorious terms, is later explained to be mere illusion, a mere magical show the Kalkin emanates to convert, not destroy, the Muslims. Furthermore, the entire myth of the external war is interpreted as allegory: the Wheel of Time yogin understands the esoteric interpretation, that the myth of the apocalyptic war in reality symbolizes the victory of gnosis over spiritual nescience.

The Wheel of Time Tantra shares a sophisticated theory of scriptural interpretation with Buddhism as a whole. Buddhists produced erstwhile utterances of the Buddha throughout the entire history of Indian Buddhism, but for the most part they debated the interpretation of scripture rather than its authenticity. The Wheel of Time Tantra pushed the limits of this openness through the wholesale borrowing of Hindu myth and imagery. Although this overt syncretism met with some resistance, in the end its power as myth and mysticism gave rise to a rich tradition that continues to this day.

The *Śrī Kālacakra-tantra* ("Splendid Wheel of Time Tantra") is the main textual source for the Wheel of Time system. Although Western scholars believe this tantra was composed long after the lifetime of the historical Buddha, the Wheel of Time tradition considers it a discourse the Buddha delivered to King Sucandra of Sambhala. The following translation consists of two excerpts, one from the first chapter (verses I.154–65) and one from the second (verses II.48–50). In the first excerpt the Buddha prophesies the exoteric eschatology, the external war in the macrocosm, and in the second he provides an esoteric interpretation that treats the war as an allegory for the inner yogic path. A brief overview of these passages will help the reader to follow the translation.

Śrī Kālacakra I.154 foretells the succession of teachers of the "barbarian" religion, that is, Islam, and demonizes the Judeo-Christian-Islamic prophetic lineage. Elsewhere in the Wheel of Time texts Muḥammad is singled out as the most important of the barbarian teachers, and al-Raḥmān (a name of Allah) is noted as their demonic deity. Verse I.155 describes the alleged culinary habits of the barbarians in terms certain to disgust Indians observing brahmanical dietary restrictions. Verse I.156 glorifies the power and omniscience of the Buddha, implicitly supporting the authority of the present prophecy. Note that the Wheel of Time claims the enlightened mind of the Buddha to be the source of the Vedas, the foundational texts of Hinduism. Verses I.157–60 prophesy the lineage of the Buddhist kings of Sambhala, beginning with King Sucandra. The eighth king,

Yaśas, an emanation of the bodhisattva Mañjuśrī, will become known as Kalkin for unifying the castes of Sambhala into a single clan. The twenty-fifth and last Kalkin, Cakrin, will be the agent of the Buddhist Armageddon. Verses I.161–63 depict the great war at the end of the eon, in which the Hindu gods will help the Buddhist army of Cakrin to defeat the army of Islam. Verses I.164–65 describe the dawning of the new age, in which Cakrin's sons Brahmā and Sureśa will reign over the northern and southern halves of the world.

Śrī Kālacakra II.48–50 correlate the elements of the Wheel of Time eschatology with its yogic path of spiritual transformation. Kalkin Cakrin symbolizes the gnosis of adamantine mind produced at the culmination of the path; the four divisions of the Buddhist army represent the four attitudes basic to the Buddhist path; and so on. Each of these has its opposite symbolized by members of the Muslim force: Kṛnmati, leader of the barbarians, represents nonvirtuous karma; the barbarian army signifies the evil attitudes of Death; and so on. Verse II.50 correlates the new age of perfection with the state of enlightenment produced by the path. Cakrin's sons Brahmā and Sureśa, emanations of the bodhisattvas Mañjuśrī and Lokanātha (Avalokiteśvara), symbolize menstrual blood and semen. In the tantric yoga of the Wheel of Time these basic components of the human body are transmuted to produce a new adamantine body.

The translation is based on my unpublished edition of these excerpts, which draws on the following editions of the Sanskrit, several manuscripts, and the Tibetan translations. Several glosses included in my translation of *Śrī Kālacakra* II.48–50 are taken from the *Vimalaprabhā* commentary.

Raghu Vira and Lokesh Chandra, *Kālacakra-tantra and Other Texts,* Part 1. Śatapiṭaka Series vol. 69 (New Delhi: International Academy of Indian Culture, 1966); Biswanath Banerjee, *A Critical Edition of Śrī Kālacakratantra-rāja (Collated with the Tibetan Version)*. Bibliotheca Indica Series no. 311 (Calcutta: Asiatic Society, 1985). Jagannatha Upadhyaya, *Vimalaprabhāṭīkā of Kalki Śrī Puṇḍarīka on Śrī Laghukālacakratantrarāja by Śrī Mañjuśrīyaśa* vol. 1. Bibliotheca Indo-Tibetica Series no. 11. (Sarnath: Central Institute of Higher Tibetan Studies, 1986).

Further Reading

See Geshe Lhundub Sopa, et al., *The Wheel of Time: The Kalachakra in Context* (Ithaca: Snow Lion Publications, 1991); John R. Newman, "The Outer Wheel of Time: Vajrayāna Buddhist Cosmology in the Kālacakra Tantra" (Ph.D. dissertation, University of Wisconsin, 1987); Edwin Bernbaum, *The Way to Shambhala* (Garden City, NY: Anchor Books, 1980); Glenn H. Mullin, *The Practice of Kalachakra* (Ithaca: Snow Lion Publications, 1991); Tenzin Gyatso the Fourteenth Dalai Lama, *The Kālachakra Tantra: Rite of Initiation for the State of Generation,* translated by Jeffrey Hopkins (London: Wisdom Publications, 1985).

Wheel of Time Tantra

(I.154) Adam, Noah, and Abraham—there will also be five others of darkness in the family of demonic snakes: Moses, Jesus, the White-Clad One, Muḥammad, and Mathanī, who is the eighth—he will be blind. The seventh, Muḥammad, will clearly be born in the city of Baghdad in the land of Mecca, where the mighty, merciless idol of the barbarians, the demonic incarnation, lives in the world.

(I.155) The barbarians kill camels, horses, and cattle, and briefly cook the flesh with blood. They cook beef and the fluid of the womb with butter and spice, and rice mixed with vegetables, all at once on the fire. Where men eat that with forest fruit, King Sucandra, where they drink bird eggs, that is the place of the demons.

(I.156) The gnosis body of the conqueror Buddha manifests on earth in these moving forms: drop, power, magic eye ointment, divine eagle, river of the gods, sage Nārada, wishing cow, fort, lightning, good science, unchanging supreme digit, divine language, and the incorporeal. It proclaims what was, what is, and what will be, and all the texts on the Vedas, philosophy, and so forth.

(I.157) O glorious King Sucandra, Kalāpa, capital of the renowned land Sambhala, surrounded by mountains, measures five hundred leagues. Soon you will establish your son Sureśa as supreme king there, then you will return to your divine abode. There will be seven kings in the splendid Śākya line, and the eighth will be Śrī Yaśas.

(I.158) He will be Śrī Mañjuśrī, saluted by the best gods, Kalkin through the adamantine lineage. He will give the adamantine initiation, and make all the brahman sages into a single clan. Elevated on the true vehicle, terrorizing the demons, Śrī Yaśas, with a short spear in his hand, will teach the Wheel of Time on earth for the liberation of sentient beings.

(I.159) At the end of the age, among those Kalkins, at the end of twenty-five reigns, the wrathful Kalkin Cakrin, lord of the gods, honored by the best gods, will appear in the lineage of Kalkins. His peaceful form will delight the righteous; he will annihilate the race of barbarians. Cakrin, mounted on a mountain horse, a short spear in his hand, radiant as the sun, will strike all the foes.

(I.160) When eight Kalkins have reigned, the barbarian religion will certainly appear in the land of Mecca. Then, at the time of the wrathful Kalkin Cakrin and the vicious barbarian lord, a fierce battle will occur on earth.

(I.161) At the end of the age Cakrin, the universal emperor, will come out from Kalāpa, the city the gods built on Mount Kailāsa. He will attack the barbarians in battle with his four-division army. The Hindu gods Śiva, Skanda, Ganeśa, and Viṣṇu will assist Kalkin, as will the mountain horses, elephant masters, kings in gold chariots, and armed warriors.

(I.162) There will be ninety million dappled mountain horses swift as the wind, four hundred thousand elephants drunk with wine, five hundred thousand chariots, six great armies, and ninety-six crowned kings. Kalkin, with Śiva and Viṣṇu, will annihilate the barbarians with this army.

(I.163) Ferocious warriors will strike the barbarian horde. Elephant lords will strike elephants; mountain horses will strike the horses of Sindh; kings will strike kings in equal and unequal combat. Hanūmān, son of Mahācandra, will strike Aśvatthāman with sharp weapons. Rudra will strike the protector of the barbarian lord, the master of all the demons. The wrathful Kalkin will strike Kṛnmati.

(I.164) Kalkin, with Viṣṇu and Śiva, will destroy the barbarians in battle with his army. Then Cakrin will return to his home in Kalāpa, the city the gods built on Mount Kailāsa. At that time everyone on earth will be fulfilled with religion, pleasure, and prosperity. Grain will grow in the wild, and trees will bow with everlasting fruit—these things will occur.

(I.165) Fifty years after eliminating the barbarian horde, Kalkin will achieve spiritual fulfillment in Kalāpa, the palace the gods built on the back of lofty Kailāsa. The sons of the guru of gods and men, Brahmā and Sureśa, will promote the dharma. Brahmā will be king in the north; Sureśa on the earth to the south.

(II.48) Cakrin is adamantine mind in one's body; Kalkin is true gnosis. The Hindu gods are the cessation of the twelve factors of worldly existence. The elephants, horses, chariots, and foot soldiers are the noble boundless attitudes: love, compassion, sympathetic joy, and equanimity. Rudra is the gnosis of the individual realizer; Hanūmān is the gnosis of the disciple. The wicked barbarian lord is living beings' sin. Kṛnmati is the miserable path of nonvirtue.

(II.49) Aśvatthāman is ignorance. The demon army is the fourfold host of Death: malice, ill will, jealousy, and attachment and aversion. Their defeat in battle is destruction of the terror of existence. Splendid victory is the path of liberation. The gift of dharma on Mount Kailāsa is elimination of the fear of existence. The earth filled with wealth is the purified collection of the body's elements.

(II.50) Cakrin's sons—Brahmā and Sureśa, to the north and south, Mañjuśrī and Lokanātha, conquerors of the three existences—are the splendid menses and semen that give bliss. The lineages of brahmans and so forth in back of the earth are the numerous pure buddhas. Thus, the war with the barbarian lord definitely occurs within a living being's body; but the illusory, external war with the barbarians in the land of Mecca is certainly not a war.

—24—

Atiśa's *A Lamp for the Path to Awakening*

Ronald M. Davidson

One of the principles of development evident during the history of Indian Buddhism is the economy of previous forms. This idea is not as well appreciated as it could be, yet is one of the keys for comprehending high monastic Buddhism during its final phases on Indian soil. Briefly stated, the principle is this: monastic life preserved, if sometimes in name only, the major theoretical and practical developments of the previous phases. The reasoning behind this process is not hard to comprehend. Institutions are inherently conservative, and Indian institutions tend to define their success by how well the past models of behavior have been integrated into present modes of operation. Thus, when the Buddhist clergy became settled in the monasteries of post-Aśokan Buddhism, they retained the "rains retreat," even though there was no longer the necessity to cease wandering temporarily during the monsoon. Mahāyāna monasteries, moreover, paid lip service to the rules of order (*prātimokṣa*) of the early tradition. Even while these same institutions became increasingly supportive of the esoteric ideology of the Path of Secret Spells (Mantrayāna), they took care that the prior forms were not entirely abandoned.

The conservatism of Indian Buddhist monasteries was grounded in a concern for survival. They depended on several elements operating simultaneously in the Indian cultural ecology—the largesse of the local community, the acceptance of religious diversity by those in power, the continuing interest in the monastic career by the young, and a sense in the surrounding culture that they were performing some vital function. The Buddhist clergy did not have the automatic role in India that was accorded brahmans by birth: they performed no essential rites of passage. Thus, Buddhist monks and nuns needed to establish their worth based on paradigms well accepted by the larger society. This primarily meant that they conducted themselves in a disciplined manner—all their other activities in education, art, medicine, commerce, and so forth, depended on the perception that the Buddhist clergy were behaving correctly.

Correct behavior, in most instances, meant demonstrating the recognizably Buddhist form of the monastic ideal, so that institutional conservatism reinforced the principle of economy and gave it a behavioral orientation. Rather than any specific confession of faith, monks and nuns took vows and accepted conditions for their continued residence in a monastic enclave. New phases in doctrine and the development of further religious forms meant that new vow structures were detailed and fresh practices were set forth. Both the Mahāyāna and the Mantrayāna specified new rites that conferred innovative forms of discipline for those who desired entrance into their visions of the Buddhist dispensation.

Although Indians proved susceptible to the claims made by the Mahāyānist and Mantrayānist factions for their practices and doctrines as "exalted," this stratification of the dharma brought about its own problems. Clearly, those adhering to the "exalted" systems became less interested in the earlier emphasis on a strict regimen, especially when the new ideologies provided a systematic critique of the earlier principles and opened the antinomian door—those with the new insight might circumvent the old norms if it serves the purpose of compassion or some other superior virtue.

The challenge to the institutions, then, was to formulate the principle of economy in a manner that would sustain the earlier ideals and preserve the institution, yet allow growth and development in response to the intellectual and spiritual vitality evident in certain quarters. Mahāyāna monasteries succeeded by identifying the bodhisattva monk as the exemplar of their system, formalized in the hagiographies of figures such as Nāgārjuna, Asaṅga, and so forth. Mantrayānist institutions had a more difficult time because of the explicit language of many of the scriptures and rituals, which drew on mythic systems spawned in village sacrifice and cemetery ghost rituals. Thus, the language of the Mantrayānist scriptures targeted attachment to correct behavior as detrimental to final realization. Although they recognized the validity of such critical techniques, those representing the institutions were caught in the middle. If the critique were physically enacted, the monastery itself would disappear, since the larger society is equally attached to correct behavior. If the critique were ignored, Buddhist monasteries could revert to the oppressiveness embodied in large institutions and suffer a slower but equally sure demise.

The solution to this dilemma was a recognizably Indian response. Rather than identify a single, fully integrated system of monastic behavior, the Mantrayānists simultaneously satisfied the principle of economy and institutional requirements by providing a stratified structure of vows. According to this solution, the different vows are adopted by Buddhists of disparate capacities. Those with lesser capacities must be content with the fundamentals of monastic decorum. Those of greater capacities may also adopt the behaviors of the Mahāyāna, while those few superior individuals may involve themselves in the practices of the esoteric tradition. As the ninth-century *Scripture of the Adamantine Pinnacle* voiced the canonical statement:

Now if he renounces, then he should correctly remain
In the triple discipline—the disciplines of the prātimokṣa,
The bodhisattva, and the highest of all,
The discipline of the holders of spells.

Vajraśekhara-mahāyogatantra, Peking Tibetan Tripiṭaka, Pe. 113.5.26.1.7–8

In many ways this solution was a profound perception of Indian monastic realities. The ideal of the triple discipline (*trisaṃvara*) provided a monastic mirror of the stratification of Indian society, but based on ability rather than on birth. Those in the upper strata demonstrated superior status by increased ritual involvement, but the increase had to be earned rather than conferred. It provided a monastic model that Indians could immediately identify and accept. Thus the triple discipline assisted the integration of Buddhist monasteries into the general trend of increasing ritualization evident in Indian society during this time.

However, the primary problem with this new organization of the religious career was the nature of the advanced rituals of initiation, or "consecrations." The ideology of the Mantrayāna indicated that the unity of opposites was to be dramatically demonstrated during the second ("secret") and third ("insight / gnosis") consecrations by means of the physical union of either the teacher or the disciple and a woman. According to the ideal of the Mantrayāna, this union displays the unity of insight and skillful means, or of emptiness and compassion, ultimately indicating that the relative and absolute levels of truth are identical. The use of sexuality for religious purposes is almost as shocking in the Indian environment as it is in the West but was considered acceptable in secrecy since the purpose of an action denotes its ethical value in the Buddhist system. Accordingly, sexuality between consenting members in a secret ritualized context leading to awakening can be considered a profoundly religious event.

Yet precisely this event was potentially destabilizing for the monastic community, which was committed to celibacy. Out of a wide variety of potential methods of interpreting or institutionalizing the event, two became standard—either sexual congress was restricted to the lay community or it became visualized in a ritual context. The first solution required that the Buddhist clergy be content with the first of the four esoteric consecrations and not receive the latter three. Conversely, the second solution redefines the nature of the consecrations so that the physicality of the sexual act is proscribed; only its visualized form is allowed to the clergy.

Atiśa Dīpaṃkara Śrījñāna (traditional dates 982–1054 C.E.) was one of the leading representatives of monastic Buddhism in India during the first half of the eleventh century. He was reputed to be from an aristocratic Bengali family and to have studied with the finest teachers of his period. In 1042 C.E., at the invitation of Tibetan kings in western Tibet, Atiśa arrived in the country to find it in the process of renewal following a hiatus precipitated by the collapse of the early Tibetan royal house in the middle of the ninth century. Atiśa elected to assist this renewal with his personal involvement in Tibetan religious life. He evidently wished to focus his followers on the monastic career rather than on the model of a lay teacher of the Path of Secret Spells. Part of his strategy was a fundamental statement of the integration of disparate threads of Buddhist spirituality under the triple discipline. This he effected with the composition of *A Lamp for the Path to Awakening,* one of the most influential of Indian texts received by Tibetans, perhaps because it was purportedly written specifically for that community.

A Lamp for the Path to Awakening implements the triple discipline by upholding the priority of celibacy as the most excellent of Buddhist virtues, a very conservative stance and indicative of the fundamentalist tenor of Atiśa's mission in Tibet. He then espouses the bodhisattva path in a manner well integrated into the celibate lifestyle, leading into a discussion of the basics of Mahāyāna dialectics, which he supplements with references. Nothing in the first two-thirds of *A Lamp* is outside of mainstream late Indian Buddhism. Yet the final eight verses (verses 60–67) of the text are devoted to a shift in definition of the Mantrayāna ritual process, first by restricting the clergy to the first of the consecrations (which includes the master's consecration) for the purposes discussed above, and second by maintaining that this first consecration is all that is necessary for the study and performance of the Mantrayāna ritual corpus.

Atiśa's autocommentary amplifies his objections to certain attitudes toward the esoteric practices. One side exaggerates freedom from rules in the pursuit of awakening and courts expulsion from the monastic enclave by defiling the vows of celibacy through the consecrations and other rituals of sexual enactment. Conversely, the other side denigrates the Mantrayāna as perverse, and espouses more limited codes of conduct for all, regardless of an individual's relationship to the monastic estate and personal capacity. Atiśa's solution—access to the higher consecrations for the noncelibate laity alone—is difficult for him to justify. Atiśa acknowledges that some will question whether his position is in contradiction to the esoteric tradition. His reply is to refer to scripture, quote from his teachers, and to use a very old Buddhist justification: if it develops the path to awakening and is in accord with the other scriptures, then there is no fault in the realization generated through these means.

For all his sophistry, Atiśa does not acknowledge that his opponents could claim that they also are without fault in their awareness of reality, thereby justifying antinomian behavior. Where they are willing to privilege ritual behavior over monastic decorum, he is willing to do the reverse; both entail a subordination of one behavioral system to the other. Atiśa, furthermore, seems to sidestep the fact that his solution allows the laity—who are theoretically ancillary to the clergy—to participate in a wider range of rituals and meditations in the "exalted" esoteric system. We may appreciate the extreme nature of Atiśa's position by understanding that although his text became the model for mainstream Tibetan monastic Buddhism for the next nine hundred years, the Tibetans almost universally elected to continue the reception of the three "higher" consecrations in a visualized rather than physical form. Thus Tibetan Buddhism retained the basic organization of the monastic lifestyle Atiśa envisioned while opting for an implementation of that career on guidelines somewhat different in letter, if not in spirit, from the statements in *A Lamp for the Path to Awakening.*

The text of the *Bodhipathapradīpa* has been critically edited and translated by Helmut Eimer, *Bodhipathapradīpa—Ein Lehrgedicht des Atiśa (Dīpaṃkaraśrījñāna) in der Tibetischen Überlieferung,* Asiatische Forschungen Band 59 (Wiesbaden: Otto Harrassowitz, 1978), pp. 104–41. The Peking edition of the work is Peking 5343.103.20.4.1–21.5.6. The Peking edition of Atiśa's autocommentary, the *Bodhimārgadīpapañjikā,* is Peking 5344.103.21.5.6–46.2.5. Verses 26–31 are taken directly from the *Mañjuśrī-buddhakṣetra-guṇavyūhālaṃkāra-sūtra,* quoted in P. L. Vaidya, ed., *Śikṣāsamuccaya of Śāntideva,* Buddhist Sanskrit Texts No. 11 (Darbhanga: Mithila Institute, 1961), 11.16–27.

Further Reading

See generally Alaka Chattopadhyaya, *Atiśa and Tibet* (Calcutta: Indian Studies Past & Present, 1967); R. F. Sherburne, *A Lamp for the Path and Commentary by Atiśa* (London: Allen & Unwin, 1983); and Helmut Eimer, "The Development of the Biographical Tradition Concerning Atiśa (Dīpaṃkaraśrījñāna)," *Journal of the Tibet Society* n.s. 2 (1982), 41–51. On Maitreya's *Stemmy Array Scripture* (verse 12), see Thomas Cleary, trans., *Entry into the Realm of Reality* (Boston: Shambhala, 1989), pp. 352–65; and Daisetz Teitaro Suzuki and Hokei Idzumi, eds., *The Gaṇḍavyūha Sūtra,* new revised edition (Tokyo: Society for the Publication of Sacred Books of the World, 1949), pp. 494–510. The received text of the *Kālacakra-tantra* (verse 64) is in Raghu Vira and Lokesh Candra, eds., *Kālacakra-Tantra and Other Texts,* Śata-Piṭaka Series vol. 69 (New Delhi: International Academy of Indian Culture, 1966), part 1.

A Lamp for the Path to Awakening

Homage to Mañjuśrī, who has been a true prince

I. THE VEHICLE OF THE DISCIPLES AND THE DISCIPLINE OF THE PRĀTIMOKṢA

1. With great reverence, I pay my respects to all the victors of the three times, their doctrine, and the community. Because I have been requested by Byang-chub 'od, the good disciple, I should illuminate this *Lamp for the Path to Awakening.*
2. Individuals may be understood as falling into three general types—lesser, middling, and excellent. Their several characteristics are clear and should be differentiated.

3. The lesser individual pursues his own benefit in the pleasures of existence by whatever means possible.
4. The middling individual pursues his own peace, turning his back on the pleasures of existence and reversing unwholesome activity.
5. The excellent individual, impelled by his own distress, seeks the perfect extinction of all the distress of others.
6. For those holy persons desiring the highest awakening, I will explain the correct ritual as detailed by the teachers:

7–8b. In front of a painting or other image of the perfect Buddha, a stūpa, and a scripture of the true dharma, one offers things such as flowers and incense, as financial resources allow. Moreover, seven kinds of offerings are mentioned in the *Kingly Scripture Concerning the Resolve toward Excellent Conduct* [*Bhadracari-praṇidhāna-rāja-sūtra,* verses 1–12; cf. Hokei Idumi, "The Hymn on the Life and Vows of Samantabhadra," *Eastern Buddhist* 5 (1930), 226–47]:

1. To all those lions among mankind who live in the three times and the ten directions, to all of them I reverentially pay homage with body, speech, and mind.
2. Making my body as numerous as particles of dust in the earth, I pay homage to the victors by imagining myself in their presence through the power of my resolve toward excellent conduct.
3. On a single particle of dust are seated buddhas as numerous as particles of dust, each surrounded by bodhisattvas. Thus I pay reverence to all the realms of reality, each full of victors.
4. With an ocean of voice in which all the notes of sound are found, I praise all those buddhas by exalting all the virtues of these buddhas, which are like the ocean of inexhaustible nature.
5. With the best flowers, wreaths, musical instruments, ointments, umbrellas, lamps, and incenses, I make offerings to the buddhas.
6. With the best garments, scented wood, powdered incense in a heap equal to [Mount] Meru, arrayed with all these excellent offerings, again I make offerings to those buddhas.
7. This is, I believe, what is to be the best, munificent offering to the buddhas; it is due to my confidence in excellent conduct that I pay homage to all the victors.
8. And all the transgressions that may have been committed by me, due to my greed, anger, and ignorance, with my body, speech, and mind, I make full confession.
9. And I rejoice in all the merits of the victors, their sons, the private buddhas, and all the world, whether they need more instruction or not.
10. And those who have come to awakening, the lumens of the ten directions of the world, who have obtained nonattachment, I entreat them to turn the unsurpassed wheel of the dharma.

11. I request all those wishing to demonstrate final nirvāṇa to remain for as many eons as there are particles of dust, for the benefit and happiness of beings.
12. Whatever merit I may have obtained, through my homage, offering, confession, rejoicing, entreating, and requesting, I dedicate it for the awakening of all.

8c–9. With mind irreversibly set until attainment of the final end, the essence of awakening, and having great confidence in the triple gem, the aspirant places the right kneecap on the ground, joins the hands at the chest, and first recites three times the refuge prayer:

I go to the Buddha for refuge.
I go to the dharma for refuge.
I go to the saṅgha for refuge.

10. Then, having developed in preparation a loving attitude toward all beings, one observes all the inhabitants of the various realms of existence in distress through birth in the three lower realms, death, and the process of rebirth. [The three lower realms are those of animals, ghosts, and denizens of hell.]
11. Impelled by one's own distress and desiring to liberate beings from both distress and its causes, the aspirant should develop the irrevocable thought of awakening.
12. Maitreya, in the *Stemmy Array Scripture,* has explained well the good qualities invoked by the generation of this thought of awakening.
13. Reading scriptures or listening to teachers, one understands the unlimited qualities of the perfect thought of awakening. For this reason, the thought of awakening is to be generated in that way again and again.
14. In the *Scripture on Vīradatta's Questions,* the merit of this thought is explained. Here I shall provide that scripture's three-verse summary [verses 15–17]:
15. "If the merit of the thought of awakening were physical, it would fill the vault of space and, indeed, overflow it.
16. "Now if a person were to fill the fields of the buddhas with jewels, and if these fields were equal in number to the grains of sand in the Ganges, and if that individual would offer all of these jewels to the Lord of the World.
17. "Superior to that would be the merit of this offering—inclining one's mind toward awakening with hands joined. This offering is without limit."
18. Having generated the thought that aspires toward awakening, one should increase that thought with intense effort. The instruction

should be preserved exactly as it was explained, so that it might be recollected even in other births.

19. Without the discipline—essentially the thought of entering into awakening—the perfect aspiration will not increase. Thus, one desiring augmentation of complete awakening's discipline will certainly take hold of it with assiduous effort.
20. Now, only the aspirant continually adhering to the primary discipline—the seven gradations of the prātimokṣa—is fit for the discipline of the bodhisattva. [The seven gradations of the prātimokṣa are: the fully ordained monk, the fully ordained nun, the female probationer, the male novice, the female novice, the layman, and the laywoman.]
21. Moreover, from the discussions by the Tathāgata on the seven prātimokṣa gradations, celibacy is clearly considered best—the discipline of the fully ordained monk is accepted as pure.

II. THE VEHICLE OF THE PERFECTION OF INSIGHT AND THE DISCIPLINE OF THE BODHISATTVA

22. Now one should accept the vow of the bodhisattva discipline from a good teacher of correct character, using the ceremony found in the *Bodhisattva Fundamentals'* chapter on virtuous conduct.
23. A "good teacher" is learned in the ritual for imparting the discipline, observes the discipline, and has the patience and compassion to instill the discipline.
24. If, however much you have tried, you cannot find a teacher, then I will explain a different ritual whereby you can obtain the discipline:
25. It is the method by which Mañjuśrī, formerly the king Ambarāja, developed the thought of awakening as related in the *Scripture on the Array of Qualities in Mañjuśrī's Field of Awakening;* this method is clearly presented thus:
26. In the visualized presence of the lords may we generate the thought of awakening, with the resolve: "I extend my invitation to all beings—may I liberate them from saṃsāra.
27. "From now until the attainment of pure awakening, I will shun ill-will, anger, avarice, or envy.
28. "I undertake celibacy, leaving behind transgression and desire. With joy in the discipline of ethical conduct, I conduct myself as the Buddha before me.
29. "I am not anxious to obtain final awakening hastily, for I will stay until the bitter end, so long as one being remains in need.
30. "I will purify unlimited unimaginable fields and make my name renowned in the ten directions.
31. "My physical, vocal, and mental acts are all to be totally purified, and unwholesome acts may not be accomplished."

32. With this attitude of entering [into awakening]—which is the cause for the purification of the body, speech, and mind—one resides in the discipline. Studying well the three curricula in ethical conduct, one's trust in them flourishes. [The three curricula in ethical conduct are an obscure list taken from the chapter on conduct in the *Bodhisattvabhūmi;* these three are disciplinary conduct, conduct preserving virtue, and ethical conduct in aid to beings.]
33. Thus, through accomplishing both vows which constitute the discipline of the perfect bodhisattva, one completes the accumulations which bring total awakening. ["Both vows" refers to the two rituals in the lineages of Asaṅga and Śāntideva.]
34. All the buddhas have held that the generation of the forms of higher knowledge is the cause of the two accumulations, knowledge and merit. [The higher knowledges are: divine vision, divine audition, knowledge of others' thoughts, recollection of previous lives, miraculous powers, and knowledge of the destruction of defilements.]
35. A bird cannot ascend into the sky without unfolding its wings. A bodhisattva cannot work for the benefit of beings without ability in the higher knowledges.
36. The merit obtained in a single day by one with the higher knowledges cannot be equaled in a hundred lifetimes by one without them.
37. The bodhisattva wishing to complete quickly the accumulations requisite to total awakening will strenuously perfect the higher knowledges. The indolent have no chance.
38. The higher knowledges will not arise for one not accomplished in pacific contemplation—exert yourself again and again.
39. A yogin spoiling the phases of pacific contemplation will not perfect concentration in thousands of years.
40. Thus, the mind should be set virtuously on any of the objects of meditation delineated in the *Pamphlet on the Accumulation of Concentration* [Bodhibhadra's *Samādhisaṃbhāraparivarta,* Peking 5319].
41. If the yogin perfects pacific contemplation, then the higher knowledges will be accomplished. If he lacks preparation in the perfection of insight, though, the obscurations will not be destroyed.
42. So, to eliminate utterly the obscurations of the defilements and the knowable, the yogin should continually cultivate the perfection of insight along with skill in means.
43. Means without insight, and vice versa, is termed bondage in the scriptures, so neither may be rejected.
44. To remove doubt concerning the nature of means and insight, I will clarify their distinction:
45. The victors have defined means as all of the virtues—such as the perfection of giving—excepting only the perfection of insight.

46. The yogin will swiftly attain awakening in cultivating insight, aided by the cultivation of means. Exclusively contemplating nonself in phenomena retards progress.
47. Insight is fully explained as cognition of the emptiness of self-existence—the realization of the nonbirth of the aggregates, the elements, and the doors of perception. [These are the three standard models for categorizing events in the continuum of experience. The aggregates are the events which constitute the categories of form, feeling, ideation, mental / emotional formations, and consciousness. The doors of perception are the six sense objects (cognitive objects are included as a kind of sense object) and their corresponding sense faculties, including the intellect as the cognitive sense faculty. The eighteen elements are the six sense objects, the six sense faculties, and the six modes of consciousness operative in each of these sensory environments. The "nonbirth" of all of these indicates the radical deconstruction of conceptual / linguistic categories as a standard tool of Mahāyāna meditation.]
48. The "birth of existence" is irrational; likewise "nonexistence" is like a celestial flower. Both of these two faulty assertions reduce independently to absurdity, yet cannot occur in simultaneous conjunction.
49. A particular does not arise from itself, from something else, or from both, nor does it arise from no cause at all. Thus, there is naturally no self-existence.
50. Moreover, if we investigate the putative unity or diversity of all phenomena, since we cannot apprehend any self-existence we arrive at certainty of their lack of this quality.
51. Particulars' emptiness of self-existence has been demonstrated conclusively in the analysis within the *Seventy Stanzas* [*Śūnyatā-saptati*] and in the *Basic Middle Verses* [*Mūlamadhyamakakārikā*] of Nāgārjuna.
52. Therefore, I will not amplify here the discussion for fear of prolixity; only the tenets already demonstrated in those works are explained for the purpose of contemplative cultivation.
53. Accordingly, the cultivation of insight is precisely the contemplation of nonself through the nonapprehension of all phenomena's self-existence.
54. Insight—by which there is no vision of self-existence within phenomena—is explained as "analysis." It should be cultivated without conceptualization.
55. This world, arisen from conceptualization, has conceptualization as its nature. Thus, the elimination of every kind of conceptualization is the highest nirvāṇa.

56. So the Lord has said, "Conceptualization is great ignorance: it brings submersion into the ocean of existence. Presence in nonconceptual concentration is lucid nonconceptualization, clear as the sky."
57. And from the *Code for Entrance into Nonconceptualization* [*Avikalpa-praveśa-dhāraṇī,* Peking 810.32.229.1.1–232.5.8], "If a son of the victor should consider this holy dharma without conceptualization, he will pass beyond the impediments of conceptualization and will gradually obtain nonconceptualization."
58. So, having arrived at certainty about the nonself-existence of all unarisen phenomena by means of both analysis and scripture, the bodhisattva should cultivate contemplation without conceptualization.
59. Having thus cultivated reality, and having gradually obtained the stages of "heat" and so on, the bodhisattva will obtain the levels of the "joyful" and so forth. Then the awakening of the buddha is not distant. [The first line encapsulates the four preparatory phases of penetration in the "path of application": heat (that is, intensity of experience), peak experience, tolerance, and the highest mundane elements of experience. Beyond these are the ten stages of the bodhisattva—beginning with the joyful—in which the ten perfections are accomplished: liberality, virtue, patience, exertion, meditation, insight, means, aspiration, power, and gnosis.]

III. THE VEHICLE OF SECRET SPELLS AND THE KNOWLEDGE HOLDERS' DISCIPLINE

60–61b. One might wish to complete easily the accumulations for awakening, whether by the incantatory power that perfects the activities of pacification, augmentation, and so forth, or through the various powers, such as the eight mundane miracles—the cornucopia and so on. [Four forms of incantatory activity are frequently enumerated: the use of spells for pacification, augmentation, subjugation, and destruction. The eight mundane miracles are powers associated with all religious accomplishment, Buddhist and non-Buddhist, and indicate the appearance of abilities or miraculous objects through ascetic practices: the cornucopia, miraculous speed, the invincible sword, the instant execution of one's commands, dominion over the netherworld, invisibility, the wishing tree, and supremacy. The supermundane miracle is awakening.]

61c–62. And should one desire to practice the secret spells spoken in the scriptures of ritual activity, practical application, yoga, and so forth, then the yogin should delight a holy teacher through rendering him service, gifts, and following his directions to obtain the master's consecration.

63. Having obtained the complete master's consecration bestowed by a teacher well pleased, the yogin becomes purified of all transgression and fortunate in the accomplishment of psychic powers.
64. Those leading the celibate life should not accept the secret or insight / gnosis consecrations since *The Scripture of the Primordial Buddha* emphatically prohibits them. [As explained in the introduction, the literal performance of these two rituals, the secret consecration and the insight / gnosis consecration, involve sexual activity, either on the part of the preceptor or by the disciple. Atiśa does not specify his source in the *Kālacakra-tantra* that "emphatically prohibits" these rituals. I have been unable to trace this prohibition anywhere in the received text.]
65. If a celibate religious accepts either consecration, then the individual's ascetic vow is spoiled, as he has engaged in forbidden behavior.
66. The fault of "defeat" will occur for that ascetic and he will certainly fall into evil states of life where there is no possibility of accomplishment.
67. Obtaining the master's consecration, the yogin may hear and explain any of the esoteric scriptures, perform the offerings or the fire ceremony; there will be no fault in his awareness of reality.
68. Based on the explanation of the dharma observed in scriptures, the elder Dīpaṃkaraśrī fashioned this summary elucidation of the path to awakening when implored by Byang chub 'od.

So is completed *A Lamp for the Path to Awakening* authored by Śrī-Dīpaṃkarajñāna. The great Indian abbot and the editor / translator dGe ba'i blo gros have together translated and finalized this translation. This teaching was performed at Tho Ling Monastery in the country of Zhang Zhung.

—25—

The Advice to Layman Tuṇḍila

Charles Hallisey

Scholars frequently contrast the Mahāyāna and the Theravāda Buddhist traditions by noting that the Theravāda has considered its scriptural canon closed, whereas the Mahāyāna had a more open conception of scripture and canon, with the result that texts were continually added to the latter's corpus of scripture. But this contrast may be overdrawn, as we can see with "The Advice to the Layman Tuṇḍila." It belongs to a group of allegedly noncanonical sūtras that have circulated for a long time in the Theravāda; the great fifth-century commentator Buddhaghosa apparently knew of such texts and accepted them as he systematized the thought of the Theravādin tradition. Such texts may still seem anomalous, especially if one approaches these Theravādin texts with knowledge of the history of Mahāyāna literature, since they do not seem to propound any new teachings in comparison to what is otherwise known from the conventionally defined Pāli canon.

We can begin to have a better estimation of the significance of such texts if we consider their possible role as instructional aids. They were apparently one response to a fundamental problem continually faced by Theravāda Buddhists. As Louis Finot said, "The Buddhist canon is not an easy study: it discourages by its mass and its difficulties the enthusiasm of the most fearless. . . . It was necessary to be concerned about making this very indigestible mass accessible, either by condensing it in the form of a summary, or by combining scattered elements from this or that part of the doctrine, or finally by simply detaching from this immense corpus some pages that interested more particularly the spiritual life or the practice of the community." (Louis Finot, "Recherches sur la littérature laotienne," *Bulletin de l'École Française d'Extrême-Orient* 17 [1917], 71).

"The Advice to the Layman Tuṇḍila" is a summary of Buddhist practice. Although it is a recent composition, probably composed in Sri Lanka in the eighteenth century, its basic structure is modeled on the "step-by-step teaching" or graduated sermon that is frequently referred to in the canon:

> The Lord gave a graduated sermon (*anupubbikathā*; Sanskrit *anupūrvikathā*) as follows: discourse on giving, discourse of morality, discourse on heavens. He displayed the danger, vanity, and defilement in desires and the benefit in renunciation. When the Lord knew that [the listener's] mind was ready, pliable, unbiased, elated, pleased, then he taught him the truth which is praised by the buddhas: suffering, its arising, its cessation, and the path to its cessation.
>
> *Dīgha nikāya,* edited by T.W. Rhys Davids and J.E. Carpenter (London: Pali Text Society, 1967), vol. 1, p. 110.

By adapting this structure of the graduated sermon, "The Advice to the Layman Tuṇḍila" illustrates one understanding of the Buddhist life as a "gradual path," to use George Bond's phrase for "the hierarchy of means and ends necessary to relate the dhamma [dharma] to a variety of people and yet to maintain the belief in one ultimate goal and one ultimate meaning of the dhamma." (George D. Bond, "The Gradual Path as a Hermeneutical Approach to the Dhamma," in *Buddhist Hermeneutics,* edited by Donald S. Lopez, Jr. [Honolulu: University of Hawaii Press, 1988], p. 34)

The function of "The Advice to the Layman Tuṇḍila" as a summary of Buddhist practice raises some questions about how we should interpret some particular points in the text. For example, the "The Advice to the Layman Tuṇḍila" frequently uses similes, a teaching technique that is very common in Buddhist literature. But what should we learn from these images? In some cases, we can see that a metaphor is meant to extend meaning from something that is known well to something relatively unknown, as when generosity is said to be a shelter. In others, the metaphors seem intended to persuade, as when desires are said to be "like a boil filled with pus because both have a stinking nature." These are familiar functions of metaphor, but neither seems to apply to the most elaborate simile in "The Advice to the Layman Tuṇḍila"—the city of perfect peace. Instead, we can suggest that this metaphor of the city of perfect peace is a helpful device for listing and linking a variety of doctrinal items and practices: the standard parts of a city are associated with different aspects of Buddhist life as a mnemonic device. It is easy to see that such a metaphor could be conducive to "The Advice to the Layman Tuṇḍila" 's functional role as a summary of Buddhist practice.

We should also note that the imagery of a city suggests a continuum between perfect peace (Pāli *nibbāna,* Sanskrit *nirvāṇa*) and the possible forms of rebirth found in the cycle of rebirth (*saṃsāra*). The same image of a city was used with other possible places where beings could be reborn, and heavens, above all, were described as cities. This homology between heavens and perfect peace as "cities" creates a double set of relations between nirvāṇa and the cycle of rebirth. On the one hand, they are still different kinds of things, and are best understood, as they are in doctrine, as opposed to one another; it is thus appropriate to contrast the bliss of nirvāṇa with the suffering of the cycle of rebirth. On the other hand, the bliss of the city of perfect peace could also be construed as merely, even if immeasurably, different in degree from that of heaven. This imagery of cities may help us to appreciate why nirvāṇa is often placed at the pinnacle of a cosmological hierarchy, as has been frequently noted in ethnographic studies of contemporary Theravāda Buddhism.

The *Tuṇḍilovādasutta* found in Charles Hallisey, "*Tuṇḍilovāda:* An Allegedly Non-Canonical Sutta," *Journal of the Pali Text Society* 15 (1990), 170–95.

The Advice to Layman Tuṇḍila

Praise to that Blessed One, the Fully Enlightened One

Thus I have heard. At one time the Blessed One was dwelling near Kapilavastu in the Banyan Park on the shore of the Rohana River. He stayed out of kindness for gods and humans in the Park of the Banyan Trees teaching the truth with a sweet voice and placing them on the path to heaven and liberation. At that same time, a certain householder named Tuṇḍila lived in that city. That householder was very wealthy with many servants, cows and bullocks, and many treasuries filled with money, grain, gold, silver, and so on. Irandatī was his wife.

One day that householder, desiring to hear the Blessed One teach, took some lamps, incense, perfumes, and flowers and approached him. After he greeted the Blessed One, he sat in the assembly and listened to the truth. Delighted by the teaching of the truth, that householder thought thus: "I was born rich and wealthy in this existence because of the merit produced by generosity in previous existences. It would now be right to be generous again." So thinking, at the end of the Blessed One's teaching, he worshiped him, and returned home with his retinue. He sent for his wife and said, "Dear, I would like to give alms," and hearing his plan, she agreed, saying, "Excellent, Lord." The two of them prepared alms and had a pavilion built in front of their own house. They invited the order of monks led by the Buddha, and had them seated in the middle of the pavilion, and they gave a great almsgiving with all kinds of food.

At the end of the meal, the Blessed One, seeing what went into the almsgiving done by that householder, thought that today Tuṇḍila—because of the fruit of almsgiving done previously—would be happy when he thought about his past, his present, and his future. So thinking, the Buddha performed a miracle, and showed his wonderful form. He sent forth the six colored rays—blue, yellow, red, white, crimson, and golden—which come from the body of enlightened ones. Those colored rays from the middle part of his body filled the universe. Those from the lower part pierced the watery edge of earth and ran down to the hell of No Pleasure (Avīci). Those from the upper part rose up to the highest pinnacles of existence. Everywhere was flooded with these rays. Then the householder Tuṇḍila, having seen his [the Blessed One's] miraculous manner, was filled with wonder and surprise, and his heart was filled with joy.

GENEROSITY

Then the Blessed One, knowing his disposition, thought that it would be proper to praise his almsgiving and said this to Tuṇḍila: "Householder, extremely great alms have been given by you today. Truly, generosity has been an ancient custom of the wise. Householder, even I, when I was a being destined for enlightenment, with knowledge still not matured and living for the sake of striving for enlightenment, gave great gifts. Now having become enlightened as the fruit of those gifts, I have received omniscient knowledge. Without generosity, it would not be possible to become an enlightened one, a solitary enlightened one, or a worthy saint. Therefore, it is said that there are great profits and benefits from generosity." To display the benefits of generosity to the householder Tuṇḍila, the Teacher said these verses:

> Generosity is a marvel of sovereignty, it is near to wealth,
> Generosity guards goods, and it increases happiness.
>
> To those who give a gift to the best, the best merit increases,
> As well as the best life, complexion, fame, glory, happiness, and strength.
>
> To those who give a gift to the best, there is the attainment of highest truth.
> Whether reborn as a divine being or a human, he enjoys the best happiness.
>
> Generosity done out of any desire achieves what is desired,
> Generosity is like a treasure pot, it is like a wish-fulfilling tree.
>
> Just as a town with a water supply never suffers from drought,
> The wealth of one who is generous never dries up.
>
> Kings, thieves, fire, and water, as well as anything that is unliked,
> These five do not destroy his wealth.
>
> Therefore alms should be given, generosity is a support to the poor,
> Generosity is a shelter for humans, generosity frees from hell.
>
> Generosity is a staircase to heaven, and the best path to liberation,
> Generosity is to be considered like the door for entering perfect peace (nirvāṇa).
>
> Generosity is increased wealth, it is running streams of wealth,
> Generosity protects material goods, and it protects life.

Whoever [gives] thinking, "whatever the life, I will have great power,"
He always receives what he desires of riches and wealth

Whether they are on top of a tree, or a mountain,
Or in between the sky and earth, or on the ocean,
[Those who are generous] have food, drink, and material goods.

Alms given with faith, they say, is what has great fruit.
Generosity preceded by faith makes whatever is done
Free from anxiety about its outcome.

Those who are at ease with their past, present, and future
Receive threefold happiness.
It gives happiness among humans and in heavens,
As well as the highest happiness.

Thus it gives the happiness of perfect peace.
Everything is received by generosity,
From local sovereignty to the splendor of a universal monarch,
Even divine kingship in heavens, all of it comes from generosity.

Whatever success there is among humans, whatever pleasure in divine worlds,
And the happiness of perfect peace, all are received from generosity.

The enlightenment of a disciple, and the enlightenment of a solitary sage,
And the enlightenment of a thus come one (*tathāgata*),
All are received from generosity.

The enlightened ones of the past, which are as numerous as sand in the ocean,
Received full enlightenment after having given extraordinary alms.

"Thus, O householder, generosity is of great advantage and is of great benefit." Thus the Blessed One taught the benefit of generosity to the householder Tuṇḍila. At the end of the narrative about generosity, he began to speak about the benefit of morality (*śīla*).

MORALITY

"O householder, morality is the root of success in this world and the next. There is no support, no help, no other shelter equal to morality. There is no ornament or decoration, no perfume like morality. There is nothing for cleaning the stains of the defilements equal to morality. There is nothing more beautiful than morality. There is no staircase for climbing to heaven like morality, no door equal to morality for entering the city of perfect peace." Then the Blessed One, teaching the benefit of morality, said these verses:

Morality is the highest source of every happiness,
The moral one goes to the three heavens because of morality,
Morality is the shelter, the refuge, the relief
Of anyone in the saṃsāra.

As the sky, though filled with a host of stars,
Does not shine without the pure moon,
So a man may be famous, distinguished by beauty and family,
But he does not shine without morality.

As the nymphs in the celestial assembly
Live there always adorned,
But without the divine lord of the city they do not shine,
So one having understanding does not shine without morality.

As with a youth adorned with jewels and pearls
And wearing good clothing, but without perfume,
So a man may be adorned with the ornament of generosity,
But he will not shine without the perfume of morality.

As a forest may have birds and bees
And in the spring may be adorned with flowers,
But does not shine without the singing of the cuckoo,
So, indeed, does he who is without morality not shine.

As a house, though filled with wife and children,
Though a house of wealth, crowded with a host of relatives,
Does not shine without the three kinds of elder,
So one with special qualities does not shine without morality.

As a city, though filled with men and women,
Though it has elephants and horses,
Does not shine without a king,
So the wealthy man does not shine without morality.

As an elephant, though strong and mighty,
Though it may be the best of elephants, perfect in every limb,
Does not shine without a tusk,
So someone good-looking does not shine without morality.

As a tank, though filled with water
And frequented by flocks of geese,
Does not shine without the lotus and water lily,
So a man, though adorned with beauty and position,
Does not shine if he abstains from morality.

Though one may have a divine form, with a divine complexion,
And be adorned with every ornament,

Without food, even with that form, one will not shine,
So a man may have wealth, grain, and money,
But he will not shine if he abstains from morality.

Those who guard morality will be freed from all suffering,
They will have long lives until they enter perfect peace.

If one might guard morality for even a moment,
It would have immeasurable fruit
Connected with infinite special qualities and praised by all the buddhas.

By a life of meager virtue, one is reborn among the nobles,
By moderate virtue, among the gods, by high virtue, one will be pure.

By abstaining from the taking of life, one will have beauty
Filling every part of the body,
One will have happiness, long life, and health.

By abstaining from stealing, one will have a lot of grain and money,
One will have wealth that cannot be taken by these five:
Kings, thieves, fire, water, and unpleasant people.

By abstaining from sexual misconduct, one will escape existence as a woman,
One will be perfect in every part of one's body, fearless, and live in happiness.

By abstaining from false speech, one will have wide wisdom and be skilled,
One's mouth adorned with the perfume of sweet speech.

By abstaining from intoxicating liquor, one will be sane, not dull,
One will have shame and scruples, and will be beautiful from speaking the truth.

"Thus, O householder, morality is of great advantage and great benefit." In this way, the Blessed One explained the benefit of morality to the householder Tuṇḍila. The Blessed One said further: "Whatever person, whether a woman or a man, a male noble or a female noble, a priest or a priestess, a male householder or a female householder, a poor man or a poor woman, one thing, O monks, is to be guarded. What one thing is to be guarded? Abstinence from taking life results in kingship among those in the Eastern Continent (Pūrvavideha), in great power and great strength. A second precept, O monks, is also to be guarded: abstinence from stealing, after having renounced taking what is not given. This results in kingship among the inhabitants of the Western Continent (Aparagodāniya; Pāli Aparagoyāna), in great power and in great strength. O monks, there is a third precept to be protected: abstinence from an unchaste life, after having renounced unchaste living. This results in kingship over the Northern Continent (Uttarakurudvīpa), in great power and in great strength. O monks, the fourth precept to be guarded is abstinence from false speech, after having renounced false speech. This results in kingship over the inhabitants of all of Rose-Apple Continent (Jambudvīpa), in the splendor of universal kingship, in great power and in great strength. O monks, the fifth precept to be protected is abstinence from the condition of indolence caused by intoxicating liquor, having renounced that condition of indolence from intoxicating liquor. This results in ruling the retinue of the four guardian gods, with great power and with great strength.

"O monks, there is a sixth precept to be guarded. It is abstinence from eating at the wrong time, having renounced eating at the wrong time. This results in becoming a king over the gods of the Heaven of the Thirty-Three (Trayastriṃśa; Pāli, Tāvatiṃsa), becoming a divine being with great power and great strength. The seventh precept to be guarded, O monks, is abstinence from dancing, singing, and music, after having renounced dancing, singing, and music. This results in becoming a strong and powerful king over the gods of the realm of death (Yama). The eighth precept is abstinence from flowers, perfumes, and ointments, after having renounced flowers, perfumes, and ointments, which results in becoming a strong and powerful king over the gods of the Happy Heaven (Tuṣita). O monks, the ninth precept to be guarded is abstinence from high, big beds, after having renounced high, big beds. This results in kingship with great power and with great strength over the gods for whom whatever they desire is created (Nirmāṇarati). O monks, there is a tenth precept to be guarded: abstinence from accepting any gold or silver, after having renounced receiving gold or silver. This results in kingship over the gods who have power over the creations of another (Paranirmitavaśavartin), with great power and with great strength. O monks, these are the ten precepts." The Teacher then said these verses:

One hundred elephants, one hundred horses,
One hundred chariots drawn by mules,
One hundred girls adorned with one thousand jeweled earrings,
All this is not worth one-sixteenth of the taking of a single precept.

Birth in two kinds of family—noble and priestly—
And never in a low family. Guard morality—this is the fruit.

They have endless wealth and endless power,
Crowds of the best women. Guard morality—this is the fruit.

They are surrounded by a fourfold army
With elephants, horses, chariots, and infantry. Guard morality—this is the fruit.

They have the scent of sandalwood on the body, and of water lily blowing
From the mouth to the extent of fifty miles. Guard morality—this is the fruit.

Great merit, great glory, great wisdom, great fame,
Great force, great strength. Guard morality—this is the fruit.

Morality is the best ornament, morality is the highest ornament,
Morality produces lack of fear about hell. Guard morality—this is the fruit.

Sandalwood, incense, lotus, and the eight kinds of jasmine,
Among these kinds of perfume, the perfume of morality is best.

HEAVENS

At the end of the explanation of the benefit of the ten precepts, he began to explain about heaven. "Śakra [Pāli, Sakka], O householder, is chief god, having the topmost, most pleasing happiness, always enjoying himself with divine fame in the realm of the Thirty-Three on top of Mount Meru [Pāli Sineru]. Endowed with a divine form and decorated with divine ornaments, and constantly hearing the five kinds of music, and finding delight in dancing, singing, and music, he perpetually enjoys divine pleasure.

"The gods of the retinue of the four guardian gods have lives nine million years in length, and throughout that time, they experience divine pleasure and happiness. The gods of the Thirty-Three have lives 30 million, one hundred thousand years in length, and throughout that time they experience and enjoy divine pleasure. The lives of gods of the realm of death are 14 million plus 4 million years in length, the gods of the Happy Heaven 57 million, one hundred thousand years, the gods whose every desire is created 132 million plus forty hundred thousand years, the gods having power over the creations of another 139 million, one hundred thousand years, and throughout that time they all experience and enjoy divine pleasure and happiness. Having been born there, they enjoy themselves for a long time.

"The palace of Śakra, chief of the gods, is surrounded by walls, has streets, a garden, ponds, a wishing tree, elephant-drawn vehicles, horse-drawn vehicles, and chariots. In that pond, there are lotuses and water lilies, white lotuses standing on the surface with many blossoms scenting the wind in all directions. The five kinds of music are made constantly and delightfully. All the musical instruments are played by gods, and they sing songs with sweet voices and they display themselves dancing day and night.

"This kind of Śakra-happiness is not received by those who have not made merit. In this world, those who do actions like taking care of parents, giving alms, guarding morality, meditating on the Buddha, his teaching, or the order of monks, those who pay respect, honor those who should be honored, those who worship, are diligent in making merit, all of these people receive divine happiness and divine pleasure and enjoy it for a long time."

Thus the Blessed One taught to the householder Tuṇḍila a sermon concerned with the qualities of the heavens.

"But this heaven is impermanent, it is not stable. All gods stay there happily for as long as they should, with merit wasting away, and they fall away from a pleasing heaven and are reborn in a birth according to their merit. Therefore, O householder, heaven is impermanent, unstable, it is suitable for making one disgusted with the constituent elements of existence, it is not to be taken as something to excite desires. Truly, it is to be held dear, it is to please, but it is also to be renounced and to be escaped from."

THE DANGERS IN SENSE DESIRES

Thus at the end of the account of heaven, the Blessed One began to teach about the fault in desires. "O householder, because of desires, one experiences great and terrible suffering. By means of desire, one has many sorrows, many troubles, much distress, one dwells with suffering, one is not freed from suffering. Always, equanimity is the best mental state [in this world], sadness is constant, sorrow is constant, being bitten [by snakes] is constant, being oppressed by other things is constant, much suffering is constant. One having desires does not survive long. He is not freed [from suffering] for even the brief moment that it takes water to drip from a lotus leaf, but is simply destroyed. Because they have the nature of being false, desires are like a dream; because they have the nature of dominating a person, desires are like a firebrand burning a forest; because they have the nature of overwhelming, desires are like a stream of clarified butter; because they have the nature of flaming, desires are like a firebrand; because they have the nature of scorching, desires are like a charcoal pit; because they have the aim of destroying life, desires are like poison; because they have the nature of clinging, desires are like quivering metal; because they have the nature of burning, desires are like a [hot] iron ball; because they have the nature of being incurable, desires are like a wound surrounded by swarms of flies. Thus all of it is suffering.

"Because they have the nature of a stench, desires are like a boil filled with pus, desires are like a man sunk in a heap of dung, desires are like a man sticking his hand in a putrid corpse, desires are like a man who puts his fingers in a bowl of coals. Thus, on account of desire, beings experience in this world exceedingly terrible suffering and great ruin. But, after having experienced the suffering of this world, in the next world, they are born in hell. They experience acute, painful, bitter sensations in that great hell."

THE BENEFITS OF RENUNCIATION

Then the Blessed One, having taught the fault in desires, began to explain the benefits in renunciation. "O householder, one in the household life has a lot of suffering, a lot of trouble, a lot of obstacles, many pains, many duties, many cares, many wants. There is only suffering in this household life, it brings one toward hell, and distances one from the path to perfect peace. Therefore, O householder, it is suitable to make one disgusted, it is not to be something that excites desire. Truly, it pleases, and is to be held dear, but it is also to be renounced and escaped from. Any person, seeing the danger in desires and the fault in household life, will practice a life of chastity, having first abandoned the delight of child and wife, gone forth from the house, and entered the realm of cold (Himavantam, that is, the Himalayas). That person will receive the great happiness of perfect peace (*nirvāṇa*)."

Then the Blessed One, having shown the fault in household life and the benefits in renunciation, displayed the benefits of perfect peace: "O householder, since this goes out, therefore it is called extinguishing (*nirvāṇa*). Because it cools the four kinds of suffering—birth, sickness, old age, and death—it is called perfect peace. Because it causes the extinguishing of the five faults—passion, anger, bewilderment, pride, and wrong views—it is called extinguishing. In that perfect peace, there is no birth, no old age, no sickness, no death, no fear, no distress.

"The great city of perfect peace which is the most excellent thing for beings, a delightful shelter, has a wall, a door, a watchtower, a moat, streets, a bazaar, a tree, a palace, a central pillar, a bed, a couch, rows of burning lamps, flowers, perfumes, and ointments, a lake with sand and filled with water in which there are lotuses and lilies of various kinds, a garden with bees, a pool with geese and cakravāka birds, frequented by flocks of pheasants, singing cuckoos, young parrots, peacocks, and heron. These are the splendors of the great city of perfect peace.

"What is the wall in that great city of perfect peace? The perfection of patience is like the wall. What is the door? The perfection of generosity is like the gate. Concentration (*samādhi*) is like the watchtower, the perfection of loving-kindness the moat. What are the streets? The twenty-four ways of exerting oneself. The thirty-seven constituents of enlightenment are like the bazaar, and the ten perfections the palace. The seven books of the higher philosophy (*abhidharma*) are like the city column. The perfection of renunciation is like the bed, the couch the knowledge of liberation. What is the brightness of the lamps? The lamps of knowledge. The flowers, perfumes, and ointments are the perfection of truth. The lake is the lake of meditation and it is filled with the cool water of compassion and morality is its lotuses and lilies. The crowd of chief disciples are the bees and diligence is the garden. The geese and cakravāka birds are the worthy saints who have removed the defilements that come with birth. What is it that is frequented by flocks of pheasants and other birds? It is the pond of perfect peace. In that city of perfect peace there is an expansive [square] in the seven books of higher philosophy.

"Truth is the highest happiness indeed. The pleasure of heaven like this is not gained without making merit. Other than this it is not possible to go to or enter the city of perfect peace. Only those people who with generosity always delight in meritorious actions will be able to go to and enter the great city of perfect peace."

Then the Teacher, praising the great city of perfect peace, said:

> Perfect peace is shown to be peaceful, excellent, pure, auspicious,
> A place without fear, permanent, without old age, without death,
> secure.

Thus the Blessed One taught a teaching on truth which is connected to various good qualities to the householder Tuṇḍila. Having heard this marvelous teaching of truth together with his wife Irandatī, and having drunk the nectar of truth, moved by joy, both of them became worthy ones (*arhat*) and other people attained many fruits, such as stream-winner and so on.

—26—

The Legend of the Iron Stūpa

Charles Orzech

The "Legend of the Iron Stūpa" recounts the origins of the Esoteric School of Buddhism and the "reappearance" of its key texts and rites contained in the *Mahāvairocana Scripture* (*Taishō* 848) and in the *Assembled Reality of All of the Tathāgathas* (*Taishō* 865–66). Together these are the foundation of East Asian Esoteric Buddhism (Chinese Mijiao, Zhenyan; Japanese Shingon). Both texts are of South Asian origin and figure prominently as root texts in Indo-Tibetan Vajrayāna. The second text, the *Sarvatathāgatatattvasaṃgraha,* is also known as the *Vajraśekhara* or "Diamond Tip." The story below is related by Bukong jingang (Amoghavajra), and is based on the oral teaching of his master Jingang zhi (Vajrabodhi). Both men came to China as missionaries from South Asia in the early eighth century. A second version by Kūkai, the Japanese founder of Shingon, relates the tale as based on the oral transmission of his teacher, Huiguo, the disciple of Bukong.

The tale of the origin of the Esoteric teachings becomes the key document in the construction of a lineage of transmission for the Esoteric School in China and Japan. Some Chinese sources and later Japanese sources trace the transmission of the Esoteric teachings from Mahāvairocana to Vajradhara, to Nāgārjuna, who is said to have fetched them from the Iron Stūpa, to Nāgārjuna's disciple Nāgabodhi, and finally to Vajrabodhi. Interestingly, this transmission is not specified in Vajrabodhi's account but first surfaces in memorial stele written by disciples of Bukong. Vajrabodhi merely says that a "great worthy" (*bhadanta*) retrieved the teachings from the stūpa.

Beyond its importance in recounting the sacred history of the Esoteric tradition, the "Legend of the Iron Stūpa" reveals a curious tension in Buddhist thought, that between the widely accepted notion that humanity had entered the last age of the teaching (Chinese *mofa,* Japanese *mappō*) and the Esoteric teaching that such notions of decline, like all notions of time, are merely mental constructions. According to the Esoteric teachings, the true teaching is always available and "has come down to this day and has not been extinguished." As Kūkai says, with the help of esoteric teaching and initiation one can eliminate the defilements and "attain buddhahood in this very body" (*sokushin jōbutsu*). Yixing, the major commentator on the *Mahāvairocana Scripture,* notes, "The three unimaginable periods of time (*triasaṅkhyeyakalpa*) are nothing other than the accomplishment of enlightenment (*bodhi*); if in the course of a single life one frees oneself from erroneous attachments, why discuss a period of time?" (*Taishō* 1796, p. 600c).

The tale has undergone some small but significant modifications in its transmission. It is particularly interesting that Kūkai's recounting of the tale, unlike Vajrabodhi's earlier version, includes Nāgārjuna's justification for being admitted to the stūpa: "After the disappearance of the Thus Come One, forests of heresies have arisen and the Great Vehicle is on the point of extinction. I have heard that the doctrines of all of the thus come ones of the three times are preserved in this stūpa. I demand to receive them for the salvation of all beings." The original version, translated below, merely alludes to the fact that in "central India the Buddhist teaching had gradually decayed."

The "Legend of the Iron Stūpa" also reflects the process of initiation into the maṇḍalas of the Esoteric School. Through the process of consecration (*guanding,* Sanskrit *abhiṣeka*) every initiate reenacts the entry into the Iron Stūpa with his or her own entry into the maṇḍala. Indeed, as Kakuban and other esoteric masters make clear, "the Iron stūpa is this very body" (*Kōgyō-daishi zenshu* [Tokyo: Kaji sekkai shisha, 1910], p. 510).

Bukong's text begins with a rather typical "outlining" discourse that both situates the reader and sets the stage for the genealogy of the text and its transmission to China. Accordingly, we are informed that the text available in China is but a superficial outline of the truly comprehensive scripture contained in the Iron Stūpa. A longer "outline" than that now extant was supposed to have been brought with Vajrabodhi from India but this text, which is described as "broad and long like a bed, and four or five feet thick," was tossed overboard during a typhoon. We are left with the obvious conclusion that the total teaching is still available, but only through initiation.

This translation is from *Instructions on the Gate to the Teaching of the Secret Heart of Great Yoga of the Scripture of the Diamond Tip [Jingang ding jing da yujia bimi shin di famen yiguei], Taishō shinshū daizōkyō* (Tokyo, 1924–1934), 1798; vol. 39, pp. 808a19–b28.

Further Reading

Chou I-liang's "Tantrism in China" (*Harvard Journal of Asian Studies* 8 [March 1945], 241–332) remains the best source on Chinese Esoteric Buddhism in English. Material on Japanese Shingon, by comparison, abounds. Yoshito S. Hakeda's *Kūkai: Major Works* (New York: Columbia University Press, 1978) gives access to the writings of Bukong's spiritual grandson, and two works give access to Japanese Esoteric thought and practice: Minoru Kiyota, *Shingon Buddhism* (Tokyo and Los

Angeles: Buddhist Books International, 1978), and Taikō Yamasaki, *Shingon: Japanese Esoteric Buddhism* (Boston and London: Shambala, 1988). The works of Tajima Ryūjun, *Étude sur le Mahāvairocana Sūtra (Dainichikyō)* (Paris: Adrien Maisonneuve, 1936) and *Les deux grands maṇḍalas et la doctrine de l'esotérisme Shingon* (Paris: Presses Universitaires de France, 1959) come from within the Shingon tradition but are more comprehensive, though hard to get. For further bibliography in French, Chinese, and Japanese see Charles Orzech, "Seeing Chen-yen Buddhism: Traditional Scholarship and the Vajrayāna in China," *History of Religions* 29: 2 (November 1989), 87–114.

The Legend of the Iron Stūpa

This scripture [which] has one hundred thousand verses in its expansive text, is unknown in this land [China]. Also, it bears the mark (*xiang,* Sanskrit *lakṣaṇa*) of the profound and esoteric realm of all the buddhas, great bodhisattvas, and so forth, and furthermore, it has not been heard of by the likes of śrāvakas, pratyekabuddhas, or people or gods of little knowledge.

This land's two-volume *Scripture of Brahma's Net* (*Brahmajālasūtra*) [contains] the abridged performances from this scripture, but in it the expanded signs and roots are inadequately [treated]. Now, as for this abridged yoga, those in the Western Land [India] who obtain consecration (*guanding,* Sanskrit *abhiṣeka*) expound it and confer it on one another. But when it comes to the expanded text, they still do not transmit it.

This one-hundred-thousand-verse text is, moreover, just the outline of the great treasury scripture of the bodhisattvas, [and] this great scripture is the scripture the teacher (*ācārya,* that is, Vajrabodhi) spoke of bringing [here]. Broad and long like a bed, and four or five feet thick, it has innumerable verses. It was enclosed in an iron stūpa in south India and during several hundred years after the Buddha's extinction, no one was able to open the stūpa, [because] iron gates and locks were used to secure it.

In this country of central India the Buddhist teaching had gradually decayed. At that time there was a great worthy (*dade,* Sanskrit *bhadanta*) [who had] first recited and held the mantra of Mahāvairocana, and attained Vairocana Buddha who manifested his body and a multitude of bodily forms. In mid-air, [Vairocana] expounded this teaching together with its textual passages and lines. He had [the great worthy] write them down in sequence. When it was finished [he] vanished. It is in fact the present *Essential Rites for Vairocana* [*Taishō* 849], in one volume.

At that time this great worthy held and chanted the "technique" [*chengjiu,* Sanskrit *siddhi,* detailed in the scripture] vowing to open the stūpa. For seven days [he] circumambulated the stūpa chanting, and taking seven grains of white mustard seed [he] threw them against the stūpa door and it opened.

Within the stūpa a multitude of spirits at once leaped forward, angrily barring [his] entry. [He] could only see the illumination of incense and candles for one or two yards in the interior of the stūpa. Exquisite flowers and jeweled canopies hung in sumptuous array, and [he] heard the sounds of praise to this king of scriptures. Then the great worthy sincerely confessed [his] sins and, giving rise to the great vow, thereafter gained entry into the stūpa. Once [he was] inside, the stūpa closed.

During the course of several days he [chanted] the praises of the expansive text of this scripture king, and each recitation was done [as if] in the space of a single meal. He obtained the instruction of all the buddhas and bodhisattvas and these [he] remembered and held and did not forget. Then he was commanded to go forth from the stūpa and the stūpa gate once again closed as of old.

At that time the transcription of the methods that were recorded and held consisted of one hundred thousand verses. This is the [scripture] entitled *The Scripture of the Diamond's Tip* and it is the expansive text preserved in the great treasury stūpa of the bodhisattvas that was cut off and missing from the world. But the light of the lamps and so forth inside the stūpa has come down to this day and has not been extinguished. This scripture—the one-hundred-thousand-verse text—is not yet available in this country. [As for] the arrival of this superficial text in this land, it was recounted by the ācārya [teacher] Vajrabodhi Tripiṭaka at the beginning of the Kaiyuan ("Opened Prime," December 713–February 742) period:

"I set forth from the western country [India] to cross the southern ocean in a fleet of more than thirty great ships, each one carrying more than five or six hundred persons. Once, when all were crossing in convoy in the very middle of the great ocean we ran into a typhoon. All the ships we depended upon were tossed about [like driftwood], and the ship I was on was about to be inundated. At that time I always kept the two scriptures I was bringing nearby so that I could receive and keep them and do the offerings. Now, when the captain saw that the ship was about to sink, everything on board was cast into the ocean, and in a moment of fright the one-hundred-thousand-verse text was flung into the ocean, and only the superficial text was saved. At that time I aroused my mind in meditation, doing the technique for eliminating disasters, and the typhoon abated, and for perhaps more than a quarter mile around the ship wind and water did not move. All on board took refuge in me, and bit by bit we got to this shore and arrived in this country.

"In the seventh year of the reign period Opened Prime (C.E. 721) [I] arrived in the Western Capital (Changan) and the Chan master Yixing sought consecration from me. When it became known that [I had] this extraordinary Gate of the Teaching, [he] commanded Iśvara to help translate it into Chinese. Yixing and the others, as it turns out, personally transcribed it. First [we] relied upon the order of the Sanskrit text and then [we] discussed its meaning so as not to lose words. [Yet] its meaning has not yet been [fully] explained."

—27—

Two Tantric Meditations: Visualizing the Deity

Luis O. Gómez

The following is an English translation of two chapters from a Sanskrit text describing the essentials of various tantric ritual and meditation sessions. The Sanskrit name for this genre of texts, and for the religious practice they describe, is *sādhana*—literally, "realization." As a text, a sādhana is presented as a description of the essential elements of a "visualization." Secondarily, a sādhana is also an iconographic description of the features of a particular deity. The description is intended as a guide for the practice of invoking, and mentally creating and retaining the visual image of, a sacred figure. But the term sādhana can be used in more general terms to refer to all of the ritual practices associated with the visualization.

Numerous sādhanas are preserved as independent texts or in collections. The one translated below forms part of an Indian anthology titled *A Garland of Sādhanas (Sādhanamālā)*. This anthology was compiled in the eleventh century C.E., but may contain sādhanas from as early as the seventh century. Each of the sections in this work describes the characteristics and features of the image that is to be visualized. Although many sections in this manual only describe the image to be visualized, the sādhanas translated below also describe the process or method of visualization—the first text does this in abbreviated form, the second is a complete visualization session, including its rituals and the content of its meditations. These sādhanas provide general guidelines that are followed in the visualization of most images.

The two sādhanas translated below are both dedicated to the late Buddhist female deity Tārā. She is often associated with the bodhisattva Avalokiteśvara, as his consort or as a member of his entourage. She shares with the bodhisattva the role of patron of compassion. Her name is usually explained as "she who saves" (or, more literally, "she who ferries [living beings] across [the ocean of saṃsāra]"), although the name probably originally meant "star," specifically the north star, which "guides [sailors] across [the ocean]." Her role as savioress (and therefore protectoress) is clearly stated in the first of the two texts translated below, where she takes on one of the major roles of Avalokiteśvara as the one to protect us from the "eight perils." Tārā, however, is more than just a feminine version of Avalokiteśvara; she comes to assume the attributes of a buddha and perfect wisdom as well, as implied by the second of the two texts translated below.

The first of the two sādhanas is an anonymous poem dedicated to Tārā as the deity that protects the worshiper from the "eight great fears" or "dangers." The details of the ritual are only suggested, but the allusions are comprehensive, so that the sādhana can be seen as a summary of a tantric ritual. This sādhana is also a classical example of the combination of religious elements forming the tantric ritual. These elements form the four axes of a visualization session: protective magic, philosophical discourse and reflection, devotion, and symbolic transformation of the self.

The second sādhana is one of the longest and most detailed in the *Sādhanamālā*. It is attributed to the Indian tantric master Anupamarakṣita, a learned monk who flourished around the year 1165 C.E. Although most of his works have come down to us only in Tibetan translation, the *Sādhanamālā* preserves two scholarly and richly detailed summaries of the tantric ritual of meditation (these same texts are also preserved in Tibetan translation). One of these texts is devoted to the visualization of Khasarpaṇa, the other to Tārā. The Tārā sādhana is translated below in full. It is a fine example of the elegant and scholarly liturgical writing that is as characteristic of tantra as the stereotypical sexual and cosmic symbolism.

The original Sanskrit text appears in B. Bhattacharyya, ed., *Sādhanamālā,* vol. 1 (Baroda: Gaekwad Oriental Series, 1925), pp. 200–206 (number 98). This sādhana was translated in part by Bhattacharyya in the first edition of his *Indian Buddhist Iconography* (Baroda: Gaekwad Oriental Series, 1928), pp. 169–75. The Sanskrit text accompanying that translation contains many errors, and makes a complicated, already defective text all the more difficult to decipher. Bhattacharyya did not explain what criteria he used in deciding which sections to omit from his translation. Both text and translation were omitted without explanation in the second, revised edition of 1968, where Bhattacharyya includes only a summary (pp. 20–23). The same author's *Introduction to Buddhist Esoterism* (2nd rev. ed., Varanasi: Chowkhamba Sanskrit Series Office, 1964) contains a paraphrase of the sādhana (Chapter II, "Procedure for Worship," pp. 104–8). Bhattacharyya's abbreviated text and translation of 1928 were also the basis for an improved, but further abbreviated, rendition by E. Conze, *Buddhist Meditation* (New York: Harper & Row, 1956), pp. 133–39 (§III.3). Kūkai's recounting of the tale may be found in Tajima Ryūjun, *Étude sur le Mahāvairocana Sūtra* (*Dainichikyō*) (Paris: Adrien Maisonneuve, 1936), p. 31.

Method for Visualizing Tārā [as She Who Protects Us against] the Eight Great Perils

Ārya Aṣṭamahābhaya Tārā Sādhana

1. I bow to her, to this one whom we only need remember to be freed from all of the eight great perils [death by fire; death by drowning; death by falling from a cliff; thunderbolts; dying at the hands of one's enemies by the sword, etc.; imprisonment or death by execution; spells and incantations, demons and ghosts; and wild beasts and vipers].

Having bowed to her, I will describe her. Listen, then, my child, to her sādhana.

2. First, one meditates on her as Tārā the Remover of the Eight Perils, [visualizing her] in the middle of the sky.

After one has worshiped her mentally, then one should confess one's transgressions.

3. After rejoicing in [the] merit [of all beings], one should offer one's own merit.

Then, one should give away one's whole person (*ātmabhāva*), and then perform the triple refuge three times.

4. After one has carried out whatever [duties one] had to perform, one should immediately [concentrate one's mind] on emptiness.

Thereupon, [one should visualize] an eight-petal lotus flower in full bloom, within the moon in one's heart.

5. In the middle of this [lotus], one imagines [the syllable] "Tāṃ," [and, then, within this syllable,] a blue-colored lotus.

In the middle of this [lotus, one visualizes] again the syllable, [now] shining with the flames of [a burning] fire.

6. With this, he generates [a mental image of] the deity [Tārā], adorned with all of her ornaments [and features].

On her right [side] she [displays the gesture of] a deity that grants all wishes, at the same time her left hand holds a lotus.

7. She has a single face, a beautiful countenance, and the appearance of fresh youth.

Her hair [is covered] with the sweetest smelling blossoms, and she stands on a moon resting on a lotus.

8. She sits in the half-lotus position, [and from this seat] will protect the three worlds.

This image of Tārā should be visualized in the midst of a group of eight other deities by the serene yogin who meditates [in this way,] pervading [all] with the power of the mantra, [he recites the following:]

Oṃ, Tāre tuttāre ture, svāhā.
Oṃ, tā, svāhā in the east.
Oṃ, re, svāhā in the south.

Oṃ, tu, svāhā in the west.
Oṃ, ttā, svāhā to Vahnikoṇa [fire, in the southeast].
Oṃ, re, svāhā to Nairṛtī [earth, in the southwest].
Om, tu, svāhā to Vāyavya [wind, in the northwest].
Oṃ, re, svāhā to Aiśāni [water, in the northeast].
"Oṃ Tāṃ. Receive the Diamond Flower—[it is for you, O Tārā,] who ferries [us across]. Svāhā.
One should offer flowers [to her]. One should present [her] with perfumes, food, and other [offerings, while holding one's hands] in the lotus gesture (*utpala-mudrā*).

9. In this way the visualization is practiced, evoking the youthful deity.
One should practice this [visualization], the highest in the world, the one that destroys the eight perils.

[Thus] concludes *The Method for Visualizing Tārā [as She Who Protects Us against] the Eight Great Perils*.

Fairly Detailed Description of the Method for Visualizing the Goddess Tārā

Kiñcid vistaraṃ Tārā sādhanam

After paying obeisance to Tārā, the great mother of the conquerors (*jina*), who is totally free from fault or defect, I now write [this account of] her sādhana, at the request of [my] friends, for the good of persons of virtue, writing with clear and beautiful words, and with devotion.

I had never before written anything at all, even at [my] teacher's behest. [I now] write in summary form what I remember from what has been taught [to me].

THE PROPER PLACE FOR MEDITATION

First of all, the person who will use mantras [for his meditation] should arise early in the morning, wash his face, feet, and other [parts of his body], and, after purifying himself, should sit in a comfortable cross-legged position in a secluded and agreeable place, where one has spread sweet fragrances and has strewn the ground with fragrant flowers.

FIRST VISUALIZATION

[Then] one should mentally perceive, [as if present] in one's own heart, the first vowel, "*A*" which gradually turns into the orb of the moon. In the middle of this moon one should see a lovely blue lotus. On the filaments of this lotus one will see the spotless orb of [a second] moon, upon which [appears] the yellow seed-syllable (*bīja*) *Tāṃ*. . . . Thereupon, [he sees rays of light] issuing from this yellow seed-syllable *Tāṃ* . . . , and [this] mass of rays, which destroy the darkness of the world's delusions, illuminate all the endless worlds that exist in the ten directions, and gather the numberless, measureless families of greatly compassionate buddhas and bodhisattvas that exist in [all] these worlds, bring them [here, before the meditator], and sustain [them in mid-air] in the sky [above him].

PRELIMINARY VISUALIZED RITUAL

1. Act of Worship

Then one should worship those buddhas and bodhisattvas who are standing [suspended in mid-air] in the sky [above him], [offering them] heavenly flowers, incense, perfumes, garlands, unguents, [fragrant] powders, robes, parasols, banners, bells, hanging cloths, and the like.

2. Act of Confession

Having done this, one should confess his sins [as follows]:

> Whatever evil deed I have committed, caused others to commit, or consented to their being committed, as I have wandered through the beginningless cycle of transmigration (*anādisaṃsāre*), whether I did so with [my] body, [my] speech, or [my] mind, all of these I confess.

After one has confessed following this prescribed [ritual], one should resolve to practice restraint and not to repeat [these evil actions] again.

3. Rejoicing

Then one should rejoice at the merit [of all beings in the following manner]:

> I rejoice at all the good attained [by living beings], whether possessed by conquerors who are full sugatas, or solitary buddhas, or disciples, or by their sons, the bodhisattvas, or by all beings in the world, with its gods and Brahmās.

4. Triple Refuge

Thereupon, one takes refuge in the triple treasure as follows:

> I will take refuge in the Buddha, until [I have myself] reached the highest awakening. I will take refuge in the dharma, until [I have myself] reached the highest awakening. I will take refuge in the saṅgha, until [I have myself] reached the highest awakening.

5. Relying on the Path

Next is the expression of reliance on the [Buddha's] path:

> I will rely on this path preached by the Tathāgata, and on none other.

6. Appeal

Following this, one should pronounce the appeal:

> May the blessed tathāgatas and their sons [the bodhisattvas], who have worked for the benefit of the world since the beginning of the cycle of rebirth, remain [in this world], without entering nirvāṇa.

7. Entreaty

Then follows the entreaty:

> May blessed tathāgatas teach such an incomparable teaching of dharma that [all] living beings in the cycle of rebirth may quickly become free of the bonds of existence.

8. Dedication of Merit

Immediately thereafter, one should perform the dedication of merit:

> Whatever merit may arise from the incomparable sevenfold act of worship and confession, I dedicate to the attainment of full and perfect awakening.

ALTERNATIVE RITUAL PROCEDURE

Alternatively, as a shorter procedure, one may recite this stanza, which expresses the sevenfold incomparable worship [in abbreviated form]:

> I confess all evil. I rejoice at merit with supreme joy. For as long as I remain in the cycle of birth, I seek the treasure of the good dharma of the Blessed One, I take refuge in the triple treasure, I dedicate my thoughts to awakening, and I rely on his path. I dedicate [all these] meritorious actions.

CONCLUDING THE ACT OF WORSHIP

After one has carried out in this manner the ritual of the sevenfold incomparable worship, one should take leave [of the buddhas and divinities invoked in the ritual] by pronouncing [the mantra] "*Oṃ Āḥ Muḥ*" . . . or else by means of the following stanza:

> Dwell in ease as you will, you whose limbs are smeared with the sandal powder of morality, who are dressed in the garments of meditation, and who are covered with [petals from] the flower that is awakening [and all its] attributes.

BEGINNING THE MEDITATION—THE FOUR HOLY ABIDINGS

Thereupon one should cultivate, in the order in which they are mentioned here, the four holy abidings, namely: friendliness, compassion, joy, and evenmindedness.

What is meant by "friendliness"? It is characterized as [feeling] toward all sentient beings the love (*prematā*) one would feel for one's only son; or else it is defined as the inclination to bring benefit and happiness [to others].

Furthermore, what sort of thing is compassion? It is the desire to remove [other sentient beings] from suffering and the causes of suffering. Or, [one also says that] compassion is the higher aspiration expressed in the thought "I will pull out even from this [prison] those persons who are immersed in [this] iron house of the cycle of rebirth—[an iron house] burning [red hot] in the fire of pain caused by all three kinds of suffering [suffering of pain, suffering of change, and suffering intrinsic to conditioned things]." . . . Or [one may also say that] it is the desire to pull out from the ocean of the cycle of rebirth those sentient beings that are suffering the three kinds of suffering.

Now, regarding joy, it is of the following nature: rejoicing is joyful enthusiasm (*pramoda*). Or [one also says that] joy is the higher aspiration expressed in the thought "I must [bring to full awakening] all sentient beings who are in this cycle of transmigration, establish all without exception firmly in the station of an awakened one (*buddhatva*) and in the means leading to that condition." . . . Or [one may also define it as] a state of mind [in which one is] drawn to [seek] full possession, [enjoyment,] and mastery of all the virtues possessed by all [beings in the universe].

What is evenmindedness? Evenmindedness is the practice of [actions that provide] the greatest benefit [equally] to those persons who benefit [us] and to those who do not, by overcoming the impediments that are hostility and attachment. Also, evenmindedness is the inclination to practice what is beneficial to others, under all circumstances, free from [any feelings of] love or resentment, [and moved by an evenminded motivation that] arises and proceeds of its own accord [without ulterior motives]. Or, again, evenmindedness is indifference toward all irrelevant concerns, chief among which are the eight worldly conditions of profit and loss, fame and disrepute, praise or blame, pleasure or pain.

MEDITATION

Following the cultivation of the four holy abidings, one should cultivate [the mind so as to realize] that all things (*dharma*) are by nature perfectly pure. [In order to do so,] one should bring [into awareness and] face-to-face reflections such as the following: "All things (*dharma*) without exception are by nature and in their own being perfectly pure. I too am by nature perfectly pure." . . .

And this [fact, that] all dharmas are by their nature perfectly pure, one should realize by means of the following mantra: "Oṃ, pure in their own being are all things, pure in my own being am I. . . ."

But, if all things are perfectly pure by nature, how is it that one brings [upon oneself this] cycle of transmigration? [This is possible] because [the original purity] is covered by the soil of [dual thoughts] such as [the duality of] subject and object. The means to remove [this covering] is the cultivation of the true path. By this [cultivation] the [cycle of transmigration] can be interrupted. Consequently, it has been established [as true] that all things are perfectly pure by nature.

After one has cultivated [this awareness of] the perfect natural purity of all things, one should cultivate [an awareness of] the emptiness of all things. Now, [with respect to] this emptiness, one should reflect in this manner: "Everything [here], moving and unmoving, is in itself nothing but the varied manifestations of the nondual, obscured by conceptualizations and discursive thought [based on constructed oppositions] such as [that between] subject and object." . . . And this same [insight into] emptiness one should realize by means of the following mantra: "Oṃ, I in my true self am of the nature of [this] diamond of the knowledge of emptiness." . . .

SECOND AND MAIN VISUALIZATION (*SĀDHANA* PROPER)

Thereupon, one should bring to mind [a] detailed [visual image of the] blessed holy Tārā. [One should see her as] proceeding from the yellow germ-syllable *Tāṃ* [one had previously visualized] resting on the spotless orb of the moon within the filaments of the full-blown blue lotus [growing] in the middle of the lunar orb [on the syllable *A*] originally visualized in one's own heart. One should conceive her to be of deep green color, with two arms, with a smiling face, endowed with all of the most incomparable virtues, and free of every defect, without exception. She is adorned with ornaments of heavenly precious substances such as gold, rubies, and pearls, her two breasts decorated with hundreds of lovely garlands and necklaces, her two arms wrapped in heavenly bracelets and bangles, her hips adorned with the beautiful splendor of the glittering rows of flawless gems on her girdles, her two feet beautified by golden anklets set with multicolored gems, her lovely matted hair entwined with fragrant wreaths made of [exquisite] flowers like those [growing in] paradise. In her resplendent jeweled headdress is [the figure of] the blessed Amoghasiddhi, the tathāgata. She [is visualized as] a shapely corporeal image, a radiant and most seductive semblance, in the prime of her youth, her eyes [the color] of a spotless blue lotus blossom in autumn, her body dressed in all [sorts] of heavenly fabrics and garments, seated in the half-lotus posture, within a circle of white rays on a white lotus as large as a cartwheel. With her right hand [she indicates that she is] granting [all] boons. In her left hand, she holds a blue lotus in full bloom.

One may cultivate such a visual image of the blessed [Tārā] for as long as one wishes.

Next, one will see this same [image of] the blessed [Tārā] being carried away by countless bundles of rays of light illuminating the triple world. [These rays of light] themselves issue from the yellow germ-syllable *Tāṃ* on the filaments of the charming blue lotus in the moon that [one had] established in [one's own] heart. [And one then] sees the blessed [Tārā], who is perfect since beginningless time, [now present] also in the form of the essence of [pure] knowledge. [And she] is brought forth from the [empty] space [in the firmament, by those rays illuminating the world]. Once she has been led forth and established on the firmament, one should [receive] this same blessed [Tārā that one visualizes, welcoming her as a guest by] offering [her] water [for the meditator] to wash her feet, scented water and fragrant flowers in a jeweled vessel. And one should worship this same Blessed One with many kinds of [offerings]—heavenly flowers, incense, lamps, food offerings, perfumes, garlands, unguents, fragrant powders, garments, umbrellas, flags, bells, banners, and so forth.

THE HAND GESTURE (*MUDRĀ*)

After worshiping her in this manner, again and again, and praising her, one exhibits the hand-gesture (*mudrā*) [appropriate to this visualization]: [first] one cups the hands [forming a hollow]. Then, one extends the two middle fingers to form a wedge. Bending slightly the three joints of these two [fingers], one keeps the two index fingers [as they were held at first]. Holding the thumbs parallel [to each other], one holds their three joints close together. Extending the two ring-fingers to form a hollow, one joins and extends out the little fingers. This is the "open blue-lotus" hand gesture.

THE INCANTATION (*MANTRA*)

After one has propitiated with this hand gesture the Blessed One [as she is] in her aspect as the essence of [pure] knowledge, one should cultivate [the repetition and visualization of] the incantation appropriate to her aspect as the essence of the symbol. In this manner one should strengthen [the] conviction that these two [aspects] are nondual.

RESTING AND RISING FROM MEDITATION

Thereupon, [the light rays] that issue from the yellow germ-syllable *Tāṃ* on the filaments of the blue lotus blooming within the orb of the moon, rays that are of unlimited range, proper to the divine Tārā, illuminate all the world spheres in the ten directions, removing, with showers of numberless precious substances and for all the sentient beings in those worlds, the suffering caused by poverty and other ills. And they refresh them with the nectar of the teachings of the dharma—such as [the teachings] on impermanence, no-self, and so forth.

Furthermore, [in connection with this], one should benefit [those in] the world with a variety [of good deeds], and at that time also produce [a visual image of] Tārā in her cosmic aspect.

Also, for as long as one does not begin to feel tired, one may continue to develop [these visualizations, focusing] on whatever [is seen] in the yellow germ-syllable *Tāṃ* in the stages of expansion and contraction, such as [the image of] the blessed [Tārā as she appears] therein.

When one feels tired from developing [this visualization exercise], one may rest by uttering the incantation [that says]: *Oṃ tāre tuttāre ture svāhā*. . . . For, it is said that this incantation is truly powerful, that even all the tathāgatas salute, worship, and honor it.

AFTER THE VISUALIZATION SESSION

Emerging from trance, the yogin sees the whole universe in the form of Tārā, and moves about freely, seeing himself as the blessed [Tārā].

BENEFITS OF THE VISUALIZATION

At the very least, the eight great magical powers [empowering a weapon, use of the magical eye ointment, use of the magical foot ointment, power of invisibility, use of the essence of all essences—either a panacea or miraculous balsam, or a solution that turns baser metals into gold, power to fly, instantaneous travel on the ground, and power to visit the nether worlds] fall at the feet of one who cultivates [the visual image] of the Blessed One following the process [described] above. What need is there to speak of the other [lesser] powers, which come to him as a matter of course? Whoever goes to a lonely mountain cave and cultivates [the visual image of] the Blessed One, will behold her with his own eyes. And the Blessed One herself will give this person her inbreath and outbreath. Why say more? In the very palm of the hand of such a person she will place even the state of a buddha, so hard to win.

CONCLUSION AND COLOPHON

May [all in] the world travel on peaceful and auspicious paths by virtue of the merit acquired by composing this *Fairly Detailed Visualization of Tārā*. This is the work of the pandit and elder Anupamarakṣita.

—28—

The Story of the Horn Blowing

Todd T. Lewis

Throughout their history, Buddhists engaged the enthusiastic devotion of all social classes through their inclusive teachings and a large repertoire of ritual practices. Buddhism attracted ascetics with myriad meditative regimes and intellectuals with vast doctrinal discourse; but it also cultivated the great lay majority with simple teachings and devotional practices, and through the efficacy of pragmatic ritual acts. This selection illustrates a popular Mahāyāna Buddhist appeal to layfolk to venerate the shrines called *stūpas* (or *caityas*).

Despite major points of doctrinal diversity among later Buddhist philosophical schools, the layman's urge toward accumulation of merit (*puṇya*) remained a consistent focus, a factor that underlies, in large part, the great similarities in lay Buddhist lifestyle and practice across Asia. The popularity of "puṇya tales"—stories (*avadānas*) and rebirth narratives (*jātakas*)—likewise represents a commonality in all Buddhist societies, regardless of the preoccupations of their respective intellectuals. Popular stories give explicit instructions on eliciting the compassionate powers of the buddhas and bodhisattvas through ritual action, and *Śṛṅgabherī Avadāna* provides a study of one such practice. This work is derived from the Sanskrit *Citraviṃśati Avadāna,* one of the popular collections of Mahāyāna-style stories preserved in Kathmandu Valley vihāra libraries.

For all Buddhist schools, the stūpa became a focal, multivalent symbol and reference point, the singular landmark denoting the tradition's spiritual presence on the landscape. Early texts and the archeological record link stūpa worship with Śākyamuni Buddha's life and especially the key venues in his religious career; one tradition recognizes a standard "Eight Great Caityas" for pilgrimage and veneration. Stūpa worship thus became the chief Buddhist ritual activity linking veneration of the Buddha's "sacred traces" to an individual's attention to managing karmic destiny and mundane well-being.

Over the centuries, Buddhist writers have advanced many levels of understanding to explain their shrine's symbolism and veneration: a stūpa is a fixed point for remembering the Buddha, a "power place" tapping a Buddha relic's presence and healing power, a site to earn merit through veneration, a monument marking the conversion and control of the serpent deities (*nāgas*) and demons (*yakṣas*). All extant books of monastic discipline except the Pāli *Vinaya* include instructions to monks on how to construct and make offerings at stūpas, and the archaeological record shows that stūpas were often built in the center of monastery courtyards, a custom still universal in Nepal.

The Mahāyāna stūpa later became a symbol conveying diverse additional views: of buddhahood's omnipresence, a center of text revelation, a center for worship guaranteeing rebirth in Sukhāvatī, and a form showing the unity of the five elements with buddha nature. The *Lotus Sūtra* (*Saddharmapuṇḍarīka*) explicitly states that relic worship itself is linked to the great upāya manifestation of the Buddha's dying; that is, by seeming to pass away, he induces spiritual self-examination on the part of the living. Mahāyāna texts also urge the creation of stūpas with "relics" in textual form (*sūtra, dhāraṇī, mantra*), and the placing of the remains of exemplary saints and subsequent bodhisattvas within them as well.

Symbiotically, great regional stūpas were pivotal in the social history of Buddhism. These monuments became magnets attracting monastery building and votive construction, as well as local ritual traditions and regional pilgrimage. The economics of Buddhist devotionalism at these centers generated income for local monasteries, artisans, and merchants, an alliance basic to Buddhism throughout its history. Thus, stūpa veneration was the most important activity that unified entire Buddhist communities; at these geographical centers arrayed around the symbolic monument, diverse devotional exertions, textual and doctrinal studies, and devotees' mercantile pursuits could all prosper in synergistic style. The great stūpa complexes—monasteries with land endowments, votive and pilgrimage center, market, state support, and so on—represent central fixtures in the Buddhist polities of Central, South, and Southeast Asia. The message of our text was part of the centripetal force that drew Buddhists toward such shrines.

The opening lines of the *Śṛngabherī* text underline a clear message: the veneration of stūpas, accompanied by a musical procession, yields a better destiny for oneself (fortune in this life, next rebirth in a noble family) and for departed relatives. No evil destinies will befall the deceased if the rite is done in their name(s). The text asserts that going for refuge at a stūpa helps to purify the mind, attain enlightenment (*bodhi*), and secure rebirth as Indra; the building and maintenance of stūpas yields even greater merit still.

The special significance of this story is in the series of linkages asserted between the Mahāyāna devotional orientation and stūpa veneration. The karmic forces released as a result of stūpa veneration are especially amplified; even more striking is the proclamation that the powers of the celestial bodhisattvas (Tārā, Supāraga) are connected to the stūpa cult. A curious feature of the *Story of the Horn Blowing* is that the relics interred in the stūpa are those of a mere buffalo, not a saint: but even these, when shaped into the archetypal Buddhist sacra and worshiped, yield a wondrous hierophony and miraculous individual destiny. Based upon this testimony, mourning Nepalese Buddhists have performed stūpa circumambulations using buffalo horns up to the present day.

A final point on the domestication of Mahāyāna Buddhism: although Buddhist texts establish the radical individualism of karmic operation and the superiority of the renunciatory lifestyle over that of the domestic householder, this Mahāyāna avadāna suggests that the celestial bodhisattvas' powers are available to reunite husbands and wives in their rebirth destiny. This wish for a conjugal connection over many lifetimes goes back to the earliest days of the tradition. In the *Aṅguttara Nikāya* (II, 61), an elderly husband Nakul Pitā addressed Śākyamuni, "Blessed One, when my wife was brought to my house, she was a mere girl, and I was only a boy. I cannot recall having been unfaithful to her, not even in thought. Blessed One, we both want to live together in this way, in this life and in our future lives." The wife expresses the same opinions. The *Śṛṅgabherī* text and its enduring Nepalese practice suggest that this is yet another hope and aspiration devout Mahāyāna Buddhists have brought to their building and veneration of stūpas.

The translation is from Badri Bajracarya, ed. *Śṛṅga Bherī (Nekū Pvīkegu Bākhaṃ)* (Kathmandu: Smṛiti Press, 1979).

Further Reading

On stūpas and their veneration, see Anna Dallapiccola, ed., *The Stūpa: Its Religious, Historical, and Architectural Significance* (Wiesbaden: Franz Steiner Verlag, 1980), pp. 112–26; P. Harvey, "The Symbolism of the Early Stūpa," *Journal of the International Association of Buddhist Studies* 7 (1984), 67–93; Akira Hirakawa, "The Rise of Mahāyāna Buddhism and Its Relationship to the Worship of Stūpas," *Memoirs of the Research Department of the Tōyō Bunko* 22 (1963), 57–106; Gregory Schopen, "The Phrase '*sa pṛthivīpradeśaś stūpabhūto bhavet*' in the *Vajracchedikā:* Notes on the Cult of the Book in Mahāyāna," *Indo-Iranian Journal* 17 (1975), 147–81; Gregory Schopen, "Burial '*ad sanctos*' and the Physical Presence of the Buddha in Early Indian Buddhism: A Study in the Archaeology of Religions," *Religion* 17 (1987), 193–225; A. Snodgrass, *The Symbolism of the Stūpa* (New York: Cornell University Press, 1985); and Giuseppe Tucci, *Stūpa: Art, Architectonics and Symbolism* (New Delhi: Aditya Prakashan, 1988).

See also John Strong, "The Transforming Gift: An Analysis of Devotional Acts of Offering in Buddhist Avadāna Literature," *History of Religions* 18:3 (1979), 221–37; and Todd T. Lewis, "Contributions to the History of Buddhist Ritualism: A Mahāyāna Avadāna on Caitya Veneration from the Kathmandu Valley," *Journal of Asian History* 28:1 (1994), 1–38.

The Story of the Horn Blowing

So I have heard: Once Śākyamuni the Lord was dwelling on Mount Gṛddhakūṭa in Rājagṛha city accompanied by 1,300 fellow bhikṣus, bodhisattvas, and mahāsattvas.

At that time also the gods and human beings all gathered there to listen intently to the discourses delivered by the sage of the Śākya clan, lord of the world.

From the audience, Śāriputra then arose and went close to the Tathāgata, knelt down before him with folded hands, and said, "O Lord! Be so kind as to tell me about those who were liberated through stūpa worship performed along with the playing of musical instruments, including the buffalo horn."

Upon hearing this, Tathāgata Śākyamuni said to Śāriputra within the hearing of all the gods and human beings in the audience, "Verily, Verily, O Śāriputra! Emancipation obtained through stūpa worship, performed with the blowing of buffalo horns, is illustrated in the following story:

In the distant past, King Suvarṇaketu and his queen Hiraṇyavatī lived happily in the city of Suvarṇavati. The king had five sons from his queen Hiraṇyavatī, namely, Puṣpaketu, Ratnaketu, Śuryaketu, Dīpaketu, Candraketu. The oldest son, Puṣpaketu, once went to his parents, paid them compliments, and asked for permission to go to Bandhumati city for listening to the discourses delivered by Vipaśvī Buddha. With their permission, he left Suvarṇavati city for Bandhumati city.

Upon reaching Bandhumati city, Prince Puṣpaketu went to see Vipaśvī Tathāgata at a monastery. Kneeling down before Vipaśvī Buddha, Prince Puṣpaketu said, "O Lord! Please tell me of those who were liberated through stūpa worship performed while playing musical instruments, including the buffalo horn."

Hearing this from the prince, the buddha said, "The month of Śrāvaṇa is considered holy for stūpa worship accompanied by music. For this, the month of Kārtik is equally holy. During these two months, after ritual bathing in the morning, if one circumambulates stūpas or monasteries playing drums and cymbals, and blowing horns, one will accumulate good fortune and religious merit here in this life and be reborn hereafter in a noble family. If one circumambulates the stūpa blowing horns and offers gifts in the name of a dead one, that one will avoid bad destinies and be reborn in a family of noble birth. And if a person seated in front of a stūpa seeks refuge in the triratna [three jewels] with a purified mind, that one will attain supreme enlightenment or be reborn hereafter in heaven to attain the title of Indra, king of the gods. Similarly if one whitewashes a stūpa with lime, decorates it with flags and garlands, and worships with a fivefold ritual, that one will accumulate a great deal of religious merit. O Prince! Please be attentive and let me now proceed to tell you how once one person was liberated through horn playing.

Once there was a king named Siṃhaketu who ruled the city of Śaśīpaṭṭana. The king had no consideration for the lives of other living beings and every day visited the forest to hunt with his bow and arrow many different wild birds and beasts such as deer, tigers, and bears.

Unable to bear the daily sight of her husband taking the lives of wild birds and beasts in the forest, Queen Sūrakṣaṇī said to her husband one day, "O my lord! Let me make a request of you. Please give up hunting the wild birds and beasts in the forest. Mind you! The wicked deed of taking the lives of living beings will subject you to a great deal of suffering in your future births." [She quoted the verses:]

> Nonviolence [*ahiṃsa*] is the best among knowledges,
> the greatest of all teachings.
> Nonviolence is the best among virtues,
> the greatest of all meditations.

[Sūrakṣaṇī continued:] "If men say they earnestly seek salvation, they should be nonviolent in body, mind, and speech toward all living beings. O my Lord! If you so wish, you may pronounce the names of the triratna seeking refuge, worship a stūpa while saying prayers and circumambulating, give liberally to the monks, the brahmans, the advanced adepts [*ācāryas*], and show compassion to many suffering ones. By so doing, your happiness here and hereafter will be assured."

Hearing this from the queen, the king replied, "Darling! What's this you are saying? Don't you know that one born in a royal family can take pleasure in hunting wild birds and beasts in the forest?"

Having listened to the king's attitude, the queen still tried her best to convince him but could not stop him from hunting in the forest.

After a certain time, the king passed away and Sūrakṣaṇī received such a mental shock at his death that she immolated herself on her husband's funeral pyre. Because of his wicked deed of so often hunting the wild birds and beasts in the forest, the king was consigned to purgatory and was afterward reincarnated as a buffalo in the same city of Śaśīpaṭṭana. But Queen Sūrakṣaṇī, as a result of her meritorious deed of sparing the lives of living beings and of being chaste and faithful to her husband, was reincarnated as a woman in a certain brahman family in the same city of Śaśīpaṭṭana.

The brahman couple became very glad when she was born to them. They celebrated the name-giving ceremony of the baby girl in accordance with their custom. The name of Rūpavatī ["Beautiful One"] was given to the child because she was very beautiful. The baby was brought up with proper care and gradually she grew up like a lotus in a pond. When Rūpavatī became a mature girl, her father gave her the job of tending a buffalo in the forest.

Rūpavatī everyday tended her buffalo, cleaned his shed, and took great care of him.

Because Rūpavatī was beautiful, many people came to propose marriage. Her parents discussed this and said to her eventually, "O Rūpavatī! Now you have come of age. People have come to us asking for you in marriage. Do you want to marry?"

Responding to her parents, the daughter said, "Dear father and mother, I do not want to be married. Please do not insist on it. I prefer staying unmarried here and devoting myself to you. I won't marry."

Hearing this from their daughter, they gave up the idea of giving their only daughter in marriage and she stayed at home unmarried.

One day Rūpavatī was in the forest as usual tending her buffalo. While she was sitting under a tree looking at the many-hued blossoms, listening to the sweet bird songs, and smelling many colorful sweet-scented flowers, a bodhisattva named Supāraga, emanating brilliant light from his body, descended from the sky and stood before her. He said, "O Rūpavatī! The buffalo you are tending was your husband in your previous birth. In his former existence, he hunted many birds and beasts in the forest. As a result of this, he is now reborn as a buffalo. For his past wicked deeds, the buffalo will be killed and devoured by the birds and beasts of the forest. O Rūpavatī! If you wish to assist the husband of your previous birth attain a good destiny, collect the mortal remains of the buffalo after it is killed and devoured by the birds and beasts of the forest, then deposit them inside a sand stūpa. One of the two horns of the buffalo may be used for offering water to the stūpa and the other horn may be used as a trumpet at the time of circumambulating it." Having said this to Rūpavatī, Supāraga Bodhisattva disappeared miraculously.

Then Rūpavatī also remembered the facts of her previous birth and took greater care of the buffalo by taking it to the forest and feeding it nutritious grasses.

One day as usual, Rūpavatī was sitting under a tree while tending her buffalo. After eating grass the buffalo wandered off to drink water from a stream in the forest. At that time, in an instant, tigers and lions came to attack the buffalo and tortured it to death. Then the tigers, lions, bears, vultures, and other birds devoured its flesh, leaving only the bones and two horns behind.

[At just this same time] Rupavatī heard a strange sound made by the buffalo, and then it did not come back as usual from the stream. Very much agitated, she went to the stream looking for the buffalo but did not find it. Instead, she saw only the dead animal's bones and two horns left behind. At the sight of the buffalo's bones and horns, Rūpavatī wept. Taking them affectionately in her arms, she said to herself, "What Supāraga Bodhisattva prophesied has come true." She then returned home with a tearful face and relayed to her parents all that had happened to her in the forest that day.

Upon hearing Rūpavatī's story, her parents comforted her, saying, "Enough, enough! Do not mourn the death of one buffalo very much. We will buy a new buffalo."

In response to her parents, the daughter cried, "O mother and father! No buffalo can be like the one that has been killed. You may buy a new buffalo but the new one cannot bring peace and consolation to my mind." The parents retorted, "Grieve no more over the dead one. It is of no use because the dead cannot be brought back to life. Get hold of yourself!"

Then Rūpavatī went again to the streamside, collected all the pieces of bone, and buried them in a sand stūpa, all as advised by Supāraga Bodhisattva. She next used one of the two horns of the buffalo for offering water to the stūpa and the other for playing while circumambulating and while performing a fivefold ritual. She regularly worshiped the stūpa in this way. One day during her stūpa worship, while Rūpavatī was offering water with one of the horns and blowing the other, a bejeweled stūpa appeared in the sky, emitting radiant light in all directions. She was surprised and with folded hands turned to the sky in great reverence.

Then the stūpa that appeared in the sky descended to the earth and merged into the sand stūpa in which the bones of the buffalo were buried. When the bejeweled stūpa entered the sand stūpa, the sand stūpa was transformed into a bejeweled stūpa.

Because of the presence of the stūpa there, stone walls and other masonry constructions came into sight by themselves around the stūpa to give it a look of a high-walled courtyard. Doorways and festoons also appeared, just as plants possessing different flowers and fruits started growing all around.

This is not all. From the horn of the buffalo that was used for blowing came out a person who grew instantly into a youthful adolescent. At that sight of the person springing from the horn, Rūpavatī became very much surprised and said, "Who are you and where did you come from?"

Turning to the brahman lady, the person who emerged from the horn said, "How could you not recognize me, O faithful woman! You liberated your husband through your conjugal fidelity and pious charitable acts. O Rūpavatī! I have been able to come out of the horn, liberated on this day. It is all due to your accumulation of merit. Have you not known that in our former existence I was the king of this city and you were my queen Sūrakṣaṇī? Although you tried to prevent me from going to the forest to hunt birds and beasts, I insisted upon doing so. As a result of these wicked deeds, I was consigned to purgatory, subjected to great suffering. Ultimately I was reborn as a buffalo. Now I am liberated through your pious meritorious worshiping of a stūpa accompanied by buffalo horn playing."

Upon hearing this from the person emanating from the horn, Rūpavatī said, "Oh! How fortunate I have been! As a result of the pious act of this stūpa worship I have been able to end the separation and rejoin my husband." Jubilant, they both circumambulated the stūpa. Then the person emanating from the horn pronounced the name of Tārā [the female bodhisattva] and remained seated before the stūpa. He recited prayers from a holy text while blowing on the horn. The whole of Śaśīpaṭṭana city echoed with the sound produced by the horn. The citizens of Śaśīpaṭṭana city heard the pleasant sound of the horn and assembled there.

All those who gathered around the stūpa were taken aback to see Rūpavatī seated beside a handsome person and so they asked her who he was. At that time, within the hearing of all, Rūpavatī related the whole story of how Supāraga Bodhisattva had prophesied strange things, how they had lived in their previous births as King Siṃhaketu and Queen Sūrakṣaṇī in Śaśīpaṭṭana, and what had happened in front of the sand stūpa.

The people assembled there became very glad after hearing this, and realized that the person emanating from the horn and the brahman lady were their king and queen in their previous lifetimes. Both of them were taken to the city in an elaborate, joyful procession. Then the person emanating from the horn was given the name of Bhadra Śṛṇga and was enthroned as the king of the city.

Then King Bhadra Śṛṇga and Queen Rūpavatī ruled over the city of Śaśīpaṭṭana happily. One day King Bhadra Śṛṇga invited the citizens to his palace to tell them the story of how his queen helped him be delivered from his sufferings in purgatory by her pious and charitable act of devotion in her former existence and how he eventually succeeded in ascending to the throne of Śaśīpaṭṭana for the well-being of the people.

King Bhadra Śṛṇga and Queen Rūpavatī lived happily for many years. King Bhadra Śṛṇga made it widely known to his countrymen how his wife delivered him from his sufferings in purgatory. He preached and propagated the significance and sanctity of stūpa worship and reigned happily over the country.

This is what was told to Prince Puṣpaketu by Vipaśvī Buddha. After hearing this from Vipaśvī Buddha, Prince Puṣpaketu returned to Suvarṇapura and relayed to his parents the same story told to him by Vipaśvī Buddha.

Upon hearing the story from his son, the King Suvarṇaketu happily ruled over the country and performed the proper worship of stūpas. And this was told to bhikṣu Śāriputra by the Lord Śākyamuni on Mount Gṛddhakūṭa.

— 29 —

A Summary of the Seven Books of the Abhidhamma

Donald K. Swearer

The Abhidhamma (Abhidharma) Piṭaka, the division of the Theravāda Buddhist canon known as the "higher teaching," has been characterized by Buddhist scholars as dry, arid, Buddhist scholasticism, preoccupied primarily with doctrinal controversy and catechetical classification. Although the scholastic nature of much of the Abhidhamma Piṭaka is beyond dispute, the texts of the Abhidhamma not only constituted the subject matter of the monastery classroom but have held and continue to hold a hallowed place within the popular Buddhist tradition. For example, in contemporary Thailand monks chant summary versions of the seven books of the Abhidhamma Piṭaka at funerals, and in Burma the last book of the Abhidhamma, the *Paṭṭhāna,* is chanted continuously for seven days and nights prior to the annual festival celebrating the founding of the Mahāmuni Temple in Mandalay. In northern Thailand, Abhidhamma texts were written as early as the fifteenth or sixteenth century and were preached to lay audiences until the turn of the present century. Copies of these texts incised on palm leaf can still be found in monastery libraries in northern Thailand.

The following translation is of one of these popular Abhidhamma sermons entitled, "A Summary of the Seven Books of the Abhidhamma" ("*Abhidhamma Chet Khamphi Ruam*"). It is a prose text inscribed in the northern Thai script on nineteen palm leaves of four lines each. The text was in the personal library of the late Singkha Wannasai, who was an unsurpassed repository of knowledge of northern Thai language and literature. As is characteristic of most popular northern Thai texts, it is written in both Pāli and Tai Yuan, the language of the Tai people who have inhabited the region of northern Thailand known as Lānnā ("The Land of a Million Paddy Fields") since the late twelfth century.

The text provides a fascinating insight into the popular transformation of the most erudite Buddhist philosophy, challenging our conventional distinctions between elite and popular, monastic and lay, Pāli and vernacular. In addition, this text also calls into question a reified, textbook understanding of Theravāda Buddhism. Elements of cosmology, cosmogony, buddhology, ethics, epistemology, and language are integrated into a yantric / mantric whole that defies precise classification.

Above all, the text provides a complex example of the performative signification of language. Syllables symbolizing the seven books of the Abhidhamma create human beings—men and women—the body, bodily faculties, and the mind. Vowels represent gross bodily parts and consonants denote the standard Theravāda analysis of the thirty-two constituent bodily parts. The mantra "Namo Buddhāya" ("Homage to the Buddha"), correlated with the five vowels, symbolizes the five elements (*dhatu*)—water, earth, fire, air, atmosphere—the five aggregates of bodily existence, the combined qualities of mother, father, Buddha, dharma and saṅgha, and the five buddhas beginning with Kakusandha and ending with Metteyya (Maitreya). The seven books of the Abhidhamma have the astrological significance assigned to the days of the week. Hearing one's birth-ascribed Abhidhamma treatise leads to a heavenly reward. The Pāli scriptures function as meditation subjects as a monk mindfully puts on his robe, and the Abhidhamma, in particular, promotes awareness of sense organs and their sense processes. Finally, the text links the Abhidhamma with meditation, study, the realization of the four paths (that is, stream-enterer, and so on), and nirvāṇa. One cannot be a true monk and be ignorant of the Abhidhamma, our text admonishes its listeners, and in even stronger terms warns that such a person is nothing but a fool.

A Summary of the Seven Books of the Abhidhamma

Let everyone—men and women, laypersons and monks—be attentive; listen and remember. I shall explain the fortunate consequences of the seven books of the Abhidhamma in relationship to the body and the faculties of human beings. In brief, they form the epigram *san-vi-dhā-pu-ka-ya-pa*, which stands for:

san = *Dhammasaṅgaṇi* [Enumeration of Dharmas]
vi = *Vibhaṅga* [Classifications]
dhā = *Dhātukathā* [Discourse on Elements]
pu = *Puggalapaññatti* [Description of Persons]
ka = *Kathāvatthu* [Points of Controversy]
ya = *Yamaka* [Book of Pairs]
pa = *Paṭṭhāna* [Book of Relations]

San. At the birth of man *san* comes into existence. It refers to the thirty-three factors of the mind in the *Dhammasaṅgaṇi*. *San* was in the right side of the first man for seven days. Then, departing from his left side, it entered the womb of the first woman through the top of her head.

Vi. Then it turned into a drop of sesame oil which stuck to the tail of a deer for seven days.

Dhā. Then for seven days it became firmer like curds.

Pu. Becoming even more solid, it turned into a clot of blood for seven days.

Ka. It grew even larger and harder for another seven days.

Ya. Then after seven more days it congealed into a lump.

Pa. Finally it turned into the five limbs as mentioned in the *Saddhāvimālā.*

There are eight vowels from *a* at the beginning to *o* at the end. The three short vowels became the connecting points. *A* became the knee, *i* became the waist, and *u* became the neck, enabling us to turn and move as quick as lightning. Of the long vowels, *ā* became the right leg, *ī* became the left leg, *ū* became the right arm, *e* became the left arm, and *o* became the body. [Furthermore], *ā, ī, ū, e, o* stand for the phrase "Namo Buddhāya" ["Homage to the Buddha"]. This in turn represents the basic elements of all things:

na = water (the twelve *āpo-dhātu*)
mo = earth (the twenty-one *pathavī-dhātu*)
bhud = fire (the four *tejo-dhātu*)
dhā = air (the six *vāyo-dhātu*)
ya = atmosphere (*ākāsa-dhātu*), in which the other four *dhātu* reside

[The consonants symbolize the thirty-two constitutive parts of the body as follows:]

k = hair of the head
kh = hair of the body
g = finger and toenails
gh = teeth
ng = skin
c = flesh
ch = tendons
j = bones
jh = bone marrow
ñ = spleen
ṭ = heart
ṭh = liver
ḍ = pleura
ḍh = kidney
ṇ = lung
t = small intestine
th = large intestine
d = food being digested
dh = excrement
ḷ = skull
n = brain

These parts of the body represent the following: form (*rūpa-dhamma*), the twenty-one elements of the earth (*paṭhavī-dhātu*), and the virtue (*guṇa*) of the father. [Correspondingly]:

n = gall bladder
p = phlegm
ph = pus
b = blood
bh = sweat
m = fat
y = tears
r = fatty oils
l = spit
v = mucus
s = joint liquid
h = urine

These are the nonmaterial (*nāma*) parts of the body, the twelve elements of water (*āpo-dhātu*) and the virtue (*guṇa*) of the mother. The two groups together total thirty-three parts. The skull and brain constitute one, thereby making thirty-two bodily parts. They are the nāma-rūpa characteristics of humankind.

[The words honoring the Buddha also symbolize the five aggregates (*khandha*):]

na = body (*rūpa-khandha*)
mo = sensations (*vedanā-khandha*)
bhud = perceptions (*saññā-khandha*)
dhā = dispositions (*saṅkhara-khandha*)
ya = consciousness (*viññāna-khandha*)

Together they are the five aggregates of the "middle way" the Buddha taught to Mahāsāriputta. We should all know the meaning of the material and immaterial constituents of existence (*nāma-rūpa-dhamma*), and the five basic elements (*dhātu*): earth, water, air, fire, and atmosphere.

The seven books of the Abhidhamma are about the body (*kāya*), the faculties (*indriya*), and consciousness (*citta*) [and can be further explicated as:]

san = the eye which sees both beautiful and ugly, meritorious and demeritorious things
vi = the ear which hears beautiful and ugly, meritorious and demeritorious sounds
dhā = the nose which smells both pleasant and unpleasant odors
pu = the tongue which tastes bitter, sour, sweet, hot, salty, delicious, meritorious and demeritorious flavors
ka = the body which touches hot and cold

ya = the mind (*citta*) which knows the meritorious and demeritorious, joy and lamentation
pa = the body and all the faculties; the body and the mind of humankind

Everyone should know them. The seven books of the Abhidhamma explain the bodily faculties, that is, the eye, ear, nose, mouth, tongue, heart—all the bodily parts.

If the seven books of the Abhidhamma were not composed, humankind would not have come into existence. All should reflect on the virtue of the seven books of the Abhidhamma, and its subject matter of the bodily faculties and the basic elements: earth, water, air, fire, atmosphere. Teach it to your fathers and mothers, relatives, older and younger brothers and sisters; teach it to all the followers of the teachings of the Buddha's middle way.

Those who do not know the characteristics of the [thirty-two] material and immaterial constituent parts of father and mother, the five basic elements, and the five aggregates are called *asaṅgha,* meaning that they are not true monks and do not teach the true dharma. It is said that they sell the dharma of the Tathāgata for their livelihood. Those who do not know the seven books of the Abhidhamma will go to hell. Therefore, men and women, laypersons and monks, be intent and listen, study and then practice the middle way teachings of the Buddha.

[Let us continue. The words honoring the Buddha also symbolize the qualities (*guṇa*) and the buddhas as follows:]

na = The twelve qualities of the mother and the destruction of all demerit
mo = The twenty-one qualities of the father . . .
bhud = The fifty-six qualities of the Buddha . . .
dhā = The thirty-eight qualities of the dharma
ya = The fourteen qualities of the saṅgha

na = The buddha Kakusandha at the right eye
mo = The buddha Konāgamana at the left eye
bhud = The buddha Kassapa at the back
dhā = The buddha Gotama at the navel
ya = The buddha Ariya Metteyya at the forehead

All men and women who know and practice this teaching continually will be released from suffering and are guaranteed the attainment of happiness. It was taught by the Buddha's disciple Kaccayana Thera in the Mulavimālā as the meritorious reward of the seven books of the Abhidhamma.

Whoever is born or dies on Sunday and hears the *Dhammasaṅgaṇi* will be released from all demerit accrued through the eye. At death this person will not be reborn in hell but will enter heaven.

Whoever is born or dies on Monday and hears the *Dhammavibhaṅga* will be released from all evil accrued through the ear, and at death will not be reborn in hell but will enter heaven.

Whoever is born or dies on Tuesday and hears the *Dhammadhātukathā* will be released from all evil accrued through the nose, and at death . . .

Whoever is born or dies on Wednesday and hears the *Dhammapuggalapaññatti* will be released from all demerit accrued through the door of the mouth, and at death . . .

Whoever is born or dies on Thursday and hears the *Dhammakathāvatthu* will be released from all evil accrued through the door of the body, and at death . . .

Whoever is born or dies on Friday and hears the *Dhammayamaka* will be released from all evil accrued through the door of the mouth or speech, and at death . . .

Whoever is born or dies on Saturday and hears the *Dhammamahāpaṭṭhāna* will be released from all evil accrued through the mind door, and at death will not be reborn in hell but will enter heaven.

Everyone listen, remember, and practice this teaching. Then when mother, father, relatives, older and younger brothers and sisters die, they will not be reborn in the four hells, as preta, phī [Thai for malevolent spirit], or asura. So all people should request the preaching of the seven books of the Abhidhamma as taught by the disciples of the Buddha in order to be released from hell.

This completes the explanation of the seven books of the Abhidhamma. Now I shall discuss the robing of a monk.

When putting on the sarong, reflect as you exhale that the five sūtras guard our out-breath. Our life depends on them, and they enable us to extend our hands and put on the sarong.

When putting on the outer robe reflect as you inhale that the seven books of monastic discipline (*vinaya*) guard our in-breath. Our life depends on them, and they enable us to extend our hands and put on the outer robe.

When putting on the shoulder robe reflect as you quiet the breath that the seven books of the Abhidhamma guard the place of air and fire in the body, and enable us to enter the state of the cessation of perception where there is no breath.

When taking off the shoulder robe reflect on the impermanence of the body; still the breath; be quiescent like the folded shoulder robe. This is called the monk's transcendent requisite.

The shoulder robe is the wrapping for the three scriptures (*piṭaka*): the belt is the cord to tie the texts together; the vest holds the palm leaves together.

Twenty-one consonants are the *rūpa-dhamma,* the virtue of the father, and the earth element. He who knows this truth is a true monk and saves his father from hell.

Twelve consonants are the *nāma-dhamma,* the virtue of the mother, and the water element. He who knows this and is ordained a novice at the age of twelve saves his mother from hell. If one is ignorant of the meaning of these truths, one cannot save his father and mother. Furthermore, taking the robe from the funeral pyre will have no [meritorious] effect.

[By way of review and elaboration:]

saṅgaṇi = the eye for seeing form
vibhaṅga = the ear for hearing sound
dhātukathā = the nose for smelling odors
puggalapaññatti = the tongue for tasting bitter and sweet tastes and the mouth for speaking
yamaka = the mind for knowing the dharma, and the difference between merit and demerit. It makes our lives stable, and provides the ability to differentiate between sleeping and waking, crying and laughing.
mahāpaṭṭhāna = the parts of the body for standing, walking, and knowing; the seven books of the Abhidhamma; the four elements [earth, water, fire, air] . . .

If you do not know the teaching of the seven books of the Abhidhamma you are not a true monk. Not knowing the way of meditation you will go to hell. One who says he follows the way of study, but does not know the four paths, the four fruits, and nirvāṇa, does not teach the dharma. Rather, he sells it for his own livelihood. The Buddha taught that such a person is a fool. Consider this warning carefully.

—30—

On Becoming a Buddhist Wizard

Patrick Pranke

According to nineteenth-century Burmese chronicles, when the hero-king Anawrahta (Sanskrit Anuruddha) came to the throne of Pagan in 1044 C.E., he found in his realm a powerful community of Buddhist monks known as the Ari. The Ari are vilified in these accounts as heretics guilty of unpardonable violations of the monastic code (*vinaya*) who officiated at animal sacrifices, were addicted to magic and sorcery, and who worshiped a pantheon of spirits and gods. Prompted by the admonitions of an arhat named Shin Arahan, Anawrahta suppressed the Ari and established Theravāda Buddhism as the official religion of the land—a religion he is said to have acquired by conquering the neighboring kingdom of Thaton and carrying off its sacred Pāli scriptures and its orthodox monks. Whatever the historical veracity of this story, and whoever the Ari might have been, it is clear that many of the beliefs and practices attributed to them have survived to the present day. In the late eighteenth and early nineteenth centuries, Burmese kings imported large numbers of Sanskrit texts from India on topics such as medicine, alchemy, incantation, and astrology. Many of these were translated into Burmese, whence they entered popular culture. The theory and vocabulary of Burmese alchemy, for example, largely derive from this source, and are in current use by large numbers of Burmese Buddhists who otherwise are entirely conventional in their Theravādin faith.

Chief among the heterogeneous systems of belief are a native animist cult of spirit (*nat*) propitiation and, more significantly for our purposes, an esoteric tradition of occult sciences dedicated to the attainment of magical powers and extraordinary long life. What is particularly interesting about this latter system, and what marks it as different from all other popular cults, is that besides its purely mundane (*lokiya*) goals of becoming physically invulnerable, and having the ability to transmute base metals into gold, and so on, it also represents a fully developed salvational path whose unconventional methods and notions of human perfection are deemed to be completely orthodox by its adherents. Known as the *weikza-lam* (path of occult knowledge), this tradition promises to deliver successful practitioners to the condition of a twet-ya-pauk, a kind of Buddhist wizard who prolongs his life for eons until finally attaining (nirvāṇa) in the presence of the future buddha, Metteyya (Maitreya). The twet-ya-pauk is a well-known figure in Burmese legend and a religious hero of considerable stature. Assured of liberation and a sorcerer without peer, he uses his great power to defend the Buddha's religion against the intrigues of Māra, the Evil One, who forever seeks to cut short the true teachings and plunge the world into darkness.

The weikza-lam, although remaining a minority movement, enjoys considerable popularity in Myanmar (Burma) today, drawing adherents from almost every social stratum and vocation, including a small but not insignificant number of Buddhist monks. Practitioners of this tradition are often organized into semisecret associations called *gaing* that function to dispense esoteric knowledge to initiates under the guidance of a charismatic teacher-adept (*saya* or *gaing-saya*). Although gaing of this sort are typically small and rarely survive the demise of their founders, over the last several decades a few have managed to attain a degree of institutional stability and even to rise to national prominence. By far the largest of these more well-established occult groups is the Manosetopad Gaing. Headquartered in the city of Pegu, where it has built a large pagoda, this gaing (whose title, Manosetopad, means "the generation of mind," from the Pāli *manocittuppāda*) currently has chapters in several cities throughout the country and an organized ministry of subordinate sayas who, besides following a course of discipline leading to their own apotheosis, perform various services for the general public such as healing and exorcism.

A useful introduction to the tenets of this group is a little manual written by one of its sayas entitled, "The Goal and Path of the Great Manosetopad Gaing" ("*Manosetopad-gaing-daw-kyi i pan-taing hning lam-zin*"). The text, which was acquired from its author in Yangon (Rangoon) in 1987, is interesting not only because it gives a fair representation of general weikza-lam theory but also because the author borrows heavily from authoritative Burmese language sources in a conscious attempt to explain Manosetopad doctrine in terms that are consistent with current standards of Buddhist orthodoxy. Instances that have been identified are noted in the translation.

Of the many marvelous qualities of the Buddha, one that is often extolled is that he possessed tremendous magical power. In the Pāli tradition, powers of this sort are exclusively the product of yoga; in particular, they result from a mastery of the four states of mental absorption called the jhānas (Sanskrit *dhyāna*). The jhānas are induced through developing concentration (*samādhi*) by means of a set of exercises that fall under the heading of tranquillity meditation (*samatha*). Samatha is contrasted in Buddhism with vipassanā, or insight meditation, which is the specific vehicle used for gaining liberating gnosis (*bodhi*) and is not productive of magical powers. Vipassanā, therefore, is regarded by Theravādins as being exclusively Buddhist, as not contained in other religions, and as the actual method used by the Buddha to gain enlightenment. Almost every adult Burmese is versed in the basics of these classifications, as they are often reiterated in religious discourses and have long been incorporated into Burmese folklore.

There is, therefore, nothing particularly Buddhist about the jhānas or the powers they produce, and many of the Buddha's contemporaries and rivals had them. In fact, the Buddha himself acquired a portion of his own samatha repertoire while still a bodhisattva under the discipleship of two heterodox yogins. But by virtue of his perfections the Buddha surpassed all others in his mastery of these attainments. The supernormal powers are variously known, and there are several classifications of them. In Myanmar they are often referred to collectively as zan, this being the popular Burmese usage of the Pāli jhāna. In this usage, the term *zan* represents a conflation of the classical notion of mental absorption with the power it delivers, as any reasonably well-educated monk will tell you. In any case, through the potency of his zan, the Buddha was able to defeat heretical magicians and perform numerous wonderful feats, such as illuminating the universe with rainbow light, reading people's minds, and flying through the air. Popular Burmese tradition has it that he flew to Myanmar on one occasion and left his footprint on Mandalay Hill. The Buddha could even have lived for an eon (*kappa,* Sanskrit *kalpa*) or more had his disciple, Ānanda, been clever enough to ask him to do so. But there was one thing the Buddha could not do, at least according to the Theravāda, and that is to communicate telepathically with anyone or to appear in their dreams. This limitation is of considerable significance, as we shall see when we consider the nature of the Buddha's teachings as conceived in this tradition.

According to orthodox opinion, when Buddha died and attained final liberation, he ceased to exist and utterly passed away. This is what happens to all perfected saints (Burmese *yahanta,* Pāli *arahant,* Sanskrit *arhat,* lit. "worthy one"), the Buddha being the chief among them, and by definition it represents the highest good. Thus, when the faithful pray to the Buddha there is no one who hears their prayers. The Burmese generally understand this and justify their devotions by saying that such prayers are nevertheless beneficial because they are motivated by faith, respect, and gratitude, all of which are virtuous states of mind and therefore merit-producing. But they also believe that relics of the Buddha (Burmese *dat-daw,* Pāli *dhātu*) are possessed of a certain kind of majestic power that he infused in them through the force of his samādhi and his resolution. Veneration of these relics is especially meritorious and physical proximity to them is supposed to imbue the devotee with a sort of subtle energy. The most famous of these relics are the hair relics enshrined in the Shwe-da-gon Pagoda in Yangon, which, because of their power, makes the platform of the Shwe-da-gon a popular gathering place for weikza-lam practitioners, as well as those who wish to cultivate zan through tranquillity meditation. Relics of the Buddha are also believed to have the ability of replicating themselves, and for this reason there are many such relics in Myanmar today. Another famous cult object possessing exceptional power is the colossal Maha-muni image of the Buddha in Mandalay. This seated statue was supposedly crafted during the lifetime of the Buddha, who then invigorated it through his resolution. The Maha-muni is highly revered throughout the country for its wish-fulfilling properties, and part of its perceived power derives from its long association with Buddhist kingship. It is adorned with the regalia of a world-emperor and was once the palladium of the kingdom of Arakan. When Arakan was conquered by the Burmese king, Bodaw-hpaya, in the late eighteenth century, the image was transported to his capital, Amarapura, for worship. Later the temple complex housing the Maha-muni was ceded to neighboring Mandalay, when that city was made the royal capital in the mid-nineteenth century.

Such was the samādhi and the zan of the Buddha that for millennia his relics and images have continued to manifest his majesty, and Buddhist kings have vied with one another for the glory of their possession. But despite all of his tremendous wonder-working abilities and yogic power, the Buddha's real importance to the world was that he taught to others the truths he realized, and established a community of ordained followers, the saṅgha, to continue his ministry after his demise. Without this teaching and without this community, his existence would have been irrelevant to history and humankind, for no one else would have benefited from his awakening. His teachings, the dhamma (*dharma*), and everything associated with them when considered as an historical entity are called the sāsana, or "the Buddha's religion." Only perfect buddhas like Gautama can teach and establish a sāsana, and as such, they are distinguished from silent or "private" buddhas (Pāli *pacceka-buddha,* Sanskrit *pratyekabuddha*) who, because of their lesser perfections, can only realize the truths themselves but not teach them to others. Private buddhas appear only during "empty periods," those dark and vast stretches of cosmic time when there is no sāsana. Buddhas of either type never overlap in time, and there is only one perfect buddha for each successive sāsana.

Since at least the fifth century C.E., the Theravāda has held that the religion of Gautama Buddha would endure for no more than five thousand years. And until very recently, it was also generally felt that the religion had already so deteriorated that nirvāṇa was no longer accessible through the practice of insight meditation as provided for in its teachings. It is for this reason that even today most Burmese believe that their best chance for liberation lies not in the present but in the future with the dawning of the next sāsana founded by Maitreya. To make oneself eligible for that opportunity, however, requires great stores of merit accumulated over many lifetimes. This is by no means an easy or certain endeavor, for should a person commit even a single misdeed, he risks a rebirth in hell. And once fallen into that state, all hope of encountering the future Buddha is lost. Hence the advantages of becoming a Buddhist wizard: having made himself immune to death, he is likewise freed from the perils of rebirth. And having equipped himself with magical powers so that he might defend the Buddha's religion, he is well positioned to earn the merit required to be liberated by Maitreya's teachings.

Further Reading

On the evolution of the arhat ideal in early Buddhism, see George D. Bond, "The Development and Elaboration of the Arahant Ideal in the Theravāda Buddhist Tradition," *Journal of the American Academy of Religion* 52:2 (1984), 227–42; and

Étienne Lamotte, *History of Indian Buddhism: From the Origins to the Śaka Era,* translated by Sara Webb-Boin (Louvain: Peeters Press, 1988), pp. 690–99.

On Maitreya and the medieval Theravāda tradition, see Walpola Rahula, *History of Buddhism in Ceylon: Anuradhapura Period 3rd Century* B.C.*–10th Century* A.D. (Colombo: Gunasena & Co., 1956), pp. 25–33; Henry Clark Warren, "The Buddhist Apocalypse," in *Buddhism in Translations* (reprint New York: Antheneum, 1963), pp. 184–96.

On alchemy and the tantric tradition, see Mircea Eliade, *Yoga, Immortality and Freedom,* 2nd ed., translated by Willard R. Trask (Princeton: Princeton University Press, 1969), pp. 274–84; David White, "Indian Alchemy," in *Encyclopedia of Religion,* vol. 1, edited by Mircea Eliade (New York: Macmillan Pub. Co., 1987), pp. 190–92.

On esoteric Buddhism in Burma, see Maung Htin Aung, "The Cult of Alchemy," in *Folk Elements in Burmese Buddhism* (London: Oxford University Press, 1962), pp. 41–50; John P. Ferguson and E. Michael Mendelson, "Masters of the Buddhist Occult: The Burmese Weikzas," *Contributions to Asian Studies* 16 (1981), 62–80; Frederic K. Lehman, "Burmese Religion," in *Encyclopedia of Religion,* vol. 2, edited by Mircea Eliade (New York: Macmillan, 1987), 574–80; Melford E. Spiro, *Buddhism and Society: A Great Tradition and Its Burmese Vicissitudes* (New York: Harper and Row, 1970), pp. 164–71.

The Goal and Path of the Great Manosetopad Gaing

I forever pay homage to the noble
qualities of the triple gem,
to my parents and my teachers.

THE GOAL. The goal of the sciences established by our benefactor, the Twet-ya-pauk [one who has attained virtual immortality] and great lord abbot, is to develop the capacity to realize nirvāṇa in this very life. Nirvāṇa is called the "truth of cessation," for it represents the utter passing away of the mass of suffering known as birth, old age, disease, and death. This cessation is achieved through eliminating, by means of the path, the defiling moral conditions that perpetuate rebirth in the cycle of existence, and so constitute the ultimate cause of suffering.

THE ORDINARY WORLDLING. In the present world-age, when the natural life span of human beings is very short, it is extremely difficult for ordinary persons or worldlings to attain nirvāṇa in a single existence through the practices of tranquillity meditation and insight meditation. This is because in order for these meditations to be effective in generating the liberating knowledge required for deliverance, the practitioner must first become well accomplished in the successive stages of moral perfection through a course of discipline that extends over many lifetimes.

In the following section on various forms of knowledge, the passages in bold type represent verbatim excerpts from Ledi Sayadaw's *Vijjā-magga-dīpanī* (1898). Ledi's purpose in writing that text was, amongst other things, to distinguish different types of worldly knowledge (*lokiya-vijjā*), such as occult sciences, from liberating knowledge (*ariya-vijjā*), that is, knowledge which pertains solely to the attainment of nirvāṇa. But here, our author uses Ledi's descriptions of life-prolonging alchemy, a worldly knowledge, as justification for the soteriology of the Manosetopad Gaing that promises deliverance in nirvāṇa through the extension of human life.

LIBERATING KNOWLEDGE. **The term "liberating knowledge" refers to perfect comprehension of the verities of impermanence, suffering, non-self, and the path, and fruit of liberation. This type of understanding is also known as "knowledge of the four truths."**

THE FIVE LIMBS. **In the *Pañcaṅguttara* and other scriptures it is stated that in order to be able to attain and master liberating knowledge within the present dispensation (*sāsana*) of Gautama Buddha, it is necessary to be endowed with the following five limbs or attributes: faith in the Blessed One, a healthy and sound body, uprightness of character, energy, and penetrative knowledge of the momentary arising and passing away of the physical and mental aggregates of existence.**

It is an extreme rarity in this era of moral decline and misfortune for anyone to be complete in the second limb; that is, to enjoy good health for a very long period of time. Quite the contrary, nowadays disease, old age, and death are all too easily encountered. To protect oneself from these disabilities, even temporarily, it is necessary to choose a suitable place to live, the proper foods to eat, and an environment favorable in terms of water, soil, and climate. Furthermore, it is always necessary to exercise caution while attempting to fulfill these needs lest the body become exhausted. Finally, should a person's physical body become contaminated, his mental capacities likewise become impaired. It is for these reasons that among the limbs enabling one to attain and master the path, this second limb of being free from disease is exceedingly important.

PREVENTING THE NATURAL DETERIORATION OF THE BODY. **There exists a way to avoid the natural deterioration of the body that occurs during old age. For people whose accumulated merits and good actions performed in previous lives are few, this cannot be achieved through natural means but only through taking the appropriate medicines. Such elixirs have the potential to extend one's maximum natural life-span of one hundred years to beyond five hundred or even a thousand years.**

THE ELIXIR OF LIFE. This point has been clarified by the Blessed One in scripture where it says, **"If a person is exceptionally intelligent and energetic, then, even if his accumulated merits and good actions be few, this type of elixir will allow him to live beyond one hundred, one thousand, or even ten thousand years by transforming the physical aggregates of his body."**

Here our author has mistakenly identified the passage he quotes from Ledi Sayadaw as canonical, when Ledi was, in fact, commenting on a much later passage from the commentary to the *Visuddhimagga.*

THE METHOD OF PHYSICAL TRANSFORMATION. Transformation of the body is brought about by gradually supplementing natural foods with stable minerals and elements, such as ruby, iron, and mercury. But these substances should not be consumed in "green" or raw form, for in that case, even though they penetrate the body's tissues, they will not have the capacity to alter its internal or external condition. In order for these substances to be efficacious, their rawness must first be removed through a process of heating and roasting. If an elixir that has been prepared in this way is repeatedly consumed over a long period of time, then the perishable matter of the body will gradually be replaced by the stable elements imbibed. And this process of mineralizing the flesh and blood of the body is precisely what enables a person to live beyond one hundred or even a thousand years.

The boldface passages in the next two paragraphs are excerpted from the official Burmese translation of the Pāli canon produced for the Sixth Buddhist Council in Rangoon in 1956. The purpose of this reference is to demonstrate that the desire for extraordinary longevity falls within acceptable orthodox boundaries.

VITAL FORCE. There is yet another way to extend one's natural life-span, and this entails the retention of the body's vital force. Evidence for how this can be brought about can be found in the Buddha's own life story. For example, just before he resolved to give up his own vital force and so live for only three more months, the Blessed One uttered these words to the Venerable Ānanda, **"Ānanda, whosoever has cultivated the four bases of psychic power and repeatedly practiced them, and having thus practiced, makes them a foundation, dwells upon, develops and strives in them, such a person could live for an entire eon or beyond that should he so desire."**

THE FOUR BASES OF PSYCHIC POWER. **"Ānanda, the Blessed One has greatly developed and striven in the four bases of psychic power. Ānanda . . . having become accomplished in this way, the Blessed One could live for an entire eon or beyond that should he so desire. . . ."** The four bases of psychic power are will, effort, thought, and wisdom.

The boldface portions of the following paragraphs concerning the "knowledge or science of the gandhāras" are again excerpted from Ledi Sayadaw's *Vijjā-magga-dīpanī.*

THE SCIENCE OF THE GANDHĀRAS (*gandhārī-vijjā*). In accordance with these teachings of the Buddha found in scripture, our benefactor, the twet-ya-pauk and great lord abbot of the Manosetopad Gaing, trained himself in a special science called "gandhārī-vijjā." Through this he was able to attain and master ten miraculous powers (*siddhis*), namely:

overcoming old age
freedom from disease
the ability to extend one's life span beyond one hundred to more than a thousand or even ten thousand years
the ability to transform nonprecious metals into gold and silver
the ability to make oneself dear to all living beings
immunity from weapons, fire and poison, whereby the body cannot be stabbed, cut by blades, nor injured by blows
the ability to pass through the earth and mountains, and to travel above the surface of the ground
the ability to fly through the sky
the ability to travel over water as if it were solid earth
the ability to disappear, and to create duplicate bodies of oneself at will

And having thus attained and mastered these ten miraculous powers, our benefactor, the twet-ya-pauk and great lord abbot, was empowered to enter upon that path of practice which ascends the stages of noble understanding and renders one capable of realizing nirvāṇa in a single existence.

At the end of the present five-thousand-year sāsana, the relics of the Blessed One will finally pass away beneath the great bodhi tree. At that time, those who have well cultivated the practice of insight will, like the powerful nats [spirits and demigods], Indra and the Brahmā gods, witness these holy relics as they magically form themselves into a likeness of the Buddha and display the "twin miracle." And having so witnessed, and having made the aspiration for liberation, these masters of insight will gain at that moment the capacity to realize nirvāṇa in a single existence.

The twin miracle occurs when the Buddha or his likeness emits fire and water simultaneously. Here we see that the Manosetopad Gaing foreshortens the career of the twet-ya-pauk to culminate at the end of the present sāsana, a mere 2,500 years in the future. With the reinvigorated teachings of Maitreya thus out of reach, the twet-ya-pauk is made ready to rely on witnessing the passing away of the Buddha's relics as a catalyst for his liberation. This configuration of ideas is unusual in weikza circles and evidently originated with the founding of this sect. Another innovation, this one introduced by the author of our text, is the addition of insight meditation to the twet-ya-pauk's repertoire of practice. Most occult groups eschew insight practice, preferring to rely exclusively on tranquillity meditation (*samatha*) instead. Indeed, earlier manuals of the Manosetopad declare insight meditation to be inappropriate for those following the weikza-lam. In breaking with his predecessors, our author is evidently attempting to rectify a deficiency he found in earlier Manosetopad theory, for in no orthodox source is it stated that those who witness the final passing away of the Buddha's relics attain any degree of sanctification, much less nirvāṇa. Although insight meditation does satisfy this lacuna, our author is careful not to affirm the views of Buddhist modernists who hold that even in the present age insight meditation can bear fruit in a single lifetime—unless, of course, that life has been greatly extended by following the weikza-lam.

THE METHOD OF OCCULT EMPOWERMENT. The method prescribed by our benefactor, the great lord abbot, uses the power of gandhārī-vijjā to render one capable of attaining liberation in the manner just described [that is, through the agency of the ten siddhis, it enables one to escape the vagaries of death and rebirth, and so guarantees one the opportunity to witness the final passing away of the Buddha's relics at the end of the present sāsana in a single—very much extended—existence].

A person wishing to practice the path of gandhārī-vijjā must first suffuse his mind with thoughts of the three jewels, and then cultivate loving-kindness toward the various grades of nats. This will cause these beings to regard him affectionately, as if he were their own son. The nats referred to here include powerful nature spirits dwelling in trees, the earth, and mountains, minor deities who preside over the use of magical incantations and diagrams, and medicine spirits whose domain includes the well-known herbs and minerals of alchemical lore. Since the knowledge-born power of gandhārī-vijjā is superior to the karmically generated powers of these beings, it is extremely important for anyone attempting this path to cultivate their goodwill. This is because nats are prone to jealousy, and often threaten the life of practitioners, or attempt to render herbal and alchemical medicines dangerous. [The recollection of the three jewels (Buddha, dharma, saṅgha) and the cultivation of loving-kindness are contemplative practices that fall under the category of samatha or tranquillity meditation.]

Indeed, such malevolent forces attacked our benefactor, the great lord abbot, U Aye, in the final stage of practice while he lay sleeping in a specially prepared coffin kept locked inside the private chamber of his monastery. But because his disciple, U Ee, thrice hurled protective alchemical pellets into the chamber as he had been instructed, U Aye was freed from danger. Thus, U Aye was able to transcend the bonds of mortality and became a twet-ya-pauk.

SELF-PROTECTION ON THE GANDHĀRĪ PATH. Through his great compassion, love and generosity, our lord abbot established the gandhārī path replete with the requisite sciences and medicines so that disciples might be protected from the dangers of evil influences such as those described above.

Science of the Final Stage of Initiation. As a foundation for disciples wishing to ascend the twet-ya-pauk path, otherwise known as the path of gandhārī wisdom, our venerable teacher carefully prescribed the "science of the final stage of initiation." It is through careful practice in accordance with this foundational science that one gains the capacity to transform the body and mind, which leads, in turn, to the attainment of the ten siddhis.

This means that male and female healer-practitioners (*sayas* and *saya-mas*) of this sect wishing to attain the ultimate goal of nirvāṇa in this life must first reach the final stage of initiation before they can progress any further along the path. Having obtained this final initiation, they must then endeavor to bring about what is called "the first transformation of mind." This attainment delivers them to the stage of "complete simplicity of character" which, when accompanied by the physical transformation of the body, endows them with the requisites of success.

The Transformation of Mind. Transformation of mind requires the skillful use of the foundational science [leading to the final stage of initiation] established by our venerable teacher. This science is delineated into two sections: the techniques used to cure patients of various ailments, and the proper method for dispensing knowledge to others.

Merit Conducive to the Perfections [Part 1]. Regardless of whether one is engaged in the treatment of patients or in dispensing knowledge, it is essential at this stage that the merit acquired through these activities be conducive to the development of the perfections. To understand how this specifically relates to the treatment of patients it will first be necessary to distinguish between that portion of the teaching which pertains to the needs of the patient and that pertaining to the requirements of the healer-practitioner.

That Which Pertains to the Patient. Out of compassion for those suffering affliction, our venerable teacher laid down the following rules so that they might easily be relieved of their maladies:

First, healers of the Manosetopad Gaing are strictly forbidden to receive the ritual offerings traditionally given as payment to other healers and herbalists. Rather, they must be prepared to treat patients for free at any time so that the poor may receive medical attention without any worry.

Second, since a patient who has been successfully cured of an ailment may still be in need of further preventative treatment to ward off possible future dangers of black magic or spirit possession, and so on, the first course of such preventatives must be administered for free if the patient was unable to pay for the initial cure.

Third, it is important to understand that the efficacy of the treatment given by healers of the Manosetopad Gaing is in all respects the same, regardless of rank of the individual healer. For example, the healing abilities of high-ranking healers who are able strictly to observe all the required precepts (*sīla*), and who can cultivate deep *samādhi* [meditative concentration] are equal to those of lower-ranking healers who are only able strictly to observe the two precepts of avoiding sexual misconduct and the consumption of alcohol. For this reason it is easy for patients to receive the appropriate treatment, since they do not have to distinguish between healer-practitioners of different rank.

THAT WHICH PERTAINS TO THE HEALER-PRACTITIONER. It is far easier for healers to treat patients successfully than it is for them to generate merit conducive to the development of the perfections. Indeed, it is ruinous for healers if they are unable to maintain a well-disciplined mind while tending to the needs of the sick. It should be noted that healers cultivate sīla and samādhi for their own sake, not for the benefit of those afflicted with diseases; for the above-mentioned sciences and medicines of our teacher are sufficient in themselves to allay the suffering of patients.

It was because our venerable teacher felt the same degree of love, compassion, and kindness for those who would take up the vocation of healer as he felt for those suffering from disease that he established a science that would suit the needs of both.

Accordingly, for the benefit of the patient, he devised the means whereby those suffering from disease could be returned to health regardless of the treatment administered by the healer, while for the benefit of the healer, he taught the importance of maintaining a proper frame of mind, of having the right intentions, and of observing the correct procedures while treating patients or dispensing knowledge. For our venerable teacher well understood that when these injunctions are not observed, then even if the patient completely recovers, the actions of the healer are unmeritorious, and thus lead him to ruin. But when these injunctions are properly observed, these same actions inevitably result in the accumulation of merit conducive to the perfections.

It is necessary for healers to be constantly mindful while engaged in mental and physical activity so as to avoid the accumulation of demerit, while at the same time generating the kind of merit conducive to the development of the perfections. In practice, this is far more difficult than actually curing any kind of ailment, for when mindfulness is not perpetually maintained, great demerit ensues. And if this occurs, the healer will fail in his objectives and fall away from the path.

In this section on the perfections, the boldface passages in the first four paragraphs represent paraphrases from Ledi Sayadaw's *Uttamapurisa-dīpanī* (1900), the remaining are verbatim excerpts from the same text. In these texts Ledi describes the role of the ten perfections in the careers of those who would attain liberation in orthodox terms as either arahant disciples, silent buddhas, or perfectly self-awakened buddhas (such as the historical Buddha, Gautama). But here, our author incorporates these perfections into the occult path of the twet-ya-pauk.

MERIT CONDUCIVE TO THE PERFECTIONS [Part 2]. **Acts of generosity or the keeping of precepts, and so on, performed with only the lower aim of attaining future wealth or worldly happiness should not be regarded as producing merit conducive to the development of the perfections. Only when a superior person performs these deeds with the aim of attaining nirvāṇa do they result in the acquisition of such kind of merit.**

BASED ON THE ROUND. **Acts of generosity, the keeping of precepts, and meditation performed with the desire for mere worldly happiness rather than for nirvāṇa, are called *vaṭṭanissita,* or "based on the round" [of rebirth]. Meritorious deeds when performed with such motivation cannot deliver the practitioner to nirvāṇa, nor to any of the four degrees of the noble path or its fruit. At most they result in future happiness experienced as a human being or a god.**

The four noble paths and their fruits represent the four degrees of holiness that an individual traverses upon gaining insight into the Buddhist truths. This intuition transforms a person into an *ārya* or "noble one" (as opposed to an "ordinary worldling"), a Buddhist saint who is assured of final liberation from the cycle of existence. The four grades of ārya are: the stream-enterer, one who will attain liberation after at most seven more rebirths in the earthly plane; the once-returner, who will return to the earthly plane only once; the non-returner, who at death will be reborn in the realm of the Brahmā gods and from there will attain liberation directly; and the arhat or worthy one, one who is liberated in this life from all moral defilement, and at death attains final liberation from the cycle of existence through the extinction of all physical and mental aggregates. The first three āryas are deemed *sekkha,* or under training, while the arhat, as a perfected saint, is no longer under training (*asekkha*).

BASED ON HALTING THE ROUND. **When the meritorious deeds of generosity, keeping of precepts, and meditation are not motivated by the desire for worldly riches and happiness, but rather by the desire to extinguish the fires of greed, ill-will, and delusion, along with the resultant fires of birth, old age, disease, and death, they are called *vivaṭṭanissita,* or "based on halting the round" [of rebirth]. This kind of meritorious activity not only leads to happiness during future existences as a human being or a god, but eventually leads the practitioner beyond the cycle of rebirth and death to nirvāṇa.**

THE TEN PERFECTIONS. When performed or maintained with a purified mind, the following ten activities and mental states constitute meritorious acts conducive to the development of the perfections.

dāna, acts of generosity
sīla, restraint or keeping the precepts
nikkhama, renunciation
paññā, wisdom
vīriya, energy or effort
khantī, patience
saccā, truthfulness
adhitthāna, resolution
mettā, loving-kindness
upekkhā, equanimity

When the perfections of patience and equanimity have been firmly established, the remaining eight perfections can be developed easily. For, having perfected these two, the practitioner can become firm in the perfection of renunciation. This perfect renunciation constitutes the basic condition whereby all subsequent meritorious deeds become automatically conducive to the development of their respective perfections.

THE PERFECTION OF RENUNCIATION. If the practitioner's renunciation is not perfectly guarded, then he will inevitably wish to enjoy the pleasurable results of his meritorious deeds. Any deeds performed in this manner, by virtue of being accompanied by craving, remain "based on the turning of the wheel" and consequently, are not conducive to the development of the perfections.

Renunciation is, in reality, nothing other than the meritorious condition of being free from greed. As such, were a householder to see an object of passion or greed and become disgusted rather than infatuated with it, then, to the extent his mind was free from greed, he would possess the merit of renunciation so long as he remained in that state.

Persons having a greater capacity for renunciation than this who, because their minds are more free from greed than average people, wish to dwell far removed from objects of the senses, don the ocher robes of an ascetic and live as hermits and wanderers. Those who possess an even greater capacity for renunciation, and who enjoy an even greater degree of freedom from greed, become ordained as novices and monks. And finally, those who surpass even novices and monks in their renunciation of the world and freedom from greed attain to the noble status of nonreturners.

The section of the Manosetopad Gaing's teaching that pertains to the relation of the perfections to the treatment of patients and dispensing of knowledge is extremely important. So that this crucial point might be clearly understood, the following passage is quoted from the venerable Ledi Sayadaw's *Uttamapurisa* [*-dīpanī*].

THE TALE OF THE BODHISATTVA MONKEY KING AND THE BRAHMAN. Once upon a time, when the Bodhisattva was a monkey king, he encountered a brahman who had fallen into a deep gorge. Having decided to rescue the poor fellow, the Bodhisattva threw the brahman on his back and carried him out of the crevasse. The Bodhisattva became very tired under this heavy load, so reaching a safe place, he promptly fell asleep in the brahman's lap. Now, all along the brahman had been thinking how pleased his family would be if he were to give them some monkey flesh for dinner. So grabbing a big rock he struck the sleeping monkey on the head. The monkey king, covered in blood gushing from his head, crawled a short distance and cried out, "Oh . . . there are still people like this in the world!" But still, being a bodhisattva, he remained determined to lead the brahman safely to his village, even though the forest was filled with lions and other dangerous animals. "Even if you see a tiger, don't worry," said the monkey, "I'll take you to your village. Just follow the path of blood dripping from my head." And so saying, the monkey king led the brahman to his village.

In this story, the great thoughts of compassion that arose in the mind of the Bodhisattva when he saw the brahman fallen in the gorge, as if that brahman were his own dear son, were an expression of mettā-pāramī, the perfection of loving-kindness.

The clever thinking required to rescue someone from such a situation was an expression of paññā-pāramī, the perfection of wisdom.

The physical effort required to carry out this well-considered plan was an expression of vīriya-pāramī, the perfection of effort.

The Bodhisattva's ability to maintain a clear and unaffected mind even though he suffered great pain by having the flesh, sinews, and bones of his head crushed and wounded by the stone's blow, was an expression of khantī-pāramī, the perfection of patience. If he were without patience at this time his mind would have been troubled.

The thought, "I will not be angry with this brahman who, even though I helped him so much, still caused me great harm," was an expression of upekkhā-pāramī, the perfection of equanimity.

If he had been without equanimity at that time, the Bodhisattva would have become angry and resolved not to further help the brahman. And becoming angry, all the merit he might have already earned would have been ruined.

But endowed with patience, the Bodhisattva was not disturbed by his pain and fatigue. And endowed with equanimity, he was neither angry nor discouraged, but willingly made a path with his own blood, and so led the brahman back to his village.

The life-saving assistance given to the brahman fallen in the gorge was an expression of dāna-pāramī, the perfection of generosity.

While protecting the brahman's life was an act of generosity, not threatening or abusing him was an expression of sīla-pāramī, the perfection of restraint.

Not being attached to the meritorious results of protecting the brahman's life was an expression of nikkhama-pāramī, the perfection of renunciation.

Finally, fulfilling the promise to assist the brahman, even though he caused great injury and pain to him, was an expression of both saccā-pāramī, the perfection of truthfulness, and adhiṭṭhāna-pāramī, the perfection of resolution.

If these two perfections are to be distinguished, then, not wavering from the decision to give assistance was an expression of the perfection of resolution, whereas not breaking the verbal promise made was an expression of perfect truthfulness. And thus it was that the ten perfections were expressed in the deeds of the Bodhisattva monkey king.

Keeping the above account in mind, practitioners should strive to develop the perfections by carefully following the points of practice and restraint outlined in the teachings of the Manosetopad Gaing.

THE VIRTUOUS WORLDLING. Through cultivating and refining the perfections, the practitioner ascends to the stage of a kalyāṇa-puthujjana, or virtuous worldling—this being equivalent to the aforementioned attainment of "complete simplicity of character." During this process of refinement, the practitioner need not give special attention to the practices of generosity, keeping of precepts, and meditation, for at this stage, all the perfections are refined simultaneously. At this stage also, greed, ill-will, and pride gradually diminish and the practitioner spontaneously begins to feel disenchantment with the world.

This degree of mental purification is the specific benefit to be gained from the foundational knowledge taught by our venerable teacher, and its fulfillment represents the completion stage of "the first transformation of mind."

LOOSENING THE FETTERS. Having thus become a virtuous worldling endowed with complete simplicity of character, the practitioner can then initiate the process that leads to the transformation of the body. For this it is necessary to first abandon, as much as possible, the fetters that bind one to the cycle of rebirth through cultivating the practice of tranquillity and insight meditation. These meditations are to be practiced while keeping the eight precepts of the Buddhist sabbath continuously for an extended period of time. The perfection of renunciation can be said to have been perfected only when these fetters, which are the ultimate cause of suffering, are completely laid aside.

TRANSFORMATION OF THE PHYSICAL BODY. The transformation of the body is induced by means of a series of magical diagrams (*sakho; sama*) drawn according to precise instructions contained in the path of our venerable teacher. These diagrams, which are rolled into "pills" and then ingested [literally "drunk"], may only be given to advanced practitioners who cultivate tranquillity and insight meditation while continuously keeping the eight precepts of the sabbath.

DRINKING SAMA. While drinking such kinds of sama, the practitioner must carefully follow the instructions given him by the current chief healer-practitioner of the Manosetopad Gaing. Furthermore, it is necessary while traversing this stage of practice that the practitioner patiently apply himself to all the disciplines prescribed by the founder and venerable teacher of our sect, the twet-ya-pauk, great lord abbot.

Through this transformation of the body and the subsequent attainment of the ten siddhis [powers], the practitioner transcends the level of normal human healers, and enters the excellent twet-ya-pauk lineage of the great lord abbot.

THE TEN SIDDHIS. After the ten siddhis have been completely developed through correct and strenuous effort, the practitioner must then cultivate the advanced stages of insight meditation with a calm and unshakable mind; for it is precisely success in this latter endeavor that will finally enable him to realize the ultimate goal of nirvāṇa.

The boldface passage in this last section is excerpted from a well-known Burmese religious chronicle, the *Thathana-linkara Sa-tan* (1831). Notice that in this account of the future disappearance of Gautama Buddha's relics, our author has interpolated references to twet-ya-pauks and the soteriological goal of the Manosetopad Gaing.

THE FINAL PASSING AWAY OF THE BUDDHA'S RELICS. When, after running its course of five thousand years, the present Sāsana becomes exhausted, **the Buddha relics enshrined throughout the realms of nāgas [subterranean deities], humans, lesser gods, and Brahmā gods will miraculously assemble under the great bodhi tree and form themselves into an exact likeness of the Blessed One. This lifelike image, seated cross-legged, will then display the "twin miracle," emitting fire and water, and radiating a six-colored light that will illumine ten thousand world systems. At that time, only the lesser and Brahmā gods hailing from these regions**, and the excellent twet-ya-pauk masters of the ten siddhis, **will have an opportunity to witness these events; ordinary human beings will not. When this miraculous apparition is finally consumed in a burst of flame, the assembled deities** and immortal weikzados [masters of occult knowledge = twet-ya-pauk] **will** perform diverse acts of **worship**, and express their aspiration for liberation. Therefore, one should strenuously practice so as to be able to witness the final passing away of the Buddha's relics, and earn thereby the capacity to attain nirvāṇa in a single existence.

—31—

Pure Land Buddhist Worship and Meditation in China

Daniel B. Stevenson

Pure Land Buddhism was not an independent school (*zong*) of Chinese Buddhism, complete with its own centrally organized canon, system of doctrine and practice, and historical lineage. Such a model is perhaps applicable for medieval Japan, where Pure Land movements such as the Jōdoshū and Jōdo Shinshū did indeed achieve a fully developed sectarian structure of this sort. But in China, Pure Land Buddhism approached this level of institutional organization only at intermittent points in its history. Even then, such movements tended to be localized and short-lived, rarely achieving a level of routinization that lasted longer than a few generations.

The selections below are chosen to focus more closely on the cultural systems and hierarchies of values through which Pure Land practice takes shape in the daily lives of individuals and communities in China. The three documents translated here, which are taken from Pure Land manuals for worship and meditation, concern the extended liturgical and institutional parameters that define Pure Land monastic and lay practice. In addition to providing representative examples from two important genres of Pure Land literature and lore—cult ritual and hagiography—these materials have been selected to allow discussion of the two familiar Pure Land motifs of rebirth in the Pure Land and "recitation of the Buddha's name" (*nianfo*).

These selections are by no means representative of the full range of institutions and cultural forms through which Pure Land practice insinuates itself into Chinese religious life. They are taken from canonical sources, which means that they are mainly composed or promulgated by eminent clergy and imbued with the normative views of the state-sanctioned monastic and lay elite. As such, these materials tell us a lot about Pure Land spirituality in established religion in China—both by what they prescribe and what they systematically excise or neglect. At the same time, there has been a long history in China of religious movements among segments of the Chinese populace that felt disenfranchised by the established monastic authority and its prominent lay patrons. Much as in Kamakura-period Japan, Pure Land soteriology has often served as a focal point for alternative socio-religious visions that articulated the religious concerns of the non- or semi-literate masses. However, because of the challenge they posed to the existing monastic and political orders, such movements have usually been greeted with animosity from the Buddhist elite and outright suppression by the government. Except for a few negative remarks in Buddhist chronicles, virtually nothing remains of them in canonical sources.

Gender represents another area within Pure Land tradition that is not adequately covered in this material. As an "easy path to salvation" that was open to anyone with faith, regardless of religious status or persuasion, Pure Land appealed a great deal to persons who were either alienated from the monastic system or for whom religious pursuits outside the family compound were not an option. Interesting work is beginning on the culture of the "inner household," with the thought that it betokens a world of religious experience and expectation quite different from that of the male-centered traditions that dominated Chinese society at large. As a form of spirituality that is the unique domain of women, the Pure Land cult of the inner household offers fascinating possibilities for study, provided one can get past the norm of the exemplary female devotee espoused in the canonical sources of the Chinese monastic system.

Nianfo or Mindful Recollection of the Buddha

If one were asked to define the single most representative feature of Pure Land practice, nianfo would probably be one's choice. As used colloquially among Chinese Buddhists today, nianfo can have two different meanings, depending on whether one takes it in its literal sense as "mindful recollection (*nian*) of the Buddha (*fo*)" or its implied sense of "intonation (*nian*) of the Buddha's name (*fo minghao*)." This divergence is not a characteristic inherent to the term's original usage but a product of its long and involved history in China. In its very ambiguity, we find a geologic record of the complex forces that shaped Chinese Pure Land in the past, as well as an emblem of the tensions that continue to animate it today.

The binome *nianfo* is originally a Chinese translation of the Sanskrit compound *buddhānusmṛti,* meaning "the recollection or the bearing in mind (*anusmṛti*) of the attributes of a Buddha." The practice of buddhānusmṛti itself has a long history in India, extending back well before the rise of Mahāyāna Buddhism. When the term and its practical lore were introduced to China, they came as a highly developed meditative system, with liaisons to a diversity of Buddhist scriptures and deities. Amitābha and the Pure Land sūtras represented but one among many such cultic reticulations.

The major Indian sources and early Chinese treatises on buddhānusmṛti treat it as a complex practice involving several different approaches to contemplation. At its most basic level, buddha-mindfulness begins with visual recollection of the thirty-two major marks and eighty minor excellencies of the Buddha's glorified body of form (Sanskrit *rūpa-kāya;* Chinese *se shen*). Progressing to successively deeper levels of practice, one may dispense with recollection of the Buddha's physical form and instead contemplate his boundless spiritual powers and omniscience, until one ultimately arrives at the Buddha's formless essence of enlightenment itself—a practice known as mindful recollection of the Buddha's "body of truth or reality" (Sanskrit *dharma-kāya;* Chinese *zhen shen, shixiang shen*). Thus, although buddhānusmṛti may take a particular buddha or bodhisattva (such as Amitābha) as its starting point, it ultimately grounds itself in universal Mahāyāna truths. This feature plants buddhānusmṛti firmly within the mainstream of Mahāyāna Buddhist practice, connecting it with the meditations on emptiness that we more often associate with the Perfection of Wisdom and other less devotional traditions of Buddhist scripture.

The immediate aim of buddhānusmṛti is to induce states of religious transport in which one comes face to face with the Buddha, either in his beatified body of form or as the incomprehensible reality of enlightenment itself. For this reason, the practice is frequently referred to as *buddhānusmṛti-samādhi (nianfo sanmei), samādhi* being a common Buddhist term for the cultivation and experience of meditative ecstasy. Yet even though meditative concentration may be the focal point of traditional Indian and early Chinese "buddha-mindfulness" manuals, this meditative element is at the same time embedded seamlessly within a complex ritual and devotional regimen. Recollection of the Buddha's form may itself be accompanied by sustained recitation of the Buddha's name or the intoning of spells. In turn, the practice will often be set within an extended ritual cycle comprising such activities as the offering of incense, veneration and prostration before the buddhas, confession, dedication of merits, profession of the bodhisattva vow, and so forth. In India this liturgical structure was eventually organized into a formal sequence known as the *saptānuttarapūjā* or "sevenfold peerless worship." Using an earlier prototype of this sevenfold scheme, Chinese masters developed a system called the "fourfold" or "fivefold penance."

Most Chinese sūtras and treatises of the North-South Dynasties period (317–589 C.E.) incorporate both mental recollection and vocal recitation of the Buddha's name within the general panoply of buddhānusmṛti procedure. The practices, however, are distinguished by two completely different names, the term *nianfo* being reserved for mental recollection of the Buddha and the binomes *chengming* (praising the name) or *chiming* (keeping the name) used specifically for intonation of the Buddha's name.

The Pure Land sūtras themselves are by no means unanimous on the practice of nianfo and just what it takes to achieve the Pure Land. The *Amitābha* (or *Shorter Sukhāvatīvyūha) Sūtra* says to "keep the Buddha's name with single-minded and undisturbed heart." The longer *Sūtra of Limitless Life (Sukhāvatīvyūha)* says, "With perfectly concentrated attention, . . . maintain mindful recollection of the Buddha

Amitāyus and vow to be reborn in his land." At one point the *Sūtra on the Contemplation of the Buddha of Limitless Life* advocates "ten moments of single-minded and sustained recitation of the Buddha's name, 'Namo A-mi-tuo-fuo.' " Yet, the bulk of the sūtra consists of meditative visualizations of Amitābha and Sukhāvatī, the content and thrust of which come right out of the buddhānusmṛti tradition. All of these have been taken as crucial passages bearing on the Pure Land practice of nianfo, but nowhere do the three sūtras in question provide a clear explanation of their meaning, much less details of practical procedure. To sort out these inconsistencies, Chinese exegetes of all periods have tended to draw heavily on the traditional culture of buddhānusmṛti, including its emphasis on the cultivation of samādhi.

Even for Shandao and his brethren in the Shanxi Pure Land movement buddhānusmṛti ritual and the effortful cultivation of samādhi continued to be of seminal importance. When one examines the liturgical writings of the Shanxi masters, one finds them to be heavily imbued with the ritual norms of the broader buddhānusmṛti culture. Even with the growing emphasis on Sukhāvatī and the salvific power of Amitābha's grace, ecstatic meditative visions of the Buddha continue to be sought and esteemed as a confirmatory sign of one's impending rebirth in the Pure Land. In many respects, vocal nianfo itself simply becomes another means to this end. In fact, nowhere do we find concrete evidence of the sort of animus against meditative buddhānusmṛti suggested either in the secondary literature on Chinese Pure Land or the Japanese Pure Land traditions on which so much of this scholarship implicitly draws.

If we look beyond the rather limited geographical and historical confines of the Shanxi movement itself, the break is even less decisive. The two interpretations of nianfo continue to persist side by side throughout Chinese history, with little uniform agreement on the relative significance assigned to them, much less the ancillary ritual and institutional culture with which they are inseparably connected. Thus, rather than being the compromise of some mythic Pure Land orthodoxy, this symbiotic tension and ambiguity in the meaning of nianfo is a defining constituent of Chinese Pure Land culture itself—a feature that has been at the heart of the tradition since its beginning, and which has allowed it continually to revitalize and reinscribe itself in response to changing historical circumstances.

The first group of documents presented below consists of three pieces on the practice of nianfo or recollection of the Buddha. They are arranged in topical rather than chronological order, beginning with two tracts from early Song Dynasty Tiantai and concluding with a short piece by the Tang-period Pure Land master, Shandao (613–681 C.E.). The purpose of this arrangement is to begin with a statement of the basic meaning, procedure, and aims of nianfo, and gradually expand the horizon of this discussion by placing nianfo within its representative liturgical and institutional setting.

The *Procedure for Mindful Recollection of the Buddha (Nianfo famen)*, the first of our three documents on nianfo, was composed by Zunshi (964–1032 C.E.), an eminent monk of the early Song period who is renowned in Chinese Buddhist history as both an influential reviver of the Tiantai school and as an ardent devotee of the Pure Land path. Zunshi probably wrote this tract on Mount Dongye between 1002 and 1014, this being the period when Zunshi himself developed a keen interest in Pure Land practice and produced various works on the subject for his monastic and lay followers. The monk Huaigan, whom Zunshi extols in the *Procedure for Mindful Recollection of the Buddha* as a leading exponent of vocal recitation, was a disciple of the Shanxi Pure Land master Shandao. Very few of Shandao's own writings survived the Tang Buddhist persecutions of the mid-ninth century, and those that did had very little influence on Chinese Pure Land thought of later periods. Consequently, it is through disciples such as Huaigan that the teachings of Shandao and the Shanxi movement were disseminated to later devotees. Huaigan's *Elucidation of Doubts Concerning the Pure Land (Shi jingtu qunyi lun)*, which is itself the focus of Zunshi's *Procedure for Mindful Recollection of the Buddha*, represents one such work that enjoyed great popularity from the Song period on. In light of our foregoing discussion of buddhānusmṛti and vocal nianfo, one should pay careful attention to the way in which the practice of recitation of the Buddha's name is treated in Zunshi's essay, noting especially the emphasis that both he and Huaigan place on samādhi and ecstatic visions of the Buddha. The *Procedure for Mindful Recollection of the Buddha's Name* has itself been republished in a number of Pure Land compendia between the Song and the Qing, thereby enjoying widespread circulation among Pure Land devotees.

The second document includes selections from another influential work by Zunshi, titled *Two Teachings for Resolving Doubts and Establishing the Practice and Vow to be Reborn in the Pure Land*. The *Two Teachings* was compiled by Zunshi in 1017 at the special behest of Ma Liang (959–1031 C.E.), a prominent Northern Song official and Pure Land devotee who served as governor of Hangzhou during the time that Zunshi was abbot of nearby Tianzhu Monastery. The text itself consists of two basic parts. The first ("Resolving Doubts") is concerned primarily with Pure Land doctrine. The second, entitled "Establishing the Practice and Vow," outlines a ritual program for daily worship and recitation of the Buddha's name. The translation presented here comprises the first two sections from the latter half of Zunshi's text: the procedure for ritual veneration and repentance, and cultivation of the ten moments of mindful recollection of the Buddha's name.

In effect, the text of the *Two Teachings* is intended primarily for lay usage. The ritual format for the vow of rebirth and meditation on the Buddha's name that is presented there, however, is typical of the Pure Land liturgical routine as a whole. Although the length, intensity, and frequency of Pure Land worship will be different for the cleric and the householder, the basic structure and intent are very much the same. Zunshi's instructions for daily worship and recitation of the Buddha's name are included here in order to provide a concise yet representative example of the ritual in which Pure Land teaching finds concrete expression.

Typically, Pure Land worship takes place in a duly consecrated altar space or daochang. *Daochang* is a Chinese translation of the Sanskrit word *bodhimaṇḍa*, which specifically means the "site where the Buddha attained enlightenment." By extension, it has also come to refer to any site where the Buddha (or the enlightenment that is the Buddha's essence) is ritually invoked, sought, or found. Hence, it may simultaneously describe an altar, a sanctuary or chapel, and a place of Buddhist practice. Where Pure Land worship is performed on a regular basis, there will usually be a permanent altar of this sort. However, if such a site is not readily available, a temporary altar may be prepared by ritually cordoning off a specific area or room, purifying its interior, and installing an image of the Buddha.

Once the daochang has been prepared, worship itself begins with a procedure known as the "incense offering," during which incense is ignited and ritually offered to the eternal essence of the three jewels throughout the universe. As the congregation chants the accompanying incense hymn, the offerer visualizes the cloud of incense, together with his or her body, spreading universally throughout the ten directions, where it produces marvelous offerings and assists the buddhas in bringing countless beings to the Buddhist path. Having thereby actualized the transcendent power of the Buddha dharma, the three jewels are then summoned into the sanctuary in the specific form of the buddhas, scriptural teachings, and saintly congregation of the Pure Land cult—that is to say, Amitābha Buddha, the bodhisattvas Avalokiteśvara (Guanyin) and Mahāsthāmaprāpta, and the denizens of the Western Pure Land. In their presence the core procedures of the worship sequence are then carried out.

Although individual adaptations will vary, this sequence typically devolves according to the following structure: After the buddhas are invoked and incense is offered, the worshipers offer veneration to each of the assembled deities, usually by simultaneously calling out their name and dropping to the ground in prostration. Then, imagining themselves to be standing directly before the all-seeing Buddha and his legions, the worshipers reveal and repent their sins through collective recitation of the confessional litany. Having purified the karmic defilements that separate them from the Buddha's grace, they secure their renewed connection to the Buddhist path by dedicating the merits generated from the ceremony toward the mutual salvation of themselves and all other living beings. For the Pure Land devotee, this concluding dedication and vow takes the more immediate form of a collective pledge to seek rebirth in Sukhāvatī. However, as Zunshi himself indicates in the litany for the closing vow, by being reborn in Amitābha's Pure Land, the bodhisattva quickly acquires the superpowers of a great bodhisattva and completes the path to buddhahood. Thus, salvation in the long term is still equated with the universal Mahāyāna goal of buddhahood. The service itself reenacts the paradigmatic Mahāyāna act of "arousing the bodhisattva's aspiration for perfect enlightenment," vivid examples of which can be seen in both the tale of Śākyamuni's original vow in the presence of the buddha Dīpaṃkara and the account of Amitābha's former career as the bodhisattva Dharmākara. Its ritual structure goes back to the beginnings of Mahāyāna Buddhism itself, but draws more immediately on the prototypes of the "sevenfold peerless offering" found in the buddhānusmṛti literature mentioned earlier. Both types of material offer an illuminating comparison with Zunshi's Pure Land rite of confession and vow.

The second section from Zunshi's *Two Teachings* contains instructions for daily practice of the so-called "ten moments of recollection or mindfulness." According to the Pure Land sūtras, even the most evil person may be reborn in the Pure Land if at the time of death he or she is able to embrace the Pure Land faith and maintain single-minded and undisturbed recollection of the Buddha Amitābha for "ten successive moments." Hence, although Pure Land Buddhism ordinarily encourages that one turn to Amitābha sooner rather than later in one's life, the ten moments of mindfulness nonetheless provide a last-minute means of assuring one's salvation. The practice that Zunshi describes here is offered as both a daily meditation and a rehearsal for that fateful moment to come.

The original references to the "ten moments or thoughts" in the Pure Land sūtras are extremely ambiguous, leaving the entire issue open as to just what a "moment" of recollection means or entails. The *Sukhāvatīvyūha* or *Sūtra of Limitless Life* states, "With complete and perfectly concentrated attention recollect the Buddha of Limitless Life and vow to be reborn in his land for [up to] ten [consecutive] moments [of thought]." The *Sūtra on the Contemplation of the Buddha of Infinite Life* says, ". . . ten moments of single-minded intonation of the Buddha's name, 'A-mi-tuo-fuo.' " Pure Land exegetes themselves have never come to a uniform agreement on their interpretation. Thus, Zunshi's approach represents but one among a range of different possibilities. In light of our previous discussions of the multivalent meaning of the term *nianfo* or "recollection of the Buddha," one should note his deliberate emphasis on single-minded concentration and, especially, the role of the breath in this practice—a feature that harkens back to a classic Buddhist method of meditative concentration known as "mindfulness of the breathing." Moreover, note how the meditation on the Buddha's name itself occurs within a liturgical framework, concluding with a dedication of merits and vow of rebirth similar to that of the preceding worship service.

The third document on Pure Land practice is taken from *The Meritorious Dharma-Gate of the Samādhi Involving Contemplation of the Oceanlike Marks of the Buddha Amitābha* (hereafter abbreviated as *The Dharma-Gate of Contemplation*), a short work on recollection of the Buddha (*nianfo*) compiled by the Tang Pure Land master, Shandao (613–681 C.E.). Two different topics are discussed by Shandao in this selection, one a seven-day retreat for the practice of nianfo, the other the procedure for attending a dying person.

The *Dharma-Gate of Contemplation* is often dismissed in scholarly literature as one of Shandao's less important works, mainly on the grounds that its meditative and ritualistic presentation of nianfo practice is at odds with the putative emphasis on faith in the original vow and vocal recitation of the Buddha's name that is characteristic of Shandao's later and more developed works, particularly his *Commentary to the Contemplation Sūtra.* Moreover, as is the case with most of Shandao's writings, the text actually had little impact on later Chinese Pure Land devotees, since it was lost during the chaotic years of the wuchang persecutions of Buddhism (845) and the collapse of the Tang dynasty.

Be that as it may, historical evidence indicates that the seven-day rite of buddha-mindfulness described in Shandao's text was a central feature in the Pure Land movement fostered by Shandao and his master, Daochuo (562–645 C.E.), in north China. Daochuo himself is known to have promoted the seven-day rite among his lay and monastic followers, as did Jiacai, another Shanxi Pure Land figure who had close contacts with Daochuo's community. Two generations later, we find Shandao's disciple Huaigan still emphasizing the practice in his writings. Thus, regardless of what Shandao may have said about the general meaning of *nianfo,* the seven-day mindfulness retreat remained one of its most distinctive institutional expressions.

Around the beginning of the Song dynasty, three hundred years after Shandao, southeast China witnessed a great resurgence of interest in Pure Land spirituality, especially among Tiantai and Chan masters of the region. Once again, a seven-day ritual retreat for buddha-mindfulness, known as the "Amitābha Repentance" or "Pure Land Repentance," proved to be an especially popular form of Pure Land practice. Various incarnations of this same basic institution can be traced, intermittently, down through the Ming and Qing periods to the nianfo qi or "Seven Days of Buddha-Recollection" that is widespread among the clergy and laity of Taiwan and Hong Kong today. It is difficult to say whether Shandao's seven-day rite of buddha-mindfulness played any direct role in the shaping of Pure Land programs of later periods. Nonetheless, it does describe an institutional and ritual paradigm that has seen repeated incarnation in Pure Land communities over the centuries.

As a rule, laity have been given free access to the seven-day retreats for buddha-mindfulness. Nonetheless, such retreats are nearly always held at Buddhist monasteries and are led by the Buddhist clergy. Moreover, their strict codes of ritual and moral purity, as well as their intensive regimen of practice, are more characteristic of monastic life than they are of lay life. In this respect, the seven-day retreat represents a unique and idealized occasion for the Pure Land lay Buddhist—one in which the ordinary householder is allowed access to an intense world of religious restraint and devotion that is otherwise the domain of the Buddhist professional. Within the world of the monastery itself, the intense devotion characteristic of the seven-day retreat becomes the norm rather than the exception.

From as early as the Tang period we hear of the existence of "Pure Land Cloisters" within larger monastic complexes, where a congregation of self-professed Pure Land mendicants could pursue a collective regimen of Pure Land practice and study. Over the centuries that follow, influential Pure Land masters have periodically sought to organize individual monasteries along Pure Land lines, at times coming close to creating an independent Pure Land "school." The Ming-dynasty master Zhuhong (1535–1615 C.E.) and Republican Period master Yinguang (1861–1940 C.E.) represent two such figures who have had a profound impact on the monastic form of Pure Land Buddhism in modern times. Both instituted comprehensive plans for adapting traditional monastic structures and routines to the specific purposes of Pure Land devotion, including the creation of halls for the concentrated recitation of the Buddha's name that were modeled on the traditional Chan meditation hall. At the same time, monks and nuns of the Pure Land persuasion have developed a number of distinctive forms of retreat that are organized along the lines of the seven-day rite of buddha-mindfulness but apply its program to a more intensive monastic setting.

Towards the end of the Tang dynasty (ca. 908), for example, it became popular for monks and nuns in southeast China to enter isolated retreat for fixed periods of three years (or a thousand days) in order to devote themselves to intensive meditation and worship of Amitābha. By the mid-Song dynasty (960–1279 C.E.), "halls for the sixteen contemplations" specially designed for this practice could be found in monasteries throughout the region. Sources from the period describe these halls as being constructed around a central courtyard, at the north end of which stood a lotus pond and, behind it, a Buddha hall. The Buddha hall contained the trinity of Amitābha, Avalokiteśvara, and Mahāsthāmaprāpta, backed by a large mural depicting the Pure Land (with its nine grades of rebirth) as described in the *Contemplation Sūtra.* To either side of the courtyard stood a long building. Each was divided into a series of eight identical apartments consisting of a small worship hall and a separate room for meditation. At six appointed times over the day and night, participants convened in the central Buddha hall for ritual worship and repentance. During the hours in between they withdrew to their individual apartments to practice concentrated nianfo. Thus a continuous cycle of meditation and worship was maintained over the day and night—just as in the week-long rite of buddha-mindfulness described by Shandao, but with greater intensity. The ritual purity of the participants and precincts was carefully guarded, and contact with the outside restricted, with major violations of the rules resulting in immediate expulsion.

Today the halls for the sixteen contemplations no longer exist, but the practice of the three-year nianfo retreat continues among Chinese monks and nuns in the form of biguan or "sealed confinement," a practice in which individuals or small groups of mendicants seal themselves in a cell or building for the purpose of uninterrupted Pure Land devotion. The Republican Period master Yinguang entered biguan for a total of six years (two periods of three years each) at Fayü Monastery on Putuo Island, and again for a period of three years at Lingyan Monastery in Suzhou.

In the *Amitābha* (or *Shorter Sukhāvatīvyūha) Sūtra* the Buddha at one point says, "If a good son or daughter, hearing of Amitābha, keeps his name with one-pointed and unperturbed mind for one, two, three . . . on up to seven days, when the time of death approaches, Amitābha Buddha and his saintly retinue will appear directly before that person." Although this passage more properly represents the locus classicus for the seven-day buddha-mindfulness retreat, it has often been taken as a succinct statement of the aims of Pure Land nianfo retreat in all its forms, whether it be the seven-day or forty-nine-day versions of the Amitābha Repentance, the ninety-day pratyutpanna or "constant walking" samādhi, or the three-year sealed confinement.

The ultimate goal of nianfo practice is to "forge the karmic connection or circumstances" that will eventuate in one's rebirth in the Pure Land. Recitation of Amitābha's name and the earnest wish to be reborn in Sukhāvatī are central to this process. However, equally key to their success is the cultivation of "a one-pointed and unperturbed mind"—a quality that admits various interpretations, but which the monastic tradition mainly takes to mean sustained meditative concentration or samādhi. In the eyes of the clerically centered Pure Land movement, samādhi is both an essential factor in and signature of the successful forging of the karmic conditions for rebirth. The seven-day retreat and its monastic variants are designed especially for this task.

Once again, the extended tradition of Chinese and Indian buddhānusmṛti is much in evidence in Shandao's *Dharma-Gate of Contemplation.* Single-minded recitation of the Buddha's name (which, incidentally, is to be accompanied by recollection of the Buddha's form) is pursued continually over the day and night, punctuated at three or six designated intervals by ritual confession and profession of vows. Shandao's *Dharma-Gate of Contemplation* gives only the barest outline of this worship service, but we may detect in it a sequence similar to the one presented in Zunshi's *Two Teachings,* as well as any number of other later ritual manuals. In nearly every case, recollection of the Buddha is integrated seamlessly within an extended framework of ritual worship and purificatory restraint, rendering it difficult to make any absolute distinction between meditative, devotional, or ritualistic aspects. Despite the rather formulaic character of Zunshi's ritual litanies, when fueled by the intense introspection and concentration of the buddha-mindfulness retreat, one can imagine that his orchestrations of obeisance, confession, and vow are capable of producing the most profound religious catharsis and reorientation.

The translations are from *Nianfuo famen* by Zunshi, included in *Lebang wenlei* by Zongxiao (*Taishō* 1969); *Wangsheng jingtu jueyi xingyuan er men* by Zunshi (*Taishō* 1968); and *Guannian A-mi-tuo-fou xianghai sanmei gongde famen* by Shandao (*Taishō* 1959).

Further Reading

On the subject of lay "Lotus" or "Pure Land" societies and their relation to Pure Land-inspired popular movements, see Daniel Overmyer, *Folk Buddhist Religion: Dissenting Sects in Late Traditional China* (Cambridge: Harvard University Press, 1976). Also, B. J. ter Harr, *The White Lotus Teaching in Chinese Religious History* (Leiden: E. J. Brill, 1992). For clerical critiques of this sort of phenomenon, see

Chün-fang Yü, *The Renewal of Buddhism in China: Chu-hung and the Late Ming Synthesis* (New York: Columbia University Press, 1981).

For examples of other forms and traditions of Chinese buddhānusmṛti ritual, see Daniel Stevenson, "The Four Kinds of Samādhi in Early T'ien-t'ai Buddhism," in Peter N. Gregory, ed., *Traditions of Meditation in Chinese Buddhism* (Honolulu: University of Hawaii Press, 1986), pp. 45–97. Also, Neal A. Donner and Daniel B. Stevenson, *The Great Calming and Contemplation* (Honolulu: University of Hawaii Press, 1993), pp. 71–96, 234–48.

Convenient, but dated, translations of the Sanskrit versions of the *Shorter Sukhāvatīvyūha Sūtra* and the *Longer Sukhāvatīvyūha Sūtra,* as well as the Chinese *Sūtra on the Contemplation of the Buddha of Limitless Life* are available in E. B. Cowell, ed., *Buddhist Mahāyāna Texts* (New York: Dover, 1969).

The Method for Mindful Recollection of the Buddha

The Enlightened Lord [Buddha] delivers animate beings by means of four basic methods. The first is by the display of [his marvelous] marks and excellencies, any of which will cause the person who contemplates them to put forth the resolution to seek bodhi [enlightenment]. The second is by preaching the dharma, the hearing of which enables beings to awaken and enter the way. The third is his display of supernatural powers, which enables those who experience them to secure all manner of benefits of the dharma. The fourth is the circulation of his name throughout the ten directions, which enables those who hear it, keep it, and concentrate their hearts on it to eliminate their sins, generate good, and achieve deliverance.

The mindful recollection of the Buddha (*nianfo*) that we refer to here [consists of two aspects]. On the one hand, one may focus on the thirty-two marks [of the Buddha's sublime form]. Through concentrating the mind [in this fashion] meditative concentration (*samādhi*) is achieved, whereupon one continually sees the Buddha [before one], regardless of whether the eyes are open or closed. On the other hand, one may simply intone [the Buddha's] name and strive to seize it firmly without letting [the mind stray]. [Through this practice] one will also be able to see the Buddha in this very lifetime.

In this day and age, most people who have experienced visitations [of the Buddha] consider intoning the name of the Buddha to be the superior [form of practice]. Dharma-master Huaigan, for example, devoted himself wholly to reciting the name of Buddha Amitābha, through which he realized samādhi and saw the Buddha manifest directly before him. As a consequence, today people everywhere teach this method of intoning the Buddha's [name].

The key is to restrain the mind and not allow it to become distracted or confused. From one moment to the next, concentrate your attention continually on the Buddha's name, as you vocally call out "A-mi-tuo-fuo" over and over. Focus your mind on the process [of recitation], keeping each syllable perfectly distinct so that mind and mouth operate in perfect coordination. So long as you are engaged in reciting the Buddha's name—whether it be for one hundred, a thousand, or ten thousand recitations, [a period of] one day, two days, or seven days, the amount makes no difference—you must always maintain a single heart and single will and [insure that] mind and mouth continuously accompany one another. When you can manage this, you will be able to "eliminate sins accumulated over eighty million eons of lifetimes in a single moment of recitation," [as it says in the *Sūtra on the Contemplation of the Buddha of Infinite Life*]. Otherwise, it will be exceedingly difficult to eradicate your sins.

If you fear that your mind is becoming scattered, rapidly call out the Buddha's name in a loud voice. It will then be easy to concentrate the mind and easy to realize samādhi. This is the reason why dharma master Huaigan, in his *Treatise on Resolving [the Myriad] Doubts [About the Pure Land],* quotes the *Divya-garbha* section of the *Mahāsaṃnipāta Sūtra,* where it says, "With a small recitation (*nian*) you will see a small buddha; a great recitation, a great buddha." His treatise explains this passage saying, " 'Small recitation' means intoning the Buddha's name with a soft voice. 'Great recitation' means recitation of the Buddha's name with a loud voice. This is the teaching of the Holy One [himself]. What could be misleading about it? I respectfully urge you students today: All you need do is recite the Buddha's [name] (*nianfo*) with a bold voice and samādhi will easily be achieved. But intone the Buddha's name with a soft voice and it will simply lead to a lot mental wandering. This is something that experienced practitioners will know, but that outsiders cannot comprehend."

It is also in perfect agreement with the interpretation that Zhiyi, the grand master of Tiantai, gives to the line in the *Contemplation Sūtra* which states that the sinner, on the verge of death, can extinguish the fires of hell and attain rebirth in the pure land by ten moments of mindful recitation of the Buddha's [name]. As [Zhiyi] says, "Even though this moment [of mindful recitation] endures for only a short period of time, its strength is vigorous, and its resolve is decisive, surpassing the power of a vow held for a hundred years. Such a mentality is called the great mind. [Because they] begrudge neither life nor limb, [persons of this sort] are referred to as virile heroes."

The one [text] speaks of "great recitation"; the other, "great mind." The one speaks of a "bold voice"; the other, "being fierce and sparing neither life nor limb." The one says that "[recitation with] a soft voice leads to much distraction"; the other that, "[great mind] exceeds the power of a vow held for a hundred years." How could they be advocating anything other than the vigorous intoning of the Buddha's name with a loud voice? Even though performed for a short time, the merits [of this practice] are numerous. But if one intones the Buddha's name with a soft voice, the merits remain meager even when it is done a lot. It is with this sense in mind that [Zhiyi says], "Ten moments [of recitation] can surpass a century [of practice]."

In this day and age, I have come across many people of the world who do not try to concentrate [their thoughts] at all, but [recite the Buddha's name] with scattered mind and languid voice. As a consequence, we find very few persons whose efforts have succeeded during their lifetime, and occurrences of miraculous response at the time of death are [for the most part] weak. For this reason I have made a special effort to explain this practice here. I urge that whenever you perform recollection of the Buddha, you do so with one-pointed mind free of confusion, chanting the Buddha's name loudly in a steady stream of invocations. Before long your efforts will bring success.

Two Teachings for Resolving Doubts and Establishing the Practice and Vow to be Reborn in the Pure Land

This second section on establishing the practice and vow [which leads to rebirth in the Pure Land] is divided into four basic sections: Veneration and Repentance, the Ten Moments of Mindful Recollection [of the Buddha], Fixing the Mind on the Final Objective, and [Cultivating] the [Ancillary] Merits.

The reason that only these four aspects are included is because these four alone are necessary for fulfillment of the practice. Why is this? One begins by venerating the Buddha and repenting, through which one purifies karmic obstructions and cleanses the body and mind. Thus, [the practices of] the first section may be likened to cleaning [and preparing] a fertile field. Next one cultivates the ten moments of mindfulness, through which one concentrates the mind, matures the practice, establishes the essential aim of the vow, and plants the efficient cause for rebirth. In this respect, the second aspect is like sowing the seed. After that one strives to focus the mind [continually on the pure land], bringing about the germination [of the lotus of rebirth] through loving protection and constant nurturement [of the final goal]. Thus, the third aspect is like moistening the ground with enriching rain. Finally, one applies the myriad meritorious deeds to help [the lotus of one's future rebirth] put on luxuriant foliage and cause it to quickly put forth blossom and fruit. In this sense, the fourth aspect is analogous to sprinkling the plant with rich fertilizer.

One should realize that being able to fulfill all four of these practices is the highest and most superior [form of cultivation]. Yet, even though they build on one another like this, if one has little time on one's hands, pursuing three, two, or even one of these practices will still bring rebirth in the [pure] land, for each of these four embraces both aspects of practice and vow and will function as the efficient cause [for rebirth].

Also, it is permissible to reserve the rite of veneration and repentance for the six [uposatha] fast days and cultivate the practice of the ten moments of mindfulness on a daily basis. However, since the ten moments [of mindfulness] are the essential element behind the efficient cause [of rebirth in the] pure [land], they absolutely must not be set aside. The last two practices should be performed as one's energy permits. Otherwise you [should] simply do what you feel is appropriate. Now I will expound on the four aspects of the practice.

THE RITE OF VENERATION AND REPENTANCE

Every morning, in a chapel (*daochang*) for regular offerings [to the buddhas], one should put on cap, sash, robe, and jewelry and, with righteous and solemn demeanor, personally offer incense before an image of the Buddha. Then, with palms joined and mind concentrated, chant the following:

> Homage to all! From the bottom of my heart I do obeisance to the eternally abiding three jewels with the crown of my head.

Mentally visualize yourself offering veneration universally to the jewels of the buddha, dharma, and saṅgha of the three periods of time throughout the ten directions. When you arise from prostration, the two knees should remain resting [evenly] on the ground. Take the censer in hand and [light] incenses of high quality. Then chant [as follows]:

> May this cloud of incense smoke spread throughout the realms of the ten directions, and in buddha lands without limit [produce] countless fragrant adornments, [causing beings everywhere to] complete the bodhisattva path and attain the [sublime] fragrance of a thus come one (*tathāgata*).

Having finished chanting [the incense hymn], pause for a moment and visualize with profound heart that the cloud of incense [suffuses throughout the universe, where it] presents offerings to the three jewels and perfumes living beings everywhere, causing them all to seek rebirth in the pure land. After putting down the incense censer, arise and perform one prostration. Once again stand up and, with palms joined and shoulders bent [in humble reverence], carefully visualize oneself standing directly before Amitābha and all the buddhas [of the ten directions]. Then sing the following praises:

> The Thus Come One's wondrous body
> Is without equal in this world;
> Inconceivable and beyond compare,
> I now prostrate to him in obeisance.
> Inexhaustible is the form of the Thus Come One,
> So it is for his wisdom as well.
> His teachings [that is, dharmas] abide eternally,
> For this reason I turn to him for refuge.
> The power of his great wisdom and vast vow
> Delivers sentient beings everywhere,
> Causing them to renounce this burning and afflicted body
> And be reborn in his cool and refreshing land.
> Having purified the three deeds, I now
> Take refuge and offer veneration and praise [to Amitābha],
> Vowing, in unison with all sentient beings,
> That we may be reborn together in the realm of ease and bliss.

Having finished [offering praises], then venerate the buddhas. Visualize each figure, one at a time. As you concentrate on [the buddha] before you, simultaneously chant [his name and prostrate] as follows:

> With all my heart I venerate the pure and marvelous dharma-body of the Thus Come One Amitābha, which resides in the pure land of eternal quiescence and radiance, together with [the dharma-bodies] of all the buddhas throughout the dharmadhātu.
>
> With all my heart I venerate the ocean-like body of infinite features of the Thus Come One Amitābha, which resides in the land adorned by the recompense [of the Buddha's attainment of] reality, together with those of all the buddhas throughout the dharmadhātu.
>
> With all my heart I venerate the body adorned with the mark of liberation of the Thus Come One Amitābha, which resides in the land of expediency where saints dwell, together with those of all the buddhas throughout the dharmadhātu.
>
> With all my heart I venerate the body of sense faculties and fields of the Thus Come One Amitābha [manifested for beings of the Great Vehicle] in the land of [highest] bliss to the west, together with those of all the buddhas throughout the dharmadhātu.
>
> With all my heart I venerate the bodies of manifestation projected by the Buddha Amitābha from the land of [highest] bliss in the west [to realms] throughout the ten directions, together with those of the buddhas throughout the dharmadhātu.
>
> With all my heart I venerate the billion bodies of purple and gold of the Bodhisattva Avalokiteśvara, who resides in the land of [highest] bliss to the west, together with all the bodhisattva mahāsattvas throughout the dharmadhātu.
>
> With all my heart I venerate the body of boundless radiant wisdom of the Bodhisattva Mahāsthāmaprāpta, who resides in the land of [highest] bliss to the west, together with the bodhisattva mahāsattvas throughout the dharmadhātu.
>
> With all my heart I venerate the pure oceanlike congregation [of saints] who are endowed with bodies of the twin adornments [of wisdom and merit] and dwell in the land of [highest] bliss to the west, together with those of the congregation of saints throughout the dharmadhātu.

Assume the kneeling posture, with the two knees held flush. Take the censer in hand; light incense; then, with utmost sincerity, chant the following words:

> On behalf of the four obligations [that is, donors, parents, monastic teachers, and sovereigns] and beings immersed in the three realms of existence everywhere throughout the dharmadhātu, I vow to eliminate the three obsta-

cles [of the afflictions, evil karma, and evil retribution]. [With this thought] I entrust my life and offer confession before you.

After arising, once again kneel down; take the censer in hand; and chant:

From the bottom of my heart I repent! Like sentient beings everywhere, I, disciple so-and-so, have been beshrouded by ignorance and deluded by inverted views since beginningless time. Through the three deeds and six sense faculties I have cultivated all manner of unwholesome habits and widely engaged in the ten evils and five heinous crimes, along with a host of other evils—so numerous as to be beyond description.

Buddhas throughout the ten directions are ever-present in this world of ours. The sound of their dharma never ceases. Their marvelously rare fragrance is all-pervading; the flavor of their dharma fills the void. Their pure radiance shines over and enfolds everything. The eternally abiding and wondrous principle [of enlightenment] fills all of space. Yet, because my six senses are internally blinded and the three activities [of body, speech, and mind] benighted, I am unable to see, hear, smell, feel, or know their presence. Because of these evil influences I revolve endlessly in cyclic birth and death, passing through all manner of evil destinies, for incalculable eons never to know a moment of release.

The *Sūtra [on the Visualization of the Bodhisattva Universal Worthy]* says, "Vairocana [Buddha] is all-pervading. The place where this buddha dwells is called [the land of] eternal quiescence and radiance." Thus we should realize that there is no object that is not inherently [identical with] the Buddha's dharma. Yet, we remain incognizant of this fact and continue to flow along in ignorance. This is tantamount to seeing only impurity when one is in the very midst of enlightenment. Or producing fetters when one is already liberated.

Now, for the first time, I awaken [to my errors]. Now, for the first time, I resolve to reform them. Standing in the presence of Lord Amitābha and all the other buddhas, I confess and repent. May he cause the grave sins committed by myself and other beings to be completely purified—regardless of whether they were done in the beginningless past, in the present life, or are yet to be done in the future; whether they were committed by myself or urged on others, passively witnessed or [actively] celebrated, remembered or forgotten, committed knowingly or not, doubtful or certain, hidden or revealed.

Now that I have repented, my six senses and three deeds are pure and without blemish. The wholesome [karmic] roots cultivated through them are likewise completely purified. All of them I dedicate toward the adornment of the pure land. May I, together with beings everywhere, thereby be reborn in [the land of] ease and succor. I pray that the Buddha Amitābha may always come to keep and protect me, and that he may enable my good [karmic] roots to manifest and increase, and prevent me from losing the foundational cause [of rebirth in the] pure [land]. As the end of my life

> approaches, may I retain perfect mindfulness in body and mind and be able to see and hear clearly. May Amitābha and his saintly assembly appear directly before me, bringing in their hands the flower pedestal with which they will greet and lead me [into the pure land]. In a flash of thought may I be reborn in Amitābha's presence, perfect the bodhisattva path, and [gain the ability to] save beings on a vast scale, causing them all to realize the omniscient wisdom [of buddhahood] along with me.

After repenting and making vows, one should entrust one's life to Amitābha Buddha and the three jewels everywhere. [This procedure for confession and vows] should be repeated three times over. But if time is short and affairs are pressing, a single recitation will suffice. After that comes the procedure for ritual circumambulation [of the altar to Amitābha], which one performs for three rounds, seven rounds, or more. Then recite out loud:

> Homage to the Buddha Amitābha. Homage to the Bodhisattva Avalokiteśvara. Homage to the Bodhisattva Mahāsthāmaprāpta. Homage to the bodhisattva mahāsattvas of the pure oceanlike assembly.

Repeat this recitation three times, seven times, or more, as you see fit. There is no requisite number. Then go before the Buddha and profess the three refuges as follows:

> I take refuge in the Buddha, with the wish that all beings may directly experience the great way and put forth the peerless resolution [to achieve perfect enlightenment].
>
> I take refuge in the dharma, with the wish that all beings may penetrate deeply into the treasury of scripture and realize wisdom [as vast as the] ocean.
>
> I take refuge in the saṅgha, with the wish that all beings may join with the great assembly and be completely free of conflict. Homage to the assembly of saints!

After [the three refuges] proceed to a seat arranged in a separate spot in order to recite sūtras. Recite the *Amitābha Sūtra* or the *Sūtra of the Sixteen Visualizations [of the Buddha Amitāyus]*. But if you have never committed these scriptures to memory, then single-mindedly intone the name of Amitābha Buddha instead. Stop when you think it is long enough. You may repeat the dedication [of merits toward rebirth in the pure land], if you wish, or incorporate [additional] concluding litanies.

THE TEN MOMENTS OF MINDFUL RECOLLECTION

Every morning, when the sky begins to lighten, having dressed and finished your ablutions, turn to face the west. Stand perfectly erect with palms joined [in reverence] and, in a continuous vocal stream, intone [the name of] Amitābha Buddha ("A-mi-tuo-fuo"). [The time it takes] to exhaust one breath constitutes one moment of recollection. Hence, ten such breaths are what we call "ten moments of mindfulness." You should chant in accordance with the length of the breath, and not set any specific limit on the number of buddha [recitations]. Draw it out for as long as you can, taking the full span of the breath as the measure.

One's chanting of the Buddha's [name] should be neither too loud nor too soft. Nor should it be too slow nor too fast-paced, but balanced comfortably between [these extremes]. Proceeding in this way, one should string together ten [cycles of] breathing, without there being any interruption. Your attention should be focused on preventing the mind from wandering, for pure concentration is what brings success. The reason we refer to this as "ten moments of mindfulness" rests in the fact that we use the breath to discipline the mind.

After you have performed mindful recollection [of the Buddha], make the following vow and dedication [of merits]:

> I, disciple so-and-so, with all my heart entrust my life to Buddha Amitābha of the realm of highest bliss. May he illumine me with his pure radiant light and enfold me in his loving vow. I have just completed ten moments of mindful recitation of the Tathāgata's name, all done with perfect mindfulness. In quest of the supreme enlightenment [of buddhahood] I seek rebirth in his pure land.
>
> Long ago, the Buddha [Amitābha] made the following basic vow: "If a being, wishing to be reborn in my land, sincerely takes faith and delights in me for up to ten moments of thought, I will not accept supreme enlightenment unless that being is assured of being reborn [in my presence]. The only exceptions are those beings who have committed the five heinous crimes or slandered the true dharma."
>
> I now resolve to myself that, from this moment forward, I will not commit the five heinous crimes or slander the Great Vehicle. I pray that these ten moments of mindfulness may enter into the ocean of the Tathāgata's great vow. And I pray that, through receiving the Buddha's loving grace, my sins may be eliminated and the foundational cause for [my rebirth in] the pure land strengthened.
>
> When the end of my life approaches, may I be aware that the moment has arrived. May my body be free of illness and suffering, and my heart without attachment or regret. May my mind be free of confusion and distraction, as though I were entered into dhyāna concentration itself. May the Buddha and his saintly assembly, bringing in their hands the golden pedestal, come to greet me and, in a flash of thought, lead me to rebirth in the land of highest bliss. When the lotus blossom [from which I am to be born] opens, may I see the Buddha Amitābha, instantaneously manifest the wisdom of a buddha, [gain the supernatural powers necessary to] save beings on a vast scale, and fulfill the bodhi vow.

After you have made this vow, bring the practice to a close. [Additional] prostrations are not necessary. For the rest of this life you must never miss this practice, even for a single day. For only through firm resolution and irrecusable [practice] will one succeed in being born in that land.

Shandao's Instructions for the Seven-Day Rite of Buddha-Mindfulness Samādhi and Mindful Recollection of the Buddha at the Time of Death

When one wishes to enter a sanctuary (*daochang*) for the practice of [buddha-mindfulness] samādhi, one must do so in complete accordance with the procedures set forth by the Buddha. First put the ritual sanctuary in order. Install an image of the Buddha. Sweep and sprinkle [the precincts] with perfumed water. If a [duly consecrated] Buddha hall is not readily available, a clean room will suffice. Sweep and sprinkle it according to the standard procedure, and enshrine a single image of the Buddha [Amitābha] against the western wall.

Four phases of the lunar month are distinguished as auspicious times [to undertake the seven-day rite]: that is to say, the period from the first to the eighth day, from the eighth to the fifteenth day, from the fifteenth to the twenty-third day, or the twenty-third to the thirtieth day of the lunar month. Aspirants should weigh for themselves the gravity of their domestic responsibilities and, at one of these appointed times, undertake the purifications and perform the rite accordingly for anywhere from one to seven days. For the entire duration [of the retreat] they must wear purified robes. Footwear should likewise be clean and new. The [prohibitions of the] extended uposatha fast should also be observed throughout the seven days—that is, one meal a day [before noon], consisting of plain biscuits or coarse rice, with occasional sauce and vegetables. In all cases [the food] should be sparing and plain.

While in the sanctuary, the participants should strive day and night to control their minds and maintain constant recollection of the Buddha Amitābha, ensuring that mental [recollection of the Buddha's attributes] and vocal recitation [of his name] proceed together uninterruptedly. One is permitted only to sit upright or stand. For the duration of the seven days sleep is forbidden. In addition, it is not necessary to observe the [usual daily] offices for veneration of the buddhas and recitation of scripture. Nor need one worry about keeping count [of one's recitations] on a rosary. Simply join the palms in reverence and, with one's attention fixed wholly on the Buddha, strive, moment to moment, to construct a mental image of the Buddha [standing before you]. As the Buddha instructs [in a sūtra], "Imagine that the Buddha Amitābha stands right before your mind's eye, his body of pure gold shining with radiant light, flawless and beyond compare." When directly engaged in recollection of the Buddha, if you [decide to] stand, perform ten or twenty thousand recollections of the Buddha while standing. If you [decide to] sit, perform ten or twenty thousand recollections while seated.

Those in retreat are forbidden to put their heads together and whisper to one another while in the sanctuary. At either the three or the six intervals [of worship] designated over the day and night, the practitioners should ritually announce [their intentions] to the buddhas, the saints and worthies, the heavenly ministries and earthly magistracies, and all [the beings of the six] karmic destinies. [Then] they should confess and repent the multitude of sins that they have committed with body, speech, and mind since birth. The phenomenal activity [of ritual repentance] depends on genuineness. When repentance is finished, they should return once again to the practice of buddha-mindfulness according to the procedure [described above]. Any visionary experiences that may occur must not be openly discussed with others. If it is something good, recognize and accept it for what it is. If it is something bad, repent. Wine, meat, and the five pungent herbs [leek, onion, garlic, ginger, and scallion] one must swear to neither touch nor eat. Make the pledge that if this vow is broken, may your body and mouth break out with severe ulcers.

In some instances practitioners may make a vow to complete one hundred thousand recitations of the *Amitābha Sūtra,* perform ten thousand recitations of the Buddha's name each day, or recite the *Amitābha Sūtra* fifteen, twenty, or thirty times a day—as their strength permits. [Whatever the pledge may be, they should dedicate this activity with] the prayer to be reborn in the pure land and received by the Buddha.

Whether one shows signs of illness or not, when a person's life is about to come to an end, he or she should resort completely to the method of buddha-mindfulness samādhi described above. With body and mind poised in perfect attentiveness, face toward the west, concentrate the mind, and mentally visualize the Buddha Amitābha. Mind and mouth should operate in harmony, the sound of recitation after recitation following one another without break. At the same time one must imagine with absolute conviction that one is bound for rebirth in the pure land and that the assembly of saints bearing the flower pedestal is on its way to greet you and lead you [there].

A dying person who sees such signs should immediately tell those nursing him. Upon hearing what he or she has to say, [the nurses] should make a record of it, just as it was related to them. Then again, if the person is so ill as to be unable to speak, the attendants should repeatedly question the dying person about what he or she sees. If the person describes signs connected with sinful [karma], those around him or her should recite the Buddha's name on his or her behalf and urge the individual to repent together with them, thereby ensuring that the sins are eliminated. If the sins are successfully removed, the assembly of saints bearing the lotus pedestal will immediately appear before the dying person. As stipulated previously, this should all be recorded.

Furthermore, if any of the personal entourage or the six relatives come to see the sick person, they must not include in their midst any individual who takes meat, wine, or the five pungent herbs. Should such a person be present, he or she must never be allowed to approach the patient's side. Otherwise [the dying person] will lose right mindfulness; demons and spirits will bring confusion; and the patient, dying in delirium, will plummet to the three evil destinies.

May all [Pure Land] practitioners take careful stock of themselves, accept and keep the Buddhist teachings, and together fashion the causal connection for seeing the Buddha. What is given above is the procedure for entering the sanctuary [to perform buddha-mindfulness samādhi] and the procedure for tending a dying person.

—32—

Āryadeva and Candrakīrti on Self and Selfishness

Karen Lang

The *Four Hundred Stanzas (Catuḥśataka)* of Āryadeva (c. 170–270 C.E.) and the commentary of Candrakīrti (c. 550–650 C.E.) present the views of the Middle Way School (Madhyamaka) on the path to the attainment of buddhahood. The first eight chapters of the root text and its commentary describe the meritorious practices that gradually prepare the aspirant to receive knowledge about the empty and insubstantial nature of persons and phenomena, which the latter eight chapters discuss in greater detail. Candrakīrti's commentary on the first half of the text aims at convincing beginners on the path of the value of Buddhist teachings by combining philosophical argument with the narration of popular stories, which provide, in a less formal manner, proof of the validity of Buddhist moral precepts.

The first four chapters deal with the importance of eradicating the four conceptual errors that impede the attainment of buddhahood. These four errors are: to mistake that which is impermanent to be permanent, to mistake that which is painful to be pleasurable, to mistake that which is impure to be pure, and to mistake that which has no self to have self. In the fourth chapter (translated below), Āryadeva examines the last of this set of four, namely, the mistaken apprehension of impermanent mental and physical phenomena as a permanent self (*ātman*). He is not concerned here with philosophical concepts about the nature of such a self but rather with the ideas that ordinary people have regarding a self or 'I' that appropriates and possesses things.

Candrakīrti's commentary presents Āryadeva's views on this topic in the form of a dialogue between Āryadeva and an unnamed Indian king—for a king, as Candrakīrti notes, best exemplifies a person under the influence of egotism and selfishness. This arrogant and egocentric king's pride in himself and his possessions comes under strong attack in this chapter. Āryadeva and Candrakīrti remind the king that since he is the servant of his people, who pay his wages from the fruits of their own harvest, he has no grounds for arrogance. Candrakīrti, in his lengthy criticism of the artificially created distinctions of the caste system, quotes the Buddhist myth of the origins of the royal class, which explains that all class distinctions were originally job descriptions. The commentary also demonstrates Candrakīrti's familiarity with the position of classical Hindu epic and legal and political treatises (*dharmaśāstra, arthaśāstra*) that the king is the embodiment of meritorious conduct (*dharma*). The king argues that his royal duties, which include the right to use force, are sanctioned by the authority of these treatises and that he has every right to be proud of his position and the duty that is his alone. The Buddhists counter with arguments designed to destroy this egotistical attitude, which they regard as a major impediment not only to the pursuit of liberation, but also to a better rebirth. The use of force in protecting his people involves the king in demeritorious actions of punishing criminals and waging war which threaten his own future, since such actions will certainly lead to an unfavorable rebirth in his next life. The king is urged to become an exemplary lay practitioner by sharing his wealth generously and by treating all people with compassion.

This translation is from the Peking edition of the *Catuḥśataka*, vol. Ya, ff. 67b–97a, published by the Tibetan Tripitaka Research Institute, Tokyo and Kyoto, 1957–1961.

Further Reading

For a complete translation of Āryadeva's *Four Hundred*, see Karen Lang, *Āryadeva's Catuḥśataka: On the Bodhisattva's Cultivation of Merit and Knowledge* (Copenhagen: Akademisk Forlag, 1986).

Showing the Method for Rejecting Egotism

Query: The method for rejecting the three [previous] conceptual errors has been explained. Now the method for rejecting the fourth error should be explained.

Reply: [Āryadeva says:]

1. What wise person would take pride in thinking "I" and "mine,"
   Since all beings have all objects in the cycle of existence in common?

Since egotism and selfishness certainly exist in abundance in the king, the king above all is advised about their removal. In this context egotism arises from the imagination of one's own superior characteristics: "I am the lord." Selfishness, however, arises in regard to the notion of power over things that are appropriated as one's own: "These are my things." The word "pride" is used here in the sense of haughtiness, conceit, and arrogance. The word "existence" refers to the cycle of birth and death, going round in the five places of rebirth [gods, humans, animals, ghosts, hell beings], with a regular succession of birth and death, on the part of someone who is subject to karma and the afflictions (*kleśa*). Under those circumstances, what intelligent person, living now, would take pride in egotism and selfishness? Of course, if there were somewhere someone whose sovereign power were extraordinary, it would be appropriate for him to have pride based on it, that is, from his perception of that power: "I alone am the master of these things; these things are mine alone." But this is impossible for a fool who goes round in the cycle of birth and death! For instance, all the objects of the senses, material form and so forth, have originated from the karma that is common to all sentient beings. Consequently, the pride that results from embracing egotism and selfishness is inappropriate [when directed] toward those enjoyable objects that are common to all sentient beings, like a common arbor formed from a group of trees.

Consider the example of a royal dancer. A royal dancer one minute assumes the role of a king; one minute he assumes the role of a minister; the next minute, the role of a brahman priest; then the role of a householder; and finally the role of a servant. In the same way, the king's role is temporary, since he dances on a stage made by the five places of rebirth.

Query: Since all undertakings are under the king's authorization, his pride, which has his authority as its cause, is appropriate.

Reply: [Āryadeva says:]

2. Supported by one-sixth of your subjects' [harvest], what pride do you have?
On every occasion your work depends upon your being appointed [by the people].

When people of the first eon began to take what had not been given to them, the majority of the populace paid a man strong enough to protect the fields with wages amounting to one-sixth of their harvested grain. Thus, he came to be called a "king" because he made the people happy with his work of protecting the fields. From that time on, the people supported each king with wages of one-sixth [of the harvest]. For this reason, it is inappropriate for a king who has been given one-sixth [of the harvest] to think "the people's work is subject to my control" and be proud. Even though a king has exercised his authority over some servant's labor, some of the king's own actions depend on him. Consequently, it is inappropriate for a king who thinks "my subjects depend on me" to be proud. Your majesty, if it is impossible to prove that the king is independent, as he is dependent on one person, why, then, bother to speak about his dependence on a great many people? Therefore, your pride is never appropriate under any circumstance.

Consider the example of the man familiar with the wilderness. A certain king set out from his own country to conquer [new territory]. With an outcaste whom he had commissioned [as a guide], he traveled across the vast wilderness. That king, along with his army, depended on him. But that outcaste should not take pride in thinking "the king, along with his army, are subject to my control" for that reason. Similarly, the king should not be proud, thinking "the people are subject to my control."

Query: The king is a generous lord, and for this reason his pride is appropriate, since he has sovereign power over the collection and donation of wealth and the circumstances [under which they occur].

Reply: [Āryadeva says:]

> 3. Just as the subjects, after they have received what he has received [from them], think of the king as a generous lord,
> Similarly, after he has given what should be given, he thinks, "I am a generous lord."

The multitude of the king's subjects, after they have received their wages or their monthly salaries, which they should be given, consider themselves inferior and the king superior. They think, "The king is a generous lord." In the same way, the king also, after he has given to the multitude of his subjects the wages and salary which he should give, takes pride in thinking, "I am a generous lord." In this situation the multitude of his subjects receive what they should receive, the wealth produced from their labor which supports the king, and they become downcast and humbled. But they do not act arrogantly toward the king. In the same way, the king also should not act arrogantly after he has given to them what he out of necessity should give.

Consider the example of a servant who should receive wages. It is necessary that a servant be given wages. It is wrong for the person who pays him to act arrogantly, and also for the servant to act arrogantly. In the same way, it is inappropriate for the king to act arrogantly when he collects or donates wealth.

Query: Since the king always enjoys the pleasures of whatever objects he desires, he is self-satisfied. For this reason, he is certainly proud.

Reply: [Āryadeva says:]

> 4. Others consider you, on the contrary, to be in a painful position.
> What produces pleasure for you, who lives on the labor of others?

People who control their senses say that having a strong attachment to such objects as women, liquor, and jeweled ornaments is a painful position to be in, since the senses are not under control. Since this sovereignty is the reason for much misfortune, it is a painful position. If it is argued that you [now] are in a high position, [we respond,] through [your] ignorance a [painful] result will be obtained [in the future]. Furthermore, when you say that people who are attracted to sensual pleasures indulge in them in order to experience pleasure, [we respond,] what pleasure can there be in being afflicted with a livelihood that has as its reward working for others and the continual pain that protecting the majority of the people produces?

Consider the example of the executioner who punishes thieves. An executioner who punishes thieves cannot be happy because of this vile work. The king is in a similar position.

Query: The king is the protector of his people. He should invariably be proud because he is their protector. If he were not and if traditional customs were not observed, all of society would be ruined.

Reply: [Āryadeva says:]

5. The king is the protector of the people but it seems that the king must be protected [by them].
   Why should he be proud because of one [reason] and not the other?

If he thinks, "the protection of my people depends on me" and becomes proud, why, then, since his own protection depends on his people, doesn't he lose that pride when he understands that he must be protected? A king who is not protected by his people cannot govern his people.

Consider the example of a married couple. "I experience pain hundreds of times," a husband complained to his wife, "while you remain in the house with no troubles at all."

His wife replied, "First, you do all the housework for twenty-four hours and then you'll understand!"

He did just that and he came to regret what he had said. Just as each one of a couple supports the other, so the king protects his people and the people protect their king.

Query: When the king protects all his people in the same way as he does his son, he is victorious and he will receive one-sixth of the merit (*puṇya*) that belongs to those who perform meritorious acts. For this reason, pride is appropriate for the king, who is abundantly endowed with good fortune because of his own and others' merit.

Reply: [Āryadeva says:]

6. It is difficult to find among all the castes people who are satisfied with their own work.
   If you incur their demerit (*apuṇya*), it will be hard for you to have a good rebirth.

Today it is difficult to find satisfaction among people whose work is based upon their caste, since human beings, their lives, their afflictions, their views, and the age in which they live have degenerated for the most part; and these people primarily seem unreliable. If you are the recipient of one-sixth of their merit, you also will receive in the same way one-sixth of their demerit. Thus, it happens that in most cases afflictions that are based upon their caste overwhelm them and they become shiftless. Those who associate with evil friends have no merit. It will be rare for you to have a good rebirth for this reason. First of all, because of his own evil, a good rebirth is impossible for a king. Alas, why even bother to speak about a good rebirth [for the king], since he shares in all his subjects' evils? Consequently, people whose intelligence is unsound will be destroyed.

Consider the example of the leper who wanted to drink milk and eat fish. Because of his error, the leper not only failed to rely on medicine for treating his illness but he also drank milk and ate fish [which aggravated it]. In the same way, because he remains in a state of carelessness, the king not only accumulates much demerit by himself but he also associates himself with the actions of those who are dependent on their caste [and shares in their demerit].

Query: Since the king is the lord of the world and independent, his pride is appropriate.

Reply: [Āryadeva says:]

7. Someone who acts after being advised by others is the [greatest] fool on earth!
There is no one else equal to you in being dependent on others.

Someone who acts after others advise him may do a little or know little but he is not independent. People call him a fool. In this world there is no one else who is under the control of others in the same way as the king is. When many associates advise him, he becomes indecisive. Most of the time he remains dependent on others. He acts only after others counsel him about what he should do and what he should not do. Because he remains dependent on others, people consider him very foolish and subject to the control of others. His pride is inappropriate for this reason.

Consider the example of trained dogs and monkeys. Dogs and monkeys listen to their master's instructions on what to seize and what to release. Similarly, the king also is subject to the control of others, since he has secret agents as his eyes.

Query: Because the protection of all the people depends on the king, his pride is appropriate.

Reply: [Āryadeva says:]

8. He thinks, "their protection depends on me,"
Receives wages from his people,
And he commits evil acts himself.
Who equals him in lacking compassion?

If the king thinks, "their protection depends on me" and takes wages from his people, then, following the tradition of virtuous kings, he must make an effort to protect the poor. He should accept that [tradition] and govern in that way. But he does not follow that rule. Thus, he commits such evil actions as executing, imprisoning, beating, threatening, and banishing criminals and people who are unable to pay his wages. He resorts to cruelty by depriving them of their lives and all their possessions. This shameless king receives wages from the people in compensation for their protection. He commits evil actions so that protection will ensue. Who else in the world apart from him lacks compassion? Because he is adept at carrying out evil actions, he alone is considered to have no compassion.

Take for example the story about the butcher's physician. When a butcher was breaking bones into pieces, a bone fragment pierced his eye. He went to a physician. This physician applied an ointment to his eye and relieved his discomfort but he did not completely eliminate the pain. Again and again the eye became irritated and the physician soothed the eye's irritation but he did not completely eliminate the pain. The patient meanwhile had parted with much of his money. Then the physician went away to another town and his son cured the butcher's painful eye. The king is just like that physician. He deprives the people of much of their wealth and does not completely carry out his obligations to his people.

Query: The king should not show compassion to people who are criminals. If he does not punish criminals, all his people will become degenerate. Consequently, he must punish criminals in order to protect his people.

Reply: [Āryadeva says:]

9. If people who do evil are not the object of compassion,
   Then all foolish ordinary people will not be the object of protection.

If this person is not worthy of compassion because he has done wrong, who, then, would be worthy of compassion? Since he is not worthy of compassion, all foolish ordinary people will not be the object of the king's compassion. In this regard the word "fool" means to have the characteristics of a fool. The expression "ordinary person" refers to someone who is not on the noble path because of committing nonvirtuous actions. Those people who are characterized in both ways are called "foolish ordinary people" by the saints (*arhat*). Compassionate people will protect them because they have compassion for them. Thus, a compassionate person thinks of stopping whatever is harmful to others. Protection is established because of compassion. Consequently, how will this king who has no compassion bring about protection, which is the result of compassion? If he receives wages without protecting his people, then surely he is a thief who lives in cities and towns without being recognized as a thief!

Consider the case of protecting life and property. If the king does not make people who do evil actions the object of his compassion, then his own life and property will not be protected because he will have harmed everyone! Now, on the other hand, when he is protected, in the same way all those who do evil will be the object of his compassion as well.

Query: If the king punishes the wicked in order to protect his people, he incurs no evil, since he is engaged in benefiting the virtuous.

Reply: [Āryadeva says:]

> 10. Where does one not find reasons for making oneself happy?
> Reasons, such as scriptural authority, do not, however, destroy demerit.

So-called reasons for making oneself happy are not lacking anywhere at all. Even those people who take pleasure in such evil actions as killing fish and butchering hogs claim that this slaughter of living beings is justified because of their caste. The lord of the people imagines that this [punishment] is his job and he thinks that there is nothing that is not virtuous about it. In this way, one may create reasons that are satisfying. But the demerit of these actions is not destroyed. It is just the same for the king. Since one observes that mainly he has done evil, he will experience the maturation of that evil in bad rebirths. His heart, overwhelmed by the fire of misery, will break into many hundreds of pieces.

In order to deny the demerit, evil people may employ the rationale of a nonvirtuous point of view to comfort themselves. But there is no destruction of demerit under those circumstances. Thus, just as superior people have the intention of benefiting others in order to do good, wicked people have the intention of harming others in order to destroy them. How can there be an opportunity for a [future] high position for those who here on earth have minds that are cruel and compassionless, who behave like demons toward others, and who are inferior? Even scripture that says, "kings who carry out royal policy through punishment and pursue what is nonvirtuous are not victorious," indicates that they are harmful. [We infer that] these kings are not victorious because they are engaged in harming others. Also, there is the analogy "they are like butchers" and the direct perception of yogins whose vision perceives the maturation of their actions. Consequently, because scripture, inference, analogy, and direct perception prove that the demerit exists, these kings have committed evil actions.

Take, for example, the story about the man who ate before [his last meal] was digested. A man thought, "I will eat [another meal] even though that [last meal] is not yet digested." He asked some brahmans, "Should I satisfy myself and eat?"

They replied, "Eat."

In the same way, they gave their consent to all the other actions he asked about, actions such as drinking water and sleeping. After he had done all this, he experienced pain.

"Why did you act like that?" his physician asked him.

"I didn't do anything without asking for advice," he replied.

This man consulted others and when he did what was wrong in order to satisfy himself, he was gripped by severe pain. In the same way, kings also do what pleases them. They use reasons for making themselves happy, and commit evil actions. Consequently, these human beings experience great suffering in hell, which this [evil] has caused. They have taken these treatises [on government (*artha-śāstra*)] as authoritative; and, because of their nonvirtuous conduct, unpleasant results will follow from their evil actions.

Query: Properly protecting his people is meritorious conduct (*dharma*) for the king, which he does so that he will reach heaven. He has no need of any other meritorious conduct.

Reply: [Āryadeva says:]

11. If this so-called protection is meritorious conduct for the king,
Then why isn't it meritorious conduct for those who create afflictions [by manufacturing weapons]?

Even though they benefit from the wages, an action that has that benefit as its motive is not meritorious conduct for carpenters and blacksmiths. In the same way, even though he provides proper protection, protecting his people is not meritorious conduct for the king who receives one-sixth [of the harvest] as his wages.

Consider the examples of Kashmiri men who dig up the earth and the men who manufacture weapons. Kashmiri men perform such actions as digging a trench [which involves them in the killing of small insects] in order to protect their cities. Although they protect their community, they have no merit because of that [act of killing]. This is also the case for kings. Also, those men who forge weapons have no merit produced by that, even though they forge them in order to protect society. This is also the case for kings.

Query: Since in this world all the people depend on the king, they all ought not criticize the king.

Reply: [Āryadeva says:]

12. The people depend on the king but the king is denounced.
Similarly, an intelligent person denounces the craving for existence, the mother of all people.

Even if all the people, householders along with wandering ascetics, depend on the king, he is still considered an evil man. For example, the craving for existence, when it causes one to go around in the cycle of birth and death, is a mother, since one observes that people who have this craving are born and people who are free of this craving are not. Nevertheless, an intelligent person whose vision is free of error denounces this craving, since it is the reason that all beings who are trapped in the prison of the cycle of birth and death wander around in that cycle. In the same way, an intelligent person will also denounce the king. Even though the king is the father of his people, he is denounced, since he is associated with violent actions, which have as their result many bad rebirths.

Consider the example of the merchants in an isolated location. A group of merchants in an isolated location depend on a trader to provide the requisites for their protection, and so forth. Because he provides them at a very high price he is criticized, but the merchants are not criticized. In the same way, even though the people depend on the king for their welfare because he is their protector, the king is still criticized because he is intent on reaping his own rewards.

Query: Since a king who is highly intelligent and compassionate properly protects his people, it is meritorious conduct for him.

Reply: [Āryadeva says:]

13. A sensible man does not acquire a kingdom.
 Since a fool has no compassion,
 Even though he is their protector, the people's lord, lacking compassion,
 has no meritorious conduct.

The so-called royal way of life has become the basis for pride and carelessness. How can one say that the king is not a fool, if he rejects the path that benefits himself and others because of his attachment to mere sovereignty? He clearly directs his mind in this way toward the excitement of worldly action. Like a blind man, he does not perceive at all that impermanence associated with him and his pleasures. With a mind that is not directed [toward worldly actions] a human being should delight in moral conduct. Its excellent pleasing results, observed and unobserved, are never destroyed, [but] the king does not perceive this. When he recognizes as good qualities a multitude of faults, which are just the reverse, he is in fact a big fool! For this reason, only a fool acquires a kingdom. The compassion of a king who is a fool does not last because his arrogance makes its appearance. There is no meritorious conduct for a compassionless king, since he engages primarily in violence. It is wrong to claim that a king who is highly intelligent and compassionate has meritorious conduct. A man who does not protect the people, even though he receives his wages, is an everyday thief and not a king!

Take, for example, the story about the minister of the merciless King Ugradatta. Since King Ugradatta's minister was unable to make the king's subjects pay their taxes by force, the king asked him: "Why weren't you able to?" He then became angry with his minister. The minister had a close friend and he told him about this. His friend advised him: "You must force them to pay." The minister then inflicted severe pain on them so that they would pay. The king appointed that same close friend as a minister. He also committed many evil actions because he wanted to please the king. Finally, when he was unable to kill all [the tax resisters] with weapons, he killed them with fire. Many thousands of living beings were killed in that fire; and the king had given his consent to it. Thus, no compassion exists where a fool is present. When there is no compassion, how can merit be acquired? All of this applies also to kings; for this reason, there is no meritorious conduct for them, even though they are protectors.

Query: There is no demeritorious conduct even for a king who engages in violence according to his duty as prescribed by the sages.

Reply: [Āryadeva says:]

14. A clear-sighted person should not undertake every action of the sages,
    Since inferior, mediocre, and superior types are found even among them.

In this world an intelligent person should not undertake every physical, verbal, and mental action of the sages because even among the sages one finds inferior, mediocre, and superior types. In this regard, a sage is inferior when in his treatises violence is explained as meritorious conduct. A mediocre sage is one who doubts: "it may be so or it may not be so." But the superior sage is one for whom violence is not meritorious conduct. For this reason, all the sages' treatises should not be taken as authoritative. It is wrong to claim that there is no demeritorious conduct for a king who engages in violence in accordance with his duty as prescribed by the sages.

Take, for example, the stories about [the brahmans] Viśvamitra, Vaiśiṣṭha, and Jāmadagnya. It is well known that the first one stole and ate dog's meat, something he should not have eaten, the second one went where he should not have gone and had sexual intercourse with Akṣamālā, an outcaste woman, who bore his sons; and the last one took life, commanded by his mother to make the earth bereft of the royal class.

Query: Since the ancient kings took the sense of that treatise [on government] as authoritative and properly protected a prosperous kingdom, the treatise is a valid authority.

Reply: [Āryadeva says:]

15. Previously the virtuous kings protected society
    Just as [they protected] a son.
    Now those [kings] who rely on the law of an age of discord
    Have made it into a hunting ground.

The virtuous universal monarchs, born before the age of discord, investigated what was proper and improper. They took as authoritative those treatises which conformed to meritorious conduct and rejected those which conformed to demeritorious conduct; and they abided by the path of the ten virtuous actions [abstention from taking life, theft, sexual misconduct, lies, slander, invective, gossip, envy, ill-will, and wrong views]. These kings who loved the people protected society just as they would a beloved son. But now kings, born in the age of discord, rely on the evil nature of their own opinions, and are devoted solely to their desire for wealth. They take as authoritative treatises that conform to demeritorious conduct and reject those that conform to meritorious conduct. In this way, these kings who have no compassion devastate this world, just as if it were a hunting ground. Consequently, a treatise that is associated with demeritorious conduct should not be taken as authoritative.

Consider the example of a foreigner squeezing an unripe sugar cane. A foreign thief squeezed an unripe sugar cane out of ignorance. He just did something that was worthless and unprofitable. Similarly, if the king does not protect those who should be protected, there will be no profit for him in this world or in the next because of his lack of merit.

Query: In this world it is not demeritorious conduct for the king to attack his enemies' weak points, since this is the opinion of [political] treatises.

Reply: [Āryadeva says:]

16. If a king who attacks [his enemies'] weak points has incurred no evil
    Then that is even more the case for others, such as thieves!

If a king who attacks his enemies' weak points or strangers' weak points incurs no evil, surely, then, because of this royal thief['s example], there is no evil for others also. Thieves who have discovered some weak points among the watchmen and then have stolen the property of others will then incur no evil, since first they have attacked weak points [like the king], and second they are better [than the king] at attacking weak points! Since this latter claim is not held to be true of the king, the earlier claim that there is no evil for a king who attacks the weak points is not true either.

Take, for example, the story about Prince Ajitasena. A king told his minister, "When I die, you will crown my brother, Prince Ajitasena." When the king died, that minister attacked [the loyalists'] weak points, killed the prince, and then seized the kingdom for himself. His infamy as an evil man was well known in this world; and in the next his demerit [was well known]. In the same way, how will there not be infamy and evil for kings who attack weak points?

Query: After a king in the jaws of battle has triumphed over his enemies, he has great satisfaction in seeing the abundance of wealth that he has acquired through his heroism. But alternatively if he dies in battle, he surely will go to heaven, since he has sacrificed himself. [The *Bhagavad Gītā* says:] "If you are killed, you will gain heaven; or if you conquer, you will enjoy the earth. Therefore, son of Kuntī, rise up, determined to fight the battle."

Reply: [Āryadeva says:]

> 17. The sacrifice of all of one's possessions for liquor and so forth is not respectable.
> I wonder why the sacrifice of oneself in battle is respectable.

In this world people who give up all of their possessions for dice, liquor, and prostitutes are not entitled to respect. Virtuous-minded people do not honor the sacrifice of these people because of the fact that they pursue an addiction. In the same way, the sacrifice of life [in battle] should not be respected, since this is basis for evil. Surely, how can it be right for someone who has no compassion, who has cruel intentions toward his enemy, who enthusiastically attacks in order to kill, and raises up his sword with a view toward bringing it down on his enemy's head, to go to heaven when the enemy kills him? Under those circumstances, it is wrong to claim that going to heaven is certain for someone who has died in the jaws of battle.

Take, for example, the story about the cowherd's wife who offered her body to her father-in-law. A certain cowherd's wife treated her father-in-law very disrespectfully while her husband was away from home. When his son returned, the old cowherd told him what had happened. He said: "If your wife ever again treats me disrespectfully, I will not stay in your house!"

The cowherd was unafraid of his wife and devoted to his father; consequently, he reprimanded his wife and told her: "If you ever again treat my father with contempt, you will not live in my house. You should do for him even what is very difficult to do, and you should give to him even what is very difficult to give."

"Yes, yes," she promised him.

The next time her husband was away from home, she very timidly and with great respect attended her father-in-law. During the day, she washed and anointed his body, presented him with garlands of flowers and offered him food and drink. At night, after she had washed his feet with warm water and rubbed them with oil, she took off her clothes, and naked she proceeded to enter into an illicit union. She began to climb into his bed. The old cowherd exclaimed: "You evil woman! What have you begun to do?"

She replied, "My husband told me that I should do for you what is very difficult to do and give you what is very difficult to give. There is nothing more difficult to do [than offer you my body] and nothing is more difficult to give."

The old cowherd angrily retorted: "This is a good strategy to make me leave! You should be pleased! I will never again stay in this house!"

After he said that, he left. His son returned; and when he did not see his father, he questioned his wife: "What did you do?"

She replied: "Husband, I deprived your father of nothing. With great respect and with pleasure, I bathed him, rubbed him with oil, and gave him food. I offered him everything!"

Her husband sharply rebuked her and drove her from his house. After he had appeased his father, he brought the old man back into his house.

Just as the cowherd's wife's behavior was wrong and her offer to give her body to her father-in-law was not honorable, so also the king's thoughts are evil and the sacrifice of his life in battle will not be honorable.

Query: In this world the fact that the king serves as lord over all the people is the cause of his pleasure.

Reply: [Āryadeva says:]

> 18. Your majesty, you are the lord of the people, yet you have no lord.
>   Who would be happy to be a master unable to master himself?

In this world the king is the lord of all the people. Thus, because of his authority, the people avoid actions that are improper and engage in actions that are proper in order to safeguard their lives and property. Because of the fact that the king experiences only pleasure, it is said that he has no teacher, no master, and that is what is meant by the expression "has no lord." That [lack of a master] is the basis for his falling [into a bad rebirth]. How will anyone who has no master and has no one to guide him have as his only pleasure doing what is proper? For this reason, when the situation calls for rejecting the [actions that are] ruinous, if he has not mastered himself, he will not be happy [in the future]! Consequently, the fact that he acts as lord over the people is not a suitable reason for his pleasure. It is, in brief, a reason for anxiety, not for joy, since the king lives in a state of carelessness!

Consider the example of prostrations made to an ordinary old monk in the monastic community. An old monk in the monastic community, an ordinary person who has no [spiritual] master, is pleased by the prostrations. Similarly, the king who has no master is pleased by people who bow and pay him homage.

Query: Since the king who resorts to mild punishment will not be notorious and the king who employs harsh punishment will be notorious after his death, the king should resort to harsh punishment.

Reply: [Āryadeva says:]

> 19. Even for a dead king there is nothing of value to be had from notoriety.
>   Being without virtue, won't you and a dog-cooker have great notoriety?

If the king were to have some advantageous distinction due to his notoriety after he has died, it would be proper for him to resort to harsh punishment. There is no advantageous distinction due to notoriety; and that notoriety cannot eradicate his evil. But if he thinks, "As long as my notoriety endures among the people, I will have the advantages of notoriety, since that will not disappear." We reply: Surely, you also have various accumulations of nonvirtuous qualities, such as being a thief and lacking in compassion. Since you have many nonvirtuous qualities, when you reach the end [of your life], you will be propelled into bad rebirths because of the evil accumulated by the great notoriety which those nonvirtuous qualities have brought about. If notoriety were to cleanse the stain of demerit, it would cleanse the stain even of dog-cookers, since these dog-cookers also have notoriety with regard to their cooking of dogs. Since this is not so, notoriety does not have any purpose at all. Consequently, the king who values his own welfare must not resort to harsh punishment.

Take, for example, the story about the girl who killed herself. A rich man's daughter had died. She was carried off [in a funeral procession] with great wealth. Another girl saw this and after she had seen it, she thought, "I will also have such riches." She strangled herself and hung by a rope. [All that happened was that] she lost her life! Similarly, the king also commits evil for the sake of notoriety, namely, that even after the king himself has died, his edicts will be notorious.

Query: The king who has the [royal] lineage is worthy of the kingdom, but not someone else. For this reason, his pride is appropriate.

Reply: [Āryadeva says:]

20. Since merit produces sovereignty over all, it cannot be said that
He [regardless of his lineage] is not the [proper] recipient of that sovereignty.

That meritorious karma which he has will provide him with the enjoyment of the earth and he will have supreme sovereignty. But that karma [which produces sovereignty] is not restricted to just one individual. It cannot be said that this human being is not the [proper] recipient of sovereignty but it is inappropriate for him to be proud because of it.

Consider the example of learning a trade. People who have learned a trade are common in society. Anyone at all who wants to learn will learn it. In the same way, when meritorious actions are performed, one will acquire a kingdom.

Query: Since it is taught that the duty of protecting the kingdom belongs just to the royal class and not to the other three, only someone of the royal class should protect the kingdom. For this reason, his pride is appropriate.

Reply: [Āryadeva says:]

21. All methods of livelihood are designated in society as "caste."
Consequently, no [intrinsic] distinction due to caste is found among all human beings.

These classes, such as the royal caste, are means of making a living. Now in the first eon all sentient beings were born self-generating because their birth was not dependent on external factors, such as semen. Because they were born only from mind, they had their own luminosity which arose from mind. They had magical powers, flew through the sky, and were nourished by bliss. They were endowed with the properties of happiness and devoid of male and female sexual organs. Since they all arose from a self-generated source, it was impossible for them to be differentiated on the basis of caste. Later, these beings were attracted to the food of the [earth] element. When they became accustomed to very coarse food, channels for urine and excrement were developed as a result of this and in order to expel that [food]. When they saw the different physiques created by male and female sexual organs, beings who had the desire for sensual pleasures set about doing together what was wrong, since they had been accustomed to it in their past lives. For this reason, birth from the womb developed. Then some among their society began to take what was not given because others were at fault in hoarding grain. Different classes came about because of the acceptance of different livelihoods. In order to protect the fields a large group of people commissioned a capable man. By accepting that work, that man became known as a person of the royal class. Those people who sought to restrain their senses in order to perform austerities, who turned their backs on the villages, became known as brahmans. Those who served the kings became known as the class of commoners. Those who engaged in evil actions such as plowing were known as the lower classes. From the differences among their differing work, there arose the different classes and the diverse castes. Thus [Āryadeva says], "All methods of livelihood are designated in society as caste." Because this is so, in society there are no [intrinsic] distinctions created by class. Because of the absence of such a distinction, class is not appropriate as a reason for pride.

Consider the example of classifying a pot according to its contents. By classifying the pot's contents, one labels it accordingly as a jar of grain or as a jar of butter. Similarly, that work which was done in the first eon become known as "class."

Query: Because the four lineages—the priestly class, the royal class, the commoner's class, and the lower class—have been established, human beings have class distinctions.

Reply: [Āryadeva says:]

22. Since the past is far gone and the minds of women are fickle,
    There is no one [certain of descent] from the class called "royal class."

In this world one is born from fathers and mothers. That so-called [royal] caste or class lineage is difficult to acquire, since one observes that women are deceitful. Because a long time has elapsed and because the minds of women are fickle, sons are born to them because they had sexual intercourse with men of other class lineages. For this reason, class is properly rejected. Pride in class lineage which [the royal] class produces is inappropriate, since these adulterous women have repudiated their class. Thus, the so-called royal class does not exist on the basis of class [alone]. The kings of today mainly have their origins in the lower class. Their pride also is inappropriate.

Take, for example, the story about [the sage] Mārkaṇḍeya leaving behind a water pot. When the world was in the process of being destroyed and Mārkaṇḍeya was wandering around, the house [he visited] and the pot [he left behind] had changed hands. He left behind for safekeeping a golden pot at a brahman's house. After a long time had elapsed, he returned to that house. At the brahman's house, he asked, "Who is here?"

"This is not a brahman's house," the inhabitants replied, "it is the house of a member of the royal class."

"There was something that I left behind for safekeeping," Mārkaṇḍeya told them. "I entrusted a golden pot to a brahman."

"There is no golden pot here," they said, "but there is one made of silver."

Mārkaṇḍeya placed that silver pot in their hands and again after a long time had elapsed he returned to that house. Now it had become a commoner's house and the pot was made of copper. Once again he placed it in their hands and returned at a later time. In the meantime the house had come to belong to members of the lowest class and the pot was made of iron. This golden pot at different times took on diverse appearances and the house also was different because of the different appearances [of its inhabitants]. In this same way, the classes of society also change. For this reason, there is no one [certain of direct descent] from the class called royal class.

Query: If someone does not become a member of the royal class because of his class [by birth], then he will become a member of the royal class because of his actions in protecting the people.

Reply: [Āryadeva says:]

> 23. If even a person of the lower classes becomes a member of the royal class by his actions,
> I wonder why a person of the lower classes does not become a brahman also by his actions?

Now, if even someone who is not a member of the royal class but who performs the actions of the royal class were to become royalty, then, of course, even a member of the lower classes who performs the actions of a brahman priest will become a member of the brahman class and he will accept gifts and recite texts! Any person who does the work of someone else will then assume that [class status]. In this connection [because of the absurdity of someone of the lowest class becoming a member of the highest class by performing the actions of a priest] it is wrong to claim that he will become a member of the royal class by his actions.

Consider the example of the boat going over to the other shore. A river is situated between two banks. [People on one bank say:] "The boat has gone to the other shore." and [people on the other bank say:] "The boat has gone to the other shore." Neither bank is proven to be the other shore. Similarly, someone is not proven to be either a member of the royal class or a member of the brahman class. If a member of the lower classes becomes a member of the royal class by his actions, then in the same way a member of the lower classes will become a member of the brahman class by his actions!

Query: The king over time is able to share his royal power with many people because of his great sovereignty. Consequently, the king should seek great sovereign power.

Reply: [Āryadeva says:]

24. Your majesty, you cannot share evil as [you can share] your sovereign power.
    Indeed, what intelligent man would destroy his future for the sake of someone else?

It is true that a king has acquired great sovereign power over a long time. It is possible that he shares it with his people but he cannot reign without oppressing the people. Much evil will of necessity occur because he has oppressed the people. The evil which he has accumulated as a result of that he cannot share in the same way as he shares his sovereign power. He alone must experience the suffering. Consequently, what intelligent man would think, "I'll share my wealth in order to benefit someone else a little," and destroy himself in the future, since he has accumulated great evil which is capable of yielding great misfortune? Consequently, this sovereign power is occasion for shame, not for pride.

Consider the example of sacrificing a buffalo. Someone killed a buffalo for his own and others' welfare. Many ate it, but the evil belonged to the man who killed it. In the same way, the king commits evil actions for the sake of his kingdom and many enjoy the result.

Query: Surely the king has great power in this world. He should be proud.

Reply: [Āryadeva says:]

25. After they have seen others who are endowed with equal or superior power
    The pride that is produced by sovereignty will not remain in people's hearts.

Pride would occur from thinking oneself superior to others. The intelligent do not become proud because this [sovereign power] is not constant, since it is dependent upon something else [namely, merit]. Consequently, someone who wants to benefit people should reject pride. He should not treat others with contempt and act as if he were an eminent person or a lord. Thus, someone who behaves in this way becomes a vessel for wealth because he is engaged in making people happy and contented.

Take, for example, the story about Vāsula's wife. His wife complained to the brahman Vāsula: "There is no woman who equals me in feminine beauty, and yet you do not honor me with suitable jewelry and clothing!" By a strategy of his she entered the female apartments of a king named Rudra. There she saw the queen's maidservants, and her pride in her beauty was shattered. Why even bother to mention how beautiful the queen was! In the same way, after the king has seen those who are equal or superior to himself, it is appropriate that he abandon his pride and egotism.

—33—

A Modern Sermon on Merit Making

Donald K. Swearer

On July 8, 1993, Buddhadāsa Bhikkhu died. Thailand lost its most distinctive and controversial monastic voice. His first translated essays, *Toward the Truth,* were published in the West in 1971. Within the past twenty years thousands of Americans and Europeans have found their way to Buddhadāsa's monastery in Chaiya, southern Thailand, and dozens of his essays and talks have been translated into English, French, German, Japanese, and other European and Asian languages, although only a relatively small number have been published in America. Buddhadāsa's distinctive interpretations of the Buddha's dharma are consistent with modern, liberal, reformist voices in Asia and the West aimed at an urban, educated audience. Buddhadāsa's teachings, moreover, also reflect his own unique personal experience living in a Thailand that has rapidly modernized since he established Suan Mokkhabalārāma monastery in 1932—the year, coincidentally, that saw the demise of absolute monarchical rule in Siam.

Some themes of Buddhadāsa's thought, such as the freed or nonattached heart / mind (*citta*), provide a continuous focus for his creative mind, a fulcrum around which he weaves his interpretations of such seminal Buddhist notions as not-self and emptiness. His identification of dharma with nature and the normal provided him with a natural vantage point from which to address important issues of Buddhism and the environment, just as his exposition of Buddhist or dharmic socialism developed logically from his application of the principle of interdependent coarising to society.

Buddhadāsa proposes both critical and constructive reinterpretations of traditional Theravāda doctrine and practice. On the doctrinal level he has been particularly critical of Abhidharma scholasticism and what he considers to be Buddhaghosa's crypto-brahmanical or foundationalist interpretation of the key Theravāda formula of interdependent coarising. On the level of popular practice he has railed against the saṅgha's and laity's preoccupation with merit making which, he argues, the saṅgha has exploited for the purposes of feathering its own nest and the laity has practiced because of a mechanistic belief that giving to the saṅgha will result in material reward either in this life or the next.

The following translation provides a flavor of Buddhadāsa's provocative style on the subject of giving. It is based on pages 5–14 of Buddhadāsa's essay, *Kan Hai Dāna Thī Mai Sia Ngœn Laew Yang Dai Nibbāna* ["Giving Dāna that Doesn't Cost Any Money and Leads to Nirvāṇa"] (Bangkok: Association for the Propagation of Buddhism, 1974).

Further Reading

For the translated works of Buddhadāsa Bhikku, see *Toward the Truth,* edited by Donald K. Swearer (Philadelphia: Westminster Press, 1971); and *Me and Mine. Selected Essays of Bhikku Buddhadāsa,* edited by Donald K. Swearer (Albany: SUNY Press, 1990). For a discussion of other modern voices in Thailand, see Peter A. Jackson, *Buddhism, Legitimation, and Conflict: The Political Functions of Urban Thai Buddhism* (Singapore: Institute of Southeast Asian Studies, 1989).

Giving Dāna that Doesn't Cost Any Money and Leads to Nirvāṇa

Thais usually interpret the benefit of giving to the saṅgha *(dāna)* as a future reward, a better life in the future or rebirth in heaven. Such a belief is childish. One still remains stuck in the cycle of rebirth. Giving can be looked at in two ways. In the first, one needs someone to receive the gift. In the other there is no recipient. The former is bound to the cycle of rebirth; the latter is not. The first involves giving a material gift to someone, and giving forgiveness in return [a process fundamental to the merit-making relationship of laity and monk]. The second is the giving of dharma. I'll call it the "giving of emptiness," which leads to release from rebirth. [Here Buddhadāsa reinterprets the traditional distinction between the giving of material goods and the giving of the gift of dharma.] Another way of talking about this kind of giving is to say that it is to give nirvāṇa as dāna.

Now some people say that I don't teach what the scriptures say, but just make things up. That's not the case. I give them different names and use different words. What giving nirvāṇa as dāna refers to is producing or giving equanimity. For example, many people come to Wat Suan Mokkhabalārāma. What they receive here is a coolness of heart because they forget themselves and their selfish interests. This is not nirvāṇa as an eternal condition, but it is a foretaste of what nirvāṇa is like.

The gift of emptiness means to give away oneself or to give up all one's selfish interests. This dāna does not need anyone to receive it, nor do we need to feel that we give it. Indeed, if we really give this kind of dāna there is no self which gives it. If you ask what is given, the answer is—the self (Thai: *tua kū*, that is, the gut sense of me / mine). What is given up is attachment to the notion of a self. What is left is freedom, consciousness composed of awareness, wisdom, purity; freedom from the attachments of the five aggregates, from grasping, and from suffering. To give with an expectation of a return is like investing with the expectation of a profit. For one to "make merit" in the truest sense, one must give with a pure heart without expectation of a return.

Actually, everything belongs to nature; it comes from nature; it returns to nature. From this perspective we can see that nothing really "belongs" to a particular individual. Only the foolish think that "this is me" or "belongs to me." The body and the mind which we think of as "belonging" to "us" we must return to nature since in reality that is where they are.

The giving up of the self is nirvāṇa. Another way of putting it is that nirvāṇa is freedom from the self, and all that attends to the self—from defilements, suffering, rebirth, thirst, and grasping. This kind of giving is peace and equanimity. When our heart is at peace and we are freed from the bases of sense obsession—that is nirvāṇa. This is what I mean by "emptiness-giving" or giving that leads to nirvāṇa. We must give up nirvāṇa in any sense that we think nirvāṇa is "ours." Likewise, a person who practices emptiness-giving doesn't practice moral virtue, meditation, or wisdom as something "other," something to be "got" or attained. S/he is [becomes] morally virtuous, meditative, wise.

What is called merit or merit making is for those caught up in the world because it tempts people to lose their way in the grasping of the senses, to look for pleasure and enjoyment in this or that. Indeed, of all the things that tempt people to be led astray and preoccupied nothing exceeds merit making. Nothing is so destructive of human freedom.

Ordinary folk think dualistically; they divide things into two sides: merit and demerit, good and evil, hell and heaven, happiness and suffering, and so on. They like one side and dislike the other. In conventional terms such distinctions are correct; however, such dualistic thinking is not correct for those who wish to eliminate suffering. In fact, what is called "merit" and "heaven" becomes another locus of attachment, thereby leading to more suffering. In order to transcend suffering we must eliminate the source of attachment. The mind must be freed from the hope of both heaven and hell, merit and demerit, happiness and suffering. A person who has merit suffers. It is not the case that one who has merit eliminates suffering. To want *anything* is to suffer simply from having the desire itself. To escape suffering, hope for merit and heaven must be totally rooted out.

—34—

Sāramati's *Entering into the Great Vehicle*

Ronald M. Davidson

By the time the Great Vehicle began significantly to demonstrate its literary vitality in the second century C.E., Buddhist scriptural and exegetical literature had already expanded extraordinarily—ultimately to become the most voluminous religious writing in the archaic world. Indian Buddhists had not felt content with a single text or closed corpus of scripture in the manner of the Semitic religions of Judaism, Christianity, or Islam. Rather, the entire enterprise of scripture was viewed as continuing to unlock the omniscient intention of the Buddha, which could not be encompassed by words and therefore could be infinitely expanded into words without exhaustion. For the Mahāyāna, this model required the generation—in a scriptural format—of the specific ideas and insights of the path of the bodhisattva, who secures illumination over multiple lifetimes for himself or herself and the entire universe of beings. Whatever well-formulated statements led to that end were definitively the "word of the Buddha."

Not all Indian monks or nuns felt the same, however, particularly with reference to much of the new language, concepts, and models of sainthood found in the scriptures of the Great Vehicle. Sainthood, in particular, was espoused as following the bodhisattva path in the manner of the myths circulating around the Buddha's previous embodiments before his final awakening. For the Mahāyāna, the bodhisattva path *was* the Great Vehicle, and any scriptural materials furthering the paradigm of the bodhisattva's activity were the word of the Buddha because they explained his own path to awakening.

The conservative response was that the Buddha's statements to his followers indicated their duty to follow the path of the "worthy" (*arhat*) leading to nirvāṇa in this life. This holy material had already been well codified into the three baskets of the canon—the discourses, the discipline, and the higher dharma—as well as the nine (or twelve) further divisions of the sayings of the Buddha. Indeed, the criteria for the inclusion of new material into the rapidly growing collections of scripture were straightforward: if the meaning of the new material was reflected in the discipline, if it might be seen in the discourses, and if it did not contradict the principle of phenomenal interdependence, then it could be considered the word of the Buddha. These three criteria were collectively known as the "seal of the dharma," whose function it was to verify the authenticity of any new teachings presented as scripture. This represented a problem for reorganization of the Buddhist path: many of the Mahāyānist scriptures did not satisfy the standard application of these criteria. Thus, over time, the exponents of the Great Vehicle had to formulate both scriptural and exegetical works—the former ostensibly by the Buddha, the latter representative statements under the names of eminent authors—which verified items on the Mahāyāna agenda. Foremost of these was the espousal of the path of the bodhisattva along with its meditative and intellectual technologies, its sense of spirituality, and its rituals imparting the vows of universal salvation. These foci were the primary orientations of the scriptures. Exegetical materials were presented to codify the Great Vehicle doctrines and scriptures, to vindicate their authenticity as the Buddha's word, and to summarize the insights of the new dispensation into simple mnemonic tools.

The mnemonic function became an integral part of the educational directions of those monasteries where the majority of the monks espoused the Mahāyāna. One of the peculiarities of the Great Vehicle was its support of large educational institutions in the Gangetic valley, although earlier Buddhist traditions had certainly initiated the institutional educational movement in Buddhism. Initially, education consisted of listening to the recitation of a text by a renowned teacher until the text was memorized. Once memorization was effected, then the doctrines were studied through questions and answers, the student asking the questions and the teacher explaining the doctrines. The teacher would frequently conclude his interpretation of the doctrines with a quotation from the appropriate scripture. On the whole this was done without physical texts, and Chinese pilgrims, who were obsessed with finding written works, wrote of their frustration in attempting to secure written materials. The issue was not the absence of writing in India, but that theoretical primacy was consistently given to the memorized, recited text, as opposed to the written, read text. Thus a learned cleric in India was *bahuśruta,* one who had "heard much," for he had accomplished the first stage of insight—insight obtained from listening to the teaching. Writing was apparently required only for certain specific incantations and epigraphs, narrower genres of literature.

*Sāramati's *Entering into the Great Vehicle,* translated here, is a work reflecting these developments. [The asterisk indicates that the Sanskrit name has been reconstructed from the Chinese.] The text is a primer from the late fourth or very early fifth century C.E., and indicates the concerns and format of a teacher of rudimentary Great Vehicle lore in the Mahāyāna monasteries of the period. Divided into four general sections, the text discusses the verification of the Mahāyāna as the word of the Buddha, the nature of emptiness and dependent origination, the path of the bodhisattva through the various stages, and the relationship between the initial vows to obtain awakening and the final embodied cognition of reality at the end of the path.

*Sāramati was clearly composing a propaedeutic work. In his initial scenario he paints a picture of a hapless novice inquiring of a conservative monk the doctrine of the Buddha. The conservative, of course, is disinterested in the Great Vehicle, which he considers the work of Māra, the Buddhist tempter who represents the idea that captivity by the senses leads to death. As a good Mahāyānist, *Sāramati has nothing but sympathy for such deluded conservatives, whom he reluctantly consigns to the depths of hell. Even more, *Sāramati maintains that individuals castigating the Great Vehicle are bound to repeat their unfortunate slander time and again, so that liberation from suffering becomes increasingly distant. All this, the listener is told, may easily be avoided by examining the arguments against the Mahāyāna with a critical perspective.

The principal thrust of *Sāramati's text is the deductive elaboration of certain axiomatic positions in Buddhism. All traditions maintained that the Buddha did not follow the path of the arhat but that of the bodhisattva. *Sāramati unites this fundamental doctrine with the Buddhist penchant for investigation by suggesting that his opponents employ the ancient Buddhist technique of doubting scriptural propositions, in this case about the Mahāyāna. Doubt is a standard Buddhist technique for eliciting interest in the practical aspects of the tradition, doubt ideally being followed by attempted verification, which Buddhists maintain is possible for anyone.

*Sāramati uses these axioms to consider the conservatives' codification of the three baskets of the doctrine (*tripiṭaka*), responding that this organization does not even take into account many of the conservatives' own scriptures. Moreover, the pronouncement of the Buddha cannot be limited to three baskets of teaching—there are in reality one hundred thousand baskets, a way of expressing the inexhaustibility of the Buddha's truth. Thus, the seal of the dharma affirms that certain scriptures normatively placed outside the three baskets are in fact included in the Buddha's truth, and this affirmation can also be extended to the Great Vehicle's scriptures.

Furthermore, *Sāramati's employment of doubt eventually leads to considerations of the meaning of the seal of the dharma and allows him to point out that the spirit, not the letter, of the dharma is under discussion. Emphasis on the spirit of the dharma dovetails with an early Buddhist tradition that the meaning of the Buddha's word is to be followed, not the mere words—a position refreshing in the Indian climate of legalistic squabbling. By the same token, the examination of intent defuses the question of whether the Great Vehicle is a fabrication of Māra, the anthropomorphic form of sensory enslavement. Clearly, if meaning is the yardstick, Māra would not espouse the Buddha's own awakening as the goal, since this would no more lead to bondage in the world than would the conservative ideal of the arhat.

Thus *Sāramati disposes of his opponent's objections by using standard Buddhist techniques and arguments against him, espousing the same ideas that initially led to the proliferation of Buddhist scriptures. *Sāramati's vindication of the path of the bodhisattva equally verifies the Buddhist focus on direct unmediated experience of the realm of awakening. Following the Buddhist path means that the saint eventually must be able to speak for the Buddha, wherever the course of that awakening leads. Consequently, *Sāramati's concluding sections—discussing the path of awakening according to the Great Vehicle—are not out of place. Indeed, they are the extensions of the same fundamental thrust: all of reality expresses awakening and all beings have the capacity to walk the path expressed by reality.

The translation below is from *Taishō shinshū daizōkyō* (Tokyo, 1924–1934), 1634; vol. 32, pp. 36a24–c24, 38a16–a19, 38c9–c29, 42b17–c3. It was translated into Chinese by the Tripitaka-Dharmācārya Dao-tai and others of the Northern Liang.

Further Reading

For an elaborate discussion of the divisions of the Buddha's sayings, see Étienne Lamotte, *History of Indian Buddhism*, translated by Sara Webb-Boin (Louvain, Paris: Peters Press, 1988), pp. 140–91; for a discussion of the problems of criteria for authenticity of the Buddha's sayings, see Ronald M. Davidson, "An Introduction to the Standards of Scriptural Authenticity in Indian Buddhism," in Robert E. Buswell Jr., ed., *Chinese Buddhist Apocrypha* (Honolulu: University of Hawaii Press, 1990), pp. 291–325.

Entering into the Great Vehicle

*Composed by the Bodhisattva *Sāramati*
Translated by the Tripiṭaka-Dharmācārya Daotai and Others of the Northern Liang

Now we might wish to penetrate the purpose of *Entering into the Great Vehicle*. What is this "purpose of *Entering into the Great Vehicle?*" First, I have composed the text for those wanting to eliminate the cause of suffering. But you should also realize that there might be someone who approaches a poor spiritual friend and takes a mistaken and partial opinion for the dharma. Then the neophyte could form a heretical view and, by means of perverted mental application, fail to penetrate the true meaning, not realize the gnosis of the Buddha, and cast aspersions on the holy pronouncement. Now, one disparaging the holy pronouncement thus destroys the true dharma, and earns an evil retribution of great magnitude. As the Blessed One has said, "the result of disparaging the dharma is heavier than that of the five sins bringing immediate retribution [killing one's father or mother, killing an arhat, dividing the holy order, or making the Buddha bleed]. Since life in evil existences is of great duration, the maturation of suffering will be experienced for a very long time." And as the scriptural verses say:

> One who slanders the dharma of the Great Vehicle certainly hastens to the lower states of existence. This person experiences the maturation of his action and its real nature should be stated.
>
> He is born sunk in hell, his body burning with a great flame, the great torture of his incineration the reliable result of sinful action.
>
> A blazing iron plow for a full five hundred [life] times furrows the top of his tongue while every part of the rest of his body is wracked with pain.
>
> If he happens to escape from hell, he still experiences other forms of evil retribution, all his faculties continually defective and defiled; he will never hear the sound of the dharma.
>
> In the exceptional case of one managing somehow to hear the teaching, again it will happen that he will slander the holy dharma. Because of slandering the dharma, he will return to birth in hell.

So all those defaming the dharma should listen to this. You should maintain an attitude of doubt toward the Great Vehicle. Just as the noble Āryadeva set forth in the verse:

> One with little merit does not even feel doubt towards this dharma. Yet existence is torn to shreds by the mere presence of doubt.
>
> *Catuḥśataka* VIII.5

If one has doubt, then, having listened to all the essential teachings of the Great Vehicle, one's intellect penetrates the topics and becomes open to awakening. Now one who has become open to awakening simply generates trust toward the doctrine, which further leads to pleasure and happiness. One generating pleasure and happiness furthermore obtains the insight developed from hearing, reflecting, and meditating on the dharma and progresses as far as full apprehension of the cognition of all modes, the same as the Buddha.

So, on one hand, one denigrates the Great Vehicle and sinks into the lower states of existence. On the other hand, one generates all wholesome actions by means of the Great Vehicle. Thus, an individual deteriorates or develops based on one's basic orientation. If the motivating concern is directed toward insight, then one treads on the path of awakening. This case is similar to that of all beings, since they equally have this capacity. If awakening were divorced from the natural capacity of sentient beings, then the path of awakening would be impossible to obtain. From the realm of all beings issues the awakening of all buddhas. Thus, the verse by the venerable Nāgārjuna:

> It does not descend from space, nor does it arise from the ground, but the direct perception of complete awakening only occurs from those having experienced the unwholesome emotional states.
>
> *Suhṛllekha* 116

Now this treatise is about correctly entering the Great Vehicle. But what sort of entity is this thing called the Great Vehicle? The collection of scripture known as the "bodhisattva basket" is the Great Vehicle.

One may object that the Buddha spoke of neither the three vehicles nor of the Great Vehicle. However, both of these were identified by the Buddha with the term "three baskets of the doctrine" (*tripiṭaka*). As it is said in the *Bodhisattvapiṭaka-sūtra:*

> The Buddha addressed Ajātaśatru, "Son of good family. There are three kinds of baskets. Which are these? There is the disciples' basket, the private buddhas' basket, and the bodhisattvas' basket. Son of good family, we identify the term 'three baskets' only by means of the Great Vehicle to be studied by all the bodhisattvas, not by means of the vehicles of the disciples or of the private buddhas. Thus we call it the 'three baskets.' Why? The expression of the dharma concerns all of the three vehicles, and this is why it is called the 'three baskets,' yet only the dharma spoken to the bodhisattvas reflects the capacity to practice the three vehicles, so it is termed the 'three baskets.'
>
> "Son of good family, there are individuals who have the capability to train in one of three ways: those undertaking the disciples' training, the private buddhas' training, or the bodhisattvas' training. Disciples do not study in the vehicle of the private buddhas since they are unable to penetrate its meaning. Likewise, private buddhas cannot penetrate the bodhisattva vehicle. Only the bodhisattvas are capable of studying the others' vehicles, yet they do not obtain realization in these paths but by means of the bodhisattva vehicle. Thus, theirs is the profound gnosis of the dharma to be practiced by the bodhisattvas. Because it has this significance, the bodhisattva vehicle is termed the 'three baskets' and not the others' vehicles."

Other scriptures also elaborate the following exhaustive distinctions, which I am now going to summarize, so please listen. You may think that the Great Vehicle is not part of the three baskets. Then, the three baskets consist of: the *Enumerated Discourses,* the *Middle-Length Discourses,* the *Long Discourses,* and the *Scattered Discourses,* constituting the one hundred thousand plus verses of the first basket; the discipline and the higher dharma, composing the two hundred thousand verses of the second basket; and the complete cultivations (?), composing the third basket. [The author's list is different from the standard one, which indicates that the three baskets consist of the discourses (*sūtrapiṭaka*), the discipline (*vinayapiṭaka*), and the higher dharma (*abhidharmapiṭaka*). It is likely that the text Daotai used was corrupt and the author meant to indicate that all practices of cultivation were found in the *abhidharmapiṭaka,* although we see that later he qualifies the abhidharma as the investigation of all characteristics of the events of reality.] This, in fact, is not to be identified as the three baskets. Why? Because many other scriptures would not be considered the word of the Buddha. Yet there are still other scriptures than those included in the discourses, the discipline, and the higher dharma. There are the works of the "scattered basket," the *Tiger Scripture,* the *Womb Scripture,* the *Advice to Kings, Prior Births of the Buddha,* the *Dependent Origination for Private Buddhas*—altogether eighty-four thousand baskets of the doctrine. [The author may have had the "smaller basket" (*kṣudrāgama*) in mind by his use of the term "scattered basket" (*samyuktapiṭaka*). The rest of his list may indicate the *Śārdūlakarṇāvadāna,* the *Garbhāvakrānti-sūtra,* the *Rājāvavāda-sūtra,* the Jātaka, and some discourse like the *Śālistamba-sūtra* as the discussion of dependent origination. Private buddhas were understood as having obtained their awakening by meditation on this principle, as delineated in treatises addressing this issue; see *Taishō* 1650.] If only the three baskets are the word of the Buddha, then we would have the problem that not everything collected by the venerable Ānanda would be considered the word of the Buddha. Thus, we should identify all of them with the term "basket," and conclude that there are over one hundred thousand baskets of the dharma. [Ānanda was the Buddha's cousin who was supposed to have memorized all the Buddha's sayings and recited them at the first recitation of the word of the Buddha immediately after his death.]

One may object that the Blessed One has previously said, "After my nirvāṇa, in the future there will come many who will sit around and argue, 'This is the word of the Buddha, this is not the word of the Buddha.'" In response to this anticipated circumstance, the Tathāgata has sealed his doctrine with the seal of the dharma. "If the meaning of a scripture is in harmony with the discourses, if it is in accord with the discipline, and if it does not contradict the nature of reality [dependent origination], then that scripture may be termed the word of the Buddha."

Our response to this objection is that the Buddha certainly did not apply these criteria to the bodhisattva vehicle while exempting the disciple's vehicle [but the application is to both vehicles]. The Buddha's word is not dissimilar in either case but indicates a single nature to be sealed by the seal of the dharma. Now, as to your means of comparison between a scripture proposed as the word of the Buddha and the three baskets, is it done by means of the letter of the texts or by the significance? If it is by the letter, then it is impossible that any of the twelve sections of scripture should be the word of the Buddha, since they all have different verses, sections, and sentences. [The twelve (or nine) branches of the dharma are standard ways of dividing up the Buddhist scriptures, although there is little concord on the precise ordering of these lists; see Lamotte, *History of Indian Buddhism,* pp. 143–49.] But if the comparison is performed by examining the meaning through reason which does not contradict the nature of reality, then a meaning which harmonizes with the significance of discourses and is characterized by reality accordingly demonstrates its own significance. So those discourses which demonstrate the significance of the disciples' dharma belong to the disciples' vehicle. Those discourses which demonstrate the significance of the private buddhas' dharma belong to the private buddhas' vehicle, and those discourses which demonstrate the significance of the bodhisattvas' dharma belong to the bodhisattvas' vehicle. . . . Now the inquiry into the perspective equal for all the buddhas in the universes (as many as are particles of dust) is also the dharma to be received from an excellent spiritual friend. It is thus the complete Great Vehicle and termed the expanded discourses—immeasurable, unlimited, and not part of the disciples' dharma. [That is, the Great Vehicle is frequently identified with one of the twelve branches of the dharma known as the extended teaching, an acknowledgment that the Mahāyāna scriptures are frequently much longer than the earlier works.] Its meaning is very profound, and accordingly all the dharma to be cultivated by the disciples is found minutely included into the path of the Great Vehicle. It is great blessedness and this is what is meant by "in harmony with the discourses."

Now we should discuss the phrase, "in accord with the discipline." The holy path of all the three vehicles equally destroys desire, anger, and hatred, which is the reason it is identified as discipline. [That is, when one obtains the level of a saint in all three systems, the unwholesome roots are destroyed. The author is using the standard explanation of discipline—to lead away from unwholesome conditions—to justify the practices of the Great Vehicle as in accord with the discipline.] Now the discourses discriminate causes and results, whereas the higher dharma discriminates the characteristics of real events, yet they both destroy the mental and emotional defilements. The Great Vehicle also speaks of the elimination of all evil events, the defilements of desire, anger, and ignorance. The Buddha taught the disciples to purify their own three varieties of action—body, speech, and mind—and called that the discipline. To the bodhisattvas, he taught them to purify their own three varieties of action—even going as far as the accomplishment of the Buddha—by generating and completing the perfection of virtue. Morality itself is to be grasped by the bodhisattvas. By generating the thought of awakening for all beings they are able to obtain the fruit called absolute truth. Thus the Great Vehicle is in accord with the discipline.

Finally, it does not contradict reality. As none of the three vehicles speaks of the contradiction of the twelve parts of dependent origination, neither does the Great Vehicle.

So, one who investigates well this issue realizes that the Great Vehicle is completely in accord with the threefold seal of the dharma. Of course, if one does not well investigate it, then neither the Great Vehicle nor any of the three vehicles is accepted. And one deprecating the Great Vehicle then commits the gravest of faults.

If you now maintain the Great Vehicle to be the word of Māra and not that of the Buddha, then we must reply that in none of the discourses do we truly find the pronouncement that the Great Vehicle is Māra's word. So, this objection cannot be trusted. If you believe that to call the Great Vehicle the word of the Buddha is like a worm in the body of the Teacher that still feeds on his corpse, then all the vehicles feed off the dharma body of the Buddha, not just the Great Vehicle. By just this token, it cannot be the word of Māra since only the Buddha is able to express it.

Bodhisattvas have immeasurable, unlimited, incalculable qualities that reach as far as the very hells. Facing nirvāṇa directly, they still return to the cycle of birth and death through their sympathy for living beings. Here they remain for an incalculable eon and experience for a very long time heroic suffering. You see, the vehicle of the bodhisattvas, the great beings (*mahāsattva*), is actually the Great Suffering Vehicle. [*Sāramati is playing with the language to make a pedagogical point. Sanskrit has a form of compound in which the central element has been elided (*madhyamalopasamāsa*), so that an "oxcart" is "a cart *pulled by* an ox" rather than an "ox's cart." *Sāramati would have us believe that Mahāyāna, the Great Vehicle, is really to be interpreted as Mahāduḥkhayāna, the Great Suffering Vehicle. Hermeneuticists frequently resort to such interpretive devices to indicate that the tradition had certain implied but unexpressed ideas from its very formation. This kind of forced interpretation frequently gives us the best understanding of the contributions authors like *Sāramati are making to their religious systems.] Their search for the highest fruit is inconceivable. They have left behind all the disciples and private buddhas, surpassing their efforts. Fulfilling all the qualities of gnosis, they transcend the stage of the facile "knowable." [The Mahāyāna recognizes two veils hiding awakening: that of the emotional directions of the mind and that of the mind directed toward intellectual objects of cognition, which are mistakenly granted the status of reality. These latter are distinguished from reality itself, which is apprehended by nondual, nonreferential gnosis.]

How is the bodhisattvas' vehicle the Great Suffering Vehicle? Suppose that a person might take a ship across the ocean. On the high seas, an evil wind arises, making the waves appear like mountains. Other countless calamities like this occur at the same time. All of his companions are anxious and develop an overwhelming fear, but the captain has long experience in handling the sails and has the merit of the ability to overcome difficulties. Transcending his troubles, he seizes the great precious gem in the ocean.

The bodhisattva, the great being, is at rest in the sea of birth and death. He does not trust the troubles that are entertained by going down the evil path on account of listening to a poor spiritual friend. During the first incalculable eon, the bodhisattva cultivates the practices associated with the stage of purity and seeks pure liberation. During the second incalculable eon, the bodhisattva cultivates the practices of pure contemplation. During the third incalculable eon, the bodhisattva cultivates the practices of pure gnosis and overcomes the obscurities of the stage of the facile knowable. Therefore, the bodhisattvas' vehicle is termed the Suffering Vehicle. Completing all the ten stages, he obtains them certainly and clearly. Because of the completion of all practices, he obtains the highest, complete, perfect awakening. Through his cognition of final gnosis, he accomplishes the great accomplishment.

—35—

Auspicious Things

Charles Hallisey

Theravāda Buddhism, like other Buddhist traditions, has an extensive body of authoritative literature and, like participants in other religious traditions with large scriptural and commentarial canons, Theravādins have frequently created functional canons within the canon. The *Maṅgalasūtraya* (Pāli *Maṅgalasutta*) or *The Scripture about Auspicious Things* is a text that is found in many of these canons within the canon. It is one of the most popular and influential texts throughout the Theravāda Buddhist world, from Sri Lanka to Southeast Asia, although it might appear, at first glance, to be a very slight text. In length, it is only twelve verses accompanied by a brief introduction, and its contents approximate a common-sense morality found in many cultures. But some indication of the significance that Theravāda Buddhists have seen in its verses can be gathered from numerous commentaries that have been written on this text over the centuries. One of the largest of these, *The Lamp on the Meanings of Auspiciousness (Maṅgalatthadīpanī)* was composed in northern Thailand in the sixteenth century and is over five hundred pages long; it continues to provide a core to monastic education in contemporary Thailand. Of more modest length is the selection presented here, a translation of a thirteenth-century commentary on the *Maṅgalasutta* found in a Sri Lankan story-collection known as *The Jewels of the Doctrine (Saddharmaratnāvaliya)*.

Before introducing the translated text, we should first look briefly at the *Maṅgalasutta* itself. It is found in two places in the Pāli canon (*Khuddaka Paṭha* 2 and *Suttanipāta* 46), but it does not seem to be among the oldest strata of Buddhist literature, and a preoccupation with it seems to be peculiar to the Theravāda; the *Maṅgalasutta* is also included in the collection of texts that are chanted as part of the protective rituals performed by Buddhist monks to ward off misfortunes. The verses are as follows:

1. Many gods and humans, desiring well-being, have thought
   about auspiciousness. Tell what is the highest auspiciousness.

2. Not to associate with fools, to associate with the wise,
   to worship those worthy of worship—that is the highest auspiciousness.
3. To live in a suitable place and to have done good deeds before,
   having a proper goal for oneself—that is the highest auspiciousness.
4. Learning, craftsmanship, and being well-trained in discipline,
   being well-spoken—that is the highest auspiciousness.
5. Care for mother and father, supporting wife and children,
   and spheres of work that bring no conflict—that is the highest auspiciousness.
6. Generosity, morality, helping of relatives, and
   doing actions that are blameless—that is the highest auspiciousness.
7. Ceasing and refraining from evil, abstaining from intoxicants,
   diligence in morality—that is the highest auspiciousness.
8. Respect, humility, contentment, gratitude,
   listening to the truth (*dharma*) at the proper time—
   that is the highest auspiciousness.
9. Patience, obedience, seeing ascetics, and
   timely discussions of the truth—that is the highest auspiciousness.
10. Ascetic practice, the religious life, seeing the four noble truths,
    and the realization of perfect peace (*nirvāṇa*)—that is the highest
    auspiciousness.
11. If someone's mind is sorrowless, stainless, secure, and does not shake
    when touched by the things of the world—that is the highest auspiciousness.
12. Having acted like this, unconquered everywhere,
    they go to well-being everywhere—for them, this is the highest auspiciousness.

Maṅgala is a concept found in many Indian religions, including Hinduism and Jainism, but it is a difficult word to translate into English, there being no close conceptual equivalent or even analogue. For lack of a better term and following the example of many others, I have translated it as "auspicious," or "auspiciousness," terms that in English can be traced back to the ancient Roman practice of interpreting omens provided by birds. But it is worth noting that there is a wide range of possible translations of *maṅgala:* luck, fortune, happiness, prosperity, welfare, auspiciousness, good omen, whatever conduces to an auspicious issue, blessing, and in some contexts, lucky object, amulet, solemn ceremony, festival, and especially marriage. In the passage presented here, we can see that questions about the meaning of the word *maṅgala* are not only a problem for the translator. The introduction sets the stage for the Buddha's preaching of this sūtra by explaining that it was occasioned by a long discussion among gods and humans about what exactly maṅgala is. It also connects the discussion of maṅgala to the contemporary context of the audience insofar as it mentions various types of good and bad omens, some of which are still noted by many Buddhists in Sri Lanka. This introduction thus implicitly acknowledges the diversity of religious practice among Buddhists in local contexts and gives us an example of how some practices are made to appear non-Buddhist by a Buddhist reinterpretation: just as the Buddha used the model of brahmanical practices to instruct about Buddhist ethics (the *Advice to Sigāla*, for example, reinterprets Vedic worship of the directions in terms of the ethical relations between people; see *The Dīgha Nikāya*, edited by J.E. Carpenter [London: Pali Text Society, 1960], vol. 3, pp. 180–93.), so here the *Maṅgalasutta* "applies" the assumptions and imagery of auspiciousness to ethical behavior to make broader points about Buddhist practice.

These broader points represent part of the significance of the *Maṅgalasutta*. It is best read not as a Buddhist perspective on auspiciousness, but as a comprehensive vision of the Buddhist religious life. In this, the *Maṅgalasutta* might be compared and contrasted with better known schema of Buddhist practice, such as the noble eightfold path described in the four noble truths, or the structuring of the Buddhist life according to morality, meditation, and wisdom, as the fifth-century commentator Buddhaghosa did in his *summa* of Theravādin thought, the *Path of Purification (Visuddhimagga)*. It could also be compared and contrasted with the vision of the Buddhist life as a gradual path, such as is found in *The Advice to Layman Tuṇḍila* that is found in this volume. The concept of maṅgala provides a thematic framework for organizing various Buddhist values as well as a consistent rationale for the performance of diverse Buddhist practices.

The commentaries on the *Maṅgalasutta* are a locus for Theravādin thought about what might be called social ethics, an aspect of Buddhist life that is often lost in scholarship because of an overemphasis on the individualism of a renouncer's life. We can see here an appealing vision of a model, if still imperfect, society, one in which care for others is part and parcel of everyday life: Buddhist values and practices of every sort are portrayed as omens of the good life. But we also see shadows of a harsher "real" world, since this text clearly assumes a world of agriculture and labor, of subsistence and hard work; this is a text that belongs to the largely rural peasant societies in which traditional Theravāda thrived for centuries. It is often said that early Buddhism appealed especially to city- and town-dwellers who suffered from a spiritual malaise and were disenchanted with the wealth displayed in city and town life. This hardly seems to be the audience of this commentary of the *Maṅgalasutta*. From a reference to hands that could become like wish-fulfilling creepers and fulfill every desire, for example, we might conclude that it belonged to a world that knew poverty all too well, a world where people too often had only dry cakes made from the husks of rice to eat.

This closeness to the world of its audience is connected to choice of language. Commentaries on the *Maṅgalasutta* have been composed in both Pāli, a learned international language, and in various vernaculars. The text translated here is from Sinhala, one of the vernacular languages used in Sri Lanka, although some verses remain in Pāli. As another translator of the *Saddharmaratnāvaliya* has said, this text "is written in an easy flowing, colorful prose, in the half-colloquial, half-literary language used by Buddhist monks in their sermons. The speaking voice and narrative persona of the author / translator cuts into the text constantly, revealing his humanity and humor, . . . and above all the intellectual and psychological subtlety with which he explores and illuminates abstract elements of Buddhist doctrine, relating them to the everyday needs and actions of ordinary people" (Ranjini Obeyesekere, *Jewels of the Doctrine,* xiii). We might keep in mind, then, that men and women have learned how to be Buddhists over the centuries through texts like this one, vernacular texts that present, often quite creatively, ideas found in canonical and commentarial literature written in Pāli.

The translation below is from Dharmasena, *Saddharmaratnāvaliya* (Colombo: Sri Lanka Pracina Bhasopakara Samagama, 1986), vol. 2, 795–800 and 827–33, with abridgments.

Further Reading

A portion of *Saddharmaratnāvaliya* has been translated by Ranjini Obeyesekere; see Dharmasena Thera, *Jewels of the Doctrine,* translated by Ranjini Obeyesekere (Albany: SUNY Press, 1991). For a series of essays discussing maṅgala in Indian religions, see *Purity and Auspiciousness in Indian Society,* edited by John Carman and Frédérique Marglin (Leiden: E. J. Brill, 1985).

The Commentary of the Scripture on Auspicious Things

Furthermore, in order to show what should be done in order to be established in what is good and what should be given up to stay away from what is wrong, we will tell stories from texts like *The Commentary on the Scripture about Auspicious Things (Maṅgalasūtra Aṭuvā).*

How do they go?

In the famous cities of the Rose-Apple Island [Dambadiva or Jambudvīpa, that is, India] and in the various provinces and territories, wealthy people would gather in prosperous times and pay for the recitation of stories which actually are a hindrance to the attainment of heaven and liberation, such as the story of Rāma and Sītā [this story is probably best known from the version in the *Rāmāyaṇa*], stories that have nothing to do with the right which is conducive to the pleasant. These stories were so long that they could not be finished in even four months' time.

One day, a certain person among those coming together to hear those stories raised the question, "what is it that is called an auspicious thing (*maṅgala*)?" when he heard people say that they were going to something auspicious. This question, once raised, was taken up by the storytellers, in between their recitations, as it happened to be a very useful topic. Now one of those there was not content to say that auspicious things are those which are conducive to well-being, nor was he willing to ask someone who actually knew, but rather announced, "I know about auspicious things." He went on, and said that an auspicious thing was something that could be seen, as when someone in this world wakes up and sees a young bird, or a woodapple stalk, or a pregnant woman, or infants decorated with necklaces and bangles, or pots full of water, or a fresh sheatfish, or a thoroughbred horse, or a chariot drawn by a thoroughbred horse, or a brahman.

Those people who knew only what they heard from him agreed, but others did not. They began to argue with the one who said that an auspicious thing is something seen: "The eye sees both the good and the bad. If what is auspicious is something seen by the eye, then whatever is seen would be auspicious. It would not be correct to say that. We, however, know what is auspicious." They said that an auspicious thing is something heard by the ear, as when someone wakes up and hears a statement like, "They increase," "They should increase," "He who is filled with," "O happy one," "O prosperity," "May prosperity increase," "Today there is a good conjunction of the stars," or "The day is good." Some people agreed with what they said. Others, not knowing themselves what is auspicious, disagreed. They started arguing, saying, "The ear hears both the good and the bad. If what is auspicious is something heard, it looks as if there is no utterance in this world which is inauspicious."

When things are discussed only for the sake of argument, one's ignorance is never apparent and the only thing that is clear is one's own bungling desires. Thus others said, "We know what is auspicious. An auspicious thing is something smelled, as when someone awakes and smells the scent of sandalwood in the nose." And others said that if one were to bite a fresh toothstick, the taste that is felt on the tongue is auspicious. Still others thought touch was auspicious, as when one handles the earth, or blue paddy, or freshly reaped wheat, or a mound of sesame seed, or the flowers of the ironwood tree, or the fruits of the jackfruit tree.

Some people accepted that smell, taste, and touch were auspicious, but others said, "What is this? If the nose smelled only good fragrance, if the tongue knew only good tastes, if everything the body touched felt good, then what you say would be correct. But the nose smells both the good and the bad and it is the same with the tongue and the body. If everything that is smelled, tasted, or touched is auspicious, why do you wrinkle your nose at a bad smell or pucker your mouth on a bitter thing? Why do you die when you eat poison? Why do you say when you carry a stone or a tree trunk that your back aches and that your sides hurt?" Thus they argued with those who said that what is auspicious is something sensed, saying that there is no justification for saying this.

In the end, there was no one who could back up what she or he said with proper proof, and since each appeared to know what he or she was talking about, there was nothing that they could do but argue with each other. In due course, this discussion about what is auspicious spread throughout the Rose-Apple Island. All the people of the continent gathered in groups and began to think, "What is really auspicious?" The gods who are guardians to the people began to think about this in their own way too. Then, tree spirits who were friendly to these deities, their friends among the celestial deities, and the gods in heavens began to ask about auspicious things, and soon the beings throughout the three worlds were talking about what is really auspicious.

In just the same way that this argument began in the Rose-Apple Island, so it continued throughout all the ten thousand world systems: there were different opinions about what is auspicious but no agreement about fact. Leaving aside those who had seen nirvāṇa, all the gods and humans divided into three factions, with one group sure that what is auspicious is something seen, another sure that it is something heard, and the third sure that it is something sensed. But they stayed divided into factions because they were not able to convince each other, and thus this brouhaha continued without resolution for twelve long years.

Then the gods, still not able to agree, said to one another, "O happy ones, just as there is a head for those in a household, and a chief for the residents of a village, and a king for the inhabitants of a country, so Śakra, king of the gods, is the leader of the deities in our divine world. It would be good to inform him about this." Putting on their finest garments and ornaments, they went before him as he was seated on his red throne and honored him. "Lord, we have something to tell you about. There has been a great furor about what is auspicious, and since we do not know if what is auspicious is something seen, heard, or otherwise sensed, it would be good if you would tell us which it is."

Since Śakra was himself intelligent, he asked where the argument had started, and when he heard that it was in the human world, he asked where the Buddha was living and whether anyone had asked him about this. "Why should we try to weigh something by hand when scales are right here? What do I know, that this question should be saved for me when no one has asked the Buddha, who is auspicious himself? He is auspicious because both worldly and transcendent prosperity are given to those who merely recollect his qualities—not to mention what happens for those who see him repeatedly, who worship him, and give offerings to him. He alone is fit to proclaim what is auspicious. All of you are like those who blow on fireflies to start a flame when there is already a burning fire nearby. If it is really necessary to know what is auspicious, then you should go to the Buddha."

Śakra then ordered a particular deity to ask the Buddha about this, because it would be impossible for all of the gods to ask together. That son of a god, bedecked with ornaments suitable to the occasion and shining like a flash of lightening, went to the Devram Monastery [the Jetavana Monastery in Śrāvastī, which was built for the Buddha by Anāthapiṇḍika] in the middle of the night, accompanied by all the gods of the ten thousand worlds who had gathered in the human world in order to hear the Buddha talk about what are auspicious things; these deities had all taken on visible forms, but there were so many that ten, twenty, thirty, forty, fifty, seventy, or eighty had to stand on the tip of a hair. This deity then said to the Buddha, "You who are a god greater than all the gods assembled here, a Brahmā greater than all Brahmās, I invite you, on their behalf. It would be good if you would tell us what is auspicious so that there might be some concurrence among humans and gods on this matter."

The noble Buddha then said, "O divine friend, those three groups gave their opinion about what is something auspicious just because they were asked, and not because they had any evidence or basis for what they said. Something is called auspicious when it is a cause for welfare in this world or the next. You have asked for one thing that is auspicious, but I will tell you thirty-eight."

So the Buddha began to speak first of what should not be done before what should be done: "Not associating with foolish, ignorant people is an auspicious thing. Friend, if someone were to do what a fool does, or say what a fool says, or think what a fool thinks, then that one will receive blame in this world, and even if they are full of regret later, they still destroy their prospects for the next world.

"But how is not associating with fools something that is auspicious? Because not associating with them is a means to welfare in this world and the next. What is the evil that results from associating with them? Just as the leaf that covers putrid meat becomes putrid, so a person possessing noble ideas of any kind eventually becomes evil by associating with fools. Moreover, as a fear of water only comes from water, not fire, and a fear of fire does not come from water, there is no fear of wise ones except for that which has ignorant people as its cause. Therefore, associating with ignorant people is evil. On account of associating with disgraceful naked ascetics like Pūraṇa Kāśyapa [a teacher who was the contemporary of the Buddha and is said to have taught a doctrine that denied karma and the fruits of actions], eighty thousand kings were born in hell. And King Ajātaśatru, who did merit and aspired to become enlightened, was deprived of seeing perfect peace (*nirvāṇa*) because of his association with Devadatta [Prince Ajātaśatru helped Devadatta in several of the latter's attempts to kill the Buddha].

"Furthermore, the future Buddha, when he was born as Akīrti, received a boon from Śakra because his fame had spread so widely: 'As there is no profit from seeing them, may there be no seeing of fools; and because there is no use in hearing about them, may I hear nothing about fools; having come together with them, may I not live with fools even for a moment; forget about actually living together with fools, may there not even be talk of seeing them.' Because he obtained that boon, he did not associate with fools, and because it was a means to prosperity in both this world and the next, it is the highest auspicious thing. [This refers to the story found at *Jātaka* IV.236. Akitti, the Pāli form of Akīrti, gave away all his wealth and retired to the forest. When gifts were brought to him as homage to his virtue, he sought obscurity and lived alone eating leaves. Because of his asceticism, Śakra's throne became hot, and Śakra gave him a number of boons, including one that Śakra should not visit him any more and disturb his asceticism.]

"Now if someone were to do just one thing, it should be just worshiping enlightened ones, silent enlightened ones, and disciples. Such beings do not do anything unless it increases merit and do not consciously do things like taking life; if they speak, they do not say lies, but only truth or something which is righteous, or an admonition; and they do not think anything that increases evil, but only things that increase merit. Associating with buddhas, silent buddhas, and disciples is the highest auspicious thing because it increases prosperity in both this world and the next. [The word for association here, *bhajana,* can also mean worshiping or serving, and it has been translated that way in the first sentence of this paragraph. It is worth noting that it is from the same verbal root as *bhakti,* a ubiquitous term in Indian religions that is commonly, if somewhat misleadingly, translated as "devotion."]

"The Buddha is supreme among those who are wise and those who have associated with him have all attained prosperity. Among those who have associated with him, there are many who have realized perfect peace (*nirvāṇa*), including the eighty great disciples, such as Śāriputra and Maudgalyāyana. Eighty times eighty thousand have been born in heavenly worlds. Therefore association with intelligent people is auspicious because it leads to one's own benefit.

"The homage paid to a buddha, silent buddha, or to disciples, all of whom should be worshiped [*pidi,* a Sinhala derivative of *pūjā*] is auspicious because it leads to both worldly and transcendent benefits. This can be seen in the story of the flower maker Sumana, who offered eight quarts of jasmine flowers to the Buddha in eight handfuls. As a result of that, he did not go to the four evil states but enjoyed heavenly pleasures and comforts in the human world, not for eight hours, or eight days, or eight months, or eight years, or eight centuries, or eight millennia, but for one hundred thousand eons. At the end of this he became the silent buddha Sumana. Further evidence is found in our great future buddha when he was born as the brahman Śaṅkha. On account of a slight offering to the shrine of a silent buddha, he received the homage of beings from the nāga world [nāgas are a class of deity in the traditional Buddhist cosmology] to the Brahmā world when he himself became enlightened, as is described in the text on the ascent of the Ganges. [A reference to the account of the Buddha's visit to Vaiśālī, where he preached the *Ratana* (Jewel) *Discourse* and ended a famine and plague. The commentary on this text describes the praise that the Buddha received when he returned to Rājagṛha along the Ganges.]

"Living in an appropriate place is auspicious because it is conducive to worldly and transcendent benefits. An appropriate place is some place like the Middle Country [north India] if the four-fold Buddhist community [renunciant men, renunciant women, laymen, and laywomen] is living there, and if occasions for the ten meritorious practices are found there, and if the word of the Buddha in the form of the Buddhist canon is there. Righteous universal monarchs, silent buddhas, and worthy ones are all born in the Middle Country. When they are alive, people adhere to admonitions and thus receive worldly comforts, but when buddhas are alive, they get both worldly and transcendent comforts. Therefore living in such a place at such a time is auspicious.

"The prior accumulation of merit with respect to buddhas, and so on, which brings one to the presence of buddhas again and again, is auspicious because it leads to worldly and transcendent comforts.

"If a person were to observe at least the five precepts—or perhaps more—while considering the bad results that come from not observing the five precepts for just a brief span of time, even one as brief as the time it takes for a cobweb to singe, it is auspicious because observing the precepts for even so brief a time leads to endless heavenly comforts.

"If one were to have faith, thinking that if one were to be devoid of faith one would not get a harvest of worldly and transcendent benefits from the karmic seed of the good deeds, just as rice will not grow on the surface of a rock, that would be auspicious because faith of that kind is conducive to merit, as was the case with Anāthapiṇḍika and Viśākhā. [These two lay disciples of the Buddha, one male, the other female, were unparalleled in the care which they gave to the Buddha and the monastic order.]

"It is also auspicious to be generous. The good deed of giving cannot be accomplished by being miserly, but only by being generous. Not only the good deed of giving, but other meritorious actions are accomplished by generosity. This can be understood by reflecting on the stories of Adattapūrvaka and Miserly Kauśika. [These two are famous for their miserliness; Adattapūrvaka's name means "Never Gave."]

"Being learned is auspicious, as can be seen in the case of the great elder Kautthila who, living in the time of seven different buddhas, practiced the religious life near them and effortlessly attained enlightenment in the dispensation of our Buddha.

"Learning any craft is auspicious because it is conducive to benefit in this world and the next, both for oneself and for others, provided that that craft is not harmful in this world or the next. Benign crafts include astrology for householders and the sewing of robes, which is appropriate for renouncers.

"If a layperson were to observe the five precepts, such as abstaining from taking life, and were to give alms and pay homage, or if a renouncer were to be established in the four pure moralities [the precepts for fully ordained men, fully ordained women, novices, and laypeople], it would be auspicious because it is supportive of worldly and transcendent benefit.

"Uttering words that are not false, not slanderous, not coarse, not surly, and not frivolous is auspicious because it is conducive to welfare in this world and the next. Preaching sermons to others with selfless thoughts is also auspicious, and it is conducive to the attainment of perfect peace for the people who preach the doctrine.

"Attending to parents by bathing them, washing their hair, giving them food and drink is auspicious because such actions bring benefits in this world and the next. Parents are of immense help to the children that they have brought forth, as when children return after playing outside and parents brush the sand from their bodies, kiss them on the heads, and thus shower them with love. This love can never be compensated even if one were to carry one's parents on the shoulders without putting them down for a hundred or a thousand years.

"If a man were to be respectful to his wife and children, and not run them down, and not attempt to override them, and were to give them wealth and make ornaments for them—if he were to treat them in this manner, then the wife of such a person would look after the household affairs carefully, and his children would be very attached to him. The servants in such a house would be loyal and faithful and not ignore the words of the master; they would protect whatever wealth has been earned against destruction and they would be diligent and energetic in all matters. Those who treat their wife and children well receive homage even from the king of the gods, since he said:

> O Mātali, I worship those people who make merit as householders,
> Pious lay disciples who look after their family in a righteous manner.
>
> *Saṃyutta nikāya,* edited by L. Feer
> (London: Pali Text Society, 1991), vol. 1, p. 234.

Treating one's wife and children well is thus auspicious.

"Being engaged in such pursuits as plowing or sowing is auspicious because it earns wealth and grain, but they should be pursued in a manner that avoids procrastination, or delay, or carelessness, or laziness. Knowing that one should engage in such actions at appropriate times, one should do so without being too lazy, since it has been said:

> The person who does appropriate action and bears the burden of work,
> Who does the work carefully, he enjoys wealth.
>
> *Suttanipāta,* edited by Dines Anderson and Helmer Smith
> (London: Pali Text Society, 1990), verse 187.

and

> Whoever's habit is to sleep by day and is seen to rise by night,
> And constantly gets drunk with wine is not fit to keep a house.
> "Too cold! Too hot! Too late!" they say;
> Saying these things, not concentrating
> On work, thus his prosperity is destroyed.
> If one were to do whatever a man should do
> Without considering cold or heat as more than straws,
> He is not separated from happiness.
>
> *Dīgha nikāya,* vol. 3, p. 185; cf. *Theragāthā,* edited by H. Oldenberg
> (London: Pali Text Society, 1966), Verses 231–32.

and

To the one who collects wealth, acting like a bee,
Wealth accumulates just as an anthill gradually grows.

Dīgha nikāya, vol. 3, p. 188.

"Giving away alms as well as believing in karma and its fruits are auspicious because they are conducive to benefits in this world and the next, because even the daughters of a garland maker were able to achieve the rank of a queen because they gave cakes made from rice bran. Moreover, people who only plucked leaves to wash a monk's bowl were reborn as tree-dwelling deities. Then there are those who merely pointed the way to a house where alms were being given, but consequently achieved everything that they desired, their hands becoming like wish-fulfilling creepers in heaven.

"Being engaged in the ten meritorious deeds, such as giving alms, being moral and keeping the precepts, meditating, transferring merit, rejoicing in the merit of others, preaching sermons, listening to sermons—all these are auspicious because they are conducive to birth in heaven. [In addition to the seven actions mentioned here, giving service, showing respect, and right beliefs are also included in the list of ten meritorious deeds.]

"Treating relatives who have come to visit well, as far as one is capable, is auspicious because it is conducive to welfare in this world and the next. Relatives are those to whom one is related up to seven generations back on one's mother's and father's sides. One should give rice, clothes, and so forth to relatives who come because they are destitute.

"Observing the eight precepts without exception on the first day of each phase of the moon, attending upon one's teachers and the elders in one's family and, for the sake of merit, planting flower gardens, building ponds, making parks, erecting waystations [this refers to a platform or support where someone carrying a load on the back or shoulders can put it down for a rest without having to place the burden on the ground], shelters, and bridges, and so on, all this is auspicious because it is beneficial in this world and the next.

"Refraining from committing wrong acts, thinking in one's mind that this is not in keeping with our family's position, with our place in society, and consequently not doing an evil deed, saying, 'From today onward, I will not do a thing of this nature'; all this is auspicious because it has benefits in this world and the next.

"Abstention from intoxicating drinks is auspicious because it is beneficial in this life and the next. Those who drink cannot understand what is good or bad, and they do not acknowledge their own parents or elders in their family or even buddhas, silent buddhas, and worthy ones. They go about now as if they were insane, and in their next birth, they suffer in horrible conditions.

"Not being indolent when it comes to doing meritorious deeds is auspicious because it brings perfect peace without delay. Thus one should do any meritorious deed well, and one should do it consistently, with effort and mindfulness and without being lazy.

"Paying respect to those who deserve respect is auspicious. If one were to pay respect to those worthy of respect and high esteem, such as buddhas, silent buddhas, and worthy ones, or parents, aunts, uncles, elder brothers and sisters, then one will be born in a heavenly world, enjoying great comfort, and when one is born among humans, then one would be born only in a noble family. In this way, paying respect is a cause for one's own improvement.

"Always being of a humble disposition is auspicious. However high a position one might have because of good qualities and intelligence, if because of one's modest nature one were to be like a doormat used for rubbing feet, being subservient to everyone, such conduct is conducive to qualities like fame, and so on. Furthermore, if a monk were to subsist on whatever he gets by way of the four requisites—namely, robes, food, dwellings, and medicine—whether they be good or bad, he should not expect anything better. If he were ill and could not wear heavy robes, partake of rough food, lie down in a dwelling because he found it uncomfortable, or use coarse medicines, he should give all these to his companions and use whatever they give in return. If he were to get very fine robes, food, dwellings, and medicine, he should give them to aged companions in celibacy and should be content with a robe from a dust heap, food from begging, the feet of trees or open space, and, by way of medicine, cow's urine or yellow myrobalan. The twelvefold noble contentment that exists in this manner, the destruction of the inclination to want each particular thing one sees, the destruction of the desire to have many things, and the ending of the pretension of having qualities that one doesn't—this twelvefold contentment and this threefold destruction is auspicious because it is conducive to the attainment of good qualities.

"Remembering the help that others gave you, whether it be big or little, and helping them in return is auspicious because through these grateful actions, one engages in meritorious deeds. The Buddha has said that those who help others and those who bear in mind the help done to them are rare indeed.

"Listening to sermons is auspicious because it is at the root of all meritorious deeds. One should listen to sermons at those times when one's mind is filled with arrogance, and if one cannot do it everyday, then one should listen to sermons at least once in every five days.

"If one could be as patient as the ascetic Kṣāntivādin who considered as help the harm done to him by the king of Banaras called Kalāpa [in order to test Kṣāntivādin's forbearance, Kalāpa had his limbs cut off], such forbearance is auspicious because it is conducive to one's own benefit, just as that forbearance brought buddhahood to the ascetic Kṣāntivādin. The future buddha Śarabhaṅga has said the following regarding patience:

> If one were to suppress hatred, one would never come to grief.
> Even sages praise the destruction of anger.
> One should be patient toward whatever is harshly spoken.
> Those at peace said, "that forbearance is supreme."
>
> *Jātaka* v.141

Even Śakra, king of the gods, has said that one should practice forbearance toward those who do harmful things even when one is able to strike back [see *Dhammapada,* verse 399]. The Buddha has also extolled in various places the virtues of forbearance.

"It is auspicious to be obedient like the venerable Rāhula [the biological son of the Buddha], and not be displeased when advice is given about how to improve one's conduct—neither with the advice nor the advisor—and not be disrespectful, because these are conducive to benefit in this world and the next.

"Seeing virtuous people is also auspicious. 'Seeing' means approaching virtuous people, waiting on them, inquiring about how they are, and looking at them, because one who looks at a virtuous person with a delighted mind will not have eye disease for one thousand births. When the Buddha was living surrounded by monks at Vediya Mountain, an owl looked at him with a delighted mind, and that owl did not go to an evil birth for one hundred thousand eons. Instead, he came to possess an appealing face, and after enjoying heavenly comforts, he became the silent buddha Saumanasa.

"The Buddha's sermons (*sūtra*), as well as philosophical texts (*abhidharma*), stories of the Buddha's previous births (*jātaka*), and the commentaries should be discussed by those who know them in the first watch or the last watch of the night. Such informed discussion is conducive to clear understanding of the scriptures (*āgama*) and other good qualities, and thus it is auspicious.

"If a person were not to be attached to the six objects of the senses, such as physical form, and were not to be repelled by unpleasant objects of the senses, that person could be said to be restrained in the senses. That restrained person would have zeal for destroying the defilements and would be able to attain profound contemplative states, and therefore such restraint of the senses is auspicious.

"If a person were to abstain from sexual relations and engage in other observances of a monk, or, if someone, having already become enlightened, were to still engage in the study and practice of Buddha's teachings, such things are auspicious for attaining worldly and transcendent good qualities.

"Realizing the path and realizing the fruits of the path by meditation is auspicious because it leads one to escape from suffering in the cycle of existence. And becoming a worthy one by means of these two—that is, realization of the path and its fruits—is auspicious because it leads one to get rid of all suffering such as birth, and so on.

"If someone, having received wealth, fame, praise, and comfort, were not to become arrogant by thinking such things are permanent but were instead to see them as an annoyance, like a louse, or a form of censure or a kind of suffering, then that person would not be grieved by discovering their impermanence. People who possess that kind of attitude are auspicious because it is conducive to becoming a buddha.

"To be free of sorrow and to be free of such blemishes as passion, and not to be tormented by the defilements that are one's enemy is an achievement that is possible only for a worthy one. Being free from sorrow and the defilements is auspicious because even if one were a scavenger, if one were also endowed with such virtues, one would be able to receive homage from Śakra and other gods."

The Buddha thus preached about thirty-eight auspicious things with eleven verses beginning with "not associating with fools." And when he preached this *Scripture on Auspicious Things,* a million gods became worthy ones, and an incalculable number became stream-winners, once-returners, and nonreturners. [Stream-winner, once-returner, nonreturner, and worthy one are the four stages of highest attainment on the Buddhist path to moral and cognitive perfection.]

On the following day, the Buddha addressed Ānanda: "Last night a certain deity approached me and asked me what is auspicious. I told him of thirty-eight things that are auspicious. Ānanda, learn this *Scripture on Auspicious Things* and teach it to the monks." Ānanda learned it and taught it to other monks. Therefore, from that day to this day, and from this day up to the end of five thousand years, this text is beneficial. [The reference to five thousand years is to the prediction that the Buddha made about how long his teachings would survive. Note that this sentence adds the text itself to things that are auspicious in this world.]

One should make one's birth fruitful by associating with intelligent people; coming to meet them; paying homage to them; living a comfortable life in an appropriate place because of meritorious deeds done earlier; learning crafts that are not harmful; becoming learned; illuminating the Buddha's teaching by one's conduct; saying something good if one says anything at all; attending upon one's parents; and, as expounded by the future Buddha when he was born as a parrot [*Jātaka* IV.276–82], paying back one's debts by treating one's wife and children well, and giving a loan that is to be collected in the future by engaging in such faultless means of livelihood as agriculture, trade, accruing wealth and grain. One should possess the essence of living by observing the precepts; win over relatives by treating them well; win over outsiders by faultless conduct; not cause oppression to others by abstinence from harmful deeds; abstain from intoxicants and thereby avoid harm to oneself; be heedful and perform meritorious deeds; and when one has a mind inclined toward merit, relinquish household comforts and become ordained.

As a monk, one should have respect for the Buddha and the rest. As haughty conduct is not in keeping with monkhood, one should be of a submissive nature to everyone at all times; observe the monastic regimen and rites assiduously; take twelvefold delight in the four requisites, thereby getting rid of greed toward them; and become a good person by knowing the good qualities in actions that have been done. If one has lost interest in doing meritorious deeds, get rid of that state of mind by listening to sermons; get rid of all misfortunes by being patient, obedient, and ready for anything. Seek out virtuous people and listen to their advice, and so become virtuous oneself. If any doubts arise regarding merit, dispel such doubts by talking to intelligent people; attain purity for oneself by establishing oneself in the fourfold morality; and attain mental purity by practicing calming (*śamatha*) meditations. As one is not able to attain purity of knowledge without purification of beliefs, investigate the characteristics and character of mental and physical things. Thus getting various states of purity for oneself, one will then become an enlightened worthy one by proceeding in the sequence of the path. Just as a mountain as big as Mount Meru cannot be shaken by the wind, so you will not be shaken by eight ways of the world. In this manner, one should make one's birth worthwhile by becoming free of sorrow and defilements, undefeated in any situation.

—36—

Tales of the Lotus Sūtra

Daniel B. Stevenson

The selections that follow are taken from a Tang-dynasty collection of pious tales and exemplary acts of devotion known as the *Hongzan fahua zhuan* or *Accounts in Dissemination and Praise of the Lotus* [Sūtra]. They illustrate some of the alternative ways in which ritual and devotional culture contribute to the construction of sacred scripture and its meaning in Chinese Buddhism.

The *Hongzan fahua zhuan* belongs to a genre of Chinese Buddhist writing known as the "record of miraculous response," or "miracle tale," for short. The Buddhist miracle tale originated during the early medieval period, taking as its model two related narrative forms of indigenous origin that enjoyed widespread popularity at that time: the Chinese "tale of the strange or extraordinary" and the tradition of the exemplary biography inspired by the Chinese dynastic histories. The Buddhist miracle tale probably stands closest in spirit to the exemplary biography. Like the latter, the miracle tale was (and continues to be) circulated primarily for reasons of spiritual edification. Behind the marvels that it recounts there lurks an ever-present injunction to faith and piety.

As a whole, the Buddhist miracle tale collections range over a diversity of topics, from karmic retribution (as in the case of the *Mingbao ji* or *Tales of Mysterious Retribution*), spiritually potent Buddhist images (Daoxuan's *Gantong ji*), and sacred mountains or pilgrimage sites (the two compendia on the Wutai pilgrimage by Huixiang and Yanyi), to cult figures such as Guanyin (Avalokiteśvara) and the pure land of Amitābha Buddha. These may appear lumped together as a miscellany (the unifying rubric being simply "numinal response") or selected and organized according to particular themes. The *Hongzan fahua zhuan* is concerned with the numinal efficacy of devotion to the *Lotus Sūtra,* a feature that places it in the company of a number of Tang-period collections dedicated specifically to promoting the cult of the book; the *Diamond, Lotus, Avataṃsaka* (or *Huayan jing*), *Suvarṇaprabhāsa* (*Jinguang ming jing*) and, to a certain degree, the Pure Land sūtras are the other notable cases in which compendia of this sort were produced.

Authorship of the *Hongzan fahua zhuan* is attributed to a Tang-period Buddhist monk from Langu (modern Taiyuan county, Shanxi province) by the name of Huixiang. There is some speculation that he is the same Huixiang who produced the *Gu qingliang zhuan,* a miscellany of miracle tales and lore concerning the pilgrimage cult of Mount Wutai. This identification sheds little light on the situation, however, since nothing substantial is known of either figure. To establish some sense of the work's provenance we must turn to the contents of the *Hongzan fahua zhuan* itself: The collection draws extensively upon earlier Buddhist biographical and miracle tale compendia, the most important sources being Huijiao's *Biographies of Eminent Monks,* Daoxuan's *Continued Biographies of Eminent Monks* (*Xu gao seng zhuan*), and Tang Lin's *Tales of Miraculous Retribution* (*Mingbao ji*). To this preexisting body of material the *Hongzan fahua zhuan* adds numerous contemporary accounts of Sui and early Tang figures who are connected specifically with Changan and its extended environs. Nearly all of these entries date from the latter half of the seventh century, with the latest recorded date in the collection being 706 C.E.

Of the miracle tales as a whole, we know that some were gathered locally from oral tradition. We know that they were selected, reworked, and disseminated by literate lay and monastic figures, some of whom were quite eminent. We also know that many of these same tales were told time and again, sometimes at formal ritual gatherings before audiences containing persons of every ilk—mendicants and laypersons, educated and uneducated. On this basis the miracle tale can be understood as "popular" in the sense of anonymous and generic—a body of literature that reflects religious motifs which are universal to Buddhist monastic and lay life rather than the province of one particular sector or stratum.

The *Hongzan fahua zhuan* organizes its contents according to eight categories of cultic activity: drawings and likenesses produced on the basis of the *Lotus,* translation of the *Lotus,* exegesis, cultivation of meditative discernment (based on the *Lotus*), casting away the body (in offering to the *Lotus*), recitation of the scripture (from memory), cyclic reading of the sūtra, and copying the sūtra by hand. Individual entries are, in turn, arranged in chronological sequence according to dynastic period.

Four of the topical sections of the *Hongzan fahua zhuan*—exegesis or preaching of the *Lotus,* recitation from memory, reading, and copying the *Lotus*—find an immediate counterpart in the famous "five practices" of receiving and keeping, reading, reciting, copying, and explicating the *Lotus Sūtra* described in the "Preachers of Dharma" chapter of the sūtra and articulated by exegetes such as the Tiantai master Zhiyi. Section 5 of the *Hongzan fahua zhuan,* on "casting away the body," contains biographies of devotees who ritually burned themselves alive in imitation of the bodhisattva Medicine King's self-immolation in offering to the dharma in chapter 23 of the *Lotus.* Various subsidiary themes of cultic and ritual activity that recur throughout the tales of the *Hongzan fahua zhuan* can likewise be traced to these chapters. One topic that is conspicuously absent from the *Hongzan fahua zhuan* is the cult of Guanyin.

Two criteria have guided the selection of tales and biographies from the *Hong-*

zan fahua zhuan that are offered below. One is to convey a sense of the scope of the collection by selecting representative entries from five of the eight topical chapters of the *Hongzan fahua zhuan.* The second is to reflect the milieu within which the text of the *Hongzan fahua zhuan* took shape by providing tales of Sui and Tang figures from the Changan area who were contemporaries of the author of the *Hongzan fahua zhuan* and whose stories are not copied from earlier collections.

The notion of "numinal sympathy or response" (*lingying* or *yingxian*) is pivotal to the thematic organization of the *Hongzan fahua zhuan* and the other works of the miracle tale genre. The Chinese concept of numinal response involves nuances of meaning and value that may not fit comfortably with conventional Western assumptions about what miracles are, how they come about, and the significance they hold for religious life. Implicit in virtually all of the miracle tales (and, indeed, Chinese Buddhist hagiography as a whole) is the age-old Chinese discursive structure of "stimulus" (*gan*), "response" (*ying*), and "causal impetus or nexus" (*ji* or *jiyuan*). In its simplest form, the structure hinges upon two basic factors. One is the arcane sacred order of the Dao or the eternally abiding three jewels. This sacred power may be localized in a particular cult object, such as the Buddha Amitābha, the *Lotus Sūtra,* Guanyin, a relic, or even the notion of an intrinsically enlightened buddha nature. The second factor is the aspirant or devotee. The two factors are conceived as being relational in nature: spiritual progress and sanctity entail a resonance between the aspirant and the sacred order at large, rather than the appropriation of one solely by or in terms of the other.

As the ganying metaphor would have it, spiritual "presence" or "manifestation" (*ying*)—whether that presence be construed as the descent of the buddhas, the arousing of the thought of enlightenment, auspicious omens, miraculous responses, even enlightenment itself—is effected by the devotee "coming into sympathetic accord" or "tally" with the hidden sacred order and forging a "causal impetus or nexus" (*ji, jiyuan*) that "stimulates" (*gan*) a flow or manifestation of sacred power. Miraculous response, as such, is the function of a commutative interaction between aspirant and the sacred order and not purely the work of either thaumaturgy on the part of the subject or numinal intrusion on the part of the cult object. Often characterized as a "manifest trace," "sign," or "event," the very concept of a stimulus working to produce a given miraculous response implies the presence of an a priori pattern or network of principles that lurks beneath the surface of manifest events, mysteriously structuring their ebb and flow.

In the indigenous Chinese tales of the strange, it is generally the taxonomical homologies of yinyang and the five elements, or Confucian and Daoist ritual, moral, and mythic norms, that serve to translate this hidden resonantal order into cultural practice. Vestiges of these earlier systems doubtless find their way into the Buddhist world of "miraculous response" in conjunction with the original Chinese concept of "stimulus and response." But, for the most part, they are reformulated in terms of distinctively Buddhist ethical and ritual motifs that serve as the normative backdrop governing auspicious response and calamitous retribution. Thus, the religious expectations expressed in the tales of miraculous response, as well as the nuances of ritual procedure, behavior, and attitude that attend these events, provide a valuable window on the everyday world of Chinese Buddhist culture.

Even though a given miracle tale or collection often involves a specialized cultic focus, some of these norms and expectations are more general. For example, such virtues as sincere faith and contrition, observance of various ascetic regimens (including a vegetarian diet, shortened sleep, eremitism, and endurance of physical hardship), concern for ritual purity, and adherence to fixed ritual cycles for veneration, confession, and so forth, are virtually universal. The tales as a whole also tend to address a common set of religious problems and themes, including the healing of illness, the obtaining of progeny and prosperity, the desire for spiritual growth, concern for spiritual offense and the averting of karmic retribution, the desire for an auspicious death and rebirth (including salvation in the pure land).

When a tale or collection entails a particular cult focus, however, more specific ritual paradigms and themes come into play. In the *Lotus* collections, for instance, we find an emphasis on the "five practices" of receiving and keeping, reading, reciting from memory, explicating, and copying the sūtra, the rudiments of which are suggested in the "Dharma Preachers" chapter of the *Lotus Sūtra.* The bodhisattva Samantabhadra ("Universal Worthy") becomes an important object of cult focus, based on the "Universal Worthy" chapter of the *Lotus* as well as *Sūtra on the Contemplation of the Bodhisattva Universal Worthy,* as do the ascetic and eremitic guidelines set forth in the "Easeful Practices" chapter. At the same time, even though the *Lotus* may provide the basic orientation for devotion, its ritual instructions are hardly complete. To fill in the details for such practices as ritually receiving, keeping, or reciting the sūtra, devotees looked to a more diffused liturgical culture and lore.

The selections translated here are from *Taishō shinshū daizōkyō* (Tokyo, 1924–1934), 2067; vol. 51. Page numbers indicated in parentheses after each selection.

Selections from the *Hongzan fahua zhuan*

I. ARTWORK AND IMAGES

Xiao Jing, the chancellor of the Directorate of Education under the Tang, was a native of Lanling. He was the great-great grandson of Emperor [Wu] of the Liang [dynasty] and the fifth son of King / Prince Gui of Liang [542–585 C.E.]. When the Liang dynasty fell and we entered the [period of the] Sui [dynasty], his elder sister became the imperial consort of Emperor Yang. Thus he grew up in a noble and flourishing line, which also held great faith in the Buddhist teachings.

During the middle of the Daye era [605–617], Jing personally learned to recite the *Lotus Sūtra* [from memory] and resolved to fashion [an image of] the stūpa of Prabhūtaratna based on its description in the scripture. It was to be constructed of pure sandalwood and stand some three feet tall, with a wooden image of Buddha Prabhūtaratna fashioned [to go inside of it]. Several years passed, however, and the project still remained uncompleted.

While staying at the family estate, Jing's elder brother Quan arose early one morning. In the grass of the forecourt he suddenly came across a sandalwood stūpa. Beneath its cover sat a single Buddha made of copper alloy. The craftsmanship was extraordinary. The image had Indian features that carried an air of majestic solemnity. Its eyes were of silver, with black pupils that glistened resplendently. It was all very lifelike. Quan, amazed at his find, went off to fetch his brother Yu [the duke of Song].

When Xiao Jing saw the image he was overwhelmed with joy. He picked up the canopy [of the pagoda] and gingerly tried to place it atop the stūpa [that he had been building]. It was a perfect fit, as though made for it specifically. Even though the tone of the wood was a little at odds, [the contrast] made the form of the stūpa look even more sublime. Next he took the Buddha image and set it inside the stūpa. It also fit perfectly, as though modeled deliberately to be placed inside it. Jing sighed with delight. He reckoned that it was his sincere devotion that had caused [the image] to materialize.

The cloth in which the Buddha image [was wrapped] was found to contain some one hundred-odd beads of śarīra (relics). Jing's daughter was a novice nun, extremely young in years. Once she stole in and took the relics out of curiosity. She tried smashing them with a mallet, but they would not break. Then she placed some thirty of the relics on a stone and struck them with an axe. The relics scattered everywhere, without one staying in place. The child got down on her knees to search for them but could only locate three or four. The rest were not to be found. Frightened at what she had done, she confessed the whole business to Jing. Jing went to examine the stūpa, and lo and behold, all of the relics were there, just as they had been previously. From that day forward Jing resolved to recite the *Lotus Sūtra* in its entirety once every day until the day he died.

In the twelfth year of the Zhenguan era [638] Jing became gravely ill. The empress Xiao came together with his younger brother and niece to see him. Jing greeted them and had each burn incense [on his behalf], whereupon they departed together. He retained only his younger brother, Yu, the duke of Song, and his novice daughter, whom he had burn incense and recite scripture. Shortly thereafter he announced to his daughter, "I am ready to depart. The bodhisattva Samantabhadra has come to meet me and is [waiting] in the eastern courtyard. Your reverence may go there to greet him."

The novice went off to welcome [Samantabhadra] as she had been instructed. When she did not promptly return, Jing said, "This courtyard is not pure. Thus [Samantabhadra] is not willing to come. I will go [to him]. You stay here."

Thereupon, he took his leave of Yu and the others, got up, assumed the full kneeling posture, joined his palms in reverence, and, facing duly west, passed away on the spot. He left instructions that [his body] should be placed by itself on a single cart, dressed in nothing more than his everyday clothing. The women of the household were not to be permitted to accompany the burial party [as mourners], nor was meat of any kind to be used in the [funerary] offerings. As soon as the tomb chamber was constructed they laid him out in the coffin. Officials and commoners alike praised his spiritual attainments. His household reverently received and carried out his instructions.

Formerly, the great being Universal Worthy (Samantabhadra), his spiritual powers being boundless, manifested himself seated atop a great [white] bull elephant and paid witness to [the supreme truth] of the *Lotus Sūtra.* Perhaps [the events recounted] here represent the expedient response of a former buddha, or the manifestation of [a bodhisattva at the stage of] one incarnation before buddhahood. It is something [bodhisattvas of] the seventh stage are unable to fathom and [beings of] the two vehicles cannot conceive.

Having themselves become enlightened to the way, when the sublime form [of these buddhas and bodhisattvas] is depicted in fine drawings and images they can also stimulate a tangible sense of faith in the ordinary person. Through [the suggestions of] the material image one awakens the spirit. By means of the traces one discerns the foundation. Features that are delightful to behold are truly the ford and pass that draw us to [enlightenment]. (13c)

V. SACRIFICING THE BODY [IN OFFERING TO THE LOTUS]

The Buddhist monk Huiyi was a native of Guangling. He left home when he was a child and followed his master to Shouzhun. During the Xiaojian reign-period [454–456] of the Song he left the capital and settled at Zhulin Monastery, where he threw himself into the relentless practice of austerities, with the pledge eventually to immolate himself [in offering to the dharma]. When members of the saṅgha learned of this, some denounced him [in disapproval]; others praised him.

In the fourth year of the Daming era [460] he began to give up coarse grains, eventually taking only hemp [buds] and barley. By the sixth year he had cut these out, too, and consumed only extract of the *zisu* herb. Before long he gave this up as well and took to swallowing nothing but pills of pure aromatic. Although his four vital elements hung by a thread, his spiritual disposition remained as determined and true as ever.

Emperor Xiaowu looked upon Huiyi with deep reverence and awe, and asked after him anxiously. He dispatched the grand steward Yi Gong, king of Jiangxia, to go to the monastery and reason with Huiyi. But Huiyi would not be swayed from his purpose. On the eighth day of the fourth month during the seventh year of the Daming era [463]—the day on which he had chosen to immolate himself—Huiyi set up a cauldron and prepared [a supply of] oil on the south [slope] of Mount Zhong. That morning he mounted an ox-carriage. Pulled along by a crowd of followers, he set out from the temple and proceeded toward the mountain.

Emperors and kings are regarded as the support of the people and the foundation on which the three jewels depend. For this reason [Emperor Xiaowu] personally [thought to] enter the terrace [and watch the event]. But upon reaching Cloud Dragon Gate, he found that [it was thronged with people and that] he could proceed no further. He ordered someone to inquire as to the reason. As it turned out, the man of the way, Huiyi, ready to renounce himself in sacrifice, had come to take his leave of the emperor officially. Being an ardent admirer of the Buddha dharma, the emperor's visage immediately changed, and he personally stepped out of the Cloud Dragon Gate [to show his respect to Huiyi]. Spying the emperor, Huiyi sternly charged him with the protection of the Buddha's dharma. Thereupon he took his leave and departed.

The emperor followed along behind him. Kings and their royal consorts, mendicants and laypersons, knights and rabble alike filled the mountain valley, where they proceeded to cast off garments and jewelry of incalculable value [in offering to the saṅgha]. Huiyi climbed into the cauldron and seated himself on a small bench. First he wrapped his upper body in bark cloth from the karpāsa tree. Over this he wound a single long [strip of cloth] in the form of a turban, which he then sprinkled with oil. As he was getting ready to add the flame, the emperor ordered the grand steward to approach the cauldron and plead with him one last time, saying, "There are many methods for practicing the way. Why must you take your life? I pray that you will think it over three times, and decide upon a different path."

But Huiyi's resolve was firm, and he had no thoughts of regret. Thus he replied, "What is worth preserving in this feeble body and worthless life? Your majesty is sagely and benevolent but shows excessive favoritism toward me. I pray that, instead, you will sponsor twenty persons to leave home [as Buddhist monks or nuns]."

The emperor issued an edict granting his request. Thereupon, taking candle in hand, Huiyi set the turban alight. As the turban caught fire he tossed the candle aside, joined his palms and began to recite the "Medicine King" (Bhaiṣajyarāja) chapter [of the *Lotus*]. The flame began to creep down over his brow, but the sound of his chanting was still clear and distinct. When it reached his eyes, all was silent. Nobleman and commoner everywhere set up a loud wail, the echo of which reverberated throughout the valley. There wasn't one among them who didn't snap his fingers and praise the name of the Buddha [in admiration], as tears of grief streamed down their sobbing faces.

The fire finally died out at dawn. At that moment the emperor heard strains of flute and pipe and smelled an exceedingly fine aroma wafting through the air around him. Not until the end of the day did he at last return to the palace. That night the emperor dreamt that he saw Huiyi. The master, shaking his mendicant's staff, approached him and charged him again with [protection of] the Buddha's dharma. The next morning the emperor convened a ceremony in order to ordain [the twenty monks, as he had promised]. He ordered the chairman of the vegetarian feast to proclaim and narrate in detail the auspicious wonders [that attended Huiyi's death]. On the site where Huiyi immolated himself, the emperor built Medicine King Monastery (Yaowangsi) in order to commemorate the deed. (24a–c)

In Jingzhou there lived two bhikṣunīs who were sisters. Their names have been forgotten, but they both recited the *Lotus Sūtra,* held a deep loathing for the physical body, and together conceived the desire to give up their lives [in offering to the dharma]. [To this end,] they set restrictions on clothing and diet and prescribed for themselves a regimen of painful austerities. They ingested various perfumed oils and gradually reduced their intake of coarse rice, until they gave up grains altogether and took only fragrant honey. [Even then,] their energy and spiritual determination remained as vigorous and fresh as ever. They announced [widely] to the monks and laity [around them] that at an appointed time in the future they would immolate themselves.

On the evening of the eighth day of the second month during the third year of the Zhenguan era [629], they set up two high seats in the middle of one of the large boulevards of Jingzhou. Then they wrapped their bodies from head to foot in waxed cloth, leaving only their faces exposed. The crowds gathered like a mountain; their songs of praise filled the air like clouds. The two women together began to chant the *Lotus Sūtra.* When they reached the "Medicine King" (Bhaiṣajyarāja) chapter, the older sister first ignited the head of the younger sister, and the younger in turn lit the head of the older sister. Simultaneously the two blazed up, like two torches in the clear night. As the flames crept down over their eyes, the sound of their voices became even more distinct. But, as it gradually arrived at their noses and mouths, they grew quiet [and their voices were heard no more]. [They remained seated upright] until dawn, linked together on their two seats. Then, all at once, the fire gave out. [As the smoke and flame cleared,] there amidst their charred and desiccated bones lay two tongues, both perfectly intact. The crowd gasped in awe. [A short time later] a tall stūpa was constructed for them.

Not far to the west of the city seat of Bingzhou there lived a sūtra copyist around twenty-four or twenty-five years of age who recited the *Lotus Sūtra.* He made a vow to immolate himself in offering [to the dharma]. Gathering up several bundles of dead stems and brush, he spread them out to sun until they were bone dry. People asked him what he was doing; but he kept his intentions secret, refusing to tell anyone. Sometime later in the middle of the night he set fire [to the pile] and immolated himself. By the time people rushed to his assistance the fire was in full blaze and he was already dead. Thereupon they added more wood to the fire to insure that his body would be completely consumed. A [strange] music and rare fragrance were detected in the air. Many people [as a result] found faith [in the Buddhist teachings]. (26a)

The Buddhist monk Tanyou had the secular surname of Zhang and was a native of Xuzhou. While traveling abroad to study in Xianyang, he suddenly conceived a profound disgust [for the world]. [Shortly thereafter] he happened to meet the dhyāna masters Wuxing and Zhi, as a result of which he left the household life and took up practice of the way on Mount Yueling.

Tanyou concentrated exclusively on recitation of the *Lotus Sūtra.* As a rule he would set up a purified altar space (*tan*) of several feet square. Only after hanging out his twenty-one banners and making formal offerings of incense and flowers would he begin to recite the sūtra. This he followed as his regular procedure.

Later You moved to Mount Xian, with the intention of reading through the *Avataṃsaka Sūtra.* Repeatedly he experienced a dream in which someone would come and teach him to recite the verses [of the sūtra]. Whenever he reached the point in his recitation [where verses occur], he found that [the verses of the dream] corresponded perfectly with the written text of the scripture.

Later You heard of the numinous Buddha image fashioned by Aśoka that had [miraculously] flown [to China] and been installed in Changsha Monastery. Numerous spiritual manifestations [were said to have been associated with it]. But the subtle sincerity necessary to tap [its supernal potency] will not be present if one is not willing to disregard one's own life and give oneself totally to religious discipline. So thinking, You decided to immolate himself in an offering [to dharma] at this site, [just as the bodhisattva] Medicine King [chose to do in the *Lotus Sūtra*].

In the first year of the Qianfeng era [666] he traveled to the spot where the image was enshrined. [Standing in its presence,] he made the solemn vow [to sacrifice himself in offering] and prayed that he might realize his aim without impediment. Thereupon, coming from in front of the Buddha hall, he heard the sound of fingers snapping [in approval]. At that moment a heavy downpour began to fall from thick and ominous-looking clouds. As this had been typical of the weather for more than ten days now, those around You sought to dissuade him, fearing that [the rain] might prove an obstacle [to the realization of his aim]. But Tanyou countered, "There is an auspicious omen in this. [My vow] will be realized. Of this I have no doubt."

When the fated night of the fifteenth day of the second month arrived, the sky cleared completely and the light of the full moon streamed forth, illumining everything. Tanyou [wrapped himself in] waxed cotton cloth and set fire simultaneously to his hands and the crown of his head. He wished for the fire to burn slowly, so that he might continue the offering for a long time. He did not want to die quickly. As the fire crept to his two wrists, his countenance showed no change whatsoever. Even as it reached his brow he continued to preach the dharma just as he had at the start. Easeful and single-minded, he kept his gaze fixed on the auspicious image before him. With the light [from the flame] as his offering, he prayed for a vision of the buddha Clear-Radiance-of-Sun-and-Moon (Candrasūryavimalaprabhāsaśrī), [to whom the bodhisattva Medicine King offered himself in the *Lotus Sūtra*].

Those around him [periodically] asked, "How do you feel?" To which he would reply, "My mind is like diamond–unflinching in its resolve. Truly I feel quite cool and pleasant. There is no pain whatsoever." Then, all at once, the blaze flared up brilliantly, consuming him entirely. Still, from the midst of the inferno [one could hear] Tanyou urging those around him to recite the Buddha's name.

When the fire first began to grow in intensity, the monks present all became quite agitated, fearing that without any skeletal remains there would be no evidence to testify to his self-immolation. Hence, they begged that at least a single token [of his saintly deed] be left behind, so that they might display it for [the edification of] the living. When it was finally over and all had been reduced to ashes, only his skull remained. As dawn arrived and word of the event spread through the prefectural seat, the local officials all flocked to the site. They prostrated in obeisance, [ritually] circumambulated the spot, praised You's devotion, and then departed. No sooner had they passed out of the monastery gate than the skull spontaneously burst apart. Some dozen of the faithful [had chosen to] remain in the presence of the sacred skull, where they prayed fervently for śarīra [relics] to appear. In all eight or so grains [of relic] descended. Sinking and floating freely [in the air], their miraculous manifestation came in answer to the heartfelt [sincerity of the onlookers]. Today the cremated remains are interred within the temple. The [miraculous] response (*ying*) of the snapping of fingers is regularly heard.

More recently, when he first took up reciting the *Lotus Sūtra* from memory, the eremite mendicant Hulun of Ximing Monastery burned one finger [in offering] with completion of each fascicle, so that by the time he reached the eighth and final fascicle, he had burned off eight fingers. Although this is not [the same as] total renunciation, it is next in status to sacrifice of the [entire] body. (26b–c)

VI. RECITATION [OF THE *LOTUS*] FROM MEMORY

The Buddhist monk Puming had the secular surname of Zhang and was a native of Linwei. He left home [to join the saṅgha] when he was a young boy. Pure by nature, he was never seen to compromise [his vow to] maintain a vegetarian diet and wear cotton robes. He took repentance and recitation [of sūtras] as his regular form of practice. The three sets of robes and rope [meditation] couch [of the mendicant] were rarely far from his person. When he wished to rest, he would take a short nap while sitting upright.

He recited the *Lotus* and *Vimalakīrti* sūtras. Whenever he chanted he would use a special robe and separate seat, which he took great care not to pollute. Upon reaching the "Exhortations" chapter [of the *Lotus*], the bodhisattva Samantabhadra would appear before his very eyes, seated atop a white elephant.

When he recited the *Vimalakīrti Sūtra* he would hear singing and music in the air.

Puming was also skilled in the use of spiritual incantations (*dhāraṇī*). Whomever he sought to save was always cured. Once there was a villager known as Wang Daozhen, whose wife came down with a serious illness. He summoned Ming to his house. No sooner did Ming enter the gate than the woman's melancholia departed. Suddenly, running from the dog entrance, they saw a creature several feet in length that looked something like a fox. As a result of this she was cured. Once when Ming was walking near a shrine by the side of the river a shaman[ess] called out, "When the spirits see you they all run away."

Later Ming developed a sudden illness. Sitting in proper meditation posture, he burned incense and quietly passed away. It was the Xiaojian era (454–457) of the Song when he died. He was eighty-five years of age. (27c)

The Buddhist monk Huiguo was a native of Yuzhou. When he was a boy he made a vegetarian diet and austerities his regular practice. During the beginning of the Song period [420] he journeyed to the capital and took up residence in Waguan Monastery, where he recited the *Lotus* and *Daśabhūmika* sūtras. Once in front of the privy he spied a ghost. With utmost reverence [the spirit] approached Guo and said, "Formerly I was a preceptor in this monastic assembly, but I committed a small irregularity and so have fallen among the excrement-eating ghosts. Dharma Master, your [powers of] religious discipline are lofty and illustrious. Moreover, loving-kindness and compassion are your aim. I pray that you may find some method to help alleviate my condition." It went on to say, "Some time ago I had three thousand in cash, which I buried at the foot of the persimmon tree [on the monastery grounds]. Please take it and make meritorious blessings for me."

Guo thereupon informed the assembly of monks and went to dig up [the cash]. Sure enough, the three thousand was there. He used the money to have a copy of the *Lotus Sūtra* made and sponsor a noon [dharma] ceremony. Afterward he saw the ghost in a dream, who told him, "I have managed to change my state of existence, and it is vastly superior to that of yesterday." Guo died during the sixth year [425] after the great founding of the [Liu] Song [dynasty], at the age of seventy-six. (27c)

There was a certain monk—his name has been forgotten—who lived in a monastery in the eastern section of Qin commandery. [In residence at the monastery] was a young novice who could recite the *Lotus Sūtra* with extraordinary fluency, except for the fact that whenever he reached the two words, "cloudy and obscure" (*ai-dai*), in the "Medicinal Herbs" chapter, he would forget them no sooner than he was taught them. This must have happened well over a thousand times. Finally his master scolded him bitterly, saying, "You are able to learn to recite the entire sūtra perfectly [from memory]. How is it that you can't muster the concentration to memorize these two words?!"

That night the master dreamt of a Buddhist monk, who told him: "You should not blame this novice. In his previous life he lived in a village on the east side of this monastery, where he had the form of a laywoman. Basically she devoted herself to reciting the single scripture of the *Lotus Sūtra.* But at that time, silverfish had eaten away the two characters "cloudy and obscure" in the "Medicinal Herbs" chapter of the household copy of the *Lotus.* Thus the two characters were originally missing from the sūtra. [As a result], when in this present life the novice monk tries to learn the words anew, he cannot do it. The surname [of the family] is such and such, and this copy of the sūtra may still be found there. If you don't believe my tale, you can go and verify it for yourself."

The very next day the master went to the village and sought out the household. After introducing himself he said to the head of the family, "Do you have a special place for making offerings?" The man replied, "We do." "What scriptures do you keep there?" he asked. To which the man replied, "We have a single copy of the *Lotus Sūtra.*" The master sent him to fetch it so that he might have a look. Sure enough, the two characters were missing from the "Medicinal Herbs" chapter. [The head of the house] went on to relate, "This is the scripture that the deceased spouse of our elder son kept devotedly while she was alive. Since she passed away it has been seventeen years now."

As it turned out, the dates corresponded perfectly with the month and year of the novice's gestation. . . . No one knows where and when he died. (28c–29a)

The Buddhist monk Jingjian. Details of his background are unknown, but he left home as a young boy and for the most part lived on mounts Chonggao and Longmen. He recited the *Lotus Sūtra* in its entirety as many as thirteen thousand times. Internally he applied himself zealously to the contemplation of the wondrous [truth], thereby becoming quite skilled in the essentials of dhyāna. However, due to having recited [the sūtra] for such an extended period of time, his physical strength was exhausted [to the point of] distress.

After [he had suffered from this illness] for more than twenty years, one day children began to gather and chatter raucously on the north side of his hut. This caused him to feel even more stressed and dispirited. Jian could not figure out where they came from. At that time a white-haired codger appeared, dressed in a short coat and skirt of crude white silk. Every day he would come and inquire [of Jian's health], asking: "How are the dhyāna master's four elements doing today?" To which Jian would usually reply, "I am feeling progressively more run down. Moreover, I have no idea where all these children are coming from; but daily their disturbance grows worse. I don't think I can bear it much longer."

The old man instructed, "Master, you should go and sit near the spot where they play. Wait for them to take off their clothes and enter the river to bathe. Then take one of the boy's garments and come back [to your hermitage]. When he comes to reclaim it, don't give it back to him. If he curses you, be sure not to respond. I, your disciple, will come to speak with him."

Jian set out to do as the old man instructed. He went and waited for the children to take off their clothes and enter the pool to bathe. Then he snatched up one of the boy's garments and returned promptly to his hut. When the child came after him looking for his robe, Jian recalled the old man's cautions and refused to hand it over. The child bad-mouthed and slandered the dhyāna master in the most vile way, even extending his remarks to his ancestors. But the master showed no response. Soon the old man arrived and said to the lad, "[I command you to] enter the master's chest." At first the boy was unwilling to do as he was told. But the old man pressed him repeatedly, until he proceeded to enter Jian's chest and vanish within his belly. The old man asked the master, "How do your four elements feel now?" To which Jian replied, "My vital energy (*qi*) is far better than ever before." The old man thereupon took his leave [and disappeared].

From that day forward Jian felt physically robust and at ease, and his practice of dhyāna and recitation doubled in intensity. Those who understand this sort of thing say that surely this was the work of the bodhisattva Samantabhadra ("Universal Worthy"). The bodhisattva had the [local] mountain spirit compel the seminal essences of different medicinal herbs to transform into the child and become absorbed into [Jian's] body, thereby curing Jian of his illness. Jingjian was the master who instructed dhyāna master Mo in the arts of dhyāna. We do not know where and how he ended his days. (29a)

The Buddhist monk Bacheng left home [and joined the saṅgha] while a young boy. His faculties were extremely obtuse, yet he faithfully kept the regular post-noon fast (*chang-zhai*) and a strict vegetarian diet. At age twenty-five he received the full precepts and resolved to learn to recite the *Lotus Sūtra* [from memory] in order to obtain rebirth in the western pure land. Daily he would memorize one line, or maybe at most a half a verse. Sometimes he couldn't remember anything. Finally, at the age of eighty, he succeeded in memorizing the entire text.

Sometime after that, while he was taking a nap, Bacheng dreamt that a person wearing a crimson robe and military cap appeared before him with an official scroll of invitation in hand. He opened it and announced to Bacheng: "The lord of heaven, Indra, has dispatched me to extend this summons respectfully to you." Cheng replied, "It is the wish of this humble monk to be reborn in the western [pure land]. Even though the Trāyastriṃśa Heaven is indeed an excellent place, it does not accord with this humble monk's vow." Thereupon the crimson-robed figure departed.

When he awoke, Cheng related his dream to his disciples. The very next day he dreamt of a stūpa of seven stories, with himself dwelling on the fifth.

Gazing toward the west he saw a staircase strung with jewels, seemingly endless in length. Two vajra protectors with staves in hand stood guard in two booths. A handful of azure-clad youths were brushing off the staircase with white whisks. Cheng asked the youths, "Where am I?" They replied, "This is the bejeweled stair that leads to the western [pure land]. We have come to welcome dharma master Cheng."

When Bacheng awoke, he related what had transpired and announced to his disciples: "You may sell my three robes and six items in order to sponsor a maigre feast and offering." They did as he instructed. Just before the maigre feast he asked the assembly, "Do you see the thousand buddhas [gathered here]?" The assembly replied, "We do not." Then again he asked, "Do you smell an unusual fragrance in the air or not?" To which they replied, "We all smell it." At the finish of the feast Cheng bathed himself, shaved his head, sat in perfect [meditation] posture, composed his thoughts, and passed away on the spot. (29a–b)

The Buddhist monk Sengding. Nothing is known of his background, but he lived at Chanjing Monastery in Jiangyang and recited the *Lotus Sūtra* [as his regular practice]. He had a particular love of popular song, which he was at an utter loss to restrain. As a result, he was given to the habit of dissipating himself in the dusty and vulgar world [of Jiangyang nightlife]. However, whenever he did so, [his devotion was such that] divine youths would regularly manifest (*gan*) and come to his assistance.

Sometimes when he had passed out blind drunk, his dharma robe cast off [in a heap] from his body, [he would awaken to find that the robe had] spontaneously pleated and folded itself and that covers had been drawn over him, properly concealing his body. If his robe had become soiled with mud when he took it off, in the twinkle of an eye it was washed clean. As he picked it up to put it on, he would find it to be impregnated with a rare and pure fragrance that lingered for a long time [without fading]. On other occasions, the water [in the vessels for offering] automatically replenished itself. Or the floor [of his chamber] always appeared cleanly swept.

One time while Ding was drooling away in a drunken stupor, he awoke suddenly to find divine deva youths standing before him. His whole body was damp with saliva. He felt immediately humbled, and from then on he regarded observance of the precepts with the highest esteem. No one knows where or how he ended his days. (30a)

During the era of [Emperor] Wu-cheng of the [Northern] Qi (562–565), a person digging on the slope of Mount Kandong near Bingzhou came upon a patch of soil—yellowish white in color—that stood out in marked contrast from the ground around it. Probing further, he turned up an object that had the appearance of a pair of human lips, with a tongue, fresh red in color, sticking out between them. He reported the matter in a memorial [to the throne]. [The emperor] made inquiries among various learned scholars but could find no one who knew [the meaning of it]. When he heard of this, the mendicant Fashang (495–580), controller-in-chief [of the saṅgha], memorialized the throne saying, "This is the recompense of nondecay of the sense faculties that is achieved by devotees who [ritually] keep the *Lotus Sūtra*. It is proof that [this individual] recited [the scripture] more than a thousand times over."

Subsequently, the emperor summoned the secretariat drafter, Gao Chen. "You are one inclined to faith," he ordered, "go personally to look into this matter. Surely [this object] will have some sort of numinous power. Place it in a duly purified place, convene a maigre feast, and make offerings to it."

Chen received the order and went to the site, where he assembled various Buddhist monks renowned for their devotion to the *Lotus*. Holding incense censers in hand and maintaining strict ceremonial purity, they circumambulated [the tongue] and offered prayers saying: "O Bodhisattva! Countless years have passed since you entered into nirvāṇa. As one who has reverently received [the *Lotus* and kept it] flawlessly during this current age of the counterfeit dharma, we beseech you to manifest for us your [marvelous] stimulus and response (*ganying*)."

The instant they raised their voices the tongue and lips began to beat about on the altar top. Although no sound came forth, it looked as though it were chanting. Of those who witnessed it, there was not one whose hair didn't stand on end. Chen reported the phenomenon. The [throne] ordered that it be stored away in a stone casket and moved to a stūpa chamber. (31c)

The Buddhist monk Lingkan. Details of his background are unknown. [His master] recognized him to be someone who was very bright and compassionate by nature and had him take up regular recitation of the *Lotus Sūtra*. However, upon first completing his memorization of the scripture, Lingkan unexpectedly came down with (*gan*) a severe illness. He informed his master of it, saying, "I have heard that if one [ritually] receives and keeps the *Lotus* one will realize purification of the six sense faculties. How is it that my recitation produces (*gan*) illness instead?"

His master replied, "When you recite the sūtra how do you go about it?"

Kan said, "Sometimes I do not wash my hands, or bother to clothe myself [with the proper robes]. I may rest the [the sūtra] at my feet, or place it at the head of my bed, as the moment moves me."

His teacher said, "In that case it is a beneficent dharma-protecting spirit that has come to inflict punishment on you. If you don't show proper care for the scripture your efforts will bring forth (*gan*) no merits. It is fitting that you repent."

Kan thereupon fashioned a plain wooden case, where he kept the sūtra and to which he [regularly] paid obeisance by touching it with the crown of his head. In the [Buddha] hall he ritually circumambulated [the sūtra]. Except for eating and relieving himself, he threw himself entirely into this painful penance, chastening himself with such intensity that his head split open and blood flowed.

For three years running he kept up this practice, until one day, just as the light of dawn was beginning to break at the fifth watch, there came a loud pounding at the door of the Buddha hall, and someone called out for it to be opened. At first Kan was reluctant, thinking, "Certainly this must be a criminal. Why else would he want a door to be opened when it is already locked tight?" But the person continued to call without letting up, so Kan finally gave in.

When he opened the door he saw an old man. His beard and temples were a hoary white, and in his hands he clutched a wooden staff. When Kan showed his face the man struck him repeatedly, saying, "Will you dare ever again to make light of the *Lotus Sūtra?*" The instant he hit him, the ulcers that covered Kan's body were healed and his four vital elements returned to their normal balance.

When the daylight finally broke Kan inspected the front of the Buddha hall, where he discovered the footprints of an elephant [in the dirt]. Thereupon he realized for the first time that the old man was the bodhisattva Samantabhadra, who had descended to eliminate his sins. From then on he completely reformed his ways and devoted himself unremittingly to the practice of recitation [of the *Lotus*]. We do not know where or when he died.

His old master, Ju, also took the *Lotus* as his main practice. Whenever he recited the scripture he felt as though an ambrosial flavor, unlike anything in the known world, would spread through his mouth. As a result, when he began reciting he never wanted to stop. (32a)

The Buddhist monk Zhiye had the secular surname of Yang. He left home as a small boy and took up residence at Changle Monastery in Yangzhou. He kept the monastic precepts assiduously and learned to recite the *Lotus Sūtra* with such fluency that the lines flowed from his mouth like a stream of water from a vase. At the end of the Daye era of the Sui [617], Yuwen Huaji committed the heinous act of murdering Emperor Yang in the palace bathhouse. Thereupon the world fell apart and the populace was thrown into famine. Residents scattered and [the region] became a maelstrom [of chaos], with the price of rice soaring to ten thousand cash amidst the tumult. Zhiye at the time was living in a small room of a detached cloister, where he was engaged in uninterrupted recitation of the *Lotus Sūtra.* Consequently, he died of starvation in his chamber. There was no one to bury him, and the room itself collapsed around him, trapping his remains beneath it.

When peace was finally restored during the Yining era [617–618], a single stalk of lotus flower suddenly appeared on the spot. Its radiantly colored petals opened forth to display the most extraordinary freshness and beauty. Monks and laity alike were struck with awe, and no one could think of an explanation for it. At that time, an old monk who was a former resident of the monastery realized what was going on and said, "There was once a monk who devoted himself exclusively to recitation of the *Lotus Sūtra* on this site. He must have perished here as a result of the turmoil of the times. Since there would have been no one to bury him, his bones are probably still here, and [this lotus has appeared] as a result of the monk's spiritual potency."

They cleared away the debris around the stalk of the flower until they uncovered his skeleton. It turned out that the blue lotus flower had grown up through the skull and was rooted beneath the tongue. The tongue itself was as though still alive, showing no sign of decomposition whatsoever. The monastic assembly took the tongue and blossom to the head of the hall. They rang the bell, gathered the monks, and performed cyclic recitation of the *Lotus*. When the tongue heard the scripture it appeared to be able to move about. Once local monks and laymen heard of it, sightseers gathered around forming a solid human wall. There wasn't one who didn't sigh in admiration. All made the supreme resolution [to seek buddhahood]. (34c)

The Buddhist monk Huijin had the secular surname of Qian, but no details are known of his background. He left home when he was a young boy and set up a fixed regimen of practice for himself at Lu grotto on Mount Kuang. No matter where he wandered or settled down, he kept up a constant recitation of the *Lotus*. This practice he maintained both day and night, never letting up except to take his meals or lie down to rest.

For reciting the sūtra he required a space of several paces in circumference. He would first purify [the ground] by sweeping and sprinkling, gather whatever flowers were in season at the time, and do his best to decorate [the sanctuary] resplendently. In the center, which was some five or six feet in width, he hung banners and offered incense [to the sūtra]. In a spot set apart [from the altar itself] he placed a single chair [for recitation]. After putting on a new and clean robe and venerating the buddhas of the ten directions, he would join his palms [in adoration] and assume the formal posture [for seated meditation]. Only then would he begin to recite [the sūtra].

One day, after he had completed some ten thousand recitations of the sūtra, everything around him suddenly became hazy, like a cloud of mist. In this cloud he saw the three transformations [of the *Lotus* assembly], together with [the stūpa of Prabhūtaratna], the jeweled thrones [for the manifestation bodies of Śākyamuni Buddha], and their jeweled trees extending throughout the eight directions. Ever so faintly, the buddhas and bodhisattvas [of the assembly] appeared before his eyes. When he reached fifteen thousand recitations, he saw them all with perfect clarity. Where and how he ended his days is not known. (38b)

There was a certain bhikṣunī, her name [long since] forgotten, who lived on the outskirts of the Kunshan district of Suzhou. She became a nun at an early age and took to constant recitation of the *Lotus Sūtra*, which she performed devotedly twice a day for some twenty-odd years. In appearance she was unusually beautiful and refined, so much so that anyone who caught sight of her was struck immediately with affection for her. During the first year of the Yongchang era [689] a certain district office manager named Zhu began to entertain wicked fantasies about her and sought to press her with his less than honorable designs. Yet the bhikṣunī remained firm in her chastity and refused to give in to him.

Angered by her rejection, Zhu made a great deal of trouble for the abbey and intentionally sought to disrupt their regular means of livelihood. The bhikṣunīs were at a total loss as to where to turn to rid themselves of this plight. Whereupon, the nun who kept the *Lotus* said, "How could the *Lotus Sūtra* fail to show its spiritual potency in this matter?" She then donned her purified robe, entered the Buddha hall, burned incense, and professed [solemn] vows.

Not long thereafter the office manager, availing himself of some official pretext, came to the abbey to pass the night. His heart, of course, harbored other intentions. But the very instant he sought to find his way to the nun's quarters, his lower extremities were seized with a burning pain and his male member dropped off. Rivulets of perspiration streamed from his skin, leprous ulcers broke out over his entire body, and his eyebrows, beard, and sideburns all fell out. The office manager grievously recanted, but even after trying a hundred remedies, he still was never completely cured. (40a)

VII. REPEATED READING OF THE SCRIPTURE

There was a certain Kim Kuayi of the [Korean] Kingdom of Silla who bore a single son. When he was a young boy the son left home [as a Buddhist monk]. He had always shown a particular delight in reading the *Lotus Sūtra*. However, in the second fascicle of his family's copy of the scripture, there was one character that had been accidentally scorched beyond recognition.

At age eighteen the young monk died unexpectedly and was reborn in the household of another Kim Kuayi who lived elsewhere. Once again he left home [as a Buddhist monk] and developed a particular affection for reading the *Lotus*. But whenever he reached the second fascicle there was one particular word that he would always forget how to read, the instant he learned it. One night he dreamed that a person said to him: "Young master, in a former life you were born into the household of a certain Kim Kuayi in such and such a region. You also became a mendicant, and in that former life read and recited the *Lotus Sūtra*. However, one character was inadvertently scorched. As a result, in this life you are prone to forget it as soon as you learn it. That old copy of the sūtra still exists. Go there; find it; and see for yourself."

Guided by his dream, the young master set off in search of the household in question. Upon finally locating it he asked tentatively if he might pass the night there. His father and mother from his previous life had a vague feeling that they knew him. [After he told them the story,] they brought out the old sūtra. Sure enough, they found that one character was scorched in the second fascicle. The young monk and his parents were joined deeply in their feelings of joy and sadness. The two households consequently became quite intimate, brought together almost as one. Their story reached the county and prefectural governments. From there, the local officials reported it to the throne. Thus it came to be transmitted and retold throughout the land. Even down to today it has not died out. All of this happened during the Zhenguan era [627–650]. (40c)

The Buddhist monk Fayan had the secular surname of Gao. He was a great-grandson of Gao Ke, who served as the duke of Qi during the Sui [dynasty]. His style name was Lijing; and he had the single personal name of Yuanyi. During the Zhenguan reign period [627–650], before he left home [to become a Buddhist monk], Lijing and his brother Lilan studied the *Lotus* and *Prajñā* sūtras at the residence of the Buddhist monk Mingzang located in Huadu Monastery. Initially Jing showed enthusiasm for his studies, but later gave them up entirely.

In the first year of the Longshuo reign period [661] the [military expedition] against Liao returned [to the Tang capital]. During the first month of the third year, Jing set off to the terrace in order to view [the ceremonies for] the decoration [of the heroes of the campaign]. As he left Shunyi Gate, two horsemen came after him, saying, "You are hereby under arrest." Jing asked, "Who are you honorable gentlemen?" To which they replied, "We are emissaries of King Yama, who has sent us to fetch you, [honorable sir]."

Jing was seized with panic. He spurred his horse and galloped off toward Puguang Monastery, thinking he might be safe there. But the emissary said, "It will do no good to rush for the monastery gate, for you still won't get in. The instant you enter you will find yourself outside again." Reaching the monastery gate Jing saw another horseman guarding the entrance. He then rushed off to the west thinking to reach Kaishan Monastery. But again he encountered a horseman at the gate. Thereupon, with his pursuers hot on his trail, he charged off in the hope of making it back to his home. But his home was east of Huadu Monastery, and, fearing it too far a journey, he thought he might [seek safety] in the ward of Sweet Water Spring. A single horseman appeared in front of him. Jing struck him with his fist and the demon tumbled from his horse. The other demon pursuing him from behind said, "What a rough one this fellow is! Let's hurry up and pull him down! Grab him by the hair!" So saying, Jing was seized by the hair on his head. The pain was as though he had been flayed with a knife. Meanwhile, another rider wearing a red robe and mounted on a white horse struck him in the chest with his fist. Jing instantly toppled from his mount and fell prone to the ground.

After what seemed a long while, he began to regain his senses. He felt as though he were sitting in a mist. Members of his family were taking him home in a carriage. When he fully came to, he related to them everything that he had experienced: [Upon being knocked from his horse and seized by the demons,] he was taken before King Yama, who said to him, "Why did you steal fruit from the monastery orchards? Why did you speak of faults [and dissatisfactions] with the three jewels?" His sins having been exposed, he dared not utter a false word. The king of the underworld said, "For stealing fruit [from the saṅgha] the punishment is to swallow four hundred and fifty [molten] iron balls. After suffering this for four years the sin will finally be eliminated. For bespeaking ill [of the three jewels] gouging out the tongue [is the appropriate punishment]." After that they let him go and he returned to life.

[Sometime after this episode,] Jing all of a sudden saw beings with horns on their heads approaching him. Each held an iron ball. They bound Jing's hands and feet and forced him to swallow them, one at a time. Those attending Jing [during his illness] could not see the iron balls. All they saw was Jing, mouth open wide and eyes glaring [in utter terror]. His body from head to foot was a crimson red. Hot breath rushed from his throat, so steamy and thick it was difficult to go near. The next day Jing awoke and said, "Already a year has passed and I have swallowed more than one hundred balls of iron. The pain is beyond compare."

Altogether four days passed like this, whereupon the swallowing of iron balls was finally declared finished. Jing went immediately to Huichang and Huadu monasteries, where he repented with utmost sincerity. On the third day of the third month, however, he was seized once again by the previous emissaries and taken before Yama. King Yama said to him, "For your sin of slandering the three jewels you must have your tongue gouged out." Two persons thereupon seized and stretched out his tongue with a pair of tongs. It seemed to extend several hundred *chi* [feet, in length]. Two more persons then appeared. Each holding a knife [in the shape of a] ploughshare, they proceeded to plow its surface. But the interrogating magistrate suddenly interrupted them, saying, "Once this fellow studied the *Lotus* and *Diamond Prajñā* sūtras."

Thus, a short time later, he returned to life. On his tongue his parents and the others around him saw what appeared to be the scores of a knife cut. Because Jing had read the two sūtras, [his tongue] had not been completely cut out. Thereafter, whenever Jing recalled or spoke of [his experiences], he would tremble with fear and break out in tears. Finally he left home as a Buddhist monk and received [the dharma name] of Fayan. His zeal in the practice was double that of the ordinary person. He lived at Baima (White Horse) Monastery in the eastern capital [of Luoyang]. No one knows when and where he died. (42a)

The Buddhist monk Daochao. Nothing is known of his secular background, but on leaving home he took up residence at Qijunshan Monastery and observed the Buddhist practices with utmost purity. He had a disciple named Wangming, who was about fifteen years of age. He set out to memorize the *Lotus Sūtra,* but upon learning the first fascicle he contracted a sudden illness and died. This disciple was particularly zealous in his studies, possessed of both character and spirit, and naturally endowed with human-heartedness and filiality. His master loved him dearly, and from the moment the boy died, he grieved over him day and night.

Qi commandery is not far from the shrine of Mount Tai. Daochao ruminated to himself, "I have often heard it said that, when a person dies, the soul must first pass through [the court of] the Lord of Mount Tai. Only after that is it able to be reborn. Even though the worlds of light and darkness are veiled from one another, a sincere heart will inevitably bring a response. I will try to ask the Lord of Mount Tai. Perhaps he will know where my disciple has been reborn."

So resolved, Daochao took up his mendicant's staff and incense [for offering] and set off for the mountain shrine. There he related in full his reasons for coming, declaring [his intentions] three times before the deity. Suddenly the wooden spirit-tablet spoke out in response, "Since you, master, are completely sincere in your observance of the precepts and your motives for coming here are so grave, I dare not tell you what you wish to know." Thereupon he ordered an attending deity from one of the adjacent placards to summon [the spirit] in charge of [the dead disciple]. The deputy deity thereupon went into a chamber in the eastern wing of the shrine and called for a particular person to come forth. The Lord of Mount Tai then asked, "Where is the disciple Wangming at this moment?" To which the individual replied, "He is being retained here. He does not yet have a place of birth."

Daochao then pleaded to see him, whereupon the Lord [of Mount Tai] had Chao follow the person back to the chamber in the eastern wing. Therein, at a distance of some ten paces away, he saw his disciple. His physical demeanor and clothing were the same as when he was alive. Master and disciple broke out in tears of grief. After a long while, Chao asked the boy, "Is your retribution painful or pleasant?"

The disciple replied, "At the moment I am being held here, so it is neither painful nor pleasant. It is just that my next place of birth has not yet been determined. I desperately need the support of religious merit. If I do not acquire wholesome karmic roots, I fear that I may be reborn in evil realms."

The master asked, "What sort of meritorious acts might I perform to enable you to obtain an illustrious [destiny]?" His disciple replied, "I pray that you might make a single copy of the *Lotus Sūtra* [on my behalf] and hold a vegetarian feast for one hundred monks."

"This can easily be arranged," the master replied.

Thereupon, Daochao parted with the disciple. When he again saw the Lord [of Mount Tai], the Lord asked him what was said during their meeting. The master related how he needed to hold a vegetarian feast and fashion a copy of the sūtra [on his disciple's behalf]. The Lord [of Mount Tai] told him, "Beings in the netherworld are in great need of spiritual merit. You should hasten to take care of this. When the task is completed, you may return to see [your disciple] again."

Chao thereupon returned home, where he immediately prepared paper and brush and hired a person to copy the sūtra. After that, he held a purificatory celebration. With the merit making complete, he returned to the shrine and announced to the Lord [of Mount Tai] that the meritorious work was finished and he had come in search of his disciple. The Lord again ordered his deputy spirit to call [the disciple's] warden. When the person arrived, the Lord asked him, "Is the disciple still here?"

The individual replied, "He has been reborn in a fine place."

"What were the circumstances that brought about this rebirth?" Daochao asked.

The warden replied, "As the copyist began to form the first character *miao*—having finished the *nü* radical but not yet having started on the *shao* part—the disciple in that split instant obtained rebirth."

"Where is he living now?" Chao asked.

The deity replied, "He has been born into the household of Wang Wu of Qi commandery. Wait for another two or three years, and then you may go to look for him."

Chao inscribed the deity's words in his heart, took his leave of the Lord [of Mount Tai], and departed. After three years had passed, he went to the Wang household and asked, "Good almsgiver, you have a little boy. This poor mendicant would like to see him."

The household in question was a truly blessed one, in which they revered the three jewels faithfully. However, hitherto they had been unable to produce a son, as everyone both far and near knew. When this child was later born, [they kept it secret] and did not even tell their relatives about it. Thus, the head of the Wang clan stubbornly refused to admit that they had a son. Chao said to him, "It has been three years now since my disciple was born in your household. Why won't you let me see him?"

Thereupon, Chao related the instructions of the Lord of Mount Tai. Having overheard him from a small side-door to the vestibule, the child's mother told her husband, "If the master has such numinal powers of invocation as this, how can we keep the boy from him?" She then picked up the child and set him down outside the entranceway, at a distance of several meters from Chao. The boy immediately ran to him and threw himself into Chao's embrace. There they remained weeping for a long time. When the child became older he left home and again served Chao as his disciple. This all took place in the fifteenth year of the Kaihuang reign-period [581–600]. No one knows when the master and his disciple passed away. (42c–43a)

VIII. MAKING COPIES OF THE SCRIPTURE

Zhang Wanfu. During the Zhenguan era [of the Tang] [627–650] [Zhang Wanfu] was transferred from the position of governor of Jinzhou to the governorship of Luozhou. By nature he was a crude and wild person, and not particularly reverent when it came to religion. When he first reached his new post he inquired among his attendants as to whether there were any monks within his jurisdiction renowned for their powers of religious cultivation. His attendants replied, "Beyond the city wall there is a bhikṣunī named Miaozhi, who is extraordinarily zealous in her practice. Moreover, she has made a personal copy of the *Lotus Sūtra*, which she keeps devotedly and to which she makes regular offerings, all according to proper ritual procedure. For this she has become famed throughout the suburbs."

At that point Fu asked, "How much expense has gone into making this sūtra?" They replied, "The bhikṣunī has used fifteen hundred duan [pieces, usually of silk]." Wanfu, somewhat taken aback, said, "The best scribes in the capital might use seven or eight duan, at the most, for copying a sūtra. How is it she uses so much? Try to bring the sūtra to me so that I might have a look at it."

The bhikṣunī, upon hearing that the governor sought to borrow her sūtra, stubbornly refused to hand it over, since neither the envoy nor the governor maintained ritual purity or ever observed the purificatory fasts. The governor was enraged at this response and dispatched the envoy again. This time the bhikṣunī did not dare keep the text. She thereupon prepared perfumed water and had the envoy wash himself. She also provided him with a new robe. Only after he put it on did she entrust the sūtra to him. When Wanfu received the sūtra he straightaway took it and opened it, without even bothering to wash his hands. But when he unrolled it, he saw nothing in the scroll but blank yellow paper—not a single word was to be found!

Wanfu exploded with rage, "That old bag! I've lost all patience with her!" So saying, he ordered his subordinate to [seize and] bring the bhikṣunī to him by force. The envoy went to the bhikṣunī and told her, "Master, your scripture is entirely blank. This has made my lord extremely angry and he has ordered me to bring you to him."

The bhikṣunī was seized with terror and completely at a loss as to why this might have happened. Perspiration streamed in torrents from her body. Nonetheless, off she went with the envoy. When they arrived at the administrative offices of the governor she saw a pair of vajra guardians [standing to either side of] the entrance screen, both of whom held out cudgels toward her as though offering her protection. Thus in her heart she felt at ease.

The instant she entered the governor's presence the written text of her sūtra appeared in the air around them, its letters taking on a brilliantly golden hue. Upon seeing the bhikṣunī arrive and the golden letters fill the air, the governor was struck with dread. He arose from his seat and descended the hall. Wailing loudly, with tears of grief streaming down his face, he humbly acknowledged his sins, confessed, and prostrated to her in reverence. Then, turning his heart toward the faith, he vowed to make one thousand copies of the *Lotus* and circulate them throughout the ten directions as a votive offering. Moreover, he personally resolved to keep the sūtra devotedly and never dare to be remiss [in his treatment of it]. He thereupon asked the bhikṣunī what procedure [she used] for making [her copy of] the sūtra.

The bhikṣunī said to him, "When I conceived the desire to make my copy of the sūtra I first planted gu trees in the hills. Everyday I watered them with fragrant water so that they grew steadily. When the trees were mature, I first mixed fragrant water and mud and constructed a room for making the paper. When finished, I collected bark from the trees, hired a craftsman, and in accordance with the proper ritual procedure, purified [the man and the materials] with fragrant water and [had him] make the paper.

"When it was done, I advertised for a scripture copyist who was able to keep [ritual] purity. I did not care whether he was skilled or clumsy, noble or mean. After three years I still had not found such a person. But eventually a scholar from Jiangnan, around twenty-four or -five years of age, wrote me in response to my inquiries.

"For the copy room, once again I mixed perfumed water with mud and went about constructing the room with the greatest purity. When the chamber was finished the copyist changed into a new and purified robe. But, before beginning the task of copying out the text, he maintained a purificatory fast for a period of forty-nine days. After that he began to write. Whenever he passed in and out of the copy room he was required to change his clothing. Only when he had bathed himself did he start to copy. As he wrote, I would kneel before the sūtra in the foreign posture [of adoration]—right knee to the ground—and make offerings with incense censer in hand. When the copyist stopped, I also would stop. And whenever the copyist went to sleep at night, I would arise alone to burn incense and ritually circumambulate the sūtra. This routine I kept up without the slightest lapse. When the sūtra was finished I made splendid accoutrements for it. And, when the ornaments were done, I fashioned special robes for the four members of the Buddhist saṅgha—bhikṣus, bhikṣunīs, laymen, and laywomen—ten sets of each. Whenever people came to use the sūtra—whether it be to read, recite, or copy it—I had them maintain ritual purity for a period of seven days beforehand and gave them these purified robes to wear. Only then would I entrust the sūtra to them. I have kept up this reverence [for the sūtra] without lapse. People far and near respect my efforts, and it has brought them great benefit."

Because of this the governor himself took refuge in the faith, after which people everywhere turned to the *Lotus Sūtra* as their principal form of religious practice. (45a)

Ma Heng was a native of Luoshui in Juzhou. When his mother and father died he built a mourning hut beside their grave site and set out to construct a tumulus of three chambers. For each of them he piled the earth into mounds all by himself. After three years he finally finished. [The tumulus] was quite high, and everyone [who saw it] was overwhelmed [with admiration for his deed].

Whenever Ma Heng bedded down for the night in his hut, a large white snake would slither its way onto the roof and drape its head down over the doorway. When he wanted to go in or out, the snake would draw its head out of the way. This happened with regularity, without the snake ever once making a strike at him. Instead, it seemed to be protecting him. There was also a lone white wolf that could often be seen lurking or dozing near the hut.

Once the tomb was completed, Ma Heng then thought to himself: "Although I have built this tomb for my father and mother, I still have not made any special effort to generate spiritual merits for their departed spirits." Thus he vowed to fashion a copy of the *Lotus Sūtra* in order to provide for them on the journey of their souls. Choosing a clean spot near the tumulus, he sprinkled the ground with perfumed water, gathered seeds of the gu tree and planted them. After they had sprouted and begun to grow, he watered them regularly with perfumed water. When they grew into mature trees, he harvested the bark and made paper according to the prescribed procedure. He also mixed fragrant water with mud to build a small hut by the side of the grave site. Then he invited a copyist to write out the sūtra. [He had the scribe] observe ritual purity and a vegetarian diet, and change his clothing whenever he entered or left [the copy chamber]. In providing offerings of the four items [of food, clothing, bedding, and medicines] he omitted nothing.

When the copying was finished but the sūtra was still awaiting its final decoration, he wrapped the scroll in three layers of paper and placed it on a ledge in the crudely thatched shed [attached to his hut]. During the night a fierce wind and rain suddenly blew up. When daylight arrived, he found that the roof of the shed had been blown off. The thatch itself was nowhere to be seen, and on the floor the water was several feet deep. He could not locate the sūtra anywhere. Two days later, after the water had finally subsided, he found the copied scripture [on the floor of the shed]. Only the first sheet of wrapping was damp. When he reached the second sheet, it was completely dry and clean, without a single blemish—neither damp nor dirtied.

When Ma Heng first lost the sūtra he wailed and worried, fretting over it both day and night. Upon discovering that the sūtra was still there he was overwhelmed with joy at this marvel. Consequently, after he finished decorating the sūtra he made offerings to it constantly. (44c)

Saṅgha

—37—

Daily Life in the Assembly

T. Griffith Foulk

Modern scholars have often presented the history of Buddhism in China in terms of "sinification"—the adaptation to the Chinese cultural milieu of a set of religious beliefs, practices, and social structures that were originally imported from India and Central Asia beginning in the first centuries of the common era. Basic Indian Buddhist beliefs in karma, rebirth, and individual salvation gradually took root in Chinese soil, but only through a process of selection and adaptation in which they were tempered by native cosmologies and beliefs in ancestral spirits. The complex, competing systems of metaphysics, psychology, and soteriology that had emerged from the Indian Buddhist scholastic tradition of analysis were even more difficult for the Chinese to grasp and accept; the process of translating, interpreting, and assimilating them eventually gave rise to new and distinctively Chinese schools of Buddhist thought. It was in the sphere of social organization and mores, however, that the Indian Buddhist model—that of a community of monks and nuns who had "gone forth from the world" to seek salvation—appeared most alien to the Chinese.

The difficulties that beset the establishment of Buddhist monastic institutions in China were formidable. In the first place, there was the problem of learning just what the "orthodox" standards of behavior were for monks and nuns. No complete recensions of the Indian vinaya, or rules of discipline for individuals and monastic communities, were translated into Chinese until the beginning of the fifth century. Well before that time a number of canonical and paracanonical vinaya texts were known to Chinese, and foreign monks had served as role models for the Buddhist monastic life in China, but the leaders of Chinese monastic communities were often forced to improvise rules. Daoan (312–385 C.E.), for example, produced a set of "Standards for Monks and Nuns" to supplement those parts of the vinaya that were not known to him.

When complete recensions of the Indian vinaya did become available in Chinese, there were many problems in interpreting and applying them. For one thing, they presented a profusion of technical terminology, which was often simply transliterated. Some of the specific rules set forth in translations of the vinaya, moreover, were incomprehensible or inapplicable due to cultural and geographic differences between India and China. To make matters worse, different recensions of the vinaya sometimes disagreed on specific procedural points. In response to these difficulties, a number of schools of vinaya exegesis arose in China, and many commentaries were produced. The most long-lived and influential exegetical tradition was the so-called Nanshan school that was based on the *Guide to the Practice of the Four-Part Vinaya* and other commentaries by Daoxuan (596–667), who came to be regarded as the founder of the school.

Finally, the establishment and spread of Buddhist monastic institutions in China was constrained throughout history, to varying degrees, by opposition from the Confucian elite and from the imperial government. Certain features of Buddhist monastic life, such as the principle of celibacy or that of subsisting on alms donated by the laity, were bitterly attacked as inimical to native Chinese values. The conception of the Buddhist saṅgha as a sacred community essentially independent of secular rule, regulated by its own distinct body of regulations laid down by the Buddha, was also perceived as a threat to the authority of the emperor and the sanctity of the imperial state.

Despite all these difficulties, the Buddhist monastic institution did manage to take root and flourish in Chinese society, and to maintain its distinct identity as an establishment ostensibly founded and sanctioned by the Buddha Śākyamuni. Given the pressures to conform to Chinese cultural norms, it is remarkable that so many features of the Indian monastic model survived in China.

The late Tang and Five Dynasties (907–960) periods represent a watershed in the history of Chinese Buddhism. The harsh suppression of Buddhism that was carried out by imperial decree during the Huichang period of the Tang (841–846), followed by the social and political chaos associated with the breakup of the imperial state, dealt the monastic institution a severe blow that it only recovered from when relative peace and unity were restored under the Song. One of the salient features of the restored institution was its domination by monks who presented themselves as members and followers of an elite lineage of dharma transmission—known variously as the Chan lineage, Buddha Mind lineage, and the lineage of Bodhidharma—which they claimed was traceable back to the Buddha Śākyamuni in India. The Chan school was so successful in promulgating its ideology and mythology that many large, state supported monasteries were designated by imperial decree in the Song as Chan monasteries, that is, establishments where the abbacies were restricted to monks certified as dharma heirs in the Chan lineage. The Chan school's main competition was from the Tiantai school, which succeeded in having a lesser number of abbacies reserved for itself. One result of this situation was that most of the saṅgha regulations compiled in the Song and later were nominally rules for Chan monasteries, although there were also nearly identical rules compiled for use in Teachings (Tiantai) monasteries and vinaya monasteries.

One of the recurrent themes that one finds in modern as well as traditional writings on the history of Chan Buddhism is the idea that the Chan school developed a unique, independent system of monastic training that allowed it to exist apart from the mainstream of Chinese Buddhist monastic institutions. According to the traditional account, this development was instigated by the Chan master Baizhang Huaihai (749–814), who is credited with founding the first Chan monastery and authoring the first Chan monastic rules (known generically as *qinggui* or "rules of purity"). Modern historians of Chan have generally accepted the traditional account, although some have assumed that independent Chan monasteries must have come into existence even before Baizhang, and others have argued that Baizhang was not so much an actual founder as a symbol, projected retrospectively, of the development of independent Chan institutions that took place in his day.

In point of fact, there is very scant historical evidence to support either the traditional account of the founding of the Chan monastic institution in the Tang dynasty or any of the modern revisions of that account. The biographies and epigraphs memorializing Baizhang that were written closest to his lifetime say nothing about the founding of an independent Chan school monastery. Nor is there mention of such monasteries, whether associated with Baizhang or not, in any other sources dating from the Tang or earlier. The oldest historical source which indicates that there were independent Chan monasteries in the Tang is a brief text known as the *Regulations of the Chan School* (*Chanmen guishi*), the same work that was responsible for establishing Baizhang's place in history as the putative founding father of the Chan monastic institution. It was written during the last quarter of the tenth century, more than 150 years after Baizhang's death.

The oldest extant Chan monastic rule is the *Rules of Purity for Chan Monasteries* (*Chanyuan qinggui*), compiled in 1103. The text sets guidelines for many aspects of monastic life and training, including the qualifications and duties of major and minor monastic officers, ritual procedures for numerous ceremonies and religious practices, and rules concerning deportment and etiquette. The table of contents reads as follows:

> Fascicle One: Receiving the Precepts; Upholding the Precepts; A Monk's Personal Implements; Contents of a Wandering Monk's Pack; Staying Overnight in a Monastery; Procedures for Morning and Midday Meals; Procedures for Having Tea or Hot Water; Requesting a Sermon from the Abbot; Entering the Abbot's Room for Individual Instruction
>
> Fascicle Two: Large Assemblies in the Dharma Hall; Recitation of Buddha Names [in the Saṅgha hall]; Small Assemblies [in the abbot's quarters]; Opening the Summer Retreat; Closing the Summer Retreat; Winter Solstice and New Year's Salutations; Inspection of the Various Quarters [by the abbot]; Entertaining Eminent Visitors; Appointing Stewards
>
> Fascicle Three: Controller; Rector; Cook; Labor Steward; Retirement of Stewards; Appointing Prefects; Chief Seat; Scribe; Sūtra Prefect

Fascicle Four: Guest Prefect; Prior; Bath Prefect; Solicitors of Provisions; Water Chief; Charcoal Manager; Decorations Chief; Mill Chief; Garden Chief; Manager of Estate Lands; Manager of Business Cloister; Manager of Infirmary; Chief of Toilets; [Buddha] Hall Prefect; Chief of Bell Tower; Holy Monk's Attendant; Chief of Lamps; Watchman on Duty in Saṅgha Hall; Common Quarters Manager; Common Quarters Chief Seat; Abbot's Quarters Acolytes

Fascicle Five: Traveling Evangelist; Retirement of Prefects; Abbot's Tea Service; Tea Service in Saṅgha Hall; Stewards' and Prefects' Tea Service; Tea Service for Assigning Places in the Common Quarters on the Basis of Seniority; Special Tea Service Sponsored by the Great Assembly of Monks; Special Tea Service for Venerable Elders Sponsored by the Great Assembly of Monks

Fascicle Six: Special Tea Service for the Abbot Sponsored by His Disciples and Trainees; Procedure for Burning Incense in Connection with a Tea Service for the Great Assembly of Monks; Serving a Specially Sponsored Meal; Thanking the Sponsor of a Tea Service; Sūtra Reading Ceremony; Special Feasts; Going Out [for a feast at a sponsor's] and Bringing In [the sponsor of a feast held in a monastery]; Signaling Activities for the Great Assembly of Monks [with bells, drums, wooden clappers, etc.]; Formal Decrees [by the abbot]; Sending out Correspondence; Receiving Correspondence; Sick Leave and Returning to Duty

Fascicle Seven: Using the Toilet; Funeral for a Monk; Appointing Retired Officers [as advisors / assistants]; Appointing an Abbot; Installing an Abbot; The Ideal Abbot; Funeral for an Abbot; Retirement of an Abbot

Fascicle Eight: Admonition [behavior models for monastery officers]; Instructions for Sitting Meditation; Essay on Self-Discipline; 120 Questions [for testing one's spiritual progress]; Disciplining Novices

Fascicle Nine: Liturgy for Novice Ordinations; Regulating Postulants; Guiding Lay Believers; Procedure for Feasting Monks; Verse Commentary on Baizhang's Rules

Within a century of its compilation in 1103, the *Rules of Purity for Chan Monasteries* had gained a wide circulation and become the de facto standard for all major monasteries in China. It was also an important vehicle for the spread of Song-style Buddhist institutions outside of China. For example, both Eisai (1141–1215) and Dōgen (1200–1253), famous Japanese monk pilgrims to China, quoted the *Rules of Purity for Chan Monasteries* frequently in their writings and used it as a basis for establishing what became known as the Zen monastic institution in Japan. The text was also transmitted to Korea. It was reedited (with new material added) and reprinted a number of times, with the result that it survives today in several different recensions.

The second oldest set of Chan monastic rules that survives today is the *Daily Life in the Assembly* (*Ruzhong riyong*), also known as the *Chan Master Wuliang Shou's Short Rules of Purity for Daily Life in the Assembly* (*Wuliang shou chanshi riyong qinggui*). The text was written in 1209 by Wuliang Zongshou, who at the time held the office of chief seat in a Chan monastery. Unlike the *Rules of Purity for Chan Monasteries,* the *Daily Life in the Assembly* was not intended to regulate all aspects of monastery life. Rather, it comprised a very detailed set of rules for the so-called "great assembly" of monks who had no administrative duties and thus were free to concentrate mainly on a daily routine of meditation, study, and devotions. As chief seat, Wuliang Zongshou was the monastic officer in charge of leading the monks of the great assembly in all of their activities. He stated deferentially in his colophon that he wrote the text for the benefit of monks first joining the great assembly, not for old hands. He also explained that he did not treat a number of activities in which the great assembly participated—including "large assemblies in the [dharma] hall, entering the [abbot's] room, small assemblies, chanting sūtras, reciting buddha names, inspecting [monastery] offices, rituals for opening and closing retreats, packing the knapsacks and donning the bamboo hat [for pilgrimage], and sending off deceased monks and auctioning off their belongings"—because detailed rules for those activities were "already included in the *Rules of Purity.*" The *Rules of Purity* that Zongshou referred to in the colophon was almost certainly the *Rules of Purity for Chan Monasteries,* for most of the activities mentioned are in fact the topics of sections of that text (see the table of contents above). Actually, some of the activities that the *Daily Life in the Assembly* does treat, such as procedures for taking meals on the platforms in the saṅgha hall and going to the toilet, are also covered in the *Rules of Purity for Chan Monasteries,* but they are scattered throughout that much longer text. The virtue of the *Daily Life in the Assembly* was that it brought together, in convenient handbook form, detailed procedures and admonitions for the activities that the monks of the great assembly engaged in most frequently. The activities that Zongshou explicitly left out, it should be cautioned, were not necessarily less important in the lives of the great assembly; indeed, they may well have been experienced as more significant. However, because they were on the order of special ceremonies rather than daily routine, the ritual procedures involved could be learned when the occasions arose, and need not have been mastered immediately by monks entering the great assembly.

Chan monasteries in Song China, following a pattern established long before the emergence of the Chan school, were organized in a way that allowed a group of monks (the so-called "great assembly") to engage in meditation and other religious practices for a three-month long retreat without having to concern themselves with practical affairs such as the provision of food or shelter. Basically, the monasteries were divided into two sectors: a practice wing, which housed the monks of the great assembly and the officers who led them, and an administrative wing, which provided living and working places for the monk officers and lay postulants and servants who handled meals, finances, supplies, building maintenance, guests, and numerous other tasks necessary for the operation of a large institution. In order to understand the physical setting that the *Daily Life in the Assembly* takes for granted, therefore, it is only necessary for us to consider the facilities that made up the practice wing, that is, the buildings that were home base to the great assembly.

The facility mentioned most often in the *Daily Life in the Assembly* is the saṅgha hall (sometimes translated "monks' hall"). Saṅgha halls were large buildings divided internally into an inner and outer hall. The inner hall was further divided into an upper and lower section, one being located in front and the other to the rear of a large central altar bearing an image of the "holy monk"—the bodhisattva Mañjuśrī dressed in monk's robes. Mañjuśrī was the tutelary deity who watched over the saṅgha hall, its occupants, and their spiritual endeavors, and was the object of regular devotional worship with offerings of incense and prostrations before his altar. The inner hall was outfitted with low, wide platforms arranged in several blocks in the middle of the floor and along the walls. Individual places on the platforms were assigned in order of seniority, based on time elapsed since ordination. It was on the platforms that the monks of the great assembly spent much of their time, sitting in meditation, taking the morning and midday meals, and lying down for a few hours of sleep at night. Their bowls were hung above their seats, their sleeping mattresses were kept on the platforms, and their other personal effects and monkish implements were stored in boxes at the rear of the platforms. The outer hall was outfitted with narrower platforms suitable for meditation and taking meals, but not for sleeping. They were mainly for use by officers of the administrative wing, novices, and other persons who did not belong to the great assembly.

Another facility referred to frequently in the *Daily Life in the Assembly* is the common quarters. Located near the saṅgha halls, common quarters were arranged internally in much the same way, with platforms on which the monks of the great assembly were seated in order of seniority, and a central altar with an image, usually Avalokiteśvara. The main difference was that the platforms in common quarters were equipped with tables for studying sūtras and writing, activities that were forbidden in the saṅgha hall. The common quarters were also used for drinking tea and medicinal potions, and for taking evening meals, which were referred to euphemistically as "medicine" (because the vinaya forbids eating after midday). Other facilities mentioned in the text are the washstands that were located behind the saṅgha hall, the toilet, bathhouse, laundry place, and hearth. All of these served the daily needs of the great assembly and thus were treated by Zongshou in his rules.

As he leads his readers through a typical day's activities for monks of the great assembly, Zongshou frequently backs up his own formulation of particular procedures and admonitions with what appear to be legitimizing quotations from a preexisting text. The quotations, which all begin "of old it was said," typically repeat points that Zongshou himself has just made. When this stylistic feature is coupled with the claim made by Zongshou in his preface, that he has "collected the standards produced by Baizhang, and has studied them thoroughly from beginning to end," the reader is left with the impression that Zongshou is actually quoting a work by Baizhang himself. In point of fact, as is explained above, no such work was available to Zongshou. I have not been able to trace more than a few of the quotations, but even that is enough to show that they derive from a number of different sources, none of which is attributable directly to Baizhang. When Zongshou speaks of "Baizhang's standards," therefore, what he means is the *Rules of Purity for Chan Monasteries* and perhaps other contemporary monastic rules (now lost) that likewise claimed to preserve Baizhang's heritage.

It is also worth noting that the *Daily Life in the Assembly* evinces a tremendous concern with "impurity" and "purity." It is tempting to see in this a concern for hygiene that would have made good, practical sense in any institution with communal facilities, but there is more to it than that. A number of rules speak not only of avoiding the contamination of neighbors' bowls, wash buckets, and so on, but of avoiding the communication of impurities from social juniors to their seniors. For example, one rule stipulates that the end of chopsticks and spoons that goes in one's mouth (and hence is polluted by saliva) must always point toward the right (where one's juniors sit) when the utensils are set down on the platform. In this respect, the *Daily Life in the Assembly* sounds very Indian, and even cites a passage to the effect that distinctions of senior and junior are necessary when brahmans gather (typically in a line) to take a meal together. The designation of the two smallest fingers of the left hand as "impure" because they are used in the toilet is also an Indian custom. At the time when Chan monastic rules were taking shape in the late tenth and eleventh centuries, there was in fact an upsurgence of interest in Indian Buddhism. Sanskrit studies were revived in China, delegations of monks were sent to India, and a number of Indian monks were received as honored guests and scholars in residence by Chinese rulers. Although Chan rules are often held up by modern scholars as epitomizing the sinification of Buddhist monasticism, the evidence of the *Daily Life in the Assembly* suggests that there may have been considerable Indian influence on Chan monasteries in the Song.

The *Daily Life in the Assembly* was originally composed as a handbook for monks newly entered into the "great assembly," but the text proved so useful that it was later incorporated into full-scale monastic rules such as the *Zongli jiaoding qinggui Zongyao*, compiled in 1274, the *Chanlin beiyong qinggui*, compiled in 1317, and the *Chixiu baizhang qinggui*, completed in 1343. Much later, in Tokugawa-period (1603–1868) Japan, the text was widely studied and commented on by both Rinzai and Sōtō Zen monks who were striving to revive Song-style communal monastic practice. That, and the similarity of many of the rules with ones laid down by Dōgen in his *Shōbōgenzō* and *Eihei shingi*, accounts for the remarkable congruence between the procedures explained in the *Daily Life in the Assembly* and those followed in contemporary Zen monastic training.

The translation is from *Dai Nippon zokuzōkyō*, 2–16–5. 472a–474b.

Daily Life in the Assembly

Having left the dust [of the world] and separated from the vulgar, we shaven-headed and square-robed [Buddhist monks], for the most part, spend our lives in monasteries. The first requirement [of monastic life] is to understand the rules clearly. If one has not yet memorized the regulations with regard to conduct, then one's actions will not be in accord with the ritual restraints. If even one's good friends and benevolent advisors do not have the heart to severely reprimand and harshly criticize, and if one continues on with one's bad habits, then reform is extremely difficult. In the end this [behavior] will bring desolation upon the monasteries, and induce negligence in peoples' minds. Because I frequently see such transgressions and evils, which are commonplace before my very eyes, I have collected the standards [for behavior] produced by Baizhang, and have studied them thoroughly from beginning to end. From morning to night, to avoid every particular offense, one must straightaway obey every single provision. Only after that may one presume to say that one has investigated the self, illumined the mind, understood birth, and penetrated death. Worldly dharmas are [ultimately] identical with supraworldly dharmas, but those who are on pilgrimage [monks] can nevertheless set a precedent for those who are not yet on pilgrimage [the laity]. May we not forsake the body and mind of monkhood, and may we together humbly repay the blessings of the buddhas and patriarchs.

Respectfully submitted.

RULES FOR [MONKS] IN THE ASSEMBLY

Do not go to sleep before others, or rise later than others. You should quietly get up before the bell of the fifth watch. Take your pillow and place it under your legs, but without folding it, lest the noise startle [the people at] the neighboring places [on the platform in the saṅgha hall]. Rouse your spirit, draw the blanket around your body and sit up straight, without fanning up a breeze that would cause peoples' thoughts to stir. If you feel sleepy, you may instead take the blanket and place it at your feet, turn your body, pick up your hand cloth and get down from the platform. With the cloth draped over your left hand, mentally recite the following verse:

> From the wee hours of dawn straight through to dusk,
> I will make way for all living beings.
> If any of them should lose their bodily form under my feet,
> I pray that they may immediately be born in the pure land.

Quietly push the [saṅgha hall doorway] screen aside with your hand, and exit to the wash stand. Do not drag your footwear, and do not make a noise by coughing. Of old it was said,

> When pushing aside the curtain, one's rear hand should hang at one's side; when exiting the hall, it is strictly forbidden to drag one's footwear.

Quietly take a basin in hand and wash your face, without using much water.

When using tooth powder, take a single dab with your right hand and rub the left side [of your mouth], and take a single dab with your left hand and rub the right side. Do not allow either hand to dip [into the powder] twice, lest there be drainage from the teeth or mouth infections passed to other people. When rinsing your mouth and spitting out water, you must lower your head and use your hands to draw [the water] down. Do not stand with the waist straight and spit water, splashing it into the neighboring basins.

Do not wash the head. There are four reasons why this is harmful to self and others. First, it dirties the basin, and second, it dirties the [public] hand cloth: these are the things harmful to others. Third, it dries out the hair, and fourth, it injures the eyes: these are the things harmful to self.

Do not make sounds within one's nostrils. Do not make loud noises clearing one's throat. Of old it was said,

> The fifth-watch face washing is fundamentally for the sake of religious practice. Clearing one's throat and dragging one's bowl [sic] make the hall noisy and disturb the assembly.

Having wiped your face, return to the [saṅgha] hall. If you are in the upper section, enter with your left foot first. If you are in the lower section, enter with your right foot first. When you get back to your blanket place, take your sleeping mattress, fold it in half, and sit in meditation.

If you change your outer robe, you must take the new one and put it around your body first. Do not expose yourself, and do not fan up a breeze.

Burning incense and making prostrations are suitable in the time before the bell rings. To don the kāṣāya [formal robe symbolic of monkhood], first recite the following verse with your palms joined and the kāṣāya resting on your head:

> Wonderful indeed is the garment of liberation,
> the robe of the signless field of merit.
> I now receive it on my head;
> may I be able to wear it always, in all worlds [of rebirth].

To fold the kāṣāya, first fold the place where it hangs on your arm, and then release the ring. Do not use your mouth to hold the kāṣāya. Do not use your chin to hold up the kāṣāya. When you have finished folding it you should bow with palms joined and proceed.

Just as when making prostrations in the various halls [such as the buddha hall or dharma hall], do not take a place in the center [of the saṅgha hall] that interferes with the abbot's coming. Do not make any sound reciting the Buddha's name. Do not walk through the area around other peoples' heads [when they are making prostrations]. Walk behind them [not between them and the image they are bowing to].

When the bell signaling the fifth watch rings, and the abbot and the chief seat are sitting in the hall, do not go out or in the front entrance.

At the preliminary signal for rising, immediately fold your blanket and gather up your pillow. The method for folding the blanket is first to find the two corners, and stretch them out with your hands. Fold it in half twice, once to the front, and then back toward your body. Do not turn it horizontally, obstructing the neighboring places. Do not shake it out and make a noise, and do not create a breeze with the blanket.

[Next] you may return to the common quarters and drink medicinal tea, or walk about in the tea hall.

When proceeding in a line back to your bowl place [in the saṅgha hall], you must follow the person [who sits] above you [on the platform]. When turning, do not turn your back toward others. If using the front entrance, enter on the south side. Do not walk on the north side or the middle, out of respect for the abbot. After the wooden fish has sounded, do not enter the hall. Either have a postulant fetch your bowl [from your place on the platform] and sit in the outer hall [to eat], or return to the common quarters. Having entered the hall and returned to your bowl place, humble yourself and bow with palms joined to [the persons at] the upper, middle, and lower seats. If you are already seated first, when the [persons on] the upper, middle, and lower seats arrive, you should have palms joined. Of old it was said,

> If one does not pay one's respects to the upper, middle, and lower seats, then there are no distinctions in a gathering of brahmans.

When you hear the long sounding of the [signal] board, take down your bowls. When raising your body, get up straight and stand still. Only then may you turn your body, making sure to follow the person above you [on the platform]. [Gesture with] palms joined and then take your bowls. One hand holds the bowls while the other hand releases the hook; the left hand holds [the bowls]. With the left hand holding [the bowls], turn your body. Lower your body in a proper crouch, and set down the bowls. Avoid bumping into others with your hips or back.

When the bell in front of the hall sounds, get down from the platform and bow with palms joined. This is for receiving the abbot. Do not wave your hands left and right. When you have gotten off the platform, step forward and bow with palms joined. Do not allow your kāṣāya to rest on the edge of the platform. Always lower it carefully.

When getting up onto the platform, do not move abruptly. Take the bowl and place it in front of your seat. When you hear the sound of the mallet, with palms joined silently recite the following verse:

> The Buddha was born in Kapilavastu;
> He gained enlightenment in Magadha;
> He preached the dharma in Varanasi;
> And entered nirvāṇa in Kuśinagara.

RULES FOR SETTING OUT BOWLS

First silently recite the following verse with palms joined:

I am now able to set out
The Tathāgata's bowls.
May I, together with all beings,
Be equal in the threefold emptiness [of giving].

Having finished the verse, remove the [bowls'] wrapping cloth. Spread this pure cloth out to cover your lap. The cloth is folded back on itself so that three edges are tucked under. Do not allow it to extend beyond your place [on the platform]. Spread out the bowl mat. Using the left hand, take the bowls, and place them on the mat. Using both thumbs, remove the bowls and set them out in order, beginning with the smallest. Do not knock them together and make a noise. Always hold back your fourth and fifth fingers; as impure fingers, they are not to be used. When folding the bowl rag, make it small. Set it down horizontally in line with the spoon and chopsticks bag, near your body. When putting them in [the bag], the spoon goes first. When taking them out, the chopsticks are first. The place where your hand grasps [the utensils] is called the "pure place" and should be pointed toward the person on your left [above you on the platform]. The swab should be placed in the second gap between the bowls, sticking out just half an inch.

When gathering up the spirit rice [the offering to hungry ghosts], do not use your spoon or chopsticks to remove it [from your bowl]. The spirit rice should not exceed seven grains, but if it is too little, that is being stingy with food.

When joining the palms while the rector chants the Buddhas' names, the fingers of the hands should not be separated. You should adjust your hands to the height of your chest. Do not let your fingers touch the area around your mouth. Of old it was said,

> Having unevenly joined palms, not aligning [the hands] with one's chest, intertwining the ten fingers, sticking them into one's nose, dragging one's sandals, lifting the [saṅgha hall] curtain, lacking courtesy, clearing one's throat, and sighing are disrespectful.

Lift the bowl with both hands to receive the food, and silently recite the following verse:

Upon receiving this food,
I pray that living beings
shall have as food the bliss of dhyāna,
and be filled to satiation with joy in the dharma.

Raise your right hand to stop [the server] when the [desired] amount of food has been received. When you hear the hammer signaling eating, look above and below you [on the platform]. Then, looking straight at it, lift your food. Do not, when you are facing forward, swing your hands to either side. Having lifted the bowl, make five reflections and silently recite:

> First, considering how much effort went into [producing] it, I reflect on where this [food] came from.
>
> Second, I consider whether my own virtue and practice are worthy of this offering [of food I am about to eat].
>
> Third, I take restraining the mind and forsaking my faults, such as greed and the rest, as the essential thing.
>
> Fourth, in principle [this food] is like good medicine, to keep my body from withering away.
>
> Fifth, I should receive this food for the sake of the work of attaining enlightenment.

Put out the spirit [rice] and chant the following verse:

> You host of spirits,
> I now give you an offering.
> May this food reach to
> all the spirits in the ten directions.

RULES FOR EATING

Bring the food to your mouth; do not bring your mouth to the food. When taking up your bowl, putting down your bowl, and the spoon and chopsticks as well, do not make any noise. Do not cough. Do not blow your nose. If you have to sneeze, you should cover your nose with the sleeve of your robe. Do not scratch your head, lest dandruff fall into your neighbor's bowl. Do not pick your teeth with your hand. Do not make noise chewing your food or slurping soup. Do not clear out rice from the center of your bowl, and do not make big balls of food. Do not extend your lips to receive food. Do not spill food. Do not use your hands to pick up scattered food. If there are inedible vegetable parts, leave them out of sight behind the bowl. Do not make a breeze that fans your neighbor's place. If you are worried about flatulence, tell the rector and sit in the outer hall. Do not rest your hands on your knees. Judge the amount when you take your food, and do not ask to throw any away. Do not fill your largest bowl with moist food. Do not use soup to clean rice out from your largest bowl. Do not wipe vegetables in your largest bowl and eat them together with the rice. During the meal, you must observe those above and below you [on the platform]. Do not be too slow, and do not swab out your bowl before seconds are offered.

Do not make any noise licking your bowl swab. When the mealtime has not yet arrived, do not give rise to greedy thoughts. Of old it was said,

> To look within grumblingly and give rise to regret and anger; to think of food and salivate; to cough; to spill gruel in one's haste [to eat]; to slurp

soup; to stuff one's mouth full; to disturb those on the neighboring seats when opening up the place mat and setting out the bowls . . .

To wash your bowls, take the largest bowl and fill it with water; then wash the other bowls in order [of size]. Do not wash the spoon, chopsticks, or smaller bowls in the largest bowl. Again, bend back your fourth and fifth fingers. Do not make any noise rinsing the mouth. Do not spit water back into the bowls. Do not fill the bowls with boiled water before washing them. When the [bowl-washing] water has not yet been collected, do not put away your lap covering cloth. Do not use the lap cloth to wipe sweat. Do not pour the leftover water on the ground. Silently recite the verse for pouring off the [wash] water:

> I now take this bowl-washing water,
> Which has a flavor like heavenly ambrosia,
> and give it to you spirits.
> May all achieve satiation.
> An mo xin luo xi suoke!

When putting away the bowls, use the thumbs of both hands to arrange them in order, then place them in the wrapping cloth.

When finished, with palms joined silently recite the verse following the meal:

> Having finished the meal, our countenance and energy are restored. We are [like] heroes whose majesty shakes the ten directions and the three times. It reverses causes and turns around effects without conscious effort, and all living beings gain supernatural powers.

When the board in front of the [common] quarters sounds, return to the quarters and bow with palms joined. Not to return is called "insulting the great assembly." The procedures for entering the door and returning to one's place are the same as in the saṅgha hall. Stand still and wait for the quarters manager to finish burning incense; then bow with palms joined to those above and below [on the platform].

If there is tea, take your seat. Do not let your robes dangle. Do not gather together and talk and laugh. Do not bow to [greet] people with one hand. Do not hoard tea leaves. Of old it was said,

> When mounting the platform and sitting in rest, it is not allowed to dangle one's robe. How could it be proper to bow with one hand [instead of with palms joined]? Privately stashing powdered tea, eliciting smiles . . .

When looking on [at a text], students who are next to each other at the tables are strictly forbidden to put their heads together and chat.

When the tea is finished, if you read sūtras, do not unfold the sūtra to a great length. That is to say, only two pages [of the accordion-folded text may be open]. Do not walk about the quarters with a sūtra in your hand. Do not allow the sūtra cord [used to tie the text when folded up] to dangle. Do not make any noise. Of old it was said,

> To make a noise holding and chanting [sūtras] is to offend people around you, and to rest one's back on the board is to be disrespectful to the great assembly.

Leave the quarters beforehand; do not wait for the board signaling sitting meditation [in the saṅgha hall] to sound.

If you need to go to the toilet, then [according to] the old custom, you wear your five-section robe. Take the pure cloth [used to cover the kāṣāya] and hang it over your left hand. [In the toilet changing room] release your sash, and tie it to the bamboo pole. Take off your short kāṣāya and outer robe, arrange them neatly, and bind them with the hand cloth. Then tie the hand cloth [to the pole so that the bundle hangs down] a foot or more. Make sure you remember [which bundle is yours]. Do not talk or laugh. Do not, from outside, importune others [to hurry and make room for you in the toilet].

Take some water in your left hand and put it in the privy. When changing shoes [prior to entering the stall], do not allow a gap between them [that is, line up the ones you have removed neatly]. Set the pure bucket in front of you and snap your fingers three times to frighten off the feces-eating spirits. When you squat, your body must be upright. Do not make a noise exerting. Do not blow your nose. Do not chat with people on the other side of the partition. Of old it was said,

> When the door is shut, just lightly snap your fingers. Even if people are concealed, who would be so bold as to shamelessly make a noise?

Upon entering the [clean-up] place, use a wiping block. Keep the used and clean ones separate. When you come out, you must have water. Do not splash water all around. Do not use water to wash both sides [of the wiping block]. Wash [the block] with your left hand, holding back the thumb and the two fingers next to it. Do not use many wiping blocks. Of old it was said,

> Use but a little warm water for washing, and refrain from taking up [too many] wiping blocks.

There are those who, when they have finished using [a block] wash it with water and set it aside in some vacant place, thereby disturbing many persons in the assembly.

It is not good to linger for long [in the toilet]. The pure bucket should be put back in its original place. Using your dry hand arrange your five-section robe, and tuck it into your breeches. Use your dry hand to open the door. Use your right hand to lift the bucket, and leave. Do not use a wet hand to grasp the leaf of the door or the door frame. With the right hand, pick out [from the container] some ashes, and afterwards pick out some earth. Do not use the wet hand to pick up ashes or earth. Do not spit out saliva and mix it together with the earth. Only after washing the hands should you use "black horn" [pod soap powder] to wash. Wash up to the elbow. You should keep your mind focused at all times on the dhāraṇī [incantation] of entering the toilet. Use water to wash the hands and rinse the mouth. In the vinaya, these purifications also apply to urinating. Next, chew on a willow twig.

Return to the [saṅgha] hall for sitting meditation before the fire board [signaling the preparation of the meal] has sounded. Do not return to the [common] quarters first.

Before the midday meal, do not wash your robes. Do not open your platform box before the morning or midday meal, or after the release from practice. If there is some pressing need, tell the officer in charge. In the [common] quarters, tell the quarters manager. In the [saṅgha] hall, tell the holy monk's attendant.

When the midday meal is over in the saṅgha hall, do not put your heads together and chat. Do not read sūtras or [secular] books in the saṅgha hall. Do not make circumambulations between the upper and lower sections of the hall. Do not pass through the hall as a shortcut [to get somewhere else]. Do not string cash on your seat. Do not sit with your legs dangling off the front of the platform.

A space one foot wide along the front of the platform is called the "area of threefold purity," [because it is the place for] 1. setting out bowls, 2. resting the kāṣāya, and 3. is the direction in which the head points [when sleeping]. Do not walk on the platform. Do not kneel to open the platform box. Do not step on the platform edge when climbing down to the floor. When wearing straw sandals and the five-section robe [that is, the robe for use in the toilet, bath, and manual labor] going about the monastery, do not pass through the buddha hall or dharma hall. Of old it was said,

> When entering the halls with the folded kāṣāya on one's shoulder, and when wearing straw sandals to go about the monastery, do not set foot in the dharma hall.

Make way for venerable elders [when going about the monastery]. Do not wear monkish shoes over bare feet. Do not hold hands [with another person] when walking, or discuss worldly matters. Of old it was said,

> What was your purpose in separating from your parents, leaving your ordination teacher and seeking the instruction of a wise master? If you have not discussed and grasped the essential matters of our school, and if when your hair is white you still have no attainment, whose fault will it be?

Do not lean on the railings in front of the halls. Do not run about in wild haste. Of old it was said,

> When going about, one should walk slowly; learn from the dignified manners of Aśvajit. When speaking, one's voice should be low; learn from the standards set by Upāli.

Do not go for leisure to the buddha hall. Of old it was said,

> One should not, for no purpose, go up into the treasure hall [buddha hall]; one must not, for leisure, go into a stūpa. If one sweeps the ground or gives perfumed water without reason, then even though there be merit as numerous as the sands of the river [Ganges], it comes to naught.

When starching garments after the midday meal, do not bare your left shoulder. Do not upset the hot water jug when dipping your robes. When you are done using the bamboo poles [for drying] and the flat-iron, put them back in their original places.

When the board signaling foot-washing sounds, do not fight to snatch the foot bucket. If you have boils or itches, then you should dip and wash [your feet] after the others have finished, or take the bucket to some screened-off place and wash. Avoid disgusting others in the assembly. Do not wait for the striking of the board signaling sitting in the [saṅgha] hall, but go back into the hall as soon as you are done and sit in meditation.

When release from practice [is signaled], take the sleeping mattress and spread it out [folded] in half. When the board in front of the [common] quarters sounds, immediately turn your body and face outward.

You must attend [the meal] with the assembly when the time arrives. While the small board is sounding, do not enter the [saṅgha] hall, and do not stand in the outer hall. When the abbot and chief seat leave the hall, open up the mattress, get down from the platform, bow with palms joined, and return to the [common] quarters.

For the evening meal, when each person is at their own table place [in the common quarters], do not be the first to rise and fill [your bowl] with food. Do not make a loud noise shouting for gruel, rice, salt, vinegar, and the like. When the meal is over and you exit the quarters, do not leave the monastery grounds, and do not go into the officers' rooms. Do not return to the saṅgha hall or walk around the corridors with your kāṣāya folded and resting on your left shoulder. Do not wait for the striking of the board to leave the quarters.

When the evening bell sounds, with palms joined recite the following verse:

> Upon hearing the bell,
> Vexations are lightened;
> Wisdom is strengthened,
> Bodhi is produced;
> We escape from hell,
> Leaving the fiery pit.
> May I attain buddhahood,
> And save living beings.

You should first return to your place [in the saṅgha hall] and sit in meditation. Do not scratch your head when on the platform. Do not make a noise fingering your prayer beads on the platform. Do not talk with your neighbors on the platform. If your neighbor is remiss, you should use kind words to help him; do not give rise to a resentful, bad state of mind.

When the bell signaling time for sleep has yet to ring, do not go out or in the front entrance [of the saṅgha hall]. When the time of the sounding of the fire [watchman's] bell has passed, then the chief seat may permit the "unfolding of pillows" [that is, going to sleep].

To burn incense and make prostrations [at the saṅgha hall altar], you must wait until late at night. When the members of the assembly are not yet asleep, do not be the first to sleep; but when the members of the assembly have not yet gotten up [for additional meditation or devotions], you should get up before them. When you arise and sit, do not startle and rouse the people at neighboring places.

When sleeping, you should be on your right side. Do not sleep facing upward [that is, on your back]. Facing upward is called "the sleep of a corpse," and facing downward is called "lewd sleep." [With these incorrect postures] there are many evil dreams. Use your pure cloth to wrap your kāṣāya and place it in front of your pillow. Nowadays many people place it at their feet. This is wrong.

If you have occasion to enter the bath, enter carrying your toilet articles in your right hand. When you get inside the threshold of the lower section [of the bathhouse], bow with palms joined and retire to an empty space. After you have bowed to the persons on your left and right, first take your five-section robe and hand cloth and hang them on the bamboo pole. Open up your bath cloth [used to carry bath articles], take out your [bathing] articles, and set them to one side. Open up, but do not yet completely remove, your outer robe. First, remove your undergarments. Take your leg cloth, wrap it around your body, and tie your bath wrap. Take your breeches, roll them up, and place them in your bath cloth. Next remove your outer robe and five-section robe and put them together in a bundle. Take your hand cloth and tie [the bundle] to the bamboo pole. If you do not have a hand cloth, use your sash to tie it. Of old it was said,

> When the drum signaling the bath sounds three times and you enter the [bath] hall, one must separate outer and under garments as "impure" and "pure."

Proceed to remove the remainder of your garments, make them into a bundle, and set them aside turned upside down [so the "impure" garments are not exposed].

Do not go about in the bath with bare feet: you must wear [wooden] clogs. Dip water at an empty place in the lower section [of the bathhouse]. Do not take the sitting places of officers or respected elders, that is, those in the upper section. Do not splash people's bodies with hot water. Do not take the buckets onto the floor and soak your feet. Do not urinate in the bathhouse, or wash your private parts. Do not rest your feet on the buckets. Do not talk or laugh. Do not rub your feet on the [drain] trough. Do not bail out water [from the trough]. Do not stand up, pick up a bucket, and pour water over your body, lest you splash the people to the left, right, front or back of you. You must keep your whole body covered. Do not use much bath water. Do not let the leg cloth become separated from your body.

If there are persons whose leg cloths should not get into the buckets, such as those with boils, those washing moxa blisters, or those using itch medicine, they should be the last to enter the bath. Do not use the public hand cloths that are on either side to wipe your head or face. In the bathhouse the hand cloths are there to use after donning your robes, to clean your hands before putting on your short kāṣāya.

When leaving the bath, bow left and right. First put on your undershirt and outer robe. When you are completely covered, then put on your lower underclothing and remove your bath wrap. Take your leg cloth and lay it inside your bath wrap, lest it moisten your bath cloth [used to carry bath articles]. The hand cloth should be held in your left hand. Do not take the wet leg cloth and drape it over your hand. Bow left and right and depart. Read the characters of the name of the donor who arranged for the bath, chant sūtras or dhāraṇīs of your choice, and dedicate the merit.

During the cold months when you face the fire, first sit above the hearth, then turn your body and enter the hearth. Bow with palms joined and then sit. If there is a place for removing shoes, leave them outside. Do not play with the incense spoon or fire tongs. Do not stir up the fire. Do not put your heads together and talk. Do not roast things for snacks. Do not make a bad smell by toasting your shoes. It is not permitted to dry such things as leggings or clothing over the fire. Do not grasp and lift your outer robe, exposing your breeches. Do not spit or throw balls of filth and grease into the hearth.

The rules of etiquette for daily activities in the assembly as collected above are not presumed as advice for old hands; they are intended for the edification of newcomers to the training. Minutely detailed rules that should be followed for assemblies in the [dharma] hall, entering the [abbot's] room, minor assemblies, chanting sūtras, reciting buddha names, inspecting [monastery] offices, rituals for opening and closing retreats, packing the knapsacks and donning the bamboo hat [for pilgrimage], sending off deceased monks and auctioning off their belongings, are already included in the *Rules of Purity*. Abbots each have [their own] special admonitions [for their monasteries], so I will not make any further statement.

Compiled on the Buddha's birthday [8th day of 4th month] in the second year of the Jiading era [1209]. Respectfully, the monk Zongjia of the chief seat's office at Qianguifeng (Thousand Tortoise Peak) [Monastery].

—38—

Deaths, Funerals, and the Division of Property in a Monastic Code

Gregory Schopen

Reading Buddhist vinaya texts as we have them can be an unsettling experience. These texts are huge compilations of rules and regulations meant to govern the lives of Buddhist monks. Though written or compiled by monks for monks, the life of a monk they envision or take for granted has little in common with the image of the Buddhist monk that is commonly found in our textbooks, or even in many of our scholarly sources. That image—which has found its way even into modern European novels—presents the Buddhist monk as a lone ascetic who has renounced all social ties and property to wander or live in the forest, preoccupied with meditation and the heroic quest for nirvāṇa or enlightenment. But Buddhist monastic literature is more gritty; it presents and presupposes a different kind of monk. The monk it knows is caught in a web of social and ritual obligations, is fully and elaborately housed and permanently settled, preoccupied not with nirvāṇa but with bowls and robes, bathrooms and doorbolts, and proper behavior in public. A French scholar, André Bareau, some years ago went so far as to say that the various monastic codes or vinayas "contain hardly a whisper about the numerous spiritual practices, meditations, contemplations, etc., which constituted the very essence of the Buddhist 'religion.' " This at least must give us pause for thought.

But even when elements of the image of the ascetic, meditating monk do appear in vinaya literature—and they do—they often appear in unexpected form. The various vinayas present the ascetic ideal, for example, in the instructions they say should be given to the candidate at his or her ordination. In the Pāli *Vinaya,* the candidate is to be told that entrance into the monastic order entails exclusive reliance on only four things, technically known as "requisites" or "means of support": begged food or scraps; rag-robes or robes of discarded cloth; the foot of trees as a place of residence; and urine as medicine. The candidate—the text says—is to be told this, and told that he should limit himself to these means of support "for as long as he lives." But then he is immediately told, in the text as we have it, that, in addition to robes made from rags, he may also have robes made of "linen, cotton, silk, wool, and so on." In a Sarvāstivādin vinaya text that describes the ordination procedure for nuns, the list of "extra allowances" is even longer and includes colored cloth, woven cloth, muslin, hemp, silk, wool, fine Banaras cloth, and linen. If this looks like a double message, another passage in the Pāli *Vinaya* puts this beyond doubt. Though the candidate for ordination is told in one place to limit himself to rag-robes, the same vinaya unequivocally says in another place that wearing only rag-robes is an "offense of wrong-doing" or a violation of the vinaya. In a late appendix to the Pāli *Vinaya* called the *Parivāra* it is even suggested that most monks who actually wear rag-robes do so "from stupidity," or "from madness, from a deranged mind," and are "of evil desires, filled with covetousness."

Other and even more extreme elements of the ascetic ideal also occur in the vinayas, but they too are treated in a curious way. The *Mūlasarvāstivāda-vinaya,* for example, knows and contains rules to regulate the behavior of monks who live in cemeteries or wear robes made from burial cloths. This text says, however, that:

> A monk who dwells in a cemetery, robing himself with burial cloth, must not enter a monastery. He must not worship a stūpa. If he should worship, he must not approach it any nearer than a fathom. He must not use a monastic cell. He must not even sit on monastic bedding. He must not sit among the community of monks. He must not teach dharma to brahmans and householders who have come and assembled. He must not go to the houses of brahmans and householders, and so on.

If in the former instances the ascetic ideal is severely weakened or rendered purely symbolic by permitting "extra allowances" or calling into question the motives that lie behind it, in the case of ascetic practices connected with cemeteries—though nothing is directly said to discourage them—a set of rules is promulgated that excludes any monk who engages in such practices from any meaningful place in normal monastic life. Such a monk cannot enter or use monastic property; he is denied full access to the object of monastic worship; he cannot engage in monastic activities or interact with fellow-monks; interaction with the laity—and therefore access to economic support—is also either denied him or seriously restricted. But notice too that the way in which these rules are framed inadvertently articulates the conception of normal monasticism presupposed by their authors: normal monks lived in monasteries and had free access to and use of monastic property and objects of worship; they lived communally and could interact with the laity. The norm here, the ideal, is not of ascetic practice but of sedentary, socially engaged, permanently housed monasticism. This same norm is equally evident elsewhere as well.

Much has recently been written about modern Buddhist "forest-monks," and the Pāli *Vinaya* also speaks of such monks. But in one of the passages in this monastic code in which the life style of such monks is most clearly described there are, again, some surprises:

> At that time the venerable Udāyin was living in the forest. The monastery of that venerable was beautiful, something to see, and lovely. His private chamber was in the middle, surrounded on all sides by the main house, well appointed with couch and chair, cushion and pillow, well provided with drinking water and water for washing, the grounds well kept. Many people came to see the venerable Udāyin's monastery. A brahman and his wife approached the venerable Udāyin and said they would like to see his monastery.
>
> "Have a look," he said, and taking the key, unfastening the bolt, and opening the door, he entered . . .

Though this is in the forest, these are not the quarters that one might expect for a monk who relied on the four requisites: he had a private room, well-appointed furniture, lock and key, and his monastery was something of a tourist attraction. And yet this, apparently, is how the compilers of the Pāli *Vinaya* saw the forest life. Their forest life was little different from their vision of monastic life in general: both, for them, were permanently housed and well appointed, well ordered, maintained, secured by lock and key, and the focal point of lay activities.

These passages from several different vinayas—and a large number of other passages—make it difficult to avoid the conclusion that if the ideal of the individual rag-wearing, begging, forest dwelling monk was in fact ever the rule in the early history of Indian Buddhism, if the ideal was ever anything more than emblematic, then it was, by the time the vinayas that we have were compiled, all but a dead letter. The vinaya texts that we know are little interested in any individual religious quest, but are very concerned with the organization, administration, maintenance, and smooth operation of a complex institution that owned property and had important social obligations.

The disinclination on the part of scholars to acknowledge fully the institutional preoccupations of the vinaya and the complexity of the institutions these texts presuppose has distorted the discussion of the vinayas' dates and disguised their historical importance. In fact, though often pressed into service to do so, our vinaya texts can probably tell us very little about what early monastic Buddhism "originally" was. They can, however, almost certainly tell us a great deal about what it had—by a certain period—become. And that, for further historical developments, is far more interesting.

Many, if not most scholars, seem to want to place the canonical vinayas in a period close to—if not even during—the lifetime of the Buddha. But this would mean that Buddhist monasticism had little or no real history or development, since by this argument monasticism appeared fully formed at the very beginning. Such an argument requires, as well, the suppression of what little we actually know about the various vinayas and the history of Buddhist monasticism.

In most cases we can place the vinayas we have securely in time: the *Sarvāstivāda-vinaya* that we know was translated into Chinese at the very beginning of the fifth century (404–405 C.E.). So were the vinayas of the Dharmaguptakas (408), the Mahīśāsakas (423–424), and the Mahāsāṃghikas (416). The *Mūlasarvāstivāda-vinaya* was translated into both Chinese and Tibetan still later, and the actual contents of the Pāli *Vinaya* are only knowable from Buddhaghosa's fifth-century commentaries. Although we do not know anything definite about any hypothetical earlier versions of these vinayas, we do know that all of the vinayas as we have them fall squarely into what might unimaginatively be called the Middle Period of Indian Buddhism, the period between the beginning of the common era and the year 500 C.E. As we have them, then, they do not—and probably cannot—tell us what monastic Buddhism "originally" was, but they do provide an almost overwhelming amount of detail about what it had become by this time. To use these vinayas for what we know them to be—documents from the Middle Period—gives to them and to this period the historical importance that both deserve but that neither has yet received.

That the vinayas as we have them do indeed belong to and reflect the Middle Period is obvious from other evidence as well. All of our vinayas presuppose a standard, well-organized, walled monastery with latrines, refectories, cloisters, storerooms, dispensaries, doors, and keys; it had more or less extensive land holdings and a battery of monastic servants and laborers. But we know from archeological sources that such an ordered and well-developed monastery did not exist before the beginning of the common era and appeared throughout India only in the Middle Period. Sources that know such monasteries, and are intended to regulate them, could therefore only date from the same period. We know, moreover, from inscriptional records that it was only in the Middle Period that Buddhist monastic groups received large donations of land and, in fact, entire villages. But the Pāli *Vinaya*, for example, already describes one such village of five hundred "monastery attendants" that was given to a single monk.

To suggest that the Middle Period saw the compilation of huge monastic codes should not be surprising. This was, after all, the period during which equally enormous doctrinal encyclopedias like the *Abhidharmakośa* were also compiled; this was the period during which the various named monastic orders—the Sarvāstivādins, Mahāsāṃghikas, Dharmaguptakas, and so on—appear in Indian inscriptions as the recipients of what must have been an enormous amount of surplus wealth. And there are no such records either before or after this period. What might be more surprising is that the Middle Period apparently not only saw the full institutional, economic, and doctrinal development of the monastic orders, it was also the period during which the vast majority of the texts that we call "Mahāyāna sūtras" were being written. And these two developments are almost certainly related; in fact, it may well be that much of Mahāyāna sūtra literature only makes good sense in light of what else was going on when it was composed. Such a possibility gives a new importance to the vinayas, and demands a new reading of them, since it seems very likely that one of the things that those groups which we call Mahāyāna were struggling with—and against—was what monastic Buddhism had become by the Middle Period. To determine what that was, the vinayas will be a major source.

We might cite a single broad example. Unless we know what landed, institutional monastic Buddhism had become when Mahāyāna sūtras were being written, it is difficult to understand the attacks on "abuses" associated with sedentary monasticism found most stridently in Mahāyāna texts like the *Rāṣṭrapāla-paripṛcchā;* it is also difficult to understand similar, if less shrill, criticisms in Mahāyāna texts like the *Kāśyapa-parivarta,* or the constant calls in such texts to return to a life in the forest, or why long sections of the *Samādhirāja-sūtra* are given over to extolling ascetic practices, and why the necessity and value of these same practices is a topic of sharp debate in the *Aṣṭasahāsrikā-prajñāpāramitā.* Unless we have a clear picture of what the authors of these Mahāyāna texts were surrounded by and reacting to, we will have little chance of appreciating what they were producing. And an important source for that picture will be the vinayas that were being compiled at the same time. It is in this light, I would suggest, that the following selections should be read.

The following selections are of interest for at least two related reasons. They provide some interesting examples of the sorts of things that institutionalized monastic Buddhism was concerned with in the Middle Period: the proper performance of funeral rituals for deceased fellow monks; the inheritance of property; the performance of death rituals for fellow monks; and negotiating ritual privileges, control of sacred relics, and economic resources. There is perhaps some added interest from the fact that such monastic concerns have rarely been identified or studied. But these selections illustrate as well how far monastic Buddhism had moved away from what we consider "spiritual" concerns—how far, in other words, it had developed strictly as an institution and become preoccupied with institutional concerns. These developments, of course, made it ripe for reformation. And this was very likely what many of the Mahāyāna groups were attempting to effect.

The selections that follow all come from a single vinaya, the *Mūlasarvāstivāda-vinaya,* or literature related to it, so at this stage one must be careful not to overgeneralize. They are—and are only meant to be—suggestive of what we still have yet to learn. The first consists of three short texts which in their original context, as here, follow one after another. They define and present as obligatory what appear to be the three main elements of a Mūlasarvāstivādin monastic funeral: removal of the body—undoubtedly ritualized; the honor of the body (*śarīra-pūjā*)—which appears to have involved bathing the body (see section III) and other preparations prior to cremation; and the recitation of some sacred or "scriptural" text, the merit from which was to be assigned to the deceased. These actions are presented here as a set of rituals that the monks must perform before any distribution of the deceased monk's property can be undertaken. They are clearly intended to effect a definitive separation of the dead monk—here presented as a club-wielding "ghost"—from his personal belongings. Keep in mind that the expression used here, "robe and bowl," was a euphemism that covered a large variety of personal property. Notice too that these passages imply a kind of exchange relationship that is also expressed elsewhere (section VII): the monks are obligated to perform the funeral and, significantly, transfer to the deceased the reward or "merit" that results from their ritualized recitation of the dharma; but the deceased, in exchange, is to allow the distribution of his estate to take place unencumbered and without interference. This conception of a set of mutual obligations between the dead and the living is almost certainly only a specific instance of an established Indian norm. Indian legal texts, for example, take as a given that the property or estate of a dead person goes to the person or persons who perform his funeral rites.

The rules regarding monastic funerals in section I were presented as a response to the problem of inheritance and the distribution of monastic estates, a problem that will reappear in other selections (sections VII and VIII). The second selection presents another set of rules as a response to a different problem—that of avoiding social criticism or censure. Buddhism has often been presented as if it had been a force for social change in early India—a reaction to and an attempt to reform established Indian norms. But again, if this were ever actually true it most certainly was not by the time the vinayas were compiled in the Middle Period. The vinayas are, in fact, preoccupied—if not obsessed—with avoiding any hint of social criticism and with maintaining the status quo at almost any cost. In terms of social norms the monks who compiled the vinayas were profoundly conservative men. Our second selection is but one particularly striking instance of this general trend. Here the institution of monastic funerals is presented and justified almost exclusively in terms of the need to avoid any offense to the social and religious sensibilities of the world outside the monastery. This world was particularly sensitive to the question of the proper ritual treatment of the dead and the need to avoid the "pollution" associated with death and dying. Our selection seems, again, to represent a Buddhist monastic expression of these same Indian concerns. Unlike section I, it explicitly refers to the means of final disposal of the body and, in fact, presents several alternatives designed to meet various contingencies: cremation is preferred, but disposal in water or burial are acceptable in certain circumstances. The text also implies that whatever means of disposal is used, a recitation of the dharma and the assigning of the resultant reward to the deceased is required. Finally, in regard to this selection it should be noted that it contains the first reference that we have seen to "the three sections" (*tridaṇḍaka*) (which is also referred to in section VII). Although it is not certain what this was, it would appear to have been a standard formulary made up of three parts that was used on a variety of ritual occasions. The first part consisted of a set of verses in praise of the Buddha, the dharma, and the saṅgha; the middle portion was made up of a canonical text suited to the ritual occasion; and the third part contained a formal transference of merit.

In sections I and II, where the rules governing monastic funerals are presented as obligatory, there is no reference to lay participation in these affairs. But in section III such participation is presented both as an obligation and as a particular privilege sought after by a number of competing groups. The beginning of the text—which is omitted here—sets the stage for the events that our selection narrates to justify an exception to established monastic rule. It was a rule that monks were not to enter towns or villages except at certain regular times. But the need to perform proper funeral rituals for a dead monk, the need to perform "the honors for his body" was apparently considered so important by the compilers of this vinaya that it was able to override or abrogate this rule. The particular case which gave rise to this exception involved the death of a monk named Udāyin, who was known as the foremost of monks who were able to convert families. A married woman who had been sleeping with the leader of a gang of thieves was worried that this monk knew what she was up to and would reveal it. She arranged with her lover to lure the monk into a house. Her lover was to wait at the door and to dispatch the monk when he came out. Our selection picks up the story from here.

In this account the Buddha begins by reiterating the obligation of monks to perform the "honors for the body" of a fellow monk. As the story develops, what starts as a monastic obligation comes to be a ritual privilege that several categories of individuals seek to secure: there is a monastic claim, but it lacks ecclesiastical specificity—these monks are presented as neither specifically coresidential monks nor ecclesiastically recognized disciples of Udāyin; there is a royal claim, but it has a purely personal or biographical basis; there is, finally, a lay claim, but one in which an institutionally recognized relationship is involved. This final claim is the one that wins. It is made by Mālikā, who declares that Udāyin was her "teacher" (*ācārya*). This would make her his "disciple" (*antevāsin*), which is an institutionally recognized formal relationship that involves a set of mutual obligations. Mālikā, however, is not a nun, but—elsewhere at least—a lay sister, and herein lies a part of the significance of the text. Elsewhere in the *Mūlasarvāstivāda-vinaya* it is made clear that monks had a series of ritual obligations in regard to lay brothers and lay sisters (*upāsaka / upāsikā*). What our text seems to be suggesting is that lay brothers and sisters might, in turn, have certain ritual privileges in regard to monks. But here this is being negotiated, not asserted or made a rule. In fact, our text seems careful to avoid making a general rule. It simply establishes a precedent—"this happened once when . . ."—that is all. Future cases, therefore, would also have to be negotiated. The ambiguity seems to be intentional, and such ambiguity or ambivalence seems to be characteristic of all those situations in which lay participation in monastic ritual is at issue, or where control of, and access to, sacred objects is involved, and is clearly visible again in section IV.

Section III also represents one of the very rare cases in which building a stūpa or permanent structural reliquary for the post-cremation remains of the deceased is specifically included as a part of the funeral. Generally these two things, although obviously related, were considered and treated separately, as in section IV. But the stūpa referred to here is almost certainly not of the monumental type; since it was, as it were, built in a day, it was probably a small structure built over a pot containing the ashes of the deceased. There is Indian inscriptional evidence indicating that small stūpas were built for the local monastic dead, and in some cases these are explicitly said to have been erected—as in our text—by a disciple of the deceased.

Section IV is particularly interesting. In Mūlasarvāstivādin literature at least—and probably in the literatures of other orders—it, and not the account of the death and funeral of the Buddha in the *Mahāparinirvāṇa-sūtra,* describes the origins of what we call the "relic cult" in monastic Buddhism. Like section III, it deals with questions of access and control, and shows the monks and the laity jockeying for position; the monks win, of course, since they wrote the account. Like several other of our selections, its denouement deals not so much with devotion as "dollars."

The selection starts with what was apparently the established monastic rule: the funeral of the monk Śāriputra was performed by a fellow monastic. The text assumes that the remains or relics of a dead monk are the property of the monastic community. However, this position becomes the initial point of friction and the point to be negotiated. For the established monastic claim cuts off a monk in death from the laity who in life may have been his supporters and followers. Such an assertion of proprietary rights by the monks has at least the potential to disaffect that lay group, and all our vinayas stress the need to avoid that.

After the novice Cunda has performed the funeral of the monk Śāriputra and handed his relics over to the monk Ānanda, the latter goes to the Buddha to express his dismay at Śāriputra's death. The Buddha then delivers a longish homily on the meaning of Śāriputra's death, which is omitted here. The householder Anāthapiṇḍada, who is the prototypical generous lay donor, then hears of Śāriputra's death and goes to the monk Ānanda to present a claim on the relics. Ānanda responds with a counterclaim in exactly the same terms, and refuses to give up possession of the relics. To this point we have monastic possession of the relics, a lay claim, a monastic counter-claim, and unresolved deadlock. Here—as in so many other cases in the vinaya involving friction between the lay and monastic communities—the Buddha himself is brought in to mediate. The layman Anāthapiṇḍada repeats his claim to the Buddha, and the Buddha sides with him. He summons the monk Ānanda and tells him to turn the relics over to Anāthapiṇḍada. The Buddha is also made to say, in effect, that when monks retain exclusive possession of monastic relics this is not beneficial to the teaching, and that monks should rather occupy themselves with the "business of a monk"—recruiting, ordaining, and instructing other monks. Here we have articulated something like a distinction that is commonly said to have existed between the religious activity of monks and the religious activity of lay persons in Indian Buddhism: monks are to be properly occupied with maintaining the institution by inducting new recruits, and in transmitting the teaching; activity in regard to relics is the concern of the laity. But note that it requires the authority of the Buddha to introduce this distinction, that it is presented as an innovation and that the prior or original monastic practice did not recognize this distinction. Also note that the account as we have it implies that there was some monastic resistance; at least the compilers of the account must have anticipated such resistance, since they apparently felt compelled to add what amounts to an editorial comment. After saying that Ānanda gave the relics of Śāriputra to the householder, the text adds: "This was so since the Blessed One when formerly a bodhisattva never violated the words of his father and mother, or of his preceptor or teacher or other persons worthy of respect." This statement is syntactically isolated and does not form a part of the ongoing narrative. It appears, rather, to be an editorial intrusion intended to make explicit how the compilers wanted the text to be read: Ānanda acquiesced not as a result of his own inclinations but strictly as a matter of obedience.

There are other indications that the compilers of the account did not see the Buddha's instructions as a satisfying solution, for the account does not end here. Both the Buddha and the reluctant monk Ānanda are presented as acceding to lay desires to have monastic relics. But—you can almost hear the editors say—look what happened. Anāthapiṇḍada takes the relics and enshrines them in his house. Although others had some access to them, the text seems to emphasize that they virtually became the object of a private household cult. The issue came to a head because lay control of monastic relics ultimately resulted in exactly what it was intended to prevent: access to such relics, when in private hands, was restricted and could be entirely shut off. Enter, again, the Buddha. He rules that lay persons can, indeed, build stūpas for the relics of the monastic dead but all such stūpas, except those for "ordinary" monks, must be built within the monastic complex, that is, must remain under monastic control. It is a clever piece. It makes it possible to present the Buddha as reasserting the right of monastic control solely for the sake of benefiting the laity.

Access and control, however, are not the only issues here. Relics gave rise to festivals; festivals gave rise to trade; trade gave rise to gifts and donations. It is this, in the end, that our text may be about. But to appreciate this particular monastic interest in monastic relics, an established principle of vinaya law must be kept in mind. Virtually all the vinayas contain rules stipulating that any donation made to the stūpa of a Buddha belongs to that stūpa, that is, to the Buddha himself, and could not, except under very special circumstances (see section VI), be transferred to, or used by, either the monastic community or an individual monk. This legal principle, which continues in effect even in Mahāyāna sūtra literature, deprived the monks of an important source of revenue, and our text is almost certainly responding to this situation. It acknowledges that a token part (the "first fruit" offerings) of the donations in question is to be given to the Buddha in the form of the "Image which Sits in the Shade of the Jambu Tree." This was, apparently, an image of the Buddha representing him in his first youthful experience of meditation. There are several references to it in the *Mūlasarvāstivāda-vinaya* (see section VIII), and an inscribed second-century image of this sort has been found at Sāñcī. A small part of the donations is also to be used to maintain the stūpa of Śāriputra. But the rest—and in this case that is a goodly amount—is to be divided among the monks. Our text hastens to add that in this instance there is no offense because the donations were not made to a stūpa of the Buddha but to a stūpa of a specific disciple. The qualification to the established rule that is being introduced here, and the full range of its applicability, is stated more straight forwardly in Guṇaprabha's *Vinaya-sūtra,* a fifth- to seventh-century monastic handbook that paraphrases our passage as: "that which is given to the stūpa of a disciple belongs indeed to his fellow monks." Such stūpas could, then, come to be a legitimate source of revenue for the monks, and such a possibility may explain what Faxian, a fifth-century Chinese monk, said he saw in India: "wherever monks live they build up stūpas in honor of the saints Śāriputra, Maudgalaputra, and Ānanda."

We have no idea, of course, if any of the things narrated in our account actually occurred. If, as seems very likely, this account was compiled in the Middle Period, then it was written hundreds of years after the events it is supposed to be describing and has, in one sense, no historical value at all. But in another sense it is an extremely important historical document: it shows us how Mūlasarvāstivādin vinaya masters in the Middle Period chose to construct and to present their past to their fellow monks; it shows us how the issue of who controlled sacred relics had—at least for this period—been settled; more generally it shows us vinaya masters in the Middle Period seriously engaged with questions of power, access, relics, and money. These monks almost look like real people.

Sections v and vi both deal with an aspect not of death but of dying, and both link it with property. Both texts reflect the importance attributed by a variety of Indian sources—Hindu, Jain, and Buddhist—to the moment of death. The basic idea is succinctly expressed in a Jain text: "as is the mind at the moment of death, just so is one's future rebirth"; or in the *Samādhirāja-sūtra:* "when at the moment of passing away, death, or dying, the thought of something occurs, one's consciousness follows that thought." The last moment or one's dying thought was believed, in effect, to determine one's next birth. However serious the difficulties such a belief might create for official Buddhist doctrine, it is obvious from our two texts that vinaya masters took it as a given. The rules they present here are solely intended either to avoid negative thoughts at the moment of death (section v) or to insure positive thoughts at such a time. The failure on the part of the monastic community to do what is required to effect either is not only a disciplinary fault but has disastrous consequences for their dying fellow monk, who is thereby condemned to rebirth in the hells.

How important such beliefs and rituals were to the monastic community is at least suggested in both texts. In section v, although the Buddha is made to rule that "excessive attachment" to some possession on the part of a monk is a fault, still the final ruling provides for the continuing existence of such a fault. In section vi the need to ensure a positive state of mind in a monk who may be on the point of death overrides not one but two otherwise firm vinaya laws. This need is apparently so important that the monks may use assets that belong to the Buddha to meet it, though this is normally strictly forbidden; to meet this need the monks are also allowed to engage in buying and selling, and this too is normally forbidden.

In terms of detail, note that section v contains a reference to the actual cremation of a dead monk as being performed by a low-caste man; this would suggest again that the monks had a purely ritual role and did not do the dirty work. In section VI, as in VIII, there is a reference to the perfumed chamber. We know from numerous references to this chamber in the *Mūlasarvāstivāda-vinaya,* and from architectural and inscriptional evidence, that it was the residential cell directly opposite the main entrance of the typically quadrangular Indian Buddhist monastery of the Middle Period. This cell was both by position and architectural elaboration set off from the other residential cells and was reserved for the Buddha himself. The latter permanently resided in such a cell in every fully developed monastery in the form of what we call an image, and there were specific monks assigned to this chamber or monastic shrine. Section VI also contains a reference to a permanent endowment for the Buddha. We know from inscriptions that Buddhist monastic communities received such endowments throughout the Middle Period. They were called "permanent" because they consisted of sums of money that could never be spent but were to be lent out on interest by the monks to generate usable income. The *Mūlasarvāstivāda-vinaya* contains a text that gives detailed instructions governing such monastic loans and the use of written contracts of debt. Note finally that section VI ends by invoking a principle of the Indian law of property. Buddhist vinaya texts, in fact, frequently reveal points of contact with Indian law, as in sections VII and VIII.

Section VII presents an interesting case of interaction between vinaya law and secular law, and involves a sizable monastic estate: "three hundred thousands of gold." The latter may appear surprising, but should not be. Reference to the private wealth of monks is frequently found. In the *Suttavibhaṅga* of the Pāli *Vinaya* it is said, for example, that if a monk asks for yarn and then has it woven into robe material, that is an offense. But if the monk does it "by means of his own wealth," the same act is not an offense. There are a dozen such references to private wealth in this section of the Pāli *Vinaya* alone. There are also clear indications in both the Pāli and Mūlasarvāstivāda vinayas that seem to suggest that monastic status or reputation was directly related to a monk's material possessions. Note that in section VI the monk who was "little known" had no medicine, and in section IX the Buddha himself and the selfish monk are each described as both "widely known" and the recipients of robes, bowls, medicines, and so on. Who you were was determined by what you received and had.

Evidence that individual monks must have had considerable private means is also available in Buddhist donative inscriptions. Large numbers of monks and nuns made private gifts to their communities, and some of these were impressive. Such wealth might very well have been of interest to the state, and establishing who had jurisdiction over, or rights of possession to, such wealth in the event of its owner's death was undoubtedly a matter of some negotiation between the state and the Buddhist monastic communities. What we see in the first part of section VII is, of course, only the monastic point of view.

The remainder of section VII suggests further that dealing with monastic estates could become a major and disruptive monastic preoccupation, and some means of sorting out the various claims was required. That is the main purpose of the second half of the text. The Buddha is made to declare that the division and distribution of a dead monk's estate was to take place on only five occasions. The first three of these correspond to moments in a Mūlasarvāstivādin monastic funeral: 1. "when the gong for the dead is being beaten"—the sounding of the funeral gong, we know from other sources (see section IX), marked the beginning of a monastic funeral by summoning the monks; 2. the recitation of the three sections—referred to in section II; and 3. "when the shrine (*caitya*) is being honored"—which seems to have marked the end of the funeral and is also referred to in section II. The order in which these occasions are listed seems to represent the order of preference, and appears to favor direct participation in the funeral. If the distribution takes place on these occasions, only those present will receive a share. The other two occasions appear to take place separately: 4. at the distribution of lottery tickets—such tickets are referred to in all the vinayas and were used for a variety of purposes; and 5. the making of a "formal motion"—such "motions" are also widely noted in vinaya literature and were used for any formal act or decision that required the consent of the entire community. Of these occasions, only the procedure for the formal motion is described in detail. Note the reference to "selling" a dead monk's property. Such references also occur elsewhere, and it appears that the property was first sold and the money realized was then divided among the monks. In Chinese sources it is clear that this involved an actual auction.

Section VIII also deals with the problem of estates, but of a particular kind. The estate in question belongs to what the text calls a "shaven-headed householder." Since monks shave their heads but householders do not, such individuals obviously represented a mixed or intermediate category. Our text, in fact, purports to describe the origin of this category: a wealthy layman decided to enter the order and approached a monk. The monk shaved the householder's head and began to train him for ordination. But the householder fell seriously ill and—in accordance with an established vinaya rule against ordaining sick people—the Buddha declared that "the rules of training" were not to be given until he recovered. He also ruled, however, that monastic attendants should be given to the sick man even when he was taken back home. The man did not recover, but at the point of death made a written will and sent it to the monastery. He died and government officials heard of it and of the size of his estate. They reported his death to the king. Since the man was sonless, and since according to Indian law the estate of a man who dies sonless goes to the king, the state should have had jurisdiction in this case and the king should have had clear rights to the property. But our monastic text has the king declare—explicitly citing the case adjudicated in section VII—that a case of this sort too falls under the authority of the Buddha, that is, under the jurisdiction of monastic law. The king, in other words, is presented as acknowledging or confirming the religious status of the category "shaven-headed householder": the estate of such an individual is not subject to secular law.

What we see here is another instance of vinaya law interacting with Indian law.

But we probably see something else as well: this vinaya passage establishes a precedent and procedure that would allow a sonless man to avoid the confiscation of his estate by the state upon his death. The procedure involves a relationship of exchange and obligation that is embedded in the text without always being explicitly stated. The layman undergoes at least a ritual or symbolic ordination—his head is shaved—but it is not completed. This ritual ordination itself, however, creates an obligation for the monastic community to provide monastic attendants to look after the layman when he falls ill, whether he remains at the monastery or returns home. In other words, it provides a kind of health insurance for the layman. But in exchange, as it were, for attending to the layman in his final days—in this case, apparently for an extended period—the monastic community receives, upon his death, his entire estate. Both parties clearly gain by the arrangement. Certain rulings in the text itself suggest that what is being proposed here was intended to apply even to laymen who might have had children—there is a provision dealing specifically with what should happen to a deceased person's sons and daughters. In a case of this sort, the shaven-headed householder would have been able to divert his estate from its normal heirs.

What we have in section VIII is, then, almost certainly a Buddhist version of a ritual practice commonly found in other monastic traditions as well. Several of the Hindu *Saṃnyāsa Upaniṣads* refer to undergoing the rites of renunciation at the point of death; Jain sources, too, speak of lay persons being initiated into the monastic order at the approach of death. But the strongest parallels are probably found in medieval Christian monastic practice: here too a layman is "ordained" at the approach of death; here too the monks are obligated to attend to him in his final days; and here too they receive his estate or substantial gifts in return.

The reference in section VIII to a written will is also of interest. Although the Pāli *Vinaya,* for example, knows and approves of the use, under certain conditions, of oral testaments or wills on the part of monks, nuns, lay brothers and sisters, or "anyone else," references to written wills are extremely rare even in Indian legal texts. There is also a reference to "written liens" or loan contracts that may form part of an estate, and to both Buddhist and non-Buddhist books. These and other such references provide important evidence for determining the history and use of writing in early India, a topic which is as yet little studied or understood. Finally, in terms of details, section VIII shows that ownership rights were clearly divided in a Mūlasarvāstivādin monastery: property belonged either to the Buddha or the dharma or the community. In each case such property could be used only for specific purposes, and normally could not be transferred to another unit or purpose (see section VI). This tripartite division of property rights, or some form of it, is in fact recognized by virtually all the vinayas.

There is one more point that needs to be noted in regard to section VIII. A Chinese monk named Yijing visited and studied in India in the last quarter of the seventh century. He wrote an important account of what he observed, which has survived and been translated into English under the title *A Record of the Buddhist Religion as Practiced in India and the Malay Archipelago.* Much of this *Record* may, in fact, be based on Yijing's observations, but some of it is not. The whole of his chapter 36, apart from the first and last sentences, for example, is nothing more than a Chinese translation of the vinaya passage that we have been discussing. The failure to recognize this, and the fact that Yijing gives the passage out of context, has misled a number of modern scholars.

Section IX does not come from the *Mūlasarvāstivāda-vinaya.* It is presented here to show how some of the concerns in the other selections were treated in more literary form. Section IX is taken from a collection of stories called the *Avadāna-śataka, The Hundred Edifying Stories,* apparently a Mūlasarvāstivādin text. Our selection appears to be in many ways only a narrative elaboration of the rules governing monastic funerals found in sections I and II. Although it is commonly asserted that Avadāna or Buddhist story literature was "popular" literature meant for the laity, there is little evidence for this, and a large number of such stories were—like our selection—explicitly addressed to monks, had monastic heroes and characters, and dealt with specifically monastic concerns that would have been of little interest to the laity. It is more likely that such moralizing story literature was written for and read by the ordinary monks who probably, at all periods, made up the largest segment of the Buddhist monastic population.

Section IX throws some further light on at least one particular detail. Sections I, II, and III all refer to "assigning" or "directing" a reward to the deceased monk as a part of a monastic funeral, but section IX alone actually describes the procedure. Like numerous passages in the *Mūlasarvāstivāda-vinaya,* section IX makes it clear that "assigning the reward" meant making a formal declaration designating who should receive the merit resulting from a specific act. When the Buddha assigns the reward in section IX, he recites a verse that says in part, "what, indeed, is the merit from this gift, may that go to the hungry ghost," that is, the dead monk. In this case the merit is formally designated for the same "person" who made the gift. In sections I, II, and III the merit results from the acts of a group (the monks), or an individual (Mālikā), but is assigned to someone else (the deceased). This practice—usually called the "transference of merit"—used to be considered a Mahāyāna innovation, but is in fact found in the Pāli sources, frequently in the *Mūlasarvāstivāda-vinaya,* and almost everywhere in Buddhist donative inscriptions that have no determinable connection with the Mahāyāna.

The selections presented here are in several senses a mere sampling: they are taken from a single vinaya or monastic code; they all deal with a single cluster of concerns; they all represent fragments of a large and complex literature. But, they also suggest at least the possibility of a new reading of the vinaya, not as sources connected with the origins of Indian Buddhist monasticism but as documents of its Middle Period. They show what is to be learned by reading the vinayas not as documents dealing with spiritual or even ethical concerns, but as works concerned with institutional, ritual, legal, and economic issues. They also show how much may have been missed or misunderstood by the modern scholarly preference for the Pāli *Vinaya.* Finally, they at least suggest how complex, rich—in several senses—and remarkable an institution Buddhist monasticism might have been.

The enormous *Mūlasarvāstivāda-vinaya* has not yet been translated. The following selections are translated from either the Sanskrit text published in Nalinaksha Dutt, *Gilgit Manuscripts,* vol. 3, part 2 (Srinagar, 1942) [I. = pp. 126.17–127.18; V. = pp. 125.10–126.16; VI. = 124.11–125.9; VII. = 117.8–121.5; VIII. = 139.6–143.14], or from the Tibetan versions published in *The Tibetan Tripitaka. Taipei Edition* (Taipei, 1991) [III. = 'dul ba, nga 65a.2–66a.4], or in *The Tog Palace Manuscript of the Tibetan Kanjur,* vol. 9 (Leh, 1979) [II. = 'dul ba, ta 352b.7–354a.5; IV. = 'dul ba, ta 354a.5–368a.5]. The last selection is translated from J. S. Speyer, *Avadānaçataka* (The Hague, 1958), i 271–73.

Further Reading

Some of the texts and topics treated here are discussed in more detail in G. Schopen, "On Avoiding Ghosts and Social Censure: Monastic Funerals in the Mūlasarvāstivāda-vinaya," *Journal of Indian Philosophy* 20 (1992), 1–39; and G. Schopen, "Ritual Rights and Bones of Contention: More on Monastic Funerals and Relics in the Mūlasarvāstivāda-vinaya," *Journal of Indian Philosophy* 22 (1994), 31–80, both of which will be reprinted in Gregory Schopen, *Bones, Stones and Buddhist Monks: Collected Papers on the Archaeology, Epigraphy and Texts of Monastic Buddhism in India,* Michigan Studies in Buddhist Traditions (Honolulu: University of Hawaii Press, forthcoming).

I. Rules Governing Monastic Funerals and the Problem of Inheritance

This took place in Śrāvastī. On that occasion a certain monk who was sick died in his cell. He was reborn among the nonhuman beings. The monk who was the distributor of robes started to enter the cell of the dead monk, saying, "I distribute the bowl and robes." But the deceased monk appeared there with intense anger, wielding a club, and said: "When you perform for me the removal of the body, only then can you proceed with the distribution of my bowl and robe." The distributor of robes was terrified and forced to flee.

The monks asked the Blessed One concerning this matter.

The Blessed One said: "First the removal of the dead monk is to be performed. Then his robe and bowl are to be distributed."

This took place in Śrāvastī. On that occasion a certain monk died. The monks performed the removal of his body but simply threw it into the burning ground and returned to the monastery. The distributor of robes entered the dead monk's cell, saying, "I distribute the bowl and robe." But the dead monk had been reborn among the nonhuman beings. Wielding a club, he appeared in his cell and said: "When you perform the honor of the body for me, only then can you proceed with the distribution of my bowl and robe."

The monks asked the Blessed One concerning this matter.

The Blessed One said: "The monks must first perform the honor of the body for a deceased monk. After that his bowl and robe are to be distributed. There will otherwise be a danger."

This took place in Śrāvastī. On that occasion a certain monk who was sick died in his cell. After having brought him to the burning ground, and having performed for him the honor of the body, that deceased monk was cremated. Then the monks returned to the monastery. The distributor of robes entered the dead monk's cell. The dead monk appeared wielding a club, saying, "You have not yet given a recitation of the dharma for my sake, but only then are you to proceed with the distribution of my monastic robes."

The monks asked the Blessed One concerning this matter.

The Blessed One said: "Having given a recitation of dharma in the deceased's name, having directed the reward to him, after that his monastic robes are to be distributed."

II. Rules Governing Monastic Funerals and the Pressure of Social Criticism

The Buddha, the Blessed One, dwelt in Śrāvastī, in the Grove of Jeta, in the park of Anāthapiṇḍada.

In Śrāvastī there was a certain householder. He took a wife from a family of equal standing and, having lain with her, a son was born. The birth ceremonies for the newborn son, having been performed in detail for three times seven or twenty-one days, the boy was given a name corresponding to his clan. His upbringing, to his maturity, was of a proper sort.

Later, when that householder's son had become a Buddhist monk, his bodily humors became unbalanced and he fell ill. Though he was treated with medicines made from roots and stalks and flowers and fruits, it was of no use, and he died.

The monks simply left his body, together with his robe and bowl, near a road.

Later, brahmans and householders who were out walking saw the body from the road. One said: "Hey look, a Buddhist monk has died." Others said: "Come here! Look at this!" When they looked they recognized the dead monk and said: "This is the son of the householder what's-his-name. This is the sort of thing that happens when someone joins the order of those lordless Buddhist ascetics. Had he not joined their order his kinsmen would certainly have performed the funeral ceremonies for him."

The monks reported this matter to the Blessed One, and the Blessed One said: "Now then, monks, with my authorization, funeral ceremonies for a deceased monk must be performed." Although the Blessed One had said that funeral ceremonies for a deceased monk should be performed, because the monks did not know how they should be performed, the Blessed One said: "A deceased monk is to be cremated."

Although the Blessed One had said that a deceased monk should be cremated, the venerable Upāli asked the Blessed One: "Is that which was said by the reverend Blessed One—that there are eighty thousand kinds of worms in the human body—not so?" The Blessed One said: "Upāli, as soon as a man is born, those worms are also born, so, at the moment of death, they too surely die. Still, only after examining the opening of any wound is the body to be cremated."

Although the Blessed One had said a deceased monk is to be cremated, when wood was not at hand the monks asked the Blessed One concerning this matter, and the Blessed One said: "The body is to be thrown into rivers." When there is no river, the Blessed One said: "Having dug a grave, it is to be buried." When it is summer and the earth is hard and the wood is full of living things, the Blessed One said: "In an isolated spot, with its head pointing north, having put down a bundle of grass as a bolster, having laid the corpse on its right side, having covered it with bunches of grass or leaves, having directed the reward to the deceased, and having given a recitation of the dharma of the three sections (*tridaṇḍaka*), the monks are to disperse."

The monks dispersed accordingly. But then brahmans and householders derided them, saying: "Buddhist ascetics, after carrying away a corpse, do not bathe and yet go about their business. They are polluted." The monks asked the Blessed One concerning this matter, and the Blessed One said: "Monks should not disperse in that manner, but should bathe." They all started to bathe, but the Blessed One said: "Everyone need not bathe. Those who came in contact with the corpse must wash themselves together with their robes. Others need only wash their hands and feet."

When the monks did not worship the shrine (*caitya*), the Blessed One said: "The shrine is to be worshiped."

III. The Death and Funeral of the Monk Kālodāyin: Negotiating Ritual Privileges

The ringleader of thieves, having pulled his sword from its sheath, waited at the door.

When the venerable Udāyin came out, the ringleader, with a mind devoid of compassion and without concern for the other world, severed his head and it fell to the ground.

An old woman saw him killing the noble one: "Who is this," she said, "that has done such a rash thing?"

The ringleader said: "You must tell no one or I will make sure that you too end up in the same condition!"

She was terrified and was then unable to speak. Thinking that perhaps someone following the tracks of the eminent one would come by later, she—given the circumstances—remained silent.

The two of them, with minds devoid of compassion and without concern for the other world, hid the body of the venerable Udāyin in a heap of trash and left it there.

That day the monk in charge of the fortnightly gathering, sitting at the seniors' end of the assembly, said: "Has someone determined the inclination of the reverend Udāyin? The reverend Udāyin is not here."

Then the Blessed One said to the monks: "Monks, that one who is the best of those who make families pious has been killed. His robes must be brought back, and the honors for his body must be performed!"

The Blessed One set forth, but was stopped by the gate of Śrāvastī. He then caused a brightness like that of gold to shoot forth. He filled all of Śrāvastī with a light like that of pure gold.

Prasenajit, the king of Kośala, thought to himself: "Why has all of Śrāvastī been filled with a light like that of pure gold?" He thought further: "Without a doubt, the Blessed One wishes to enter!"

Together with his retinue of wives, and taking the key to the city, he unlocked the gate and the Blessed One entered.

Prasenajit, the king of Kośala, thought: "But why has the Blessed One come into Śrāvastī at an irregular time?" But since buddhas, blessed ones, are not easy to approach, and are difficult to resist, he was incapable of putting a question to the Buddha, the Blessed One.

The Blessed One, together with the community of disciples, having gone ahead, Prasenajit, together with his retinue of wives, went following everywhere behind the Blessed One, until they came to that heap of trash.

The Blessed One then addressed the monks: "Monks, he who was the best of those who make families pious is hidden here. Remove him!"

He was removed, and those who had depended on the venerable Udāyin, seeing there what had truly happened in regard to the noble one, said: "Since he was our good spiritual friend, does the Blessed One allow us to perform the honors for his body?"

The Blessed One did not allow it.

Prasenajit, the king of Kośala said: "Since he was a friend of mine from our youth, does the Blessed One allow me to perform the honors for his body?"

The Blessed One did not allow it.

Queen Mālikā said: "Since he was my teacher, does the Blessed One allow me to perform the honors for his body?"

The Blessed One allowed it.

Queen Mālikā, then, having had the dirt removed from the body of the venerable one with white earth, had it bathed with perfumed water. Having adorned a bier with various colored cotton clothes, she put the body onto it and arranged it.

Then the Blessed One, together with the community of disciples, went ahead and the king, together with his retinue of wives, followed behind them.

Having put the bier down at an open, extensive area, Queen Mālikā, heaping up a pile of all the aromatic woods, cremated the body. She extinguished the pyre with milk, and having put the bones into a golden pot, she had a mortuary stūpa erected at a crossing of four great roads. She raised an umbrella, a banner, and a flag, did honor with perfumes, strings of garlands, incense, aromatic powders, and musical instruments. When she had venerated the stūpa's feet, the Blessed One, having assigned the reward, departed.

IV. Śāriputra's Death and the Disposition of His Remains: Negotiating Control and Access to Relics

After the venerable Śāriputra had died, the novice Cunda performed the honors for the body on the remains of the venerable Śāriputra and, taking the remains, his bowl, and monastic robes, set off for Rājagṛha. When in due course he arrived at Rājagṛha he put down the bowl and robe, washed his feet and went to the venerable Ānanda. When he had honored with his head the feet of Ānanda, he sat down to one side. Being seated to one side, the novice Cunda said this to the venerable Ānanda: "Reverend Ānanda, you should know that my preceptor, the reverend Śāriputra, has entered into final nirvāṇa—these are his relics and his bowl and monastic robes."

*

The householder Anāthapiṇḍada heard it said that the noble Śāriputra had passed away into final nirvāṇa and that his relics were in the hands of the noble Ānanda. Having heard that, he went to the venerable Ānanda. When he had arrived there and had honored with his head the feet of the venerable Ānanda, he sat down to one side. Having sat down to one side, the householder Anāthapiṇḍada said this to the venerable Ānanda: "May the noble Ānanda hear! Since for a long time the noble Śāriputra was to me dear, beloved, a guru, and an object of affection, and since he passed away into final nirvāṇa and his relics are in your possession, would you please hand them over to me! The honor due to relics should be done to his relics!"

Ānanda said: "Householder, because Śāriputra for a long time was to me dear, beloved, a guru, and an object of affection, I myself will perform the honor due to relics for his relics."

Then the householder Anāthapiṇḍada went to the Blessed One. When he had arrived there and had honored with his head the feet of the Blessed One, he sat down to one side. Having sat down to one side, the householder Anāthapiṇḍada said this to the Blessed One: "May the Reverend One hear! For a long time the noble Śāriputra was to me dear, beloved, a guru, and an object of affection. His relics are in the hands of the noble Ānanda. May the Blessed One please grant that they be given to me! I ask for the honor due to relics for his relics."

The Blessed One then, having summoned Ānanda through a messenger, said this to him: "Ānanda, give the relics of the monk Śāriputra to the householder Anāthapiṇḍada! Allow him to perform the honors! In this way brahmans and householders come to have faith. Moreover, Ānanda, through acting as you have there is neither benefit nor recompense for my teaching. Therefore you should cause others to enter the order, you should ordain them, you should give the monastic requisites, you should attend to the business of a monk, you should cause [the teaching] to be proclaimed to monks as it was proclaimed, cause it to be taken up, teach it, and through this, indeed you profit and give recompense for my teaching."

Then the venerable Ānanda, by the order of the Teacher, gave the relics of Śāriputra to the householder Anāthapiṇḍada—this was so since the Blessed One, when formerly a bodhisattva, never violated the words of his father and mother, or of his preceptor or teacher or other persons worthy of respect.

The householder Anāthapiṇḍada took the relics of the venerable Śāriputra and went to his own house. When he got there, he placed them at a height in the most worthy place in his house, and together with members of his household, together with his friends, relations, and older and younger brothers, undertook to honor them with lamps, incense, flowers, perfumes, garlands, and unguents.

The people of Śrāvastī heard then that the noble Śāriputra had passed away into final nirvāṇa in the village of Nalada in the country of Magadha, that the noble Ānanda, after having obtained his relics, presented them to the householder Anāthapiṇḍada, and that the latter, together with members of his household, together with his friends, relatives and acquaintances, and elder and younger brothers, honored them with lamps, incense, flowers, perfumes, garlands, and unguents. When Prasenajit, the king of Kośala, heard this, he went to the house of the householder Anāthpiṇḍada together with his wife Mālikā, the kṣatriyā Varṣākārā, both Ṛṣidatta and Purāṇa, and Viśākhā, the mother of Mṛgāra, as well as many of the devout, all of them carrying the requisites for doing honor. Through paying honor to the relics with the requisites of honor, several of them there obtained accumulations of good qualities. But, on another occasion when some business arose in a remote village, the householder Anāthapiṇḍada, having locked the door of his house, went away. But a great crowd of people came then to his house and when they saw the door locked they were derisive, abusive, and critical, saying, "In that the householder Anāthapiṇḍada has locked the door and gone off, he has created an obstacle to our merit."

Later the householder Anāthapiṇḍada returned and members of his household said: "Householder, a great multitude of people carrying the requisites of honor came but, seeing the door locked, they were derisive, abusive, and critical, saying, 'Anāthapiṇḍada has created an obstacle to our merit.' "

Anāthapiṇḍada thought to himself, "This indeed is what I must do," and went to the Blessed One. When he had arrived there and had honored with his head the feet of the Blessed One, he sat down to one side. Seated to one side he said this to the Blessed One: "Reverend, when a great multitude of men who were deeply devoted to the venerable Śāriputra came to my house carrying the requisites of honor I, on account of some business, had locked the doors and gone elsewhere. They became derisive, abusive, and critical, saying, 'In that the householder Anāthapiṇḍada has locked the door and gone away, he has created an obstacle to our merit.' On that account, if the Blessed One would permit it, I would build a stūpa for the noble Śāriputra in a suitably available place. There the great multitudes of men would be allowed to do honor as they wish."

The Blessed One said: "Therefore, householder, with my permission, you should do it!"

Although the Blessed One had said, "with my permission, you should do it," Anāthapiṇḍada did not know how a stūpa should be built.

The Blessed One said: "Make four terraces in succession; then make the base for the dome; then the dome and the harmikā and the crowning pole; then, having made one or two or three or four umbrellas, make up to thirteen, and place a rain receptacle on the top of the pole."

Although the Blessed One had said that a stūpa of this sort was to be made, since Anāthapiṇḍada did not know if a stūpa of such a form was to be made for only the noble Śāriputra or also for all noble ones, the monks asked the Blessed One concerning this matter, and the Blessed One said: "Householder, in regard to the stūpa of a tathāgata, a person should complete all parts. In regard to the stūpa of a solitary buddha, the rain receptacle should not be put in place; for an arhat there are four umbrellas; for one who does not return, three; for one who returns, two; for one who has entered the stream, one. For ordinary good monks the stūpa is to be made plain."

The Blessed One had said, "In regard to a stūpa for the noble ones it has this form, for ordinary men this," but Anāthapiṇḍada did not know by whom and in which place they were to be made. The Blessed One said: "As Śāriputra and Maudgalyāyana sat when the Tathāgata was seated, just so the stūpa of one who has passed away into final nirvāṇa is also to be placed. Moreover, in regard to the stūpas of each individual elder, they are to be arranged according to seniority. Those for ordinary monks are to be placed outside the monastic complex."

The householder Anāthapiṇḍada said: "If the Blessed One were to give permission, I will celebrate festivals of the stūpa of the noble Śāriputra."

The Blessed One said: "Householder, with permission, you should do it!"

Prasenajit, the king of Kośala, had heard how, when the householder Anāthapiṇḍada asked of the Blessed One permission to institute a festival of the stūpa of the noble Śāriputra, the Blessed One had permitted its institution. Prasenajit, having thought, "It is excellent! I too should help in that," and having had the bell sounded, proclaimed: "Sirs, city dwellers who live in Śrāvastī, and the multitudes of men who have come together from other places, hear this: 'At the time when the festival of the stūpa of the venerable Śāriputra occurs, for those who have come bringing merchandise there is to be no tax, no toll, nor transportation fee. Therefore, they must be allowed to pass freely here!' "

At that time five hundred overseas traders who had made a great deal of money from their ships arrived at Śrāvastī. They heard then how the king, sounding the bell in Śrāvastī, had ordered, "Whoever, at the time when the festival of the stūpa of the noble Śāriputra occurs, comes bringing merchandise, for them there is to be no tax, no toll, nor transportation fee. Therefore, they must be allowed to pass freely here!" Some thought to themselves: "This king abides in the fruit of his own merit, but is still not satisfied with his merit. Since gifts given produce merit, why should we not give gifts and make merit?" Becoming devout in mind, on the occasion of that festival they gave tortoise shells and precious stones and pearls, and so on.

The monks, however, did not know how to proceed in regard to these things.

The Blessed One said: "Those gifts which are the 'first fruit' offerings are to be given to the 'Image which Sits in the Shade of the Jambu Tree.' Moreover, a small part is to be put aside for the repair of the stūpa of Śāriputra. The remainder is to be divided by the assembly of monks—this is not for a stūpa of the Tathāgata, this is for a stūpa of Śāriputra: therefore one does not commit a fault in this case."

V. The Death of a Monk Who Was Excessively Attached to His Bowl

This took place in Śrāvastī. A certain monk was afflicted with illness, was suffering, seriously ill, overcome by pain. His bowl was lovely and he was excessively attached to it.

He said to the attendant monk: "Bring my bowl!" The attendant did not give it to him. The sick monk, having become angry in regard to the attendant, died attached to his bowl.

He was reborn as a poisonous snake in that same bowl.

The monks, after carrying his body to the burning ground, after performing the funeral rites, returned to the monastery.

The monks assembled. The belongings of the deceased were set up on the elder's end of the assembly by the distributor of robes. At that moment the Blessed One addressed the venerable Ānanda:

"Go, Ānanda! Declare to the monks: 'No one should loosen the bowl-bag of that deceased monk. The Tathāgata alone will loosen it.' "

The venerable Ānanda told the monks. After that the Tathāgata himself loosened it. The poisonous snake, having made a great hood, held its ground. Then the Blessed One, having aroused it with the sound ṛvraṭa, harnessed it. "Go!" he said, "you stupid fellow. Give up this bowl! The monks must make a distribution!"

That snake was furious. He slithered off into a dense forest. There he was burnt up by the fire of anger and that dense forest burst into flames. Because at the moment when he was consumed by the flames he was angry with the monks, he was reborn in the hells.

Then the Blessed One addressed the monks: "You, monks, must be disgusted with all existence, must be disgusted with all the causes of existence and rebirth. Here, indeed, the body of one person was burnt up on three different occasions: in the dense forest by the fire of anger; in hell by an inhabitant of hell; in the burning ground by a low-caste man. Therefore, a monk should not form excessive attachment in regard to a possession. That to which such an attachment arises is to be discarded. If one does not discard it, he comes to be guilty of an offense. But if a sick person asks for one of his own belongings, it should indeed be very quickly given to him by the attendant monk. If one does not give it, he comes to be guilty of an offense."

VI. Undertaking Acts of Worship for Sick or Dying Fellow Monks

At that time a monk was afflicted with illness, was suffering, seriously ill. He was little known; there was no medicine for him. Realizing the nature of his condition, he said to the attendant monk: "There is nothing that can be done for me. You must perform worship for my sake!"

The attendant monk promised, but the sick monk died. He was reborn in the hells.

Then the Blessed One addressed the monks: "Monks, the monk who died, what did he say to the attendant monk?"

They related the situation as it had occurred.

"Monks, that deceased monk has fallen into a bad state. If his fellow monks had performed worship to the three precious things, his mind would have been pious. Therefore, a monk should never ignore a sick fellow monk. An attendant should be given to him. When he asks for it, if there is no medicine for him, a donor is to be solicited by the attendant monk. If that succeeds, it is good. But if it does not succeed, what belongs to the community is to be given. If that succeeds, it is good. If it does not succeed, that which belongs to the Buddha's permanent endowment is to be given. But if that too does not succeed, an umbrella or banner or flag or ornament on a shrine of a tathāgata or in the perfumed chamber which is to be preserved by the community is to be made use of. After selling it, the attendant monk should look after him and perform worship to the Teacher.

"To a monk who has recovered this is to be said: 'What belongs to the Buddha was used for you.' If that monk has any means, he, making every effort, should use it for repayment. If he has none, in regard to that used for him it is said: 'The belongings of the father are likewise for the son. Here there should be no remorse.' "

VII. The Death and Property of the Monk Upananda

When he died the monk Upananda had a large quantity of gold—three hundred thousands of gold: one hundred thousand from bowls and robes; a second hundred thousand from medicines for the sick; a third hundred thousand from worked and unworked gold. Government officials heard about it. They reported it to the king, saying: "Lord, the noble one Upananda has died. He had a large quantity of gold—three hundred thousands of gold. We await your orders in regard to that!"

The king said: "If it is so, go! Seal his residential cell!"

The monks, having taken up Upananda's body, had gone to the cremation.

The government officials came and sealed Upananda's cell.

After having performed the funeral ceremonies for him at the cremation ground, the monks returned to the monastery. They saw the cell sealed with the seal of the king. The monks asked the Blessed One concerning this matter. On that occasion the Blessed One said this to the venerable Ānanda: "Go, Ānanda! In my name, ask King Prasenajit concerning his health, and speak thus: 'Great King, when you had governmental business did you then consult the monk Upananda? Or when you took a wife or gave a daughter did you then consult Upananda? Or at sometime during his life did you present Upananda with the standard belongings of a monk—robes, bowls, bedding and seats, and medicine for the sick? Or when he was ill did you attend him?' If he were to answer no, this is to be said: 'Great King, the affairs of the house of householders are one thing; those of renouncers quite another. You must have no concern! These possessions fall to the fellow monks of Upananda. You must not acquiesce to their removal!"

Saying "Yes, Reverend," Ānanda, having understood the Blessed One, approached Prasenajit, the king of Kośala. Having approached, he spoke as he had been instructed.

The king said: "Reverend Ānanda, as the Blessed One orders, just so it must be! I do not acquiesce to their removal."

The venerable Ānanda then reported to the Blessed One the answer of the king.

Then the Blessed One addressed the monks: "Monks, you must divide the estate left by the monk Upananda!" Having brought it into the midst of the community, having sold it, the return was divided by the monks. But the monks from Sāketā heard it said: "Upananda has died. He had a great quantity of gold—three hundred thousands of gold—which was divided by the monks." Making great haste, the monks of Sāketā went to Śrāvastī. They said: "We too were fellow monks of the reverend Upananda. The possessions belonging to him fall to us as well!"

Having reassembled the estate, the monks of Śrāvastī divided it again together with the monks of Sāketā. The same thing happened with monks from six great cities, since monks from Vaiśālī, Vārāṇasi, Rājagṛha, and Campā also came. The monks, having reassembled the estate on each occasion, divided it. Reassembling and dividing the estate, the monks neglected their exposition, reading, training, and mental focus.

The monks asked the Blessed One concerning this matter.

The Blessed One said: "There are five occasions for the distribution of possessions; which five? The gong, the three sections (*tridaṇḍaka*), the shrine, the lottery ticket, and the formal motion is the fifth. He who, when the gong for the dead is being beaten, comes—to him a portion is to be given. It is the same when the three sections (*tridaṇḍaka*) is being recited, when the shrine is being honored, when lottery tickets are being distributed, when a formal motion is being made. Therefore, in the last case, monks, after making a formal motion in regard to all the estate, it is to be divided. The formal motion should be a fixed procedure and should be done in this way: having made a provision of seats and bedding . . . and so forth, as before, up to . . . when the entire community is seated and assembled, having placed the estate of the deceased at the senior's end of the assembly, a single monk seated at the senior's end should make a formal motion: 'Reverends, the community should hear this! In this parish the monk Upananda has died. This estate here, both visible and invisible, is his. If the community would allow that the proper time has come, the community should give consent, to wit: that the community should take formal possession of the goods of the deceased monk Upananda, both visible and invisible, as an estate of the deceased—this is the motion.' This, monks, is the last occasion for the distribution of the estate of the deceased—that is to say, the formal motion. A monk who comes when this motion has already been made is not to be given a portion."

The venerable Upāli asked the Buddha, the Blessed One: "Wherever, Reverend, there is no one who makes a motion through lack of agreement in the community—is an estate to be divided there?"

The Blessed One said: "It is not to be divided—Upāli, after having performed 'the first and last,' it is to be distributed."

But the monks did not know what 'the first and last' was.

The Blessed One said: "After selling as a unit the deceased's belongings, and then giving a little to the seniormost of the community and to the juniormost of the community, it is to be distributed agreeably. There is in that case no cause for remorse. When a formal motion has been made, or 'the first and last,' then the possessions belonging to the estate of a deceased monk fall to all pupils of the Buddha."

VIII. The Death and Distribution of the Estate of a Shaven-Headed Householder

This took place in Śrāvastī. At that time in Śrāvastī there was a householder named Śreṣṭhin who was rich, had great wealth, possessed much property, whose holdings were extensive and wide, and who possessed the wealth of Vaiśravaṇa, equaled in wealth Vaiśravaṇa. He took a wife from a similar family. Being sonless but wanting a son, he supplicated Śiva and Varuṇa and Kubera and Śakra and Brahmā, and so on, and a variety of other gods, such as the gods of parks, the gods of the forest, the gods of the crossroads, the gods of forks in the road, and the gods who seize offerings. He even supplicated the gods who are born together with individuals, share their nature, and follow constantly behind them. It is, of course, the popular belief in the world that by reason of supplication sons and daughters are born. But that is not so. If it were so everyone—like the wheel-turning king—would have a thousand sons. In fact, sons and daughters are born from the presence of three conditions. What three? Both the mother and father are aroused and have coupled; the mother being healthy, is fertile; and a gandharva is standing by. From the presence of these three conditions sons and daughters are born.

But when there was neither son nor daughter even through his propitiation of the gods, then, having repudiated all gods, the householder became pious in regard to the Blessed One. Eventually he approached a monk: "Noble One," he said, "I wish to enter the order of this well-spoken dharma and vinaya."

"Do so, good sir!" said the monk, and in due order, after shaving the householder's head, he began to give him the rules of training. But the householder was overcome with a serious fever that created an obstacle to his entering the order.

The monks reported this matter to the Blessed One.

The Blessed One said: "He must be attended to, but the rules of training are not to be given until he is again healthy."

Although the Blessed One had said that he was to be attended to, the monks did not know by whom this was to be done.

The Blessed One said: "By the monks."

The doctors treated the man during the day, but at night his debility grew worse. They said: "Nobles, we treat him during the day, but at night his debility grows worse. If he were taken home we could treat him at night as well."

The monks reported this matter to the Blessed One.

The Blessed One said: "He should be taken home, but there too you must give him an attendant!"

His debility turned out to be of long duration. His hair grew longer and longer. It was in regard to him that the designation "shaven-headed householder, shaven-headed householder" arose.

When he did not get better although treated with medicines made from roots, stalks, leaves, flowers, and fruits, then, realizing the nature of his condition, he said, "I am dead." After that, at the time of death, he made a written will containing all the personal wealth belonging to him and sent it to the Grove of Jeta. And he died.

His government officials reported to Prasenajit, the king of Kośala: "Lord, a shaven-headed householder without a son has died, and he had a great deal of gold and silver, elephants, horses, cows, buffaloes, and equipment. Having made a written will containing all of that, it was sent to Jeta's Grove for the noble community."

The king said: "Even in the absence of a written will I did not obtain the possessions of the noble Upananda, how much less will I obtain such goods when there is a written will. But what the Blessed One will authorize, that I will accept."

The monks reported this matter to the Blessed One.

The Blessed One said: "Monks, what is there in this case?"

The monks fully described the estate.

The Blessed One said: "It is to be divided according to circumstances. Therein, property consisting of land, property consisting of houses, property consisting of shops, bedding and seats, a vessel made by an ironworker, a vessel made by a coppersmith, a vessel made by a potter—excepting a water pot and a container—a vessel made by a woodworker, a vessel made by a canesplitter, female and male slaves, servants and laborers, food and drink, and grains—these are not to be distributed, but to be set aside as property in common for the community of monks from the four directions.

"Cloths, large pieces of cotton cloth, a vessel of hide, shoes, leather oil bottles, water pots, and water jars are to be distributed among the entire community.

"Those poles which are long are to be made into banner poles for the 'Image which Sits in the Shade of the Jambu Tree.' Those which are quite small, having been made into staffs, are to be given to the monks.

"Sons and daughters are not to be sold at will within the community, but when they have gained piety they are to be released.

"Of quadrupeds, the elephants, horses, camels, donkeys, and mules are for the use of the king. Buffaloes, goats, and sheep are property in common for the community of monks from the four directions and are not to be distributed.

"And what armor and so forth is suitable for the king, all that is to be handed over to the king, except for weapons. Having made knives, needles, and staffs with them, they are to be handed out within the community.

"Of pigments, the great pigments, yellow, vermilion, blue, and so on, are to be put in the perfumed chamber to be used for the image. Khaṃkhaṭika, red, and dark blue are to be distributed among the community.

"Spirituous liquor, having been mixed with roasted barley, is to be buried in the ground. Turned into vinegar, it is to be used. Except as vinegar it is not to be used but is to be thrown away. Monks, by those who recognize me as Teacher spirituous liquor must neither be given nor drunk—even as little as could be held on the tip of a blade of grass.

"Medicines are to be deposited in a hall suitable for the sick. Thence they are to be used by monks who are ill.

"Of precious jewels—except for pearls—the gems, lapis lazuli, and conch shells with spirals turning to the right are to be divided into two lots: one for the dharma; a second for the community. With that which belongs to the dharma, the word of the Buddha is to be copied, and it is to be used as well on the lion seat. That which belongs to the community is to be distributed among the monks.

"Of books, books of the word of the Buddha are not to be distributed, but deposited in the store house as property in common for the community of monks from the four directions. Having sold the books containing the treatises of non-Buddhists, the sum received is to be distributed among the monks.

"Any written lien that can be quickly realized—the share of the money from that is to be distributed among the monks. And that which is not able to be so realized is to be deposited in the storehouse as property in common for the community of monks from the four directions.

"Gold and coined gold and other, both worked and unworked, are to be divided into three lots: one for the Buddha; a second for the dharma; a third for the community. With that which belongs to the Buddha repairs and maintenance on the perfumed chamber and on the stūpas of the hair and nails are to be made. With that belonging to the dharma the word of the Buddha is to be copied or it is to be used on the lion seat. That which belongs to the community is to be distributed among the monks."

IX. Monastic Rules Expressed in Story: The Death and Funeral of a Rich Monk in the *Avadānśataka*

The Buddha, the Blessed One, honored, revered, adored, and worshiped by kings, chief ministers, wealthy men, city dwellers, guild masters, traders, by gods, nāgas, yakṣas, asuras, garuḍas, kiṃnaras, and mahoragas, celebrated by gods and nāgas and yakṣas and asuras and garuḍas and kiṃnaras, and mahoragas, the Buddha, the Blessed One, widely known and of great merit, the recipient of the requisites, of robes, bowls, bedding, seats, and medicines for illness, he, together with the community of disciples, dwelt in Śrāvastī, in Jeta's Grove, in the park of Anāthapiṇḍada.

In Śrāvastī there was a guild master who was rich, had great wealth, possessed much property, possessed the wealth of Vaiśravaṇa, equaled in wealth Vaiśravaṇa. He on one occasion went to Jeta's Grove. Then he saw the Buddha, the Blessed One, fully ornamented with the thirty-two marks of the Great Man, his limbs glorious with the eighty secondary signs, ornamented with an aureole of a full fathom, an aureole that surpassed a thousand suns—like a moving mountain of gems, entirely beautiful. And after having seen him, after having worshiped at the feet of the Blessed One, he sat down in front of him to hear the dharma. To him the Blessed One gave an exposition of the dharma instilling disgust with the round of rebirths. When he had heard this, and had seen the faults of the round of rebirth and the qualities in nirvāṇa, he entered the order of the Blessed One. When he had entered the order he became widely known, of great merit, approached, a recipient of the requisites, of robes, bowls, bedding, seats, and medicines for illness. He, having accepted the requisites, obtained more and more. He accumulated a hoard but did not share with his fellow monks. He, through this selfishness which was cultivated, developed, and extended, and being obsessed with personal belongings, died and was reborn in his own cell as a hungry ghost.

Then his fellow monks, having struck the funeral gong, performed the removal of the body. Having performed the honor of the body on his body, they then returned to the monastery. When they unlatched the door of his cell, and began to look for his bowl and robe, they saw that deceased monk who was now a hungry ghost, deformed in hand and foot and eye, his body totally revolting, standing there clutching his bowl and robe. Having seen him deformed like that, the monks were terrified and reported it to the Blessed One.

Then the Blessed One, for the purpose of assisting that deceased son of good family, for the purpose of instilling fear in the community of students, and for the purpose of making fully apparent the disadvantageous consequences of selfishness, went to that place, surrounded by a group of monks, at the head of the community of monks. Then that hungry ghost saw the Buddha, the Blessed One, fully ornamented with the thirty-two marks of the Great Man, his limbs glorious with eighty secondary signs, ornamented with an aureole of a full fathom, an aureole that surpassed a thousand suns—like a moving mountain of gems, entirely beautiful—and as soon as he had seen him, piety in regard to the Blessed One arose in him. He was ashamed.

Then the Blessed One, with a voice that was deep like that of a heavy thundercloud, like that of the kettledrum, admonished the hungry ghost: "Sir, this hoarding of bowl and robe by you is conducive to your own destruction. Through it you are reborn in the hells. Indeed, your mind should be pious in regard to me! And you should turn your mind away from these belongings lest, having died, you will next be born in the hells!"

Then the hungry ghost gave the bowl and robe to the saṅgha and threw himself at the Blessed One's feet, declaring his fault. Then the Blessed One assigned the reward in the name of the hungry ghost: "What, indeed, is the merit from this gift—may that go to the hungry ghost! May he quickly rise from the dreadful world of hungry ghosts!"

Then that hungry ghost, having in mind become pious toward the Blessed One, died and was reborn among the hungry ghosts of great wealth. Then the hungry ghost of great wealth, wearing trembling and bright earrings, his limbs glittering with ornaments of various kinds, having a diadem of many-colored gems and his limbs smeared with saffron and tamāla leaves and spṛkka, having that very night filled his skirt with divine blue lotuses and red lotuses and white lotuses and mandāra flowers, having suffused the whole of Jeta's Grove with blinding light, having covered the Blessed One with flowers, sat down in front of the Blessed One for the sake of hearing the dharma. And the Blessed One gave him an appropriate exposition of the dharma. Having heard it and become pious, he departed.

The monks remained engaged in the practice of wakefulness throughout the entire night. They saw the blinding light around the Blessed One, and having seen it—being unsure—they asked the Blessed One: "Blessed One, did Brahmā, the Lord of the world of men, or Śakra, the leader of gods, or the four guardians of the world approach in the night for having the sight (*darśana*) of the Blessed One?"

The Blessed One said: "Monks, it was not Brahmā, the Lord of the world of men, nor Śakra, the leader of the gods, nor even the four guardians of the world who approached for having sight of me. But it was that hungry ghost who, having died, was reborn among the hungry ghosts of great wealth. In the night he came into my presence. To him I gave an exposition of the dharma. He, becoming pious, departed. Therefore, monks, work now toward getting rid of selfishness. Practice, monks, so that these faults of the guild master who became a hungry ghost will thus not arise for you."

This the Blessed One said. Delighted, the monks and others—devas, asuras, garuḍas, kiṃnaras, mahoragas, and so on—rejoiced in what the Blessed One spoke.

— 39 —

A Rite for Restoring the Bodhisattva and Tantric Vows

Donald S. Lopez, Jr.

Throughout the Buddhist traditions, one of the most important tools for the formation, continuity, and sense of identity of a Buddhist community has been vows. In addition to taking refuge in the three jewels, laypeople took up to five vows: not to kill, not to steal, not to engage in sexual misconduct, not to lie about spiritual attainments, and not to use intoxicants. Some laypeople would take eight vows which they would maintain for two days or four days each month. These were vows not to kill, steal, engage in sexual activity, lie about spiritual attainments, use intoxicants, attend musical performances or adorn their bodies, sleep on high beds, or eat after noontime. This same set of vows, with the addition of a vow not to handle gold or silver, constituted the vows of novice monks and nuns. Fully ordained monks and nuns held many more vows; under one of the codes, monks held 253 vows, nuns 364. All of these vows, whether lay or monastic, are called prātimokṣa vows, vows of liberation. These vows were regarded as the foundation of the life of a Buddhist. For laypeople, maintaining vows was a way to accumulate virtuous karma that would bring happiness in the future. For monks and nuns, vows were regarded as defining monastic identity, a lifestyle designed by the Buddha himself as most conducive to the pursuit of liberation from rebirth.

It was the maintenance of these vows by monks and nuns that was said to justify the alms they received from the laity. Hence, perhaps the most important of monastic ceremonies was the upoṣadha ceremony, in which the monks of a given monastery or area gathered together to recite their vows. Prior to the ceremony, monks would gather in small groups of two or three to confess any transgressions of the monastic code to each other. The senior monk would then recite each of the categories of vows, asking three times at the end of each category whether there were any transgressions to be revealed. Hearing none, because whatever transgressions had occurred would already have been confessed privately, he declared the saṅgha to be pure.

With the rise of the various groups that came to be called the Mahāyāna, we find the development of more vows, the bodhisattva vows. It seems that in the early Mahāyāna, persons publicly took the famous bodhisattva vow, promising to achieve buddhahood in order to liberate all beings from saṃsāra. In time, a more formal code of conduct was developed, derived from a number of sources, with categories of root infractions and secondary infractions, which are listed in the text translated below. The bodhisattva vows, however, could be taken equally by laypeople and monastics, men and women, and formal ceremonies are set forth in a number of Mahāyāna treatises. In addition, there appear to have been ceremonies for the confession of infractions, modeled on the upoṣadha; the text translated below is one example.

There is a great deal that could be said about the content of the bodhisattva vows. Some of the vows have to do with interpersonal relations, prescribing the kind of altruistic behavior that one might expect from a bodhisattva. Others are more grand, such as the vow not to destroy cities. There is also the suggestion that the bodhisattva vows supersede the prātimokṣa vows, for one of the infractions of the bodhisattva code is not to engage in killing, stealing, sexual misconduct, lying, divisive speech, harsh speech, or senseless speech if it would be beneficial to do so. And, as with all ethical formulations, one might attempt to draw inferences about the historical circumstances that led to the formulation of the infractions. Working under the assumption that activities that are not being performed at a given historical moment are not proscribed through the formulation of a vow, we can conclude, for example, that at the time of the formulation of the bhikṣu vinaya, certain monks were working as astrologers—because monks were forbidden to engage in such activity. Similarly, the great weight given to the bodhisattva's vow not to reject the Mahāyāna as the word of the Buddha suggests that throughout the history of the Mahāyāna in India, as we know, there were many who held the Mahāyāna sūtras to be of spurious origin.

With the rise of Buddhist tantra, one sees again the importance of vows. Initiates into the cults of various tantric deities were enjoined to follow a certain mode of behavior, sometimes presented in terms of vows. These disparate rules were later codified more systematically into the kind of formula translated below.

At the conclusion of his massive *Great Exposition of the Stages of the Path to Enlightenment* (*Lam rim chen mo*), the author of our text, the Tibetan monk Tsong kha pa (1357–1419 C.E.) offers a very brief discussion of tantric practice, a topic to which he would later devote an equally massive companion volume, the *Great Exposition of the Stages of Mantra* (*sNgags rim chen mo*). The passage is worth quoting at some length:

> After training in the paths common to both sūtra and mantra, you must undoubtedly enter the secret mantra because that path is very much rarer than any other doctrine, and because it quickly brings the two collections [of merit and wisdom] to comple-

tion. If one is to enter it, initially one must please the guru by respecting him and practicing his word, as Atiśa's *Lamp on the Path to Enlightenment* (*Bodhipathapradīpa*) says; this was explained earlier, but [in tantra] it must exceed that. Furthermore, the way [to rely on a guru] with all the limitless qualities explained [in the tantras] is [explained] there [in Atiśa's text]. Then, at the outset, the mind should be ripened through the ripening initiation explained from a source tantra. Then, at that time, you should listen to the pledges and vows to be taken, understand them, and maintain them. If you are defeated by the root infractions, they can be taken again. However, doing so greatly delays the creation of the qualities of the path in one's mind; you should strive fiercely not to be tainted by them. Strive not to tainted by the large infractions, but even if you are tainted by a hundred of them, use the methods for restoring [the vows]. Since these are the basis of the practice of the path, without them you will become like a dilapidated house whose foundation has collapsed. The *Root Tantra of Mañjuśrī* (*Mañjuśrīmūlatantra*) says, "The Munīndra [that is, the Buddha] did not say that someone of confused ethics achieves [the attainments of] mantra." It says that none of the great, intermediate, and low attainments (*siddhis*) [are achieved]. And it says in the unexcelled yoga (*anuttarayoga*) tantras that those who do not protect their vows, who have inferior initiation, or who do not understand reality, do not achieve anything, even though they practice. Therefore, someone who talks about practicing the path without protecting the pledges and vows has completely strayed from the mantric way. Thus, in order for a person who keeps the pledges and vows to practice the path of mantra, at the outset, on the stage of generation one should meditate on a pure divine maṇḍala explained from a source tantra. The unique object of abandonment of the mantric path is the idea of ordinariness which conceives of the aggregates, constituents, and sources to be common. It is the state of generation itself that abandons that [conception of the ordinary] and transforms those [aggregates] to appear as special abodes, bodies, and resources [of a buddha]. The person who abandons the conception of ordinariness in that way is continually blessed by the conquerors and their children and joyfully brings to completion the limitless collections of merit, thereby becoming a suitable vessel for the stage of completion.

Tsong kha pa, *mNyam med tsong kha pa chen pos mdzad pa'i byang chub lam rim che ba* (mTsho sngon mi rigs dbe skrun khang, 1985), pp. 808–9.

One is immediately struck by Tsong kha pa's emphatic statement of the centrality of the tantric vows and pledges. In the text translated below, we find a ceremony, again modeled on the upoṣadha, for confessing infractions to the tantric vows. The tantric infractions to be confessed are of three types. Although not identified in this text as such, the first thirty derive from the *Fifty Stanzas on the Guru* (*Gurupañcaśika*), a work traditionally ascribed to Aśvaghoṣa. Infractions 31–46 are a modified list of the fourteen root infractions of the Vajrayāna vows. The final list of twenty-eight infractions confessed at the end of the text are the so-called "gross infractions" of the Vajrayāna vows. There is a host of issues to be considered here. For example, the Indian origins of these various infractions need to be explored in an effort to identify the process of consolidation that led to these particular sets of infractions in these particular forms. One might explore the issue of why Tsong kha pa combines the list of infractions from the *Gurupañcaśika* with the presumably more important root infractions: one would assume that abandoning emptiness (38) would be more consequential than cracking one's knuckles in the presence of the guru (18). In the case of the Vajrayāna, one might speculate about the possible meaning of the pronounced presence of infractions that do not strike us as particularly tantric but that could just as easily be placed under the bodhisattva or even the prātimokṣa vow. At the same time, while the bodhisattva infractions seem to go to great length to defend the integrity of the śrāvakayāna, the vehicle of the Hīnayāna disciples, perhaps because monks of both the Mahāyāna and Hīnayāna persuasions inhabited the same monasteries in India, the tantric infractions take a much dimmer view of the lesser vehicle, prohibiting the tāntrika (tantric practitioner) from spending seven days in the dwelling of a śrāvaka (Hīnayāna practitioner). Indeed, the relation among the three vows is a topic that received a great deal of comment in the exegetical literature. It was the opinion of the author of our text, however, that there were no contradictions between the prātimokṣa vows, the bodhisattva vows, and the tantric vows. In his view, monks could and should take and hold the bodhisattva and tantric vows. Although the prātimokṣa were not required for them, lay people could take both of "the higher vows." However, the bodhisattva vows were an essential requirement for receiving tantric vows.

The infractions seem to fall into various categories. For example, many of the infractions seem designed to promote a certain etiquette. In the case of the bodhisattva vows, this etiquette is often of a pedagogical sort, whereas in the Vajrayāna it is largely directed toward the guru. Certain other infractions seem intended to preserve and protect the institutional identity of the sect. For example, in the prātimokṣa, the crime of parricide would strike us as more serious than causing dissension in the saṅgha, yet both are deeds that send the doer immediately to the most tortuous of hells. And we see in the tantric infractions repeated and redundant injunctions against revealing secrets to the uninitiated. Finally, we can identify infractions that seem to be more closely connected to issues of "practice": the reminders not to lose sight of bodhicitta (the altruistic aspiration to enlightenment), not to have doubts about emptiness, not to misuse sexual union. Such a typology might divert us, however, from the larger issue of the function of these vows, apparently so difficult to keep that they must be retaken six times a day (and one takes a vow to do so) and that the recitation of the fault is itself the repair. We might ponder how all of this might relate to Tsong kha pa's contention that what the mantric path destroys is the idea that one is ordinary, suggesting finally that vinaya, whether prātimokṣa, bodhisattva, or tantric, is more fruitfully understood not as that which restricts individuals and their actions but that which creates them.

This translation is from *sDom pa gong ma gnyis kyi phyir bcos byed tshul rje'i phyag len bzhin bkod pa.* The work (Tohoku Catalogue no. 5279) occurs in the second volume (*kha*) of the Lhasa (also known as Zhol) edition of his collected works. See *The Collected Works (gsuṅ 'bum) of the Incomparable Lord Tsoṅ-kha-pa bLo-bzaṅ-grags-pa (Khams gsum chos kyis* [sic] *rgyal po shar tsong kha pa chen po'i gsung 'bum)* (New Delhi: Mongolian Lama Guru Deva, 1978), 1–5b6 (Guru Deva, 793–802). In the Tibetan text, the instructions for the rite appear in a smaller script, which will be rendered here in a smaller bold typeface. The numbers of each of the infractions do not appear in the original Tibetan text and are added here for convenience.

Further Reading

Mark Tatz, *Asanga's Chapter on Ethics with Tsong-kha-pa's Commentary* (Lewiston, NY: Edwin Mellen Press, 1986).

Procedure for Restoring the Two Higher Vows According to the Practice of the Foremost One

Everyone bows down three times [and then] says: I beseech all the buddhas and bodhisattvas who reside in the ten directions and the saṅgha of bodhisattvas, the principal of whom is the bodhisattva master [who bestowed the vow], to direct their minds to the rite for the restoration of infractions. **Sit down and say:** I beseech all the buddhas and bodhisattvas who reside in the ten directions and the sangha of bodhisattvas, the principal of whom is the bodhisattva master, to take heed of the rite for the restoration of infractions. From among [the deeds] set forth that are bases of defeat, the transgressions that go against the bodhisattva vinaya are the actual [transgressions]–the first root infraction through the eighteenth root infraction—and the transgressions that are the small and intermediate contaminations. [The root infractions are]: 1. to praise oneself and slander others out of attachment to profit or fame; 2. not to give one's wealth or the doctrine, out of miserliness, to those who suffer without protection; 3. to become enraged and condemn another, without listening to his or her apology; 4. to abandon the Mahāyāna and teach a facsimile of the excellent doctrine; 5. to steal the wealth of the three jewels; 6. to abandon the excellent doctrine; 7. to steal the saffron [robes] and beat, imprison, and expel a monk from the life of renunciation, even if he has broken the ethical code; 8. to commit the five deeds of immediate [retribution, that is, kill one's father, kill one's mother, kill an arhat, wound a buddha, or cause dissent in the saṅgha]; 9. to hold wrong views; 10. to destroy cities and so forth; 11. to discuss emptiness with sentient beings whose minds have not been trained; 12. to turn someone away from buddhahood and complete enlightenment; 13. [to cause someone] to abandon completely the prātimokṣa vow in order to practice the Mahāyāna; 14. to believe that desire and so forth cannot be abandoned by the śrāvakayāna [the Hīnayāna] and to cause others to believe it; 15. to discuss one's own virtues and to slander others for profit, fame, or reputation [This infraction, which seems to be identical to the first infraction, causes the standard list of eighteen root infractions of the bodhisattva vow to be expanded to nineteen here.]; 16. to claim falsely, "I have withstood the profound [emptiness]"; 17. to impose fines on renunciates, [and] to take donors and gifts away from the three jewels; 18. to cause [meditators] to give up [the practice of] quiescence (*śamatha*); [to take] the resources of those on retreat [and] give them to reciters [of texts]; 19. to abandon the two types of bodhicitta.

In what I, so and so, have done, from among [the deeds] set forth that are bases of defeat, limitless actual [transgressions] have occurred which go against the bodhisattva discipline—from the first infraction to the eighteenth infraction—as well as transgressions that are small and intermediate contaminations. Those transgressions committed by me, so and so, are disclosed and revealed in the presence of all the buddhas and bodhisattvas who reside in the ten directions and the saṅgha of bodhisattvas, the principal of whom is the bodhisattva master. I do not conceal them. By disclosing and revealing them, I will abide in happiness; if I do not disclose and reveal them, I will not abide in happiness. **Say this three times.**

After that, the master asks, Do you see those as faults? Will you refrain [from them] hereafter? **The person who has disclosed the transgressions says,** I do see. If I watch with vigilance, I will take them to the crown of my head in accord with the dharma and in accord with the vinaya. **Repeat the question and the answer three times.**

There is also a way to restore the faulty deeds of a bodhisattva. As before say: I beseech [all the buddhas and bodhisattvas who reside in the ten directions and the saṅgha of bodhisattvas, the principal of whom is the bodhisattva master, to take heed of the rite for the restoration of infractions]. From among [the deeds] set forth which are bases of faulty deeds, the transgressions which are faulty deeds contrary to the bodhisattva discipline are: 1. not to make effort when one should make effort in order to provide others with requisites and food; 2. to be biased [for or against] others based on one's judgment that they have benefited or harmed one and to prejudicially regard them with attachment, hatred, or dismissive neutrality; 3. not to teach the excellent; 4. not to listen to and contemplate the profound and vast bodhisattvapiṭaka; 5. not to be imbued with altruism when making use of food, clothing, and dwelling place; 6. not to be imbued with bodhicitta when practicing the six perfections, such as giving; 7. not to abandon the four black qualities that defile bodhicitta; 8. not to practice the four white qualities that benefit [bodhicitta] [The four black factors, taken from the *Kāśyapaparivarta,* are: lying about one's practice of the bodhisattva vows, discouraging others from the practice of virtue and causing those who have performed virtuous deeds to regret having done so, insulting bodhisattvas, having ulterior motives for the practice of the path other than bodhicitta. The four white factors are the opposite of these.]; 9. not to strive to bring about the benefit and happiness of others and the eradication of their suffering; 10. not to worship the three jewels with the three [body, speech, and mind]; 11. to indulge in desirous thoughts; 12. not to respect elders; 13. not to answer a question; 14. not to accept an invitation; 15. not to accept such things as gold; 16. not to give gifts to those who desire the dharma; 17. to reject those who have broken the ethical code; 18. not to practice in order [to conform to what] others have faith in; 19. to do little for the welfare of sentient beings; 20. not to perform [one of the seven nonvirtuous deeds of body and speech] with love and mercy; 21. to take on wrong livelihood; 22. to become agitated and laugh loudly; 23. to intend to travel solely in saṃsāra; 24. not to avoid disrepute; 25. not to nurture [someone] even by using the afflictions; 26. to respond to abuse with abuse; 27. to neglect the angry; 28. to reject another's apology; 29. to indulge in anger; 30. to gather a circle [of disciples] out of desire for fame; 31. not to eliminate laziness, and so on; 32. to be addicted to idle talk; 33. not to seek the aim of samādhi; 34. not to eliminate the obstacles to concentration; 35. to see good qualities in the taste of concentration; 36. to reject the śrāvakayāna; 37. to strive [exclusively] in that [śrāvakayāna] while being in one's own [bodhisattva] mode; 38. to strive after the treatises of outsiders, which are not to be strived after; 39. to strive after [those treatises] and to take delight in them; 40. to abandon the Mahāyāna; 41. to praise oneself and belittle others; 42. not to go [somewhere] for the sake of the dharma; 43. to belittle [a teacher] and rely on the letter; 44. not to go to a friend in need; 45. to neglect to serve the sick; 46. not to dispel suffering; 47. not to teach what is fitting to the unconscientious; 48. not to help in response to a [good] deed; 49. not to dispel the sorrow of others; 50. not to give to those who desire wealth; 51. not to act for the welfare of your circle of followers; 52. not to act in accordance with others' expectations; 53. not to praise good qualities; 54. not to destroy in accordance with the conditions; 55. not to use supernormal powers [against] the sinful.

In what I, so and so, have done, limitless transgressions that are faulty deeds such as these which go against the bodhisattva vinaya have occurred. Those transgressions committed by me, so and so, [are disclosed and revealed in the presence of all the buddhas and bodhisattvas who reside in the ten directions and the saṅgha of bodhisattvas, the principal of whom is the bodhisattva master. I do not conceal them. By disclosing and revealing them, I will abide in happiness; if I do not disclose and reveal them, I will not abide in happiness. **Say this three times.**

After that, the master asks, Do you see those as faults? Will you refrain hereafter? **The person who has disclosed the vow says,** I do see. If I watch with vigilance, I will take them to the crown of my head in accord with the dharma and in accord with the vinaya. **Repeat the question and the answer three times.**]

I beseech all the buddhas and bodhisattvas who reside in the ten directions and the saṅgha of vidyādharas, the principal of whom is the vidyādhara master [tantric master, who bestowed the vow], to direct their minds to the rite for the restoration of infractions. **Sit down and say:** I beseech all the buddhas and bodhisattvas who reside in the ten directions and the saṅgha of vidyādharas, the principal of whom is the vidyādhara master, to take heed of the rite for the restoration of infractions. From among [the deeds] set forth that are bases of defeat, the transgressions which conform to the category that go against the Vajrayāna vinaya, from the first root infraction through the fourteenth root infraction are: 1. not to make obeisance, together with the offering of a maṇḍala and flowers to the glorious excellent guru six times each day; 2. to listen to or explain the dharma without analyzing the connection between master and disciple; 3. to scorn and slander the guru; 4. to disturb the mind of the guru; 5. not to offer him or her pleasing things; 6. not to protect one's pledges constantly; 7. not to worship the Sugata [Buddha] constantly; 8. not to worship the guru constantly; 9. to imagine that the guru and Vajradhara [tantric form of the Buddha] are different; 10. to step on the guru's shadow, shoes, seat, [or use his or her] conveyance, and so on; 11. not to listen respectfully to his instructions; although it is suitable to explain [to the guru] that one is unable [to follow his or her instruction], [it is an infraction] not to do [what he or she says] without explanation; 12. not to consider the guru's property as [as valuable] as one's life and not to consider his circle as one's relatives; 13. to sit on the bed or seat where he is present and to walk in front of him without receiving permission to do so; to place one's feet on a seat prior to the guru and to sing; 14. to remain lying down or sitting when the guru has risen [and] to lie down when he is sitting; 15. in the presence of the guru to spit, stretch one's legs, walk about, or dispute his or her authority; 16. to rub one's limbs, dance, sing, make music, or talk foolishly; 17. not to rise respectfully; 18. to twist one's body, lean against pillars, or crack one's knuckles in the presence of the guru; 19. not to perform prostrations before and after washing him, massaging him, and so forth; 20. to utter the name of the guru without using honorifics and not to use [additional] special words in order to create respect in others; 21. not to cover one's mouth with one's hand when laughing or coughing; when one has done [what one was told to do], not to indicate that, using soft words; 22. not to sit before him with discipline and not to be restrained in the mode of dress, and so on; 23. when listening to the excellent dharma of the secret mantra, not to request [the teaching] three times kneeling with the palms together; 24. not to accompany [the guru] with restraint and conscientiousness, having given up all pride and affectation; 25. in the area where the guru resides to perform a consecration, [create] a maṇḍala, perform a fire offering, gather students, or teach without receiving the guru's permission; 26. for disciples [when one oneself is] a guru, to act as disciples [in the presence of one's own guru]; 27. not to offer to the guru whatever one receives [from ceremonies] such as "opening the eyes", and when he has taken the gift, not to do whatever one wishes with the rest; 28. not to bow [the head] and use both hands [when] something is offered to the master or something is bestowed by the guru; 29. not to stop others from bowing [to oneself] in the presence of one's guru; 30. not to stop fellow disciples from going beyond [the suitable] in their own behavior by striving in everything one does; 31. to transgress the word of the Sugata guru; 32. to become enraged at one's [vajra] siblings and speak of their faults; 33. to speak cuttingly to qualified [vajra] siblings; 34. to abandon love for sentient beings; 34. to abandon the two types of bodhicitta; 35. to disparage the tenets of one's own [Buddhist] and others' [non-Buddhist] schools; 36. to proclaim secrets to the unripened; 37. to scorn the aggregates; 38. to abandon emptiness; 39. to love the vicious; 40. to use deceitful love; 41. not to contemplate emptiness continuously; 42. not to seek emptiness and instructions on the great bliss; 43. to disillusion the faithful; 44. to speak of the faults of yogins; 45. not to use the excellent substances properly; 46. to disparage women.

In what I, **say your secret name**, so-and-so Vajra, have done, limitless transgressions such as these have occurred. Those transgressions committed by me, **say your secret name**, so-and-so Vajra, are disclosed and revealed [in the presence of all the buddhas and bodhisattvas who reside in the ten directions and] the [vajra] master [from whom one took the vows] **or the** elder vidyādhara [present]. I do not conceal them. By disclosing and revealing them, I will abide in happiness; if I do not disclose and reveal them, I will not abide in happiness. **Say this three times.**

After that, the master asks, Do you see those as faults? Will you refrain [from them] hereafter? **The person who has disclosed the vow says,** I do see. If I watch with vigilance, I will take them to the crown of my head in accord with the dharma and in accord with the vinaya. **Repeat the question and the answer three times.**

The restoration of the gross infractions. As before say: I beseech [all the buddhas and bodhisattvas who reside in the ten directions and the saṅgha of vidyādharas, the principal of whom is the vidyādhara master, to take heed of the rite for the restoration of infractions.] From among [the deeds] set forth that are bases of gross infractions, the transgressions which go against the Vajrayāna vinaya are: 1. to use an unqualified consort; 2. to engage in union inappropriately; 3. not keeping secrets from the unripened; 4. to argue in an assembly; 5. to teach the faithful a doctrine different [from that which they requested]; 6. to stay seven days with a śrāvaka; 7. to claim falsely to be a yogin; 8. to teach the doctrine to the faithless; 9. to display secrets to the unripened without preparing them well; 10. to enter a maṇḍala without purification, such as approximation; 11. to transgress the two vows [prātimokṣa and bodhisattva] without purpose; 12. not to promise to restrain oneself from the root infractions and the gross infractions six times a day; 13. to go against the three ethical codes; 14. not to go for refuge six times a day; 15. not to rely on the pledge of the mudrā, vajra, and bell; 16. not to give the gifts of requisites, nonfear, the doctrine, and love six times a day; 17. not to create the wish to uphold the excellent doctrines of the three outer and secret vehicles; 18. not to make effort at the vows and make offerings six times a day; 19. not to give up what is unsuitable except in order to tame sentient beings; 20. not to make offerings to yogins; 21. not to strive to practice the ten virtues; 22. to desire the Hīnayāna; 23. turning one's back on the welfare of sentient beings; 24. to abandon saṃsāra; 25. to be constantly attached to nirvāṇa; 26. to scorn gods, demigods, and secret deities (*yakṣas*); 27. to walk over or eat [in the presence of] mudrās, conveyances, weapons, and hand implements [of deities]; 28. to step on the shadows of ancient deities.

In what I, so-and-so Vajra, have done, limitless forms of transgressions that are gross infractions which go against the Vajrayāna vinaya have occurred. Those transgressions which are gross infractions committed by me, so-and-so Vajra, [are disclosed and revealed in the presence of all the buddhas and bodhisattvas who reside in the ten directions and the vajra master or the elder vidyādhara. I do not conceal them. By disclosing and revealing them, I will abide in happiness; if I do not disclose and reveal them, I will not abide in happiness. **Say this three times.**

After that, the master says, Do you see those as faults? Will you refrain from them hereafter? **The person who has disclosed the transgressions says,** I do see. If I watch with vigilance, I will take them to the crown of my head in accord with the dharma and in accord with the vinaya. **Repeat the question and the answer three times.**]

Stand up and do three prostrations. Say: All the buddhas and bodhisattvas who reside in the ten directions and the saṅgha of vidyādharas, the principal of whom is the vidyādhara master or the elder vidyādhara, have with great kindness directed their minds to the rite for the restoration of infractions. **They say:** It is most wonderful to be in accordance with the dharma and in accordance with the vinaya.

May the teaching of the Muni hereby long remain. Sarvamaṅgalaṃ.

—40—

Awakening Stories of Zen Buddhist Women

Sallie King

The status of women in Buddhism has been problematic throughout Buddhist history. According to scripture, the Buddha was approached early in his career by his aunt, Mahāpajāpatī, at the head of a delegation of women who wished him to institute a Buddhist order of nuns. The Buddha initially declined to institute such an order. But when the Buddha's close disciple, Ānanda, asked him whether women were able to attain the fruits of spiritual practice, the Buddha unhesitatingly answered that women could attain such fruits. This affirmation on the part of the Buddha has been of the first importance to Buddhist women throughout history, while his reluctance to establish an institutional place for women has haunted them.

The ordination of the first Buddhist nuns followed shortly after this interview. In the order instituted, all nuns were formally subordinated to all monks by means of the "eight weighty rules," which forbade nuns' admonishing or teaching monks and declared the most senior nun to be subordinate to the most junior monk in the monastic seniority system. As reflected in their place in the monastic hierarchy, the social standing of nuns as a group has always been inferior to that of monks. The nuns' order died out in Theravāda countries and in Tibet, but has continued to the present in East Asia. But in East Asia as well, the nuns' order has been subjected to unequal treatment. For example, in 1913 in the Japanese Soto Zen sect, from which the translations here derive, the sect annually spent 600 Japanese yen per nun and 180,000 yen per monk or male priest. With such poor institutional support, it is obvious that the social standing of nuns was far inferior to that of monks and that provisions for their education and training were minimal. Social reform came to the Soto sect, as to much of the rest of Japan, in the Meiji era and especially after World War II. But it was not until 1970 that nuns were formally permitted to hold meditation retreats by themselves, without male supervision. The selections below give accounts of women-only meditation retreats held in the 1940s and 1950s, led by a nun ahead of her time.

These selections are excerpted from a text entitled *A Collection of Meditation*

Experiences, published in Japan in 1956. The book records the meditation experiences of laywomen and nuns practicing under the Zen master and nun, Nagasawa Sozen Roshi. (Her family name means Long Valley; her Buddhist name means Zen-ancestor.) Nagasawa Roshi was in her time perhaps the only nun directing a Japanese Zen nunnery and practice center and holding meditation retreats without the supervision of a male Zen master. She was a disciple of the famous Harada Daiun Roshi, who, though a member of the Soto Zen lineage, supplemented traditional Soto practices with Rinzai Zen koan practice. The present selections show Nagasawa Roshi at work, training nuns and laywomen in the Tokyo Nuns' Practice Center. Her nun disciples themselves had previously undertaken an extensive alms-begging tour in order to raise funds to build the meditation hall in which the retreats were held.

It is noteworthy that Nagasawa Roshi is depicted as training her disciples in the same manner as other teachers in her line. Though a number of contemporary Western feminist Buddhists have criticized aspects of Zen training as "macho," and some modern Zen masters have dropped some such practices, Nagasawa Roshi seems to employ them all. She is depicted as being quite stern and even fierce with her disciples before they make a breakthrough in their practice, shouting at them and abruptly ringing them out of the interview room with her dismissal bell; she relies heavily on a koan practice in which the disciple aggressively assaults the ego, suffering a roller-coaster ride of blissful highs and despairing lows in the process; and she uses the "encouragement stick," a flat hardwood stick with which meditators may be slapped on the shoulders during prolonged meditation sessions to help them call up energy for their practice (it functions much like cold water splashed in the face and is not a punishment). This severity is what Zen calls "grandmotherly kindness": the teacher's aid to the student working to free herself from the limitations of ego. The atmosphere of the meditation retreats is portrayed as taut and austere; Nagasawa Roshi herself is described as possessing exalted experience and, though hard and demanding before a disciple makes a breakthrough, warm and gentle when the breakthrough is achieved. It is clear that her students deeply respect her and are grateful to her. All this is classic Japanese Zen. Thus, while Nagasawa Roshi does represent for her time a female incursion into a male world, she makes no changes in behavior within that world other than the significant change of inviting other women into it.

The text from which these selections are drawn contains some sixty accounts written by laywomen and nuns studying under Nagasawa Roshi. In the Zen sect, it is believed that enlightenment comes in varying depths and is subject to ever greater deepening. In the lineage which Nagasawa Roshi represents, it is customary upon attaining kensho, the first awakening experience, to write an autobiographical account of the events that led one to practice Zen and a description of one's practice, culminating in an account of the kensho itself. Two such accounts follow.

These accounts depict students working with koans, meditation devices which give the practitioner a puzzle that cannot be resolved by rational means. It functions as both goad and carrot to the inquiring mind. The accounts translated below show one nun and one laywoman working with the well-known koan "*Mu*." This is very frequently given as the first koan to serious practitioners; it is believed to be a good tool for helping the practitioner to make the breakthrough to a first awakening, or preliminary enlightenment, experience. The *Mu* koan reads: "A monk once asked Master Joshu, 'Has a dog the Buddha nature or not?' Joshu said, '*Mu!*' "

A koan is assigned by a Zen master with whom a student has an ongoing relationship; the teacher assesses the student's character and degree of understanding and assigns a koan which he or she believes will best work for the student at his or her current stage. The teacher may or may not give additional instructions or explanations to the student. The student then meditates on the koan for a period that may last hours or years, attempting to resolve the puzzle embedded in it. Periodically, the student returns to the private interview with the teacher, or dokusan, to demonstrate his or her progress in working with the koan. These interviews are not the time for casual discussion; they are the student's opportunity to demonstrate understanding and ask for specific instructions, and the teacher's opportunity to test the student and give further instruction. Their atmosphere is extremely formal and intense.

As the following selections demonstrate, students working with *Mu* frequently concentrate their minds entirely on the *Mu* itself, repeating the word *Mu* over and over to themselves with great energy as an aid to concentration. When the student working on the koan *Mu* returns to the private interview with the teacher, any answer spoken from dualistic thinking will be rejected; an answer that is an expression of buddha nature, in whatever form it takes, will be accepted.

In the following selections, both students work on the koan *Mu*, most importantly in the setting of sesshin. In this tradition, sesshin are severe and intensive week-long meditation retreats. In a typical day at such a retreat, all present rise well before the sun and spend the entire day in meditation. Most of the day is given to formal zazen, or sitting Zen meditation, done usually in the full- or half-lotus position, sometimes in kneeling Japanese style. The rest of the day is occupied with light meals, chanting, a work period (mostly cooking and cleaning), usually one talk per day by the teacher, and mandatory private interviews with the teacher. The student is expected to maintain a meditative state of mind throughout all of these events. Strict silence is required and eye contact is avoided at all times, except in the private interview room. Formal rules of decorum and ceremony cover all movements and interactions, contributing to the taut and intense atmosphere. The programmed part of the day ends around 9:00 or 10:00 P.M., but many students stay up later, sometimes through the whole night, to continue working on their meditation practice.

In reading the following accounts one should recall the dual heritage of Buddhism for women: the Buddha's affirmation of women's spiritual ability paired with the weighty neglect of women in Buddhist institutions. In Nagasawa Roshi and her lay and nun disciples we see three modern Japanese women encountering this heritage, embracing what helps them and transforming what could hold them back.

The translations are from Iizuka Koji, ed., *Sanzen Taiken Shu* (*A Collection of Meditation Experiences*), with a Foreword by Nagasawa Sozen (Tokyo: Chuo Bukkyosha, 1956), pp. 30–38 and 242–46.

Further Reading

On the *Mu* koan, see Zenkei Shibayama, *Zen Comments on the Mumonkan*, translated by Sumiko Kudo (New York: New American Library, 1974), p. 19.

Remembering My Child

In the first account, written in 1949, a laywoman named Nakayama Momoyo shares with us her life before and during Zen practice. We are given a picture of a woman who manages impressively as virtually a single mother in prewar and wartime Japan, but who finally cannot cope with her grief over her son's death. Her initial encounter with Zen is instructive in its outsider's perspective and skepticism. Her experiences in retreat, with her roller coaster of emotions, are typical. Finally, however difficult it is to understand her awakening experience, it is at least clear that her broken spirit has been healed.

My beloved son, my only son, for whom there is no replacement in heaven or earth, him I lost in the war. Just three days after graduating as a reservist from Tokyo Imperial University, he left for the front in high spirits. In a corner of a northern island his life came to an end; this young sapling of just twenty-six years died.

Our son had cultivated his parents' fields—his father's as a man of religion, mine as an educator. . . . From the time of his childhood, idealizing his good but ordinary father and mother, he had cherished the hope of inheriting the child-care center which I ran and becoming a religious educator. His smaller motives were to give joy to the children and to express his filial piety toward his mother; his greater concern was, as a true man of religion, with the people of the world and, by extension, with the religious path. Thus he revered all buddhas and patriarchs. . . .

As a consequence, his personality was easy-going and generous. I, on the other hand, who was raising and guiding children, was always being taught and purified by him. I never stopped reflecting, "Can this child have developed in my womb? Can he have been born and raised by a mother with such deep sins as I? There must have been some mistake for me to come to be his mother."

After his preschool days, and throughout his school days, many people—teachers, classmates, all who knew him—loved him for his personality. From the bottom of their hearts, they grieved over his death in battle. A wounded soldier who had miraculously returned alive and who had served under my son from beginning to end called on me after the war was over. Kneeling before the Buddha altar, he spoke to me for thirty minutes, hands palm-to-palm and tears flowing:

"He was truly a kind commander. He loved his subordinates. No matter what, he never reprimanded us. In other squads, the commander always ate first, but our commander always gave food to his subordinates first. Consequently, all his subordinates adored him and had confidence in him. In the end, when we knew there was no hope, no one spoke of giving up. There wasn't a single person who didn't want to share the fate of the commander. I myself was wounded in the chest, but when I told the commander that I absolutely must die with him, I upset him. Uncharacteristically angry, he admonished me, 'Dying is not the only way of serving your country and your parents. You're young; your wound will certainly heal. Take responsibility for the seriously wounded; take them to the rear for me.' Then he put in good order all the mementos, charms, and photographs he had from you. He threw away his saber, saying, 'This kind of thing is why we've lost,' and calmly walked, unarmed, toward the enemy camp. This is what I have to say to you, his mother."

. . . As a foreign missionary, my husband lived [away from the family] for a long time in a temple in Hawaii. During his absence, in addition to running the child-care center, I had put my whole heart into raising my son; his growing up had filled me with delight. This great objective of my beloved son's adulthood, had been the one and only shining light in my life; whatever pain, whatever sorrow I experienced were nothing. My life had been full to bursting, like an always full moon.

The day I can never forget arrived! May 7, 1945: while I still held in my hands the news of my son's death in battle, his remains were ceremoniously delivered. The agony and grief I felt as I held in my arms the small box of plain wood cannot be expressed with such phrases as "I felt like vomiting blood," or "my heart was broken." Only another mother who has experienced it can know.

I was pushed from a world of light into a world of gloom. I lost all desire to live; every bit of happiness was taken away in grief and hopelessness. A soulless puppet, I mourned day in and day out, wretched with the loss of my son. How many times did I decide to follow my beloved son in death? In my need, I could clearly hear the longed-for voice of my son come back to me: "Mother, you must not die! Please, be happy! Please, live in happiness!"

So my son would not permit me to die, suffer, or sorrow. But I . . . would cry until I was emptied. People criticized me as a foolish mother, a prisoner of my emotions. I fell to a very low place. I felt it would be best if my life would end. I cried on and on for over three years. Day and night I consoled myself at the family altar, offering scripture readings, flowers, and incense before his spirit. Thus passed the dreary days and nights. I realized that I had been a teacher to over two thousand pupils and young mothers, but now my life took on a pitiful appearance.

On June 3, 1949, I met the nun-teacher Nagasawa Sozen of the Nun's Practice Center (*dojo*) and listened to her give a talk. At first I thought, "How could she understand this pain, this suffering? She's never given birth to a child or raised a child, much less had a child be killed." My hard heart was shut tight, leaving me without a soul in the world to turn to. However, as I listened to the talk, and was touched by her character, I felt somehow that there was dragged out from me some kind of innocence free of poison which was just on the other side of my deep and relentless bitterness. My feelings toward Nagasawa Roshi changed a little, and as I was pulled along more and more by her lecture I decided, "maybe I'll give meditation (*zazen*) a try." The upshot was that I tried meditating for two days, then three, and finally completed a week's retreat (*sesshin*). As the retreats piled up, my shallowness bored deeply into me, by which I mean I realized that though it was true that Nagasawa Roshi had not borne a child, raised him, and had him die, with respect to the search for knowledge she possessed exalted experience surpassing that of the world's mothers.

I was bitter. And yet, wasn't there deep within me a great, shining compassionate heart which spontaneously wrapped itself around humankind in all their infinite variety? Yes, a compassionate heart! I made my decision: "I too will be the disciple of this teacher. I'll break through the barrier!" Henceforth, as I pressed ahead on the path, I depended upon the teacher in my literally do-or-die struggle. However, I did not escape from the saying, "It's easy to say but hard to do." During the retreats, my pain and sorrow, my melancholy and wretchedness were beyond words; those who haven't had this experience cannot know what I suffered.

As a beginner, jumping headfirst into this world without knowing the first thing about it, my first surprise was a big one. When I saw the group earnestly taking up the practice of *Mu,* I didn't know whether to think it was a joke, or some kind of stupid incompetence, or perhaps that I was in a mental hospital and they were psychotics. Meals were even more surprising. When we received two slices of pickle, we reverently joined our palms in thanks. How often we joined our palms—for the rice gruel, the water, the clearing up—from beginning to end, the whole meal seemed like it was taken with joined palms! These harmonious manners were truly graceful and beautiful, but on the other hand, I felt that the solemnity brought with it an oppressive restraint.

In the search for *Mu,* I didn't relax my meditation posture, I didn't sleep, and I lost sensation in my whole body from the pain in my legs. But despite the fact that I was struggling with the misery of a thousand deaths and ten thousand pains, just when I wished for some mercy, I was hit from behind [with the encouragement stick], making sparks fly from my eyes. It was the first time in my life that I had ever been hit by anyone. "How barbaric!" flared up my rebellious thoughts. I went furiously into the private interview with the teacher (*dokusan*).

"Don't spout logic! It's just your ego!" she thundered at me, driving me out with the ringing of her bell.

"*Mu—, Mu—, Mu—*" with all my might. I thought, "I am driving myself to death or insanity knocking up against this." But each time the teacher would crush me with, "That's emotion! That's theory! That's interpretation! What are you waiting for?" My faith, my ideas were demolished. "*Mu—, Mu—, Mu—,*" while sleeping, while eating, while in the toilet room, just *Mu*.

As time passed, I lost my appetite. At night I couldn't sleep, but sat up in meditation. The fatigue of body and mind reached an extreme. I was seized, tormented by *Mu* to the extent that during walking meditation, my feet could not take a single step forward. Though *Mu* was in my tears, I could not seize *Mu*. Private interview was always, "That's an hallucination! That's just a belief! That's just an idea! That's just a blissful feeling!"—an unbearable, merciless, cutting whip of words.

Soon all means were exhausted and I had nothing left to cling to. "Oh, I'm no good. I'm an evil person totally lacking the necessary qualities to be helped." How many times I gave up, sinking to the bottom with a sorrowful "thud"! I even thought, "My son disappeared with the dew of the battlefield, but I don't think his suffering was worse than mine is now."

At one time I clung to the Roshi, overflowing with hope, believing that only she was capable of being my spiritual teacher; but after all, that was still my ignorance. Another time I decided to run away as fast as I could from this practice center. I went to my room, and as I was tearfully packing my bag, I heard a voice from deep within my heart saying: "Under the sky of a far-away foreign land, no food, nothing to drink, lying down in a field, sleeping in the mountains, how many times did he dream of his home? I'm sure he wanted to see his father and mother, his beloved younger sister. Cutting off his unsuppressable personal feelings, fully aware of the preciousness of his life, with no way to advance and, following his superiors' orders, no way to retreat, what was his distracted state of mind like?"

"I must think of my child's death in war!" I thought. "What is my hardship? It doesn't amount to a thing! If I don't open up the way here and now, when will my dead son and I be released from the world?" Instantly, all thought of fleeing vanished. Greatly stirred and with courage renewed, I picked up the practice again.

Previously I had been cramped, immobilized in my own narrow and rigid shell. As my practice progressed, I gradually got rid of my egotism, freed of my distracting thoughts, and able to emerge out into a bright and wide-open world. For a slice of pickle, a morsel of rice-gruel, even the intense "whip" of words, from deep in my heart a grateful prostration came. Heretofore, as the wife of a religious man, I had eaten Buddhist food, was taught Buddhism and read Buddhist books; I thought of myself as having understood Buddhist thought. But I had come to realize keenly that since I had never really suffered, never really tasted experience, I couldn't stand up to a real battle in a crisis. I was truly abashed and could hardly bear my shame. Now this realization soaked into the marrow of my bones.

In high spirits I went into the private interview, but once again, "You're just finding religious joy in the world of faith. . . . Hey, reluctant one, where are you? Come out! Come out! Come out and grab *Mu!* Don't be unwilling! Come out naked and exposed! Come on out and grab it! Come on! Come on!" she pressed her urgent command. She sent me staggering away, thrown back upon my own resources and writhing in pain.

"Now I have arrived here where there is only death. . . . It is death, it is *Mu,* it is death, it is *Mu,* it is *Mu,* it is *Mu.*" Soon I forgot all about the private interview. *Mu*—, *Mu*—, *Mu*—, there is only *Mu.* . . . I went out into the yard and quietly sat down. Before the temple house one great tree stood alone, reaching to the clouds. In harmony with my chant of *Mu*—, *Mu*—, *Mu*—, the earth trembled and urged me on. Azalea leaves and small flowers spoke to me one by one. The bright moon laughed and became one with me.

Night passed. How pleasant the morning practice, how sweet the little bird's song! The crisp crunch, crunch, crunch of the kitchen master at the cutting board, the sound of the mallet as a woman out back hammered away cracking soybeans—from everywhere I could hear wonderful, indescribable music. Was this a visit to the paradise of the pure land? I didn't know, but it was the greatest of joys. No longer was there either a corrupt and troublesome world nor an honored teacher. My clinging to my beloved dead son vanished, and the painful search for *Mu* also disappeared in this ecstatic, exalted state of mind (*samādhi*).

However, later, I was again slapped in the face by the teacher's ferocious roar and returned, startled, to *Mu*. Again, *Mu*—, *Mu*—, *Mu*—. A tiny insect flew onto the paper door; it was *Mu*. An airplane flew through the sky; it was *Mu*. The whole universe was nothing but *Mu*. In the midst of this, the wooden frame of the paper door fell away and vanished. My body felt as if it were being dragged up from deep within the bowels of the earth. "Gong!" rang the temple bell, and suddenly, I cried out and returned to myself. It was attained! "Heaven and Earth are of one piece. The universe and I are one body. I am the Buddha! We're joined in one!" It was *Mu*.

This greatest of treasures, which I hold, is without a shred of falsehood, even of the size of a cormorant's down; no one could ever harm it. This treasure, which I hold, transcends death; even the teacher herself could never damage or destroy it.

"It's nothing, it's nothing, it's nothing." . . . Imperturbable, I at long last went into the private interview as my original self. Now, for the first time, the teacher herself smiled warmly and I received formal approval. Then she gave me various instructions and advice.

The joy itself passed in a moment. When I was made aware of the responsibility and difficulties of those who aspire to the way, I fully understood what the teacher meant in the private interview when she said, "That's just religious joy." I was introduced to koan practice as the way to the most exalted spheres. And while it is a path of trials, there is all the difference in the world between it and the suffering I formerly experienced within my narrow and rigid shell. These are the hardships one suffers while punting one's boat over to the territory of the buddhas and patriarchs; in reality this is the greatest of joys.

Eternal life presents me with ongoing, daily occupations. Words cannot express what it is like to live and work together with my dead son. That is buddha mind. This too is buddha mind. Apart from buddha mind, there is nothing. That is joy. This too is joy. My life is full in this vast, delightful and pure world. In one of my teacher's lectures she spoke the lines,

> My clear dew mind
> Is a ruby
> When amongst the autumn leaves.

It's because my mind is clear or colorless that it can adapt to any and all circumstances.

Because of the kindness of the buddhas and patriarchs, a life worth living, a life that requires only the slightest effort, has begun. I can never in my life forget the austerities of the retreat. For the trouble taken by my teacher I have truly deep gratitude which I can only express with hands palm to palm. I bow to you.

Seizing the True Body

The following account is the story of a nun, Nachii Keido, who manages through sheer persistence to overcome the limitations of her background. Born and raised in rural Japan, she was almost completely uneducated; the prewar educational neglect of girls and of nuns was her daily experience. She attained a somewhat minimal literacy largely through her own determined efforts; in the same way, she rebuilt a deteriorated shrine with little community support. Lacking in training herself, she soon found herself the head of her convent. Her sincere spiritual questioning led her to seek doggedly the training she was never given, culminating in her encounter with Nagasawa Roshi. Unlike the laywoman in the previous account, the now elderly nun who speaks to us in this account is not surprised by what she finds at Nagasawa Roshi's retreat, but is delighted to have found what she has sought throughout a lifetime as a nun. Note that her long-held personal devotion to the bodhisattva Kannon, the female embodiment of perfect compassion, becomes transformed through Zen practice into an experiential sense of ongoing union.

I know that our world is full of heavenly beings living in peace, but at the same time, I see that sentient beings are being endlessly consumed in a great fire. I have eaten Buddhist food for forty-eight years, hoping to escape from this burning house of the triple world. When I look back on those years, there is nothing that does not move me to deep gratitude. My motive for leaving home and becoming a nun was rooted in my horror of the burning house. In the spring of my twentieth year, I wrenched myself away from my loved ones. Crying and begging, I finally obtained my mother's consent and hurried to the village convent.

At the time that I grew up, there were no schools like today's schools. In those days only special people went to school; girls especially were thought to have no need for schooling. So in the daytime I worked for a teacher and in the evenings I went over to my elder brother's house in the neighboring village to study basic reading and writing. I still remember how happy I was when I received an inkstone case as a reward for being able to write the Japanese syllabary without looking. With this background, my struggles to learn the Buddhist scriptures were indescribable. While unflaggingly laboring at this, I grew accustomed to a nun's life, and was fortunate enough to be sent to school in Toyama for four years.

From this time on, I gradually began to scrutinize myself and ask myself: What is human life? What is the mission of one who has left home? In the midst of this, the management of the convent was turned over to me and my responsibilities piled up. If I didn't work, there wouldn't be any food even to offer the Buddha. The convent was in a state of deterioration unworthy of the enshrinement of revered Kannon, the object of everyone's faith. Somehow or other, I wanted to build a shrine for Kannon; this would be the great undertaking of my life. I vowed before the Buddha, "From now on, I dedicate my life to revered Kannon. I offer to her the greatest effort I can possibly make." From then on, I was quite literally stirred up. I begged for monthly contributions that people would not give. Evil things were said about me, and I became physically and mentally exhausted. How many times I went before revered Kannon with tears pouring down my face! When I think about it now I realize that I did a good job, and what's more I can clearly see that that hard struggle became a great shining light for me.

I breathed a sigh of relief when I accomplished the enshrinement of revered Kannon in her new shrine without going too far into debt. But as I did this, the questions from my youth that I had forgotten in the interim rose up in my mind. What is the purpose of going around begging (*takuhatsu*)? What is the point of reading scriptures? What in the world is revered Kannon? I accosted the heads of four or five neighboring temples with these questions. Once or twice a year we studied how a nun should progress on the path and I proposed setting up some kind of association for this purpose.

My elder brother who, happily, had become a monk and was chief priest in a nearby temple, shared a great deal of wisdom with me. With his assistance and that of an abbot whom he knew, a training institute for nuns was organized. This institute was made possible by the great efforts of everyone, but since I was the eldest attending, I was always made to sit in the seat of honor, raised above the rest. I didn't know anything, though, so while my body was raised in a position of status, my embarrassed mind always took a low seat. No matter how many scriptures I heard or books I read, I didn't understand anything. This worried me; I always felt uneasy because I didn't understand anything. Once while visiting a Buddhist friend's sickbed, I was deeply struck: "All his distress, all his grumbling—it's common enough in this world, but he's a monk!" I trembled as if I were the one who was sick. My uneasiness grew.

Three years ago in May, I heard that the nun teacher Nagasawa of the Tokyo Nuns' Practice Center (*dojo*) would be coming to the area for a meditation retreat. Deciding I must by all means go, I waited impatiently. Unfortunately, I had to do some temple business which made me miss the first two days of the retreat. When I, white-headed and knowing nothing, first went into the midst of them, they all seemed as young to me as my own novices. I felt embarrassed, but even more I feared that I might hinder them in their zealous practice. But as I got used to it, I felt, "How wonderful! Thank goodness! This is what I've been searching for all these years! I understand, I understand! Well, if it's a matter of sitting in meditation, I'll sit! I'll sit until I understand the true body of Kannon!" Taking courage, I embraced my faith and forgot my years. I returned home, aiming for that bright light of hard struggle I had previously discovered.

I had heard that practice in the midst of activity surpasses practice in inactivity a hundred-, a thousand-, ten thousand-fold, so when going and coming from reading scripture at parishioners' houses I purposefully took the long way around. I also chose quiet places to practice, such as while weeding, sweeping the garden, caring for the Buddha altar, and so on. I tried hard to practice in the midst of all these activities. I struggled to keep this up, but I just couldn't do it. How my mind wandered! I was thoroughly disgusted with it. Just as a monkey leaps from branch to branch, my mind grasped at the branches of desire for sense experience. It was pathetic. In the face of this unconscious and unknown bad karma which I had created in former lives, I could do nothing but press my palms together and bow my head.

I had not been able to attend all of the previous year's retreat, but had had to miss a little. At the time of the following year's retreat I had to stay in bed with an intestinal problem and was unable to attend. And so another year went by. But anyway, there was no other way than this. "If I don't cross over to liberation in this body, in this lifetime, then I'll cross over in some other lifetime," we say; all things are impermanent and ephemeral.

This year, though, I attended the retreat from the day before it began, together with a novice. I helped out as my age allowed and at long last the opening day arrived. From the three o'clock bell to the unrolling of my bedding at nine P.M., I exerted myself with enthusiasm. I sat in meditation with all the zeal I had, but I didn't make much progress. The young people were full of energy as they practiced. Whatever face or figure I looked at, all were strained, as if pulled taut. Such austere, yet noble figures! Forgetting about myself, how many times I revered them as I sat behind them, thinking, as tears welled up, "these are truly living buddhas."

One day, two, three, gradually the days were gone.

> Life and death is a great concern,
> All things are impermanent and ephemeral.
> Each of you must quickly wake up!
> Be careful, don't miss your chance!

The verse recited at bedtime echoed on and on in my ears. I couldn't sleep.

It was the middle day of the retreat. I was sitting in meditation with fresh spirits. I don't know how or why, but all of a sudden, out of the blue, a happy feeling came over me, and I cried out. I realized: "It's *Mu*, it's *Mu! Mu* is overflowing! I understand *Mu!* I understand Kannon's true body, my true body, no—the true body of all things! It's all one! No matter what anyone says, I have penetrated to my original self (*honrai no jiko*). How wonderful! How wonderful that even I could have such an exalted experience!"

At the private interview, I presented the important points. The teacher smiled. In gentle words such as she had not used before, she said this experience was a matter of paradoxical self-knowledge that was completely inexpressible.

The uncertainty I had felt before this experience has been swept away and I have become constantly one with Kannon. I pass my days in peace and gratitude. Since the joy of realizing that the triple world is composed of mind only, I clearly understand that all things, from the doors and windows and the straw floor-mats to Kannon herself, all things that strike my eyes, indeed, all invisible things too, are full of life and vigor. It's strange: the triple world has remained the same before and after I experienced myself, before and after I experienced the truth, but since I woke up and saw, the triple world seems so different.

Wanting even one more person to penetrate to the bright light of this great truth, I have forgotten my white hair and sixty-eight years, and related my foolish feelings. Please, dear readers, be my companions on the path for life after life. We will strive to advance on the path toward the realization of buddhahood and to send a refreshing breeze to the countless sentient beings. I bow to you, hands palm to palm.

—41—

The Chinese Life of Nāgārjuna

Roger Corless

The Chinese *Life of Nāgārjuna* depicts him as a tantric master rather than as a logician. He first learns worldly (*laukika*) magic and then gives it up in favor of the dharma, and his death, or disappearance, is mysterious. His literary output, for which he is usually best known, is here described in a quite perfunctory manner, and he convinces a proud brahman of the truth of Buddhism not by debate but by the manifestation of superior powers.

There are many structural similarities to the traditional accounts of the life of Śākyamuni Buddha, and the text might be read as a biographical manifestation of the dharma. Like Śākyamuni Buddha, Nāgārjuna is represented as precociously bright, becoming learned in early youth, and disporting himself with the pleasures of the senses. He then realizes an aspect of the first noble truth—that is, that grasping at sensual pleasure produces suffering—and forsakes it, becoming a śramaṇa (monastic practitioner) under a teacher who, however, he finds inadequate. He then gets caught up in a doctrine of deep meditation, in exact opposition to his life of sensual indulgence, somewhat as Śākyamuni tries the teachings of Ārāḍa Kālāma and Udraka Rāmaputra. Such teachings and practices are regarded, in Buddhism, as inadequate for liberation and as even delaying liberation; they are associated with immobilizing (*āniñjya*) karma, and lead to rebirth either in the formless realms or the top level of the realm of form, where beings reside in a state of mental hibernation for a very long time. Then, just as Śākyamuni Buddha finds the median between sensual gratification and sensory denial, and proclaims the Middle Way in the four noble truths, Nāgārjuna, with the help of a *nāga* (Chinese *long,* dragon; Sanskrit *nāga,* snake deity) who is unaccountably roaming in the high Himalayas far from his undersea home, is rescued from his practice of radical enstasis, meets the true teaching, attains enlightenment, and proclaims that the middle way is emptiness (*Mūlamadhyamakakarikāḥ* 24:18). Then he occupies himself with propagating the dharma. Finally, just as Śākyamuni passes into parinirvāṇa because Ānanda, although given the opportunity, does not request him to remain until the end of the eon, Nāgārjuna passes away when a

Hīnayānist truthfully says that he would not wish Nāgārjuna to remain. Nāgārjuna's death, or departure, however, is very Chinese: it is a Daoist "parting from the world" (*qushi*). As the Daoist immortal "drops the body" and, after his spirit (*qi*) has left it, his body is found by his disciples to be feather-light, so Nāgārjuna invisibly flies away and leaves behind the husk or exoskeleton of a cicada.

The *Taishō Tripiṭaka* prints two versions of the *Life of Nāgārjuna.* The first, which I call A, is a single recension and is therefore printed without notes on variants. The second, which I call B, is a family of texts: the Ming dynasty edition (c. 1601 C.E.) is printed, with textual notes on the Yuan (c. 1290), Song (c. 1239) and "Old Song" (1104–1148) editions. The chief difference between A and B is in the story of the doubting king. In both versions, the story begins with Nāgārjuna drawing the attention of the king. In B, he does it simply by carrying a red banner around until, after seven years, the king asks him for an explanation. In A, the method of drawing the king's attention is complicated and curious, and the text is often unintelligible: my translation is something of a guess. Further, B places the story immediately after Nāgārjuna returns from his submarine study session with the dragon, whereas A has it following the story of the proud brahman, which itself is put after the study session. The Old Song edition omits the story of the doubting king entirely. I have translated A and referred to B only when I think the variants are significant, since A is used as the basis for the standard Japanese rendering in the *Kokuyaku Issaikyō,* whose reading I have sometimes preferred over that of A. We can, with some certainty, date the original manuscript on which the texts are based to within fifteen years, between 402 and 417 C.E. The section headings are my own.

The translation is from *Taishō shinshū daizōkyo* (Tokyo, 1924–1934), vol. 50, pp. 184a–185b (version A); and 185b–186c (version B).

The Life of the Bodhisattva Nāgārjuna
translated during Yao Qin by the Tripiṭaka Master Kumārajīva

EARLY YEARS AND EDUCATION

Nāgārjuna Bodhisattva came from south India and was of the brahman caste. He was an acute listener and unusually intelligent: things did not need to be repeated for him. At his mother's breast he heard the holy sounds of the four Vedas, forty thousand verses of thirty-two characters each. He could chant them all, and he understood their meaning. [While yet] uncapped [that is, about twenty years old] he was famous and unrivaled in all the land. In astronomy, geography, prediction, and all the sciences, there was nothing he did not know fully.

A YOUTHFUL ADVENTURE

Once, he made a pact with three friends to do something daring. They said to themselves, "Have we not finished [our study of] all the truths under heaven which can uncover divine wisdom and enlighten the dark decrees? Now, we want to [find out] how to enjoy ourselves. We are excited and extremely aroused: we very much desire a life of pleasure. However, we are brahmans and are of the priestly class, not the nobility: so how do we obtain it? Only by having the art of making our bodies invisible can we manage to get that pleasure."

The four men consulted with each other and no one was opposed to the idea that they should go to a magician and request a formula for invisibility. The magician reflected, "These four brahmans are proud and famous—throughout their whole lives they have treated the people as grass. Now, for the sake of magic, they have humbled themselves and come to me. These brahmans are skillful enough to destroy the world, the only thing they do not know is this trifling formula. If I give it to them, they will abandon me and not supplicate me again. But if I give them this medicine [already prepared from the formula] to use, they will not know what to do when it runs out, and must come to see me constantly, and then I will be their teacher." [So] he gave each man one pill of dark-colored medicine and instructed them, "In a secluded place, grind this up with water, then smear [the mixture] on your eyelids. Your form will become invisible and no one will see you."

When Nāgārjuna ground up this medicine he smelled its fumes and recognized everything about it: the number of the ingredients, and their quantities in zi and zhu, [small units of measure], without error. Returning to the doctor, he said, "In regard to the medicine I received, it has seventy ingredients—this is what they are, and their quantities, and this is the recipe." The doctor asked him, "How did you find this out?" He replied, "The medicine has distinctive fumes—how could I not know what it is?" The doctor sighed [to himself], "If this man understood this difficult thing by himself, then, when he meets the others, will they not despise my trifling magic?" And so he gave it all to them.

The four men, having obtained the magic, entered the king's palace freely, constantly, and whenever they wished, and violated all the ladies in the palace for more than a hundred days. Then, those in the palace who had become pregnant shamefacedly petitioned the king, "If it please your majesty, let us not be punished." The king was greatly displeased, "What ill luck has caused these strange events?" He summoned all his knowledgeable ministers to devise a plan in regard to this matter. The wise ones said, "Generally, matters like this are of two kinds: [caused by] demons or [caused by] magic. Let fine soil be spread inside the doors, and command an officer to guard them and prevent anyone from passing. If there are bewitched men, you will see footprints, and the soldiers can eliminate [the men]. If demons have entered there will be no footprints, and we can destroy the magic." So it was decreed that the gatekeeper prepare things this way. He saw the footprints of four running men, and informed the king. The king commanded a hundred powerful knights to enter the palace, and all the doors to be locked. He ordered the powerful knights to wield their swords in the air: they beheaded three men, who died. Only Nāgārjuna was left alive. He had hidden his body and saved his life by standing near the king's head: the swords did not come within seven *chi* of the king's head [about eight feet].

Then he [Nāgārjuna] awoke to [the truth that] desire is the origin of suffering and the root of the crowd of calamities, and that from this comes moral ruin and bodily peril. Then he resolved in himself, "If I escape then I will go to a śramaṇa (monastic practitioner) and 'leave home' " (*chujia,* that is, *pravrajyā*).

SEARCHING FOR THE TRUE TEACHING

Then he escaped and went into the mountains. He visited a certain pagoda and received the "leaving home" precepts. Within ninety days he completed the chanting of the Tripiṭaka. Then he sought other texts, but completely failed, so he went to the Himalayas. In those mountains there was a pagoda, and in that pagoda there was an old bhikṣu who gave him the Mahāyāna texts. By chanting them he obtained rapture and delight, but he was not able to understand their true meaning. He wandered around in many countries still seeking other texts. He circled Jambudvīpa, searching without success. He refuted all the non-Buddhist teachers and the propositions of the śramaṇas' systems.

A non-Buddhist disciple spoke to him straightforwardly: "Teacher, you are an omniscient one and are presently a disciple of the Buddha. But if the disciple's [that is, your] way is not transmitted and received fully, will I not be unfulfilled? And if I am unfulfilled about something, you are not omniscient." When [the disciple's] words were finished, [Nāgārjuna's] spirit became debased, his mind filled with false pride, and he thought to himself, "Worldly teachings lead in many directions and the Buddhist texts, although wonderful, are incomplete, and need to be taken further by means of reasoned argument. At the points where they are deficient they could be taken further and expanded, and with this updated teaching, one could be enlightened. Theory would be without error and practice without fault. What could be wrong with that?" Having thought of this, he wanted to effect it. He set himself up as a master of doctrine and precepts, and went on and designed robes. His teaching was close to the Buddha's dharma but had some differences: he wanted people to rid themselves of feelings, so he expounded the doctrine of nonsensation.

At the appointed day and time the disciples received the new precepts and put on the new robes, individually in a secluded ice cave.

THE GIFT OF THE TRUE TEACHING

A great dragon who was a bodhisattva saw Nāgārjuna doing this, and regarded him with compassion. He invited him to come into the ocean, into his palace, where he opened a very precious treasure house and took from it a very precious and ornate book chest, and gave him the profound vaipulya sūtras [which contain] the limitless, true teaching. Nāgārjuna accepted them and read and analyzed most of them for ninety days, his mind profoundly penetrating their essence and attaining to their true meaning. The dragon, reading his thoughts, asked him, "Have you looked at all of the texts?" He replied, "The texts in your book chest are many, limitless, and inexhaustible! [Even] what I have been able to read is ten times that [available] in Jambudvīpa!" The dragon said, "Were I to bring here all the texts in my palace and let you compare them with these [in this one chest], you would find them to be even more innumerable." Nāgārjuna acquired the texts [in the chest, thoroughly understood emptiness, which was their] main point, and completely entered into [the calm acceptance of] the nonarising [of phenomena], the second of the two acceptances.

THE PROPAGATION OF THE TRUE TEACHING

The dragon then dismissed him and he emerged in southern India, where he propagated the Buddha's dharma widely and defeated the non-Buddhists. He clarified the Mahāyāna at length in an expository commentary of one hundred thousand verses. He also wrote a treatise in five thousand verses on the ornament[s] for the way of the Buddha, and a treatise in five thousand verses on great compassion, that is, skillful means. The "Treatise on the Middle," in five hundred verses, enabled the Mahāyāna teachings to spread widely in India. He also composed the "Treatise on Fearlessness" in one hundred thousand verses: the "Treatise on the Middle" is in this.

THE PROUD BRAHMAN

Once, there was a brahman who was well versed in spells and magic and wished to use these to defeat Nāgārjuna. He said to a king of south India, "I am able to defeat this bhikṣu: let the king hold a contest." The king said, "You are very foolish. He is a bodhisattva whose knowledge shines more brightly than the sun and moon, and whose wisdom is as radiant as the mind of a sage. Why do you not humble yourself? How can you dare not to honor him?" The brahman said, "In order to be sure about the man, why does not the king put him to the test in a debate? Then he will witness his downfall!" The king saw [the truth of] these words and summoned Nāgārjuna: "At dawn, attend us at the palace administration hall." The brahman arrived later and, casting a spell, he created a large lake—broad, long, and clear. He sat in the middle of it on a thousand-petaled lotus and bragged to Nāgārjuna: "You are sitting on the ground just like a dog and you desire to match words on the meaning of the treatises with me, a man of great virtue and knowledge, who is sitting on a pure lotus!" Then Nāgārjuna used a magical spell in his turn, and produced a white elephant with six tusks. Walking on the water of the lake, it went up to the lotus seat, lifted [the brahman] up high with its trunk, and flung him to the ground. The brahman, whose hip was injured, bowed down and took refuge with Nāgārjuna, saying, "I am of no account and have been humiliated by a great teacher. Take pity on me and enlighten my ignorance!"

THE DOUBTING KING

Then, there was a king in south India who greatly honored countries which had faith in heretics, and who had never seen a single disciple of Śākyamuni. The citizens from far and near all converted to his way. Nāgārjuna thought to himself, "If the root of a tree is not destroyed, its branches cannot be killed. If a people's leader is not converted, the way will not prosper." [Now,] the government of that country was financed [entirely] by the royal household. Nāgārjuna hired men from the lodging houses and recruited them, with himself as their commander. He arranged them into a squad, properly marshaled, with those in the van holding lotus spears. The parade was not magnificent, yet the ranks were ordered; the regulations were not elaborate, yet everything was concordant. The king marveled at this and asked, "Who is this man?" His attendants replied, "This man must have been recruiting, but he does not have a government stipend nor has he received any money. Yet his servants are respectful and well trained like this! We do not know what he is thinking, what he is seeking, or what he wants." The king summoned him and asked him, "What kind of a man are you?"

He replied, "I am an omniscient one." The king was startled and asked him, "There is only an omniscient one every once in a very long while. If you say this of yourself, how can you prove it?" He answered, "If the king wishes to know the wisdom of which I speak, let him ask a question." The king reflected, "By assenting to question him, I would be regarding him as a chief among wise ones, a great teacher of the meaning of the treatises. But, he is insufficiently famous. Maybe I should not ask just now. This is no small matter. [But,] if I do not ask him, I shall be shamed." He hesitated for a long time, and could not make a choice. Finally, he questioned him: "What are the deities doing at this moment?" Nāgārjuna said, "The deities are fighting the asuras." The king heard mutterings like people choking without being able either to spit or to swallow. But these noises did not convince him. There had to be either something definite or nothing at all in order for him to be certain: noises were no proof. So Nāgārjuna said, "I do not seek to win the argument merely with noise. Let the king wait a little while. Soon he will have proof." As he finished speaking, shields, spears, and other weapons fell from the sky. The king said, "Even though there are weapons—shields, spears, lances, and battle-axes—how can you know for certain that the deities are fighting the asuras?" Nāgārjuna said, "Investigating mere noises does not compare with the real thing." When he had finished speaking, hands, feet, fingers, ears, and noses of asuras came down from the sky, and the king with his ministers and brahmans were enabled to see, in a clearing in the sky, two battle lines facing each other. The king kowtowed and converted to the dharma. There were [also at that time] ten thousand brahmans on [the roof of] the palace: they all cut off their topknots and received the complete precepts (*upasaṃpadā*).

DISAPPEARANCE

There was a Hīnayāna dharma master who was always angry. When Nāgārjuna was close to death, he asked [the Hīnayānist], "Would you like me to remain for a long time in this world?" [The Hīnayānist] replied, "Truthfully, I do not wish it." [Nāgārjuna, therefore,] retired into a locked room and did not come out for a whole day. A disciple broke down the door and looked in, and the husk of a cicada came out. From that leavetaking until today one hundred years have passed. In many regions of south India temples were established for him and he is worshiped as a buddha.

THE MEANING OF HIS NAME

Because his mother gave birth to him under an [arjuna] tree he was called Arjuna. Because a dragon perfected his knowledge [literally, "completed his way"] he is fittingly called Dragon (*nāga*). His style (*hao*) is Long Shu [Dragon Tree, that is, Nāga-arjuna].

APPENDIX

According to the "Record of the Transmission of the Dharma Treasure" [*Fu Fazang Juan*, i.e., *Fu Fazang Yinyuan Juan*] he was the thirteenth patriarch. Had he eaten immortality cakes he would still be alive, [as it was, he] attained longevity and lived over two hundred years, transmitting the Buddha dharma. The number of those he liberated is incalculable.

— 42 —

Atiśa's Journey to Sumatra

Hubert Decleer

According to his traditional biographies, the Indian master Atiśa (the author of the text translated in Chapter 24) left India for some years in order to study under the tutelage of the monk Dharmakīrti (also known as Guru Suvarnadvīpa) on the island of Sumatra. This is an account of his voyage. The story is noteworthy for a number of reasons. First, it is an example of an account of a Buddhist traveler who sets out on a long and perilous journey in search of the dharma. The most famous of these journeys are those of Chinese monks going to India or Japanese monks going to China. Here, however, we have a case of an Indian monk leaving India, the homeland of Buddhism, to seek a teacher more learned than any to be found in India. This may suggest something of the state of Buddhist learning in India at the beginning of the eleventh century. Indeed, at the time of his departure for Tibet, Atiśa is reported to have stated: "In all of India, those who knew all the subtleties in the philosophical systems of both Outsiders [non-Buddhists] and Insiders [Buddhists] were only four: Guru Suvarnadvīpa of Golden Island [Dharmakīrti], Śāntipa [Ratnākaraśānti], myself, and my disciple Kṣitigarbha; besides these four, there was no one else."

Like the journeys of other pilgrims, Atiśa's route is fraught with dangers from supernatural forces. On the journey to Sumatra, Atiśa's ship was tossed about in a great tempest and then becalmed by the god Śiva, here called Maheśvara, the "Great Lord." Śiva is apparently angry that Atiśa has left India in pursuit of the Buddhist dharma and is seeking to stop him. In response, Atiśa, who was to become renowned in Tibet as a teacher of compassion, performs a wrathful act of destructive magic. He and his disciple Kṣitigarbha manifest themselves as wrathful tantric deities to defeat Śiva and his consort. After this immediate threat is averted, Kṣitigarbha, with the blessings of the female bodhisattva of compassion, Tārā, launches a preemptive strike against the enemies of Buddhism, including Hindus, Muslims, and practitioners of the Bön religion of Tibet. Atiśa, living in the century that saw the beginnings of what was to be the wholesale destruction of the Buddhism on the Indian subcontinent, is portrayed as the last champion of the dharma.

In the account, when Atiśa correctly identifies the danger as Maheśvara, the god Śiva, he tries to appease him by entering a samādhi from which he could not be disturbed by normal means: a meditation on loving-kindness (*maitri*) and compassion (*karuṇā*). His disciple knows better, and realizes he has to call in all the deities with whom he has established a relationship by previous meditational practice. They include first, the Slayer of Death (Yamāntaka), the bull-headed wrathful form of the bodhisattva of wisdom, Mañjuśrī, who appears to be Kṣitigarbha's personal deity, and the ten Wrathful Ones of his entourage, with two mentioned specifically: the Invincible by Others (Aparājita) and the Immovable (Acala). Next Kṣitigarbha calls on Tārā, the goddess famed for fast response in situations of extreme danger, as well as various protector deities, such as Dharmarāja with the buffalo head. Kṣitigarbha's prayer is, however, in the first place addressed to his guru, Atiśa, who now responds by transforming himself into the Red Slayer of Death (Yamāri). When the sea monster appears as an emaciated girl, she is in fact Carcika (Caṇḍikā, a form of Śiva's consort Durgā), the goddess mentioned later and against whose promises the Tārās give Atiśa a serious warning. It is Maheśvara, the Great Lord himself, who next appears from the kitchen hearth on board, and with an unusual foreknowledge he proposes a deal to Atiśa: if Atiśa promises not to go to Tibet (something which Atiśa himself has no idea about as yet), or to visit islands like Sri Lanka, Maheśvara will end the storm and allow him to return to northern India. Mistakenly viewing Atiśa in his appearance of the Slayer of Death as a mere yakṣa (a minor earth spirit) Maheśvara rounds off his discourse with a mantra addressed to a yakṣa and becalms the ship.

In reply and while still manifesting himself as the Red Slayer of Death, Atiśa emanates one of his wrathful entourage, Acala the Immovable, to get the ship to move. At this moment, the personal deity of Atiśa since innumerable lifetimes, who had manifested herself since his early childhood, Tārā the Savioress, appears in all her twenty-one forms simultaneously, and Atiśa offers salutation to four of the forms. They mildly rebuke him for not having called on them in his moment of danger, especially since shipwreck is one of the eight terrors against which Tārā specializes. Fortunately his disciple Kṣitigarbha had called on them, hence their response. To Kṣitigarbha they entrust the wrathful action against the main enemies of the dharma—at which point we must remember that in his earlier urgent prayer the disciple of Atiśa had first invoked his guru, immediately followed by an appeal to the same Slayer of Death, two of whose ten Kings of Wrath attendants (Invincible by Others and Immovable) he mentioned by name; here a third one, Horseneck Hāyagriva, later mentioned in the "Words of Divine Pride," seems to perform the action, with the disciple staying himself in self-generation as the Slayer of Death Yamāntaka, and emanating that particular attendant, whose mantra is spelled out.

Not all of the enemies that Kṣitigarbha attacks can be clearly identified. The Tīrthika (non-Buddhist) temple of Maheśvara could be situated just about anywhere; the site is first given as *Svabha-thana,* apparently *Svabhāva-sthāna,* "the Self-Arisen Throne Seat," and later as *Svabhanatha,* apparently *Svabhāva-Nātha,* "The Spontaneously Arisen Lord" or "The Self-Existing Lord." The Carcika image appears to be in the same temple complex and is destroyed first, possibly as it is closely associated with heavy blood sacrifice. The Turuka palace of the Mongol hordes relates to the Afghan borderlands: "Turuka" refers to their ancestral lands some centuries before. His "stopping them from reaching [and raiding] the Vajra Throne" refers to the eventual attack of these troops on the temples at Bodhgayā, the site of the Buddha's enlightenment. Shang-shung, the location of the Black Tent palace of the king of Shang-shung, is the traditional place of origin of Bön, Tibet's pre-Buddhist religion, variously situated anywhere between southwest Tibet and Iran. The famous Tibetan epic *Gesar of Ling* is in fact devoted to a hero who wipes out entire cultures obsessed with the blacker forms of magic. The poison lake (or sea) in the south, from which leprosy spread, remains a mystery, but the country Lanka of the rakṣasa cannibal-demons is Sri Lanka, which had a long tradition of such practices; the hero Siṃhala, after whom the island used to be called Ceylon, escaped the enticing sirens that were in fact cannibal-demonesses, and later returned to rid the island of this plague. By the time of Atiśa, they seem to have returned and taken up the ancient custom again.

As an introduction to the account of Atiśa's journey (which is recounted in the first person), here is what Atiśa's biography says about the reasons for the voyage:

> From among all these gurus, the one unencompassable by thought, absolutely matchless, without rival, was Guru Suvarnadvīpa, "the Golden Islander." His name was Dharmakīrti, "Dharma Fame." Although he lived on Golden Island [Sumatra], his fame pervaded the entire [Buddhist] world and he was like the crown jewel of all Buddhists. It was said that he was the foremost teacher of [the training in] loving-kindness and compassion, and when the Lord [Atiśa] heard about him, [he was confident that] the Golden Island teacher had been his guru over innumerable previous lives. Merely by hearing his name, an extraordinary faith and devotion arose in him. Greatly affected in mind, he joined a group of merchants on their way to get precious stones from Golden Island, and set out in a great ship. They sailed through the poisonous ocean, through the milky ocean, through the ocean invading the land, and so forth.
>
> *Jo bo rje dpal ldan mar me mdzad ye shes kyi rnam thar rgyas pa* (Varanasi: E. Kalsang, 1970), p. 132.

The translation below is from 'Brom ston pa, *Bla ma'i yon tan chos kyi 'byung gnas* (Varanasi: E. Kalsang, 1969), section 2, *Jo bo gser du byon pa'i rnam thar.*

How the Guru, in His Search for the Dharma, Coped with Difficult Circumstances

The Story of How, In the Ocean, He Conquered the Deity Maheśvara

To the precious lords Maitreya and powerful Avalokiteśvara, in full prostration I offer salutation.

I, the monk Dīpaṃkara Śrījñāna [Atiśa], for thirteen months was on board a ship, on my way into the presence of the guru of Golden Island.

When five months had passed [on board], a son of the gods (*devaputra*), Maheśvara [Śiva], in order to destroy my aspiration to achieve enlightenment for the sake of others (*bodhicitta*), caused a storm to move in, blowing in the wrong direction. Changing himself into the great Makara ["Fish Swallower"] sea monster, he obstructed [our passage] in front. From the sky he caused a thunderbolt to fall right on top of me. At that time, due to my meditating on loving-kindness [wishing all beings to be happy] and compassion [wishing no living being to experience suffering], the tempest was completely calmed and I saw six great bolts of lightning stuck motionless in the sky.

Yet the Makara sea monster was still blocking [our progress] in front, and the surface of the ocean was being churned about by this strong wind with such force that this ship of ours, too, like a prayer flag flapping in a strong wind, was rocking and rolling all about. One moment it was lifted toward the sky, the next moment it seemed to be plunging into the very depths of the ocean. The four great banners, one in each direction, broke off. Although four massive iron weights had been let down [as anchors] into the depths of the ocean, from each of the four directions, it was as if a massive drum was being beaten, with a howling noise, a thundering sound, light [at the horizon] and great flashes of lightning erupting, all of which made every one of the companions extremely frightened. As they were thus trembling in fear, again I entered into equipoise, meditating on loving-kindness and compassion.

Then Paṇḍita Kṣitigarbha, the great scholar, addressed his guru [me] with the following prayer:

> Arise, please arise [from your meditation], compassionate guru,
> If indeed you are without rival on earth.
> This terror and agitation [of ours] caused by evil forces—
> Out of your great compassion please pacify it; thus we pray.
>
> If you [can] liberate all living beings from the ocean of existence,
> [intervene here, because]
> These evil forces threaten us now.
> E MA! A tempest is moving us about and "the sky-metal" of thunder is
> coming down on us like hell.
> A colossal Fish Swallower is causing terror right in front.
> Most Precious Lord, from these terrors be our refuge; thus we pray.

Moved about by the ocean winds, the waves reach up to heaven,
A terrible noise resounds, hurting the ear, and there is the moving light of lightning,
While the ship too is rocking this way, rocking that way, rolling and rolling from side to side, in endless motion,
Rising up into the sky on a great wave, then flung down again into the depths.
O may this Most Precious Lord be our refuge from these terrors; thus we pray.

In the vast sky of your excellent qualities,
The close helpers: dharma protectors and guardians, entire assemblies like sky-soaring garuḍas,
All-pervading, surrounding [you], if they do indeed clear away obstacles
Yet ignore our present hindrances without being a haven of protection—
That compassion [of theirs] dwelling in the sphere of isolation, how poor it is!
So now, assemblies of ḍākinīs and dharma protectors, inner, outer, and secret,
Arhats, heroes, heroines, and wisdom deities,
All the divine assemblies who rejoice in the forces of goodness,
On all sides surround you; here and now in this great ocean [assisted by them],
O guru, with the mass of your compassion, drive back [this evil]; thus we pray.

To the Lord Red Slayer of Death (Rakta-Yamāri),
Surrounded by the entourage who terrifies the Lord of Death [Yama]: Invincible By Others [an epithet of the King of Wrath (Krodharāja)],
Together with the Immovable Lord [Acalanātha and the others of] the assembly of the Ten Wrathful Ones,
And the Goddess [Tārā] who protects from the eight terrors, [in your form as] Lady Blazing Forth Auspiciousness and Splendor,
[And] King of Dharma; Guru, in great numbers drive back [this evil]; thus we pray.

Lord of the Teachings, Precious Bhagavān Buddha,
Precious Avalokiteśvara, with your maṇḍala devoid of all impurity,
Dharmarājas, father and son, who clear away the misery of transmigrators,
The time has come! Bring forth your compassionate family in great numbers!
Extend the river of your stainless blessings; thus we pray.

In this way, with a clear voice he spoke his special prayer and I heard it. Then I [turned into] the Bhagavān Slayer of Death [Yamāri], [my] body red, with a fat belly, dark brown hair waving upward, with reddish eyes wide open looking into the ten directions. As soon as this was seen, I let all the other hand-emblems fall, I raised the vajra cudgel into the sky [with my right hand] and with the left [hand] in threatening [mudrā] I swung a lasso. With a blow of the vajra cudgel I struck the world mountain, thereby smashing the world mountain to pieces, and below the world mountain, all the way down to the golden foundation [of the world], I cut open and laid bare. Back and forth the great ocean was roiled and became like boiling blood. This fish-swallowing Makara sea monster was [soon reduced to] pure white bones, then suddenly changed into a child, a young girl, completely emaciated and of blue color. Suddenly appearing on board ship, she offered prostrations, then with her palms joined in front of her, she spoke:

> King of Wrath, mighty in powers and forces, Krodha rāja,
> Mahākaruṇika, Great Compassionate One, sole refuge for
>   transmigrators,
> I, now terrified, I who truly committed so many mistakes,
> Now pray to you, out of your great compassion, please protect me.

Thus she spoke; and I, still wielding the vajra cudgel, [replied]:

> Huṃ! I am the great master over the life of living beings!
> Being the power of compassion, I,
> Out of pity for you, did not liberate [kill] you.
> Now do not teach the erroneous religion of the Tīrthikas
> To my disciples!
> Girl, do not expound the false religion of Bön!
> Your life, your survival is in my power.

Thus I spoke. She said:

> These melodious verses I offer,
> Great Compassionate One, please listen, thus I pray.
> To these disciples of yours [in Tibet],
> No erroneous teachings will I give;
> Please have kind thoughts toward me;
> Over my life you are the master indeed.

In this way she spoke. Then from the bottom of the fire hearth [on board], one human figure of white complexion suddenly arose, [telling me:]

> Do not [ever] travel to the Land of Snows [Tibet];
> And stop your journey on this Nepalese ship.
> Do not go to either Copper Island [Sri Lanka] or any of the other small
>   islands.

Stop this continuous roaming!
Bhrum hṛi yakṣa, listen to this!

Thereupon the stormy weather calmed down altogether, the waves, the light [of far-away lightning], the noise all became pacified. The great ship too quietly resumed its course, while all on board gave out a sigh of relief and engaged in joyful conversation among themselves.

Yet I, without breaking up my generation stage [visualization] of [myself as] the wrathful Slayer of Death, Yamāri, from the back of the ship I settled the clear appearance of the deity, like an image of bronze with the nature of rainbow light. Then, I fixed the vajra cudgel to the mast.

Then the great vessel did not make the slightest movement any more but remained steady like a residential building. As this occurred, I wondered: "What's this?" and went to have a look, then heard some girls engaged in joyful talk and laughter. As soon as I looked in that direction, now [manifesting myself] as the king of the wrathful [circle of protector deities], Acala the Immovable, I waded through the depths of the ocean, which only reached up to my knees. Then like a young man picking up a wooden trough by starboard and port, I made it move. With my crown amidst the clouds, I caused a wind to arise.

All around the ship there were twenty-one girls who now turned their heads, speaking: "If it had not been for us sisters, would you have been such a great lord today?" to which I [replied]:

To the lady guarding from the eight terrors, I offer salutation in full prostration.
To the lady who makes auspiciousness and good fortune blaze forth, I offer salutation in full prostration.
To the lady shutting the gate to [rebirth in] evil existences, I offer salutation in full prostration.
To the lady guiding us to heavenly abodes, I offer salutation in full prostration.
May you at all times accompany us and assist us.
At present, out of compassion, please protect us, I pray.

I addressed this prayer [to the twenty-one Tārās]. These girls spoke: "Had it not been for the presence of [our] son Kṣitigarbha, we were just thinking: "Let's reduce that Tīrthika city Svabhanatha to ashes," when we heard his voice in prayer. Father [Atiśa], you are supreme among all sentient beings, yet he is a mahāsattva, a great hero. In fact we have come here because of his strong request and invitation. [Also] if that child with the blue face again recovers, beat her!" they said, [adding]: "From this day forward, do not allow her outside this ship of Nepal!"

Next they exhorted Kṣitigarbha: "Most venerable one, scatter these flowers from the sky onto Svabhanatha. We girls will take upon ourselves the [karmic] responsibility [of your breaking your vows of] refuge and the altruistic aspiration to enlightenment [by engaging in this violent act]. The paṇḍit Kṣitigarbha with a threatening mudrā cast one lightning flash. Having gone around in a circle, at the northern side of the Tīrthika city Svabhanatha, it came down right on top of the [image of] goddess Carcika that was the established there, crushing the Tīrthika temple, including the [image of the] goddess. He shot forth another [flash of lightning] and it hit the sacred image of Maheśvara itself and cracked it to dust.

One shaft of light from it hit the Tīrthika king and burned dry his right side; another shaft of light hit the Turuka palace in the [Afghan] borderlands, and for thirteen years the Mongol hordes were stopped from reaching [and raiding] the Vajra Throne [Bodhgayā]. Yet another light ray struck the Black Tent palace of the king of Shang-Shung, causing the teachings of Bön to go down. Only a couple of their [teachers] here and there survived, and in distress they fled into the Himalayan mountain ranges. One light ray, directed at the poison lake in the south, hit the palace of Kṛṣṇa, stopping short the burning disease of leprosy. One ray of light struck Lanka, the country of the rakṣasa cannibal-demons, and put a stop to the cannibal-demons' tradition of eating human flesh. Then he spoke these words of [divine] pride:

Of this maṇḍala-residence of the earth, am I the master; therefore,
Evil circumstances and conditions, scatter, disperse, be reduced to dust!
The Great Hero [Slayer of Death] is my master.
In Uddhyana country, Hāyagriva, King Horseneck neighs with a voice of a horse.
Destroy, destroy Maheśvara, reduce him to ashes;
Eliminate the gods of Bön and the magic that is their essence!
Oṃ padmāntakṛta vajrakrodha hāyagriva hulu hulu huṃ phaṭ!"

Thus I heard him say. Next the king of wrath Acala the Immovable, and the Bhagavān [Yamāri Slayer of Death] himself suddenly became invisible, and I showed again forth my own form as a monk and remained as such.

All the followers in my entourage greatly rejoiced:
"Spontaneously arisen, not fabricated
King of dharma, similar to a hill of precious stones,
On account of this ultimate wisdom, [as revealed by] signs supreme,
All of us are extremely pleased.
E ma ho! Lord with powers and strengths,
Tathāgata from the ocean
That terrified us, please hear us,

And under the protection of your compassion,
Without error, gave us shelter, thus we pray!"

Thus they spoke. For twenty-one days we were utterly unable to continue, but as soon as we were truly safe from further fear, on each of the four directions [of the ship] we raised the great wind banners, we hauled up the four massive iron [anchor weights]. Then, as an opportune wind arose for one and a half months without break by day or night, we remained on the great ocean and proceeded.

After seven months had passed, again, from in front, a storm arose and we were driven back by the wind over the distance of one day's travel. I prayed to my guru, to the precious three, and to the ḍākinīs and dharma protectors. Soon the storm subsided by itself, yet a strong wind in the right direction failed to arise. Because of the [little] merit of the sentient beings [on board], half a month was lost there, during which I meditated on the aspiration to enlightenment based on loving-kindness and compassion. Eventually a right wind arose and we took off again. It took us a further two months and twenty-six days to reach the shore across the ocean.

[Colophon] From the exposition of how the Guru, in his search for the dharma, coped with difficult circumstances: the exposition of the story of how, in the ocean, he conquered Maheśvara.

— 43 —

Bimbā's Lament

Donald K. Swearer

In the Theravāda Buddhist tradition the first continuous narrative of the deeds of the Buddha was the *Nidāna Kathā,* a fifth-century C.E. introduction to the Pāli commentary on the stories of the former lives of the Buddha (*Jātaka*), compiled in Sri Lanka. The narrative brings together episodes from the life of the Buddha found in the Pāli canon, such as his enlightenment and his first postenlightenment teaching, with cycles of legends that had probably developed around major Buddhist pilgrimage sites in India. One of the episodes in this tale portrays Prince Siddhārtha's wife's distress at the sight of her husband collecting alms in the royal city of Kapilavastu. It was the first time Yasodharā, referred to as Bimbā in some of the Pāli commentaries, had seen her husband since his renunciation of the householder life.

Within the context of the story of the Buddha's life from his birth as Prince Siddhārtha until his death, Bimbā's lament occurs within a series of "conversion" stories following Prince Siddhārtha's enlightenment as the Buddha. These include the conversions at Varanasi, Uruvela, Rājagṛha, and Kapilavastu. The Kapilavastu cycle includes the conversion of the Buddha's relatives—his father, his wife, and his son. Even though the conversions are central to the Buddha's career and the early development of the saṅgha, the episode also brings to life the realistic human feelings attendant to Siddhārtha's renunciation: Bimbā's natural resentment at being deserted by her husband; the disappointment felt by Bimbā and Suddhodana, the Buddha's father, at Siddhārtha's decision to eschew the privilege and prestige of kingship; the offense experienced by the Kapilavastu elites when the Buddha refused to favor them on his alms rounds. Even the necessity felt by the Buddha to perform an impressive miracle in order to overcome the doubts of the people from his home town has the ring of historical reality. In short, in the Kapilavastu episode the Buddha legend seems to reach out toward history. Furthermore, in the light of the patriarchal background of the text's composition, the unknown author, most certainly a monk, should be applauded for his sensitivity to the plight of a royal wife deserted by her husband.

We begin the story after the Buddha has accepted King Suddhodana's invitation, conveyed by his councilor, Kāḷudāyin, to visit Kapilavastu. The citizens of the capital made preparations for the Buddha's arrival and the Blessed One started out on his journey.

The event appears in other Pāli, Sanskrit, Prakrit, and vernacular biographies of the Buddha, including the *Mahāvastu* (from the Mahāsaṅghika canon); Kṣemendra's eleventh-century *Dasāvatāracarita;* the *Jinacarita,* a thirteenth-century Pāli composition written in Sri Lanka (*Journal of the Pali Text Society,* 1904–1905, translated by W. H. D. Rouse); and biographies of the Buddha written in Burma and Thailand; see the *Mālālaṅkaravatthu,* translated by Chester Bennett, *Journal of the American Oriental Society* 3 (1852–1853); see also P. Bigandet, *The Life or Legend of Gaudama: The Buddha of the Burmese,* reprint edition (Varanasi: Bharatiya Publishing House, 1979); and the *Paṭhama Sambodhi* (*The First Enlightenment*), compiled by Phra Paramanuchit and published in Bangkok in the late nineteenth century. Phra Paramanuchit may have based his life of the Buddha on the sixteenth-century *Paṭhama Sambodhi* composed in Chiang Mai, incorporating other manuscripts such as *Bimbā's Lament,* a popular story in the north written in both prose and poetry. The following exegetical translation, based on a microfilm copy of a palm leaf manuscript in the Chiang Mai University Social Research Institute's archives, is excerpted from the prose text copied in 1799 C.E. written in northern Thai (Tai Yuan) and Pāli.

Further Reading

For a brief discussion of the development of the Buddha legend see Étienne Lamotte, *History of Indian Buddhism,* translated by Sara Webb-Boin (Louvain: Université Catholique de Louvain, 1988), pp. 648–62. See also Frank E. Reynolds, "The Many Lives of the Buddha: A Study of Sacred Biography and Theravāda Tradition," in *The Biographical Process. Studies in the History and Psychology of Religion,* edited by Frank E. Reynolds and Donald Capps (The Hague: Mouton, 1976); and A. Foucher, *The Life of the Buddha According to the Ancient Texts and Monuments of India,* translated by Simone B. Boas (Middletown, Conn.: Wesleyan University Press, 1963), chapter 9.

Bimbā's Lament

Having decorated the road, princes adorned in beautiful costumes, holding flowers, candles, incense, and sweet-smelling garlands in their hands, approached the Buddha and paid their respects to him. Their elders then did likewise.

The Lord Buddha, radiating the six rays of omniscience, the eighty majestic victorious powers, and the thirty-two marks of the Great Person, arrived at the Rohini River which flowed between the cities of Mathura and Kapilavastu. Eighty thousand friends and relatives from the two cities gathered there. Upon seeing the leonine form of the Lord Buddha they praised him with heartfelt joy.

The Blessed One, with complexion beyond comparison, bathed in the river. He emerged shining like a lion king of old, and radiated the six rays of omniscience, inspiring the faith of his family, relatives, and friends. [The Buddha is often likened to a lion, and his preaching to a "lion roar." One of the most famous Buddha images in northern Thailand is called the "Lion Buddha." In popular Buddhist literature such as the Jātaka, the Buddha's enlightenment is symbolized by a halo of bright rays, traditionally six but as many as a thousand. Buddha images may include a halo. In contemporary Sri Lanka and Burma this often takes the form of blinking neon lights, an attenuation of the solar symbolism in which the notions of *raśmi* (Sanskrit) and *ramsi* (Pāli) are rooted.]

The Lord Buddha, the perfected one, together with 60,000 male and female followers, entered Nigrodhārāma and sat down on the seat prepared for him by his family and relatives. Looking at the Blessed One, the royal retinue headed by King Suddhodana were filled with pride and conceit: "We are older than Prince Siddhārtha. He is very youthful, more like our child or nephew [than a royal lion]." Consequently, they sat down without paying respects to the Buddha.

The Blessed One, filled with every auspicious quality, knew their feelings and thought to himself, "Because of my youth my relatives consider that I am unworthy of their respect. But that will soon change." By his magical power he created a crystal path in the sky from the eastern boundary of the city of Kapilavastu to its western perimeter. Then, ascending into the air, the Tathāgata, surrounded by many previous buddhas, walked on the sky-bridge he had miraculously created. The Lord Buddha, filled with splendor, extended his arms until he touched the sun and the moon. Then, from a teaching platform that he created in the sky, he told the assembled crowd, "Here there is no place for dust to settle." He also performed numerous other miracles, such as appearing to walk above the heads of the Śākyans.

Upon witnessing all of these miracles, King Suddhodhana, overwhelmed with happiness, raised his folded hands above his head in abject respect and begged the Lord Buddha's forgiveness, "O Blessed Lord Buddha, sublime and of great compassion, please forgive your old father and all of those assembled here. . . ."

"I take refuge in you, Lord Buddha, in your transcendent teaching and in your order of monks." At these words, all of the Śākyan people bowed in respect before the Lord Buddha.

After the Buddha's kinsmen and women had worshiped him he descended from the sky and took his seat among them. A lotus-petal rain fell from the sky. [This is portentous rain in which only those who wish to get wet are rained upon. Others shed the water as does a lotus petal.] Then the Lord Buddha, radiating a halo of omniscience preached the *Vessantara Jātaka*. King Suddhodhana and the assembled Śākyan clan had never heard this sermon and were overcome with joy. Leaping from their seats, they bowed down before the Lord Buddha. None of the Śākyans invited him to receive food from them the next morning because they assumed that he would go on his alms rounds in the city and nowhere else.

At dawn the next morning the Lord Buddha, glowing with the six rays of omniscience, took his robe and bowl and went out on his alms rounds with 60,000 arhats to the city of Kapilavastu. He experienced the same sort of happiness he had known eight years earlier when he had departed. Then Kapilavastu had appeared to him as a funeral ground, an ancient city without inhabitants.

Miraculously, wherever the earth was uneven it became level; dense forests became smooth like the head of a victory drum and were resplendent with bright rows of variegated flowers. Some were in full bloom; others were just beginning to open. When the wind blew, the trees and flowers bent down to pay respects to the Buddha.

The air was perfumed and fragrant. Flowers of gold and silver, pearls and rubies, diamonds and emeralds descended from the sky to honor the Blessed One. It was as though the flowers were clever artisans decorating ceiling, chair, and dwelling place for the splendid, august Lord Buddha. One of the breezes carried away everything that was not beautiful and unsuitable for the occasion; another breeze blew soft sand to cover the ground; and yet another breeze scattered scented water everywhere as a sign of respect [to the Blessed One].

Under a bright and shining sun flowers bloomed in ponds and lakes, sending fragrances in every direction. The earth trembled for a distance of 240,000 yojana [one yojana = 9 miles]; the oceans churned; Mount Sumeru, that incomparable king of mountains, bowed down as a palm tree bent by the wind. All the gods played melodious, joyful music with drums and gongs and presented offerings of sweet-smelling garlands as the Buddha entered the city of Kapilavastu. Such was the nature of this miracle.

When the fully enlightened Lord Buddha approached the city gate at the edge of the river and stood by the city pillar he reflected, "Did the more than two-hundred thousand buddhas who have preceded me go on alms rounds to other places before their own clans? Although they gave their own families the opportunity to make donations, customarily they also [went on alms rounds among] the townspeople. My disciples and I will do likewise." [This is apparently a reference to a dispute regarding the merit-making donations to the saṅgha. The text implies that the Buddha and the saṅgha should function as a field of merit for everyone and not just for their own kin. In regard to alms rounds especially, monks should not restrict themselves solely to their own families. This statement might be directed specifically at practices among northern Thai monks, since it is said that prior to the late nineteenth-century reforms of the Thai saṅgha, northern monks were lax in observing this rule and were even known to take the noon meal at their own home.]

When the villagers, both men and women and those who dwelt in the palace, looked out of their windows and saw the Buddha proceeding on his alms rounds, they all exclaimed, "Bhanto . . . Prince Siddhārtha, the son of our king, long absent from our kingdom, is as handsome as a star come down from heaven. He has taken his robe and bowl and has granted us the favor [of going among us for alms]." All the villagers went out to observe the Buddha. There was tremendous excitement throughout the kingdom. Some ran back and forth; still others shouted, making a noise as loud as a hurricane hurling ocean breakers over the land.

Bimbā, the mother of Rāhula, hearing the loud noises and the excitement of the people, asked her ladies in waiting, "O attendants, what is it I hear? What is happening?" Her servants replied with respect, "O Queen, you hear no ordinary noise. It is the return of the king's son, your husband. At this very moment he is going barefoot on his alms rounds throughout the city."

When Bimbā heard this news she covered her face with her scarf and sobbed uncontrollably, her heart filled with pain. "When my lord was ruling the city," she exclaimed, "he was a mighty warrior. Wherever he went he rode in a carriage or on an elephant. He was surrounded by a retinue of soldiers carrying royal umbrellas and rare and precious things. Wherever he went he was honored. Now he has discarded all signs of his royal status. He wears a monk's robe and goes begging for food like a poor, starving person with no sense of shame. Such behavior brings disgrace upon me as a royal princess. People will think that my husband has deserted me. Having been abandoned by his father, Rāhula is forced to live only with me. Is it the consequence of some bad karma in a previous life that this has befallen us?

"Being a wife without a husband is a sorrowful state. I have been deserted and am bereft of merit. Woe is me; my life has surely come to an end!" Bimbā sobbed and sobbed, "I was once beautiful, but I'm now an ugly hag." Her skin grew mottled, and her hair fell in disarray. With her left hand she covered her face with her scarf. With her right she beat her breast, falling down on her side, unconscious, hardly breathing.

When Bimbā regained consciousness she went to the window, where she beheld the handsome form of the Buddha radiating the splendor of his enlightenment like the rays of the sun shining throughout the ten thousand worlds. She was transfigured by his beauty, the thirty-two marks of the great person, and the eighty minor signs, the splendor radiating between his eyebrows like the stars in the heavens.

Praising the Blessed One, she exclaimed, "You are like the bright clear sun, with the visage of a lion king." And then turning aside to her son, Rāhula, she said, "O child, look at your father. Now you know how handsome he is. He has a radiance like the shining sun without blemish or imperfection. His soft and supple hair is collyrium in color; his face is bright and shining like a brilliant fire; his eyes are round and beautiful like those of a calf; his eyebrows have the arch of a fine bow made by a skilled craftsman; his perfection and valor is like that of a lion king emerging from Sattapanni cave." [The entrance to this cave in the Rājagṛha hills is reported to have been the site of the first council after the Buddha's death.]

"[Your father's] golden complexion resembles the color of linen cloth washed a hundred times; his pleasing voice is like the beautiful sound of the karavika bird; his ruby lips have the burnished sheen of the fruit of the nigrodha tree; his pink skin, soft like the petals of a budding flower, emits rays that fill the sky like the full moon on a cloudless night; and his two feet resemble white fans. Altogether he is of unsurpassing beauty.

"The Lord achieved enlightenment. Now when he walks among the people he is like the full moon attended by a company of stars. He was born of noble lineage with the power to dispel all enemies like the royal elephant.

"*Vandāmi* . . . I am the lady Bimbā. I have come to pay respects at the feet of my husband whose beauty surpasses all others. O, please extend your compassion to your bereaved servant, queen Bimbā. I praise you, O my lord."

Bimbā, knowing that the Buddha had gone many places on his alms rounds, exclaimed, "I'm upset and brokenhearted that Rāhula's father has behaved in this dishonorable way." Bimbā then approached Siddhārtha's father and, after paying her respects, said, "I honor my father and mother. Your son has gone far and wide for alms. His actions disgrace and dishonor our family name. My heart is broken, and I am ashamed. People criticize us saying, 'The son of our king acts in an unbecoming manner. It is a loss of face for the king and the royal family.' " Then, tearing off her veil, she fell in a swoon on the ground. "O, my lord," she gasped, "you know the cause of my distress."

Upon hearing his daughter-in-law's confession, Suddhodana was likewise troubled that the Buddha's extensive alms tours would prompt gossip and reproach. "People will think we have fallen on hard times and have inadequate wealth to support the triple gem, or that we are selfish and refuse to provide food for the Buddha and his followers." But in truth, the Buddha harbored no such thoughts toward his father. Even when the monks were in need, the Tathāgata never condemned his family.

The Tathāgata is of the lineage of the buddhas beginning with Dīpaṅkara until the buddha Kāsyapa reached enlightenment. The buddhas overcame the five hindrances [sensuality, ill-will, torpor, worry, and doubt] through the four right efforts [to prevent, to overcome, to develop, to maintain]. They destroyed all of the defilements, and developed the seven factors of enlightenment [mindfulness, truth-investigation, effort, joy, tranquillity, concentration, equanimity]. The buddhas reached the highest, supreme enlightenment. The buddhas depended on alms for their food. It was their tradition to devalue status and wealth, and to depend upon alms for their livelihood.

"O King, the home of the Tathāgata is in the forest where the Buddha's visions occurred, illuminating the ten thousand worlds. In this manner, the Tathāgata followed the lineage of the buddhas. While the Tathāgata was engaged in meditation he was attacked by the forces of Māra as he sat on the crystal throne. Having been defeated by the Tathāgata, Māra's army fled. This followed the tradition of the buddhas.

"O King, in the last watch of the night, as the sun was about to rise, the Tathāgata contemplated the law of dependent coarising, beginning with ignorance as cause, and attained to the enlightenment of the four noble truths and the nine factors of supreme truth [that is, the four stages of the path and their fruits, and nirvāṇa]. The Tathāgata thus attained the most sublime royal treasure."

Having explained this tradition, he then preached to his father, "O King, and all the people, be diligent in the pursuit of the good and truth. Observe the ten royal virtues [charity, high moral character, self-sacrifice, honesty, kindness, self-control, nonanger, nonviolence, patience, conforming to righteousness. *Jātaka* v.387] in every respect in order to overcome rebirth and attain nirvāna ['the crystal realm']. If one continues in the cycle of birth and death, one will enjoy happiness and will be honored by every human and celestial being in the world." At the conclusion of the Tathāgata's sermon, the king reached the stage of stream-enterer.

On the second day, the Buddha proceeded to the palace of his stepmother. After eating, the Buddha preached the follow verses:

Dhammam care ca sucaritam, na tam duccaritam care;
Dhammacari sukham seti, ittham loke param hi ca

Follow the law of right conduct; never that of wrong conduct.
One who lives the dharma is happy in this world and the next.

At the end of the sermon, his stepmother reached the stage of the fruit of the stream-enterer. King Suddhodhana also listened attentively to the sermon and attained to the state of fruit of the once-returner.

On the third day, the Buddha preached the Jātaka before his relatives. Suddhodhana attained the state of the fruit of the never-returner at the conclusion of his sermon. Then the Buddha gave his blessing regarding the meritorious consequences of giving alms. His stepmother, who was moved by the Buddha's sermon, remained with her female attendants. Then King Suddhodhana, looking at the assembled female attendants and not seeing his daughter-in-law, Bimbā, told his maid, "Go to Bimbā. Tell her that her father wants her at the palace. The Buddha himself has entered the palace and extended his blessing to his father, stepmother, Bimbā, and Rāhula, from whom he has been separated for seven years. The Buddha has returned in order to console us ['wipe our tears'] with his sermon."

Having received the order from the king and paid her respects to him, the servant went to Bimbā's palace to inform her of the king's wishes. Bimbā, broken-hearted, wailed and lamented [at the memory] of having been abandoned. After Siddhārtha left, Bimbā took Rāhula and confined herself to her sleeping quarters. She became pale and emaciated, weak and feverish. She sobbed uncontrollably and lost her appetite because the Buddha had deserted her. Her eyes were always filled with tears, like the sun and the moon entering into the midst of clouds during the rainy season. She cared nothing for her appearance: her hair and clothing were disheveled; her body became withered like a small, dried-up river during the hot season.

Having approached Bimbā, the servant paid her respects and asked, "O queen, why are you so sad and emaciated?" Bimbā, looking at the maid, replied, "O servant, come in. I shall tell you why I am so sorrowful nowadays. I am sad because the Lord Buddha, the founder of the religion (*sāsanā*), no longer loves me even though I have done nothing wrong. I faithfully performed all my wifely duties toward him. I must be a person of little merit. I can accept being abandoned, but the Buddha should have sympathy for his son, Rāhula. He is lovable and innocent. His perfection is like that of a lotus standing above the surface of a pond. We have suffered greatly as if crushed by a mountain.

"O, my beloved Rāhula. You were a misfortune for your father from the very beginning. I have suffered as a widow. Men look down on me; they do not respect me. A royal carriage is symbolized by its banner; a flame depends upon fire; a river exists because of the ocean; a state devoid of a ruler can not survive. Just so, Rāhula, you and I, having been abandoned, are persons of no account [that is, no merit]. Everyone accuses you of being illegitimate; and people look down on me as a widow. My suffering brings only tears. How can I continue to live? I am ashamed before everyone. It is better for me to take poison and die or to put a rope around my neck and hang myself from the palace." Bimbā continued to sob uncontrollably.

(Here ends the first chapter of *Bimbā's Lament*. I copied this text in the afternoon of Culasakarāja 1161 [1799 C.E.], the year of the snake, the eleventh lunar month, the first day of the waning moon, corresponding to the fifth day. Novice Suriya copied this dharma text, the first chapter of *Bimbā's Lament* in order that the tradition (*sāsanā*) might prosper for another five thousand years [rains retreats, *vassa*]. I copied this text in order that I, my teacher, father, mother, brothers, sisters, and everyone might be delivered from suffering and attain the three kinds of happiness, with nirvāṇa as the highest. In my next rebirth may I be blessed with a wisdom surpassing the five oceans. May my wish be fulfilled without exception. I wrote this text when I was a disciple of the venerable Isara of Maena Monastery.)

And so Bimbā related her tale of woe to her servant. Hearing this sad account of the queen's abandonment, she consoled Bimbā, saying, "O Queen Mother, don't be sorrowful. In fact, we are people of little merit." Having expressed her sympathy, the servant then told Bimbā that Suddhodhana had invited her to listen to the Buddha's sermon at the quarters of the king along with Gotamī

(Sanskrit Gautamī), Siddhārtha's stepmother. Bimbā, hearing the request, asked, "O servant, has my father-in-law really requested my presence?" "Yes, indeed," she replied, "the king has invited you to join him."

Then Bimbā said, "I'm such an unworthy person. I am unable to perform my duties toward my husband. There is nothing left for me to do. Everyone will blame me for being abandoned by my husband. When I heard that the Buddha had returned, I thought he must still love me and I eagerly rushed to see him. O servant, my husband departed without even saying good-bye. He then returned unannounced and did not come to see me. I am so ashamed. In the past my Lord came to my quarters without telling anyone and came into my bedroom even when the bed was unmade. He was kind to me and was never harsh or angry. . . .

"O servant, we are confidants. Let us keep these secrets between us. In the past when my Lord came he smiled and talked to me in an affectionate and playful manner. I prepared the water for washing his feet, but if he came unannounced he would wash them himself. If the towels were in disarray, my Lord would fold them neatly. If my Lord did not arrive in time to sleep in the bed, I would make sure that he was covered. I would do everything to please him. But no one knew about these things. They thought that Siddhārtha left me because I failed to be a dutiful wife.

"Now the Lord Buddha has come to see his father, but did not visit Bimbā, the mother of Rāhula. O servant, there is an ancient saying that a poor man who has nothing finds a wife who is wealthy and beautiful and lives with her for a long time. Later he says she is no longer beautiful, like a withered flower [and he abandons her]. Although I, Bimbā, married a handsome lord, I have truly suffered just like the old saying. This story will be told to future generations. O my servant, I'm not an evil person. This must be the consequence of evil karma in a past life. I'm like a tree that has lost its flowers and its fruit. I have been abandoned but not because of anything I've done.

"My lord decided to take up the religious life and has reached enlightenment. Nothing that I have wanted has come to pass. My husband deserted me a long time ago and became a mendicant, leaving me filled with sorrow for the rest of my life.

"O servant, tell my father-in-law what I have said, and that I, Bimbā, am unable to come and pay my respects. The king's son entered the court three nights ago. My father-in-law did not send a servant to summon me. Now my Lord has left and did not come to visit me. My Lord was not gracious enough to come to my palace. The king knew the reason for this. I do not want to live any more! O servant, please ask my father-in-law to forgive me." The servant took Bimbā's message to the king.

Having heard the message from Bimbā brought by her servant, King Suddhodana invited the Lord Buddha to go to his daughter-in-law's palace. Paying respects to the Lord Buddha, he said, "O Lord Buddha, handsome and pure beyond comparison, if you do not go to Bimbā's palace she will certainly die."

The Blessed One said, "O king, you speak the truth. If the Tathāgata does not visit Rāhula's quarters, Bimbā will weep and die from a broken heart." The Tathāgata remembered that Bimbā had accumulated countless virtuous qualities over a hundred, thousand, ten thousand, one hundred thousand lifetimes. "Before I reached enlightenment I gave up my children and wife as dāna (a gift) [a reference to the *Vessantara Jātaka*]. So now I must see Bimbā."

King Suddhodana said to the Lord Buddha, "O, Venerable One, take your forty thousand monks with you." The Buddha had the forty thousand monks stay outside while he entered Bimbā's sleeping quarters with Śāriputra and Mahāmaudgalyāyana. The Lord Buddha then said, "Śāriputra, the mother of Rāhula was very helpful to the Tathāgata. If Bimbā receives me by massaging my feet with her soft hands out of her compassion toward the Tathāgata, the two of you should not stop her from doing this. If you forbid her she will die of a broken heart. Because of Bimbā's great virtuousness, she can not abandon her duty. O, Maudgalyāyana, the Tathāgata has overcome the defilements—greed, hatred, delusion—so this act of Bimbā's will not trouble me." Having spoken to Śāriputra and Maudgalyāyana, the Buddha entered Bimbā's palace.

The Lord Buddha radiated six bright colors from his body with hundreds and thousands of rays like the sun and the moon rising above Yugandhara Mountain. The Blessed One then went up to the throne that was covered in a red cloth protected by a canopy decorated with seven kinds of jewels [diamond, ruby, emerald, gold, opal, sapphire, amethyst]. Upon seeing the Buddha sitting on the throne, her attendants approached Bimbā and said, "Oh mistress, you no longer need to be sad. The Lord Buddha has come into your palace and is sitting on the throne."

When Bimbā heard the attendants' message, she suddenly felt hot and short of breath. She then fanned her face with her scarf, dressed, arranged her hair, and finished her toilette. Taking Rāhula by the hand, she went into the palace. Upon seeing the Lord Buddha she felt angry and resentful. Falling down at his feet she sobbed and sobbed, crying out her unhappiness: "O, I, Bimbā, have been abandoned. I have no husband by my side."

Her attendants tried to calm her. "Bimbā, your anger caused you to cry. But now that the prince, your husband, is here, you should feel content and at peace." Distraught and with tears streaming from her eyes, Bimbā turned her head and looked at the Lord Buddha, saying, "Why do I cry? I'm angry because my husband has not even greeted me. We were married for only seven years and he abandoned me. I was still young. It was not as though my Lord was leaving me in his old age. I felt very lonely." Bimbā's attendants, unable to relieve her sorrow, wept with her.

Bimbā then slowly came forward. She bowed her head down to the Lord Buddha's feet and paid respects to him. Unfastening her hair, she dusted off his feet and then embraced them. She fanned his feet back and forth, moving tenderly like the fronds of a banana tree in the forest. Sobbing, she spoke to the Enlightened One, "*Bhante* . . . O, my Lord, I pay my respects to you. I am unlucky and ashamed before you, O Lord of Jambudvīpa. You abandoned me and our child without any compassion. In the old days I never considered myself unlucky. You never gave any indication that you would leave me alone for such a long time. Prince Rāhula was just born, but you left without any concern for me. You made your departure at midnight on your bejeweled horse, Kanthaka.

"Even though you were married to me, Bimbā, I was left deserted. O, my Lord, you are a person of merit with a father, mother, family, and friends in a large palace. An astrologer had once predicted that in the future Bimbā would experience suffering. O my Lord, when I heard this ancient wisdom I knew that it was foolhardy to think that mother, father, or king could escape from suffering. As the astrologer foretold, I suffered when you abandoned me for six years. I thought of you every day, morning and night."

After she had spoken, Bimbā took Rāhula, a handsome jewellike boy of golden complexion, put him on her lap and kissed him on the top of the head. She asked Rāhula to bow in front of the Buddha, and then said, "O, Prince Rāhula, child of this gentle mother, your birth was of little merit and inauspicious for your father. From now on I shall be considered a widow, one ashamed before villagers and townspeople. I cannot remain here. From today your mother who loves you so much will be as your father. If I were to die I would attain nirvāṇa (Thai *yọt kaew,* 'the diamond peak'). O, Rāhula, let us go and die together. We will be released from all our suffering."

. . . After Bimbā's sorrowful lament of pain and suffering, King Suddhodana spoke to the Lord Buddha, "*Bhante Bhagavā* . . . O, Blessed One, Bimbā loves you very much. When you renounced the householder life Bimbā thought of you night and day and cried continually after you left at midnight. She stared at your bed under the royal umbrella decorated with the nine jewels. Bimbā cried and cried when evening arrived and you had not yet returned. She opened the windows and looked far and wide, overcome with sadness. She stared at your throne and then returned trembling to the window once again. Having heard that the Lord Buddha did not eat for seven days, that he wore a saffron robe, and that he slept on a bed of grass on the ground, Bimbā told others to spread out grass for her to sleep on. Bimbā followed the example of the Lord Buddha."

. . . Bimbā's sorrow gradually disappeared. She regained her composure and took delight in the Lord of Jambudvīpa's [the Buddha's] teachings. She attained to the stage of the fruit of the stream-enterer. All of the kings and others assembled there reached the highest states of spiritual realization.

Prince Nanda and Prince Rāhula were ordained by the Buddha into the *sāsanā* [religion]. They left for the city of Rājagṛha. They entered the Veḷuvana forest hermitage with a large number of the Buddha's followers. Wherever the Lord Buddha stayed he helped those who lived in the area. After five years the Buddha had five hundred disciples. . . .

The final portion of the text relates King Suddhodana's death and cremation. It becomes an occasion where the Buddha performs a healing miracle and also preaches a funeral sermon about the inevitability of death and the universality of impermanence, as Theravāda monks do today at funerals. Before he dies, Suddhodana gains arhatship after reflecting on the Buddha's teachings of the four noble truths. Gotamī, the Buddha's aunt, and his wife, Bimbā, join the Buddha's order along with various other Śākyan officials.

The text concludes with the transcriber of the text wishing the highest happiness of nirvāṇa to his family, teachers, and all living beings:

sukham vata nibbānam, sāram vata nibbānam, nibbānam paramam sukham.

—44—

Hagiographies of the Korean Monk Wŏnhyo

Robert E. Buswell, Jr.

The Buddhist scholiast Wŏnhyo ("Break of Dawn," 617–686 C.E.) was the Korean monk who contributed most to the development of an indigenous approach to Buddhist doctrine and practice. Wŏnhyo wrote some one hundred treatises and commentaries on virtually all of the East Asian Buddhist materials then available to him in Korea. Over twenty of the works in this extensive oeuvre are still extant and tell us much about Buddhism during its incipiency on the Korean peninsula.

As is all too common with the lives of Buddhist monks, however, we know comparatively little about Wŏnhyo the man. Virtually everything available about his life derives from two sources: the Chinese hagiographical anthology *The Song Biographies of Eminent Monks* (*Song gaoseng zhuan;* hereafter *Song Biographies*) and the Korean quasi-historical miscellany *Memorabilia and Mirabilia of the Three Kingdoms* (*Samguk yusa;* henceforth *Memorabilia*); the portions of both of these dealing with Wŏnhyo will be translated in full below. These biographies are emblematic of the approaches East Asian hagiographers took toward Buddhist biography, and display the type of symbolism and imagery often used in such works.

East Asian hagiography was principally intended to preserve for posterity the achievements of an eminent individual who personified a particular spiritual ideal, cultural symbol, or religious accomplishment. Hagiography also functioned as a didactic tool, offering a spiritual exemplar for religious adherents, a model of conduct, morality, and understanding that could be imitated by the entire community. East Asians tended consciously to emulate the lives of past moral paragons, which meant that religious virtuosi tended to follow strikingly similar patterns in their vocations. This penchant for sacred biography to become self-perpetuating and mutually imitative is what Ernst Kris has termed "enacted biography." Hence, Wŏnhyo's biographies should give implicit indications about the character of Korean Buddhism as a whole, for Wŏnhyo became a cultural archetype of the entire Korean tradition, not solely because of his religious and scholastic achievements but also because his character as recounted in these biographies exerted a profound influence on the personal development of religious adepts on the Korean peninsula.

The first of Wŏnhyo's biographies translated here appears in the *Song gaoseng zhuan,* compiled in China between 982 and 988 by Zanning ("Extolling Repose," 919–1001), a noted Buddhist historiographer and polemicist. The anthology is typical of the East Asian Buddhist hagiographical tradition in typecasting its eminent monks as models worthy of emulation. Hence, we should not expect to find much information on Wŏnhyo the man in this hagiography; rather, the stories about him will have explicit didactic purposes. The short introduction to the biography, full of literary allusion and martial euphemism, is little more than the stereotyped encomium appropriate to any respected teacher, and its style betrays the biography's lack of concern with Wŏnhyo himself.

The *Song Biographies'* treatment of Wŏnhyo is a quintessential example of the way in which East Asian Buddhist hagiography employs folkloric topoi to present a stereotyped characterization of an eminent religious personage. The incurable sickness of a female member of the royal family, the scriptural repository in the dragon king's palace, the use of the thigh as a secret hiding place, the theft of a sacred book—all these are common topoi found in folklore throughout Asia.

Rather surprisingly, the single strand of the *Song Biographies'* narrative concerns not Wŏnhyo's religious career but instead the question of the scriptural authenticity of the *Book of Adamantine Absorption* (*Jingang sanmei jing,* or *Vajrasamādhi-sūtra*), a Buddhist apocryphal text that I have shown elsewhere to be of Korean provenance and probably composed toward the end of Wŏnhyo's lifetime. Only after the long description of the rediscovery and promulgation of the *Book of Adamantine Absorption* does Zanning once again return to Wŏnhyo the man. But there too he is content to summarize in just a few short phrases some of the other legends that circulated about Wŏnhyo, even though in a real biography these should have been of intrinsic interest equal to the story surrounding this apocryphal text. So little of Wŏnhyo himself emerges from this hagiography that Zanning clearly appears to have used Wŏnhyo primarily as a stratagem for discussing the legend about the recovery of the *Book of Adamantine Absorption.*

Sacred biographies often explicate the mythic trials of a religious hero in three major stages: the exile of the subject from his community, his trials and tribulations to redeem himself, and his eventual reinstatement in the community, often at heightened status. In Wŏnhyo's hagiography, the community of monastic elders first tries to bar him from participating in the prestigious state-protection ritual using the *Book of Benevolent Kings* (*Renwang jing*). While Wŏnhyo is out traveling among the people, as the Korean version of his biography tells us, the dragon king calls on Wŏnhyo to write a commentary to the *Book of Adamantine Absorption.* His lecture on this scripture redeems his reputation and restores Wŏnhyo to his rightful place in the Buddhist community.

Wŏnhyo also appears prominently in several sections of the Korean *Memorabilia and Mirabilia of the Three Kingdoms,* compiled sometime during the thirteenth century by the Buddhist monk Iryŏn ("The Blazing of Oneness," 1206–1289), of which only the main entry on Wŏnhyo is translated here. Although Iryŏn culls passages from earlier Chinese hagiographical anthologies in writing his hagiographies, he also incorporates stories from local legend and regional biographies into his accounts. Because of his interest in stories about the actual events in a subject's life, Iryŏn's accounts tend to convey a genuine sense of flesh-and-blood individuals who achieved their renown through personal trial and tribulation. Thus Iryŏn's biographical style offers a somewhat more vivid sense of the personalities who helped to forge the Buddhist tradition than is usually found in Chinese hagiographies.

Iryŏn's tendency to place greater focus on the individual is probably attributable to the fact that one of the purposes of *Memorabilia* was to preserve all Buddhist lore then extant on the Korean peninsula that had not been preserved in the major historical records. The only other systematic account of Korea's ancient period, the *Historical Record of the Three Kingdoms* (*Samguk sagi*), a Korean secular history written in 1145 by Kim Pusik (1075–1151), included minimal references to Buddhist personages or ceremonies in its treatment of early Korean history. (Wŏnhyo, for example, is given just one line in the biography of his literatus son, Sŏl Ch'ong ["Sŏl the Astute," date unknown].) Iryŏn was concerned that this lore not be lost, and packed his miscellany with any and probably all stories circulating about the past eminences of Korean Buddhism.

Although the *Memorabilia*'s biography gives us a somewhat better sense of Wŏnhyo the man, like any East Asian hagiography it also is not immune to pious embellishment of his life, and is still prone to portray Wŏnhyo as embodying the ideals of his religious community. The ideal Iryŏn most emphasizes is "unhindered action," in which enlightenment is said to liberate the saint from such dualistic concepts as right and wrong or good and evil, freeing him from the normative standards of morality. This liberty to frequent even bars and brothels with impunity was obviously a controversial matter within the ecclesia of the Silla kingdom of Korea.

The fusion of mythic and historical elements in Buddhist hagiographical writing is crucial to remember in examining the following biographies of Wŏnhyo. Although it is common for most hagiographers to treat Buddhist eminences as epitomes of specific religious qualities, whether that be talent in theurgy, erudition, or proselytization, this depiction is often corroborated by anecdotes presumably taken from the personal life of the subject. Both *Song Biographies* and *Memorabilia* are episodic in their treatments of Wŏnhyo, but the overall concerns of the two biographies are somewhat different and convey distinctly varied impressions of their subject. *Song Biographies* adheres more closely to the Confucian biographical tradition in presenting its subjects more as types than as individuals. Zanning offers little information about Wŏnhyo's personality; indeed, *Song Biographies* explicitly typecasts Wŏnhyo as "certainly in the same class with Beidu ["Cup-crosser", d. 426] and Zhigong ["The Gentleman Precious Expression"]," two well-known theurgists during the Chinese Liang dynasty. *Memorabilia*, by contrast, is more apt to expand its accounts to include anecdotes that illustrate the day-to-day life of Wŏnhyo rather than simply recounting his emulation of a given ideal. Iryŏn provides only minimal details regarding Wŏnhyo's ancestry, training, and awards, and prefers instead to focus on Wŏnhyo's debauchery and his exploits among the ordinary people of Silla. By adopting such an approach, Iryŏn's compilation is lively, robust, and even ribald on occasion.

These translations are from *Tang Xinluoguo Huanglongsi Yuanxiao zhuan* ("Biography of Wŏnhyo of Hwangnyong Monastery in the Tang Dominion of Silla"): *Song gaoseng zhuan* 4, *Taishō shinshū daizōkyō* (Tokyo, 1924–1934), 2061; vol. 50, p. 730a6–b29. *Wŏnhyo Pulgi* ("Wŏnhyo, the Unbridled"): *Samguk yusa* 4, *Taishō* 2039; vol. 49, p. 1006a7–b29. The section titles have been added.

Biography of Wŏnhyo of Hwangnyong-sa in the Tang Dominion of Silla
From Song Biographies of Eminent Monks

INTRODUCTION

Shi Yuanxiao's [Sŏk Wŏnhyo, "Break of Dawn"] patronym was Xue [Sŏl]; he was a native of Xiangzhou [Sangju] on the Eastern Sea. During his queued-haired youth, he willingly entered the law [and became a monk]. He traveled around the country without any constancy, studying under various teachers. He valiantly assaulted the ramparts of meaning, and heroically thwarted the marshaled lines of text. Resolutely, martially, he marched forward without retreating. He covered the depth and breadth of the three trainings [morality, concentration, wisdom]. In his country, he was known as a "match for myriad people." Such was his mastery of doctrine and his attainment of mystery.

Once, together with the master of the law Ŭisang [alt. "Marks of Meaning," 625–702 C.E.], he tried to go to Tang China, longing to join the canonical master Xuanzang's ["Mysterious Stoutness," d. 664] school at Cien ["Loving Grace"] Monastery. But as his conditioning was discrepant, he was content just to wander around for a while.

His utterances were mad and outrageous, and his conduct perverted and remiss. Together with householders, he entered bars and brothels. Like Zhigong ["Gentleman Expression," viz. Baozhi ("Precious Expression,"), 418–514], he carried a metal knife and an iron staff [when he traveled]. Sometimes he composed commentaries in order to explicate the "Assorted Flowers" [of the *Flower Garland Scripture, Huayan jing*]. At other times, he plucked the zither in order to enliven the shrines and temples. Sometimes, he dwelled overnight at the village gate. At other times, he sat in meditation in the mountains and along the streams. He followed the turn of events in any way that he pleased, completely without any fixed regimen.

RECOVERY OF THE BOOK OF ADAMANTINE ABSORPTION

At one time, the king of the Silla kingdom inaugurated a Great Assembly of One Hundred Seats [for eminent monks] for the recitation of the *Book of Benevolent Kings* (*Renwang jing*), and sought out everywhere learned venerables [to participate]. Wŏnhyo's native province, on the basis of his reputation, nominated him, but the other venerables despised his personal character and recommended that the king not accept him.

Wŏnhyo had not been present long [at the convocation] before the brain of the king's queen-consort was afflicted by a tumorous swelling that had exhausted all the doctors' remedies. The king and the crown prince, the vassals and subjects, prayed and petitioned at the numinous shrines in the mountains and along the streams; there was no place that they did not visit. There was a shaman who said, "Only if you dispatch a person to a foreign kingdom to seek medicine will this illness be cured." The king then ordered an envoy to sail across the sea to Tang [China] and seek out their medical arts.

While en route over the murky swells, [the envoy] unexpectedly saw an old man jump up from the billowing waves and climb aboard ship. He invited the envoy to enter into the sea, where he saw the awesome splendor of the palace basilica. There he had an audience with the dragon king, whose name was Qienhai ["Holder of the Seal of the Seas"]. He told the envoy, "The queen-consort of your country is the third daughter of Jingdi [the Green Emperor, ruler of the east, who controlls the spring season]. Since times of old, [the scriptural repository in] my palace has contained a copy of the *Book of Adamantine Absorption* in which the two enlightenments [innate and actualized] are completely imparted and which discloses the practice of the bodhisattva. Now, taking the queen's illness as an ideal pretext, I wish to entrust you with this scripture so that it may be circulated and disseminated in your kingdom." He then took the thirty-some folios, which were loosely stacked in unbound form, and entrusted them to the envoy.

He said again, "While this scripture is being taken across the sea, I fear that it might incur some interference from Māra [the devil]." The king then commanded that the envoy's thigh be slit with a knife and [the scripture] placed inside. [Surgeons then] used waxed paper to wrap and bind up [the scripture] and spread his thigh with unguents so that it was just like before.

The dragon king said, "Have the saint Taean ["Great Peace"] collate [the loose folios] and sew them together [into a bound volume]; ask the dharma master Wŏnhyo to write a commentary explicating [the scripture]. Then the queen's illness will undoubtedly be cured. Even the efficacy of the agada [herbal] panacea of the Snowy Mountains [the Himalayas] does not surpass this."

The dragon king saw him off to the surface of the sea, where [the envoy] then climbed aboard ship and returned to his kingdom. At that time, the king was delighted to hear [of his adventure], and summoned first the saint Taean to bind and collate the [folios].

Taean was an unfathomable person. His appearance and dress were unusual and bizarre. He was constantly among the shops of the marketplace striking a bronze alms bowl and calling out, "Taean! Taean! ['Great Peace']." This was how he earned his sobriquet. The king summoned An, but An said, "Just bring the scripture; I don't wish to cross the threshold of the royal palace." An received the scripture and arranged [the folios] into eight chapters, which were all in accordance with the Buddha's intent.

An said, "Quickly take it and entrust it to Wŏnhyo to lecture; don't let anyone else have it." Hyo, who was just then residing at his birthplace of Sangju, received the scripture. He said to the messenger, "The theme of this scripture is the two enlightenments—innate and actualized. Prepare an animal cart for me." Taking his writing table, he set it between [the ox's] two horns and laid out his brushes and inkstone. While riding continually on the ox-cart, he wrote the commentary, complete in five fascicles.

The king requested that, on a given day, a lecture be convened at Hwangnyong ["Yellow Dragon"] Monastery. At that time, a menial lackey [of Wŏnhyo's opponents within the order] stole the new commentary. The matter was therewith reported to the king. [Wŏnhyo] delayed [the lecture] for three days and re-recorded [his words, this time] complete in three fascicles, and called it the abbreviated commentary. Then the king and his vassals, the monks and laypeople, thronged like clouds into the Hall of the Law. Hyo then expounded [his commentary], which was elegant, elucidated disputed points, and could serve as an exemplar [for commentarial writings]. The sound of the praise, acclaim, and snapping fingers [signaling approval] welled up into the sky.

Hyo then spoke openly:

"Although I was not welcomed at the convocation when a hundred rafters gathered, I am the only one qualified here this morning to lay a single beam."

At that time, all the famous venerables bowed their heads, embarrassed and ashamed; humbled by their pettiness, they were repentant and contrite.

CONCLUSION

From the first, Hyo's appearances were unpredictable and his method of proselytism was variable. Sometimes he rescued people [monks threatened by an impending earthquake] by throwing his tray. At other times he put out [monastery] fires by spitting water. Sometimes he displayed [transformation] bodies at several locations. At other times he announced his extinction at six regions. He was certainly in the same class with Beidu and Zhigong! When it came to understanding people's temperament, that would become completely clear to him in a glance.

His commentary [to the *Book of Adamantine Absorption*] had two versions: an expanded and an abbreviated one. Both are in circulation in their native land. The abbreviated version was transmitted to China. Later, a canonical master who was a translator of scriptures finally changed [the title from a commentary] to an exposition [thereby placing the status of Wŏnhyo's text on a par with that of Indian scriptural exegeses].

CLARIFICATION

In connection [with the above story]: How is it that there are scriptural texts in the dragon king's palace?

Explanation: The scriptures say that in the basilica of the dragon king's palace there is a reliquary adorned with the seven precious jewels. All the profound principles spoken by all the buddhas—such as the twelvefold chain of conditioned origination, mnemonic devices, meditative concentrations, and so forth—fill completely a separate trunk adorned with the seven jewels. Truly, it was fitting that this scripture was put into circulation in the world and, moreover, it revealed the theurgic uniqueness of Taean and the venerable Hyo. [The dragon king] then used the sickness of the queen-consort as a great pretext to propagate the doctrine.

Wŏnhyo, the Unbridled

From Memorabilia and Mirabilia of the Three Kingdoms

INTRODUCTORY REMARKS AND ANCILLARY STORIES CONCERNING WŎNHYO'S NATIVE REGION

The holy master Wŏnhyo's patronym was Sŏl. His grandfather was Baron Ingp'i, who was also known as Baron Chŏktae. Now, beside Chŏktae pool there is an Ingp'igong shrine. His father was the eleventh-degree bureaucrat Tamnal.

[Wŏnhyo] first displayed birth beneath twin sal trees in Yulgok ["Chestnut Valley"], north of Pulchi ["Stage of Buddhahood"] village, in the south of Amnyang district [now Changsan'gun]. This village was called Pulchi or Palchi ["Arising of Wisdom"].

[Note:] In the local dialect, it is called Pultŭngŭlch'ŏn.

[Note:] "Sal trees": A folk tale says that the master's family originally resided in the southwest of this valley. When his mother's pregnancy had reached full term, she happened to be passing through this valley and, under these chestnut trees, she unexpectedly went into labor. Due to the urgency of the situation, she was not able to return home; so, draping her husband's raiments from a tree, she lay amid [her makeshift screen and gave birth]. It is for this reason that these trees were called sal trees. The fruits of those trees are also out of the ordinary, and even now are called sal chestnuts.

[Note:] "Yulgok": There is an old legend that, long ago, a monastery abbot gave each temple serf a ration of two chestnuts per evening. A serf lodged a complaint against him with the [local] magistrate. The magistrate thought [this story] strange and, taking up a chestnut, examined it. One nut filled an entire bowl! He then ruled instead that [the serfs] should be given only one chestnut. It is for this reason that [the valley] was named Chestnut Valley.]

Once the master had left home [to become a monk], he converted his residence into a monastery, which he named Ch'ogae ["First Opening"]. Beside the tree he established a monastery, named Sara ["sal trees"].

The master's *Account of Conduct* (*Haengjang*) states that he was a person from the capital [of Kyŏngju], following [the records available for] his grandfather and father. The *Tang Biographies of Eminent Monks* [sic] states that he was a native of Hasangju.

[Note:] During the second year of [the Tang Chinese] Linde ["Felicitous Goodness"] reign-period [665], King Munmu ["Civil and Martial," r. 661–681] redivided the regions of Sangju and Haju and established Samnyangju. Haju then became what is now Ch'angnyanggun. Amnyanggun was originally an affiliated county of Haju. Sangju now [has the alternate name] Sangju, which is also written [with the logographs] Sangju. Pulchi village now is part of Chain district. Hence, it is right on the border with Amnyang [district].

The master's childhood name was Sŏdang ["Sworn Banner"]; his local name was Sindang ["New Banner"] [both suggesting that Wŏnhyo's family had military connections].

[Note:] "Banner" in the vernacular means "hair."

Initially, his mother dreamed that a shooting star entered her bosom; as a result of that, she conceived. Just as he was about to be born, five-colored clouds blanketed the earth. This was in the thirty-ninth year of King Chinp'yŏng's ["True Peace"] [reign, 617], the thirteenth year of Daye ["Great Enterprise"], during the cyclical year changch'uk.

Congenitally, [Wŏnhyo] was shrewd and unusual. He studied without following a teacher.

A complete account of his pilgrimages and his luxuriant accomplishments in proselytization appears in full in the *Tang Biographies of Eminent Monks* [sic] and in his *Account of Conduct,* and need not all be recorded here. But there are one or two other notable events that are only recorded in the *Local Biography* (*Hyangjŏn*).

SELECTIONS FROM THE LOCAL BIOGRAPHY

One day the master's air was perverted [by spring fever] and he sang in the streets:

> Who will loan me a handleless axe?
> I would hew a heaven-supporting pillar.

No one could understand his analogy. At that time, T'aejong ["Great Ancestor", King Muyŏl ("Martial Majesty"), r. 654–661] heard [this song] and said, "It would appear that this monk is saying that he wants a noble woman to bear him a sagacious son. There would indeed be no greater benefit than for the kingdom to have a great sage."

At that time in Yosŏkkong ["Prasine Palace"] (note: now an academy) there was a widowed princess. [The king] ordered the palace officials to find Hyo and escort him back. The palace officials honored the order and went in search of him, but he had already come from Namsan ["South Mountain"], crossing Munch'ŏn'gyo ["Mosquito Stream Bridge"], and met them there.

[Note:] Sach'ŏn, in the local dialect, is Yŏnch'ŏn, or Munjŏn. The bridge is also named Yugyo ["Elm Bridge"].

He deliberately fell into the water, soaking his clothes and trousers. The officials led the master to the palace, where he removed his clothes and dried them in the sun. Under that pretext, he stayed overnight there and the princess ended up becoming pregnant; [later] she gave birth to Sŏl Ch'ong ["Sŏl the Astute", fl. ca. eighth century].

Congenitally, Ch'ong was astute and clever, and had extensive understanding of the [Confucian] *Classics* and *Histories*. He was one of the Ten Sages of Silla. He set up equivalencies for the names of things which figured in the local customs of China (Hua) and the Eastern Tribes (I, viz. Korea), in order to inculcate and explain the *Six Classics* and belles lettres. Even today, those in Korea (Haedong; lit. "East of Parhae") who devote themselves to interpreting the *Classics* have transmitted these [annotations] without interruption.

Since Hyo had broken his precepts in begetting Ch'ong, he subsequently changed into lay clothes and called himself Householder Sosŏng ["Humble Commoner"].

By chance one day, he came upon an actor who was dancing with a large gourd [mask], the appearance of which was bizarre and strange. He made his own religious requisite in the same shape, and ordered that it be named Muae ["Unhindered"] after a [passage in] the *Flower Garland Scripture:* "All unhindered men leave birth and death along a single path." He then composed a song that circulated throughout the land. He used to take up this [gourd] and sing and dance his way through thousands of villages and myriad hamlets, touring while proselytizing in song. He prompted all classes of "mulberry door-posts and jar windows" [the destitute] and even "gibbons and macaques" [youth and country bumpkins] to recognize the name "Buddha," and recite together the invocation "Homage." Hyo's proselytizing was great indeed!

A CHRONOLOGY OF WŎNHYO'S LIFE

The village of his birth was named Pulchi ["Stage of Buddhahood"]; his monastery was called Ch'ogae ["Initial Opening"]; he called himself Wŏnhyo ["Break of Dawn"], which refers to the first shining of the sun of buddhahood. [The name] "Wŏnhyo" is also the Silla pronunciation. People of his time all referred to him in the vernacular as Sidan ["First Dawning"].

When he resided at Punhwang ["Fragrant Sovereign"] Monastery preparing his *Commentary to the Flower Garland Scripture,* he reached the fourth [fascicle of the commentary] on the "Ten Transferences Chapter" (*Shi huixiang pin*) and, having completed it, laid down his brush.

Furthermore, because of the reproach he had suffered, he divided his body among the hundred pines [and appeared everywhere]. Everyone considered his status and position to be that of a first-stage (*bhūmi*) [bodhisattva].

Also, due to the inducement of the dragon of the sea, he received a royal command while on the road, and wrote his *Commentary on the Book of [Adamantine] Absorption.* He placed his brushes and inkstone between the two horns of an ox; because of this, he was known as Kaksŭng ["Horn Rider"] [a name homophonous with Enlightenment Vehicle], which also expressed the recondite purport of the two types of enlightenments—innate and actualized. The master of the law Taean collated the folios and then pasted them together. This [felicitous arrangement] also was "knowing the sound and singing in harmony."

After [Wŏnhyo] had entered quiescence, Ch'ong crushed his remaining bones and cast them into a lifelike image which he enshrined at Punhwang Monastery—this in order to show his reverence and affection [for his father] and his intent [to mourn his father until] the ends of heaven. When Ch'ong prostrated beside it, the image suddenly turned its head [to look at him]; still today, it remains turned to the side.

The site of Ch'ong's house is beside a cave monastery where Hyo used to reside.

EULOGY

Horn Rider first opened the hub of meditative concentration.
His dancing-gourd was finally suspended in the wind of myriad streets.
At moonlit Prasine Palace he was deep in spring sleep.
The gate is closed at Punhwang Monastery, his glancing image is hollow.

—45—

The Illustrated Biography of Ippen

Dennis Hirota

In the figure of Ippen (1239–1289 C.E.) we find a form of Pure Land tradition in which various strands of Buddhist thought are fused with a wide range of popularly accepted religious practices. Ippen studied in the lineage of Hōnen and is regarded as the founder of the Ji school, one of the major new traditions that emerged during the Kamakura period. His basic message is framed in terms of the Pure Land path: in the utterance of the nembutsu, "Namu-amida-butsu," persons become one with Amida Buddha, so that their own realization of buddhahood is settled. At the same time, however, his religious attainment was recognized by the Zen master Kakushin, from whom he received certification, and he also felt strong ties with the temple complex on Mount Kōya, one of the major centers of esoteric Buddhism.

In addition, he adopted a number of activities ultimately rooted in indigenous and non-Buddhist practices: mountain austerities; pilgrimages to sacred sites, including major shrines and temples throughout the country; retreats at such sites undertaken in the hope of receiving divine revelations and dream messages; an itinerant life of propagation as a "wandering holy man who had abandoned all attachments"; the use of verse as religious offerings at temples and shrines; distribution of fuda (slips of paper bearing a sacred inscription and often regarded as possessing protective powers); ecstatic dancing; and the keeping of a register for recording the names of the faithful.

Further, Ippen's life of constant travel brought him into contact with a diversity of people—of various classes and livelihoods—in all parts of Japan, and the events of his biography reveal the religious climate of the times. In his admonitions against self-drowning in order to be born in the Pure Land, for example, or the numbers of men and women who received the tonsure from him, we sense both widespread disquiet and intense energy, arising from the harsh conditions of daily life, radical social and political changes, and such extraordinary pressures as the Mongol invasion attempts.

The following selection consists of passages drawn from the *Illustrated Biography of Ippen* (*Ippen Hijiri-e*), a set of twelve horizontal handscrolls in which forty-eight sections of written narrative alternate with painted illustrations. It was completed in 1299, just ten years after Ippen's death, and both the text and the paintings are regarded as invaluable resources for the study of the daily life of the period. The text, by Ippen's half-brother, Shōkai, records not only details of Ippen's life and his teaching in the form of his poems, letters, and spoken words but also background explanations of religious sites and practices. Here, we will focus on the depiction of Ippen's activities.

The passages are translated from Asayama Enshō, ed., *Ippen Hijiri-e: Rokujō engi*, revised edition (Tokyo: Sankibō Busshorin, 1976; first ed., 1940).

Further Reading

For a complete translation of Ippen's extant writings and recorded sayings, along with a study of his thought from the perspective of the Japanese Pure Land tradition, see Dennis Hirota, *No Abode: The Record of Ippen* (Kyoto: Ryukoku University, 1986). Two articles treat the *Illustrated Biography of Ippen* in James H. Sanford, William R. LaFleur, and Masatoshi Nagatomi, eds., *Flowing Traces: Buddhism in the Literary and Visual Arts of Japan* (Princeton: Princeton University Press, 1992): Laura S. Kaufman, "Nature, Courtly Imagery, and Sacred Meaning in the *Ippen Hijiri-e*," pp. 47–75; and James H. Foard, "Prefiguration and Narrative in Medieval Hagiography: The *Ippen Hijiri-e*," pp. 76–92.

Early Training

Ippen was born into a provincial warrior family, the Kōno, on the island of Shikoku. Although his clan had once held extensive power, in 1221, less than two decades before Ippen's birth, his grandfather Michinobu supported the retired emperor Gotoba in an unsuccessful uprising against the military government in Kamakura and was exiled after suffering defeat. Of Michinobu's sons, two had not participated against the government and therefore escaped punishment; the elder took over the leadership of the clan, and the younger, Ippen's future father, entered the priesthood with the name Nyobutsu, probably in order to pray for family members.

Nyobutsu studied in Kyoto under one of Hōnen's leading disciples, the Pure Land teacher Shōkū, then returned to Shikoku, where he married. In a mode of life seen increasingly in the period, particularly among Pure Land Buddhists, he maintained his status as a priest, performing rites in the family temple, and also openly fulfilled the role of head of a warrior household. Ippen was his second son (the name "Ippen" was not adopted until after a revelation at Kumano, described below).

When Ippen was ten years old by traditional Japanese count, his mother died, and shortly thereafter Ippen also entered the priesthood. The *Biography* states that with his mother's death, he "awakened to the truth of impermanence," but no doubt Nyobutsu played a large role in the decision. At the age of thirteen, Ippen journeyed to Kyushu to begin his studies in the Pure Land tradition under a colleague of his father.

In 1263, when Ippen was twenty-five years old, his father died. On learning of the death, Ippen returned home to Shikoku, eventually reverting to lay life as a warrior and taking a wife. Problems arose, however:

At times he entered the gate of truth and endeavored in practice; at other times he mingled in the dust of worldly life and turned his thoughts to familial love and affection. Then he would play with children, even spinning a spool-shaped top in the air for them. On one occasion, the top fell to the ground and lay still. Later he would say: "Going over this in my mind, I saw that if you spin a top, it will turn, but if you do not go about spinning it, it won't. Our turning in transmigration is precisely so. With our activities of body, speech, and mind, there can be no end to transmigration in the six paths. But how would we transmigrate if our self-actions ceased? Here for the first time this struck my heart, and realizing the nature of birth-and-death, I grasped the essence of the Buddha's dharma."

Seeking liberation from saṃsāric existence, Ippen resolved to "sever emotional attachments and enter the realm of the uncreated." The *Biography* comments: "The Buddha taught that even sleeping in the mountains and forests is superior to diligence while in home life. Moreover, there was an incident that reminded him of the admonition, 'If they linger long in the village, holy men and deer meet with disaster.' " The nature of this incident is not known, but there appears to have been a serious feud within the clan.

In 1271, at the age of thirty-three, Ippen set out for Kyushu once more to consult his former teacher, then made his way to distant Zenkōji temple. He was later to speak of his earlier decade of doctrinal study as nothing but "an exercise in self-will"; it seems likely, therefore, that at this point he was determined to pursue his religious quest by other means. Zenkōji was a popular pilgrimage site and a center for wandering nembutsu monks. Its sacred image of Amida, thought to have arrived in Japan from India, was regarded as the living Buddha himself; hence, the *Biography* speaks of the temple as "auspicious ground for the decisive settlement of birth in the Pure Land." Seeking a direct encounter with the Buddha, Ippen remained in retreat at Zenkōji for a number of days. He then returned to Shikoku, where,

in autumn of the same year, at Kubodera, he made a clearing in a secluded spot covered with blue moss and verdant ivy. There he built a hermitage with a pine gate and brushwood door. . . . Cutting off all outside contact, he carried on his practice in solitude. Abandoning all affairs, he solely recited the name of Amida. With no impediments to his practice . . . , he greeted and passed the springs and autumns of three years. At that time, he made a verse in seven-character lines expressing dharma as he understood it in his own heart:

> Perfect enlightenment ten kalpas past—pervading the realm of sentient beings;
> Birth in one thought-moment—into Amida's land.
> Where ten and one are nondual, we realize no-birth;
> Where land and realm are the same, we sit in Amida's great assembly.

In this verse, "ten" signifies Amida's enlightenment, realized ten kalpas ago when his vow to liberate all beings who say his name was fulfilled, and "one" signifies our attainment of birth in Amida's pure land in the utterance of the name. The inseparability of Amida's buddhahood that transcends time and beings' attainment in the immediate present would remain the foundation of Ippen's thought for the rest of his life.

In order to verify his realization, Ippen went to Sugō, a mountainous region on Shikoku favored by yamabushi or "mountain ascetics" because caves and precipitous peaks made it an ideal site for rigorous practices, and also because of the lore associated with the place. The *Biography* relates in detail how a bodhisattva had manifested himself there before the spread of Buddhism. One night when a hunter touched and drew his bow against a rotting tree, the tree began to glow. Looking the next day, he found beneath the moss a golden figure in human form, and realized at once it was Kannon. Eventually he built a hall to enshrine the bodhisattva and, vowing to protect it, became the guardian deity of the place. Among the legendary ascetics who practiced austerities in caves in the area seeking the aid of Kannon was a woman who, through chanting the *Lotus Sūtra,* had overcome the hindrance of a female bodily existence and gained the ability to fly. Ippen remained in a hermitage for six months:

> Here the hijiri secluded himself and prayed for the fundamental resolve of renouncing this world. Revelations in dreams appeared to him frequently. . . . After going out from this place he abandoned house and property forever, detached himself from desires and family, and relinquished all temple halls and buildings to the three treasures of the dharma realm. . . . He selected and arranged only the most essential scriptures, furnishing himself thus for his practice.

At this point Ippen seems to have made a major decision to cease his solitary discipline as a recluse and to take up a life of wandering that combined renunciation of any settled dwelling—whether house or temple—with travel throughout the country to bring people into living contact with dharma.

Spreading the Dharma

From Sugō, Ippen returned home briefly then, in the second month of 1274, set out once more accompanied by two nuns, who may have been his wife and child. They remained with him until his revelation at Kumano. He first made his way to Shitennōji temple, a popular pilgrimage site associated with Prince Shōtoku, who was worshiped as a bodhisattva. People entered retreats there in the hope of gaining his guidance and aid. It was also a site for Pure Land devotions, particularly the practice of one million recitations of the nembutsu, and its western gate was thought to be "the eastern gate of the land of bliss," for the sun setting to the sea seen from the temple grounds inspired pilgrims with thoughts of Amida's land in the west.

On this site, Ippen attained true faith. Making fast his aspiration for birth, he submitted priestly vows to refrain from the ten grave transgressions, received the Tathāgata's precepts, and began to propagate the ippen [one-utterance] nembutsu for the salvation of sentient beings.

Ippen is depicted standing at one of the temple gates surrounded by people. Here he probably first engaged in the method of propagation he was to employ throughout his life. There were two basic elements. One is suggested by the term *ippen-nembutsu,* in which *ippen* literally means "once" or "one time," indicating utterance of "Namu-amida-butsu." As a concrete activity, it seems to have been an "exchange" or "bestowal" of utterance in which Ippen, reciting the name himself, would urge a passerby to follow his example. The significance of the person's utterance was monumental in Ippen's eyes, for Amida Buddha had vowed not to attain enlightenment unless he brought to birth in the pure land—the realm of enlightenment—every person who said the name even once. "One utterance" does not, however, refer to a numerical count; rather, it indicates the instant of the immediate present that becomes, through utterance, the point in which the person's emancipation and Amida Buddha's enlightenment are both fulfilled simultaneously. The "one-utterance nembutsu" never becomes two or three utterances, but is always the present moment rooting itself in Amida's enlightenment, or the Buddha's enlightenment emerging into the present moment of the person's utterance. When a person responded to Ippen's utterance with his own, Ippen presented a fuda—a paper strip three or four inches high on which the six Chinese characters making up "Namu-a-mi-da-butsu" had been block-printed. This is the second element of his method of propagation. It is not certain what significance he attached to the fuda, but he speaks of using the written name as the central buddha image in the altar, so they were probably used as sacred objects of worship. Further, since the name embodied the oneness of a person's attainment and the Buddha's enlightenment, the fuda were probably regarded as concrete evidence that the person's birth into Amida's pure land was completely settled. Basically, however, the fuda lent a tangible form to utterance of the nembutsu, and for the ordinary people Ippen encountered, it made acceptance of Amida's name a bodily rather than chiefly intellectual act. The distribution of such fuda bearing holy inscriptions had been practiced before him and continues down to the present at temples and shrines, where they are widely sought as amulets and charms for a variety of benefits.

In addition to the name, Ippen's fuda carried the inscription, "Decisive settlement of birth for sixty myriad people." "Sixty," the approximate number of provinces of Japan, signified the whole land; "myriad" implied all the people. The inscription expressed Ippen's aspiration to take his propagation efforts to everyone in the country. Before him, there were others who devoted themselves to the immense undertaking of bringing Amida's name to all people. One of these was Ryōnin (1073–1132), the founder of the "nembutsu of interpenetration" (*yūzū-nembutsu*), in which, under the influence of Kegon and Tendai thought, the nembutsu recitation of a single person was considered the practice of all, and vice versa. Ryōnin toured the country writing the names of those who promised to recite the nembutsu in a record book. This register was regarded as proof that practice had been performed and that birth in the pure land was thus assured for all enrolled. In this way, Ryōnin created a body of nembutsu practice that could extend to all beings, transcending the bounds of time and space, and his record gave a count of the actual number of people who had been saved through interpenetrating nembutsu. Ippen also had a register kept of the names of followers who, with death, had attained birth in the pure land. Further, his use of fuda allowed him to assess his propagation activity. The *Biography* states that the total number of fuda distributed reached 251,724, probably based on records of the number he block-printed.

From Shitennōji, Ippen traveled to Mount Kōya, whose monks also influenced Ippen's decision to use fuda in his propagation. There, in profound samādhi,

Kūkai awaits the spring when Maitreya will appear in this world and preach beneath the dragon-flower tree. Leaving behind a printing block of the six-character name, Kūkai provided the altar image for sentient beings of the five defilements who are ever floundering [in the sea of birth-and-death]. For this reason Ippen went to pay his respects at the place where that great bodhisattva manifested himself, making his way far into the mountain so that he might seal his bonds for the same birth in the pure land.

Mount Kōya was one of a number of religious centers that took on intense Pure Land Buddhist coloration during the Kamakura period, and it was even popularly identified with the pure land itself. It became the home of wandering monks who, while based at special areas on Mount Kōya, traveled through the country collecting donations, performing rites for the dead, and practicing Shingon-influenced nembutsu, in which Amida was identified with Dainichi, the central buddha of esoteric Buddhism. One method of propagation was the distribution of rubbings made from blocks attributed to Kūkai himself, like the one mentioned here, although there is no evidence for the use of the name of Amida on such fuda before Ippen.

From Mount Kōya, Ippen went on toward Kumano, an ancient Shintō shrine-complex whose central deity had come to be regarded as a manifestation of Amida Buddha. On the way, however, he was thrown into a profound quandary:

There was a monk. Ippen said, "Please accept this fuda, awakening one thought (*ichinen*) of faith and uttering 'Namu-amida-butsu.' "

The monk refused, saying, "At present faith that is single-minded (*ichinen*) does not arise in me. If I accepted your fuda, I would be breaking the precept against lying."

Ippen said, "Don't you believe in the Buddha's teaching? Why can't you accept the fuda?"

The monk replied, "I do not doubt the teaching, but there is nothing I can do about faith not arising in me."

The problem presented here seriously challenged Ippen, for it posed the question of the necessity of faith in utterance, an assumption he had not probed adequately. The problem is crystallized in the term *ichinen,* which, as a Pure Land term, had come to mean "one utterance" of the nembutsu, and also implied "single-mindedness" or "wholeheartedness" of faith. In offering the fuda, Ippen uses it with the sense of "even once"—even a single moment of faith and utterance. For the monk, however, *ichinen* meant wholeness of heart, a total entrusting. Ippen hastily grasped for a solution:

By that time, a large number of pilgrims had gathered. If the monk did not take the fuda, neither would the others, so with great reluctance Ippen said, "Please accept it even if faith does not arise in you," and gave him the fuda. Seeing this, the other pilgrims all took one, and the monk went on his way.

Ippen realized that if faith was necessary, the distribution of fuda to which he had resolved to dedicate his life was not only meaningless, but deceptive. He decided to seek the guidance at the main shrine at Kumano.

When he had closed his eyes but not yet fallen asleep, the doors of the sacred hall were pushed open and a mountain ascetic with white hair and a long hood emerged. On the verandah three hundred other mountain ascetics touched their heads down in obeisance. At that moment Ippen realized that it was the Manifestation himself and entrusted himself completely. Then the mountain ascetic stepped before Ippen and said, "Wandering monk spreading the nembutsu of interpenetration, why do you go about it mistakenly? It is not through your propagation that sentient beings come to attain birth. In Amida Buddha's perfect enlightenment ten kalpas ago, the birth of all sentient beings was decisively settled as 'Namu-amida-butsu.' Distribute your fuda regardless of whether there is faith or not, and without discriminating between the pure and impure."

Then Ippen opened his eyes and looked around. About one hundred children of twelve or thirteen came up and, holding out their hands, said, "Let us have your nembutsu." Taking the fuda, they uttered "Namu-amida-butsu" and went off.

Whereas other monks stressed the orthodoxy of their teachings by tracing them to the sūtras and the Buddhist masters of India, China, and Korea, Ippen later asserted, "My teaching is the oral transmission bestowed in dream by the Kumano deity."

Life of Wandering

On receiving this revelation at Kumano, Ippen resolved to carry on his itinerant propagation activity alone.

While Ippen was undertaking practice in Kyushu, few gave alms. When his food ran out as he savored the spring mists, he passed the long day mindful of the birth in the pure land that is no-birth. . . . A monk he encountered as he spread the nembutsu gave him a torn surplice, which he wrapped around his body as he continued walking on as his steps led him. When the sun set on the mountain paths, he brushed off the moss and lay down in the dew.

Speaking of these years, the *Biography* further records his reverence for Kūya (or Kōya, 903–972), a Heian-period holy man who spread the nembutsu:

When he first embarked on a life of renunciation, he announced, "Master Kūya is my teacher and model." Kūya's words imbued his heart and were constantly at his lips. Among his sayings:

> When one seeks fame or leads a following, both body and mind grow weary. When one accumulates merit and practices good, desires and ambitions increase. Nothing is comparable to solitude, with no outside involvement. Nothing surpasses saying the name and casting off all concerns. The recluse leading a tranquil life rejoices in poverty; the contemplative in his dim cell makes a companion of stillness. Hempen clothes and paper bedding are robes of purity; they are easily acquired, and engender no fear of thieves.

Complying with these words of dharma, Ippen first spent four years forsaking body and life in the hills and meadows, taking shelter where wind and cloud led him and spreading the teaching alone in the dharma realm. He entrusted the work of saving beings to opportunities and conditions, and though he had followers as the occasions arose, in his heart he was far removed from all entanglements. He possessed not a particle of money; for the rest of his life, no silk or cotton cloth touched his skin. He never took gold or silver objects in his hand and strictly refrained from liquor, meat, and the five forbidden flavors, observing fully the jewels of the ten major precepts.

He composed the following poem:

> In the way of things, we meet and we part,
> yet each person invariably remains alone.

After several years of solitary wandering, Ippen began to attract disciples who traveled with him, known as *jishū*. The term *jishū* (literally, "time-group") had been used to refer to groups of practicers who, during sessions of uninterrupted nembutsu, took turns in leading the recitation during the six "times" or four-hour periods of the day. Although there are various interpretations, Ippen probably adopted the term from this usage, for nembutsu sessions, particularly during a seven-day period at the end of the year, were an important activity among his followers. During this period, participants, both tonsured and lay, would bathe each dawn to purify themselves, then seek to devote themselves wholly to recitation, taking only one meal a day. At the beginning, this occasion was used for self-reflection and assessment of the practicers' level of faith, but toward the end of his life Ippen abandoned such discussion as meaningless.

By 1278, when he was thirty-eight years old, Ippen had a following of seven or eight, and later scenes in the *Biography* show the number increasing to twenty or thirty. They are clothed in distinctively austere gray robes with black surplices, and in some scenes nearly half appear to be nuns. In addition, he successfully propagated the teaching, and many people asked to receive the tonsure from him, though they remained living in their homes.

Dancing Nembutsu

In 1279, while chanting the nembutsu, Ippen suddenly began to dance, and others joined in, waving their arms in the air or beating out a rhythm using whatever implements were at hand. The *Biography* explains:

> Dancing nembutsu was first practiced by Master Kūya, who said: "My meditative practice lies in letting my lips freely utter Amida's name; hence, even the marketplace is my practice hall. My contemplation of the Buddha lies in following after my voice [in utterance of the name]; hence, my breath is a rosary. . . . To the course of nature I give charge of my thoughts, words, and deeds, and to the working of enlightenment leave all my acts." After Kūya, imitators spontaneously appeared, but the benefit [of dancing nembutsu] did not spread widely. Perhaps now its time had come. . . .

At a warrior's residence, Ippen began dancing, and many monks and laypeople gathered, all making their bonds with the dharma by joining in the dance. This practice was gradually taken up and became an activity that Ippen carried on for the rest of his life.

The *Sūtra of Immeasurable Life* states:

> Persons who have beheld a world-honored one in a past life
> Are now able to entrust themselves to the teaching of Amida's vow;
> Humbly revering it, they devoutly practice what they have heard,
> And they leap and dance, rejoicing greatly.

. . . This is not at all our own activity, but is entirely the inconceivable benefit of Amida Buddha, of other power. . . .

Once a man named Shigetoshi, an officer-monk of [the Tendai temple] Enryakuji, came to see what Ippen was like, but was scandalized to see people dancing while reciting the sacred name. Ippen responded:

> If they leap, let them leap! If they dance, let them dance
> like spring colts on the road:
> The path of dharma is known to those who know.

Shigetoshi responded:

> If you mounted and quieted the heart's colt,
> surely it would not dance and leap thus.

Ippen answered:

> But leap still! And yet dance! My heart's colt—
> joyful to hear it's Amida's teaching.

Later, the *Biography* indicates that raised platforms were constructed for dancing nembutsu where Ippen and his followers stayed, and the dancing itself appears to have become organized, with the use of gongs and the group, usually restricted to the jishū, moving in a circle.

At His Grandfather's Grave

Ippen led his group far to the north, and took the opportunity to seek out the burial mound of his grandfather, who had died in exile. The *Biography* notes that he kept the company of people in the lowest strata of society, whose occupations were regarded as entailing destruction of life or deceit and were therefore inherently sinful. At the same time, he is depicted in the role of a traveler-poet at a site with classical literary associations:

Fisherman and itinerant peddlers were his companions on the road. He talked together with lowly people whose names he did not know, and even before he spoke of the teaching, tough village elders made their bonds with the dharma through him. Upon nearing the checkpoint at the Shirakawa Barrier, he wrote the following poem and attached it to a post of the holy shrine of the barrier's deity:

> That those who pass beyond this gate
> not slip from the working of Amida's vow,
> let his name be halted here:
> the barrier of Shirakawa.

On reaching the Esashi district, he visited the grave of his grandfather Michinobu, reflecting that human beings do not live forever, that families do not endure. . . . He cleared away the briar and bramble, then performed a service out of filial gratitude, chanting sūtras and reciting the nembutsu as he circumambulated the mound. Truly, when a child renounces home to become a monk, seven generations of ancestors gain release [from the pain of hell]; thus, for the departed spirit of Michinobu, lingering dreams filled with yearning for home were surely brought to an end, so that he could reach the land of everlasting bliss.

Ippen composed a poem:

> This vanity! For the little while that corpse is undecayed,
> earth of the meadow appears to be something other.

Outside Kamakura

Ippen's goal was to spread the nembutsu to all people. Although he had considerable success in his travels, he felt it necessary to bring his propagation activity to Kamakura, the vital political center of the country. Support from the warrior government and the people of the city would advance his cause immensely, as it had the work of a number of other monks. He saw Kamakura as the test of his entire effort. Samurai there, however, were under orders to clear the road of beggars and other rabble.

In the spring of 1282 Ippen stayed three days at a place called Nagasago with the intent of entering Kamakura. He told his followers, "Depending on the conditions of our entrance into Kamakura, we will decide whether or not to continue our propagation activity. If our work to benefit beings is obstructed here, we must realize that it is over."

He attempted to enter Kamakura from Kobukuro Hill, but was told, "Today, the regent is going to Yamanouchi; you cannot use this road." Replying that he had his own plans, he continued on. A warrior confronted them and blocked their path, but they tried to force their way past. The warrior had his henchmen attack the jishū and called for the leader of the group. Ippen stepped forth to face him.

"This lawlessness cannot be allowed in front of the regent," the warrior said. "It's solely for your own notoriety that you lead these people along. Trying to force your way in despite the prohibition is outrageous."

Ippen answered, "I have no need for fame or anything else. I simply encourage people to say the nembutsu. How long will you be alive to assault and revile the dharma thus?—even though it is the nembutsu that can save you when, drawn by your evil karma, you are about to head down the path of darkness."

The warrior, without the slightest reply, struck him twice with his staff. Ippen, out of the great compassion that does not abandon those possessed of anger and hatred, showed no sign of pain. Acting to bring the teaching to every living being, he spoke only from the joy in linking another with the dharma: "The propagation of the nembutsu is my life. If, in spite of this, I am prohibited in this way, where should I go? I will face my death here."

The warrior replied, "There is no restriction concerning the outskirts of Kamakura."

Thus, Ippen passed the night in the hills, reciting the nembutsu at the side of the road. Monks and laypeople came from Kamakura and gathered like clouds to offer alms.

Despite Ippen's failure to enter the city, he seems to have been successful in gaining the devotion of the citizens, and from then on crowds of people from all classes gathered wherever he went.

In the fourth month of 1284, Ippen arrived at the Hall of Śākyamuni in the center of Kyoto. People of all ranks—noble and humble, high and low—came to him in such throngs that it was impossible even to turn around or for carts to move.

The *Biography* shows Ippen being carried on the shoulders of a follower so that he could distribute the paper fuda to crowds of people.

The next day he moved to the Inaba hall [founded by Kūya]. While there, the lay-priest Tsuchimikado, former minister of the Imperial Household, came to see him in order to secure his bonds with the nembutsu and later sent the poem [using the plaintive call of the hototogisu, a bird associated with the heat of summer, as an image for utterance of the name]:

> Although I hear faintly a single call of the hototogisu,
> still I do not waken from my dozing dream.

Ippen responded:

> The call of the hototogisu and the hearing of it
> are both nodding dream:
> beyond this sleep of dream and reality
> is the solitary voicing.

Also, Ippen replied to a letter from Tsuchimikado requesting an explanation of liberation from birth and death:

> Simply say the name embodying the primal vow with your lips, giving no ear to the attainments of enlightenment in the various teachings, and put your mind to no use other than saying the name. . . . Our hearts and minds vanishing as we say "Namu-amida-butsu" is right-mindedness at the point of death. At that moment we are blessed with Amida Buddha's coming to receive us and are born into the Land of Bliss: this is birth through the nembutsu. Namu-amida-butsu.

Continuing Journey

Undistracted by his successes from his life of itinerancy, Ippen formulated rules for his followers and even designed a wooden backpack to carry the minimal possessions permitted each person. "Verse of Aspiration" (1286), which the jishū probably chanted together, begins:

> We disciples of the Buddha
> Vow that from this point of our existence
> Until all the future is exhausted
> We will not cling to body or life
> But turn to and enter the primal vow;
> And to the very cessation of life
> We will wholeheartedly say the name.

Toward the end of his life, however, Ippen expressed feelings of discouragement:

In 1289 Ippen crossed to Shikoku Island and made pilgrimages to Zentsū Temple [which Kūkai founded at his place of birth] and Mandara Temple. . . . Though it is difficult to know his thoughts, he said, "The conditions for my propagation have already grown weak; people no longer put my teaching and precepts into practice. Little remains to my life; the time of death is approaching." People were apprehensive, and before long he became ill and could neither sleep nor eat normally. . . . He composed the verse:

You are born in the name of Amida said without a sayer:
in the solitary voicing—all that remains
of pronouncing and letting go.

On a slip of paper he attached at the front of the Ninomiya shrine:

The heart in accord with the name has passed into the west—
Escaped from the cast-off cicada's shell:
How cool and fresh the call!

Last Days

Eighth month, second day (1289). Ippen sat on a rope mat facing south and spoke of dharma. . . . Priests and laypeople beyond number listened. . . . He said repeatedly: "After I die, some of you will want to throw yourselves into the sea [in order to attain the pure land with me]. If the settled mind has been established in you, your birth is certain whatever you may do. But if your self-attachment has not been exhausted, you must not take your own life. It is rare and difficult to receive an existence in which one encounters the Buddha's way. How lamentable it would be to cast it away in vain!" With tears falling he went on, "This is the reason for having this written down and leaving it behind. You should well take heed." With this, he put it in his wooden pack. . . . His final instruction:

> Among the five aggregates there is no sickness afflicting sentient beings; the four elements include no blind passions that torment us. But we turn our backs on the one thought-moment of our original nature, and making the five desires our home and the three poisons our sustenance, we take on the pain and anxiety of the three evil paths: this is the truth of receiving the fruit of our own acts. Thus, apart from awakening in ourselves the mind taking refuge, there is no way we can be saved even by the compassion of the buddhas of past, present, and future. Namu-amida-butsu.

People came to him reporting dreams in which he had appeared as a bodhisattva, and miraculous signs of Amida Buddha's closeness such as purple clouds in the sky. Since it was popularly believed that Amida came to receive the truly faithful, concrete signs at the time of death were considered auspicious, but Ippen denied their significance:

Unthinking people, apprehensive about the mischief of demons [at the time of their death], turn their attention to omens and do not entrust themselves to the true Buddha's dharma. This is altogether meaningless. There is only Namu-amida-butsu to depend on.

Concerning the transmission of his teaching:

Tenth day, morning. Ippen gave a few of the sūtras he possessed to a monk from Mount Shosha. He had always said, "My propagation is for this lifetime only," and now, while chanting the *Amida Sūtra,* he burned the writings he possessed with his own hands. Seeing this, people deeply grieved that there was no one to transmit the teaching and that it would perish with the teacher. Ippen said, "All the sacred teachings of Śākyamuni's lifetime have wholly become Namu-amida-butsu."

Further, he said:

After I die, my disciples are not to mourn with funeral rites for me. Abandon my body in the hills, leaving it for wild beasts. There is no need, however, to apply this prohibition to laypeople who seek to effect bonds with dharma.

Concerning the moment of death:

Someone asked what would take place at the time of his death. Ippen said, "Good warriors and people of the way do not make their final moments known to those about them. Others will not be aware of my end." His death exemplified these words.

—46—

Account of the Buddhist Thaumaturge Baozhi

Alan J. Berkowitz

By the twelfth century, accounts of the life of the Buddhist thaumaturge Baozhi state that he was found as a baby in a falcon's nest atop an old tree near the capital. Earlier sources, however, record nothing strange about how he came into existence. That an uncommon individual should be accorded an uncommon birth is a mark of retrospective hagiography. In the case of Baozhi, the story of Baozhi's origin also contains a sign of Baozhi's nascent bodhisattvahood, for it is said that the Buddha preached the *Lotus Sūtra* on Vulture Peak.

Time and hagiography often enhance accounts of the lives of individuals, and Song dynasty accounts of Baozhi differ substantially from earlier accounts in content and length. Some additions are the result of purposeful fabrication or amplified hearsay, with little basis for credence. Others come from conflating anecdotes concerning the monk that had been culled from a variety of sources, some of which are traceable, some now lost. Others yet are the result of the accretion of accounts of several persons with the same name into the account of the life of a single man.

Huijiao (497–554 C.E.), himself a Buddhist monk and a younger contemporary of Baozhi, included an account of Baozhi's life in his *Lives of Eminent Monks (Gaoseng zhuan),* in a section devoted to "Miraculous and Strange Monks (Theurgists)." This earliest account of Baozhi, translated below, is largely corroborated by the account of his life contained in the early seventh-century *History of the Southern Dynasties* (*Nan shi*). The accounts obviously are of the same person, yet the two accounts write his name differently: the earlier account gives his name as "Preserving the Insignia," whereas the *History* writes "Precious Insignia" ("preserving" and "precious" both are pronounced *bao*). The thaumaturge has most commonly come to be known by the latter name, although he often also is referred to simply as Zhigong ("Master Zhi") and occasionally as Baogong ("Master Bao," "Precious").

Anecdotes concerning another Buddhist monk who was referred to as Baogong, Master Bao ("Precious"), sometimes have been ascribed to Baozhi because their names were similar and because this Baogong's enigmatic prescience was also characteristic of the thaumaturge Baozhi. The longest account of Baozhi, from the tenth-century *Taiping guangji*, simply appends accounts of this Baogong to those of Baozhi, saying that it is uncertain whether they concern one man or two. However, Baogong was a northerner active at the close of the Northern Wei (c. 528; he perhaps was the same as one or both men called Baogong in the early years of the Northern Qi and the Sui), whereas Baozhi was from the south and died in 514 at an advanced age.

The account of Baozhi is intrinsically interesting, but also reflects the awe accorded to "men of miracles" and their conspicuous role in the Buddhist tradition in China, as in other religious milieus. Baozhi was trained and ordained as a Buddhist monk. He was knowledgeable in the Buddhist sūtras, and in traditional scholarship as well, but his fame was due to his being "miraculous and strange." He worked miracles for the emperor and offered cryptic auguries to the elite, speaking in conundrums or poems that events proved to have been prophetic; his renown even attracted an emissary from Korea. His strangeness was manifest in being able to be in several places at the same time, and in eccentric conduct and manners. Although his head was generally shaved in the Buddhist manner, he often wore a cap or let his hair grow out; although he sometimes dressed in a Buddhist robe, he often was scantily dressed or clothed as a layman. His eating habits were irregular, and his hygienic practices peculiar, yet he did not transgress his religious precepts. According to an anecdote, which is of relatively late fabrication, and reflects the popularizing of stories about Baozhi in the manner of other, later, "strange" monks:

> He was fond of using urine to wash his hair, and someone among the common monks secretly jeered and scoffed. Now Zhi equally knew that many of the monks had not forsaken wine and meat, and that the one who had ridiculed him drank wine and ate pork intestines. Zhi of a sudden said to him, "You scoff at me for using piss to wash my head, but why is it that you eat bags full of shit?"

Baozhi foresaw his own death, and passed away without illness near the end of 514 (one source writes that Baozhi was buried in 506, but this is due to faulty editing of a local gazetteer). The emperor gave him a sumptuous burial, spending 200,000 cash and founding a temple at his tomb on a hill at the foot of Zhongshan Mountain, just outside the capital in modern Nanjing. This temple, first called the Kaishan Temple and known as Baogong yuan during the Tang, is the most important of the several that Emperor Wu of the Liang had founded in honor of Baozhi. It is the predecessor of the grand Linggu Temple at Zhongshan park in Nanjing. Its original site, and the site of Baozhi's grave, however, was where the tomb of the first emperor of the Ming is now located: that emperor rebuilt the temple at its present location in 1381 so that he could avail himself of the geomantically perfect location for his own burial spot. Monuments to Baozhi still are to be found at the temple, including a shrine and a commemorative stele.

At the time of Baozhi's death, the emperor had portraits of the thaumaturge circulated throughout the land. Baozhi had been the subject of portraits since being captured on silk by his younger contemporary Zhang Sengyao (c. 480–post 549), the artist of whom the famous story is told about adding the life-imbuing final touches to the eyes of a painted dragon. Portraits of Baozhi always picture him with his long staff and its dangling accoutrements, and this is how he is depicted on a celebrated stele known as the Stele of the Three Incomparables (*Sanjue bei*), a monument bringing together works of the greatest in portraiture, poetry, and calligraphy. This stele bears Baozhi's portrait by Wu Daozi (Wu Daoxuan, c. 685–758), with a poem about the monk by Li Bai (701–762) engraved in the calligraphy of Yan Zhenqing (709–785). The original stele no longer is extant, but there is a Ming replica in the garden of the Yangzhou Historical Museum and a Qing facsimile at Baozhi's shrine at the Linggu Temple. Engraved on the stele also are twelve Buddhist poems known as "Songs of the Twelve Temporal Divisions [of the Day]" attributed to Baozhi, done in the superlative calligraphy of Zhao Mengfu (1254–1322).

The portrait of Baozhi engraved on the stele is a further example of hagiography, reflecting the popularization of Baozhi's image and the enhancement of his prophetic powers through time. The earliest accounts of Baozhi describe him holding on his shoulder his long staff, from the top of which hang scissors, mirror, and cloth strips or, in some accounts, also pincers. The portrait, however, depicts the staff's accoutrements as scissors, a ruler, and a fan. These accessories are symbols for the three successive dynasties that Baozhi ostensibly foretold, as indicated in Li Bai's accompanying poem: the scissors, which cut things into a uniform height (*qi*), stand for the Qi dynasty; the ruler, which measures (*liang*), stands for the Liang dynasty; and the fan, which fans away dust (*chen*), stands for the Chen dynasty.

The fan in some accounts was a "duster" (*fu*), a rebus for "Buddha." The ruler may also have had another significance, relating to the founding of eras other than the Liang: according to one account a jade foot-measure was fashioned by Baozhi and sent to the northern Zhou court to be presented to "an elderly fellow with plentiful whiskers"; both the founder of the Zhou and the founder of the Sui assumed that they were meant. The mirror (a symbol of prophetic omniscience) originally adorning Baozhi's staff came to represent in Ming dynasty accounts the monk's prophetic symbolization of their own epoch: the mirror indicates brightness (*ming*), the name of the dynasty. Further "evidence" was educed from the fact that Baozhi was raised by members of the Zhu family, Zhu also being the surname of the founder of the Ming; the intervening dynasties between the Chen and the Ming presumably were not predicted by Baozhi because they had their capitals in the north, whereas Baozhi was active in Jiankang (Nanjing), the capital also of the early Ming.

Baozhi's legacy and accuracy of prophesy were incorporated into popular Buddhist tradition, and Baozhi still plays a role in popular religion and religious iconography, both in China and Japan. His image has frequently been painted on temple walls at least since the Tang. The Boston Museum of Fine Arts holds a

Southern Song painting in which Baozhi appears as one of five hundred Lohans, and Baozhi was commonly considered an incarnation of Guanyin; one anecdote describes him showing his "true" appearance as the Eleven-faced Guanyin connected with tantric performances. A wall of a cave in Dunhuang (cave 147A), depicts him with his cloth cap (the head attire sometimes still worn by priests, known as the "Zhigong cap," and at least in the eleventh century worn to indicate the death of a priest), thus referring to the anecdote that Baozhi once wore three of these caps when foretelling the imminent deaths of three members of the imperial family. A fragmentary manuscript also from Dunhuang concerns Emperor Wu of the Liang seeking spiritual guidance from Baozhi; this anecdote is recounted in the translation below; his enigmatic responses to the emperor have earned him a niche in the patrimony of the Chan (Zen) sect. And the Water and Land Convocation Ceremony (*Shuilu hui*), a rite of propitiation by alms to departed souls still performed today, is generally presumed to have its origins with Baozhi.

Huijiao, the compiler of *Lives of Eminent Monks,* was himself a learned Buddhist monk from Guiji (or Kuaiji) in Zhejiang, a locale famous for its eminent monks and lay Buddhists. His *Lives* records accounts of two hundred and fifty-seven men from 67 to 519 C.E., with appended accounts of two hundred and fifty-nine others. The accounts are categorized under ten major headings: translators (*yijing*), exegetes (*yijie*), theurgists (*shenyi*), meditators (*xichan*), disciplinarians (*minglü*), self-immolators (*yishen* or *wangshen*), cantors (*songjing*), promoters of works of merit (*xingfu*), hymnodists (*jingshi*), and sermonists (*changdao*). The *Lives* is a valuable source on the five first centuries of Buddhism in China, documenting the accomplishments and merit of those men of religion whose contributions to the introduction and spread of the faith left an indelible mark on the religious culture of China. Valuable as it is as an historical document, it also is an elegant piece of polished literary prose.

The translation below is from: Huijiao (497–554 C.E.), comp., *Gaoseng zhuan* (Nanjing: Jinling kejingchu, 1885; reprinted by the same from the original blocks, 1986), 11.17b–20b. This version has slight orthographic variances from the text reprinted in the *Taishō shinshū daizōkyō* (Tokyo, 1924–1934), 2059; vol. 50, pp. 394–95.

The Account of the Buddhist Thaumaturge Baozhi

The Buddhist Baozhi was originally surnamed Zhu and was [of a family living in the capital but hailing] from Jincheng [near modern Lanzhou in Gansu province]. At a young age he left his family [for the priesthood], taking up residence at the Daolin ["Forest of the Way"] Temple in the capital [Jiankang, modern Nanjing in Jiangsu]. He served as his Master the śramaṇa Sengjian and became a monk, cultivating and practicing the meditative endeavor [that is, the Buddhist way].

At the beginning of the Taishi ["Great Incipience"] reign (465–471 C.E.) of the Song (420–479), he suddenly became eccentric and strange: he kept no fixed place of residence, had no regularity in his eating and drinking, and his hair grew several inches long. He often freely roamed the streets and alleys, clutching a monk's staff from the point of which dangled a scissors and a mirror, and sometimes also a strip or two of silk. During the Jianyuan ["Founding the Commencement"] reign (479–482) of the Qi (479–502), signs of his strangeness were increasingly to be seen. He would not eat for several days, yet he had no appearance of being undernourished. When he spoke with others, his sayings at first seemed incomprehensible but later all were found to be effectual and verified. At times he expressed himself in poetry, and his words were as prophetic accountings.

As all of the scholars and commoners of the capital district rendered him esteem and services, Emperor Wu of Qi declared that he was confounding the masses and had him detained in Jiankang [the capital]. The following morning people saw him [Baozhi] enter the marketplace, but when they returned to inspect the jail, Zhi was still there inside. Zhi told the jailer, "Outside the gate there have arrived two cartloads of food, with gold bowls brimming with cooked grains; you might take them in." It happened that the Qi heir designate Wenhui [Xiao Changmao] and the King of Jingling [Xiao] Ziliang jointly had sent food as a banquet for Zhi, and sure enough, it was as he had said. Lü Wenxian, magistrate of Jiankang, brought the affair to the attention of Emperor Wu, and the emperor then invited [Baozhi] into [the palace], lodging him in the posterior apartments.

One time when [the emperor] dismissed a banquet in the palace, Zhi also left [the hall] along with the crowd. Subsequently on Jingyang Mountain (outside of the imperial compound) there was seen another Zhi together with seven Buddhist priests. The emperor became angered and dispatched [his men] to investigate Zhi's having left his station. The officer of the hall entry reported, "Zhi left long ago and presently is in his quarters smearing ink on his body." At that time the Buddhist priest Zheng Faxian wished to present to Zhi a garment, and sent a minion to look for him at both the Longguang and the Jibin temples. Each said that [Zhi] had passed the previous night there and had left at daybreak. He also went to look for him at the home of Li Houbo, where Zhi often frequented. Bo said, "Last night Zhi was here practicing his faith. I went to sleep at daybreak and was not aware [that he had left]." The minion returned to relate all this to Xian, and only then was it known that Zhi could divaricate himself to pass the night at three locations.

Zhi once went about in the full of winter with bared flesh. The śramaṇa Baoliang wished to present him with a Buddhist robe, but before he had said a word Zhi suddenly arrived, brought out the robe, and left. Also at that time [Zhi] approached someone and asked for minced raw fish. The man undertook to prepare this for him and went to find some [live fish]. When he had gotten his fill, he [Zhi] left. When [the man] turned his gaze back to the basin, the fish was alive and swimming as before. Zhi later provided his spiritual power for Emperor Wu: he saw Emperor Gao [Emperor Wu's deceased father] beneath the ground in constant pain from an awl [an instrument used in a form of capital punishment]. From this time on the emperor forever banned awls [and capital punishment]. Hu Xie, chamberlain for the palace garrison of the Qi, was ill and sought [assistance from] Zhi. Zhi went, but withdrew saying, "will submit tomorrow." The next day he did not go at all, and on that day Xie died. When his [Hu Xie's] corpse had been carried back to his [Hu's] residence, Zhi said, "What I meant by 'will submit tomorrow' was that on the next day his corpse would go forth" [the character "submit" could be construed as being composed of the characters for "corpse" and "go forth"].

Yin Qizhi, commander-in-chief of the Qi, accompanied Chen Xianda in guarding Jiangzhou [in 490]. When he parted from Zhi, Zhi painted on some paper a single tree with a bird atop it and said, "In times of exigency, you can climb this." Later, when Xianda went against his duties [in revolt against an unrightful and tyrannical ruler], he left Qizhi to guard [Jiang]zhou. When he [Xianda] was defeated, Qizhi rebelled and took refuge at Lu Mountain. When the pursuing riders were about to overtake him, Qizhi saw a single tree amid the forest with a bird atop, just as Zhi had painted. Having understood, he climbed it; the bird unexpectedly did not fly off. When his pursuers saw the bird, they thought that there could not be a man present and turned back. In the end, [Qizhi] was pardoned.

When Sang Yan, commandant of garrison cavalry of the Qi, was considering planning a revolt [also hoping to restore order], he happened to go pay a visit to Zhi. Zhi looked off to the distance and walked away, saying with a great sigh, "He'll be encircled at Taicheng Fortress, desiring of rebellion: they'll chop off his head and split open his guts." Less than a week later, the events began to unfold. Yan revolted and headed [downriver] toward Zhufang, but was captured by others; the result was his head being chopped off and his gut split open.

Xiao Hui, the Zhonglie king of Boyang in the Liang, once constrained Zhi to come to a gathering at his residence. Zhi suddenly ordered that some thistles be found with great haste; when he got hold of them he fixed them on the door. None could guess his reason. A short time later the king was appointed as regional inspector of Jingzhou [Thorn Province]. There were more than one example of this kind showing the palpability of his [Zhi's] prescience.

Zhi often frequented the Xinghuang and Jingming temples. When the present emperor [Emperor Wu] rose [to assume the rule] in the manner of the dragon, Zhi was accorded great reverence and ceremonial attentions, but earlier during the Qi, Zhi often was forbidden free access [to the imperial residence]. When the present emperor ascended the throne, he issued an edict stating:

> Master Zhi's tangible traces are confined to the dust and dirt [of the mortal world], but his spirit roams in the Profound Stillness. Water and fire cannot

> wet or burn him; snakes and tigers cannot harass or scare him. In speaking of his Buddhist principles, then what one hears from him is unparalleled. When discussing the way he is seclusive and submerged, then he is a withdrawn immortal, one of lofty ways. How could one ever hope vainly to constrain and restrict him with the common sentiments of an ordinary man? How could one's vulgarity and narrowness coalesce to such a point? Effective from the present onward, he shall enter and leave according to his will. He is not again to be prevented.

From then on Zhi often came and went within the forbidden imperial quarters.

There was drought during the winter of the fifth year of the Tianjian reign [506–507]. Sacrifices for rain were executed to the fullest, yet rain did not fall. Zhi suddenly petitioned, saying, "When I, Zhi, am afflicted with illness that does not abate, I go to my [local] official to beg for sustenance. If he does not petition on my behalf, then the official is deserving of [punishment by] the cane and the staff. I wish for you to solicit rain by having the *Śrīmālā-devī-siṃhanāda-sūtra* (*Shengmanjing*) recited in the Huaguang hall." The emperor forthwith had the śramaṇa Fayun [Dharmamegha or "Dharma cloud"] recite the sūtra, and when he had finished, that very night there was a great snowfall. Zhi also said that he needed a bowl of water. He cut across the top [of the water] with a knife, and a moment later a great rain fell, sufficient for locales of both high and low elevation.

The emperor once asked Zhi, "I, your disciple, have not yet rid myself of vexation and perturbation. What may I do to cure this?" Zhi responded, "Twelve." Ones who understood took this to mean the medicine of the twelve nidānas for curing perturbation. When further asked for direction about the twelve nidānas [links in the chain of existence], he responded, "It is to be found in the written characters, in the temporal divisions, and in the water clock." Ones who understood took this to mean that it was written in [his "Poems on] the Twelve Temporal Divisions [of the Day"] (*Shi'er shi shi*). He [the emperor] further asked, "At what time will I, your disciple, attain a tranquil mind so as to cultivate and practice [the precepts of Buddhism]?" Zhi responded, "When ease and joy are proscribed." Ones who understood took this to mean that "proscribe" meant "cease," and that it was simply that at times of ease and joy he should desist.

Later, when Fayun was reciting the *Dharma-Flower* (*Fahua;* that is, the *Saddharma-puṇḍarīka* or *Lotus Sūtra*), when he came to "and was caused a dark wind [and storm to arise]," Zhi suddenly asked whether the wind existed or not. Fayun replied, "It is a 'worldly truth,' and thus exists; but in terms of 'supreme reality,' then it does not." Zhi walked back and forth three or four times and then laughed, saying, "That's as if form presumes existence. It permits it but does not allow it; it's an explanation that is difficult to explain." The purport of his words was obscure and cryptic, with many examples just like this.

There was a certain Chen Zhenglu, whose entire family served Zhi with great devotion. Zhi once made manifest to him his [Zhi's] true presence: his radiant "distinctive indication" [sign of buddhahood] was just like that of a likeness of a bodhisattva. Zhi gained a prominent reputation, displaying his uncommonality for over forty years. One could not measure the number of men and women who paid him reverence and service. In the winter of the thirteenth year of the Tianjian reign [late 514 or possibly January 515], he told people in the rear hall of the palace complex, "the bodhisattva is about to leave." In less than a week's time, he came to his end without illness. His corpse was fragrant and soft, and he had a radiant and pleased appearance.

When he was near to death, he personally lit a single candle and gave it to the houseman of the Entry to the Rear [apartments], Wu Qing. Qing brought this to the attention of the emperor, who sighed and said, "Our grand teacher will not be staying with us any longer. As for the candle, doesn't it signify that the matters to come will be consigned to me ['candle' was a homophonic equivalent to 'consign']?" Thus, the emperor generously provided for the encoffining and funeral procession, burying Zhi at Dulong ["Lone Dragon"] Hill at Zhongshan Mountain [just outside the capital]. He further had the Kaishan ["Unfolding of Goodness"] Hall of Contemplation erected at the place of his grave, and ordained Lu Chui to compose the funerary tablet inscription to be placed in the tomb and Wang Jun to engrave the stele inscription at the gate of the temple. He disseminated a posthumous likeness of Zhi, which was to be everywhere preserved.

Earlier, when signs of Zhi's prominence were first noticed, he was perhaps around the age of fifty or sixty; yet at his demise he still was not aged. Nobody at all could guess his age. A certain Xu Jiedao, who lived north of the Jiuri ["Ninth Day"] Pavilion in the capital, said personally that he was Zhi's younger maternal uncle, younger than Zhi by four years, and that calculating from the time of Zhi's death, he should have been ninety-seven [*sui,* or ninety-six years of age in Western reckoning].

—47—

Buddhist Chaplains in the Field of Battle

Sybil Thornton

The Japanese civil war of 1331–1333 C.E. witnessed the development of a new type of ministry in Buddhism: providing chaplains to warriors in the field. The leaders in this movement were the very recently established itinerant-mendicant orders claiming Ippen Shōnin (1239–1289) as their founder, of which the Itinerant School (Yugyō ha) became the most prominent. The monks (and, very likely, nuns) of the Itinerant School were not the only ones in the field, but they appear very quickly to have played the dominant role. By 1400, however, the heads of the order had effectively withdrawn them from such service. The two documents translated below illustrate the Itinerant School's struggle against the abuse of monks and nuns by their warrior parishioners.

Ostensibly, the chaplains went with the warriors to make sure that they chanted the ten invocations of Amida Buddha's name (*nembutsu*) before death (*saigo no jūnen*); the invocation was the principal practice of the order, for which the members of the order were called "community which chants the invocation of Amida Buddha's name six times a day" (*rokuji nembutsushū*), shortened to jishū. But contemporary sources indicate that their activities expanded: not only did they burn, bury, and pray for the dead, but they cared for the sick and wounded, amused the men with poetry, probably served as personal servants, informed relatives, supervised taking the tonsure, and aided noncombatants and the defeated. Often the battle came to the temples: bodies were brought for burial; men came to have their heads shaven or to commit suicide.

Itinerant School jishū in the field were referred to either as "same-road jishū" or as "accompanying jishū." Following the early custom of the order, they were assigned to warriors (rather than to a temple), at first only by the head of the order (the Yugyō Shōnin) or by the retired head (Fujisawa Shōnin), but later by the head of the local Itinerant School or related temple. Once assigned to a patron, the jishū stayed with him: he witnessed his death and sometimes died with him.

However, by the 1350s Itinerant School jishū in the field were subject to so many abuses that in 1350–1351 the seventh head of the order, Takuga, was forced to circulate a directive. This has not survived. In 1399, the eleventh head of the order and current retired head, Jikū, reissued the directive, known as the "Jikū letter," translated below. Jikū reasserted that the "purpose of jishū going on the same road is to administer the ten nembutsu at the time of death." Jishū are to secure the rebirth in the pure land of their patrons and of themselves. They are to perform religious ceremonies. They are permitted to do what is necessary to protect themselves in battle and to protect noncombatants. They may not touch weapons, they may not act as couriers, they may not act as their patrons' servants. Any infringement of the rules will result in the loss of rebirth in the pure land, both for the jishū and for his patron.

The secondment of jishū for paramilitary services was seen initially as a problem for internal regulation, where the main point of contention was the transfer of commitment from the head of the order and religious guide to the warrior patron, at the risk of both their souls. But the problem had been present from the very beginning, when Ippen-school jishū were first assigned to adherents as chaplains. In order that the jishū experience as much as possible the discipline and hardship of itinerancy, it had been stipulated that the jishū should be dependent in every way upon the patron, who, apparently, had to provide food, clothing, and housing. Not only was it difficult to refuse a powerful patron, especially if the jishū was entirely dependent on him, it was difficult to define the line between commitment to the head of the order and that to the patron, if both were dictated by the head of the order. Takuga and Jikū determined to resolve the conflict by insisting that the jishū recognize his principal commitment as that to the head of the order and by giving him a standard set of regulations.

Internal regulation alone would not solve the problem. This became all too clear in 1353. Nikki Yoshinaga, constable of Ise Province, tried to have the jishū of the Nagano temple Senjuji expelled and replaced because they had protected some of the defeated in the aftermath of the siege of Nagano Castle. Takuga immediately despatched a letter, the "Nagano missive," also translated below.

In this letter, Takuga stressed that it was a common assumption of both warrior and jishū that the jishū would, if necessary, aid and protect the warrior patron. The right to save lives was based on the vow of every Buddhist monk or nun not to take life. Ippen himself is credited with the abolition of animal sacrifice at certain Shintō shrines. The Itinerant School monks and nuns, following Ippen's regulations, carried strainers to sift insects out of their food and water.

The members of the Ippen School order were rigorous in keeping their vows. One who did not was no longer a jishū and lost rebirth in the pure land. Even if exposed after death, a jishū could expect to have his rebirth in the pure land canceled by the head of the order.

The jishū's failure to act in a strictly religious capacity was fraught with implications. By the time of Takuga, the head of the order was seen as the Buddha on earth and responsible for securing the rebirth in the pure land of one and all as Amida dictated. To the members of the order he had particular responsibilities. Upon taking final vows, the jishū exchanged absolute obedience to and dependence on the head of the order (later, as the order expanded, the head of the temple) for an absolute guarantee of rebirth in the pure land, as it were, on this earth; they were considered to be as one. Thus, the lapse of a jishū, the action of a person not in the pure land, reflected on the head and religious guide of the order as a failure to meet his responsibilities, as the heir of Ippen, to the jishū. Furthermore, the warrior parishioner stood in relation to the jishū chaplain as the jishū to the head of the order; since the head of the order and the jishū were in effect one and the same, there was an equal responsibility to prevent the warrior parishioner from doing what might lose him his rebirth in the pure land. This reciprocity of responsibility and obedience to secure rebirth in the pure land was the very essence of the order and the doctrines it preached. Nothing was allowed to threaten it.

The prohibition of paramilitary functions was meant to prevent the jishū from following, however inadvertently, his patron instead of the head of the order and thereby losing his rebirth in the pure land. At the same time, it was difficult for even Takuga to draw the line between religious duties and paramilitary functions: commitment to save the life of a warrior might be seen as aid to the enemy. Therefore, it was absolutely crucial that the warrior recognize the neutrality of the Itinerant School and its right to offer asylum as part of its religious duties.

But, as the need to reissue Takuga's directive indicates, one could not rely exclusively on the warrior's faith, understanding, or good will. One of the principal reasons that the Itinerant School was able to protect its jishū is that the order won the protection of the Ashikaga shogun. The heads of the order, especially the eleventh, thirteenth, fourteenth, fifteenth, and seventeenth (as now numbered), had particularly strong influence over the Ashikaga shogun Yoshimitsu, Yoshimochi, Yoshikazu, and Yoshinori, who ruled at the height of Ashikaga power. This influence was based on the above-mentioned belief that the head of the order was the Buddha on earth and had the authority to guarantee and to deny rebirth in the pure land. Following the lead of the Ashikaga shogun, many shogunate warriors of this period became parishioners of the head of the order, based in Kyoto. Their names are listed in the death register carried by the head of the order: entry, whether before or after death, guaranteed rebirth in the pure land.

The conflict over control of jishū in the field was apparently resolved in favor of the Itinerant School. Jikū's 1399 directive is the last reference to jishū activity in the field. In addition, propaganda material based on this activity is limited to fourteenth-century works such as the *Chronicle of Great Peace* and *Chronicle of the Meitoku Period.* Although most scholars would assume that the activity was so prevalent that it hardly merited mentioning, it seems more likely that the activity was sharply curtailed. If the warrior could not command the services of his jishū—if he could not force him to engage in paramilitary activities or prevent him from aiding the defeated enemy—the warrior would cease to employ the Itinerant School jishū and turn to the jishū and monks of other schools.

As long as the Itinerant School had enough influence over the Ashikaga shogunate and the shoguns were strong enough to support the Itinerant School in its conflict with shogunate warriors over the abuse of the jishū's services, then it seems only reasonable to assume that warriors ceased to look to the Itinerant School for their accompanying jishū. Even after the collapse of the Ashikaga shogunate, awe, and perhaps a little fear, of the authority of the acting and retired heads of the order persisted among the warriors of the provinces as well as at court. For the head of the Itinerant School, as the chief representative of itinerancy, toured unhindered throughout Japan inspecting his temples and no doubt defending the interests of his community with the implicit threat of denying or canceling rebirth in the pure land. There is no evidence that the jishū of the Itinerant School were forced, as were the religious of other schools, to provide warlords "camp-priests," who acted as couriers, bodyguards, and body servants to warriors in the field during the sixteenth century. The Itinerant School, because it remained faithful to its religious mission, was protected by the national hegemons Oda Nobunaga and Toyotomi Hideyoshi, notorious for suppressing and even wiping out Buddhist institutions. Under the Tokugawa shogun, the Itinerant School was supported in its mission and recognized as an independent sect, the Jishū.

The Jiku letter translated below is from *Shichijō monjo [Documents of the (Temple on) Seventh Avenue]* no. 9, in *Teihon Jishū shūten [Standard Edition of Collected Works of the Jishū]*, 2 vols., edited by Teihon Jishū Shūten Hensan Iinkai [Committee to Edit the Standard Edition of Collected Works of the Jishū] (Tokyo: Sankibō busshorin, 1979; Fujisawa: Jishū Shūmusho [Jishū Sect Office], 1979). The Nagano missive is from *Shichidai Shōnin hōgo [Sermons of the Seventh Patriarch]*, ibid.

Further Reading

See James Harlan Foard, "Ippen and Popular Buddhism in Kamakura Japan," Ph.D. dissertation, Stanford, 1977; Laura S. Kaufman, "Ippen Hijirie: Artistic and Literary Sources in a Buddhist Handscroll Painting of Thirteenth-Century Japan," Ph.D. dissertation, New York University, 1980; and Sybil Anne Thornton, "The Propaganda Traditions of the Yugyō Ha: The Campaign to Establish the Jishū as an Independent School of Japanese Buddhism (1300–1700)," Ph.D. dissertation, Cambridge, 1989.

Jikū Letter

Item: As for the rules for jishū accompanying armies, although a letter was sent from [the head of the order] the Yugyō [Shōnin] to several places during the Kan'ō period [1350–1351], there must now be not a single jishū who has been able to see it or heard about it from others. Therefore, because there are those who have acted as they pleased, saying it was the wish of their masters or that it was convenient at the time, they have ended up as objects of scorn of followers of the order and have lost their own rebirth in the pure land. Even though they have made themselves useful to their masters, because they have broken the rules of the order, the path of the jishū is cut off to them and, moreover, suffering will result even for their masters. Thus, the following articles must be understood both by laity and religious.

Item: The purpose of the religious going on the same road is to administer the ten nembutsu at the time of death. When in times of war, free passage is denied to the warrior, the religious must never be sent to carry a message or a letter for the purposes of battle because, as a jishū, he will be allowed to pass freely. However, if the reason is to rescue people, women, children, and noncombatants, there must be no objection.

Item: In the field, there will be times when you hold your master's armor. There is no objection concerning articles such as cuirasses and helmets. That is because they are things which protect the body. But jishū must never touch things like bows and arrows and weapons. That is because they are used to kill.

Item: As for the Special Ceremony at the End of the Year (*Saimatsu betsuji*), there is of course a rule that even if you are in the field, you must perform cold-water austerities, prepare the foods, wear jishū robes, and chant the nembutsu. However, depending on the situation, water may be hard to find. You may not be able to serve the foods you wish. Again, it does no good to be so weak that you cannot attend your master properly at his death; since you have followed him, eat whenever you can, and perform cold-water austerities, and prepare the proper foods as well as you can according to the conditions. In the situation [where there is difficulty in getting food or water], perform the ceremonies according to the rules.

Item: When a battle is about to begin, you must think. When you joined the jishū, you turned over to the head of the order your very life. Knowing that the reason for which you did this is the rebirth in the pure land at hand, you must not only lead your master in chanting the nembutsu but achieve your own rebirth in the pure land. These instructions must be proclaimed to jishū who may not be aware of them, that they might understand them well.

Respectfully
Namu Amidabutsu
Sixth year of Oei, eleventh month, twenty-fifth day
Ta'amidabutsu

Nagano Missive

Letter dispatched concerning Nagano in the province of Ise. Second year of Bunna, ninth month, last day.

In regard to the news that the jishū of the Nagano Temple (*dōjō*) must be expelled and replaced; what is the reason for this? For, to call one among the jishū friend and one foe is by no means the way of one who has entered religious life. This is the work of devils. However, since there is no estrangement among jishū in different places in the many provinces, clearly they all follow the same way. When during times of warfare, jishū and their patrons hide their traces in mountain and field, accompanying nuns come to their aid. Probably because our monks and nuns follow the same principle, even now warriors requesting our monks and nuns are very many. If they were to abandon this principle, what would happen in the end? That, not knowing the reason, you have tried to make jishū your enemy, I feel is most regrettable. Accompanying jishū who, in this way, with prejudiced minds, do not teach this principle and give the patrons the idea that they are on the same side, are not jishū. That it results in your becoming an unbeliever is a very sad thing for you. I must submit this religious instruction. As for the shogun [Takauji], I see only that he surpasses men in bravery. When I last met him in Karazu, I saw that he knows [the difference between] good and evil. If he should agree with you on such an issue, it would be most regrettable. You must discuss this affair with him at a time convenient to you.

Respectfully
Namuamidabutsu

—48—

Death-Bed Testimonials of the Pure Land Faithful

Daniel B. Stevenson

These three documents from Pure Land hagiographical compendia illustrate some of the paradigms and rhetoric that attend Pure Land notions of sanctity, as well as various ways in which the goal of rebirth in Sukhāvatī (the pure land) organizes the everyday expectations of Pure Land believers.

As a tradition whose soteriological concern is manifestly directed to the afterlife, one might expect Pure Land Buddhism to take a special interest in death and dying. The second half of the selection from Shandao on "the Seven-day Rite of Buddha-Mindfulness Samādhi and Recollection of the Buddha at the Time of Death" (Chapter 31) is taken up with instructions on how to negotiate this crucial passage successfully, thereby ensuring that the dying person is delivered from evil destinies and reborn in Amitābha's pure land.

In literary and oral Buddhist lore, it is commonly claimed that the last thoughts of a dying person have a direct influence on the status of rebirth in the next life. While this may seem a fairly straightforward matter of self-control—just "think good thoughts"—it is complicated by the belief that, with the waning of one's conscious powers, the mind is overwhelmed by subliminal karmic propensities or "memories" that manifest as visions before the dying person. In this way, the habits and events of one's current and previous existences quite literally draw one toward one's future destiny. As frightful and unpredictable as it might seem, this liminal moment of transition between death and rebirth is considered a time of enormous spiritual potential. For at no other time (except, perhaps, upon attaining the knowledge of former lives that comes to accomplished meditation masters) is a person afforded such a chance to remove the veil between the conscious and unconscious dimensions of self, review directly his or her karmic stock, and refashion one's being. Shandao's rites for the dying person, as well as the diverse repertoire of funerary ceremonies that are performed for the deceased over the forty-nine days following death, devolve around a common belief in the potency of this moment.

The primary aim of Shandao's deathbed procedures is to ensure that the dying person successfully forges what is known as *jingyin* or *jingyuan,* "the connection or nexus of conditions that will bring rebirth in the pure land." The ritual process itself unfolds as a fluid symbiosis between the two complementary activities of divination and ritual response. Throughout the last days or minutes of life, a careful watch is maintained for any signs of visions that may be indicative of the dying person's spiritual disposition. On the basis of these divinatory clues, different modes of ritual procedure—confession, nianfo (reciting the Buddha's name), reading of sūtras, and the like—are applied accordingly, the ultimate aim being to absolve the mind of worldly attachments and karmic obstructions, and direct it toward rebirth in the pure land. The successful forging of this "connection with the pure land" is itself indicated by the appearance of the desired auspicious signs at the time of the person's death or, as the case may be, during the weeks of funerary observances that follow.

Precedents for such a concept can be found in the Pure Land sūtras themselves. The *Sūtra on the Contemplation of the Buddha of Limitless Life,* for example, distinguishes various visionary signs that will confirm for the dying person that he or she is destined for the pure land. Having set this prognostic tone, the "ten moments of recollection of Amitābha" are touted as the only effective means for turning the situation around should less desirable omens appear and salvation be in doubt. At the same time, other sources are also at work in Shandao's system, including forms of ritual penance and prognostication traditionally associated with Chinese buddhānusmṛti practice. One will notice, for example, that Shandao's procedure for dealing with manifestations of evil karma entails an orchestration of invocation or veneration of the Buddha, confession, and vow—the three basic building blocks of Chinese Buddhist liturgy and cult devotion.

It is one thing for the individual Pure Land practitioner to seek an auspicious vision or sign as confirmation of having secured a "connection with the pure land," but something quite different is at stake when Shandao insists that these "signs" (*xiang*) and the entire deathbed drama should be written down "just as they happened." For rather than the deceased, it is the generations who survive him or her that become the point of focus here. This unusual practice brings us to another important aspect of Pure Land culture and representative genre of Pure Land literature—namely, the writing of exemplary testimonials and creation of hagiographical collections for the purposes of spreading the faith.

Records of auspicious wonders and exemplary devotees are as old as Pure Land practice itself in China. As early as the Shanxi Pure Land masters Daochuo and Shandao, we find dedicated collections of rebirth testimonials attached to or circulating alongside of the more familiar treatises on Pure Land doctrine and practice. Nearly every generation since has seen the publication of some compendium or other of this sort, usually by persons bent on promoting a particular redaction or movement of Pure Land teaching. Individual records or entries may involve a diversity of religious themes. Some of these, such as the healing of illness, the averting of evil reciprocity or demonic influence, are perennial concerns of Chinese religion. Others, such as meditative visions of Amitābha and the deathbed conversion of sinners, are more peculiar to Pure Land. Throughout these narratives, however, exclusive devotion to the Pure Land path and omens verifying a successful "forging of the connection with the pure land" are bedrock elements.

Among the signs that confirm rebirth in these tales, deathbed and mortuary anomalies are certainly popular. Some involve the dying person, such as visions of Amitābha and his retinue coming to greet one with a lotus pedestal, as described in the *Sūtra on the Contemplation of the Buddha of Limitless Life*. An unusually peaceful death (often while seated erect in meditative posture) or the hearing of marvelous strains of music, the smell of rare fragrances, or the sight of unusual auroras on the part of friends and relatives are also common features. Another variety of post-mortem omen centers around the disposition of the corpse or the experience of the mourners over the weeks of mortuary observance that follow. One phenomenon that is a universal sign of sainthood or high spiritual attainment in Chinese Buddhism is the discovery of auspicious relics (*sheli* in Chinese, from the Sanskrit *śarīra*) amid the ashes of the cremated corpse, usually in the form of glassine or jadelike beads. If burial is chosen over cremation, natural mummification of individual bodily organs or the corpse itself will be taken as an indication of sanctity. Another frequent occurrence, but one which seems to be more peculiar to Pure Land devotees, is the experience of visitations from the deceased to the surviving relatives or friends. Usually these occur in dreams and take the form of either a vision of the beatified dead person or a "spirit-journey" with the dead person to the pure land. Upon occasion, however, a layperson or cleric of highly developed religious ability will have a vision of the deceased while in a state of samādhi or meditative transport.

Although death signs are an important and frequent topic of discussion among Pure Land believers, it is essential to realize that great emphasis is placed on confirmatory signs for the living practitioner as well. After all, when one has decided to devote a lifetime to Pure Land practice rather than wait until the last breath to turn to Amitābha, it is perfectly natural to expect some confirmation of spiritual progress along the way. Following the cue of such Pure Land scriptures as the *Sūtra on the Contemplation of the Buddha of Limitless Life*, together with various other buddhānusmṛti sūtras popular in China, Pure Land practitioners looked to two sorts of visionary phenomena as assurance of their future rebirth in Sukhāvatī: One was auspicious dreams of Amitābha and the pure land; the other, visitations from Amitābha and previous saints or "spirit journeys" to the pure land experienced in a state of samādhi or meditative ecstasy. Both forms of experience were considered valid proof that the "connection with the pure land" was or would soon be secured—provided, of course, that the character and behavior of the individual who claimed the experience fit the profile of a dedicated Pure Land devotee. Nevertheless, in Pure Land hagiography and doctrine, samādhi is given precedence over dreams. The biography of nearly every major Pure

Land saint—especially the patriarchal figures—is marked by the watershed experience of a vision of this sort.

Here we find an important point of soteriological convergence between the Pure Land ritual and meditative manuals and the Pure Land hagiographical collections. In certain respects, it requires us to reevaluate the way in which the long-range goal of rebirth in the pure land actually functions within the lives of Pure Land believers. It is easy, but perhaps ultimately misleading, to think of Pure Land spirituality as having a morbid obsession with death and the afterlife just because its stated aim is rebirth in Sukhāvatī. This is especially so if we are to take Zunshi and Shandao seriously when they claim that sustained practice of nianfo will bring a vision of the Buddha in this very life. In effect, such a vision of Amitābha does more than confirm that one is destined for the pure land in the near future, for it implies that one already has access to the Buddha now. Thus it becomes a mark of sainthood that is virtually equivalent (in anticipated form) to the irreversibility on the bodhisattva path that will be formally achieved when one is reborn in the pure land itself. In this respect, it represents a kind of Pure Land "enlightenment" experience that is equally compelling and equally vital to establishing religious identity and authority as the "seeing into one's original nature" of Chan / Zen.

The three pieces below are representative of the testimonials that one finds in Pure Land miracle tale and hagiographical anthologies. The first, which is taken from the thirteenth-century *Comprehensive Record of the Buddhas and Patriarchs (Fozu tongji),* concerns the life of the late Tang-period monk, Shaokang. Shaokang is regarded variously as the fifth or sixth "patriarchal ancestor" (*zu*) of the Chinese Pure Land tradition. Hence, his story gives a sense of the paradigms associated with Pure Land monasticism and patriarchal sanctity.

The remaining two testimonials, the "Record of the Lady Yueguo," by Huang Ce, and the "Record of the Parrot of Hedong," by Yi Weigao of Chengdu, are taken from Zongxiao's *Topical Selections on the Land of Bliss (Lebang wenlei),* another influential thirteenth-century Pure Land anthology. Both pieces are acknowledged to have circulated as independent testimonials prior to being collected by the anthology's author. Thus, in addition to touching upon dimensions of Pure Land spirituality that extend beyond the Buddhist monastic system, they give us some insight into the process by which many such miracle tales and exemplary original biographies came into being.

The tale of the Lady of Yueguo is especially pertinent, for it deals with an exemplary woman who dedicates herself to the Pure Land faith within the cloistered environment of an aristocratic Song dynasty household (she was the wife of one of the younger brothers of Emperor Shen). The testimonial itself is written by the Buddhist layman and literatus, Huang Ce (1070–1173), which obviously shapes the Lady Yueguo to norms of female virtue representative of Chinese society and the Buddhist monastic system at large. Although we can sense various ways in which her role as a woman of aristocratic birth may have contributed to a distinctive form of Pure Land spirituality, it is difficult if not impossible to obtain any immediate sense of this religious world through the materials at hand. One can, however, raise the issue of divergent or multiple cultural domains within Chinese Pure Land tradition, as well as the corollary question of just what certain documents can and cannot tell us about Chinese religion. As a backdrop to Lady Yueguo's story, one might begin with the narrative setting of the *Sūtra on the Contemplation of the Buddha of Limitless Life* itself. The sūtra, one will recall, devolves around the suffering figure of Queen Vaidehī. Imprisoned in the palace by her evil son Ajātaśatru, she beseeches the Buddha to grant her a teaching that will enable her to endure her torment, eliminate her sinful karma, and lead to life in a "pure" world free of all such wickedness. The Buddha Śākyamuni appears and preaches the meditation on the pure land of Amitābha specifically in response to her request. This narrative and its accompanying paradigms provide material to explore Lady Yueguo's understanding of sin, suffering, purity, and salvation.

The translations are from *Fuozo tongji* by Zhipan (*Taishō*, vol. 49.264a–b); *Jingwang yüeguo furen wangsheng ji* by Huang Ce (*Taishō*, vol. 47.189c–190a); and *Hedong yingwu sheli ta ji* by Yi Weigao (*Taishō*, vol. 47.191a–c). The latter two are found in *Lebang wenlei* by Zongxiao (*Taishō* 1969).

The Biography of Dharma Master Shaokang

The dharma master Shaokang was from the Zhou clan of Jinyun. His mother was of the Luo clan. Once she dreamed that she journeyed to Dinghu Peak, where a jade maiden gave her a blue lotus blossom, saying, "This flower is auspicious. You are destined to give birth to a precious son." When [Shaokang] was born, a radiant blue light filled the room, and there was a pervading fragrance of lotus blossoms in full bloom.

Even at seven years old, Kang still did not speak. Prognosticators thought it very strange. Once his mother took him with her to Lingshan Monastery. Directing him to the Buddha hall, she said, "When you reverence the Buddha, don't be hasty." To which he replied, "Who wouldn't be reverent toward our Lord Buddha Śākyamuni?" [After this episode,] his mother and father looked upon him with even greater respect and awe. Ultimately, they allowed him to leave home [as a novice monk].

By age fifteen he had perfectly memorized five scriptures, including the *Lotus* and *Sūraṅgama* sūtras. Later he set off for Jiaxiang Monastery in Kuaiji to study the vinaya codes. After that, he went to Longxing Monastery in Shangyuan, where he attended lectures on the *Avataṃsaka [Sūtra]* and various treatises such as the *Yogācārabhūmi*. At the beginning of the Zhenyuan reign-period of the Tang [785–805 C.E.] [he was residing] at White Horse Monastery in Luoyang. There he once saw light radiating from a text [stored] in the hall. He picked it up and found it to be the venerable Shandao's *Tract on Converting to the Way of the Western [Pure Land] (Xifang huadao wen)*. Master [Shaokang] thereupon proclaimed, "If I have a karmic connection with the pure land, may this [text] again put out radiance." No sooner did he speak these words than [the text] again blazed with light. Kang said, "Though stones may grind me for an eon, I will not deviate from my vow."

Subsequently he proceeded to Shandao's mortuary hall at Radiant Light Monastery (Guangming si) in Changan. There he set out a great array of offerings. All of a sudden he saw [Shandao's] commemorative image rise up into the air and address him, saying, "By relying on my teaching you will widely convert sentient beings. On a select day [in the future] your meritorious efforts will bear success and you will assuredly be born in the land of ease and succor."

The master heard the voice of the Buddha, which seemed to be a confirmation [of Shandao's charge]. Thereupon he set off southward for Jiangling. On the road he met a monk who told him, "If you wish to convert people you should go to Xinding [the present-day Yanzhou]." As soon as he finished speaking these words, he disappeared. When the master first entered [Xinding] commandery, no one there knew him. So, he begged money and enticed little boys saying, "The Buddha Amitābha is your teacher and guide. Recite the Buddha's [name] one time and I will give one piece of cash." Setting his sights on the money, the boy would recite along with [Shaokang].

After a little more than a month, he had gathered a considerable crowd of urchins who would come to recite the Buddha's name for cash. The master thereupon said to them, "To anyone who can do ten recitations of the Buddha's name [without interruption] I will give one coin." He continued this for a full year, [after which] there was no person—young or old, nobleborn or mean—who didn't intone "A-mi-tuo-fuo" whenever they met the master. [Thus,] the sound of reciting the Buddha's name (*nianfo*) filled the streets.

In the tenth year [of the Zhenyuan reign period], [Shaokang] built a Pure Land chapel (*jingtu daochang*) on Mount Wulong. He constructed an altar (*tan*) of three levels, where he gathered his followers to perform ritual services and circumambulation. Whenever the master ascended the high seat and chanted the Buddha's name out loud, the congregation would see a single buddha issue from his mouth. When he strung together ten such recitations, they would see ten buddhas. The master said, "Those of you who see these buddhas are certain to achieve rebirth [in the pure land]." At that time the group numbered several thousand. Those among them who failed to see [the buddhas] wailed and reprimanded themselves, [resolving] to persevere even more zealously [in their practice].

On the third day during the tenth month of the twenty-first year [of the Zhenyuan reign], [the master] called together his lay and monastic followers and charged them [saying]: "You should engender a heart that delights in the pure land and despises [this deluded world of] Jambudvīpa. [If] on this occasion you can see [my] radiant light then you are truly my disciple." Thereupon, the master put forth various unusual beams of light and passed away. The people of the local commandery built a reliquary (*stūpa*) for him at Terrace Crag. During the third year of the *qianyu* reign period of the Posterior Han [950], the state preceptor Chao of Mount Tiantai urged that his pagoda be renovated. People who came after him often point to the master as a latter-day Shandao.

The Record of the Rebirth of the Lady Yueguo, Wife of the King of Jing

I have observed that beings caught up in deluded thinking and enmeshed in the five desires ordinarily give no thought to escape and are almost never able to make a decisive resolution to seek rebirth in the land of highest bliss to the west. However, when faced with something unbearable—such as malicious intentions or an unfavorable turn of events, separation from their loved ones, signs of [oncoming] old age, sickness, and death, pressing danger, or being overcome by pain and poison—they suddenly weep and wail out loud and turn to the Buddha for refuge. Hoping to escape death's grip, they recite a few words out loud with their profane minds, professing their refuge in the Compassionate Lord and praying that he might greet and lead them to rebirth in the pure land.

The lady Yueguo from the Wang clan is the only person I know who was not like this. Her ladyship was the wife of the king of Jing [paternal uncle to Emperor Zhe of the Song dynasty]. Seeing that [her husband] was caught up in the five desires and had no interest in departing from them, she kept her thoughts to herself. [Inwardly] she took refuge in the Buddha of Infinite Life and made the vow to seek rebirth [in his pure land] to the west. When someone has suffered a host of tribulations, faced the unbearable, and begun to seek release, how can one speak with that person about commonplace things?

People say that her ladyship planted the roots of virtue in former lives and had already received prophesy [of her future] buddhahood. For eons since, she has taken birth among human beings as a preacher of the way in order to establish the teaching in the Buddha's stead. [Since we know that] she personally enjoined the noble and well-to-do, both within and outside [of her household], to practice Pure Land meditation together with her, and together take refuge in the land of the Buddha, doesn't this [claim] make sense?

In her ritual service to the western [pure land], her ladyship was tried and true, never missing [the appointed hour of worship], whether it be day or night. The people who scurried about in attendance on her had no other thought in their minds [than to serve her and her religion].

There was only one maidservant who was indolent and refused to respond [to her commands]. One day her ladyship scolded her, saying, "My entire household is diligent. Only you are lazy and will not do what you are told. If delusion is present in the group I fear that others [also] lose their determination for the way. I cannot permit [such a person] to be part of my retinue."

The maidservant suddenly awoke to her errors and recanted with deep remorse. Thereafter she dedicated herself to contemplation and strove to maintain thought of the pure land at all times. After a long while she finally confided to one of her fellow servants, "I too am a [Pure Land] practitioner." One evening an unusual fragrance filled her room, and she passed away without any sign of illness. The next day her fellow servant informed the lady of the house, "Last night I had a dream of our late maidservant who just passed away. She came to me and said, 'The lady of the house once admonished me to dedicate myself to cultivation of the western [pure land]. Today I have been reborn there, thereby realizing incalculable meritorious virtues.' "

Her ladyship responded, "When I also have a dream like this, I will believe it."

That very night her ladyship dreamed that she met the dead maidservant, who spoke to her much as she had the previous woman. Her ladyship said, "Can the pure land be reached [by the living]?"

The maid said, "If your ladyship will come with me . . ."

The lady of the house set off with the maid, and in time they came to two pools of water, both of which were filled with white lotus blossoms of varying size. Some were glorious. Others were withered or drooping. However, each one was different. Her ladyship said, "Why are they like this?"

To which the maid replied, "They all represent persons of the mundane world who have made the resolution to seek rebirth in the western pure land. With the arousing of the [first] flicker of thought [of the pure land], one's wholesome [karmic] roots will have already sent forth a sprout. Eventually it will form a single blossom. However, because people's degrees of diligence are not the same, there are differences in the quality of the blossoms. For those who are unrelenting in their efforts, [the blossom] is fresh and resplendent. For those who are sporadic, it is withered. If people continue to practice for a long time without giving up, to the point where their mindfulness becomes stabilized [in samādhi] and their contemplation reaches fruition, then when their physical bodies perish and their life [in the mundane world] reaches its end they will be reborn by miraculous transformation in the center [of one of these lotus blossoms]."

In the middle of the pool there was one particular blossom, the calyx of which suddenly fell away, showing a person dressed in courtly garb seated in the midst [of its newly opened petals]. His robes were whisked away by the breeze, revealing a body bedecked with jeweled crown and intricate necklaces. Her ladyship asked, "Who is that?"

The maid replied, "It is Yang Jie [Cigong] [a famous Pure Land devotee, 980–1048]."

Another flower then opened, revealing a person in courtly dress seated in its center. However, soon thereafter the blossom withered away, leaving nothing but the sepals. Her ladyship again asked who it was, to which the maid replied, "It was Ma Gan [another famous Pure Land devotee]."

Her ladyship asked, "Where might I be reborn?" The maid led her ladyship forward another several leagues, then had her look off into the distance. She saw nothing but a single sprawling altar (*tan*) which glistened resplendently of gold and azure, with splinters [of rainbow] light intertwining in intricate patterns. The maid said, "This is the spot where your ladyship will be reborn by spontaneous transformation. It is the golden altar that represents the highest level of the highest grade of rebirth."

When [her ladyship] awoke she set out, with mixed feelings of joy and grief, to visit the homes of Yang Jie and Ma Gan. Jie had, in fact, passed away. Gan was free of misfortune.

On the day when her ladyship herself finally realized rebirth, she took her censer in hand, lit incense, gazed toward the Guanyin Pavilion, and stood up. At that moment, the grandchildren and attendants approached her ladyship to receive her ceremonial blessing [of long life]. As soon as it was done, she passed away while standing there. The birds all gave out a cry, which was very strange indeed.

As a rule, fortunate and happy people will find little time for Buddhist matters. Those who do are often lost for lack of faith. The few who are capable of belief are plagued by the inability [fully] to resolve their doubts. Those who embrace the faith when confronted with distress and suffering for the most part fail because it is just too late. How, then, could knowing true faith, manifestation of true mindfulness, and cultivation of the wholesome conditions [that lead to rebirth] be considered such an easy thing? Yang Jie Cigong had a keen understanding of the teachings of this Chan school, but people did not know that he practiced Pure Land meditation in secret. On his deathbed he revealed his mistakes and composed his verse on "going from mistake to mistake." [According to his biography, Yang experienced a vision of Amitābha coming to greet him when he died. The verse that he composed upon departing the world reads: "Although I take birth, there is yet no place to dwell. Although I die, there is nothing to relinquish. One who abides in the grand void on the basis of error goes to error—the land of highest bliss to the west."] When I heard the tale of her ladyship's experience, I weighed it and set it down in writing, primarily to help those who have already aroused faith in [the pure land]. However, nonbelievers will surely be moved to faith by this text as well, and thereby turn to pure meditation on the Buddha's land.

Recorded by Huang Ce, [also known as] the Buddhist layman Suiyuan.

Inscription for the Reliquary of the Parrot of Hedong

The primal essence gave form to the myriad species by means of the five elemental energies. Even though some creatures may have scales, and others shells, fur, or feathers, there are sure to be some whose [sentient] endowments are keen and pure. Whether resplendent like fire or an unusual pure green in color, all respond to human culture. If [the training] that they receive is timely and orderly, there will be instances where their animal nature is transformed and they learn the ability to speak. Upon coming to understand single-minded [absorption in] emptiness, they [may] leave behind genuine relics after they die.

Most likely these will not simply be manifestations produced by the primal sage [that is, a buddha such as Amitābha], but something [instigated by] the stimulus of the human heart. We are the same [in essence], but different by circumstance—transformed on the basis of a single reality.

Some years ago there was a man who had a parrot for sale, claiming that "in this parrot's call one could detect the sounds of Chinese." Mr. Pei of Hedong had a keen love for the way of the immortals. He had heard that, in the western [pure land of Sukhāvatī or highest bliss], there was a type of precious bird that would flock together with its fellows, harmonize its call, and warble forth songs of the dharma. The name of this bird is recorded in the Sanskrit sūtras.

Seeing that [this bird's] perspicacity far exceeded that of the common species, Pei figured that it was produced deliberately from the Buddha's own essence. Thus, he constantly kept it nearby [or tended it closely] and showed great reverence toward it. First he taught the bird to keep the prohibitions of the six monthly uposatha fast days, so that the bird would not even look at food from the time noon approached until the night was ended. [If an animal is capable of this,] surely it is possible to bring the wayward and vulgar populace to uprightness and the observance of brahma purity!

Pei also taught the bird to keep the Buddha's name, explaining to it, "Through mindful thought (*nian*) [of the Buddha], one reaches no-thought (*wunian*)." In response, the bird thereupon raised its head and spread its wings, as though it were ready to listen attentively to his instructions. Thereafter, whenever Pei commanded the bird to perform recollection or recitation of the Buddha's name (*nianfo*), it would stand there silently and not respond. But when he told it to not recollect the Buddha's name, it would immediately cry out, "A-mi-tuo-fuo, A-mi-tuo-fuo." Pei tested the bird many times over, and it was always the same, never different.

I believe that, since [Pei told the bird] that having thoughts led to existence [in saṃsāra] and no-thought was absolute reality, the bird would not respond to [the command to recollect the Buddha], because to do so entailed conditions for dependent origination [in saṃsāra]. Although the bird chattered away when ultimate reality [was mentioned], [he was justified in doing so because he knew that] words are fundamentally empty.

Every morning the parrot would signal the approach of day from its empty room by calling out in harmonious song. Keeping time with his beak, he would lightly drum out the beat in the air, while at the same time he would raise and lower his voice in a continual stream of recitation. Whoever heard it never failed to feel cleansed and delight in the good.

Coming to birth, do desport [oneself in life] and proceed by the stars. But these circumstances must also come to an end. [Or: Does the sport of life proceed by the planets? Or does it come to an end by cause and condition?] During the seventh month of this year, the bird became weak and unresponsive. After several days, the keeper knew it was going to die. He struck the sounding stone and called out to the bird, "Are you getting ready to return to the western [pure land]? I will keep time on the sounding stone, and you maintain recollection [of the Buddha] accordingly."

Each time he struck the stone, the bird would recite "A-mi-tuo-fuo." When Pei had struck the stone ten times and the bird had completed ten recitations, it smoothed its feathers, tucked up its feet, and, without wavering or fidgeting, serenely ended its life.

According to the Buddhist scriptures, with the completion of ten recollections or recitations [of the Buddha's name] one may achieve rebirth in the western [pure land]. It is also said that one who has acquired the wisdom of a buddha will leave śarīra relics when he dies. One who really understands this concept certainly will not make distinctions based on species! Consequently, Pei ordered a fire to be built and immolated [the bird] according to standard cremation procedure. When the blaze finally died out, lo and behold, there were more than ten beads of śarīra relics. They glistened brightly before the eye and felt smooth to the palm, like fine jade. Those who saw them gaped in amazement. Whoever heard about them listened with alarm. Everyone agreed that if the bird was able to entice the wayward and bring benefit to the world [like this], how could it not have been the manifestation of a bodhisattva!

At that time there was a certain eminent monk named Huiguan, who had once made a pilgrimage to Mount Wutai to pay reverence to the sacred sites [connected with the bodhisattva Mañjuśrī]. Hearing people speak of this bird, he wept tears of compassionate grief and begged that he might erect a porcelain [stūpa] for the relics on the holy mountain in order to commemorate the wonder.

I say that this creature was able to keep and follow the way, and when it died, [these relics] verified it. In ancient times, beings that penetrated the level of the sages and worthies and appeared as manifestations include Nügua, who came with a serpent's body to instruct the emperor [Fuxi], and Chongyan, who had the body of a bird and came to establish the marquis [of Qin]. They are recorded in the secular annals. Who says that these tales are strange? How much the less should it be so when this bird spread the way and left such clear proof of its sagehood? How could one remain silent? Hence, there is no reason to think it strange that I set it down in words.

This record was made on the fourteenth day of the eighth month of the nineteenth year of the Zhenyuan reign period (803).

INDEX

This index covers the introductions to the translations only. It includes the names of selected historical figures, deities, titles of works, and technical terms. Place names and the names of historical periods are not included.